THE RECEIPT OF THE EXCHEQUER
1377–1485

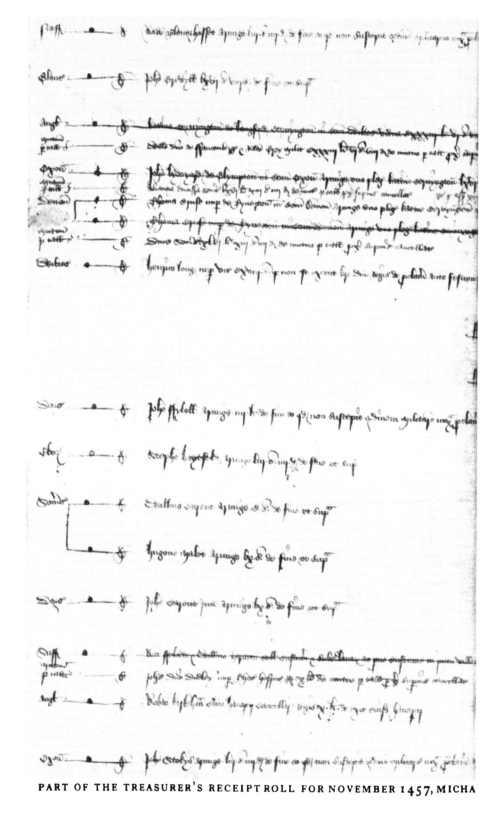

PART OF THE TREASURER'S RECEIPT ROLL FOR NOVEMBER 1457, MICHA

THE RECEIPT OF
THE EXCHEQUER
1377–1485

BY

ANTHONY STEEL

Principal of University College, Cardiff, and
Fellow of Christ's College, Cambridge

Laissons d'abord parler les chiffres. Ils
ont une sorte de brutale éloquence.
MARC BLOCH

CAMBRIDGE
AT THE UNIVERSITY PRESS
1954

CAMBRIDGE UNIVERSITY PRESS
Cambridge, New York, Melbourne, Madrid, Cape Town,
Singapore, São Paulo, Delhi, Tokyo, Mexico City

Cambridge University Press
The Edinburgh Building, Cambridge CB2 8RU, UK

Published in the United States of America by Cambridge University Press, New York

www.cambridge.org
Information on this title: www.cambridge.org/9781107600102

© Cambridge University Press 1954

First published 1954
First paperback edition 2011

A catalogue record for this publication is available from the British Library

ISBN 978-1-107-60010-2 Paperback

CONTENTS

PREFACE

Although this book has taken nearly a quarter of a century to write, it probably would not have needed more than two or three years if it had been possible to make it anything like a whole-time occupation. But from the moment when it was first conceived in 1926 to that of its present much-belated delivery I have never been able to treat it as more than a somewhat desultory piece of research, taken up from time to time in free moments like a piece of knitting, and sometimes laid aside for years. Subject to the usual imperative demands and interruptions of university and college teaching, examining and administration, progress was reasonably continuous until 1935, but at that point I took a sabbatical leave of nine months, which I spent on other interests in the eastern Mediterranean, while on my return to Cambridge I was quickly engrossed in new administrative duties, as well as in the writing of my book on Richard II, for which I had been collecting material for some time.

Hence by 1939 the work was little more forward than it had been in 1935, although a number of preliminary articles, to which I refer later in this preface, had been published, and about three-quarters of the primary research done. There supervened six years of war, during which the receipt rolls on which I was working were dispersed throughout the country—and indeed buried underground in steel cylinders!—while in any case I myself had other obligations. In September 1945 I was, however, able to resume my part-time work on the subject, thanks to the remarkable speed with which the Public Record Office was reopened for the use of students, though once more my efforts were to some extent frustrated by new calls on my interests and energies. None the less I should perhaps have started on this final presentation of my results in 1947, but for the fact that I was then called on at short notice to make contributions in a wholly different field of learning. Even now—in the interval between two appointments—it has been difficult to find enough time in which to write.

Like so many other students I was first directed towards exchequer material by the present Deputy Keeper of the Public Records, Sir Hilary Jenkinson; and indeed all my work on the receipt rolls is little more than a logical development of his four seminal papers on medieval tallies, communicated to the Society of Antiquaries in 1911 (*Archaeologia*, LXII); 1913 (*Proceedings*, XXV and XXVI); and 1925 (*Archaeologia*, LXXIV). It was, however, through the medium of a course of lectures delivered on the F. W. Maitland Memorial foundation in Cambridge (1925) that Mr. Jenkinson (as he then was) first interested me in the subject. When I expressed to him my desire to research, he suggested that I should begin by ascertaining at what date the receipt roll developed marginalia distinguishing between cash entries (marked *sol'*) and certain other entries (marked *pro*), which recorded not a cash receipt but the fact that there had been 'assignment' or anticipation of the revenue. He thought that I should then go on to count the numbers of each kind of entry up to the year 1399 or later and establish finally the numerical relation between them. I remember feeling that this somewhat simple task seemed well within my powers and wishing that I had been given a rather more ambitious programme. But I have no doubt that, quite apart from his wish to discover whether the *sol'* entries really disappeared to all intents and purposes during the fifteenth century, as he was then inclined to think, Mr. Jenkinson had a shrewd idea that I would in fact be led from one thing to another until I had made a much more profitable examination of the rolls. It is certainly true that even while I loyally completed the chore which he had asked of me, I became more and more convinced that the results obtained were not of great value.

It was not long before I had begun publication with a rather general paper on the background of the subject, which I communicated to the Cambridge Historical Society in March 1927. This was subsequently printed in *History*, XII (January 1928), under the cautious title of 'Some Aspects of English Finance in the Fourteenth Century'; I have used the substance of it in my Introduction to the present work. While this was in preparation I had been carrying on with Mr. Jenkinson's suggestion and had found that it involved me in a fairly close study, not of two kinds of entry but of a whole mass of highly complicated and varied marginalia for the years 1349–99. There was so much of this material and it was so difficult to interpret that I decided to make 1399 the closing year of my research for the time being, in order that I might evolve an appropriate technique to tackle the recesses of the fifteenth century. It was as well I did so, for all the time I was working I became increasingly uneasy about the real value of *sol'* and *pro* tables based on frequency alone—that is, tables showing the *number* of cash entries irrespective of their *value*, and the *number* of assignments without reference to the *volume* of revenue assigned. It did not seem to me that tables of this kind would really reveal anything of any very great importance, while if by any chance certain items of revenue were habitually paid in cash and others were always assigned, they would tell us hardly anything at all. To remove this second doubt I took a cross-section, more or less at random, through the series of receipt rolls and published the results in the *Cambridge Historical Journal*, II (1927): the title of this article was 'The Distribution of Assignment in the Treasurer's Receipt Roll, Michaelmas, 1364–5'. It proved conclusively, for that particular term, what all my subsequent experience with receipt rolls confirmed, viz. that almost any item of revenue could either be assigned (that is, anticipated) or paid in cash, according to convenience. Fluctuations in the frequency of *sol'* and *pro* entries did not, therefore, mean a great increase or decrease in one of the heads of revenue, as might have been the case; but did mean that the amount of general revenue anticipated by the crown before reaching the exchequer could vary pretty widely. This was a sufficiently encouraging result to make it worth while to complete and publish my frequency tables for 1349–99, and these duly appeared under the title of 'The Practice of Assignment in the Later Fourteenth Century' in the *English Historical Review*, XLIII (April 1928). Both this article and the previous one contained a good deal of special pleading, intended to convince myself as well as my readers that this mere counting of entries was worth while. I felt, and indeed wrote quite clearly, at that time that an attempt to establish, over any long period of years, the actual volumes of cash and assignment—that is, the amounts in pounds, shillings and pence per term; not the mere number of entries—would be hopelessly time-wasting and laborious: but it was not long before I changed my mind.

In the meantime I had card-indexed all my notes on marginals for this same period 1349–99 and had come to the conclusion that there was a good deal to be learned from them about the nature both of assignment and of many other forms of entry on the rolls: in fact, instead of a simple division into *pro* and *sol'* entries it now seemed that there were eight or nine major classes and quite a number of subdivisions to be made. I accordingly persuaded the editor of the *Bulletin of the Institute of Historical Research* to publish a long article of an extremely technical nature, which appeared in three instalments, viz. in November 1929 and February and June 1930. This will be found, more or less unchanged, in an appendix to the present work.

During this time I had also prepared a general survey, which I called 'The Present State of Studies on the English Exchequer in the Middle Ages', for the International Congress of Historians held at Oslo in 1928, but I was not able to attend this congress when the time came, so the paper was not communicated: however, it appeared in the *American Historical Review*, xxxiv (April 1929). I am glad to mention it now, although it was no more than a detailed bibliography in narrative form, because my doing so gives me an opportunity to apologize, belatedly of course but still wholeheartedly, to Professor Sidney R. Packard for some discourteous references to him and to his work. My only excuse is that Professor Packard had himself, as I thought, written rather rudely of Mr. Jenkinson, and it will be clear enough by now that in exchequer matters I thought Mr. Jenkinson at that date—as indeed I still do—the 'master of those that know'. He had told me that he was aware of what Professor Packard had said but would not personally reply to him, so I took it on myself in my turn, without any authorization of any kind from Mr. Jenkinson and indeed without his knowledge, to write rudely of his critic. I have not ceased to regret this action, for which I was rightly reproved in due course by the late Professor Willard, since I believe Professor Packard wrote in good faith, however erroneously, and had no intention of giving offence, and I hope that this confession may be taken as amends. Apart from this blemish the paper was, for that time, an up-to-date critical account which may still be of some use to students, though I have not incorporated any part of it in the present work. Not a great deal on the subject has been published since, but a few of such additions as there have been are clearly of the first importance. For example, between 1928 and 1933, Tout completed his great *Chapters in Mediaeval Administrative History*, which throws a flood of light upon exchequer personalities, among others, up to 1399 and will always be indispensable to the exchequer student. Then in 1934 came Willard's valuable *Parliamentary Taxes on Personal Property*, 1290 *to* 1334, while in 1940 the latter part of the same period was illuminated, as never before, by the same scholar's editing of that great composite, *The English Government at Work*, 1327–1336. Unfortunately both Willard and his co-editor, W. A. Morris, died while this important work was in process of publication, but the second and third volumes were in fact completed by their colleagues, J. R. Strayer and W. H. Dunham (1947 and 1950). These are all major works, but there have also been articles of importance by Willard, e.g. in the *Bulletin of the Institute of Historical Research*, VIII (February 1931), and the *English Historical Review* (January 1933); by R. Fawtier in *Le Moyen Age*, January–April 1928; and by G. O. Sayles in the *Economic History Review*, III (October 1931). In addition the Pipe Roll Society and Sir Hilary Jenkinson's special interest, the Surrey Record Society, have intermittently continued publication, while in 1929 H.M. Stationery Office published a facsimile edition of the pipe roll of 31 Henry I (1130), which had long been out of print. This list is not exhaustive, but it serves to show that a steady interest in exchequer studies, or in studies closely related to the exchequer, has been well maintained since I surveyed the field; for my present purpose, however, it is unfortunately true to say that, with one exception, the fifteenth century has remained unrepresented, and that none of the work listed except Tout's has been of any direct value to me. For the fifteenth century, on the other hand—neglected as it still is—we now have Mr. K. B. McFarlane's very interesting paper on 'Loans to the Lancastrian Kings: the Problem of Inducement', which was published in the *Cambridge Historical Journal*, IX (1947), after being communicated to the Cambridge Historical Society. This is the most up-to-date and authoritative piece of writing on the subject and rests on many years of unpublished research: I shall have occasions to refer to it again.

But to return to my own work. Somewhere about 1930 I had decided that with the help of a small pocket calculator of a simple mechanical nature it might, after all, be possible to add up the actual money value of the different classes of entry in the receipt rolls over long periods without undue waste of time and labour. My original idea was to start at the year 1399, where with the completion of Tout's work the really uncharted area in English administrative history began. I could then work towards 1485, treating everything which I had previously discovered about the fourteenth-century receipt rolls as merely introductory to and explanatory of later forms. It had long been known that Henry VII had introduced sweeping changes into exchequer procedure, although exactly what he did was (and still is) obscure, so that 1485 seemed a good date at which to stop: moreover F. C. Dietz's work on *English Public Finance, 1485–1558*, starts at that point, which is in short in exchequer history, as in so much else, the evident beginning of a new epoch. Apart from this it was already clear, simply from the much-reduced bulk of the Yorkist and later Lancastrian receipt rolls that something had already happened to the number and importance of the payments they recorded. I hoped to determine the nature of this change as I went on, and also to discover if it was really related, as it seemed to be, to the outbreak of the wars of the roses. Then besides this there was Sir Hilary Jenkinson's original point about the supposed disappearance, or virtual disappearance, of the cash entry: I had proved that this was very far from taking place during the last years of the fourteenth century, but it remained to be seen whether it had not in fact occurred by 1485.

In pursuit of these remote objectives I published in the *English Historical Review*, XLVII (April 1932), an article upon 'Receipt Roll Totals under Henry IV and Henry V'. This article broke down the nominal totals term by term into cash receipts, assignments, and the various forms of book-keeping which were not really revenue at all. It was some advance on anything which had previously been published on the subject, and certainly a great improvement on my own previous article about assignment in the later fourteenth century, but I was still dissatisfied. Feeling that there was in fact more than this to be extracted from the rolls, I had begun to keep another card-index, dealing this time not with marginals but with the names of all persons concerned in any book-keeping transactions, such as loans, together with the sums and dates involved on each occasion. This was of such immediate interest when tabulated that I at once went back to 1377 in order to obtain the same kind of information from the book-keeping entries made during Richard II's reign; and I was rewarded with a most illuminating picture of the financial antecedents and results of the Lancastrian revolution. The men and institutions I was dealing with seemed to fall into ten main classes, viz. household officers, chancery and exchequer clerks, local officials of the crown, bishops, monks and other clergy, magnates, country gentlemen, burgesses and aliens. It was fascinating to calculate the extent to which these several classes, and individual persons prominent among them, either lent money to the crown, were entrusted by it with the administration of large sums, or were unable for long periods to recover other sums which the crown admitted that it owed them. I believed that I had evolved an entirely new technique (which I describe in greater detail in a later part of this book). I immediately applied it to the writing of a long article on 'English Government Finance, 1377–1413', which was published in the *English Historical Review*, LI, in two instalments (January and October 1936); and I decided to incorporate it permanently with my earlier form of analysis when working on the long list of rolls from 1413 to 1485.

Naturally this meant my rate of progress became even slower, but, if only for the element of human interest now imparted to my work, I felt that the increased delay was well worth while. But there was more to come; for the ambitious nature of my latest article had provoked constructive criticism. Professor Postan (as he now is) had seen it at an early stage and had asked me whether the great increase I was discovering after 1399 in the number of assignments which went wrong did not merely reflect the falling volume of the wool trade and the rise of a native cloth industry with but a small export surplus of its own. He suggested in brief that most assignments were merely drafts upon the customs, which meant primarily the wool customs, and that as these declined in value the number of drafts which the collectors could not honour would be automatically increased. Now, as Sir Hilary Jenkinson, and before him Sir James Ramsay, discovered long ago, the most usual procedure when a draft could not be cashed was for the payee to be credited with a 'loan' to the crown for the amount in question, and this 'loan' would be paid off in due course by fresh drafts or in cash. The technical name for such a 'loan' was *mutuum per talliam* and it was conspicuous upon the rolls because in practically every case the original unsatisfactory draft had been cancelled and an interlineation made establishing the 'loan' which took its place. It was therefore a comparatively simple matter for me when Professor Postan made this point to look through all the rolls from 1377 to 1413 with the sole object of noting and recording details of fictitious loans, though it must be admitted that, for Richard II's reign, it meant going through the series for a third time. By doing this, however, I soon collected details which showed conclusively that there was *no* correlation in that period between changes in the incidence of *mutua per talliam* and the rise or fall of either cloth or wool exports. It was true that the vast bulk of assignment was certainly and steadily made upon the customs under Henry IV as under other kings; but that such assignments went wrong to an unprecedented extent under Henry IV alone was evidently caused not by any change in the volume or the character of exports but by civil disorder and the general contraction of all trade which resulted from it, more particularly in the early years of the reign. This conclusion I published in the *Bulletin of the Institute of Historical Research*, XIII (November 1935), as a preliminary to the other article, and I accompanied it for good measure with three tables, each showing in money values, as well as in number of tallies, all the *mutua per talliam* produced by drafts upon at least nine different sources of the revenue for the periods 1377–89, 1389–99 and 1399–1413 respectively. At the same time I prepared another table, showing the different incidence of all the customs *mutua* on the main ports of the kingdom; and I also kept a record of the names and stations of all collectors of the customs concerned, but these were not published. I felt, however, that all this additional information in respect of *mutua per talliam* might ultimately prove of value, and I therefore added the entire technique of analysing such *mutua* along these lines to the already complicated methods of analysis which I was now proposing to adopt for the entire period 1413-1485. The results will be found here in another appendix to this book.

It was unfortunate that just as my technique had reached its maximum elaboration I should enter on the period I have mentioned earlier in this preface, when from 1935 to 1939 I was either out of Cambridge or had many other matters on my mind. None the less I was able to produce by 1938 another article upon the lines of 'English Government Finance' entitled 'The Receipt of the Exchequer, 1413–32'. This was published in the *Cambridge Historical Journal*, VI (no. 1), and ought to have included supplementary sections on the volumes of cash, book-keeping and assignment during those years, together with a note on the *mutua per talliam* of the period; but lack of space made this impossible. As it happened, this turned out to be my last article, although by August 1939 I had just accumulated but not properly prepared enough material to write another one, carrying the subject up to 1452 or 1453.

When I picked up my research again some six years later, on the ending of the war, I soon found that I was able to make very rapid progress. The two years 1453–5 proved laborious but, thanks to the wars of the roses, from then on nearly every roll was comparatively easy going, and within a year or two I had arrived at 1485. But looking backward from this vantage point, which at one time I had scarcely hoped to reach, I realized with some dismay that at the other end of the period there was still a great omission to be made good, which would involve going through the long and numerous rolls of Richard II's reign for yet a fourth time. The trouble was that in writing 'English Government Finance' I had deliberately pushed back the starting-point of my book from 1399 to 1377 as far as the analysis of ordinary loans and *mutua per talliam* was concerned, but I had omitted to accompany this new piece of work with the complementary breakdown of the roll totals into cash, assignments and book-keeping. All I had for Richard II was the frequency table of *pro* and *sol'* entries constructed in the early days of my research at a time when I had thought the working out of actual money totals under these various heads was not worth the labour involved. I now knew better, for these totals had not only proved to be much easier to extract than I had imagined, but had come to play an essential part in the picture I was building up; and indeed my failure to make more use of my own exchequer studies in my book on Richard II, which had puzzled one of my reviewers, was perhaps attributable to the fact that I did not then possess these figures and unconsciously felt rather lost without them.

There was nothing for it then but to start again in 1946–7 on rolls which I had already been through three times and had first used twenty years before. Fortunately I was able to obtain the totals I required within six or seven months and had then only to decide whether, having gone back so far, I would now push my opening date back further still—say to 1355, when the number of 'blank' (that is, unclassifiable) entries on the rolls first drops consistently below an average of twenty-five per cent. From that point, it is true, with the exception of only two terms, *sol'* and *pro* are pretty well established for the rest of Edward III's reign; yet the baffling 'blank' entries still average slightly over four per cent to 1377, when there is another abrupt change and they virtually disappear for good. The year 1377, coinciding as it did with the opening of a new reign, therefore seemed to be the more logical starting-point of the two, and it must be noticed that from that date onwards my original article on the practice of assignment has therefore been completely superseded by the much more close and accurate analysis incorporated in the present book.[1]

Altogether it has been a long and rather lonely furrow to have ploughed, and unlike the many writers who become attached to their subjects I am more surprised than sorry to have reached the end of it. What I have achieved seems to me to be, if anything, a kind of calendar of the receipt rolls: and in this connection I would like to state emphatically what I reassert elsewhere, that I have *not* been trying to calculate the total revenue of the crown (which is certainly not confined to sums mentioned on the receipt rolls in this period). Another point which I should stress is the misleading nature of the air of accuracy and precision which hangs about my figures—very largely because they are expressed not merely in round numbers of pounds, but in broken numbers of pounds, shillings and even pence. The alternative, since true accuracy was impossible for reasons which I shall shortly describe, would have been to work in pounds only and in round figures, but it seemed to me that, though I knew that I was going to be relatively inaccurate in any case, this was no reason why I should go out of my way to be more inaccurate than was absolutely necessary.

The causes of this over-all inaccuracy, to which I now confess, are numerous and for the most part, I believe, inevitable. To begin with, there is the sheer bulk of the rolls. I once measured an average-looking roll from the middle of Richard II's reign and found that it was 66 ft. long—the length of a cricket-pitch. It is true that, while there are a few still longer rolls, there is a marked tendency for them to get shorter as time goes on, especially after 1454. Yet even after allowing generously for this tendency I calculate that I must have read well over ten thousand feet, or upwards of two miles, of roll. This figure again takes no account

---

[1] The many recensions of the receipt rolls for Richard II's reign also resulted in some substantial modification of the figures previously published in the double article in *Eng. Hist. Rev.*, LI (Jan. and Oct. 1936), referred to above.

of the fact that the series was originally in triplicate, and that wherever one particular roll was deficient I had to collate it roughly with one or both of its fellows. This of course did not happen every term, for where the master roll (the treasurer's) exists and is in order it is hardly necessary to compare it with the inferior rolls produced for the chamberlains: none the less, the occasional need for collation, which becomes more frequent towards the end of the series, has undoubtedly extended the two miles in question to, say, two and a quarter miles, perhaps more.

Secondly there is the fact that each contracted Latin entry contains a figure embedded in it in Roman numerals at almost any point in the line: tabulation is unheard of. In these circumstances errors of reading and translation, transcription and addition are always possible, considering the vast number of such entries involved. I should put this number, rather conservatively, at something like 150,000 (there are nearly 82,000 for the 100 surviving rolls between 1349 and 1399 alone), and I may add parenthetically that among these about 10,000 of the more unusual entries have been noted on the 3,000 cards or so of my card-index. When one is dealing with figures of this magnitude mistakes will creep in: moreover it has been necessary to make some use, however cautious, of the medieval day totals to be found in most of the rolls. Repeated checking of specimen totals of this kind proved them to be in general so accurate that the temptation to save time and labour in this way was not to be resisted: on the other hand I must admit that the medieval scribe, being both human and not, I think, really very interested in day totals which can have had little use or meaning for him, was also capable of error: I have caught him out in a small number of them, which I have listed, and have always checked his calculations whenever there was any reason to be suspicious, but there are no doubt several mistakes from this source which have slipped through my net.

Thirdly there is the artificial character of my own calculations, which depend on the correctness of my ascription to different headings of all the 150,000 entries concerned. Many of them, especially assignments, were on a border-line and had to be broken up: some of these may conceivably appear twice over, while others may have been wrongly ascribed. Cancelled entries which have, and others which have not, given rise to fictitious loans are another fruitful source of confusion, for whereas the main object of the fictitious loan seems to have been to avoid changing totals already written into the roll, I have found many cancellations *without* 'loans', of which the totals therefore ought to take account—yet it is not until the middle of the fifteenth century that they begin to do so! In other cases it is the actual cancellation implied by a recorded 'loan' which the clerk has forgotten to make; or a fictitious loan has been entered twice over, or a fictitious has been confused with a genuine loan. It will readily be seen how in such circumstances mistakes amounting to hundreds, or in rare cases to thousands, of pounds may easily arise, and how two modern scholars may work through a receipt roll without arriving either at each other's exact totals or at those of the medieval scribe.[1] None the less, there is a broad field of agreement, and even if the details are blurred the outlines of the various readers' and compilers' pictures will be much the same.

To the modern statistician, it is true, this enormous margin of error may appear to render my results almost worthless. But I would remind him that, even if my particular totals and ascriptions were all a hundred per cent accurate, the completely unbridged gaps in the receipt rolls—not to mention the long stretches where we have to depend on relatively incomplete chamberlains' rolls— are sufficiently serious, especially under Henry IV and Edward IV, to make absolute accuracy impossible. Where we have to guess so much anyhow, owing to lack of evidence, it matters less if the treatment of such evidence as we have got is not completely satisfactory. On the other hand, while it is true that the receipt roll data for the whole of this long period are not complete, infinitely more survives than has been lost and it is a pity not to take account of what is left merely for the reason that in doing so we can never reach a state of scientific exactitude in our conclusions. After all, why should we not use inexact historical 'facts' expressed in figures with as small compunction as we use inexact historical 'facts' expressed in words? Provided that we remember that there is no special sanctity about figures merely because they are figures, and that they can be as vague as any literary statement and fully as misleading, their use by the historian simply means that in place of the broad brush strokes and pigments of the literary master we

---

[1] Thus my totals often differ quite substantially from a number kindly given me by Professor Richard A. Newhall of Williams College, Williamstown, Mass., U.S.A.

shall achieve a kind of *pointillisme*: yet *pointillisme*, too, may have its place in art.

And there is another consideration. Fifteenth-century England was rich in government records, nearly all of which survive in bulk but very few of which have been put, by calendaring or other means, into a condition fit for use by the historian. It is difficult to imagine from their structure—which the end-paper depicts— any means by which the receipt rolls with their single-line entries could be calendared in the same sense as the great chancery enrolments, and yet no historian trying to obtain a wide and balanced view of the century as a whole could afford the time and energy to plough his way through this exhausting series. He will want to know briefly what the receipt rolls say and do not say, and possibly where and how to look for any special information he may need from them—and this is what I have tried to tell him. If it be further argued that what I have sought to do cannot be done convincingly, or even usefully, by confining one's investigations to this solitary class of record: if it be urged that I should have also worked through issue rolls, enrolled accounts, pipe rolls, memoranda rolls and so forth, in order to discover more exactly what receipt rolls mean—I would reply that this is no doubt very true, but that in that event I might have covered in the same space of time, say, eight years of exchequer history instead of a hundred and eight. The fact is one can either know a lot about the working of the whole machine over a short period, or rather less about a single part of it over a long period. The editors of *The English Government at Work* chose the one method and I have chosen the other: there is obviously scope and, as I think, necessity for both.

In any case I am fortunately not alone, either in my somewhat mystical approach to medieval figures or in my belief in the utility of monographs. Both points have been expressed for me more forcefully than I myself can state them—and with more authority —by Professor E. A. Kosminsky in the *Economic History Review*, III, 37–8, and I can do no better in conclusion than to quote his words.

> The figures at which we arrive by means of calculations often represent not real values but conventional valuations, and can only be compared with other conventional figures, after thorough testing of the possibility of error on either side. Naturally conclusions drawn from such figures are of a very uncertain character and allow for the

presence of possible variations and error . . . The patient statistician
. . . will find his satisfaction in the realization that the results he has
achieved can only be reached by the way which he has chosen for
himself, and that what he sees, dim as it is, is something very different
from what is apparent to those who have not carried through this
difficult work. I recall the words of the late Professor Savine . . .
After he has described the tendency of present-day historians to
limited specialization, to a preoccupation with the criticism of sources,
and to 'tedious calculations', he remarks: 'Those who occupy themselves with tedious calculations are only striving after probable,
approximate conclusions or explanations of a dominating tendency,
but they know no shorter or more reliable way towards this goal than
that of tiresome calculation.'

I must admit the inevitability and justice of criticisms on the score
of method . . . Would it not be right to use in the treatment of this
subject as many contemporary sources as possible? No doubt it would
be possible by this means to avoid many mistakes and difficulties, and
to find confirmation where our source is vague and doubtful. Nevertheless certain arguments in defence of a monographic investigation
of one main source can be advanced. I can quote Professor Savine's
exemplary elucidation, by means of a monographic study of the great
government survey (the *Valor Ecclesiasticus*), of the question of
monastic economy shortly before the Dissolution . . .

I certainly would not presume to put myself in the same distinguished category as Professors Savine and Kosminsky, but my
case, such as it is, seems to wear some resemblance to theirs. And,
as Bracton says, *si autem aliqua nova et inconsueta emerserint et quae
prius non fuerint usitata in regno, si tamen similia evenerint, per simile
judicentur.*

A.S.

Christ's College, Cambridge.
University College, Cardiff.

ACKNOWLEDGMENTS

I am indebted to the editors of the journals I have referred to for
permission to reprint all or part of my contributions, and also to Mr.
J. R. Lander, M.Litt., for a few points taken from his unpublished
thesis, 'The Administration of the Yorkist Kings', which is deposited
in Cambridge University Library. The section of a fifteenth-century
receipt roll is reproduced by permission of the Public Record Office.

A.S.

INTRODUCTION

Somewhere between the constitutional and economic camps of English medieval history lies that vague financial and administrative No-Man's-Land whose Ulysses was T. F. Tout. Thanks mainly to the Odyssey he gave us in the six volumes of his *Chapters in Mediaeval Administrative History*,[1] the outlines of that country as it existed in the twelfth, thirteenth and fourteenth centuries have taken shape and form. We have, too, the labours of Round, Poole and Willard on exchequer procedure, Mr. J. Conway Davies's book on Edward II, and the more scattered researches of such scholarly and patient workers as Sir Hilary Jenkinson, Mr. K. B. McFarlane, Dr. Dorothy M. Broome and Miss Mabel H. Mills.[2] These and many others have between them greatly supplemented and corrected even works of such permanent value as those of Madox[3] and Stubbs; they have added immensely to our knowledge of English medieval finance and administration, and above all have taught us to regard those important subjects in a new light and from a different angle. But the main wave of research has for some time checked its course at the revolution of 1399, so that, while we now know a good deal about the Plantagenets in this relation, we continue to know far too little about the Lancastrians and Yorkists. Although much remains to be done, the Tudor epoch has found its own specialists, and it is therefore only the fifteenth century which is still a relatively unworked field for the financial and administrative historian. The materials are there, but in so far as they have been explored at all they have frequently been misinterpreted; while the sheer bulk and intricacy of the surviving documents makes it unlikely that any scientific or final interpretation will emerge for some years. It is the object of this book to attempt a new analysis of one class of record only, the receipt rolls of the exchequer, but before that task can be proceeded with it will be necessary to say something of the work already in existence, and to

[1] Manchester University Press, 1920–33.

[2] See my 'Present State of Studies on the English Exchequer in the Middle Ages', *American Historical Review*, xxxiv (1929), 485–512, and the additional references in the preface to the present work, above, pp. x–xi. We should now add Dr. S. B. Chrimes's *An Introduction to the Administrative History of Mediaeval England*, Oxford (Blackwell), 1952.

[3] *History of the Exchequer* (second edition), 1769.

explain the unsatisfactory character which some of it unfortunately bears.

With the exception of the admirable and up-to-date volume edited by Professor Eileen Power and Professor M. M. Postan in 1933 and entitled *Studies in English Trade in the Fifteenth Century*, not all of which is relevant to the receipt rolls, the only work of outstanding importance on a major scale[1] appears to be that of Ramsay in the financial chapters of his *Lancaster and York* (1892), considerably expanded from some earlier papers on the accounts of the same kings, which were published in the *Antiquary* between September 1882 and December 1888. For Richard II's reign we have an earlier paper from the same authority in the *Antiquary* of November 1881, which formed the basis of the 'financial view' printed at the end of his *Genesis of Lancaster* (1913), just as that in turn led up to the last chapter of his *History of the Revenues of the Kings of England* (1925), which stops at 1399. The earliest of all Ramsay's papers in the *Antiquary* (April 1880)—one on the accounts of Edward III—is similarly expanded, first in his *Genesis of Lancaster* and again in his *History of the Revenues*. The whole forms at first sight a rather impressive body of work, though of course there is much repetition in it, and it appears to bear out the claim that the 'Scholar's History of England' deals particularly with financial as well as with Ramsay's favourite military subjects. It is all the more unfortunate that his purely financial results do not stand up to elementary analysis and can only be used piecemeal with the very greatest reserve, though I have used his great work freely on its political side.

Ramsay's basic error was undoubtedly that of continually tending to accept financial records of the period at face value, that is of reading into them modern habits of balancing and accurate arithmetic. In this connection it may be excusable to quote as a corrective—though the correction is admittedly overdone—a somewhat highly coloured passage from Werner Sombart's *Quintessence of Capitalism*.[2]

> To be exact, to make calculations balance, is something modern. In all previous ages numerical statements were always only approximate.

[1] If we also except the special studies of the customs made by Dr. Hubert Hall (*History of the Customs-revenue of England*, 2 vols., 1885) and Professor N. S. B. Gras (*The Early English Customs System*, 1918).

[2] Translation by M. Epstein, 1915, p. 18.

Anyone who is at all acquainted with calculations in the Middle Ages knows that if you check the columns the general thing is to find the totals quite incorrect. Mistakes in arithmetic were common occurrences. So was careless usage of figures in calculating prices . . . All these errors are clearly seen in the so-called book-keeping of the Middle Ages. If you look through the books of a Tölner, a Viko von Feldersen, a Wittenborg, or an Ott Ruhland you will find it exceedingly difficult to believe that the writers were great merchants in their generation. All their calculations amount to this: they just note down the sums paid and received, without any attempt at order, much like the small country trader does today . . . There is no conception of exact statement, nor any effort to make clear how much is owed or owing. 'Item, a box of gloves—but I do not know how much they were.' Or, 'Item, one owes me 10 gulden . . . but his name I have forgotten.'

Sombart, of course, is speaking of commercial houses on the continent of Europe, not of English government finance. Yet, although he grossly overstates his case, much of what he says in this passage is, *mutatis mutandis*, true of the receipt rolls. I do not forget that the late Professor Tout and Dr. Dorothy M. Broome believed that they had found an example of a 'national balance-sheet', drawn up in 1362–3 for their own use by the clerks of the exchequer.[1] But in his introduction to that document Tout, too, emphasized the faulty arithmetic against which one must be ever on one's guard in the receipt rolls and even in this 'balance-sheet' itself: while my own personal experience is much the same. I certainly do not think one finds such mistakes on anything resembling the Sombartian scale, but mistakes do occur and one must watch for them. Again, the statement that 'they just note down the sums paid and received, without any attempt at order', might have been made of the receipt rolls: they are essentially registers of tallies with some other items added, rolls of record not of audit.

Sombart, however, is exaggerating when he goes on to say that 'there is no conception of exact statement, nor any effort to make clear how much is owed or owing': to imply, in fact, that the medieval business man could not be accurate, because he did not

[1] Published, with comments, in the *English Historical Review*, XXXIX (1924), 404–19. Miss Mabel H. Mills's article, 'Exchequer Addenda', ibid., XL (1925), 229, deals with the same subject. There were three or four similar attempts in Edward IV's reign, *c.* 1464, 1469 and 1478–9: J. R. Lander, 'The Administration of the Yorkist Kings', M.Litt. thesis in C.U. Library.

know what accuracy meant. The sentence just quoted would in fact be totally untrue of many English financial records. Miss Mills, for example, in her analysis of the Surrey membrane[1] of the pipe roll for 1295, shows again and again in great and complex detail the infinite pains taken and skill used by successive generations of exchequer clerks in recovering bad debts: such as that of Geoffrey de Cruce, which attained an age of over eighty years before it was settled, or that incurred by a prior of Newark early in the thirteenth century, when he acquired a small holding already burdened with a huge debt of over £450, obscurely connected with arrears of the farm of Southampton and dating from the reign of Henry II. It was not until 1339, over 170 years after this debt had originally been incurred, that the exchequer's attempt to exact full payment from successive occupiers of the land (though without, of course, the modern burden of compound interest) was finally abandoned. The pipe rolls, in fact, are full of exact balances struck with individual debtors; but then the pipe rolls were essentially rolls of audit as well as of record. Sombart's generalization is therefore only of any force in so far as it goes to show that medieval business men, possibly under the influence of canonist teaching, were perhaps not primarily obsessed with balances and accuracy. The English exchequer clerks at least were capable of both in some degree, when they saw occasion for them, and the difference from the modern angle lies not so much in competence as in the point of view: individual accounts with the crown could be, and usually were, strictly audited, but there was no conception of balancing royal or national revenue against expenditure as a whole. Tout himself took this view: he thought that the solitary 'balance-sheet' he discovered was a very rough, and perhaps a quite intentionally misleading, estimate of the true position—in fact a piece of propaganda designed merely to convince parliament of the unlimited needs of the king.

Ramsay, on the other hand, had apparently little inkling of the mixed character of the entries upon the receipt rolls—or perhaps it would be more exact to say that he habitually gave too little weight to the inklings which he did possess.[2] In order to arrive at an estimate of the gross revenue of the crown he was content to

[1] *Surrey Record Society*, vol. XXI.
[2] See the reviews of his *Revenues* by Miss Mills in *Eng. Hist. Rev.*, XLI (1926), 429–31, and by Dr. Dorothy M. Broome in *History*, XI, 276.

use totals often inaccurate in the way just suggested and still more often in ways to be described; selected totals, too, taken at random from enrolled accounts, from wardrobe and other household accounts; from the receipt rolls themselves. These, not without further slips in his own arithmetic, he simply added up, ignoring the inflationary effect, of which, both in *Lancaster and York* and in the *Genesis of Lancaster* he was none the less aware,[1] of the fictitious loan. In taking the result as real revenue in any one year he also ignored the influence of assignment, or anticipation of the revenue, which, while not necessarily affecting the gross total over a period of years, continually distributes annual 'revenue' over more than one year. Furthermore, he apparently took no account of the vast prests, or advances in goods and cash to royal officers, which were made and repaid so often during Richard II's reign and can hardly be regarded as revenue, while even where he was consciously dealing with genuine loans, which again are not revenue, he omitted to make any adequate deductions under that head and on the contrary assumed far too easily that a high percentage of these loans was not repaid. Lastly he did not allow sufficiently for the fact that, quite apart from the special parliamentary grants he mentions for the fifteenth century, some at least of the crown's ordinary revenue habitually escaped record at the receipt of the exchequer: Miss Mills, for example,[2] knows of orders issued to the sheriffs—and the same may well be true of other local officers—to pay out large sums for the expenses of the central administration; sums which none the less never appeared in either pipe, receipt or issue rolls, or in wardrobe accounts, though the orders for them may be traced in the memoranda rolls, under the heading of *precepta*.

It would be a tedious and ungrateful task to pursue Ramsay's errors in financial history through the whole of his published work, which in fact contains much that is still of value under this head, but it may be of assistance to the student who would like to learn how to separate the possibly correct from the obviously incorrect in Ramsay to say something by way of criticism in rather greater detail on his approach towards the finances of the first two Lancastrians. It may be admitted at once that he is an improvement

---

[1] *Lancaster and York*, I, 144–5; *Genesis of Lancaster*, II, 94–5. Cf., too, his paper on 'Accounts of Henry V', *Antiquary*, VIII (1883), 95–100.

[2] *Eng. Hist. Rev.*, XLI, 430.

on his predecessor, J. H. Wylie,[1] the historian of Henry IV, for Wylie simply took at face value[2] any surviving totals he could find at the end of the receipt and issue rolls and made no attempt at systematic study of either series. However, beyond drawing attention to the obvious financial necessities of Henry IV, Wylie did not try to arrive at a general estimate of revenue and expenditure for the reign, though he used issue roll totals, once more at face value, to illustrate the declining expenditure of Henry's later years.[3] Ramsay was more ambitious. Already in 1882, two years before the appearance of Wylie's first volume, he had published his 'Accounts of Henry IV',[4] followed in 1883 by the 'Accounts of Henry V'.[5] These purported to give a more or less exact statement of income and expenditure under these two kings, but the results arrived at were largely vitiated by the means employed. For while in the first of these two papers Ramsay advanced beyond Wylie in discerning that the receipt and issue rolls not only do not as a rule approach a balance but are frequently not even added up, he was completely unable to account for the first fact and often employed simple guesswork to remedy the second. Thus in order to arrive at a missing total for an issue roll, 'in one or two cases' he takes an extant total for the same term *from the other series* (i.e. the receipt rolls), though he is continually noting with surprise that there are occasions when the totals in the two rolls differ. By such means he produces a complete table of (nominal) *issue* roll totals for the reign, but confesses frankly that the labour of adding those *receipt* rolls whose totals are missing is too great. No receipt roll table is therefore given. One important feature of the receipt roll, however, which appears to have escaped Wylie, is rightly noted by Ramsay as a possible key to the discrepancies which he has admitted but has also so magnificently disregarded: 'the systematic erasures and

---

[1] *History of England under Henry IV*, 4 vols., 1884–98.

[2] Ibid., I, 60–1: 'for all practical purposes, however, a good working estimate may be formed as to the annual Receipts and Expenses of the Public Exchequer by consulting the Pells Rolls'. He proceeds to quote a figure which is approximately that of the nominal receipt (or 'pells') roll totals for the first year of the reign, and to deduct from it the corresponding issue roll totals, 'leaving a balance on the right side at the year's end of £243 4s. 6d.'

[3] Ibid., 114–15.

[4] *Antiquary*, VI, 100–6.

[5] Ibid., VIII, 95–100.

interlineations on the Pells Rolls, of which I have not yet found the interpretation, may account for some inflation of the figures'.

The next paper, on Henry V, shows some advance in discovering the answer to this particular conundrum (the fictitious loan), but unfortunately no use is made of it; on the other hand, there is still the same preoccupation with balances and the same haphazard methods of arriving at misleading 'totals'. Once more the issue rolls alone are tabled, but this time the missing totals are roughly 'calculated' instead of being taken from the receipts, though in such cases shillings and pence have been, quite excusably, omitted and only a 'summary total' given. The reason is that 'the Receipt Rolls, which we do not publish, are in a very incomplete state; only five of them give full totals'. Ramsay, it is true, proceeds to add up eight others 'privately', but only in order to convince himself that there would be no balance with the issues—really an example of misdirected labour. For even then he is unconvinced that this monstrosity can be: 'possibly, if we had the full totals of all the Rolls, the amounts might be found to balance after all'.

In 1892, as we have already seen, Ramsay published his *Lancaster and York*, appending to each reign a 'financial view' expanded from his older papers in the *Antiquary*. Unhappily, much the same misconceptions and the same tendency to guesswork still prevail. In the case of Henry IV[1] he notes that in fifteen terms only out of twenty-seven (which these terms are he does not say) do both receipt and issue roll totals occur, and then states that on summing them apparent receipts exceed apparent issues by £55,000. Ignoring the remaining twelve terms, he then proceeds to make the bland assumption that this excess, 'if real', is equivalent to another £4,000 revenue *per annum* for the entire reign! The existence of numerous and heavy loans, both genuine and fictitious, is realized, but it is claimed that 'by a curious coincidence' fictitious loans at least are compensated for by the omission of 'direct payments made by Revenue officers to individuals under royal grants, without the intervention of the Treasury; as in the case already noticed of the special war grants'.[2] The coincidence of these two amounts,

[1] *Lancaster and York*, I, 143–60.
[2] Ibid., 74. It is said that in the Easter term 5 Henry IV parliament only granted the abnormal tax of 1s. in the pound rental of land on condition (among others) that no record of the tax should be allowed to live as a precedent. Cf. Stubbs, *Constitutional Hist.* (1896), III, 46 n.

the first of which Ramsay had not bothered to ascertain while the second is probably unascertainable, is certainly curious and has yet to be proved.

It is unnecessary to weary the reader still further by going on to criticize in detail the equally unsure foundations—most of the weaknesses in which are fairly obvious—of Ramsay's full analysis of annual revenue, but attention must be drawn to yet one more assumption, which again is arbitrary, viz. that we may calculate another annual addition to the revenue, this time of £500 *per annum*, from free gifts to the exchequer and from loans supposed not to have been repaid because not entered as repaid in the receipt roll.[1] Calculations of this sort hardly inspire confidence in the summary 'Table of Revenues of Henry IV (estimated average)', which ends the chapter.

It is equally unnecessary to exhibit all the defects in Ramsay's 'financial view' of Henry V's reign,[2] though this, too, is largely a tissue of assumptions based upon a misconception of the evidence. The desire to balance the receipts and issues is still present, and inevitably leads him into the same morasses as before. Much the same is true of what he has to say about Henry VI and the Yorkists, about Edward III and Richard II: a great deal of interesting material has been looked at and there is information here and there of use, but the conclusions are incredibly slapdash: almost any 'totals' which are found are accepted superficially at face value; gaps and difficulties are cheerfully bridged by guessing; and 'averages' for whole reigns are often based on totals for a year or two. The fact is that Ramsay was attempting too much. In addition to writing from the primary authorities a general history of England in the Middle Ages, he was trying, almost incidentally, to do something which the whole-time modern specialist cannot do with any certainty, that is, to construct an accurate table of revenue and expenditure, itemized under many different headings, for the medieval kings of England. Even Ramsay's courage, industry and enthusiasm would probably have shrunk from such a task, despite his very real endowments as a scholar, if he had realized its full complexity and magnitude; but, though he certainly observed that

---

[1] Ramsay probably never had occasion to collate the three receipt rolls with any care or frequency, or he would have known that such omissions from any one roll generally have small significance.

[2] *Lancaster and York*, I, 310-21.

there were odd things in the records he was studying, it apparently did not occur to him that methods of accounting and the ideas which underlie them might have radically changed between the fifteenth and the nineteenth centuries. Ideas of balances, of exact totals meaning what they say, in fact of totals at all, as any necessary part of a receipt roll, must be swept away before we can begin to reconstruct, brick by brick, a much humbler edifice than Ramsay so magnificently tried to build. Having cleared the ground in this way, we may pause before beginning our constructive labours in order to describe more closely the tools which we propose to use.

English medieval finance was built upon the tally and the assignment. Tallies were a kind of receipt, as the official catalogue of the Record Office Museum explains:[1] 'narrow shafts of hard wood on which notches were cut to denote particular sums of money . . . inscribed with the name of the accountant . . . After being split longitudinally, one section was retained by each of the parties to an account.' Assignment was once described by Tout as a 'pernicious process . . . by which, all through the period of war, the crown sought to stave off present disaster by imposing severe penalties upon the future'.[2] It was, very roughly, 'a system of anticipatory drafts on the . . . revenues', but it was a system which might take a number of forms. The most usual process was for a writ to issue to the collectors of the customs, or of a subsidy, or to a sheriff or to any other royal official who might be expected to have money in hand, ordering them to satisfy one of the king's creditors on his production, together with the said writ, of a tally for the amount involved—a tally, however, made out not in the creditor's name but in the names of, let us say, the collectors of customs at Newcastle-on-Tyne. When the collectors came to account, therefore, at Westminster, they would produce as many of such tallies as they had accumulated in lieu of moneys they had already paid on order to the king's creditors. Alternatively, there might be no tally, and therefore no entry to begin with on the receipt roll, but a writ of privy seal, or some other small seal, might be issued, of which there is no register or enrolment, simply

[1] P. 27; cf. plate vi. On tallies in general see Sir Hilary Jenkinson's four articles, cited in the preface of this work, above, p. viii.
[2] *Eng. Hist. Rev.*, xxxix, 411. A later and more sympathetic account of the system is to be found in Willard's article, ibid., xlii, 12. See also his 'Exchequer Tally', *Bulletin of the John Rylands Library*, vii (1923), 270.

ordering the collectors to pay a specified sum to the holder of the writ, who would surrender it on receiving the money, so that the collectors might have something to show in their account at the exchequer. Or again, officials of the wardrobe, chamber or some other household department, might request and receive cash from the collectors, giving them in exchange bills, also known as debentures, of the wardrobe, which would ultimately be presented at the exchequer. Or again, letters under the great seal, duly recorded and enrolled, might issue for much the same purpose, or the collectors might get a different form of receipt for what they had paid out, such as the half of an indenture. Whatever it was they would never fail to bring an assorted bundle of evidence of this kind to Westminster to explain why they could not bring as much cash as was expected of them, and as soon as this evidence had been sifted and allowed they would receive a tally or tallies, quite distinct from the simpler type of tally they got when they paid in cash, but none the less a kind of tally of receipt for revenue, which had indeed been collected but had already been spent.

Whatever the means adopted, the practice meant that the exchequer of receipt was tending to become more and more of a clearing-house for writs and tallies of assignment and less and less the scene of cash transactions. This tendency is a very old one: Sir Hilary Jenkinson has found it at work as early as the twelfth century.[1] But alongside it always persisted the still older habit of paying a good deal of the revenue in cash into the exchequer, and the continually changing relation between these cash payments and the credit transactions is of obvious importance. The labour of establishing this relation for many years prior to 1349 is probably not worth the result: it took Willard an infinite deal of trouble to do it for two years, 1327–8 and 1332–3.[2] But from 1349 at least, though the first traces occur twelve or thirteen years earlier, it is possible to discover with increasing speed and only some slight loss in accuracy how many entries represent cash and how many credit or

[1] 'William Cade, an Early Financier', *Eng. Hist. Rev.*, XXVIII, 209–27, 731–2. This is supplemented by the same author's 'A Moneylender's Bonds of the Twelfth Century' in *Essays presented to R. L. Poole* (1927), especially pp. 197–9.
[2] *Eng. Hist. Rev.*, XLII, 12. I have an unqualified admiration for this article: the statement in the text refers to *many* years (say fifty or a hundred), which is a different matter.

book-keeping transactions. This can be done, as has already been explained, with the help of certain marginal annotations which establish themselves on the receipt rolls about the middle of the fourteenth century. From 1349 to 1355 seventy-five per cent of all entries are thus annotated; from 1355 to 1377 some ninety-six per cent; and after 1377 practically a hundred per cent. They creep into the rolls as follows. First, on the issue roll for the Michaelmas term of the exchequer, 1332–3, cash payments begin to be distinguished from drafts by the annotation *sol'* or *soluc'*, as opposed to *assign'*, *ass'n*, *ass'*.[1] Then on the receipt roll for the Easter term of 1336 we begin to get the annotation *pro* for draft entries, though it is not at all frequent before the Michaelmas term of 1337–8, i.e. in the period of the great wool pre-emption[2] at the beginning of the Hundred Years' War. Ten years later (2 August 1346) there occurs the first entry of *sol'* on the receipt roll, and this in turn becomes common in and after the Easter term of 1349. We have here in fact a reflection of the new *pro* and *sol'* tallies, whose introduction is attributed by Sir Hilary Jenkinson[3] to 'some time in the reign of Edward III'; but we have more than that, for the convenience of this annotation was so quickly realized by the clerks of the receipt that almost from the first the notes are used even of entries for which no tallies were cut.[4]

The effects of assignment on the financial machine were many and various. True, Willard himself has warned us against carrying the contrast with cash payments too far: 'writs of assignment were after all only a slower form of payment'.[5] But he himself describes the inconvenience which this method caused to creditors, and that inconvenience was to have important consequences, among which may be reckoned the habit of discounting tallies of assignment. I shall soon go on to deal with that development; at the moment it is enough to say that the motive for attempting something of the sort is clear enough. Otherwise, instead of being paid in cash at Westminster, the creditor might have to make a difficult, expensive journey, possibly of many weeks' duration, to make contact with

[1] Willard, *Eng. Hist. Rev.*, XLII, 12.
[2] *Finance and Trade under Edward III*, ed. G. Unwin, pp. 181–94.
[3] In 'Medieval Tallies, Public and Private', *Archaeologia*, LXXIV, 298–9.
[4] E.g. loans, genuine and fictitious, and the other types of entry mentioned in the last three paragraphs of this introduction.
[5] *Eng. Hist. Rev.*, XLII, 21.

some harassed royal officer, it might be at the other end of England. Even if he found his man, it was uncertain whether he would be paid, for the exchequer might have overdrawn on that particular official, or the official might not have got all his money in himself as yet. Or again the king might order, as in August 1327, the collectors of customs at a certain port (in that case Southampton) to send all their money in hand to the king, *previous assignments notwithstanding*.[1] On 6 May 1339 all outstanding assignments were revoked, 'other than for the defence of castles and towns in Scotland and to the Bardi and Peruzzi',[2] while a little later the patent roll states that certain merchants have agreed that they will make further loans of sums assigned *when they have obtained these*.[3] The implied uncertainty of assignment is interesting: one wonders, too, what happened to assignments when the subsidy upon which they were made was converted into something else; for instance, when the ninth of sheaves, fleeces, lambs and movables of *1340 was* converted into a grant of a definite number of sacks of wool by the parliament of 1341. It is amusing to find in the close roll of 1343 mention of an assignment which 'the king and council had agreed to keep',[4] almost as if it were an exception!

In short, tallies of assignment were frequently dishonoured, as appears from the receipt rolls themselves. Here again and again at all periods we meet entries recording the receipt of a certain sum from some accountant, followed by the marginal note *pro* somebody else, the sure sign of an assignment to the latter. Afterwards the entry has been struck through and an interlineation made which records the receipt of a so-called 'loan' from the individual mentioned in the margin. The 'loan' is, of course, a fictitious one: the king's creditor had been marked as paid (by the *pro* entry), but in reality had failed to cash his tally. To save trouble with the totals, therefore,[5] the original entry was cancelled, and the amount

---

[1] *Finance and Trade under Edward III*, p. 103. My italics.

[2] Ibid., p. 122. For the priority given to the claims of the Bardi and Peruzzi cf. Sapori, *Crisi delle compagnie dei Bardi e dei Peruzzi*.

[3] *Finance and Trade under Edward III*, p. 117. My italics.

[4] Ibid., pp. 118, 122.

[5] In view of the not infrequent inaccuracy, already mentioned, of the daily and weekly totals, this policy is at first surprising. But the clerks seem to have aimed at a rule-of-thumb exactness, and the attainment of even that modest ideal would have been impracticable without some such system as this.

in question recorded over again as a 'receipt' in the form of a 'loan' from the creditor, which in a sense it was, as the king still owed him the money. This is usually followed by an attempt to pay off all or part of the 'loan' with fresh tallies of assignment, so that the same amount of money does duty as revenue twice over; perhaps oftener, as the process is repeated.[1] Hence any student of the receipt rolls in this period will soon come to associate considerable confusion, cancellation, and in general bad finance with the practice of assignment, and on the other hand will always find clarity, order and simplicity accompanying the record of cash payments.

It seems, then, that a high percentage of assignment must naturally be a feature of any period during which there is a strain on the revenue produced by abnormally large expenditure or by an equally abnormal reduction in the revenue itself: not having the cash to meet its obligations, the exchequer will anticipate revenue, and in a phase of falling income confusion may result. Conversely, when the revenue is buoyant and expenditure is relatively low, we may expect to find that most transactions are in cash. Now it is obvious that periods when the country is at war will normally fall into the former, and periods when it is at peace within the latter, category. It is all the more surprising to find that Willard's very scholarly and detailed analysis has proved conclusively that in 1327-8, a year of peace, it was assignment which prevailed, while in 1332-3, a year of war, cash payment was considerably more common.[2] Whatever the explanation of this particular phenomenon may be, it illustrates the dangers of generalization on the basis of a study, however thorough, covering only one or two years. For if we take the whole series of the receipt rolls in the later fourteenth and the fifteenth centuries we get a very different, and much more rational, result. So far from a period of war being a

---

[1] See, for example, Ramsay's analysis of the payments to a single creditor, John Neville, in the period 1340-7 (*Genesis of Lancaster*, II, 94-5). In this case, as was not uncommon, several tallies were levied in succession over many years, in order to effect a single payment, before the sum was fully paid. Many of these tallies were bad ones, so that in this way an actual £1,231 18s. 9d. did duty for a nominal £1,911 18s. 9d. But even genuine loans were capable of falsifying the revenue. See my 'Distribution of Assignment in the Treasurer's Receipt Roll, 1364-5', *Cambridge Historical Journal*, II, 182.

[2] *Eng. Hist. Rev.*, XLII, 12-19.

THE RECEIPT OF THE EXCHEQUER, 1377-1485

period of cash payments, the war-disturbed years 1349–60 mark the lowest ebb of cash transactions in the century, and the cash percentages are also low in general during the by no means peace- ful reigns of those insecure monarchs, Henry IV and Henry VI. Cash predominates, it is true, during Henry V's reign, in spite of the French wars, but even then there are some significant and sudden relapses into assignment, for example in the Easter terms of 1415 and 1421. On the whole, then, we may conclude that while a strong and popular king did not need to practice assignment on a great scale, except for brief periods in acute emergencies, weaker governments were always driven to it when subjected to the slightest financial strain, and the commonest of such strains was civil or foreign war. Assignment, in its turn, though not *necessarily* 'pernicious', easily became so: tallies of assignment always *tended* to become worthless, and at the best were often very difficult to cash, except at heavy discount: hence, no doubt, the growing popular dislike of them which may be noticed here and there in fourteenth-century literature.

Thus in Coulton's *Chaucer and his England*[1] attention is thrice drawn to a significant extract from a London chronicle: 'This same year (1359) the King held royally S. George Feast at Windsor, there being King John of France, the which King John said in scorn that he never saw so royal a feast and so costly *made with tallies of tree, without paying of gold and silver.*' We may put this in the context of a complaint made by Londoners in 1357: 'Whereas the good folk of the City had been charged for taxes and tallages above all others of the Commons, and whereas they had lent the king (sums varying from £2,000 to £60,000) . . . which had not been repaid . . . they pray the king to take these matters into con- sideration.'[2] In such circumstances king John's remark was likely enough to be appreciated two years later. Again, as early as the reign of Edward I the 'Song against the King's Taxes' remarks,

---

[1] Pp. 33, 194, 197 in the edition of 1908; quoting *A Chronicle of London* (1827), p. 64. (My italics.) Coulton did, however, adopt my view in a subsequent edition of this work. C. L. Kingsford, in the introduction to his *Chronicles of London* (p. x), pointed out that the chronicle cited above (MS. Harl. 565) 'is throughout of a distinctly civic character'. Thus, though its composition may be dated precisely to 1443–4, it may well enshrine a sufficiently accurate tradition of an earlier age.

[2] R. R. Sharpe, *Calendar of Letter-Book G among the Archives of the City*, p. 85.

Est vitii signum Pro victu solvere lignum.[1] So, too, among the
English works of Wyclif there is a tract called 'Servants and Lords',
written shortly after the peasants' revolt, which refers to 'lords
who take the goods of the poor and pay for them with white sticks'.
There are parallels to this in the anonymous 'Lantern of Light',
viz. 'other payment get they none but a white stick', and in 'God
speed the Plough', the unknown writer of which, after mentioning
that the king's purveyors want bread and meat, adds:

> And to the kyngis courte we moste it lede,
> And our payment shalbe a styke of a bough,

which I would certainly interpret with H. B. Workman as a tally,
and not with Skeat as a beating![2] I owe these three quotations to
Workman's *John Wyclif* (ii, 244). He refers them to 'the king's
right of purveyance when travelling, for which only a tally was
given', which seems to me unexceptionable; but, much as I should
like to, I cannot find in 'God speed the Plough' any evidence for
his further interesting statement that 'these tallies were then
bought up at a ruinous discount by sharpers'; the word 'sharpers',
moreover, begs the question.

In the Good Parliament, it is true, lord Latimer and Richard
Lyons were actually charged with thus discounting tallies of assignment[3] as a grave offence, but it is natural to suppose that under
such conditions so obvious a business had long existed and even
flourished. The rise of the self-made layman from obscure origins
is an important feature of the fourteenth and fifteenth centuries,
and Sir Hilary Jenkinson has pointed out the number of such
men who seem to spring from what he has called 'the floating civil
service'. Great merchants could not afford to be put off again and
again by the exchequer with what might frequently be bad tallies,
which would none the less drive them up to Yorkshire perhaps for
their encashment, or to Cornwall; and it is natural to suppose that
individuals, or groups of individuals, might be found to undertake
the discounting of such dubious tallies, for a consideration, on the
spot. Nor were these people necessarily 'sharpers': the demand

---

[1] *Political Songs*, Camden Society, p. 186.
[2] *English Works of Wyclif* (ed. Matthew, Early English Text Society),
p. 233; *Lantern of Light* (ed. Swinburne, ibid.), p. 113; *Pierce the Plough-
man's Crede* (ed. Skeat, ibid.), appendix, 11, 29-30.
[3] *The Anonimalle Chronicle* (ed. V. H. Galbraith, 1927), p. 87.

was a genuine one and they were taking the real risk of locking up their fluid resources for a long time in meeting it, so that according to modern ideas they were certainly entitled to some financial reward. The step is an important one in English economic history, for the tally thereby becomes one of the earliest known negotiable instruments and in effect it expanded the currency. There is nothing improbable in the theory, in spite of the scarcity of direct evidence: indeed the innumerable *per manus* entries in the margin of the receipt rolls, though not always attributable to this cause, strongly support it. After all, the *pro* tally never bore the name of the payee, which was always theoretically the crown, but that of the prospective payer, so that it could easily change hands. There is now positive evidence, some of which I have printed,[1] that wardrobe debentures had been negotiated in this way at least as early as the beginning of Edward III's reign and probably far earlier: the tally was a still more ancient and familiar instrument and can hardly have failed to set the debenture an example which its holders were not slow to follow; and so small men became rich out of meeting the immediate necessities of greater ones, and richer men made fortunes. It is not surprising that there is less trace of the process in the records than the historian could wish, for discount is after all only a fixed form of interest taken in advance (in this age for an uncertain period), and the canon law rigidly, though ineffectively, condemned all forms of usury. But this was a method which was fool-proof and left no written evidence of canonical misdemeanour: it is true that the exchequer clerks might conceivably have insisted that evidence of local payment could only be accepted when accompanied by proof that it had been made to the actual person for whom the original assignment had been meant, but they were far too deeply involved in the business themselves to do anything of the sort and in any case the payee often seems to have been quite legitimately represented by another party. Probably the whole complicated business will never be completely disentangled, but that is not to say that it did not exist.[2]

---

[1] In *Eng. Hist. Rev.*, XLIV, 439–43, under the title of 'The Negotiation of Wardrobe Debentures in the Fourteenth Century'.

[2] Dr. S. B. Chrimes has recently suggested to me, and I agree, that the long delays in payment may also be explained by tallies passing through the hands of a whole succession of discounters, with perhaps a diminishing rate of discount. Mr. Lander (loc. cit.) points out that the traffic in house-

Much the same considerations apply to the problem of inducement in the case of the genuine loan. Why did so many persons and so many institutions, small and great, lend so much money so often to the crown? This problem has been exhaustively examined by Mr. K. B. McFarlane[1] with extremely interesting, if not quite conclusive, results. It may well be that an element of strong persuasion, though not actual force, habitually entered into it: a great council or parliament would authorize the raising of a large loan, and then commissioners would be appointed, county by county, to see the loan was raised: fifteen-century patent rolls are full of such commissions. Yet in such cases some sort of security for repayment was nearly always given, usually in the form of tallies of assignment but sometimes in the shape of letters patent, or more concretely in plate or jewels. Ramsay again has noted more than once that it was very common for collectors of clerical tenths to be asked to advance immediately from their own resources most of the money that they were about to collect, receiving in return tallies of assignment on themselves in their capacity as collectors! But, particularly in the case of the big lender, such as cardinal Beaufort, or the merchants of the staple or the city of London, there must have been other inducements, some of which are sometimes openly stated to have been trading or other privileges or liens on the customs for a term of years. Even this, however, would not account for the obvious fact that certain frequent and heavy individual lenders, of whom cardinal Beaufort is the prime example, were obviously getting richer and richer all the time and making larger and larger loans, each loan being, as it seems, an immediate source of profit for them and enabling them to make a larger loan next time. It is in this context that Mr. McFarlane repeats Ramsay's suggestion[2] that the actual cash advanced to the exchequer may have regularly been very much less than the sum recorded on the rolls and ultimately repaid: thus the archbishop of Canterbury or

hold debentures, as well as in bills and tallies of assignment, *obligaciones* and so forth, eventually reached such proportions that it was strictly forbidden to all household officers by the ordinances of 1478.

[1] 'Loans to the Lancastrian Kings: the Problem of Inducement', *Cambridge Historical Journal*, IX, 51–68.

[2] *Lancaster and York*, II, 465. This was a stroke of genius on Ramsay's part, but, as so often happened with him, he did not follow it up; and Mr. McFarlane deserves the greatest credit for working out all the implications.

the duke of York may have been credited with a loan of £1,000 on such and such a date and repaid with tallies of assignment for the full amount within a day or two, but what the exchequer actually got out of it may have been, say, £666 13s. 4d. in cash down, the lender pocketing the difference. In other words, the exchequer, always desperately in need of ready cash, may well have got into the habit of discounting its own tallies on the spot in the way in which it knew other persons were already in the habit of discounting them: there would naturally be no written evidence of this practice in its records, where the full face value of the loan is invariably assumed throughout, but evidence may yet be found in private local records of the lenders that they made a profit. So far, it is true, such evidence is not forthcoming,[1] but when due allowance has been made for the pressure of the usury laws and the necessity for eliminating any written evidence at any point of such transactions the hypothesis becomes extremely plausible. It would at any rate explain the steady rise to really great wealth of persons associated with such loans, many of whom started as quite humble officials or small squires or merchants with little visible means of support.

We have now exhausted the main types of entry that appear on the receipt rolls through the whole period 1377–1485. In the earlier part of that period, it is true, *prestita restituta* also play a large part, but they are not of much importance under the Lancastrians and of none at all under the Yorkists. Entries of this sort, for which no tallies whatever appear to have been struck, simply record as a 'receipt' the 'repayment' of what are sometimes very large sums originally advanced to usually rather minor clerks and serjeants of the crown at some earlier date, not necessarily in cash but frequently in goods or simple credits, e.g. for 'wages of war', the commonest of all such entries. Under Richard II in particular these officials seem to have acted somewhat like paymasters of the forces: that is, they were loaded with immense responsibilities, proof of the discharge of which they clearly had to bring to the exchequer. This is the *prestitum*, prest, advance or obligation to the crown which is *restitutum* when the obligation is discharged: sometimes it might take the form of the repayment of an unexpended cash balance into the exchequer, or perhaps of small sums

---

[1] I have now found some supplementary evidence in the receipt rolls themselves. See below, pp. 18–20.

made from goods or services belonging to or under the control of the crown, for which some capital outlay had originally been required, but more commonly it must have represented little more than a quittance, that is proof that the official had duly spent the money for which he was responsible and was no longer liable for it. This, I think, is the only explanation when the sum concerned turns out to be a really large one, running into several thousands of pounds, as happens in the earlier part of the period. Possibly that may account for the fact that a tally was not given in exchange: in other words, even the exchequer clerks, accustomed to fictions as they were, recognized after their own fashion that such 'payments' were not really receipts at all.[1] I have accordingly extracted them from the receipt roll totals wherever found and have made a separate record of them—a thing which Ramsay never attempted to do—but, as I have said, they rapidly become of small importance in the fifteenth century.

Finally there are two other classes of infrequent entry, hardly ever very large, which I have also thought it best to make a note of wherever they occur: for these, too, no tallies were levied, though unlike *prestita restituta* they are both true revenue. As such they are included in my totals, nearly always under cash, though the second of them is occasionally assigned. These are the *donum*, or free gift to the crown, to which may be related the benevolence, which occasionally occurs from Edward IV's time onwards; and, secondly, the *remissio*, or abandonment of a claim against the crown, which gracefully acknowledges the fact by an entry in the receipt rolls. How far any of these gifts, benevolences or remissions were really voluntary it is impossible to judge: *dona* and *remissiones*, at any rate, occur from the beginning and continue sporadically throughout the whole series, and the only surprising thing about them is that, like the benevolences, they are comparatively rare and nearly always small,[2] apart from a few large *dona* which I shall mention when I come to them in the latter part of Henry VI's reign and, rather more, under Edward IV. The reason why no

---

[1] Or rather were appearing in the receipt roll for the second time, since the funds out of which such prests were made must normally have figured as revenue at some earlier date.

[2] Mr. J. R. Lander (loc. cit.) says that the household, not the exchequer, handled the benevolence of 1475; and this was probably true of most benevolences. Hence there is little record in the receipt rolls.

tally was levied is clear: it was because neither the crown nor any third party could have any future claim, concerning which a dispute could arise, over what by definition was a free gift, nor did the giver need to be protected by a tally from the consequences of his voluntary surrender. The very rare assigned *remissio* is a freak which can only be explained by the use of a writ or other instrument without a tally: the assignment is usually in favour of the remitter, which simply means that his remission has not been accepted: otherwise it could hardly be anything but a clerical error.

But in reaching these refinements I feel I have come to the end of my introduction and have passed, almost insensibly, into the region of technique, which will be the subject of the next chapter.

CHAPTER I

TECHNIQUE

The method of analysis adopted has already been described in general terms, but may be briefly recapitulated as follows.

The gross total of each roll was first ascertained and the separate totals of the *sol'*, *pro* and book-keeping entries were extracted from it, together with the percentages of the gross total which they represented in each case. Tables giving these results for the whole period, both in detailed and in summary form, will be found at the end of the book.

In the course of these operations separate notes were made of *dona*, benevolences and *remissiones*—all of which were included under revenue and were found to be predominantly *sol'*—as well as of loans, genuine and fictitious, and *prestita restituta*, which between them constitute a further breakdown of the book-keeping totals under three distinct heads. A card-index was kept of the names of all persons concerned in these unusual entries, together with a note of the amounts and dates involved on each occasion. In the case of fictitious loans note was also made of the particular branch of revenue on which the original assignment had been levied, and, wherever this turned out to be the customs, both the port and the collectors' names, and of course the nature of the particular customs-due in question, were also recorded. Special tables of the results will be found under the title of *Mutua per talliam*, together with an explanatory introduction, in appendix B.

In arriving at the *sol'*, *pro* and book-keeping totals day by day throughout each term certain abnormalities were not infrequently encountered and were noted wherever they occurred. Their sum total was certainly not enough to invalidate the general method of analysis or the broad assumptions on which that method rests, but it may be said of them that, taken as a whole, they do suggest certain minor qualifications of my results, while in any case they throw additional light upon the make-up of the rolls as well as on the different types of entry to be found in them. I have therefore used them freely for the basis of this chapter on technique, which may itself be regarded as a kind of continuation to 1485 of the earlier notes I made on fourteenth-century marginals and have reprinted in appendix A. The discussion is, however, rather intricate in places and before embarking on it I propose to make some other and more elementary observations.

To begin with, something should be said of the exchequer terms and of the staff and working of the lower exchequer or 'receipt'. The exchequer year was divided into two terms. The first, or Michaelmas, term began any time in September and usually extended into March or even April. There was a break of two or three weeks about Christmas, known as *medium tempus* or mid-term, but there was usually no separate totalling of the receipt roll at that point: it was totalled, if at all, at the true end of the term, and there was invariably only one roll, kept in triplicate, for the entire term. The second, or Easter, term tended to be rather less important—probably because it coincided with the campaigning season and the general quickening of medieval life in summer: thus summer was more commonly the time for action and expenditure, while winter was the season for recuperation and thrift. But the rule was not invariable and in some Easter terms the receipts were greater than at Michaelmas. This second term generally ran from the end of April to the end of July, with quite often a few scattered days of business during August and even in September. Its *medium tempus*, break or close season, was normally from about the middle of June to the second week in July, but the interruption was once more not a serious one. It will therefore be seen that, even allowing for the two mid-term periods, the exchequer of receipt was open in effect during every month in the year, though there were short breaks at midwinter and in the spring, midsummer and early autumn. This is not to say, however, that apart from these brief close seasons it was open every day. It is rare, though not unknown, for business to be done on a Sunday or on any important feast day, such as Christmas, but even on week-days and in the fourteenth century, when the receipt was at its busiest, the average number of days of business done annually under Richard II, for example, was only 164 (counting both terms together) during the first half of the reign, and 103 during the second half. It fell to 52·5 under Henry IV, and though it rose to 66 under Henry V it collapsed to 48 during the first ten years of his successor. In the second and third decades of Henry VI's reign, it is true, it recovered slightly to an average of just over 55, but in the fourth decade it was only

42, while under the Yorkists it dropped to 23, and even 21 (after Edward IV's earlier years). The fact is very significant, but it should not be overstressed, for the unit of one 'day' at the receipt is not a constant but can vary from a single entry to a hundred or more, so that fewer days might mean longer days and more days shorter ones. Broadly speaking, however, this is not the case: long and short days are found at all points in the series, and there is no doubt at all that the fourteenth-century rolls not only have more days but are in general really longer than those of at any rate the later fifteenth century. For the period before 1455 this is not quite so true—thus Henry V's rolls will compare in length with those of any king, and even his son's officials occasionally produced a long roll—but the Lancastrian *average* in over-all length remains lower than that of the Plantagenets, and there is certainly no doubt at all about the exiguousness of the Yorkists'.

Before leaving this subject it will be convenient to mention here that I propose to save time and space henceforward by simply giving a double notation, e.g. '1384–5', to all Michaelmas rolls I may refer to, and a single notation to all Easter rolls, e.g. '1443'.

Unlike the volume of business, the staff and procedure of the lower exchequer changed very little, if at all, during the whole period. Both remained relatively simple compared with the complicated business of the audit, or upper, exchequer. The treasurer of England, who was head of the whole department, upper and lower, does not seem to have concerned himself much with the receipt, where he was represented by a clerk, known as the clerk of the receipt rolls or pells. This clerk was an important official and was responsible for the preparation of the treasurer's roll, the actual writing of which was performed by a separate scribe or scribes. The two chamberlains of the receipt, on the other hand, although they also had their clerks and scribes and rolls, and were themselves sometimes people of importance in the outer world, appear to have attended the receipt in person, at any rate on numerous occasions. One of them was always appointed, for a long but indefinite period of office, by the crown, and (in the fifteenth century at least) would be a man of some standing, while the other post was in the hereditary gift of the Beauchamp family and until quite a late date was always filled by relatively unimportant people. None the less the P.R.O. notation for the Beauchamp (or Warwick) chamberlain is always C[1] in its catalogue of rolls, and C[2] for the royal chamberlain, with the exception of the two terms 1439 and 1439–40, when it is temporarily and unaccountably reversed. Theoretically both chamberlains represented the lay element in the exchequer, being more concerned with actual tallies (originally designed for the illiterate) than with the versions of the receipt roll kept by their respective clerks, yet they were not all laymen, particularly in the first half of the period. However, in the 1430's the office undoubtedly becomes more important, when it is held by Sir John Hotoft, a future treasurer of the household, who of course is royal chamberlain and is succeeded in the 1440's by no less a figure than the exchequer expert Ralph, lord Cromwell. Cromwell had in fact been treasurer of England some ten years before, yet he did not disdain to hold the post of royal chamberlain in the receipt for another ten years, and even reappears as such, after a brief interval, during the early years of Edward IV. The Beauchamp chamberlains, on the contrary, seem to have been relatively insignificant until the end of Edward IV's reign, when the office was held first by Sir John Pilkington and then by Sir James Tyrell, both *ex parte* the duke of Gloucester.

Other officers of importance in the receipt included the auditor or writer of the tallies (*scriptor talliarum*), the tally-cutter, the doorkeeper or usher, who found the wood for the tallies, and the four tellers (*numeratores*). Their various functions are best described in a seventeenth-century document first discovered and quoted in the *Proceedings of the Society of Antiquaries* (xxv, 29–39) by Sir Hilary Jenkinson: I have consulted the original in the Public Record Office (E 369/117), but cannot find anything of importance there which Sir Hilary has missed.

This document is 'the first of a series on the Exchequer, written in defence of the official practice': it was prepared in 1670 in answer to a request from the treasury. It is evident from the account contained in it that the exchequer of receipt was held in two rooms, one above the other, and that anyone having business at it came at first into the upper room, in which sat the tellers.

The Four Tellers attend their offices above Staires and receive the King's money within their respective Assignments and give a Bill in Parchment that Teller subscribeing his name to it who received the money.

Here we may note in passing that from the middle of the fifteenth

century at least, if not earlier, either the tellers themselves or, as
we shall see, the auditor on their behalf, kept a roll or rolls on
which the bills they gave to their visitors—whom it will be convenient to refer to as 'accountants'—were recorded. In the second
volume of his *Lancaster and York* Ramsay uses some of these rolls
for the Yorkist period, whenever the receipt rolls proper are
deficient, and it is obvious that they were potential rivals to the
'pells'.[1]

But to continue with the procedure—the teller's bill, when
ready, is given to the accountant, and he in turn

> puts it downe through a Trunke for that purpose made unto the
> Tally Court, the Chamberlains being there present . . .

Many bundles of these tellers' bills, as originally dispatched down
this 'trunke' or chute, survive in the Public Record Office.

The chamberlains received the bill and delivered it to the tally-
cutter, who then made a tally, notching it in accordance with
prescribed and ancient rules to represent the exact sum of money
mentioned in the bill; and he in turn passed it on to the auditor
or *scriptor*, who made the inscription on the tally recording the
same sum in writing. The auditor now

> enters the Bill in his Booke and then delivers it to the Clerk of the
> Pell who doth the like in his Parchment Booke called Pellis Recepte
> and haveing endorsed Recordatur upon the Bill returns it back to the
> *Scriptor Talliarum* who . . .

proceeds to file it. In this passage 'Booke' clearly means a roll, and
in this roll kept by the auditor or scriptor we may perhaps see the
true origin of the mysterious 'tellers' rolls' already mentioned. If
so, this gives additional point to a long and complicated quarrel
which took place between the auditor and the clerk of the pells at
the extreme end of Elizabeth's reign (P.R.O., E 407/71), the gist
of which seems to have been not only the relative importance of
the two officials concerned but also the validity of the 'tellers'
rolls', compared with that of the receipt rolls. The quarrel is of

---

[1] Or, more accurately, to the *issue* rolls. Thus Mr. J. R. Lander (loc.
cit.) points out that the issue rolls cease entirely after 1479 (which the
receipt rolls of course do not) because they have become 'superfluous
since the development of the Tellers' Rolls in the early part of the century'. He himself makes much use of the tellers' rolls in describing the
preparations for the French expedition of 1475.

additional importance in that in the course of it a full description seems to have been given of Henry VII's little-known but sweeping reform of the exchequer. The documents are numerous and difficult, and have never been edited, but it is clear from even the most superficial inspection of them that the tellers were allied with the auditor against the clerk of the pells.

The prepared tally is now returned to the *deputy* chamberlains of the receipt, who together perform the operation of splitting it longitudinally into a 'stock' and 'foil'.

> Then the Senior Chamberlaine taketh the longer part of the Stick called the Stock and the Junior Chamberlaine the shorter called the Foyle And the Scriptor Talliarum taketh the Bill and the Clerke of the Pell his Bookes wherein the said Tellers Bill is Recorded and the Senior Chamberlaine biddeth Examine and then readeth the Stock with a loud voice.

The stock is then given to the original accountant, who may or may not have descended to the tally court to receive it—the record does not say—and the foil is put away in the chamberlains' chest, until the deputy chamberlains remove it for preservation in their office 'as a Comptroll or Checque', to be 'joyned' on occasion with the accountant's stock; 'to the true performance of which duty', says Sir Hilary Jenkinson, 'they are sworn at their appointment'.

The exchequer was so conservative in its habits during its long history that there is little doubt that the 'ancient practice' of 1670 was the actual practice of the fourteenth and fifteenth centuries. At first sight, it is true, it seems to be only the making of a simple cash payment into the receipt and the levying of a *sol'* tally in return which is being described, but it is possible to imagine that even if the original accountant had come equipped with armfuls of tallies of assignment, writs, debentures and so forth, instead of actual cash, much the same procedure would have been followed, though, where tallies were produced, it may well have been preceded by the 'joyning' of stocks and foils already mentioned. An ordinary tally of assignment (*pro* tally) might also have started life in much the same way; only in such a case the prospective accountant, instead of having anything to pay in, would have had to start by convincing the officers of the receipt that he was entitled to a draft upon some local source of revenue. This of course would be a form of issue as well as an anticipated receipt. We know much less at the moment of procedure in the lower exchequer on the issue side, except that it was conducted by the same officials and would normally involve a writ of *liberate*, or authority for making the payment. But it is clear that the ordinary assignment contained both elements in itself, and it is therefore a fair inference that the two processes were not dissimilar. However, having described what was theoretically the ordinary procedure, we must now return to the make-up of the receipt rolls themselves and to the difficulties to which certain bastard or unusual forms of entry on them occasionally give rise.

First, as regards make-up, it may be assumed that what is rather inaccurately known as the 'treasurer's roll'—it is actually the clerk of the pells' roll—was the most complete and carefully constructed of the three. For example, it is the only one to mark with a large dot on the left of the main column every entry for which a tally had been struck—a practice which makes it easy to tell at a glance whether any given receipt roll is a 'treasurer's' roll, or one of the chamberlains'. Although more trouble was taken with the master roll, I do not think that the other two were necessarily copies of it: my impression is that rough notes were made by all three scribes during the proceedings, and that these were subsequently written fair, perhaps after more than one attempt. Thus for 1447, though for no other term, I have found what appear to be first drafts of both chamberlains' rolls—drafts in which there were later so many alterations that the membranes were detached and fair copies inserted in their place, but it was forgotten to scrap the originals. I shall return later to the difficult question of the exact relation between the three rolls in point of fullness and accuracy and the comparative authority of each. All I need say now is that all three, but particularly the 'treasurer's', were continually being over-hauled and checked with other records, e.g. with the issue rolls and registers of writs, as well as with the stocks of tallies. Thus in 1384–5 we begin to get, in a later ink and hand, the letter 'e' (certainly standing for *exitus*, or issue) against every genuine assignment. Two years later this begins to be accompanied by a small dot before the word ·*pro*, whenever an assignment follows it. Then from 1406–7 to 1441–2 other letters regularly make their appearance besides 'e', viz. an unmistakable 't' (evidently for *tallia*) and what might be either a 'b' or a 'v', but I think must be a 'b' standing for *breve* (writ) or just possibly for *billa*. Here we evidently

7

have traces of three successive checks upon assignments, viz. entry at some time in the issue roll (not necessarily on the same day) as well as in the receipt; the cutting of a tally; and the production of a written instrument of some sort ordering the payment to be made: and that in turn proves some serious attempt to avoid the worst abuses of Tout's 'pernicious process' and to place some control upon assignment.

As regards totals, these are found in the proper place reserved for them, viz. the centre of the column at the end of each day, but only up to the end of Richard II's reign. In 1397–8 we get the first appearance of small marginal day totals—rough jottings or scribblings, which gradually replace the official totals, whose place is soon left blank. These marginal—and even 'ultra-marginal'—totals are, however, remarkably accurate, and even bear comparison with the centralized totals which on one occasion only (1423–4) actually appear on the royal chamberlain's but not on the treasurer's roll. 1431–2 is an illuminating term in this connection: for this again we have a royal chamberlain's roll, in which the totals have been centralized, but only as far as 20 February, after which they break off and there are simply *provisional* week and term totals in the margin, together with rough notes of what later on will probably have to be added to them. Another kind of marginal total which appears regularly from 1443, and occasionally earlier, is the totting up of large assignments composed of several tallies: I have found this, too, to be accurate, except where cancellations have occurred, but unfortunately all these practices, which are most helpful to the modern computer, are at best irregular and tend to die away completely in the second half of Edward IV's reign, when marginal totals of any kind are rare and centralized totals non-existent. One curious phenomenon peculiar to the end of Richard II's reign and the beginning of Henry IV's may be mentioned at this point, viz. the appearance of proper names, scribbled in as ultra-marginals on the extreme right of the roll. These are all names of various exchequer officials—e.g. 'burgh', 'somer'—and may have been those of the tellers concerned: on the other hand, 'prest' ' perhaps and 'jocal' ' (jewels) certainly—both found in 1396—must clearly have a different significance, the exact nature of which remains obscure: I shall, however, return to the point rather later in this chapter.

The usual custom of totalling a roll only at the end of a term is occasionally modified when there is a change of treasurer. For example, in 1450 separate totals are produced for the portions of the term falling within the treasurership of lord Saye, which terminated shortly after 12 June, and that of his successor. Special notes were also made of the amount of cash remaining in the treasury at the beginning of the Michaelmas term 1433–4, when lord Cromwell first took office, and again of what was left in it when he gave place to Ralph, lord Sudely, in July 1443: the second of these notes comes three-quarters of the way through the term. The amounts are curiously similar in each case, viz. about £175 in cash and another £200 in the shape of an 'obligation' charged against Thomas Burgh esquire (*armiger*), which was still unpaid in 1443. By 1449, when Marmaduke Lumley, bishop of Carlisle, retired from the treasurership, the position was very slightly better: Burgh's 'obligation' had been reduced to £20 and cash had risen to £480. But when the office again changed hands a year later, as already mentioned, at lord Saye's retirement, the cash balance had fallen back to £350; and, after all, none of these figures can be regarded as anything other than a perilously small margin, especially when they are contrasted with Richard II's 'hoard' of £14,000 (actually his child-queen Isabella's dowry), taken over by Henry IV.

It has been explained that the dot on the treasurer's rolls makes them easy to identify, but it is often much more difficult to distinguish the two chamberlains' rolls from one another. These difficulties are not made any lighter by the occasional raiding of the receipt rolls for parchment, from which even the treasurer's roll is not exempt; I have noticed at least eight glaring instances of mutilation for this reason at various dates throughout the fifteenth century. On the other hand there was a curious practice, which helps to counteract any embarrassment caused by mutilation, of recording either the chamberlain's name or his scribe's name or both upon the back of the roll inside the actual join where two successive membranes have been stitched together. I have in fact found it practicable to construct an almost complete table of chamberlains' scribes in this way from 1415–16 to 1484–5, and this has enabled me to identify every roll but one with absolute certainty, and to correct the P.R.O. catalogue (which was very uncertain) accordingly.

Having thus established the identity of the treasurer's and the two chamberlains' rolls in almost every case, we now come to the much more difficult problem of determining the exact relation between them. This is best tackled by first testing the alleged superiority of the treasurer's roll to both the others, and then by trying to determine which, if either, of the two chamberlains' rolls is consistently the more authoritative. In 1414–15 and 1415—the first sample year I have chosen—the evidence in favour of the treasurer's roll is perhaps a little inconclusive: it contains more entries on occasion than does the Beauchamp chamberlain's, but on the other hand certain marginalia which have been the subject of doubt and correction in the treasurer's roll are right the first time in the chamberlain's: this, however, may merely mean that the second roll was copied from, or at least made up later than, the first. In 1433–4, 1446–7 and 1449 the treasurer's roll is definitely superior to both the other two in accuracy as well as fullness. Disconcertingly, in 1450 the royal chamberlain records a small fictitious loan unknown to the treasurer, but this seems to have been the exception which proves the rule, for again in 1452, 1455, 1459–60 and in 1462 the treasurer's roll is easily and demonstrably the best. In 1470, it is true, the royal chamberlain adds three whole days to his roll which are not found at all in the treasurer's, but this can be explained by the fact that there was a change of treasurer at that point and the three days in the chamberlain's roll belong to the new treasurer only, whose copy of them has evidently been lost. On the whole, then, the tradition that the treasurer's roll is regularly the best, the fullest and most trustworthy of the three is well maintained under collation: it is therefore especially disturbing that in 1471 there is some temporary uncertainty over the employment of its distinguishing mark or dot: luckily, however, this shaking of the foundations does not persist.

The relation of the chamberlains' rolls with each other is a tougher question. In the fourteenth century, it seems fairly clear, the royal chamberlain's roll was, as might be expected, habitually the better of the two, but this is by no means true of the middle and later years of the fifteenth century. As early as 1428 the Beauchamp roll seems to improve, though in that term its sole superiority consists in having marginal day totals, which the royal chamberlain's, though still fuller in certain other respects, has not; and as late as 1444 the royal chamberlain's is still in general the better and fuller roll. In 1444–5 and 1445, on the other hand, the balance is more even: each roll from time to time contains some important item which is either not found at all or is stated wrongly, and left uncorrected, in the other one; and it is really necessary to use both. This tendency to diverge has become very noticeable by 1449–50, and for the next fourteen years and again from 1472–81 it is absolutely essential for the student to supplement the one roll with the other. Generally speaking, the royal chamberlain's remains the fuller and more accurate roll, but again and again the Beauchamp chamberlain's roll, while itself omitting much it should include, contains entries, sometimes of the first importance, not found on the other roll at all. The two, in fact, are obviously not copies either of each other or of the treasurer's roll, but give the impression of being two sets of notes taken during the same proceedings by two different clerks showing different degrees of competence and of what one might call interested attention to what was going on. One curious feature which occurs in 1456–7 (only) is that several lines left completely blank by the royal chamberlain's clerk are filled up by his colleague, while conversely many *later* interlineations in the royal chamberlain's roll do not occur at all on the other one! On 11 July 1457 the entire order of the entries is different in each roll—a thing hitherto unheard of. A year later (1458) the actual wording of some entries starts to differ: for example, on 13 July the Beauchamp chamberlain, who in this term really seems to be the better of the two, refers to two London messuages *situat' super Ripatu vocat' Toure Wharffe*, whereas the royal chamberlain refers to them as *situat' super Ripatu Turr' Lond'*. By 1458–9 the discrepancies are positively alarming, for instance upon 5 and 28 December. Often, too, entries have been begun in both rolls but not finished, which in itself suggests a dangerous incompleteness in comparison with the (unfortunately lost) treasurer's roll. Both rolls again give the impression of having been broken off suddenly, though at slightly different points, before the end of the term; and this general condition of affairs persists through 1459, though with Edward's victory in the civil war (which is clearly the disturbing factor) there is an immediate improvement. Minor variations, however, are resumed very quickly, especially in the later part of his reign, and whenever there is no treasurer's roll it is still unsafe to abandon all collation of the two chamberlains' rolls. In this late phase the Beauchamp chamberlain was of course rising rapidly in importance, so that it is not surprising to find that his roll is now of much the same weight as the royal chamberlain's. What is really disturbing is the fact that for so many terms in the entire series from 1377 to 1485 (forty-seven altogether) only *one* chamberlain's roll (and *no* treasurer's roll) survives: this may not matter quite so much for the first half of the period, but it is apt to lead to much inaccuracy and understatement in the second half. None the less it is still better, on the principle of half a loaf being better than no bread, to have even one unsatisfactory, and perhaps mutilated or fragmentary, chamberlain's roll than, as sometimes happens, to have no roll at all, provided one remembers that, compared with that of the treasurer's roll the record will be incomplete and relatively unsatisfactory.

There is, however, another kind of inaccuracy which is unfortunately not limited to those terms represented by a single chamberlain's roll but may occur even in a treasurer's, and that is clerical error. Without attempting to make an exhaustive list I have noted at least 150 instances of proved mistakes on the part of clerk or scribe, not counting the extremely numerous occasions on which the marginal totals have been left uncorrected after an entry has been cancelled *without* having given rise to a fictitious loan. These mistakes are, however, highly variable and many of them do not affect my calculations. One of the commonest, for example, is a mistake in dating, as for instance when Tuesday, 15 May, is followed by Wednesday, '17' May, and so on for perhaps a week or more before the mistake is discovered. Usually the error is not more than one day late or early and is soon corrected, but there are occasions when the roll is temporarily as much as four or five days out, while a run of false dates may, exceptionally, persist for several weeks on end (as in 1390–1). Occasional errors in the marginal totals (apart from cancellations), whether for a day's 'takings' or for a single large assignment, are more serious, but also much less common: I have checked for them as much as possible, but it may well be that many have eluded me. Discrepancies between the totals of fictitious loans and those of the cancelled entries which they are supposed to replace are also not infrequent and, though usually small, will now and then amount to a large sum. The effect of this unfortunately is to prevent the self-balancing of some of my own calculations, since for certain purposes I have had to take the total of the cancellations and for other purposes the total of the fictitious loans. It may be noted, however, that the total 'loan' exceeds the cancellation almost as often as the cancellation exceeds the 'loan', so that the two sources of error tend to negative each other: moreover, in the vast majority of instances the two are properly identical. Then there are plain omissions, as for example when the *amount* of an entry is unfortunately left out or when it is not stated whether some such figure as 'lx' represents pounds or shillings! Proper names are also deficient now and then in some respect, though very rarely, or else erroneously given; while there is clearly something wrong with a few small loans which are said to have been repaid before they had been raised! Several entries which, from the context, obviously ought to have been cancelled have been left untouched, and on at least two occasions fictitious loans have been accidentally made, in each case for the *same* small cancellation.

All this sounds rather seriously discouraging, but it must be remembered that the period studied is a long one and that the mistakes I have discovered and enumerated so far do not average in general more than one or two a roll. It is obvious that this figure might be much increased by more laborious checking, but considering that there are several hundred entries on each roll I doubt if it would ever rise as high as 1%; and that complex rolls like these should be as much as 99% accurate is a tribute to the medieval scribe. On the other hand, the fact that, being human, he could sometimes make mistakes, is worth recording, if only because it justifies the modern student in assuming that at least a few of the worst puzzles he may find are possibly to be explained by nothing more recondite than contemporary error. This, however, is an explanation which the historian must obviously be very chary of using, and then only in the last resort. For in fact the rolls are full of difficulties, and as regards by far the greater part of them the medieval scribe was clearly well aware what he was doing. To these special difficulties we must now turn.

The first point to be made is, I think, that the medieval clerk does not seem to have attached as much importance as one might expect to making any very sharp or clear-cut distinction between his *sol'* or cash tallies and his *pro* tallies of assignment. Had it been otherwise he might have tried a good deal harder than he did to organize his work in such a way that on one day he would be dealing exclusively with cash and on another day with loans or with assignment. For short stretches of a term or two, as a matter of fact, *sol'* and *pro* entries do tend to run in solid, separate blocks, and every day's entry is almost or entirely one kind or the other. But this reform (for to the modern worker it is so convenient that it seems no less) was never persisted in, and the general rule throughout the whole series is that *sol'* and *pro* and loans and so forth all occur quite indiscriminately. This, though rather tiresome for the student, would not really matter so much if the medieval clerk had only made a little clearer to posterity what was no doubt quite clear to himself, namely whether certain dubious entries were in fact really *sol'* or really *pro*. But he seems to have thought it so unnecessary to do this, particularly early in the period, that an appreciable number of entries has been left without any marginal notation whatsoever, and the research worker must therefore simply guess the category in which to place them. This, however, is not quite so dangerously an unscientific process as it sounds; for, given long familiarity with the general structure and appearance of receipt rolls, the student will be able to guess right nearly every time, as can be proved when a 'control' exists in the shape of another, and fuller, roll for the same term.

By far the largest number of these 'blank' entries (it is only the margin which is blank, of course) are *sòl'*: in the whole period there are two or three hundred such of which I feel so sure that I have ventured to include them outright in my cash totals. It is true that their total value comes to well over £30,000, which may seem a large assumption to make—and yet again it is not so large when spread out over something like 200 rolls. About 'blank' entries which I am convinced are really assignments, and have therefore reckoned as such, I have been much more cautious, though there are certain indications, such as the presence of an empty bracket in the right margin, ready for the names of the assignees to be written in, which are a certain guide. However, I have confined myself to adding only 30 or 40 tallies, worth about £3,000 in all, to the grand total of assignment over the entire period, and this at least will be conceded to be almost negligible.

This leaves only one more category of this kind, viz. that of entries, 'blank' and otherwise, about which I feel a really serious doubt but which I have none the less assigned, somewhat tentatively, to either *pro* or *sol'*. There are between 150 and 200 of these, of which I am reluctant to treat more than a quarter to one-third

as genuine assignments: in money values this works out at about
£4,000 tentatively *pro* and some £6,500 (rather less tentatively)
sol. Actually, very few of these tallies are either 'blank' or illegible:
the main reason for my doubts, in other words, is no longer the
absence of any marginal, so much as the obscure or unusual nature
of existing ones. Here again the obscurity consists for the most
part in many of them containing both *sol'* and *pro* elements simultaneously, which in turn is yet another illustration of the medieval
clerk's frequent failure to distinguish sharply between *pro* and *sol'*.
It will, however, be better not to enter upon any detailed discussion
of these cases at this point, but instead to comprehend them one
by one as they occur in the systematic analysis of difficult, hybrid
and generally abnormal types of *sol'*, *pro* and so forth on which we
must now embark.

To start with abnormal cash entries, there is a whole group
which, though obviously cash, does not carry the marginal *sol'* at
all. It is most commonly replaced by the words *in manibus*, followed
by a proper name or title (e.g. *in man' thesaurarii*) and is usually
self-explanatory. Then again there is the small class already mentioned in connection with the 'ultra-marginals' of the late fourteenth and very early fifteenth centuries. Every one of these was
originally marked *sol'*, but these curious little scribblings—usually
of a proper name—have been added on the far right, e.g. (1387)
'cholmeley'. Reference to the roll of 1401–2 suggests that when,
but only when, these names are preceded by the dotted ·*pro* these
entries were in some way converted into assignments and the *sol'*
later erased. This is also true of certain *sol'* entries in the same roll
marked ' 'hosp',' ''hospic' ', etc. (as the issue roll confirms), and
it may possibly be true of the grouped *sol'* entries very faintly
marked 'prest' ' in the same way in 1396, though certainly not of
the single entry marked 'jocal' ' in the same term. The only way
in which this conversion can have been carried out would seem to
have been by refunding the original in-payment in cash and then
drawing tallies of assignment for the payers for the same amounts,
which appears to be extremely cumbrous, though one can imagine
possible reasons for it: 'jocal' ', on the other hand, is probably no
more than a memorandum that an in-payment in cash had been,
or was going to be, spent on jewels—or it may mean that somebody was simply using the receipt as a safe place for the deposit
of jewels valued at that amount. This, however, would be more

likely to figure as a 'loan', whereas, as I show below, it was quite common for marginalia to refer to a proposed or actual object of expenditure.

This last point leads us towards one possible explanation of the not really uncommon, but always baffling, entries marked with *both* a *sol'* and a *pro!* Here, I think, a good deal depends upon the order of the words: thus *pro* . . . *sol'* generally, but not invariably, means that an assignment has taken place, but that a small cash balance is also being paid into the receipt by the accountant against whom the assignment had originally been drawn. *Sol'* . . . *pro* on the other hand simply means, as I have already hinted above, that a genuine in-payment in cash has been earmarked by someone in the exchequer for some particular, and probably immediate, purpose: thus *sol'* . . . *pro pergamena* (i.e. cash received and then paid out again for the purchase of parchment) is quite common. Similarly *sol'* . . . *pro* X (where X is a proper name) simply means that X has been paid in cash and not by an assignment: where *pro* X becomes *pro eodem* the inference is that the cash paid in has been handed back, no doubt for good and sufficient reasons which are not stated, to the payer. In the same way *pro div' sol'*—although here *pro* precedes *sol'*—simply means that a cash payment—often a very large one where this formula is used—has been earmarked for immediate expenditure on sundry (*diverse*) objects: *sol' pro liberate* (1398—unique) means the same, but probably for one purpose only: other early variants are *sol'* . . . *pro diversis operibus*, *sol'* . . . *inde pro*. In other words most, but by no means all, of the *sol'* and *pro* combinations are fundamentally based upon cash payment, and at least some element of cash always enters into them; whereas *pro* may mean *either* an assignment in favour of some person or institution *or* simply an object of expenditure in some form into which the idea of assignment simply need not enter at all.

This completes the notes I have to make on the types of entry which are regularly associated with tallies, but we have still to examine certain variations of those different classes of entry for which no tally was made. The first of these is the genuine loan, which is normally a *sol'* entry without tally. None the less I have found at least one instance ('22' (23) June 1380) in which a genuine loan has been assigned: this is, however, so extremely rare that it may fairly be called a clerical error. If it is accepted as meaning what it says, it looks suspiciously like a forced loan of the kind whose existence Mr. McFarlane at least is disposed to deny: for by definition the first that any lender would know about a tally of assignment would be the presentation to him of the *pro* tally involved by the person in whose favour the assignment had been made, and he would then presumably have to pay up. This, as I have said, is so unusual that, in spite of any appearance to the contrary, it may in fact never have happened. On the other hand there is a fairly large number of cases in which the presence of the treasurer's dot implies that, contrary to normal practice, at least a *sol'* (though not a *pro*) tally has been levied for a loan. The first of these which I have noted is a solitary example from 26 November 1421, and I believe it, too, to have been entered by mistake, since this particular loan is really quite normal in all other respects save one, viz. the mention of the county of origin (Staffordshire) in place of the word *mutuum* in the left-hand margin. It is more difficult to suppose that there were thirty-one such mistakes running on 26 July 1426, yet I do not think that even this is impossible; for once a clerk had started to record something erroneously he was apt to go on doing so automatically for some time before he caught himself out, as in the case of false dating, and it was not a great matter after all for a careless or sleepy scribe to put in a vertical row of dots which ought not to have been there. The last example I have found (from 11 December 1473) is, it is true, more complicated, since it seems to be a really complete hybrid of an ordinary entry with a loan, but this too, I am convinced, is nothing but a clerical muddle and no theory can be built on it. In short, I am quite certain that, whatever mistakes the clerks made—and it will be seen that these are very rare, considering the thousands of loans—it was never seriously intended to give *sol'* tallies in return for genuine loans, much less to assign them.

Though tallies were not given for genuine loans, letters patent under the great seal were often given in their place, more particularly in the fifteenth century. A lender wishing to recover his money would present such letters on the proper date at the receipt, but if the receipt was unable to repay him then and there he would retain them, and the loan would be prolonged as a 'fictitious' one: that is, the dishonoured letters patent would be treated exactly like dishonoured tallies of assignment. Instances of this elaborate fiction can be found in 1435 and 1444–5, while an example of the method working properly is given in a detailed note of 9 August 1451. This explains that the bishop of Winchester had lent £300, for which he had received letters patent, but that he is now returning these to the receipt because the loan has been repaid by the hands of the collectors of the great and petty customs in the port of London, i.e. by assignment. Had it not been so repaid the bishop would either have received cash or else would have been credited with a 'fictitious' loan—actually a simple prolongation of his real one!

The other thing that might happen of course was that, for one reason or another, the original lender might despair of ever being repaid. In that case the loan would automatically become a *donum* or free gift, as happened to the abbot of Ramsey on 3 June 1435 and to the citizens of Worcester on 22 August 1444. Alternatively, as Sir James Ramsay noted, a loan might be simply something in the way of cash in advance on account of future taxation: good examples can be found on 1 June and 6 July 1400 (abbots of Reading and Darley, on account of clerical tenths). More concrete forms of security than a future tax liability are, however, also to be found, and among these the pledging of jewels, plate, etc., was perhaps the favourite: thus in February 1450 the Londoner John Poutrell lent £600, and then a further £18, on the security of plate and precious stones. But the most important question of all in relation to the genuine loan is undoubtedly that of interest or inducement, and here I have some new evidence to offer in favour of the theories mentioned in the introduction to this book.

All this evidence comes from the eight years 1379-86, but for that short period at least it seems to me conclusive. Thus on 23 September 1379 that well-known 'captain', Sir Robert Knolles, banneret, was credited with a loan of £2,703, to be repaid in two equal instalments at the following Easter and Candlemas respectively, and there is nothing to show that he did not in fact get repayment at those dates of the entire sum. But had he really lent as much? The entry goes on, *Inde sol' £2,000 et pro eodem £703*, which looks as if £2,000 was all that Knolles had actually paid over. In other words he made an apparent profit of substantially over 25 % on the transaction, but in this particular case the evidence is not quite so watertight as it is in others, for the issue roll shows that the £703 marked *pro eodem* in the receipt roll was at any rate supposed to be for 'war expenses'. It is therefore an open question whether Knolles may or may not have spent this sum (which in any case he eventually recovered) on national rather than on his own private account. But even this shadow of doubt—for I do not think it is much more—fails to linger round the somewhat similar cases I have found in 1384-6. These are so important that I make no excuse for tabulating them:

30 March 1384:
    Loan of £2,645 from the Lombard Matthew Cheyne, of which £645 is marked *pro eodem*.

27 June 1384:
    One loan of £2,133 6s. 8d. from the Bardi, marked *de mutuo . . . sol'*; and another of £533 6s. 8d. from the same, marked *de mutuo . . . pro eisdem*: the whole £2,666 13s. 4d. repaid 5 July.

26 July 1384:
    Loan of £600 from Thomas, earl of Warwick. £200 *pro eodem*.
    Loan of £544 from the Lombard Antony Pynell. £144 *pro eodem*.

4 March 1385:
    Loan of £3,111 2s. 3d. from Walter de Bardi. *Inde sol'* £2,333 6s. 8d. et £777 15s. 7d. *pro eodem*.
    Loan of £1,333 6s. 8d. from Antony Bache by the hands of Guy de Synoche. *Inde sol'* £1,000 *et pro eodem* £333 6s. 8d.
    Loan of £884 17s. 9d. from Matthew Cheyne. *Inde sol'* £666 13s. 4d. *et pro* Anton' Bache £224 4s. 5d.

18 March 1385:
    Loan of £1,250 from the Lombard Arnald Martyn. *Inde sol'* £1,000 *et pro* Anton' Bache £250.
    (In the last two entries it is fairly obvious that Antony Bache was acting as a man of straw or agent for his fellow Lombards.)

27 June 1385:
    Loan of £2,666 13s. 4d. from Antony Bache by the hands of Guy de Synoche. *Inde sol'* £2,000 *et pro eodem* £666 13s. 4d.

27 June 1385:
    Loan of £766 13s. 4d. from Thomas, earl of Warwick. *Inde sol'* £666 13s. 4d. *et pro eodem* £100 (half the usual rate).

19 August 1385:
Loan of £2,200 from Cheyne. *Inde sol'* £1,600 *et pro eodem* £600.

18 December 1385:
Loan of £400 from Antony Bache by the hands of Guy de Synoche. *Inde sol'* £300 *et pro eodem* £100.

8 June 1386:
Loan of £1,333 6s. 8d. from Walter de Bardi. *Inde sol'* £1,000 *et resid' pro eodem.*

(There are two similar cases in May 1386, but the above should be more than enough to establish the practice. It should be noted that in every instance the *full* nominal sum is repaid upon a definite date.)

All this seems to me to be quite conclusive evidence for the habitual taking of a discount or interest at rates averaging about 25% for an indefinite period. The only strange thing is that this method, which was an easy and indeed an obvious manipulation of the ordinary machinery of the receipt, does not seem to have practised after 1386. The most likely explanation is that it was leaving much too clear an indication of an openly usurious transaction in the rolls, and that for the remainder of the period it became the custom to adopt the thoroughgoing fiction of recording all these loans at face value, wherever they were mentioned, while discounting them in practice at the usual 25%. After all, it was only necessary to omit the one word *inde* before *sol'*, together with the tell-tale *pro eodem*. If this confirmation of Mr. McFarlane's theory is accepted it does, however, carry with it an important modification of the figures I present for loans elsewhere, viz. a 25% reduction in the actual cash value to the exchequer of most, if not all, of the 'genuine' loans I have recorded for the whole period 1377–1485.

So much for the 'genuine' (or 75% genuine) loans. We have now to consider the openly fictitious ones (other than those few already mentioned which simply extended the life of real loans under letters patent). Some of these present peculiar difficulties of their own: for example, just as 'genuine' loans should never be assigned, so fictitious loans should never be marked *sol'*; yet I have found at least one, and that a very large one, which is so! On 25

September 1378 Nicholas Brembre and John Philpot are credited with £2,666 13s. 4d. in the shape of an ordinary fictitious loan following a cancellation, but the entry is nonsensically marked *sol'*. As a 'loan' which, by definition, was fictitious could not possibly have been received in cash, I assume that this is another *lapsus calami*: the scribe must have nodded for the moment and thought that he was dealing with a real loan. In normal circumstances there is not—and obviously cannot be—any marginal of any kind to a fictitious loan, except the date at which it was paid off, and I have found no other instance of any; *pro*, of course, in this connection (except *pro eodem* or *eisdem*) would be almost as meaningless as *sol'*. On the other hand a fictitious loan may occasionally masquerade under a form which, as I have just suggested, permits of reflex if not of true assignment. Thus on 3 December 1394 tallies worth £7,957 in all out of a still larger assignment to the treasurer of Calais had to be cancelled, whereupon the officer in question would normally have been credited with a fictitious loan or loans for them. Instead of this, however, he was supposed to have made an in-payment equal to the total of the cancelled tallies (*per div' tall'*—each of them described in detail) and then to have had the whole of it assigned back to himself (*pro eodem*). This of course was merely a book-keeping device for preserving the nominal accuracy of the day total in the roll, but it was a device of an even more cumbrous nature than the ordinary fictitious loan: and it is not surprising that it did not establish itself.

That the fictitious loan could often be of very long duration is a matter of common knowledge: many indeed could only be paid off at all after several abortive efforts, and I have found one of only £26 13s. 4d. which none the less ran continuously from 1439 to 1456. In spite of this disadvantage this curious method of recording crown debts seems to have gone on being widely practised until 1455, after which it suddenly becomes much rarer. Indeed, by 1484–5 it is possible to doubt whether the proper way of working the fictitious loan is any longer fully understood, for in that term (7 December 1484) six tallies, worth in all £50 0s. 4½d., are first cancelled and then re-entered, while a meaningless and inaccurate fictitious loan of £49 19s. 11½d. (5d. short of all the cancellations to which it specifically refers) is none the less allowed to stand. This, however, is perhaps mere carelessness, for although fictitious loans do become rather uncommon during the Yorkist period they are certainly not unknown and, though generally for insignificant amounts, are usually entered quite correctly whenever they do occur.

What took the place of the fictitious loan under the Yorkists seems to have been simple cancellation of unsatisfactory entries, with or without adjustment of the various totals in the rolls. Such cancellations may be found, of course, in relatively small numbers from the beginning; and one whole class, which I have hitherto omitted to note, arose out of lost and automatically replaced, or 'innovated', tallies. Obviously such a concession was not made without stringent inquiry, but in a fair number of cases the accountant who had lost his stock seems to have been able to persuade the receipt to cut a new tally for him without any special difficulty. A note was then made opposite the entry on the receipt roll, consisting of a brief and simple form of words to the effect that the tally represented by this entry had been 'innovated' on such and such a date: in which case, it may be assumed, the original foil held by the exchequer was destroyed and the new foil substituted for it. In such cases the 'cancellation' involved was merely nominal; the receipt roll entry was in fact as good as ever, and it was only the original tally which was 'cancelled' and replaced. As all totals, real and nominal, were completely unaffected by the transaction I have not troubled to record the number of occasions on which it occurred: they may be found intermittently, if not very commonly, in almost any roll throughout the period. Usually the difference in date between the original entry and the 'innovation' is small, but I have noted one *sol'* tally the original entry for which was made on 22 October 1472, while the 'innovation' did not take place until 22 May 1508. It seems almost incredible that nearly thirty-six years after this small sum had been paid into the exchequer the original accountant, or his executors or heirs, should still have been concerned about an inability to produce proof that the entry on the receipt roll meant what it said, but such appears to have been the case.

From time to time, however, there were variations in this well-established procedure. Thus in 1384-5 a *pro* tally for £5 was cancelled with a note to the effect that the foil had accidentally been lost, but instead of the tally being 'innovated' in the normal way a fictitious loan was recorded, and the writer of the note goes on to say that, since allowance for the tally has been taken in this way, the foil must be destroyed if it is found again. Exactly the same is done with an accidentally lost 'bill' in 1462: for 'bills' (that is, written documents) were always used in every way in place of tallies for certain royal appanages, such as north and south Wales, Cornwall, the earldom of Chester and (after 1399) the duchy of Lancaster. In this case the bill had represented an assignment drawn in favour of Sir John Fogge, treasurer of the household, *super expensis*, on the official 'issues' or profits of Nicholas Sharp, receiver-general for the duchy; but Sir John Fogge had lost it, and so for that reason it had been 'renewed' (*reformata*—it is interesting that *innovata* seems to be confined to tallies) with the proviso that, if the original bill is ever found again, it must be condemned and held as valueless.

We now come to a very difficult class of cancelled entry—one moreover which, as time goes on, seems to assume more and more importance. This is the 'vacated' tally, with or without special reason, which has *not* been innovated. Plain 'vacation' of, or striking through, the entry without a reason given is comparatively rare; but there is another and much larger group of cancellations whose outstanding characteristic lies in the addition of a note to the effect that the tallies (or the bills) they represent have been returned to the receipt of the exchequer to be cancelled and condemned—in the case of tallies, *cum foliis*, with their foils. There is not only no 'innovation' in such cases; there is normally no fictitious loan; so that there is clearly no remaining obligation left on either side and absolute 'vacation' of the entry is intended. Where the case differs from unexplained 'vacation' is in the almost invariable use of the 'returned-for-cancelling-and-condemning' formula, which is itself accompanied in some cases by a direct statement of the reason for this action or, more commonly, by a reference for the explanation of it to some other group of records. I have found instances from March 1380 to December 1484; but they tend to be both heavier in value and a good deal commoner for the last forty years of that period.

An early example comes from 13 December 1383, when a cancellation worth £664 18s. 6d. is declared to be in virtue of an exchequer suit (*processus*) affecting the executors of the will of Robert Assheton: details, it is suggested, may be found *inter recorda* in the treasurer's remembrancer's memoranda roll for 1393–4, to which a reference is given. In the fourteenth century, however, such detailed references are comparatively scarce compared with the unvarnished statement 'cancelled because returned and condemned'. Altogether I have noted some twenty-seven instances from Richard II's reign, including the special case already quoted: the total comes to some sixty-five tallies and the sum involved to just about £10,000. In three cases (£276 in all in seven tallies) *remissiones*, or abandonments of a claim against the crown, have been noted as the explanation of such entries, but this is obviously not the general explanation and in itself is not of any great significance. What is more interesting from my point of view is the fact that throughout the reign the totals in the rolls have not been altered to correspond with cancellations, and, since no fictitious loans have been recorded in this particular connection to correct them, they are therefore some £10,000 larger in the aggregate than they really ought to be. I may add that I have not included in this rough computation seven other cancelled tallies for £360 in all, because in their case it is just possible, in default of any other evidence, that it *was* intended to record fictitious loans which simply got omitted by mistake, though I am not much in favour of that theory.

Under Henry IV these mysterious cancellations are continued, but they amount to only £3,022 in 19 tallies, though it must be remembered that many of the rolls for this reign are missing. There is only one special note of any interest, made on 2 September 1410, when it appears that 14 *pro* tallies for £1,548 are extracted (*extrahuntur*) and condemned, together with their foils, because nothing has been heard of them on the issue side (*in exitu*). On 28 September another *pro* tally, worth £666 13s. 4d., was returned and later (*postea*) condemned because no payment had been made on it—apparently the normal occasion for a fictitious loan. Yet no such loan is recorded for any of these cancellations, and the roll totals still remain unaltered.

During Henry V's reign there is only one small and rather doubtful instance of a cancellation of this kind, and there are none at all that I have noticed for the first ten years of Henry VI, unless we except a *sol'* entry of 28 April 1430, which was cancelled without explanation but re-entered shortly afterwards. In 1432-3, however, the trouble starts again. Thus early in November 1432 John Merston, *armiger*, keeper of the king's jewels, received two £100 tallies of assignment on successive days, each of which was returned, cancelled and condemned, because he had already had a tally on the same collectors of customs four or five days earlier. On 6 February 1433 another of these cancellations carries a reference to that section of the memoranda rolls known as *status et visus compoti* for Easter 13 Henry VI; while two more of 23 February relate to tallies on the London customs totalling £456 odd in favour of Richard Bukland, treasurer of Calais, which had been cancelled on 13 March 1443 (incidentally this shows that such notes were often added at a much later date) by consideration of the barons of the exchequer, to be found *inter recorda* on the treasurer's remembrancer's roll of that term. Finally, on 27 February, yet another cancellation of an assignment made in favour of the archbishop of Canterbury, for attending the king's council, is explained by the fact that neither the archbishop himself *nor anyone else in his name* has received or is entitled to receive that sum or any part of it, for reasons which are more fully set forth in *status et visus compoti* on the treasurer's remembrancer's roll for October 1437. The receipt roll totals, however, are still ignoring these cancellations, and for none of them is there any fictitious loan.

After this there is a lull for ten years, but in 1443 the cancellations start again and occur in every year to 1450. There are frequent references to the memoranda rolls as before, but from June 1443 a new note is also struck by a deliberate reference to a writ under the great seal as the cause of cancellation, while for the first time in this series the recipient of the assignment thus cancelled is credited with a fictitious loan and the failure to adjust the roll totals is by this means made good. The same thing happens twice in October 1444, but in November of the same year, on a somewhat similar occasion, the fictitious loan has disappeared again: yet the 'loan' returns with other cancellations made in February 1445. There is the same oscillation between the two techniques during the summer of that year, but from 1446 onwards the rolls seem to settle down to the new procedure, viz. cancellation because the bills or tallies have been returned and condemned (or some other variant of the formula), followed by a reference to the memoranda rolls and accompanied by evidence of a fictitious loan.

The mystery is finally solved by an entry of 2 May 1447 which states that 11 tallies of assignment, totalling £3,499 13s. 4d., in favour of Sir Roger Fenys, treasurer of the household, have been cancelled and condemned in virtue of a writ under the great seal, *because they have been paid by letters patent*, as may be seen by reference to the section called *mandata* in the memoranda rolls of Easter 33 Henry VI. This recalls the use of letters patent in this same period as a security for real loans; and it suggests that, whether out of departmental jealousy of chancery or for other reasons, the exchequer clerks were for a long time most reluctant to accept letters patent and writs under the great seal as valid financial instruments, whose use should be recorded in their rolls. It may well have been that it was only under pressure, and because the receipt roll totals were becoming meaningless with all these uncorrected cancellations, that they grudgingly agreed to accept letters patent as authority for the repayment of fictitious, as well as of genuine, loans. But they did not do this without a struggle, for genuine cancellations continue side by side with this new type of fictitious loan: thus on 25 July 1447 the new treasurer of the household, Sir John Stourton, surrendered eight tallies worth £2,055 3s. 0d. because he had from them, as the roll says, neither payment (*solucionem*) nor contentment (*contentacionem*). In this case there was no fictitious loan but the whole transaction was at last excluded from the roll totals; and the same seems to be true of ten tallies for £3,657, drawn in favour of queen Margaret but cancelled on 1 January 1449; of a single small assignment upon 18 February 1449; and of no less than 29 tallies worth £6,000 on 29 July 1449. Finally, there were two more small but genuine cancellations without fictitious loans when, firstly, on 23 January 1449, John Wode, the clerk of the pells, cancelled an assignment he had just made on himself in favour of the great wardrobe and 'restored it to the king's use'; and, secondly, when on 3 March 1450 another small cancellation was, like all the others I have mentioned, deliberately omitted from the roll totals.

After this there is nothing to report till 1462, and it may therefore be convenient to pause at this point and attempt a rough calculation of the numerical effects of this disturbing influence during the whole of Henry VI's reign. This of course can only be approximate, but for what it is worth it works out somewhat as follows:

	Value in £ s. d.	Tallies
(1) Totals uncorrected after cancellations, and without fictitious loans	996 17 3½	12
(2) Totals uncorrected after cancellations, but set right by fictitious loans	4,578 0 0	33
(3) Totals given correctly after cancellations, of which they take no account. (No fictitious loans)	11,787 0 11	49

The almost geometrical progression in the increase of these figures and the overlapping of techniques which they suggest are both extremely interesting. It should be noted that the first group is found *only* between 1432 and 1446; the second *only* between 1443 and 1448; and the third *only* between 1447 and 1450. All alike represent assignments which have somehow gone wrong, but whereas the first two groups should both have given rise to fictitious loans—and should perhaps be added to the totals which I give elsewhere under that head—the third and largest group seems to me to suggest merely optimism—a rather desperate optimism perhaps—on the part of the exchequer at a time of grave financial stringency, and to be nothing more than, so to speak, a programme of assignment, rather than assignments actually made and then repudiated. My reason for this revolutionary suggestion is the fact that on the one hand the perfectly correct totals of uncancelled entries in the roll now simply ignore the existence of these large cancellations, while on the other hand they are not really justified in doing so, as in the past, by the presence of fictitious loans to cover cancelled entries. I believe that the explanation is that the tallies were already cut and the receipt roll entries made, when someone in the exchequer pointed out that there was not the slightest chance of these assignments being cashed—or perhaps the creditors in whose favour they were made found they could not even discount them, and so flatly refused to accept them. They were therefore cancelled (being useless)—but *before*, instead of after, presentation to the officers against whom they were drawn; and this enabled the roll totals, which might not have been inserted at that stage, to be written in correctly. Had events followed their more normal course the cancellations would have come too late and the totals, instead of excluding, would have included them. An alternative explanation is, of course, that there had been real assignment but that the date at which receipt roll totals were put in suddenly became much later at this point—so much later, in fact, that when the time came at which somebody did finally decide to tot them up it was already known that these assignments had been made and failed. This explanation seems to me incredible in view of the fact that by this date the totals have long been nothing more than a hasty marginal scribble, suggesting anything but long and cautious delay and elaborate preparation, while in any case the failure of each separate tally helping to make up a large assignment was generally not known in the exchequer for a matter of months, or even years, after the event, and then only when the particular accountant against whom that particular tally had been drawn chose to come into the exchequer. If the fate of every genuine *pro* tally was to be awaited in this way before a day total could be calculated, such totals would have been too stale, when reached, to be of interest to anyone: yet since in these cases the totals are in fact correct, the only possible explanation is that the clerks knew *from the start* (or almost from the start) that certain *pro* entries were no sooner made than cancelled. Such at any rate is my belief, but in any case and whatever the true answer may be, it is pretty clear that these cancelled entries which do not appear at all in the roll totals really *were* cancelled, without reserve, and therefore should not be included in any of my own calculations.

We have now reached the Yorkist period, during which a good many tallies were still being returned and cancelled and condemned, and the entries recording them struck through, on very much the same lines as before. Such incidents are found, in fact, all the way from 1462 to 1485, but with a broad peak or plateau of maximum activity between 1466 and 1477. They seem to pass through something like the same stages of development as under Henry VI, but with one important difference, viz. that there are now no references at all to writs under the great seal as authority for cancellations, but (e.g. in 1462, 1468 and 1484) to writs of privy seal instead. Apart from this feature, the earlier Yorkist cancellations at first resemble the later Lancastrian ones in not being included in the roll totals, but this is only true of twelve entries cancelled in the roll for 1462-3. In the next roll (1463) six cancelled entries for a total of £300 are in fact included in the totals—that is, the totals are now incorrect again—and the same is true of 1465-6, which includes one such entry for £100 in one place and eight others, for the large sum of £4,487 18s. 11d., in another. These last, however, have been marked *quod gratis restituuntur*, which suggests that they were possibly *remissiones*. The roll totals might therefore seem to be excused for taking account of them, since *remissiones* were true revenue, though I feel that if these sums had really been remitted—that is, if the claim they represent against the crown had been withdrawn—they would have appeared quite frankly as *remissiones . . . sol'*. As it is, the evidence merely shows that the recipients of these *pro* tallies did not like the look of them and returned them into the exchequer: there is nothing, however, to show that they did not press their claims against the crown as hard as ever, or that they did not get satisfaction for them in a different way upon a subsequent occasion.

In November 1466 we find a rather different case, in which certain tallies of assignment were cancelled, as in Henry VI's time, because their recipient had had satisfaction of his claim elsewhere. The details are worth quoting owing to the amount of substitution involved among successive holders of these instruments of credit, for that is what the *pro* tally had quite obviously become. Thus the original assignment for £100 is made in favour of earl Rivers, but it is cancelled because William Kerver of London (into whose hands earl Rivers's tally had evidently passed, presumably at a discount) now confesses that he could get payment to that amount on certain letters patent, dated 10 September 11 Edward IV and made by various royal officials, such as Richard Fowler, the king's solicitor, Morgan Kidwelly, king's serjeant and attorney-general in all his courts of record in Wales, and various others—all *ad usum dicti Willelmi Kerver*. On the same day there is a somewhat similar cancellation of two more tallies of assignment in favour of Sir John Say, but in this case there is no substitution and Say himself figures throughout.

All these cancellations, as already stated, seem to be included in the roll totals, but in 1468 the technique begins to change again, as it had done before under Henry VI, and then assumes a shape which it retains, practically without any variation, for the rest of the Yorkist period. To begin with, in July 1468 there are two large cancellations (nine entries for £1,000 in all and fourteen for £1,833 6s. 8d.) which are made by virtue of writs of privy seal but are none the less included in the uncorrected roll totals as before. But in another cancellation of the same month, involving no less than 18 entries for the relatively small total of £388 11s. 9d., the same is only partly true: some of the 18 tallies are included in the roll totals and some are not. The August and September cancellations of this year, which again are of no great importance, tend to be included, but when the Michaelmas term, 1468–9, gets under way the practice is virtually discontinued, and from October 1468 to March 1469 there are at least 44 cancellations which are specifically marked *non in summa huius diei*, and only three small ones in November 1468 upon the old model. I have not systematically noted the money values of the new cancellations, though they are often large, because it is so definitely stated in the above note, which becomes common form, that they are true cancellations and not to be brought into any reckoning—even the misleading reckonings of the rolls. There are seventeen more of them in 1469, followed by a drop to only two or three during the next two terms, which of course were those of renewed civil war, and to none at all during the brief period of Henry's restoration in 1470–1. But in June 1471 there is an unprecedented increase to the huge total of £23,281 9s. 6d. in 58 tallies, all of which are completely ignored by the roll totals—and in the same term there are literally no fictitious loans.

What are we to make of this? Fictitious loans, it is true, do not seem to occur in connection with tallies returned to the exchequer for cancelling and condemning at any time during the Yorkist period, but they are found, though in small numbers and usually for small amounts, in association with the ordinary type of cancellation. I think myself that it is too easy an explanation to suppose that the large new cancellations under the 'returned-for-cancelling-and-condemning' formula—cancellations which, as we have seen, are now always omitted from the roll totals—merely take the place of the increasingly old-fashioned fictitious loan. I believe that on the contrary—for reasons which I have already mentioned in writing of Henry VI's reign—even the big assignments of June 1471 were really never issued; that they remained a programme or an aspiration, which was quickly recognized to be so hopeless that again no real attempt was ever made to translate them into fact. It was Edward's most difficult summer: after crushing the Lancastrian counter-revolution he had to re-establish his own power and he needed money quickly for his allies, friends and creditors. This was some of the money that he hoped to raise by means of large assignments, but it was realized by someone, as in Henry's time, that he had little chance of doing so and that to let these large drafts on non-existent funds go forward was merely to invite disillusionment with his régime. So the drafts were quietly cancelled at an early stage—so early that even the hasty scribblers of the roll totals knew that they need take no account of them. There are few remaining cancellations of this size after 1471, but there are three or four that possibly deserve some notice. Thus in March 1474 twenty-five tallies for £751 3s. 9d. in all, in favour of Edward's faithful supporters, the Italian firm of the Caniziani, were cancelled for the well-established reason that the payees were to have their satisfaction *aliter*. In December 1476, and again a year later, two tallies for £200 and ten tallies for £1,000 respectively were cancelled, and seven for £2,000 in March 1483. But the roll totals know nothing of all this, and there is only one small instance from June 1481 of a cancellation being made *after* the total (which is left uncorrected) had been reached. Generally speaking, enough accuracy had been achieved under the late Lancastrians and the Yorkists for the clerks to know at a comparatively early stage whether an assignment had any chance of being effective, or discountable, or not. If not, it was very quickly cancelled and so fictitious loans were usually unnecessary: their mechanism was still understood, but it was getting rusty and was out of date. What is unfortunate for my purpose is that from the middle 1440's onwards the new exchequer techniques tend to make my calculations much more difficult and, by spoiling their self-balancing, to make them seem a good deal more inaccurate than they are. For when we begin to get cancellations which are not cancellations, and yet remain uncorrected by fictitious loans, it becomes necessary for me to show a book-keeping total much of which is not reflected in any of the traditional fourteenth- and early fifteenth-century forms, and more particularly not in *mutua per talliam*. What is worse, I have had to use my own judgment to decide in every instance when a cancelled entry, which is none the less included in a day total, is rightly included and on what occasions it is not. With the Yorkists things are easier, since practically all their cancellations, other than the small ones where the old machinery of the fictitious loan is still employed, are excluded from their roll totals, and in my view need not therefore be brought into account. In general I have not even troubled to assess their value, though I have made a rough count of their numbers, which work out at round about two hundred entries—perhaps less rather than more. I did, of course, mention for their general interest the large figures of this sort which occur in March 1466, June 1471 (especially) and in 1474, 1476-7 and 1483, but they have none the less not been included in my calculations because they are specifically excluded from the rolls. Those I have counted are the much smaller numbers of entries (about sixty in all) which, in spite of cancellation, do seem to have been allowed for in the roll totals: they come entirely from the short period 1463-8 and on a rather rough computation their total value is perhaps £5,000. It is not a very serious matter, but possibly, before leaving the subject, I should also mention that I have noticed one freak cancellation of a tally (dated 21 January 1473) because returned and cancelled and condemned, which is actually marked *sol'*. All the rest, however, are assignments.

There are some other curious hybrids which cannot be dismissed so readily, but they are all of small importance. On 31 October 1377, for example, right at the beginning of the period, there is what looks like an ordinary *prestitum restitutum* of £100 from Sir Guy de Brienne, yet it is assigned (*pro eodem*) to Sir Guy himself and is furthermore marked *mutuum* in the margin. Ten and a half years later there are several such entries on a single day (2 March 1388), but they are no longer marked *mutuum* though still *pro eodem*. The difference (if there is a difference) may lie in the fact that in the second batch of entries it was merely found convenient to pay off certain creditors or servants of the crown by cancelling sums which these persons themselves owed, no doubt in some quite different connection, to the exchequer. In the case of Sir Guy de Brienne, on the other hand, it may perhaps be assumed that more was owing to him on the crown's part than he owed to the crown, and that he was being credited with a 'loan' for the difference: however, as the entry is unique, it is also possible that the word *mutuum* in the left-hand margin is just a clerical error. In any case these are all clearly book-keeping transactions in which no cash passed, but that was certainly not true of all *prestita restituta*, for one entry of the sort in 1433 is labelled *denar' restit'*, which implies that actual money (*denarii*) was repaid into the receipt. This may also be true of an entry made on 22 November

1437 crediting an ambassador to Arras with an in-payment of £20 *de remanencia compoti sui*: it is true that this is not specifically described as a *prestitum restitutum*, but all the same it seems to be a perfect example of one. Finally, there is an unusual entry of somewhat the same kind on 25 February 1434, when Hamo Sutton, mayor of the Calais staple, William Estfeld and other merchants of the same staple, return into the receipt £107 8s. 2d. from excess money accruing to them out of divers assignments which they had received in repayment of loans made to the crown. Here there is a special marginal note to the effect that part of this repayment took the form of the return of two actual tallies of assignment, one for £68 6s. 2d., levied on 1 June 9 Henry VI, and the other of £4 5s. 8d., levied on 20 June of the same year. It may be assumed that the balance of the £107 8s. 2d. was repaid in cash, since the care taken to avoid any appearance of usury is remarkable: on the other hand it is quite probable that, as usual, the exchequer had never actually received more than some seventy-five per cent of the face-value of the original loan which had just been overpaid. Be that as it may, the merchants of the staple were clearly very anxious to avoid the *appearance* of usury by way of overpayment.

This leaves for consideration only the small group of voluntary payments to the crown, beginning with *remissiones*. These, of course, one would normally expect to be *sol'*, and the fact that, as with genuine loans, 'bills' and *prestita restituta*, the treasurer's dot was withheld from *remissiones*, shows that no tallies as a rule were given for them. There are, however, numerous exceptions in this case; for example, in 1379 and 1381–2 certain *remissiones* have been assigned, but only back to the 'remitter', who, in the second of the two instances quoted, happened to be William de Windsor, then captain of Cherbourg. As far as I can see this simply means that the exchequer took the initiative in cancelling an obligation to the crown instead of the 'remitter' doing so; in de Windsor's case he was receiving a very large assignment for the defence of his fortress, only a small part of which took the peculiar form of 'remitting' an obligation in which he was already bound to the crown. Not unlike these two are the entries in a small group coming from about the same period (1382, 1385, 1387–8, 1388) in which tallies of assignment have been cancelled, presumably as worthless, but have then been labelled *remissiones* from the persons in whose favour they had originally been drawn. This, however, is a rather more normal

33

type, in that the initiative clearly came not from the exchequer but from the recipient of the worthless tallies, who, rather than pursue them any further, had obviously agreed to write them off and make a free gift of his claim against the crown. This may seem a little strange, but the amounts were seldom very large: indeed the total for all forms of *remissiones* for the entire period 1377–1485 is only £2,371, of which £1,178 in all, or almost exactly half, is *pro* (usually *pro eodem*) and the rest *sol'*. These figures may be compared with a total of £15,736 in free gifts (*dona*) over the same period, only £53 6s. 8d. of which is marked *pro*, the whole of the rest being *sol'*. Benevolences, it may be noted, hardly found their way at all on to the receipt rolls, at any rate under that name, and then only in minute quantities: I have noticed a few very small ones in 1478 and 1482, but their grand total is no more than £17 14s., which affords a ludicrously inadequate explanation of the outcry these exactions caused. It must therefore be assumed that the great bulk of them appeared in some disguised form which cannot now be traced or else were not entered at all: it seems improbable that there was any tally given for them.

This completes the enumeration of what might be called the 'technical hitches' and difficulties in the procedure which I have devised for dealing with the receipt rolls. If the various gaps and uncertainties seem at times unduly large I can only reply that, considering the length of the whole period covered by the investigation and the infinitely larger sums and numbers of entries about which there is little or no doubt, I see small cause for alarm. As I have already said before, anything even remotely approaching a hundred per cent accuracy in this kind of statistical impressionism is utterly impossible in any case, and I make no claim to have established anything more than what it is now the fashion to describe as 'secular trends'. These at any rate stand out extremely clearly, as will be seen from the tables and, especially, the graphs at the end of this book.

Secular trends, however, while of interest in surveying the whole field, are of smaller use for close analysis. For this purpose I have had to break up the period into manageable sections, whose size has been dictated partly by the facts and landmarks of political history and partly by the distribution of surviving evidence in my particular field. In the end the most suitable unit to adopt seemed to be the decade, with its ideal complement of 20 rolls. This means two units for Richard II's reign, conveniently divided at the close of the appellant revolution (April 1389), and represented by 22¼ and 21 surviving rolls respectively. Henry IV's reign is longer, but its 13½ years can be treated as a decade from the point of view of the receipt rolls owing to the large gaps in his series—gaps so substantial that the surviving weight of evidence does not in fact amount to more than 21 rolls, together with four fragments, mostly small. Much the same is true of the longish period from 1462–75 (21 surviving rolls at most, some of them mutilated); while all but one of the remaining sections are in fact exact decades, each with 20, or at the worst 19, rolls. The solitary exception is Henry V's reign of only 9½ years, but in his case not a single term is unrepresented by at least one complete roll in really good condition, so that his 19 rolls compare favourably with the total weight of evidence to be found in any other section. All in all I have therefore been content to divide my 108 years into not more than ten sections, each of which is approximately equipollent with the others as far as the surviving weight of evidence from the receipt rolls is concerned.

Having established this division into 'decades' or near-decades my next task was to analyse them. I decided to adopt the comparative method (using gross totals from each section in their various breakdowns for the purpose), but since it would have been very unwieldy, and indeed almost impossible, to compare all ten at once I determined to divide my sections into four groups of three, two, two and three 'decades' respectively. This enabled me to begin by comparing my findings for the first half of Richard II's reign with those for the second half and for the reign of Henry IV, and incidentally to estimate in this way the financial causes and effects of the revolution of 1399. After this I proceeded to compare Henry V's reign with the period of conciliar government during the early minority of Henry VI. This was followed by a comparison of the later minority and coming of age with the decade of Henry's marriage and attempts at personal government—stopping well short, however, of the outbreak of actual civil war in 1455. Finally I compared Henry's last ten years, during most of which there was a good deal of fighting and disturbance, with the somewhat similarly disturbed first part of Edward IV's reign, and then both of them with the final phase of established Yorkist government.

Since that is my arrangement for analysis, it has also had to be my arrangement for what I call the calendar of, or running commentary on, the rolls, which I have thought it desirable to prefix to each of my analyses. These 'calendars' will not be found easy reading and are really meant only for reference on the part of any student interested in some particular term or year falling within the periods covered by them: the analyses, on the other hand, form chapters of continuous argument which will, I hope, be of a more general interest.

I begin then with the 'calendar' preceding my first analysis, viz. that for 1377 to 1413.

CHAPTER II

CALENDAR, 1377–1413

EASTER 1377 (quarter-term):		£	s.	d.	%
	Cash	14,227	16	6	93
	Assigned	649	5	1	4
	Book-keeping	492	8	4	3
	Total	15,369	9	11	100

The largest single *sol'* was a sum of £5,766 13s. 4d., contributed by the London wool customs on 26 August. Other substantial payments included one of £2,626 8s. 4d. from the property of Alice Perrers, made on 13 July, although her existing banishment was not followed by a formal sentence of forfeiture until the following December.[1] There was also a belated payment of £1,019 13s. 4d. on account of the ransom of David II, king of Scots, who had died in 1371:[2] in this, as in other respects, it is obvious that this fragment of a roll really belongs financially to the previous reign. However, when Richard II became king on 22 June the Easter term was, very exceptionally, broken into two rolls, the second of which runs from 29 June to 26 August: there are no entries between 22 and 29 June.

MICHAELMAS 1377–8:		£	s.	d.	%
	Cash	127,541	1	7	77
	Assigned	28,528	12	0	17
	Book-keeping	9,265	6	8	6
	Total	165,335	0	3	100

---

[1] Ramsey, *Genesis*, II, 114; quoting *Rot. Parl.*, III, 12-14; Walsingham, *Hist. Anglic.*, I, 343. This payment is not actually marked *sol'*, but there is no evidence that it was assigned and in the circumstances it is particularly unlikely to have been so.

[2] The ransom had been negotiated as far back as 1357: see Ramsay, *Genesis*, I, 422. Its terms had been modified in 1364–5 (ibid., 457) and in 1369 (ibid., 457, 495). In his *Revenues* (II, 287) Ramsay calculates that by the end of 1376 £52,666 13s. 4d. had been paid towards the £66,666 13s. 4d. assessed in 1357. See *Genesis*, II, 130 n., for the final settlement in February 1379.

Very heavy cash payments were made, especially during February 1378. They came predominantly from the double fifteenth and tenth granted by the parliament of October 1377, and from the double tenths granted by the two convocations a few weeks later. In March the wool customs, notably of London and to some extent Southampton, were also contributing heavily. But the London customs were quite as freely used for assignments, e.g. in favour of the household and the garrison of Calais (£3,000 on 25 November 1377). They were also employed on 9 March 1378 to repay a loan of £5,000 advanced by the mayor and citizens of London on 10 October 1377. This was the only large loan raised.

		£	s.	d.	%
EASTER 1378:	Cash	33,779	17	11	73
	Assigned	9,961	11	1½	21
	Book-keeping	2,736	11	1	6
	Total	46,478	0	1½	100

Cash payments remained large and were drawn mainly from the still outstanding clerical subsidies, though the wool customs also accounted for a good deal, e.g. over £4,000 on 3 June from London alone, with a further £1,365 on the 15th. Boston, Lynn and Hull customs on the other hand were heavily assigned, generally in favour of the household. No large loans were raised, unless the curious *mutuum per talliam* of 25 September for £2,166 13s. 4d., in the names of Nicholas Brembre and John Philpot, can be so described.[1] But although this *mutuum* is marked *sol'*, as if it were genuine, it follows the common form of the fictitious loan in all other respects and the unique—and apparently nonsensical—*sol'* attached to it may be only a clerical error. Two days later (27 September) there was an abnormal windfall for the receipt of just under £4,000 in cash from the sale of jewels belonging to the young king. This payment was made by the hands of John Bacon, king's chamberlain in the exchequer and keeper of the king's jewels and plate; he used the proceeds to pay off sundry royal creditors forthwith, as appears from the issue roll of the same day, to which there is a reference in the receipt roll.

[1] This entry has already been discussed above, p. 21.

		£	s.	d.	%
MICHAELMAS 1378–9:	Cash	40,111	3	4	61
	Assigned	15,086	18	3½	23
	Book-keeping	10,743	12	6	16
	Total	65,941	14	1½	100

The only important cash payment in the ordinary receipt roll was one of £1,000 from the London wool customs (17 March 1379), but the special receivers, Walworth and Philpot, drew heavily in cash, not only from the same source but also from the wool customs of Boston, Hull and, in one instance, Chichester. Assignments were on the light side until 25 January 1379, when several were made on royal lands and tenements in Wales, while on 5 April miscellaneous royal farms were assigned up to a total of £2,606 13s. 4d. in favour of the household. The special receiver's roll on the contrary shows only one day of heavy assignment (11 December 1378)—in this case mainly on the London wool customs, in favour of various beneficiaries. Two-thirds of the book-keeping entries are accounted for by the 'repayment' of large prests—one of over £4,500, made on 11 September 1377 to John Hermesthorp[1] and associated clerks, and the other of approximately £2,100 to the king's clerk William de Lokyngton (7 October 1377).[2] There are indications that both these advances had been made for sailors' wages—the second certainly so. Loans were unimportant in the ordinary receipt roll, but the special receivers raised £3,715 in continuous daily borrowing between 19 February and 7 April 1379. This sum was made up of 114 small loans—none larger than £100 —made by all monied classes in the community. They represent the first instalment of the loans authorized by the great council on 7 February 1379.[3]

		£	s.	d.	%
EASTER 1379:	Cash	43,501	3	10	59
	Assigned	13,429	9	3	18
	Book-keeping	16,421	9	2	23
	Total	73,352	2	6	100

[1] Beauchamp chamberlain of the exchequer.
[2] For these *prestita restituta* see above, pp. xxxviii–xxxix, and also the detailed commentary in the present chapter under 1379–80, 1380 and (especially) 1381.   [3] Ramsay, *Genesis*, II, 129.

Nearly nine-tenths of the cash payments came from the special receipts of Walworth and Philpot. These were drawn at first from the wool-customs of London, Hull and Boston, but in August (especially) and September large sums appear from the collectors of the poll-tax voted in the April parliament.[1] There was moreover a windfall of about £4,000 in cash, paid on 23 September, from the £15,000 ransom of the count of Saint-Pol. Assignments from the ordinary revenue were levied to a limited extent on the wool and wine customs (14 May—slightly over £1,000), but easily the largest item came from further sales of the king's jewels by John Bacon (25 September—£4,042 1s. 10d. in two tallies). As usual, there was little assignment of the special receipts, except for the Saint-Pol ransom, which carried two assignments totalling a further £5,000 from this source (16 August) in favour of Sir Thomas de Felton.[2] Book-keeping entries consisted almost entirely of the loans still being raised by Walworth and Philpot. There were only thirty-four of them in this term, counting a small one in the first or ordinary part of the roll, but the total yield jumped to £13,229 2s. 2d. This was caused by a £5,000 corporate loan made by London on 28 April, followed by two other large loans on 23 September—one from Sir Robert Knolles (£2,703) and one of £4,185 10s. 8d. from John Sandes and Richard Craddok, esquires of the chamber. It is to be noted, however, that the odd £703 of Knolles' nominal loan was immediately assigned back to him—though 'for war expenses' it is true—so that he did not actually advance more than £2,000 in cash while being repaid £2,703.[3] The whole of the other large loan made on the same day was similarly assigned back to the lenders, Sandes and Craddok, who were probably mere agents of the chamber, which may have been temporarily providing funds out of its own resources for purposes normally financed by the exchequer: in any case there is a note, which the issue roll confirms, that this loan was repaid early in the next term. The book-keeping total is, however, further swollen by the 'repayment' on 7 May of a prest of £2,366 13s. 4d. advanced to the well-known soldier, Sir Hugh Calverley, *super certis secretis*

[1] Ramsay, *Genesis*, II, 130.

[2] Seneschal of Aquitaine and justice of Chester; *Cal. Pat. Rolls*, 1377–81.

[3] This entry is discussed in greater detail in connection with the problem of interest or inducement, above, p. 18.

negotiis regis on 12 June 1378, when he was captain of Calais.[1] Finally, this is the first term of the reign in which the 'remission' of a claim against the crown has been noted (7 May). Such *remissiones* were indifferently in cash or assigned, as has been seen in the previous chapter, but when assigned they were usually assigned back to the 'remitter' (in this case the keeper of a royal manor) as here. The transaction can be regarded as a windfall for the crown, even though no cash passes: on this occasion, however, the amount was only £17 19s. 4d.

		£	s.	d.	%
MICHAELMAS 1379–80:	Cash	17,180	8	7½	21
	Assigned	54,410	4	3½	65
	Book-keeping	11,317	19	9	14
	Total	82,908	12	8	100

The only sizeable cash payments were one of £1,000 from the London wool customs (26 January 1380) and another, in the special receipts, of over £2,000, mainly from the Boston customs (19 February). Assignments on the ordinary receipts included one of £3,450 for the household, levied on hereditary revenues of the crown (15 October 1379); nearly £3,000, again for the household, on the London wool customs (23 January 1380); just over £2,000 for the great wardrobe, on a variety of sources (24 January 1380); and a further £1,160 for the household (27 January), mainly on the Hull and London customs. In the special receipts for the war, John, lord Neville de Raby, received assignments on the Hull and Boston customs for £2,000 (12 October 1379) and Sir John Harleston, captain of Cherbourg, others for £2,850 made upon a large number of ports (24 October). All these were dwarfed, however, by five assignments totalling £10,000 on the customs of London, Hull and Boston in favour of the treasurer of Calais (10 November 1379). The keepers of Berwick and Brest were financed in the same way to the much smaller total of £1,500 between them (26 November) and Brest again on 23 February 1380; while on 10 December 1379 other numerous assignments were made, totalling £5,562 11s. 2d., to several crown creditors, mainly from the

---

[1] *Genesis*, II, 115. There may well be a connection with Calverley's raid on Boulogne later in the year; in which case the money was probably spent on wages of war.

customs revenue of various ports. On 6 February 1380 the treasurer of Calais received a further £5,000 on the same wool customs as before, and on 5 March 1380 about half the last London loan was repaid from the customs of the same city. On 8 March 1380 lord Neville de Raby again received some £3,000 worth of assignments, mainly on various ports, while finally on 17 March the earl of Northumberland received assignments of the order of £2,000 on the proceeds of the poll-tax, which were not normally assigned to this extent—at any rate in the south of England. The book-keeping total is largely accounted for by the 'repayment' on 23 March 1380 of nearly £9,000, advanced in eight prests to Lokyngton at various dates during the previous two years, for the payment of wages of war to men-at-arms, archers and sailors. The only other large item is provided by the first sizeable fictitious loan of the reign, viz. one of £1,000 from among the sums assigned to lord Neville de Raby on 8 March (above): this particular assignment was levied on the Boston customs, which should normally have been good for that amount.

		£	s.	d.	%
EASTER 1380:	Cash	81,958	15	6	47
	Assigned	32,051	13	5½	19
	Book-keeping	59,001	18	4	34
	Total	173,012	7	3½	100

The only large cash item in the ordinary revenue was a further payment on 12 September of £2,835 10s. 9½d. produced by yet a third sale of jewels belonging to the king. John Bacon was still the agent and the proceeds were immediately used, as in September 1378, to satisfy some of the more pressing crown creditors. On the other hand the special receipts for the war, which exceeded the ordinary revenue in this term by over £157,000, showed a steady influx of cash payments, at first from the London and Southampton wool customs but later (on and after 12 April) from the yield of the one and a half subsidies granted by the January parliament.[1] By 12 May clerical tenths appear alongside the lay contributions and predominate from 28 June. Large assignments were comparatively rare in both sections of the roll, but there was one of

---

[1] *Genesis*, II, 133. The clergy granted only one-tenth, and that a little later.

rather under £3,000 for the household on the hereditary revenues (16 April), and another of £1,000 for Calais from the London wool customs (in the special receipts, 5 May). This was followed on 26 July by an additional £4,000 for Calais, drawn on Boston, Southampton and Hull, as well as on London. Meanwhile on 23 June a further £4,500 had been raised from the same ports (except Southampton) to help finance the great Brittany expedition,[1] while on 26 July not only Calais, as already stated, but Cherbourg, too, received assignments totalling another £2,333 6s. 8d. from the same ports, Southampton now included. Towards the end of the term (8 September) the duke of Lancaster, the archbishop of York and the earl of Warwick shared still more assignments of £1,353 in all, drawn mainly against the clerical subsidy, which was not often assigned to this extent. The heavy book-keeping totals nearly all come from the end of the special receipts, starting on 26 July with £1,000 in six fictitious loans from the earl of March. Heavy borrowing of a more genuine order begins with three loans on 7 September, including £2,000 from London and £1,000 from Philpot. Three days later Thomas, earl of Buckingham, William lord Latimer, Ralph de Basset and others 'lent' no less than £14,480 3s. 10d., but this was on account of their war service in Brittany and, as I have explained in the next chapter, should really have been entered as a *prestitum restitutum* by the hands of John Hermesthorp. On 12 September Hermesthorp also 'repaid' other recent prests amounting to some £9,000, and another exchequer clerk, Thomas Restwold, various others reaching £7,000; while on the 13th John Lincoln[2] contributed well over £20,500 on account of 27 large prests for sailors' wages. Other clerks of less importance 'repaid' another £2,000 or so between them, with the result that the receipt roll total was inflated by nearly £39,000 under this one heading. This was money whose original receipt must have already been recorded upon earlier rolls, and its reappearance here probably means nothing more than that certain paymasters of the forces had been cleared of liability for the large sums they had been handling in the king's name.[3]

---

[1] Ibid., 135.

[2] Clerk of the king's ships, *Cal. Pat. Rolls*, 1377–81.

[3] For these *prestita restituta* see above, pp. xxxviii–xxxix, and also the detailed commentary in the present chapter under 1378–9, 1379–80 and (especially) 1381.

MICHAELMAS 1380–1: No surviving roll.

		£	s.	d.	%
EASTER 1381:	Cash	28,965	4	2½	47
	Assigned	17,298	12	7½	28
	Book-keeping	15,712	13	5	25
	Total	61,976	10	3	100

Since the mob failed to break into the exchequer[1] it is unlikely that the disappearance of all rolls for 1380–1 can be connected with the peasants' revolt. However that may be, the proceeds of the famous poll-tax granted by parliament and the convocations in November 1380 were still flowing strongly in the last week of April 1381, when in seven working days some £17,000, mainly from this source, was paid in cash into the exchequer. After this there was a steep fall in cash receipts until on 23 September a further £3,600 or so was raised by Bacon on the crown jewels, as before. Assignment was relatively light until 13 May, when the household received some £3,000 by this means out of the hereditary revenues: a further £1,000 went to Alan Stokes, keeper of the great wardrobe, from the same source on the 20th. On the 31st £1,000 out of the London poll-tax was assigned towards the repayment of the last London loan, while towards the end of the term (30 July and 19 August respectively) first Cherbourg and then Brest received about £2,000 worth each of tallies on the leading wool ports. As regards book-keeping entries, John Philpot lent £800 on 13 May and the Lombard, Matthew Cheyne, £2,666 13s. 4d. on the 31st,[2] but the largest items were again not loans but 'repayments' to the crown of balances created for wages of war—that is, for seamen, men-at-arms and archers—more especially in connection with the earl of Cambridge's expedition to Portugal in May 1381.[3] This alone accounted for nearly £7,000 under the head of prests, 'repaid' by the hands of 'Robert'[4] Grill on 2 August, while on the same day Lokyngton accounted for a further £1,770 on account

[1] Tout, *Chapters in Administrative History*, III, 370.

[2] Much of this was assigned back to the lender in lieu of interest. This is one of the key loans in the discussion of the subject: see above, p. 18.

[3] *Genesis*, II, 140.

[4] Probably Reginald Grill, the well-known Genoese merchant, is intended.

of seamen's wages. What seems to have happened in such cases was that the money, when originally collected, was issued to certain king's clerks as paymasters, and these became personally responsible for it. In due course, however, evidence would be produced by them at the exchequer that the expected payments of wages had actually taken place, whereupon they would be cleared of liability and the receipt roll would note that the 'prest', or sum advanced, had been 'restored'. This of course only referred to the paymasters' accounts, not to any repayment of actual cash into the exchequer, although it was not by any means impossible that a small cash balance might be used in squaring them.[1] On the other hand the ten *remissiones* of the term, totalling some £725, represented the abandonment of real claims against the crown and so were genuine windfalls for the revenue.

		£	s.	d.	%
MICHAELMAS 1381–2:	Cash	7,137	13	6½	11
	Assigned	47,501	2	7½	76
	Book-keeping	7,857	10	7½	13
	Total	62,496	6	9½	100

For the first time in this reign there are no sizeable cash payments at any point during the term. Assignment dominates the situation from 10 October 1381 (some £1,000 for Sir John Harleston on the wool custom of four ports) to 25 March 1382 (about the same amount each, from much the same sources, for the earl of Northumberland and lord Neville as keepers of the marches). Towards the end of October upwards of £5,000 was assigned to the household out of general revenue, while on the last day of the month Calais received tallies for no less than £14,000, mainly on London, but also on Boston and Hull. The great wardrobe, which had had tallies for about £2,000 out of general revenue on the same date, was given at least as much again on 13 March 1382 by the hands of its clerk or keeper, Alan Stokes, while on 14 March Cherbourg got over £3,000, drawn upon three wool ports. This was followed on the 24th by a slightly smaller sum for Brest, distributed between the wool customs of six ports. Book-keeping totals on the other

---

[1] See the whole discussion of *prestita restituta* in the introduction above, pp. xxxviii–xxxix, and also the detailed commentary in the present 'calendar' under 1378–9, 1379–80 and 1380.

hand were inconsiderable, with the exception of four loans totalling £5,333 6s. 8d. upon a single day (25 March)—of these, easily the largest was a further £2,000 from the Lombard, Matthew Cheyne.

EASTER 1382:		£	s.	d.	%
	Cash	7,094	3	10	25
	Assigned	14,948	18	7	53
	Book-keeping	6,082	0	5	22
	Total	28,125	2	10	100

The only large item in the cash account came from the now almost annual selling or pledging of crown jewels by John Bacon on 24 September (£2,913 10s.), while the only outstanding assignments were one for the repayment of £1,000 to London out of London's own wool-customs (20 June) and another totalling very little more, from general revenue, in favour of Alan Stokes and the great wardrobe. Book-keeping is more than half accounted for by two large loans—one of £1,333 6s. 8d. from Nicholas Brembre (23 August) and another of £2,200 (23 September) from the indefatigable Cheyne: the rest of it is also mainly borrowing from a variety of lenders, but on a much smaller scale.

MICHAELMAS 1382–3:		£	s.	d.	%
	Cash	39,230	17	2½	45
	Assigned	45,808	6	3	53
	Book-keeping	2,147	17	7	2
	Total	87,187	1	0½	100

The relatively large cash payment came principally from the lay subsidy granted in October by the third parliament of 1382:[1] the proceeds of this subsidy were flowing strongly into the exchequer from 20 January to 23 February 1383. The still larger total of assignment is accounted for, first and foremost, by a sum of nearly £20,000 drawn on 23 October in only five tallies on the London and Boston wool customs in favour of the treasurer of Calais. This was followed on 18 November by a further £1,000 for the same

---

[1] Ramsay, *Genesis*, II, 188. The clerical half-tenths voted by the two convocations in November and December seem to have come in more slowly.

purpose, drawn on London. On 8 December the same two wool ports, together with Hull and Southampton and with some further assistance from the issues of the hanaper,[1] provided over £5,000 for William de Windsor,[2] while on 19 February upwards of £2,500 from five wool ports went to Robert Knolles. On the 26th Thomas Percy and Alan Stokes shared another £1,000, found mainly by the wool customs, with some support from general revenue. Book-keeping entries throughout the term were obviously insignificant.

EASTER 1383:		£	s.	d.	%
	Cash	16,412	6	4	39
	Assigned	19,927	3	10	48
	Book-keeping	5,553	12	0	13
	Total	41,893	2	2	100

Although the cash percentage is fairly high there are no particularly large entries for any single day: there is merely a steady flow of rather small cash payments from the belated clerical half-tenths and from ordinary revenue. A few assignments are worth noting —two of about £1,000 each (7 April and 1 June) on five wool ports in favour of the household; another of about £1,500 (20 May) from the same source in favour of lord de la Sparre;[3] one of about £1,500 (8 July) and another of £1,000 (29 July) both drawn for William de Windsor, who is still at Cherbourg, on the customs of Southampton; and a final £1,000 (27 August) taken from the clerical subsidy for the bishop of Norwich's ill-starred 'crusade' to Flanders.[4] There were also numerous other assignments for considerably smaller sums, but book-keeping provides nothing of any interest in this term, except a loan of £2,666 13s. 4d. from London on 26 September.

MICHAELMAS 1383–4:		£	s.	d.	%
	Cash	25,681	9	7½	30
	Assigned	47,111	13	1	56
	Book-keeping	12,227	7	3	14
	Total	85,020	9	11½	100

[1] I.e., profits of the great seal.
[2] Captain, or keeper, of Cherbourg at this date.
[3] One of the lesser-known titles of the earl of Huntingdon.
[4] For this episode see my *Richard II*, 101–2.

Cash payments were again well maintained, but present nothing out of the ordinary until the end of January 1384, when the proceeds of the half-subsidy voted in the parliament of October 1383[1] begin to figure noticeably in the rolls: the clerical subsidy granted in December is not similarly conspicuous before 1 March. On 9 January the credit side of the bishop of Norwich's operations is illustrated by in-payments of about £1,000 in cash from the sale of goods captured from the enemy. The wool customs again bear most of the assignments, such as one of well over £1,000 for Thomas de la Peye[2] (19 October); another of nearly £3,000 (16 December) for William le Scrope, seneschal of Gascony; another £3,000 divided between William de Windsor and the king's butler (8 January 1384) and about £1,000 worth of small loan repayments (5 March) based entirely on the customs revenue of Chichester. But £2,000 out of a large assignment of some £14,000 (20 November) for the treasurer of Calais merely took the form of writing off that officer's exchequer liabilities to an equivalent extent (*de remanencia compoti sui*), and on 19 December something over £4,000 for half a dozen leading creditors of the crown was assigned on the lay subsidy as well as on the wool customs. Book-keeping mainly took the form of loans, mostly made during the second half of December and in early January: on 30 March, however, there was another large one of £2,645 from Matthew Cheyne (of which £645 was immediately assigned back to him).[3] Among other lenders, Knolles and Philpot, who joined together to advance £1,000 on 16 December 1383, and Andrew Michell with other Lombards, who lent £1,166 4s. on the same date, were particularly prominent. There were more fictitious loans than had been customary hitherto during this reign, but none was of any individual importance.

		£	s.	d.	%
EASTER 1384:	Cash	8,456	19	5½	13
	Assigned	35,157	10	3½	55
	Book-keeping	20,707	0	6½	32
	Total	64,321	10	3½	100

[1] *Genesis*, II, 208. The Canterbury convocation granted a half-tenth in December; ibid., n.

[2] Possibly identical with Thomas Peytevyn, knight of the chamber, 1383–90: Tout, *Chapters*, IV, 346.

[3] See the discussion of these loans in the preceding chapter, pp. 18–20 above.

Cash is almost negligible, in spite of the fact that by the beginning of July the lay and clerical subsidies granted by the Salisbury parliament and by the two convocations during the spring and early summer were being mobilized: the fact is that, for the first time in the reign, they were being used largely for assignments. These begin with £1,000 for Alan Stokes, keeper of the great wardrobe, on 5 May (from general revenues), and another £1,000 for William de Windsor from four wool ports (7 May). On 23 June Calais received £5,500 by this means from the customs of Boston, Hull and London, but on 5 July it was the lay subsidy which provided security for the repayment of £2,666 13s. 4d. recently advanced by the Bardi, and the customs actually played a dwindling part in other miscellaneous assignments of the 12th. So, too, when the Bardi received a further £1,000 in assignments on 6 August and the earl of Northumberland £4,047 on the same date, it was the lay subsidies which principally contributed to the cost, together with general revenues. Lay subsidies and the London wool customs between them were charged with £2,645 for Matthew Cheyne on 13 August, but on 1 September it was the clerical tenths which assisted the lay fifteenths and tenths in financing further large payments of the same order to Cheyne. Book-keeping entries, too, are of some interest during this term, for about half the large total of £20,707 is accounted for by heavy new borrowing from the Bardi (£2,666 13s. 4d. on 15 August); and from many other smaller lenders. Moreover, as noted in the previous chapter, a semi-concealed form of interest can be detected, at least in several of the larger transactions. The remainder of the book-keeping total is almost wholly accounted for by the clearance of several prests, totalling nearly £9,900, made to John Hermesthorp, Beauchamp chamberlain of the exchequer, in connection with the king's current expedition to Scotland.

		£	s.	d.	%
MICHAELMAS 1384–5:	Cash	15,990	3	3	18
	Assigned	53,569	1	5½	61
	Book-keeping	18,991	16	10½	21
	Total	88,551	1	7	100

Cash entries are fairly heavy again (e.g. on 19 October) until after the middle of November and come largely from the remnants of

49

the half-subsidy granted in the Salisbury parliament. There was only one important windfall at a later date, namely £900 on 15 December from the farm of the lands and tenements of the late earl of March: the heir, Roger, was a minor. Assignments open, as usual, with £1,333 6s. 8d. for the household (8 October) secured on general revenue; this is followed on the 18th by £1,000 for the earl of Arundel from the issues of the late earl of March, as aforesaid. On 9 November Calais received £4,709, principally from the wool customs of five ports; on 15 December Cherbourg was assigned £1,000 on the Southampton wool customs; and on the 20th the earl of Northumberland received tallies for about £2,000, mainly on the clerical subsidy. On the same day £993 was assigned to the king personally *per signetam* (an extremely rare—I think unique—entry) from the forfeitures of John of Northampton,[1] while only two days later the household was refreshed with a further £2,200 (of which the queen got £100) mostly from the wool customs of as many as seven different ports. All through the first three months of 1385 assignments continued at an exceptionally high level: thus on 21 January John lord Neville got over £2,700 in effective tallies (a further £333 6s. 8d. was, however, uncashable) from both lay and clerical subsidies and from the wool customs: this was in his capacity as keeper of Carlisle and of the west march towards Scotland. Two days later William le Scrope, still seneschal of Gascony, got tallies, mainly on the wool ports, for £3,110, and was disappointed in a further £369. The chamber was allotted £1,000 from the London wool customs on 31 January, while a final burst of activity in March saw large assignments, mainly from the lay subsidies and totalling some £1,500, in roughly equal shares for the keeper of Roxburgh castle and the lieutenant of Ireland. There was a general repayment of loans on the 13th and 16th to a total of nearly £6,000, secured on the lay subsidy and the customs, and there were various assignments adding up to over £3,646 on the 18th. Most of this was accounted for by a payment of £3,425 to Simon de Burgh, treasurer of Calais, *pro diversis actualibus*—towards this sum the lay subsidy contributed £2,305 and the London wool customs £826 odd: the rest came from the Sandwich customs, with a little from the clerical subsidy. It is obvious from these figures that the extra

---

[1] For the career of this contentious citizen of London see Tout, *Chapters*, III, 391, 393, and other references in his index (vol. VI).

half-subsidy conditionally promised by the April parliament and confirmed in November 1384[1] was now beginning to come in. The high book-keeping total of just under £19,000 was caused partly by the financial transactions of the earl of Northumberland: thus on 30 December he was cleared of five recent prests for the Scottish expedition, amounting to just under £7,951, and on 18 January 1385 he was credited with a fictitious loan on two bad tallies for £1,000. Most of the remaining £10,000, however, took the form of genuine loans, and of these many were openly subjected to a heavy discount in lieu of interest, notably those provided by Walter Bardi (now described as master of the king's mint in the tower of London), and the Lombards Antony Bache and Arnald Martyn,[2] while on 13 March there were again fictitious loans.

		£	s.	d.	%
EASTER 1385:	Cash	33,475	15	1	35
	Assigned	37,341	19	11	39
	Book-keeping	24,114	19	11	26
	Total	94,932	14	11	100

Over three-quarters of the cash received came in during the second half of April from the extra half-subsidy conditionally promised by the Salisbury parliament and confirmed by the November parliament of 1384. The assignment of about £1,000 on general revenue now regularly made to the household early in the term appears on 18 April, and the Calais assignment, nominally £5,000, of which £400 could not be collected, on the 22nd. The great wardrobe received its quota of £1,000 from general revenue on the 29th, and the earl of Northumberland £1,000—levied from the clerical subsidy—on 2 May. On 14 June there was an attempt to allot a further £2,000 to his son (Hotspur) as keeper of Berwick and the east march, but £1,012 of this, assigned upon the wool customs, could not be cashed, though the household successfully cleared a similar assignment made on the following day. On 27 June the treasurer of Calais collected about £3,600 out of a £5,000 assignment on the Hull and Boston customs, but Cherbourg, now

---

[1] Ramsay, *Genesis*, II, 215–6.
[2] See the detailed discussion of these loans in the preceding chapter, pp. 18–20 above.

in the hands of Thomas, earl of Kent, was left £100 short of the £1,000 assigned to it from the same general sources on 11 July. Four-fifths of a new £5,000 loan from London was 'repaid' in tallies on the London customs dated 3 July, but £1,071 odd of this could not be collected, even by the Londoners themselves. Antony Bache, on the other hand, had a loan of £2,666 13s. 4d. repaid in full, partly from the customs but also from the clerical subsidy (13 July), and Robert Knolles all but £393 out of £2,000 (14 July). Finally, on 20 September, Matthew Cheyne received assignments on the Southampton wool customs for the full amount of a new £2,200 loan (mentioned below) made just a month earlier, although only £1,600 had actually been paid in by him.[1] Apart from three or four days of heavy borrowing, the book-keeping total was considerably swelled for the first time in this reign (it had been common enough under Edward III) by the incidence of a really large number of bad tallies and the fictitious loans resulting from them. Several of these have been referred to already, but ten tallies totalling £1,173 10s. 8d., cut for John lord Bourchier on 15 July, should now be added to the list. In addition to all this there was at least one large prest of £2,000, made on 8 July for reasons unspecified to Durant and Howelot, tellers of the receipt, and cleared (restitutum) on 20 September. There were also one or two small dona, but these of course represented genuine, if abnormal, revenue.

		£	s.	d.	%
MICHAELMAS 1385–6:	Cash	35,125	17	11½	28
	Assigned	57,643	17	10	45
	Book-keeping	34,223	4	11½	27
	Total	126,993	0	9	100

The rise in real income to nearly £93,000 is largely accounted for by the subsidy and a half granted in the October parliament of 1385—'the money to be received by commissioners named by themselves', i.e. by parliament.[2] In accordance with this stipulation Hermesthorp acted as special receiver of fifteenths and tenths from 11 to 15 December 1385, and John Haddele and Nicholas Exton

---

[1] See my previous analysis and discussion, *Richard II*, 101–2. Note that this latest loan of Bache's, referred to in the text, also figures in the interest-bearing list.　　　[2] Ramsay, *Genesis*, II, 227.

(jointly) during February and March 1386. The first period was used wholly for assignment, but the total was only £8,606 18s. 9d.: Haddele and Exton, on the other hand, did nothing but receive cash amounting to £29,208 10s. Cash yields from the normal revenue were insignificant; but assignment in the main body of the roll was heavy, starting with about £1,000 on 19 October from the wool customs for Thomas Percy as captain of Brest. The household received its usual quota of approximately the same amount, this time also from the customs, upon 3 November. On the 13th lord Basset received the best part of another £1,000, partly from the customs, and lord Neville rather over £1,000 from the Hull customs and lay and clerical subsidies on 2 December. On the 7th Thomas Percy got as much again from the customs, but on the 8th the usual Calais assignment of £5,000 on the same source went badly astray; less than £2,000 could be collected and the rest appeared as a fictitious loan. On 18 December the money-lender Cheyne received tallies on the clerical subsidy for some £2,500, while on the 21st the household again drew tallies, principally on the customs of seven ports, for another £2,500. This concludes the first part of the roll and Hermesthorp's brief period as special receiver follows: during it £5,000 was assigned to Walter Bardi, £1,520 to the Scottish marches, and nearly £2,000 to the repayment of sundry small loans. In the second part of the roll assignment was renewed on 25 January with security for a £1,000 loan from William Venour of London, while on 8 February lord Neville got another £1,000 odd for the west march: both these were drawn on miscellaneous sources. On 9 March the London and Boston customs provided a further £1,000 for Neville, and general assignment continued at a fairly high level for the rest of the month: thus on 29 March London received about £1,000 in tallies on the lay subsidy in repayment of previous loans. On 4 April the household again drew upwards of £1,000 on Hull and London, and about the same amount was secured to the Genoese merchant, Reginald Grill,[1] upon the 12th, entirely on the customs of Southampton. This concludes the process of assignment in this long roll, since the special receipts which follow were all cash, as already explained.

---

[1] It is interesting to note from the receipt roll that on 23 July this financier and his associates advanced £200 in cash, *payable in Rome*, to Sir Nicholas Dagworth and Master Henry Godebarne, ambassadors to the papal curia.

Book-keeping first becomes important with the £3,000 fictitious loan from Calais on 8 December. On the 23rd the total rises steeply, owing to the clearance of eleven prests amounting to £5,136 8s., made probably in connection with the Scottish expedition;[1] the Beauchamp chamberlain of the exchequer and special receiver in this term, John Hermesthorp, together with Thomas Durant, one of the tellers, was responsible for most of it, while on 6 January 1386 the earl of Northumberland cleared a further £1,237 11s. 8d., presumably in the same connection. Meanwhile, Hermesthorp, in his other capacity as special receiver, had accepted three genuine loans of some size on 11 December 1385—£1,000 from London, just over £2,000 from the Bardi, and yet another £2,666 13s. 4d. from Matthew Cheyne. William Venour advanced his £1,000 on 25 January 1386, only two days before he received tallies for the amount, as already mentioned: on 8 February the duke of Lancaster lent £2,000 and lord Neville £1,333 6s. 8d. on the 10th. On 31 March there were five smaller loans totalling £1,254, and finally on 10 April seven more lenders produced £3,166 13s. 4d.: among these both Walter Bardi (£1,200) and Matthew Cheyne (£900) appear yet again.

EASTER 1386:		£	s.	d.	%
	Cash	11,458	18	3	18
	Assigned	29,914	11	10	48
	Book-keeping	21,661	12	7	34
	Total	63,035	2	8	100

Receipts of the subsidy and a half granted a year earlier were still coming in and are again listed separately at the end of the roll, though the special receivers are not mentioned by name and presumably remained unchanged. They account for rather more than half the cash total for the entire roll, which is, however, relatively small and contains no specially heavy days. As regards book-keeping and assignments, which are more than usually intertwined this term, the roll begins on 1 May with two large loans—one of £2,444 8s. 10d. from Walter Bardi and the other of £2,533 6s. 8d. from Matthew Cheyne. Both of these seem to have been subject to a substantial discount, and a good deal of the security for the

[1] This was one of the 'wars' specially sanctioned by the parliament of October 1385: Genesis, II, 229.

former was given in the shape of tallies on the clerical subsidy as early as 5 May.[1] A further £1,333 6s. 8d. was raised from Walter Bardi on 8 June and was discounted by the exchequer for an immediate cash payment of £1,000. On the following day another £1,500 was raised from three lenders, and tallies of assignment on the London wool customs were levied for most of Bardi's loan. Although borrowing of this sort continues fairly steadily, the high book-keeping figures in the latter part of the roll are mainly caused by *prestita restituta*. Easily the most important individual accountant under this head was the clerk 'John Hatfield',[2] who on 23 July was cleared of responsibility for £1,600 advanced to him on 19 May 1386 *super diversis solucionibus apud Plymouth pro passagio ducis Lancastrie versus Ispaniam faciendo*.[3] The same 'Hatfield' reappears with six *prestita restituta* (all of recent date), totalling £3,750, on 18 September and again for £248 on the 20th: there were also many other clerks figuring in similar transactions on a smaller scale. The special receipts on the other hand show only one book-keeping entry. It takes place on 27 July, when another king's clerk, John Benteley, 'restores' a prest of £1,180 5s. 10d., made to him in connection with the war only twenty-four hours earlier. These special receipts were, however, in contrast with most previous practice fairly heavily assigned: thus on 19 May nearly £4,000 went in this way to Walter Bardi, Matthew Cheyne and Hatfield, and on the 28th just under £3,000 to the garrisons of Berwick, Carlisle and Roxburgh.[4] The only other heavy day's

---

[1] For both these references see the discussion in the previous chapter, above, pp. 18–20.

[2] There is a mystery about this individual, for sources quoted by Tout, *Chapters*, IV, 459–60, make it clear that he resigned his keepership of the privy wardrobe in the Tower to Hermesthorp in 1381 and died very soon afterwards. In 1382 this keepership passed to Randolph Hatton, who held it until his death in 1396, ibid., 462. Whether we are here dealing with the executors of John Hatfield, as sometimes happens—in which case the recency of the prests raises almost insuperable difficulties—or with repeated clerical errors for Randolph Hatton, is not clear, but I much prefer the second explanation. (I have been unable to find any trace of any other John Hatfield.)

[3] This of course refers to John of Gaunt's well-known Castilian expedition, for which see my *Richard II*, 106–9.

[4] This shows that the entering of receipts from the lay subsidies separately at the end of the roll really meant very little: they could be, and were, treated precisely as if they had been entered in the ordinary way.

assignment in this term fell on 15 September in the main body of the roll, when profits of some £1,837, derived from the sale of enemy merchandise captured at sea, were assigned to William More, citizen and vintner of London, William Venour (another Londoner) and other persons.

		£	s.	d.	%
MICHAELMAS 1386–7:	Cash	25,583	6	9	36
	Assigned	33,548	14	8	47
	Book-keeping	11,884	11	4	17
	Total	71,016	12	9	100

Cash payments were on a small scale until 25 January 1387, when the London wool customs contributed £1,483 6s. 8d., followed by a further £1,000 on 4 February. From 9 February onwards until the end of the term there was a steady flow of cash from the first of the two half-subsidies reluctantly granted by the stubborn parliament of October 1386.[1] The lands of the young earl of March were also still yielding some substantial cash payments, while eccentricities are represented by three *dona* totalling £233 6s. 8d. and made on 17 December 1386 and 14 and 27 February 1387 respectively by the Ricardian Londoner, Brembre, who was to suffer death at the hands of the 'merciless' parliament a year later. Assignment was heavy from an early date: thus on 18 October Cherbourg received over £2,000 from six wool ports, while on the 23rd there were many smaller assignments on various sources, totalling over £1,200. On 27 November some £3,000 of another London loan was secured upon the London customs (with some help from the lay subsidies collected in that neighbourhood), and on three more days in December and January miscellaneous assignments rose to between £1,000 and £2,000. On 24 January 1387 the king's butler received tallies for over £1,000 on seven wool ports, while at the end of February no less than ten ports contributed tallies totalling almost as much in favour of John Benteley. On 11 March Calais got £3,000, assigned entirely on the London wool customs, and on the 21st le Scrope received £1,000 on three ports in his capacity as keeper of the castle of Fronsac in the Gironde; he was still, presumably, seneschal of

---

[1] Ramsay, *Genesis*, II, 239.

Aquitaine. There was a fairly steady flow of small book-keeping entries throughout the whole term, but the only really heavy day was 29 October 1386, when London lent £3,184—followed by a further £150 two days later.

		£	s.	d.	%
EASTER 1387:	Cash	30,759	0	2½	77
	Assigned	6,211	15	0	15
	Book-keeping	3,089	4	10	8
	Total	40,060	0	0½	100

There was only one day (22 July) in the whole term when there were no cash payments whatsoever: the heaviest were on 30 April (£2,000 from the Hull customs), 3 May (£1,000, of which £700 came from the Lynn customs), 15 May (£2,000 from the Boston customs), 18 May (£1,500 from Hull again), 24 May (£977 still from the same source, out of a total of £1,257), 11 June (£1,000 from the Boston customs), 6 July (£1,000 from the London customs and another £500 from Boston), 28 July (£1,000 from various sources), and 27 July, 19 and 21 August, which yielded £2,410, £2,216 and £2,676 respectively from general revenue, in which the customs, especially those of London, continued to play a large part. There were no outstanding assignments and very few book-keeping entries of any kind during the term: it was, of course, the period in which the whole government was in the hands of a baronial commission and little attempt at raising, or even spending, revenue was made by them.

		£	s.	d.	%
MICHAELMAS 1387–8:	Cash	18,324	19	10½	32
	Assigned	31,563	9	5	55
	Book-keeping	7,637	16	1	13
	Total	57,526	5	4½	100

The flow of small cash payments remained steady until the middle of November, when some irregularity set in. It was not until the 13th that any day total passed the £1,000 mark: this in turn was mainly owing, when it came, to a £600 receipt from the London wool customs. The same source contributed the greater part of

£1,937 on 23 January 1388, while on 6 March the customs of Hull, Boston and Southampton produced some £1,500 between them. A further £1,500 on the 14th, however, came from the forfeited possessions of the Ricardians Sir John Beauchamp and Nicholas Brembre, and constitutes perhaps the earliest positive evidence in the receipt rolls of the first great political crisis of the reign. It is interesting that the method of assignment was not at first used in this connection: thus when, on the very same day, the duke of Gloucester, one of the appellant leaders, was assigned £333 6s. 8d. *de superplusagio*, it was to be drawn merely from the farmers of the lands and lordships of the late earl of March—an entry which is exactly repeated on 14 May 1388 in the middle of the 'merciless' parliament. Assignments in this Michaelmas roll in general show a convenient, but unfortunately short-lived, tendency to congregate on special days: thus there were only four days in the autumn months of 1387 on which any assignments at all were made, but in each case a day-total of £1,000 to £1,600 was reached. On 21 October lord Neville was the chief beneficiary with £666 13s. 4d. assigned to him on three wool ports; on the 26th (£1,024) the assignments were miscellaneous, and again on 5 November (£1,626). On the 14th they reached £1,574, of which Neville took £500, partly from the customs of Hull and partly from ordinary revenue. The next day worth noting was 27 November, when Calais got £2,000, £1,500 of which came from the London wool customs and £500 from Boston: other assignments brought the day total under that head to £2,593. This was dwarfed, however, by a further assignment on 3 December of no less than £10,000 to Calais, drawn on five wool ports: evidently the regular replenishment of the treasurer of Calais's resources had been neglected under the appellant régime. Even this substantial compensation was still not enough, for on 21 February 1388 another £1,000 had to be assigned on the Boston customs to this always harassed official, and on 2 March more than £4,400 from the proceeds of various ransoms: other assignments brought this last day-total up to £5,112 under that head. Book-keeping during the term is almost wholly accounted for by some heavy borrowing on 6 March 1388, totalling £5,433 6s. 8d.: another corporate loan from the now predominantly pro-appellant city of London produced the bulk of this (£5,000), while the wealthy individual London citizen, William Venour, found the rest.

		£	s.	d.	%
EASTER 1388:	Cash	33,493	12	5	40
	Assigned	27,010	4	0½	32
	Book-keeping	23,982	8	0	28
	Total	84,486	4	5½	100

During this term the proceeds of lay subsidies—specifically those of the half-subsidy voted by the 'merciless' parliament in March 1388[1]—reappear on the receipt rolls: there are substantial cash payments from this source on 17 April (£1,200), 20 April (the larger part of £1,321), 24 April (part of £1,248), 28 and 29 April (part of £1,230 and of £3,520 respectively), 4 May (part of £2,284) and 8 May (most of £1,544). Clerical subsidies, on the other hand, predominate in the £1,711 paid in on the 11th and in the £2,011 of 13 May, while by 15 May (£2,092) and 23 May (£1,142) the flow of cash is coming from more miscellaneous sources, with a strong infusion of wool customs. Towards the end of the term the only heavy days are 20 July (£2,544 from general revenue) and 11 September (£1,197, including a good deal from forfeitures). Assignment begins seriously on 10 April with some tallies drawn entirely on the lay subsidy for the benefit of London: on the 13th le Scrope, now at Cherbourg, got £1,000 on the tunnage and poundage of London. On 14 May various assignments for war purposes, mainly on the London wool customs, produced £1,767, and on the 16th an entirely miscellaneous batch reached the high figure of £3,894, drawn from all sources. Out of £2,672 assigned on 19 June the mayor of London drew £1,463 6s. 8d., secured upon the London wool customs: on 25 June Henry Percy got some £1,500, mainly from the clerical subsidy but including £333 6s. 8d. from the wool customs of Hull. Again on 11 July le Scrope got about the same amount for Cherbourg, secured wholly upon customs, while two largish totals (£1,625 and £1,270) for 17 and 18 July were wholly miscellaneous in origin and purpose. There were only four days of heavy book-keeping, of which two were wholly devoted to genuine loans: thus on 2 June £1,400 was raised from various lenders, and on 8 June £3,586 13s. 4d., including £1,000 from the appellant chancellor, Thomas Arundel, then bishop of Ely, and a further £1,000 from his chancery staff. On

---

[1] Ramsay, *Genesis*, II, 254.

17 July, on the other hand, some real financial stringency was reflected in a number of fictitious loans totalling £2,470, of which the unfortunate treasurer of Calais, and future Ricardian, Roger Walden, carried £2,000. All these items put together are, however, easily exceeded by the £11,402 of *prestita restituta* which appear on 14 September, mostly in the name of Thomas Durant, one of the tellers of the receipt, while the balance is in that of Thomas Restwold, another teller. The main advances had been made to Durant as recently as 11 May 1388 (£1,300) and 2 June (£8,666 13*s.* 4*d.*)—probably in connection with the renewal of the Scots war, but there is nothing to indicate the precise reason.

		£	s.	d.	%
MICHAELMAS 1388–9:	Cash	22,365	3	2½	33
	Assigned	37,665	11	11½	56
	Book-keeping	7,639	4	0½	11
	Total	67,669	19	2½	100

Cash flowed in steadily until almost the end of November: especially heavy days were 30 October (£1,000 from the London wool customs) and 6 November (£1,864, mainly from the Hull customs but also including £477 from the earl of Kent for the marriage of the infant Roger, earl of March—that is, for the lucrative right to find a bride for him). On 16 November Brembre's forfeited property yielded £787 out of a day-total of £1,410, but the £1,195 brought in on the 27th came chiefly from such orthodox sources as the London and Southampton customs. On 28 November the tunnage and poundage of Bristol, London and Lynn accounted for over half the £1,000 total, but a similar sum paid in on 10 December was drawn mainly from farmers of the earl of March's lands. In the early part of 1389 cash payments, though numerous, were of smaller size and added little to the total for the term: the sole exception was the £1,781 which came in on 20 March as a special receipt springing from the lay subsidy granted in the autumn parliament of 1388 held at Cambridge.[1] Assignments, still tending to be made on special days apparently reserved for the purpose, were first heavy on 30 November (£1,954) and 9 December (£1,710)—both composite sums of miscellaneous origin and destination. By far the most costly of the government's commit-

---

[1] Ramsay, *Genesis*, II, 263.

ments continued to be Calais, whose treasurer now had to be assigned as much as £19,000 (of which he was able to collect less than £16,000) upon seven wool ports on 3 February, and a further £5,478 *de remanencia compoti sui*—probably a mere book-keeping transaction—on the 22nd. Compared with these, the remaining assignments were relatively insignificant: £1,580 was drawn on miscellaneous sources (of which £522 was earmarked for the duke of Gloucester) on 12 February, and £1,675, of a highly varied nature, on 9 March. Finally, on 29 March, there were mixed assignments totalling £1,598, of which the most important was £635 for the household from the customs of Southampton. Book-keeping was trifling until 3 February 1389, when the larger of the two great masses of assignments made to Calais went so much astray that the treasurer of that fortress was credited with fictitious loans amounting to £3,137. There was not much genuine borrowing: the only large loan was one of £1,000 made on 23 February 1389 by the hands of Lambert Fermer, receiver of the chamber[1] —that is, in effect, by the king himself. The only other sizeable item in the small book-keeping total came from various short-dated *prestita*, amounting to some £1,820 in all, cleared by Thomas Restwold, teller of the receipt, on 1 April: the reason for the original advances is not given.

		£	s.	d.	%
EASTER 1389:	Cash	29,034	18	0	54
	Assigned	12,301	11	5	23
	Book-keeping	12,236	14	8½	23
	Total	53,573	4	1½	100

Over three-quarters of the cash payments were made to the Beauchamp chamberlain, John Hermesthorp, and to his colleague, Nicholas Exton, in their capacity as special receivers of the subsidy granted in the Cambridge parliament 'for the war against the Scots'.[2] These receipts came in between 27 April and 1 June and were taken wholly in cash, without any book-keeping or assignment. Even in the main body of the roll assignment was on the light side. It is true that on 17 May about £1,000 from the London wool customs was earmarked *super sustentac' galearum*, while on

---

[1] Tout, *Chapters*, IV, 336 and n. 3.
[2] Ramsay, *Genesis*, II, 263.

the 31st Henry Percy received tallies for £1,504 on the Hull and Boston customs for the east march towards Scotland, together with a further £500 upon the London customs on 15 July *de dono regis* (a most unusual entry), but these were the only outstanding assignments of the term. Book-keeping was mainly represented by some £8,500 in 27 *prestita restituta* on 28 August, nearly all of them in the name of John Benteley: but on 14 June there was also a substantial contribution of £1,633 6s. 8d. in the shape of fictitious loans from Richard, earl of Arundel, to cover four bad tallies drawn on London, Boston and Southampton. It is worth noting, however, that the sole surviving copy of this roll ends somewhat abruptly on 28 August and, late as that date is, it is just possible that a day or two may be missing.

		£	s.	d.	%
MICHAELMAS 1389–90:	Cash	18,802	8	10½	35
	Assigned	29,044	18	6½	55
	Book-keeping	5,227	15	8½	10
	Total	53,075	3	1½	100

Although there were only three days of special receipts in 1389 and one in 1390, they were again all in cash and accounted for nearly a third of the total under this head. The rest was fairly evenly distributed over the main body of the roll, though there were particularly heavy cash receipts in the last week of October, and again on 30 December when £1,940 6s. 8d. was received *pro diversis solucionibus*. Assignment begins early on 7 October with the writing off of over £1,000 due from Sir John de Windsor, nephew of William de Windsor, now dead, by the simple process of assigning it back to him. Exactly a fortnight later the duke of Gloucester *et alii* received nearly £2,000 in tallies on the customs —mainly those of London. Heavy drafts on 5 November were more miscellaneous in character, but included £666 13s. 4d. on the Hull customs for the chamber; while on the 11th Hermesthorp got well over £3,000 on London—probably as a prest. All these were dwarfed, however, on 30 November by the usual heavy assignment, this time of some £8,000, in favour of the treasurer of Calais: it was secured principally upon the wool customs of Boston and Hull, with a little help from Lynn and butlerage dues. No other assignment reached £1,000 in this term, though there were very many smaller ones, which helped to swell the total. Book-keeping on a large scale began with the appearance of £1,300 in fictitious loans made on account of seven bad tallies by le Scrope, still captain of Cherbourg: the only other items of importance took the shape of three *prestita*, totalling £1,275 17s. 6d., which were cleared on 28 March 1390 by two tellers of the receipt, William Howelot and (especially) Thomas Restwold.

		£	s.	d.	%
EASTER 1390:	Cash	13,528	1	10½	50
	Assigned	11,765	4	9½	43
	Book-keeping	1,941	9	10	7
	Total	27,234	16	6	100

The only heavy cash payments occur, as usual, in the special receipts paid to William Fulbourne and John Haddele, and were derived from the restricted grant of customs dues at reduced rates made by the January parliament.[1] The proceeds from the duty on wool, wool-fells and hides, as well as from tunnage and poundage, on the new but strictly temporary basis, amounted to rather over £3,000 paid on 30 May and just over £6,000 paid on 9 July; but these two days alone (which represent the entire sum of the special receivers' activities) account for two-thirds of all the cash received in the exchequer during this unusually inactive term. Assignments on the other hand were fairly evenly distributed through the whole term in relatively small packets—several of them, e.g. one on 19 July, in favour of that eminent controller of the customs, Geoffrey Chaucer. The only large payments made by assignment took place on 18 June, when the household received tallies for £2,350 on the lands of the infant Roger Mortimer, earl of March, as well as for a further £500 on the wool customs of London and Southampton. Book-keeping for the term was almost negligible and contained no item of outstanding interest or importance.

		£	s.	d.	%
MICHAELMAS 1390–1:	Cash	40,609	0	7½	57
	Assigned	20,467	18	1½	29
	Book-keeping	10,253	10	6	14
	Total	71,330	9	3	100

[1] Ramsay, *Genesis*, II, 272.

Early in October three more days of special war receipts, apparently left over from those of the previous term—for the receivers are the same—accounted for considerably more than two-thirds of the cash total. In the main body of the roll there is only one large item paid in cash, namely £5,031 from the sale of forfeited lands, which accrued in mid-December through the bishops of Durham and St. David's 'and others' assigned for that purpose, by the hands of John Hermesthorp. Assignment first exceeds the £1,000 mark in favour of the household, which on 15 November secured tallies on a variety of sources for rather more than that amount, as it regularly used to do before the appellant revolution. On 20 March 1391 about the same amount was assigned to Richard, earl of Arundel, but as the tallies were drawn against the same earl's indebtedness to the crown in connection with his newly purchased manor of Mereworth,[1] it seems to have represented little more than a rather complicated way of bestowing crown lands on a subject free of charge. In any case both these sums were easily surpassed by the assignment on 21 March of £4,666 13s. 4d. out of the wool customs and tunnage and poundage of London, Boston and Southampton to Sir John Stanley, lieutenant of Ireland, which was the most important transaction of this type in the term and perhaps the first hint of the coming Irish expedition. The book-keeping total is mainly accounted for by the clearance of nearly £6,500 in prests on 20 March: of these, two standing in the name of John Hermesthorp accounted for some £4,377, while Roger Walden, still treasurer of Calais, was responsible for another £2,000. The only other item of interest was the duke of Lancaster's failure to collect on three tallies drawn against the Hull and Boston customs on 21 February for a total of £1,000. However, this roll again is cut off sharply after the day total on 21 March: it is therefore possible, though not likely, that another day or two may be missing.

EASTER 1391:		£	s.	d.	%
	Cash	6,912	18	5½	26
	Assigned	15,583	8	7	57
	Book-keeping	4,615	4	7½	17
	Total	27,111	11	8	100

[1] In Kent, one of the forfeited manors of Nicholas Brembre, and in the king's hand since 1387: *Cal. Fine Rolls*, 1383–91, 221, 247.

There was a fairly steady flow of small cash payments throughout the term, but never as much as £1,000 on any one day. Large assignments began on 18 April with about £1,000 from general revenue for the household, followed by a further £1,666 13s. 4d. on 10 May from the profitable issues of the March earldom. During May and June Calais received only £3,100 in sizeable assignments, mainly on the London wool customs, while failing to collect a further £800 on Southampton, Hull and Yarmouth, but small as these were no other assignment even approached them in amount. Among book-keeping entries a fictitious loan of £66 13s. 4d. from Geoffrey Chaucer, caused by his failure to cash a tally drawn on the farmer of Rockingham forest, is worth mentioning for its extraneous associations, but there is little else of interest, except for a few small *prestita restituta* on 28 September, the total of which just passed £1,100.

		£	s.	d.	%
MICHAELMAS 1391–2:	Cash	15,264	10	5	28
	Assigned	32,428	17	10	59
	Book-keeping	6,911	16	11	13
	Total	54,605	5	2	100

The only substantial cash payments came from customs on 24 November (some £2,000 from London) and on 5 March (nearly as much again from various ports). Punctually on 9 October the household received a large mixed assignment for £1,476, and Calais its first large subvention of the term (£1,200 from London and Southampton) on the 26th. The household again got nearly £1,000 from various sources on 14 November and slightly more than that on 4 December; while successful assignments for Calais on the usual wool ports suddenly jumped to £6,300 on 24 February —though a further £4,700 levied on them at the same time could not be collected. Other substantial assignments on the customs went to the duke of Lancaster in his capacity as duke of Guienne and peacemaker with France[1] (£2,666 13s. 4d. on 21 November) and to the Percy earl of Northumberland for the east march (about £1,000 on 1 December). On the other hand, it was the sale of forfeited lands and tenements which provided the duke of Gloucester with £916 13s. 4d. on 19 January 1392. As for the book-keeping

---

[1] Ramsay, *Genesis*, II, 284–5.

total, it was mainly accounted for by the large fictitious loan of 24 February from Calais already mentioned above.

		£	s.	d.	%
EASTER 1392:	Cash	38,539	0	9	76
	Assigned	11,738	3	9	23
	Book-keeping	316	1	8	1
	Total	50,593	6	2	100

Receipts this term were dominated by the cash proceeds of the one and a half subsidies granted in the November parliament of 1391 and followed in December by the usual clerical grants.[1] These were pouring in from 22 April, together with some customs and other revenue, to such effect that well over £30,000 in cash had been received by the end of May, and nearly £39,000 by the end of the summer. Assignment was comparatively restricted, but the household drew nearly £1,150 from various sources in this way on 29 April and more than twice as much again on 8 July: Calais, on the other hand, got only £1,000 by this method (on 8 May) during the entire term. There was no appreciable book-keeping.

		£	s.	d.	%
MICHAELMAS 1392–3:	Cash	20,430	16	9½	35
	Assigned	38,089	10	9½	65
	Book-keeping	279	8	0½	—
	Total	58,799	15	7½	100

The cash total in this term was swollen mainly by the customs, which exceeded the £1,000 mark on four occasions between October and March. The only other high scorer was the hanaper, or sealing department of the chancery, whose income from fees seems to have been rising steadily throughout the reign: thus on 4 November £1,000 in cash was paid into the exchequer from this source alone. Assignment was throughout fairly heavy, beginning with £1,176 for the household on 1 October and £1,114 on the 3rd, both from general revenues with some help from customs. The household appeared again with £1,038 on the 15th and £1,116 on the 22nd, while on the latter day the closely related chamber

[1] Ramsay, *Genesis*, II, 280–1.

received tallies of its own, all on the customs, for a further £1,702, and the duke of Lancaster £1,000 from the same source (supported by the hanaper). On 24 October Roger Walden got £7,148 on the London and Boston customs for Calais, and a further £3,361 (on the east coast ports) upon the 29th. The duke of Lancaster appeared again with £940 on 6 November, and the earl of Northumberland with £1,425 on the 12th: the first of these payments was made exclusively, and the second principally, through the customs. The same source of income, particularly at London, produced £2,516 for Richard Clifford, keeper of the great wardrobe,[1] on 14 November, and £1,305 for the household again on 2 December. Early in 1393 the household got another £800 (16 January) and £908 (21 February)—both on the customs. Finally on 5 March there were miscellaneous assignments totalling just over £2,000, drawn mainly on the same source. Book-keeping was less than 1% of the whole, and the main feature of the term remained the strength of customs for all purposes. This may obviously be dated from the parliamentary grant of these revenues for three years at increased rates in November 1390, and from the renewal of that grant for another three years in January 1393.[2]

EASTER 1393:		£	s.	d.	%
	Cash	40,171	6	10	64
	Assigned	19,839	16	3½	31
	Book-keeping	2,897	8	8½	5
	Total	62,908	11	10	100

As in the previous term, cash entries were throughout well nourished by tbe customs which on six occasions between 8 May and 22 July rose above £1,000 a day. But from 25 June there was also the powerful reinforcement of the immediate half-subsidy granted in the January parliament of 1393 and of the clerical grants made in March of that year.[3] By the end of the term considerably over half the high cash total could be attributed to these two sources of supply alone, especially to the lay half-subsidy. The first assignment to exceed £1,000 went as usual to the household (on 29 April); it was drawn on general revenue. On 12 May the

---

[1] Tout, *Chapters*, III, 464, for his appointment in 1390.
[2] Ramsay, *Genesis*, II, 275, 287.
[3] Ibid., 287.

earl of Northumberland received £1,320, nearly all of it from the customs, while on the 14th the Genoese financier Cataneo got £679 on Southampton, and the chamber £630, principally on London. The household scored again with £910 odd, mainly from the customs, on the 21st, and with a further £1,100 from various sources on 4 June. On the 14th Richard Clifford got £1,033 6s. 8d. for the great wardrobe from the customs, and on the 17th a further £1,166 13s. 4d. from the same source. After this various assignments of miscellaneous origin and destination topped £1,000 on only four more days in the term: the largest single item was one of £900 odd for the household, mainly from customs, on 12 July. Book-keeping would again have been trifling but for two unusual loans made on 12 September by Sir William le Scrope and the duke of Lancaster respectively in the form of specie and foreign exchange. The first was for £466 13s. 4d. *de prec' div' pec' arg' in massa ponder' per pondus de Troy* £353 18s. 8d. *qualibet libra computata ad* £1 6s. 8d. *sterlingorum*; the second for £2,000, by the hands of Thomas Tuttebury, the duke of Lancaster's treasurer, *de prec' div' pec' arg' in massa et div' monetar' fabricat' vocat' Reales et Cynkeyns de Ispann' et Juliakes de Naples.* Apart from the interesting equation in the first loan, it is noteworthy that le Scrope at least seems to have incurred a loss of about £5 over this transaction.

		£	s.	d.	%
MICHAELMAS 1393–4:	Cash	45,273	15	7	61
	Assigned	20,915	17	2	28
	Book-keeping	8,556	0	6	11
	Total	74,745	13	3	100

For the first half of the term the heavier of the cash payments came exclusively from the customs, which were still being levied at the higher rates granted in November 1390, although the conditions then imposed, notably in the case of tunnage and poundage, had not been fulfilled.[1] 7, 13 and 14 October, 18 November and 6 December were especially fruitful days in this respect, but from 19 January 1394 'the second of the half-subsidies voted conditionally in the last Parliament'[2] was already beginning to come

---

[1] Ramsay, *Genesis*, II, 275, 287, 294.
[2] Ibid., 294.

in, though parliamentary sanction for this step was not formally given until parliament met again at the end of that month. The subsidy continued to flow strongly, assisted by the customs and to some extent by clerical tenths, until 11 February, but a month later the cash revenue was again mainly dependent on the customs, supplemented by one large payment of £880 from the hanaper. The household received the unusually large assignment of £3,023 from various sources as early as 6 October, and £1,474 in the same way on the 15th, but the east march and Calais got substantially less than usual. On 15 January 1394 the household again obtained £800 from the customs and £1,100 from the lands of the earl of March: the sole remaining assignment of some size was one of £1,800 on 11 March in favour of the duke of Lancaster and drawn on the London wool customs. Book-keeping was almost entirely accounted for by the sum of £7,894 in fourteen *prestita restituta* on 6 December: easily the two largest items contained in this were a short-dated £4,000 cleared by Thomas Stanley, clerk,[1] and £3,854 from the procurators of the king of Navarre, which had been outstanding since 1 June 1378. Loans of all kinds were negligible, but it is perhaps worth noting that on 6 December 1393 Matilda, countess of Oxford, made a cash payment of £466 13s. 4d. into the exchequer—not, apparently, by way of loan—the reason for which is not given.

		£	s.	d.	%
EASTER 1394:	Cash	23,131	4	7½	60
	Assigned	14,773	8	11½	38
	Book-keeping	888	1	5	2
	Total	38,792	15	0	100

Customs accounted for nearly all the larger cash payments between 14 May and 8 August. Yet again assignment on a big scale started with the household, viz. on 2 May with £1,351 from general revenue. Calais, which had not been receiving large assignments for some time, got £2,048, entirely on the Hull customs, on 26 May, and the earl of Northumberland £1,300 on London, Boston and Hull upon 3 June, but there was only one other day during

---

[1] For the different Thomas Stanleys, all connected with the chancery, see Tout, *Chapters*, IV, 51 n. This is probably the Thomas Stanley who was shortly to become treasurer of Calais (1395).

the term (viz. 8 August) when miscellaneous assignments reached £1,000, while book-keeping for the entire term failed to attain this figure.

		£	s.	d.	%
MICHAELMAS 1394–5:	Cash	35,765	19	11½	29
	Assigned	35,819	1	5½	30
	Book-keeping	49,035	1	10½	41
	Total	120,620	3	3½	100

The unusually large gross total for this term, inflated as it is by book-keeping, must none the less be attributed to the necessities of the first Irish expedition. The cash total was raised mainly from the customs between 28 October and 30 November 1394 and throughout the whole of February 1395. On and after 1 December there was also much help from clerical tenths—presumably those voted in 1394, though there were fresh grants in February 1395.[1] The lands of the late queen Anne also yielded large cash payments in November and February, amounting to £2,666 13s. 4d. For the first half of the term assignment tended to be concentrated heavily on certain days. Thus on 7 November alone Calais got £2,624 on the Hull customs and £832 on Boston; the earl marshal £1,000 on Hull; and the great wardrobe (Clifford) £700 on London, followed by £800 on three ports on the 10th. On 13 November the earl of Northumberland received £833 odd out of assorted customs, and Richard Clifford another £1,070 for his department on the 24th, together with £1,127 on 3 December from the same. But the still larger assignment of £7,597 made to the treasurer of Calais on the same day seems to have been more in the nature of book-keeping, since it was drawn on the treasurer himself for his own benefit (*pro eodem*) *per div' tall' canc' et dampn'*, etc.[2] Genuine assignment was resumed on 7 December with £1,000 for the duke of Lancaster on the London customs, after which there was a lull until 11 February, when the earl of Northumberland got £1,850 on London, Boston and Hull. He received another £1,000 on 1 March out of the lay subsidy—presumably the third half-subsidy conditionally voted in January 1393 'in the event of a renewal of the war, and of an actual expedition having been undertaken by the

[1] Ramsay, *Genesis*, II, 294 n., 302 n.
[2] This entry is discussed in the preceding chapter, above, p. 21.

king'.[1] On 12 March the earl of Arundel had tallies for some £1,350 on the same source, but the last assignment of the term— £3,333 6s. 8d. for London on 3 April in part payment of a loan —was based as usual on the Londoners' own customs revenue. Book-keeping was fairly evenly divided between *prestita restituta* and a great series of genuine loans—the first for many years. Thus on 27 November the aged William of Wykeham, bishop of Winchester, lent £1,000, to be followed on 1 December by the archbishop of Canterbury with a similar sum, not to mention several smaller lenders. On the 5th London advanced £6,333 6s. 8d., and there were other, but much smaller, loans both on that day and on the 7th. On 10 December the bishop of Salisbury, who was also treasurer of England, lent £1,000 and lesser folk a further £633 6s. 8d. Small loans reappeared in February 1395, but it was not until the 27th that they once more reached four figures, mainly owing to the loan of £1,000 by the Percy earl of Northumberland. Two days later (1 March) there were no less than 23 loans totalling £6,300, of which the three largest were another £1,000 from Wykeham, as much again from the chancellor-archbishop of York, and £1,333 6s. 8d. from Richard, earl of Arundel: for this last the earl, as has been seen, received tallies on the lay subsidy within a fortnight. This practically concluded the great borrowing operation, which had produced something well over £20,000. But even this figure was surpassed by the remarkable short-term prests entrusted for a matter of only two or three days in each case to Laurence Dru, king's esquire, and John Elyngeham, king's serjeant-at-arms,[2] together with a clerk or two. Thus from 7 to 10 December 1394 these two, with their clerk, were responsible for handling no less than £16,000, and again from 1 to 3 April 1395, with another clerk, for £10,730. The other half-dozen prests of the term taken together did not amount to as much as £1,000 and can be ignored: what is so remarkable about the Dru-Elyngeham prests is, firstly, that so much ready money could be found, presumably for wages and material of war, and secondly that it should

---

[1] Ramsay, *Genesis*, II, 287—but cf. 294.

[2] The use of military laymen in this connection for the first time, instead of entrusting the entire responsibility to clerks, is a good example of the rising importance of the *miles litteratus*. Cf. the militarized chamber, first devised by Simon Burley in 1386 (Steel, *Richard II*, 114–15) and reintroduced in the last years of the reign.

have been thought necessary to pass it through the hands of pay-masters for such extremely short periods. However this may be, the £27,000 in question cannot be regarded as a receipt in any real sense of the word: on the contrary it constitutes from the modern point of view an immense 'watering', not to say falsification, of the ordinary revenue. It must be remembered, however, that the medieval exchequer clerk was not interested in accurate assessments of the crown's real income, nor was such an estimate the object of the records kept in the receipt rolls.

		£	s.	d.	%
EASTER 1395:	Cash	36,791	7	9	71
	Assigned	13,202	4	10	25
	Book-keeping	1,876	13	4	4
	Total	51,870	5	11	100

About half the high cash total came from customs, notably before 11 June and again at the extreme end of the term (19 and 29 July and 9 September; there were no August entries of any kind). Between these two phases—that is, for about a month from 11 June onwards—as much again was contributed from the lay subsidy voted in January 1395, together with some small help early in July from the clerical tenths granted that February.[1] Assignment, based chiefly on customs, was of a somewhat scattered, miscellaneous nature, except on 15 July, when Walden's successor at Calais, Robert Selby,[2] received tallies on Hull for the peculiar amount of £2,001 0s. 0½d. Book-keeping was almost wholly sustained by a large *prestitum restitutum* on 26 June for £1,066 13s. 4d., which was cleared by Richard Cliderowe and other executors of the will of Robert Folkyngham, clerk, yet another ex-treasurer of Calais: this illustrates the normal perseverance of the exchequer in bringing even deceased officials to account. The only other point worth noting about this term is that the only surviving receipt roll is that of the royal chamberlain (Arnold Brocas), which contains only two

[1] Ramsay, *Genesis*, II, 302. The single lay subsidy was to be raised 'half at Whitsuntide and half at Martinmas' (11 November). The proceeds during this term therefore represented the first half only.

[2] Himself superseded (after only a very short period in office) by Thomas Stanley as treasurer and victualler of Calais, September 1395: *Cal. Pat. Rolls*, 1391–6, 620.

day-totals and no term total: moreover, it is possible that at least one day (17 July) is incomplete, even if nothing else is missing, about which it is difficult to be sure.

		£	s.	d.	%
MICHAELMAS 1395–6:	Cash	55,047	9	2	86
	Assigned	9,156	16	5	14
	Book-keeping	280	11	2	—
	Total	64,484	16	9	100

Though not comparable with the high cash figure for 1377–8 or even with that for 1380, this is none the less the highest cash total for the second half of the reign. Customs revenue was particularly prominent in this respect during October, but at Martinmas the second half of the lay subsidy voted in the previous January punctually appeared, together with more clerical tenths, and proceeded to dominate the cash receipts until 7 December, after which the customs took first place again. The only other cash item of importance was a further £1,000 from the estate of the late queen on 27 January. There were only two days of really heavy assignment —viz. 22 October, when the earl of Northumberland got £1,475 from three wool ports, and 27 November, when the treasurer of Calais received £1,355 from Hull. The insignificant book-keeping total was made up entirely of several small *prestita restituta*.

		£	s.	d.	%
EASTER 1396:	Cash	28,711	17	8½	50
	Assigned	25,178	9	10	44
	Book-keeping	3,491	17	9	6
	Total	57,382	5	3½	100

All the larger cash payments, which were well distributed throughout the term, came only from the customs, though on 18 May the hanaper contributed as much as £800. The greater assignments, too, came entirely from the same source, notably £1,000 for the great wardrobe (Clifford) on 3 July and £1,013 for the household on the same day; £2,000 for the duke of Lancaster and £1,200 for Calais on the 7th; and another £1,200 (approximately) for Calais and £1,006 for the great wardrobe on the 10th. On 19 July the great wardrobe got another £2,800, while the household and the chamber received only £300 each: finally, on 12 September, miscellaneous assignments on three ports reached a total of £2,761. Book-keeping was increased to appreciable proportions by twelve genuine loans totalling £2,353 6s. 8d., all made on 7 September: of these, Wykeham's contribution of £1,000 was easily the largest.

		£	s.	d.	%
MICHAELMAS 1396–7:	Cash	20,857	13	4½	29
	Assigned	36,189	4	7½	51
	Book-keeping	14,244	19	11½	20
	Total	71,291	17	11½	100

There were only three days of really heavy cash payments, viz. 26 October, 16 December and 15 March: of these, the first and last were due to customs, and the December payments to miscellaneous revenue, much of it from Wales. The first large assignment, on 8 November, was one for £1,300 on three wool ports in favour of Henry Percy: this was followed on the 28th by the assignment to the household of £1,200 drawn against the receiver-general of the late queen Anne—the first time that this estate had been at all heavily assigned. On 29 January Wykeham received, as security for his recent £1,000 loan, tallies on Southampton, but about one-third of all the assignment in the term was reserved for only four days of business, viz., from 23 February to 19 March inclusive. On the first of these the earl of March, who had now come of age, received £4,000 on four wool ports, while on 26 February Henry Percy got £750, also on customs. On 15 March the chamber was credited with more customs tallies for £2,500 and the great wardrobe with £1,814 worth of the same, while on the 19th the chamber got another £2,800 and Thomas Stanley, now treasurer of Calais, £3,000 on London and Southampton. Finally, on the same day another £2,333 6s. 8d. was assigned *pro operibus*, about half of it *de remanencia compoti* of the clerk of the works concerned and the rest again from customs: presumably the first half of this assignment was technically a book-keeping transaction. Indubitable book-keeping took the form, firstly, of fictitious loans made by the treasurer of Calais (19 March) on six bad tallies, totalling £2,000, drawn on London and Southampton, and secondly of heavy genuine loans. Nearly £12,000 was in fact raised by this means over the entire term, but out of thirty-four such loans in all there was only one large one, viz. the £6,666 13s. 4d. lent on 19 March by the king himself, through the chamber, in the shape of 40,000 French crowns, valued at 3s. 4d. a crown and thus producing exactly 10,000 marks, or £6,666 13s. 4d. There is the following marginal note on this loan: *inde recepit* £2,000 (but without the usual date of repayment) *et habet lit' pat' pro restitucione eiusdem summe de terris et diversis que fuerunt Anne nup' regine Anglie.* In view of the fact that the 40,000 crowns advanced to the exchequer for conversion into sterling clearly represented the first instalment of the new child-queen Isabella's dowry,[1] there is a certain irony in the fact that the king was to reimburse himself from the estates of the late queen, to whom he had been so deeply attached. It is also noticeable that the dowry is being treated as more private to the king than the late queen's estate, which is evidently reckoned as in some sense public money. The point perhaps illustrates the vexed distinction between the public and private capacities of the crown, at least in matters of finance and of the king 'living of his own', and if this distinction seems at times a fine one it is only because its nature was still extremely nebulous and indeed a matter of contention.

		£	s.	d.	%
EASTER 1397:	Cash	9,583	19	0	13
	Assigned	41,728	13	9	56
	Book-keeping	23,480	13	6	31
	Total	74,793	6	3	100

Major items in the greatly reduced cash percentage came entirely from the customs, e.g. on 21 May and 1 September—on the latter day with a little help from belated clerical tenths. Customs again supported most of the heavier assignments, beginning with £4,166 13s. 4d. on 12 May in favour of the duke of Lancaster: on 17 May several small loans totalling £1,484 were repaid by the same means. On 1 June the great wardrobe got £1,547 and on the 18th the household received nearly £2,700, with a further £2,625 on 14 July. On the same day Calais drew rather over £2,000 on Hull and Lynn, and a further £1,550 on as many as five ports upon 9 August, when yet another £3,950 could not be collected. Before the term was over the household, whose expenditure was already

---

[1] Ramsay, *Genesis*, II, 306.

rising very rapidly as the final crisis of the reign set in, got still more assignments for £2,500 (22 August), of which £400 came from the late queen and the rest from customs. Miscellaneous assignments were made to a greater or lesser extent on every single day throughout the term and helped to produce the high total under that head. There was again much borrowing: thus on 6 June the Lombard Laurence Janyn lent £666 13s. 4d., while between 9 August and 1 September there were no less than 166 genuine loans, producing nearly £18,000.[1] Most of these were from a host of small lenders, but two of them are outstanding, viz. yet another £1,000 from Wykeham on 9 August, and (on the 22nd) £6,666 13s. 4d. from the city of London. 9 August also saw the heavy fictitious loans already mentioned from the unfortunate Thomas Stanley at Calais, who was unable to collect on eleven tallies drawn on Lynn and Boston, Hull and London.

		£	s.	d.	%
MICHAELMAS 1397-8:	Cash	12,343	17	4½	18
	Assigned	44,927	4	8	67
	Book-keeping	10,330	7	9½	15
	Total	67,601	9	10	100

4 December, the first of two outstanding days contributing between them nearly half the cash total, was marked by heavy customs payments, supported by clerical tenths: 26 December, on the other hand, saw the raising of almost £1,000 in cash from 66 small forfeitures,[2] the first-fruits of Richard's 'second tyranny'. Assignment was considerably more active, but while both the household and the chamber benefited steadily from quite early in the term, the first really large sum (£1,041 on 26 October, from the customs) was credited to Henry Percy. On 8 November Calais got £1,350 in successful, and £650 in unsuccessful, assignments, mostly on five wool ports; and on the 26th the earl of March received £1,073 from three ports. On 1 December Thomas Stanley made good some of the Calais deficit by drawing £2,225 against customs,

---

[1] At least one of these loans, from Thomas Coggeshall, a country gentleman of Essex, was converted into a *remissio*. He had lent £66 13s. 4d. on 22 August 1397 but subsequently surrendered the letters patent which he had received in exchange for his money, *de mera sua voluntate*, thereby renouncing all claim to the repayment of his loan.

[2] Two more of these forfeitures were assigned, making 68 in all.

while on the same day the chamber got £1,000 from Boston. Another attempt to finance Calais by assignment, made on 5 December, was again only partially successful: tallies for some £2,500 on the customs were cashed, but others for over £3,500 were not. At the same time the great wardrobe and the household drew over £1,000 each against customs and the late queen Anne's estates. On the 24th Stanley got another £1,100 from customs, while he and Clifford (for the great wardrobe) shared a further £2,000 or so upon the 26th: at the same time Edward, earl of Rutland, was credited with nearly £1,600 *de remanencia compoti sui*. On 19 January 1398 there was a windfall of about £1,000 for the household, assigned upon the duke of Gloucester's forfeited property, but on 1 March, when the household got another £1,600 from the deceased queen Anne, the widowed duchess of Gloucester was allowed £666 13s. 4d. from her late husband's estates. Some borrowing continued, though on a reduced scale: thus on 4 December fifty genuine loans produced £4,092 13s. 4d., though no individual contribution reached £1,000.[1] Fictitious loans were also fairly numerous: thus on 8 November 1397 the incoming treasurer of Calais, John Bernard, whose term of office seems to have overlapped with that of Thomas Stanley, failed to cash six tallies on the London and Bristol customs totalling £650, while on 5 December the collectors at the same two ports, together with those of Lynn and Hull, defaulted on as many as 35 tallies, reaching a gross total of £3,957: the principal sufferer, as has already been seen, was again the treasurer of Calais.

		£	s.	d.	%
EASTER 1398:	Cash	14,698	4	5	27
	Assigned	33,393	15	$2\frac{1}{2}$	61
	Book-keeping	6,383	4	7	12
	Total	54,475	4	$2\frac{1}{2}$	100

The flow of cash payments was sustained on every day but two throughout the term: 22 June and 13 July, however, were the only days which just exceeded £1,000—mainly owing to a £600

---

[1] The largest were £800 from Bristol and £666 13s. 4d. from Richard Whittington, citizen and mercer of London. The latter was, as Wylie (*Henry IV*, I, 64) says, 'influential enough to secure repayment in three annual instalments', even *after* the revolution of 1399.

contribution on 22 June from the hanaper (which had already paid £500 on 3 May), while on 13 July seven fines *coram concilio* produced £813 6s. 8d.,[1] and the forfeiture of the late archdeacon of York a further £133 6s. 8d. Assignment was of course correspondingly heavy: the first notable payment was one of £1,193 on 4 May to the earl of March in Ireland from the Hull and Boston customs. Henry Percy got £1,650 for the east march on 8 May from the ports of north-east England, while on the 11th the chamber, great wardrobe and household shared nearly £1,000 of customs revenue. On 21 May two ports contributed over £2,300 to the duke of Lancaster as lieutenant of Aquitaine, but Southampton failed to produce a further £1,000 for him. On 22 June the household received nearly £1,200 from customs and clerical tenths, but the apparently large assignment of £4,450 to John Bernard, now indisputably sole treasurer of Calais, on 24 July was drawn from the issues of his own office and is suspect on that account. Yet there may have been some genuine revenue from Calais to counterbalance the large sums continually assigned to it, for on 31 July £4,950 assigned to Thomas Stanley, now elsewhere, was drawn partly against the revenues of Calais, though the bulk of it came from four wool ports in England, together with £200 from clerical tenths and a little from other sources: possibly the Calais portion was in the nature of a *de remanencia compoti sui* from his former treasurership, though this is not stated. Finally, on 13 August, Stanley got another £1,000, this time from the London customs, and the household £1,370 from miscellaneous revenue. One-third to one-half of the book-keeping total was represented by fictitious loans, of which the most important was a bad tally for £1,000 on Southampton levied on 21 May for the duke of Lancaster, though there were also six more of this type from London on 13 August to the detriment of John Lowick, receiver of the chamber. Most of the remaining book-keeping was covered by a genuine loan of

---

[1] Among those fined on this occasion was that ancient and loyal servant of the crown, John Hermesthorp, the Beauchamp chamberlain, who had to pay as much as £250, which he did in three instalments between 1397 and 1399. This suggests that he must have made some profit out of his office, which is not wholly surprising in view of the large prests he had handled for so long. It is noteworthy that the king's esquire, Laurence Dru, who had been responsible in part for the large prests made in connection with the first Irish expedition, was also fined, though only about a third as much as Hermesthorp.

£2,000 from London, made on 31 August, and another of £666
13s. 4d. from the chamber on the same date. One relatively small
loan of £278 odd was raised by the clerk of the king's council,
John Innocent, *de diversis personis in civ' Lond'*.

		£	s.	d.	%
MICHAELMAS 1398–9:	Cash	46,706	10	8½	63
	Assigned	26,396	9	2½	35
	Book-keeping	1,695	15	9	2
	Total	74,798	15	8	100

Cash payments, though at first sustained especially by customs
(e.g. 9 October), soon came to depend on the first of the three half-
subsidies voted in the Shrewsbury parliament of January 1398[1] and
on the clerical grants also associated with the counter-revolution.
The former was coming in rapidly from 16 October to the end of
November, while the clerical tenths appear mainly in the last
three weeks of that period and continue well into December. From
2 December, however, until 27 March (the last day of the term)
customs again predominated on heavy days, with some assistance
from the hanaper (two payments of £500 each), the lands of the
March earldom, which were once more subject to a minority after
the killing of the young earl in Ireland—that is, in the hands of
the crown—and from general revenues, e.g. those provided by the
chamberlain of south Wales. Assignment was small and infrequent
until 7 November, when Calais got some £850 from the customs
of Chichester and Lynn, followed on 2 December by £1,333
6s. 8d. from no less than six ports. On the same day the new duke
of Surrey drew £916 13s. 4d. on Boston, and the household, which
had already received £700 on 29 November, £400 from the
customs: the first large assignment in its favour came, however, on
11 December when it received nearly £2,000, partly from customs
and partly from the still buoyant revenues of the late queen. Also
on 11 December Henry Percy got £750 from customs and clerical
subsidies for Berwick and the east march, and another £50 for
himself (*pro feodo*, fee). Early in 1399 (8 January) the old duke of
Lancaster was credited with £1,000 on Lynn and Ipswich *pro*

---

[1] Ramsay, *Genesis*, II, 335. A great deal of the lay half-subsidy (some
£11,188) was entered without any marginal on the treasurer's roll, but on
previous analogy may safely be reckoned cash (*sol'*).

79

restitucione unius tallie dated 21 May 1398, but by far the biggest assignments of the term came on 30 January 1399 in connection with the second Irish expedition, towards the expenses of which (*pro viagio versus Hiberniam*) the household and the chamber between them got £7,000, nearly all out of 'customs not yet levied, but to be levied in future': for the first time this new formula was used.[1] Assignment continued at a high level through February and March until the end of the term, but became more miscellaneous in character. The only important book-keeping operation during the term was a small group of four genuine loans on 8 November totalling £1,400: of these, the largest was one for £666 13s. 4d. from Richard Whittington. It is notable that no prests were created, as on similar occasions in the past, for this Irish expedition.

		£	s.	d.	%
EASTER 1399:	Cash	35,560	7	9½	57
	Assigned	26,354	8	9	42
	Book-keeping	493	19	11	1
	Total	62,408	16	5½	100

This was an unusually short term of only 24 days: the roll has, however, been cut into two parts, so that it is possible that a few days are missing between 13 and 30 May. On the other hand the recorded term total at the end of it is only about £1,000 more than that obtained by adding up the roll in its existing condition, so that the gap, if any, is of no great importance, and in fact it is more than covered by a large cancellation on 5 May which the clerk, as usual at this date, has wholly failed to take into account. Cash revenue was well sustained by the lay subsidies (especially in April) and the customs;[2] there were also smaller contributions from clerical tenths and the hanaper. The first large assignment was one of £2,000 on 3 May in favour of the emperor of Constantinople,

[1] This was apparently connected with the grant of the customs for the king's life made by the Shrewsbury parliament in January 1398. See below under Easter, 1399.

[2] In January 1398 the Shrewsbury parliament had granted Richard the customs for life, at a slightly increased rate for aliens—and also three half-subsidies, to be raised at intervals of six months. One of these had already been collected, and it is therefore the second which figures in this roll. Before the third fell due the king had been deposed and it was consequently remitted: see below under Michaelmas, 1399–1400.

for whom £560 was also collected in five *dona*, paid in cash by a few magnates and (at a slightly lower rate of subscription) by some bishops. On 5 May the household, chamber and wardrobe, all still in Ireland, shared assignments totalling well over £6,000, for which the new formula anticipating future customs revenue was used: of this sum, the wardrobe, with £4,800, received the largest share. It is noteworthy that on 20 June the exiled duke of Hereford was assigned the considerable sum of £1,566 13s. 4d. out of the Lancastrian inheritance, which may have done something to alleviate its disastrous confiscation by the crown. Three days later Bolingbroke's fellow exile, the duke of Norfolk, also had part of his lost inheritance assigned to him, but in this case the amount was only £666 13s. 4d. The Ricardian magnates naturally fared better; thus the new marquis of Dorset got £2,066 13s. 4d. on future customs on 23 June, when in addition John Macclesfield, the new keeper of the great wardrobe,[1] received £1,010 from the Boston customs on the old formula, together with a little help from Hull. On 9 July the Londoners were assigned £2,000 out of their own customs towards the repayment of their recent loans, while the politically doubtful earl of Northumberland twice got assignments of £750 each on the customs (13 May and 4 July)—the second group of tallies included some drawn, rather exceptionally, on sheriffs, but only in the two northernmost counties. Finally, amid over £3,139 worth of mixed assignments on 12 July, came the last large individual draft of the reign in the shape of some £1,026 for John Carp, keeper of the wardrobe,[2] drawn (unusually) on the butlerage dues payable by alien merchants (£960) together with £66 13s. 4d. from general revenue. As against these high figures book-keeping was negligible; it consisted of eleven small *prestita restituta*.

	£	s.	d.	%
MICHAELMAS 1399–1400: Cash	20,860	4	2	31
Assigned	36,011	3	6½	54
Book-keeping	10,015	8	11½	15
Total	66,886	16	8	100

Nearly three-quarters of the cash total came from a payment by

---

[1] For this officer's career see Tout, *Chapters*, IV, 385–6 nn.

[2] Tout, *Chapters*, III, 464.

the new king into the exchequer on 10 December of £14,664 13s. 4d. in French crowns, amounting to 87,988 crowns at 3s. 4d. each, the previous rate of exchange: though sometimes described erroneously by Ramsay as Richard II's 'hoard', this large sum presumably represented arrears of queen Isabella's dowry. It is noticeable that payment was not made until the French had sent an embassy to England to inquire after the welfare of the young queen. Henry saw these French envoys on 1 November; 'gave them a hearty welcome and access to Isabella . . . and shortly after sent ambassadors of his own to treat for a marriage between Isabella and the Prince of Wales'.[1] Meanwhile, parliament had guaranteed the wool duties for three years (though not for life) at the rates fixed in January 1398, and had also confirmed the collection of arrears on the two half-subsidies 'which Richard had been authorized to raise at Michaelmas 1398 and at Easter 1399; the third half-subsidy, which had just fallen due, being cancelled'.[2] Nothing was said about tunnage and poundage, although Henry had 'ordered the collection of these dues to be suspended on the 15th September . . . As a matter of course all the blank bonds and recognisances issued by Richard were called in and destroyed.' Genuine loans during the term amounted to £3,526, of which the two largest (amounting to £666 13s. 4d. each) were those from Thomas Arundel, the new archbishop of Canterbury, on 3 October, and from Richard Whittington on 7 April, in spite of the fact that the latter, who from now on is one of Henry's principal financial backers, had also lent money to the crown under the old régime. Fictitious loans stood at £6,476, mostly at the expense of Calais. Thus on 17 December Nicholas Usk, the new treasurer of Calais, was unable to cash tallies on the customs for £2,840, while on 26 January the retiring victualler of the same place, Reginald Curtays—for the two offices, though frequently combined, could be separated—failed to collect on five London tallies worth £1,200.

---

[1] Ramsay, *Lancaster and York*, I, 17. In this passage Ramsay's treatment of the £14,664 13s. 4d. is obviously correct, but elsewhere in his writings he forgets himself and refers to it as Richard's 'hoard', disregarding its French currency and origin. When the marriage between Isabella and the prince of Wales did not take place the French, of course, as Ramsay points out, claimed repayment of the entire dowry.

[2] Ramsay, *Lancaster and York*, I, 13.

EASTER 1400:		£	s	d.	%
	Cash	5,988	10	7	14
	Assigned	17,077	3	3	40
	Book-keeping	19,289	1	2	46
	Total	42,354	15	0	100

One-third to one-half of the small cash total came on 3 July alone from forfeitures imposed on the rebel Ricardians, especially the earl of Kent:[1] the day-total was in fact £2,467, but this included a few other sources of revenue. During May there was a good deal of petty borrowing, especially from the clergy, *pro viagio regis versus Scotiam*. There were also several instances of money paid in by some clerk, specifically on account of clerical tenths, being treated as a loan and subsequently repaid to him: yet by no means all payers of clerical tenths were treated in this way, and in only one instance (6 July) did the marginal note of repayment definitely describe the transaction as having been a loan and not a tax-payment. There seems little doubt in fact that the persons singled out in this way were the *collectors* of the tenth, who had advanced money on the security of what they were about to collect and were naturally repaid: this is not to say, of course, that they did not also contribute their share of the tax in due course, but that was another matter.[2] Some of the other loans were also rather curious: e.g. two justices of the common bench lent £80 each, £60 on account of overdue salaries and £20 in cash: similarly a justice of the king's bench 'lent' £100, of which only £40 was in cash. In these cases it is obvious that the real loans were only £20 and £40 respectively, or even less (for that is the repayment figure): the balances merely represent an attempt on the part of the judges to get it put on record that the king really did owe them certain sums on account of salary which he had hitherto omitted

[1] A year later (23 July 1401) £14 odd out of the forfeited issues of the former Ricardian sheriff of Cambridgeshire and Huntingdonshire, Andrew Newport, was still being assigned (to the wardrobe).

[2] Ramsay notes this practice and refers to it more than once as common form: indeed, he seems to think that all clerical tenths were habitually anticipated in this way, but in fact entries of precisely this type are found only during this term, though that is not to say that *normally entered* loans were not raised from collectors of clerical tenths from time to time on subsequent occasions.

to pay! The sum total of 'genuine' loans was over £11,000, mostly in small packets from 176 lenders: the only really large loans were one of £1,333 6s. 8d. made by London on 6 July, and one of £1,038 from the king's esquire, John Norbury, now treasurer of England (25 September). *Prestita restituta* were very few and small, but fictitious loans came to over £8,000 and there were fifty-three of them. The principal sufferers were the two Percies, father and son —Hotspur with £600 drawn on London (26 June), and his father with £540 drawn mainly on Hull and Boston (6 July): on 15 July Wykeham also failed to collect £500 from customs revenue.

		£	s.	d.	%
MICHAELMAS 1400-01:	Cash	6,357	9	4½	11
	Assigned	28,706	16	7½	50
	Book-keeping	22,019	9	6½	39
	Total	57,083	15	6½	100

The small cash total includes a further £615 received on 11 December towards the fund which had been started in Richard II's time for the emperor of Constantinople. Some deterioration of the revenue was reflected by the steep rise in fictitious loans from £8,000 to almost £17,000: the principal sufferers were Sir John Stanley, lieutenant of Ireland, with £2,500 in seven tallies on the customs (26 October and 26 February); the chamber, with £2,000 in one tally on London (22 November); and Richard Whittington (8 February) with ten tallies on assorted customs, worth £1,000. Apart from these large defaults, the shortage of money is well illustrated by the fact that from this term onwards it was quite common for the exchequer to fall into arrears of salary not only to the judges but to numerous small officials of its own (e.g. 25 February), all of whom are credited with 'loans' for the petty amounts owing to them. 'Genuine' loans were in fact fairly high this term at £5,049, of which the chamber advanced £1,000 (11 December) and Whittington and Sir Hugh Waterton[1] another £666 13s. 4d. each (both on 5 February 1401).

[1] At one time chamberlain of Henry (when still earl of Derby) and a prominent landowner on the Welsh marches, *Cal. Pat. Rolls*, 1396-9; 70-1. He is also found acting with Whittington and others in London (1406): *Cal. of Select Pleas, etc., of the City of London*, 1381-1412, p. 279.

		£	s.	d.	%
EASTER 1401:	Cash	20,904	12	5	30
	Assigned	32,933	7	6½	46
	Book-keeping	17,149	16	4½	24
	Total	70,987	16	4	100

This term showed some financial recovery, for the parliament of January 1401 had voted a subsidy, to be raised half at Trinity (29 May) and half at All Saints (1 November), together with tunnage and poundage for two years, though at slightly reduced rates.[1] The first half of this subsidy was clearly coming in well in cash during June, even though there had been heavy advance assignments on it as early as 16 May to the extent of £4,000. It was overlapped as usual by the less valuable clerical tenths, payment of which persisted into July. The numerous assignments, which on nine days out of 25 exceeded, sometimes very largely, £1,000 in value, included £1,000 apiece for the prince of Wales and the earl of Rutland on 2 September, the last day of the term. Many more assignments miscarried and appeared as fictitious loans, totalling £14,235: thus on 6 May the chamber failed to collect £1,600 from London customs, while on 13 May even the mayor and aldermen themselves were unable to recover £1,333 6s. 8d. assigned to them on the same source. On 30 June the London customs again failed to honour no less than 17 tallies, totalling £1,000, in favour of the chamber. There were no really large genuine loans, however, except one of £666 13s. 4d. from John Norbury and Laurence Allerthorp, the new treasurer of England, made through Whittington on 20 July.

		£	s.	d.	%
MICHAELMAS 1401–2:	Cash	14,530	3	10½	22
	Assigned	39,823	5	0½	60
	Book-keeping	12,380	1	6½	18
	Total	66,733	10	5½	100

Cash included a £500 fine on a certain Robert Goushull and his wife *pro transgressione* (31 October—there are no details). Assignment was even heavier than before: thus as early as 7 October

---

[1] Ramsay, *Lancaster and York*, I, 30.

some £1,500 odd was assigned to the chamber, though not much more than £1,050 was actually collected. In fact most of the second half-subsidy voted in the previous January was, rather unusually, assigned, with the exception of a large cash payment of £2,000 or so on 8 November. At the other end of the scale there was a single entry of as little as 4d. (sol') paid in by the collectors in the West Riding on 22 November. On the last day of the term (14 March) assignments rose to £7,153, over £5,000 of which was in favour of Henry Percy, earl of Northumberland; in spite of this, however, the same earl received £700 worth of bad tallies on the same day, whereas his rival Ralph Neville, earl of Westmorland, got the same sum cashed without any difficulty and further contributed a *donum* of £66 13s. 4d. towards the expenses of Roxburgh castle. Genuine loans at £2,390 showed little change from the previous term; the largest lenders were William Parker and Thomas Oyster, both citizens of London, with £700 between them on 28 February, and the bishop of Bath and Wells with £666 13s. 4d. on 14 March. Fictitious loans fell to just under £10,000: among these the chamber failed (15 December) to cash 45 tallies on the customs, worth £1,686 13s. 4d., and William Loveney[1] eleven on the same (30 January) worth just over £900; while on 14 March the earl of Northumberland experienced the inconvenience (four bad tallies on the customs for some £700) already mentioned.

		£	s.	d.	%
EASTER 1402:	Cash	4,076	7	7½	7
	Assigned	29,209	7	4	48
	Book-keeping	26,873	2	11	45
	Total	60,158	17	10½	100

Cash was obviously negligible and no detailed note has been taken of the large assignments which persisted from the first to the last day of the term. Fictitious loans were very little more than in the previous winter, but genuine loans jumped from £2,390 to £16,284, which is the highest total recorded during the reign. Most of them were raised on 11 May, when some sixty-one loans produced £14,020. The chief lenders were John Hende, citizen and draper

---

[1] Clerk of the great wardrobe and one of the alleged murderers of Richard II; Wylie, *Henry IV*, I, 115.

of London, with £2,000; the bishop of Bath and Wells (treasurer of England) with over £1,000, raised partly by pledging his own plate; Richard Whittington (£1,000); and the city of London (£1,333 6s. 8d.). The crown jewels and plate were freely pledged in order to increase the total: thus a London goldsmith, Christopher Tildesley, advanced £500 on the security of two pairs of golden basins, one gilt cup and one gilt salt-cellar. Tildesley also accepted jewels for a further £300, while more 'vessels' and a cross were pledged to other Londoners. One of these, Richard Whittington, mislaid a collar of SS pledged to him in this way and agreed to pay £8 for it. This desperate activity should all be connected with the progress of the dangerous Welsh rising, which had started in the previous year; the rumour that Richard II was still alive in Scotland, which reached London early in May;[1] and the imminent threat, shortly to be realized, of a full-scale Scottish invasion. On 15 July twenty-two more loans were raised, but these were on a small scale and produced rather less than £1,200. It was unfortunate that the largest of the fictitious loans were almost all at the expense of the Percies, who were to break the Scots on 14 September at Homildon Hill. Thus as early as 8 April Hotspur had had two bad tallies on the customs for £1,526, while on 10 July he got three more for over £2000: his father got two bad tallies for another £1,000 on the same day. These defaults to the Percies, constituting nearly half the total value of all the bad tallies levied during the term, may have played some part in the quarrel which began that autumn and developed into the revolt of 1403. The only other creditors who suffered on anything like the same scale were officials, such as Nicholas Usk, the treasurer of Calais, with £666 13s. 4d. in five bad tallies on 21 July, and William Loveney, for the great wardrobe, with just over £800 in a single tally on Ipswich (26 September): once again it was the customs which were unable to bear the heavy burdens imposed on them.

		£	s.	d.	%
MICHAELMAS 1402–3:	Cash	19,910	9	11	27
	Assigned	32,455	4	11	44
	Book-keeping	21,174	13	9½	29
	Total	73,540	8	7½	100

[1] Ramsay, *Lancaster and York*, I, 44.

Henry's financial difficulties were to some extent eased by the parliament which met at Westminster on 30 September, for it continued the existing customs duties to Michaelmas 1405 and granted a fifteenth and tenth, to be raised in three instalments during 1403.[1] The first of these was coming in well by the first half of February and accounted for two-thirds to three-quarters of the cash total for the term. It is possible, but not probable, that this total should be doubled, since at one time or another three-fifths of the assignments were also marked *sol'*, but this seems to have been either an oversight or some experiment in method which was not persisted in, for reference to the issue rolls shows that in practically every case it is correct to treat these entries as assigned. The overburdening of the revenue with large assignments became marked during December: once again the earl of Northumberland was a sufferer, with £750 in two bad tallies on the customs on the 7th, but the fact that the crown itself could not always secure payment, in spite of the new parliamentary grants, was shown on a much bigger scale upon the 9th, when the king's second son, Thomas, now the nominal lieutenant of Ireland,[2] failed to collect ten tallies on the customs worth £5,000, while William Loveney was presented with no less than 45 bad tallies on the same for the great wardrobe, to a total of £5,800. Genuine loans came to about £5,500, among which the only large items were two loans from Whittington, made on 9 December and 26 March and adding up to £1,666 13s. 4d., and a third, value £666 13s. 4d., also dated 26 March, from John Norbury.

EASTER 1403:

(Fragmentary—gross total £16,814 10s. 1½d.)

Only part of one receipt roll survives, beginning on 4 May and terminating abruptly in the middle of 30 May, so that the breakdown totals and percentages are meaningless. There may be some connection with the fact that this Easter term coincided with the second, and major, crisis of the reign—the Percy rebellion: the decisive battle of Shrewsbury was fought on 21 July. In such

[1] Ramsay, *Lancaster and York*, I, 50. About the same time the clergy of the southern province granted one-and-a-half tenths, though with considerable reluctance.

[2] He was only fourteen at this date; became duke of Clarence in 1412; and was killed at Beaugé in 1421.

entries as remain assignment is four times as heavy as cash and book-keeping combined. The most notable payment by this means was one of £2,500 made to John Hende on 21 May *pro certis debitis regis Ricardi II*, contained in two tallies of Richard II's time. Henry's honouring of his predecessor's obligations to this extent at such a moment is, however, less surprising than at first sight appears when it is remembered that Hende was one of his main financial supporters among the Londoners. The only other item worth mentioning is the failure on 4 May of the executors of Nicholas Usk, late treasurer of Calais, now deceased, to collect £833 owing to them, for which they had received seventeen bad tallies on the customs.

		£	s.	d.	%
MICHAELMAS 1403–4:	Cash	7,222	13	0	11
	Assigned	39,470	14	9	58
	Book-keeping	20,637	11	9	31
	Total	67,330	19	6	100

By 2 September, Henry, who had reached Worcester and was hoping to deal with the smouldering revolt in Wales, 'found his movements paralysed by absolute want of means'.[1] The southern clergy were persuaded to grant half a tenth, but this did little to ease the situation, and unfortunately parliament did not meet again until January 1404. In the meantime 30 loans, totalling £4,023, were raised on 15 October; the chief contributors were the mayor and aldermen of London with £2,000, and Whittington with £1,000. A further £700 was raised from nine more lenders on 10 December, and the Percy forfeitures, which began to come in from 20 November, were another small source of comfort. There is, however, surprisingly little trace of what should have been the third instalment of the subsidy for 1403, voted in the autumn of the previous year: perhaps most of it had been anticipated in assignments. When parliament met, it did so in an ugly mood and Henry was obliged to make numerous concessions, including a display of clemency towards the captive earl of Northumberland, before he obtained a special land-tax of 1s. in the £ on rents, to be received and expended by four special treasurers of war. This was granted only on condition that no record of the tax should be

[1] Ramsay, *Lancaster and York*, I, 66.

'allowed to live as a precedent':[1] it was therefore not entered on the receipt rolls and its yield is unknown. Though the recorded cash receipts throughout the term remained anaemic, assignment flourished strongly: thus on 20 October the loyal earl of Westmorland had tallies for rather over £1,000, while on the 25th the Londoners got security for their £2,000 loan; and payments on this scale, or larger, continued to be common for the rest of the term. Many more attempts to make assignments went astray, amounting to some £15,000 in all. The chief sufferers were now the royal family, beginning with the new queen, Joan, whose financial agent, Galvan Trent of Lucca, failed on 27 October to cash £1,666 13s. 4d. in ten tallies on the customs made out in her name. This, however, was easily excelled on 6 March by the inability of her unhappy stepson, Thomas, lieutenant of Ireland, to collect some £6,517 in a rather larger number of tallies on the same general source. In addition, the earl of Westmorland himself experienced really serious trouble of this kind for the first time on 25 February 1404, when he was unable to cash £2,633 6s. 8d. in 14 tallies drawn on Hull, London and Southampton. The difficulties of the collectors of customs in meeting these large drafts are well illustrated by a special note on the conduct of Simon atte Ford, collector at Melcombe in Dorset, who on 6 March seems to have been fined an unstated amount for concealing sums collected by him on account of customs: the total is given as £266 13s. 4d., but this included both the money he had concealed and the fine *pro concelamento*. Whether this was actually collected, however, remains doubtful, since the entry was struck through and a note added that the tally had been cancelled by virtue of a writ of great seal recorded *inter mandata* on the memoranda roll for 1405–6. The reason given was that, whereas this tally had been assigned to William Loveney, in order to pay for harness bought for the wardrobe from William Tristour, saddler and citizen of London, the said Tristour had received letters patent authorizing him to collect the farms of two alien priories (Lodres and Carisbrooke) in Dorset and the Isle of Wight, until the amount owing to him should be satisfied. Simon atte Ford's fate is not mentioned.

E A S T E R 1404 :
          (Fragmentary—gross total £7,477 1s. 8d.)

[1] Ramsay, *Lancaster and York*, I, 74–5.

Only a small fragment, covering the period 9 June to 9 August, survives. In the seven days during which business was done cash slightly exceeded the other two totals combined, particularly on 17 June and 17 July, when nearly £3,700 was paid into the exchequer. Assignment was fairly heavy on the first and last days mentioned, when cash receipts were small, but book-keeping was negligible. It is perhaps worth noting that the last entry on 9 August records a payment of £70 *de pretio cert' bonor' que fuerunt Thome Tuttebury clerici defuncti*: presumably this well-known official[1] had died in debt to the crown and his executors were trying to clear his account.

MICHAELMAS 1404–5 :
(Fragmentary—gross total £17,915 16s. 2½d.)

This roll ends abruptly on 2 December, which is a pity as it was excellently kept. The fact that in two terms running no chamberlains' roll survives and we have only fragments of the treasurer's rolls may again bear some relation to the troubles of the time, for all through 1404 the 'hostile influences' at work were building up to the great crisis of the following year,[2] which ended with the crushing of the rebels, the reduction of the Northumbrian castles and the famous execution of the rebel archbishop of York. There were heavy cash payments of just over £3,000 on 20 October (only), while assignment reached £1,526 on 6 November and £8,489 on 2 December. The fact was that the 'unlearned' parliament, from which lawyers had been excluded, met at Coventry on 6 October and proved unusually generous: thus not only were the customs duties prolonged at the existing rates for two years from Michaelmas 1405, but a double subsidy was also granted, 'to be raised by three instalments within twelve months, and expended by Lord Furnival and Sir John Pelham as war treasurers'.[3] Henry may therefore have been rather less than normally pressed for means, although the following terms do not show any great prosperity. Book-keeping in what is left of this roll is principally

[1] He had been treasurer of John of Gaunt and later became keeper of Henry IV's wardrobe: Tout, *Chapters*, IV, 202 n.
[2] Ramsay, *Lancaster and York*, I, 83, quoting Stubbs, *Const. Hist.*, III, 48.
[3] Ibid., 81. The southern clergy, in addition, voted a tenth and a half, and the northern clergy a tenth.

sustained by only two items, viz. a fictitious loan of just under £800 for two bad tallies on the London customs, made on 21 November by Thomas More,[1] and a *prestitum restitutum* for the same amount on 2 December in the name of William, lord Ros. The last is of some interest, as lord Ros was treasurer of England. in 1404 and had received his £800 prest on 17 June from John Oudeby, Haddeley and the other special treasurers of war appointed in the January parliament: this suggests that the conditions attached to the grant made on that occasion could not have been very embarrassing in practice to the crown. Those made by the October parliament must have been even less so, for as has been seen one of the new war treasurers was lord Furnival, who himself became treasurer of England during 1405.

EASTER 1405:		£	s.	d.	%
	Cash	6,632	17	10	13
	Assigned	34,304	17	5	67
	Book-keeping	10,745	15	1½	20
	Total	51,683	10	4½	100

The already mentioned troubles of this summer may account for the fact that there were only ten days of business in the receipt between 1 May and 20 July (in itself an unusually early date for the ending of an Easter term) and yet the rolls (two of which survive) are in good order and appear to be complete. Not much cash entered the exchequer after the first week in May, which brought in nearly £3,600 in two days, but assignment was heavy from the first on every day but one, and reached an exceptionally high level (£12,703) on 1 June. Over £5,600 was raised in genuine loans, of which the war treasurers, Furnival (now also treasurer of England) and Pelham, advanced £1,440 on 1 June—presumably on the security of the double subsidy they were collecting—while John Hende, now mayor of London, produced £3,194 in all, mainly on 20 July (all but £500). Fictitious loans came to about £4,800: among these, the king's third son, John, afterwards duke of Bedford, was the only sizeable loser, with £700 in two tallies on Bristol

---

[1] Formerly receiver-general of queen Anne, and subsequently cofferer and then keeper of the king's wardrobe: Tout, *Chapters*, IV, 201. He is described as 'late keeper' in the receipt rolls from July 1404, but continued to account for some time after that date.

and Melcombe (23 May). Now aged sixteen, he was perhaps already on the Scots marches, iearning his trade under the earl of Westmorland.

MICHAELMAS 1405–6:
(Fragmentary—gross total £18,296 1s. 8½d.)

This is another treasurer's roll, ending in the middle of 10 December. Less than £800 cash was received by that date, but assignment was throughout extremely heavy. As might be expected, book-keeping consisted almost wholly of fictitious loans, rather more than half the total of which was produced by the failure of an attempt made on 9 November to pay off the £2,694 17s. 8d. advanced by John Hende in July. None of the numerous tallies on the customs which this process involved could be honoured and Hende, although he got something on account in the following August, was not finally paid off until December 1407. There is also a curious note, scribbled on the left margin of the roll on 20 November, to the following effect—*memorandum de quodam mutuo facto de domino de Furnyvall de £1,849 5s. 2d.*—but there is no trace of this in the surviving portion of the roll, and if the loan was made at all it must have been after 10 December 1405.

		£	s.	d.	%
EASTER 1406:	Cash	10,922	1	8	22
	Assigned	24,644	10	3	51
	Book-keeping	13,169	2	7½	27
	Total	48,735	14	6½	100

The solitary roll for this term (the royal chamberlain's) is in excellent order, apart from the day-totals, though the number of days of business fell to twelve. The fairly good cash receipts were spread evenly over the term: book-keeping and assignment, on the other hand, present a strange appearance. There was no assignment at all until the last three days of the term, when tallies were suddenly levied for as much as £5,239, £8,905 and £10,499 respectively. Almost the same is true of book-keeping, with the exception of a genuine loan for £600, made on 18 May by Thomas Fauconer, mercer and citizen of London. Then on 28 July—which is also the first day of assignment—comes the raising of £12,085 in 26 genuine loans, an unusual proportion of which consisted of really large ones. Thus John Hende made two separate loans of £1,040 and £1,000 each; and Whittington one of £1,000 and another of £666 13s. 4d.; while lord Furnival (still treasurer of England) lent £2,824. In addition, there was a corporate loan of £1,333 6s. 8d. from London, and a loan of £666 13s. 4d. from the executors of Walter, late bishop of Durham. The sudden burst of financial activity between 28 July and (counting the activity in assignment) 14 August may be accounted for by the obstinate refusal of the March parliament to make any grant until its demands had been satisfied. The result was that the rest of the year was spent in interminable wranglings with the crown, which were not finally resolved until the king had made various important concessions. One of parliament's minor concerns had been the status of foreigners, notably French and Bretons, whom they wanted expelled from the country. Henry steadily refused to take this step, but it is noteworthy that as early as 14 August the receipt rolls contain a list of 106 fines paid in cash by aliens sojourning in London, Kent, Surrey and Middlesex, *pro mora sua habenda infra regnum Anglie*. The average fine paid, however, was only about 20s., which may explain the commons' reluctance to accept this rather mild alternative to banishment: indeed they did not finally consent to it until the end of December,[1] by which time the king, in order to secure a grant, had given way on other, and more important, issues.

		£	s.	d.	%
MICHAELMAS 1406–7:	Cash	40,025	5	8	63
	Assigned	15,915	7	8½	26
	Book-keeping	7,146	11	9½	11
	Total	63,087	5	2	100

This is the first term in Henry's reign during which there were any really heavy cash receipts, and, though better sustained from this point onwards, they never reached this level again in his day. They came in mostly during February and the first four days of March 1407 and evidently represented the proceeds of the subsidy granted in the previous December. In fact there was practically no assignment at all after 13 December (up to which date it had been fairly

[1] Ramsay, *Lancaster and York*, I, 102.

heavy) apart from a very little early in March. Book-keeping, on the other hand, was always on the light side: it included some £5,000 of genuine, but only £2,000 of fictitious, loans. The latter were all small and scattered, but among the genuine lenders the treasurer, lord Furnival, was outstanding with £2,448, advanced on 11 December; while on 4 March the earl of Westmorland lent £902. Meanwhile, on 13 December, William Tristour, saddler and citizen of London, had produced £533 6s. 8d., repayment of which was secured, like his bills for harness supplied to the wardrobe, on the farms of alien priories in Dorset and the Isle of Wight (Lodres and Carisbrooke) granted him by letters patent until all the debts owing to him should be satisfied.

		£	s.	d.	%
EASTER 1407:	Cash	21,022	19	5	49
	Assigned	4,716	13	4	11
	Book-keeping	17,173	17	0	40
	Total	42,913	9	9	100

The continuance of the high cash percentage (though not of the abnormally large cash total) in this term can be attributed only in part to the final payments made on account of the subsidy, which took place early in April: the fact that 1407 was perhaps the most peaceful summer which Henry had yet enjoyed[1] may have had something to do with it. There were only four days on which any assignments were made, while fictitious loans declined in sympathy to a little over £1,200. On the other hand there was another considerable burst of real borrowing, caused no doubt by the fact that actual revenue, although principally in cash, was at its lowest for seven years. Thus on 9 May Richard Whittington, now mayor of the staple, together with other merchants of that body, lent £4,000 to the crown, followed by a further £4,000 on 12 June, when other large loans brought the total for the term up to nearly £16,000. In particular, John Hende lent £2,500; John Norbury £2,000; and Whittington again, in his other capacity as mayor of London (for he seems to have held the two mayoralties simultaneously) an individual loan of £1,000. Recourse was also had for the first time to alien financiers in the persons of the Albertini of Florence, who

---

[1] Ibid., 108.

produced £1,000 and were 'at hand' for household needs[1] in the later part of the summer. Smaller loans on 12 June included £500 from the earl of Westmorland and £333 6s. 8d. in a joint loan from various clerks of the chancery. This last was paid by the hands of Robert Claydon, clerk of the hanaper, and obviously represented something more than the arrears of salary (less than £20 in all) 'lent' on 15 June by individual officers of the exchequer: it is in fact the first of several interesting demonstrations during this and the following reign of the small fortunes being made in one way or another by even the humbler members of the civil service.

		£	s.	d.	%
MICHAELMAS 1407-8:	Cash	33,166	12	7½	37
	Assigned	47,272	11	9½	52
	Book-keeping	9,960	13	2	11
	Total	90,399	17	7	100

The treasurer's roll for this term has been cut into two separate parts between 14 and 17 February and is unique in that each part has also been totalled separately: the term total, however, at the end shows that nothing is missing. Parliament met at Gloucester in October and was induced, after some trouble with the commons, to grant a subsidy and a half, together with prolongation of the customs duties for two years from Michaelmas 1408.[2] Mention was made by the chancellor, archbishop Arundel, of the loans which had had to be raised during the summer, with special reference to those advanced by members of the king's council, though these do not seem to have totalled more than £900. Payment of the subsidy was made mostly during February 1408 and helped to produce the large cash total: assignment, on the other hand, was even heavier, touching £9,000 on 20 January alone, £6,000 on 4 March, £18,000 on the 5th of the same month and nearly £13,000 on the 12th, besides smaller figures on two other days. This as usual brought a crop of fictitious loans: thus as early as 16 November the king's fourth son, Humphrey, later duke of Gloucester, made his first appearance with £866 13s. 4d. in three bad tallies on Hull, and on 4 March Sir John Tiptoft, the new keeper of the wardrobe, failed

[1] Wylie, *Henry IV*, III, 65.
[2] Ramsay, *Lancaster and York*, I, 109-10.

to collect £2,246, also on the customs. The next day the prince of Wales was £1,000 out of pocket and Ralph, earl of Westmorland, £300—again owing to the failure of three tallies drawn on Hull—while on the 12th the same earl lost a further £200; the king's second son, Thomas, £666 13s. 4d.; and the treasurer of Calais, Richard Merlawe, £1,500 in seven tallies: all these were again failures of the customs. Genuine loans stood at no more than £1,930, rather more than half of which was produced by Whittington and Hende between them.

		£	s.	d.	%
EASTER 1408:	Cash	27,830	0	6½	66
	Assigned	13,616	19	3	32
	Book-keeping	840	10	9	2
	Total	42,287	10	6½	100

The high cash figure undoubtedly reflects the continued collection of the grant made at Gloucester, which seems to have been unaffected by the old earl of Northumberland's final rising during February and his defeat and death at Bramham Moor. Ramsay thinks[1] that, in spite of failing health, Henry actually discharged the duties of treasurer himself for part of this term, but Sir John Tiptoft was certainly treasurer by 14 July. Assignment was fairly steadily employed after the first day or two, but never on a really large scale: as a result of this discretion, fictious loans shrank to less than £700 in all, and there was hardly any genuine borrowing.

		£	s.	d.	%
MICHAELMAS 1408–9:	Cash	22,880	16	3	35
	Assigned	37,737	17	4	57
	Book-keeping	5,382	9	8	8
	Total	66,001	3	3	100

Though the percentage fell sharply, it will be seen that the actual amount of cash received was only about £5,000 less than in the summer, but, since there was no parliament during the whole of this exchequer year and the subsidy and a half was practically exhausted, the cash inflow must have come principally from

[1] Ibid., 113.

customs. Assignment, though continuously employed at a fairly high level through the entire term, was singularly successful in attaining its objects, for there were hardly any fictitious loans, although nearly £5,300 worth of genuine ones. Almost all of these were raised early in the term (e.g. 27 October), and Whittington was once again responsible for almost half the total, viz. £2,433 6s. 8d. in all. Hende and Norbury contributed £1,000 apiece, and the balance came from smaller lenders.

		£	s.	d.	%
EASTER 1409:	Cash	10,201	4	9	24
	Assigned	25,815	11	11½	62
	Book-keeping	5,893	11	8½	14
	Total	41,910	8	5	100

Cash receipts, though they occurred on every day of business, continued to shrink steadily in value. Assignment, which was also fairly evenly spread, remained relatively high but was beginning to feel the strain again, for whereas genuine loans fell to only £650 odd (of which Hende lent £533 6s. 8d. on 4 May) fictitious loans rose sharply to £5,240. Most of this was for the account of Thomas, lieutenant of Ireland, who on 27 May was unable to collect on twenty-seven customs tallies totalling £4,666 13s. 4d., but his brother Humphrey was also in difficulties, though to a much smaller extent. He was in fact still trying to obtain the money owing to him since November 1407, but two of the fresh tallies he received in May 1409, value £533 6s. 8d., again went wrong, and he had five new ones on Boston, Hull and Ipswich in their place. As will be seen below, these too were dishonoured by July 1410, and he did not finally secure payment until December of that year.

		£	s.	d.	%
MICHAELMAS 1409–10:	Cash	6,909	14	3	16
	Assigned	21,871	13	10½	49
	Book-keeping	15,324	16	0	35
	Total	44,106	4	1½	100

The steady fall in cash receipts can be explained by the fact that, although parliament met in January and again granted one and a half subsidies, their collection was to be spread over three years.[1] Although customs duties were as usual prolonged for two years from the following Michaelmas and the clergy of both provinces made a grant, there is no doubt that the king was gravely disappointed and financially embarrassed: Ramsay, for example, stresses[2] the inadequacy of the revenues in comparison with the high cost of naval defence and of garrisoning Ireland, Wales and Calais. It is true that from this time until November 1411 the prince of Wales and his party on the council virtually took over the government, for the king was now a permanently sick man, but it is more than doubtful whether this temporary change did much to ease Henry's mind. The new government, like the old. had to have recourse both to borrowing and to continuous assignment—not without the usual, if not invariable, rise in fictitious loans. As early as 10 October a group of Venetian and Genoese merchants had advanced £600, but the first really large loan was not raised until 22 November, when the city of London produced £4,666 13s. 4d.: a further £666 13s. 4d. was lent by John Norbury and as much again by John Hende, both on 30 January. There was also a scattering of smaller loans, which brought the total up to £7,676. Fictitious loans were only £200 less: the most important of them took place on 22 and 30 November and were only three in number. On the 22nd, Thomas Brounflete, the treasurer of the household, was unable to cash some thirty-five tallies on the customs, worth £2,591, while on the 30th three similar tallies, given to the Londoners as security for their recent loan, failed to repay £2,666 13s. 4d. of it: finally, on the same day, the king himself was unable to collect £1,000 owing to him from the exchequer.

		£	s.	d.	%
EASTER 1410:	Cash	7,974	12	10½	18
	Assigned	26,652	13	8	59
	Book-keeping	10,655	13	8	23
	Total	45,283	0	2½	100

This roll presents much the same picture as that of the previous term, except that while cash is only slightly higher, assignment

[1] Ramsay, *Lancaster and York*, I, 124.
[2] Ibid.

shows an increase of nearly £5,000: both were spread fairly evenly over the whole period. Fictitious loans fell to £2,800, but Thomas Brounflete was still finding difficulty in cashing tallies for the household or wardrobe:[1] thus on 8 May he had five bad tallies on the customs for £833 6s. 8d. and on 31 July four (rather unusually) on the hanaper for £252 10s. 4d. On 16 June the Albertini failed to secure repayment of their £1,000 loan through the customs, while on 8 July, as has been seen above, the king's son Humphrey, who had long been trying to collect a debt of £533 6s. 8d., was disappointed for the second time. New loans, on the other hand, were slightly higher than before at £7,826: the first contributor was the king himself (27 May) with £1,000 from the chamber. On 9 June £4,340 was raised in 21 loans, including the first £1,000 from the young Henry Beaufort, bishop of Winchester and supporter of the prince of Wales's party, now in power: as bishop, and later as cardinal, he was destined to be the main financial prop of the crown, on a scale unequalled in England during the Middle Ages, for the whole of his generation. On 17 July 27 more loans were raised, but these produced only £2,486 in all: John Hende, with £666 13s. 4d., was the only sizeable lender.

		£	s.	d.	%
MICHAELMAS 1410–11:	Cash	10,670	13	10	29
	Assigned	25,256	19	5½	69
	Book-keeping	665	5	3	2
	Total	36,592	18	6½	100

The roll for this term suggests that something may perhaps have been done by the prince's party to ease the perpetual straits of the crown, for book-keeping of all kinds was reduced almost to vanishing point. Yet the cash revenue was little increased and assignment actually fell by £1,400, so that the relief, if any, can only have been temporary and was probably brought about by drastic economies, such as suspending payment of pensions, which in their nature could not be kept up for long. It is unfortunate that no roll survives for the next term, Easter 1411—the last in which the prince's party was in power.

[1] He is described indifferently as treasurer of the household or keeper of the wardrobe.

EASTER 1411: No surviving roll.

		£	s.	d.	%
MICHAELMAS 1411–12:	Cash	19,877	16	3½	61
	Assigned	12,773	17	1½	39
	Book-keeping	102	5	0	—
	Total	32,753	18	5	100

If the prince's party had indeed initiated any new financial policy involving the virtual elimination of what I have called 'book-keeping' entries, it looks as if, for this term and indeed for the brief remainder of the reign, it managed to survive the party's fall from power. It was in fact with some apparent reluctance that the parliament which met on 3 November saw Henry's reassertion of himself and the dismissal of the prince. None the less it renewed the customs for a year from Michaelmas 1412 and voted 'an immediate supply in the shape of an impost of 6s. 8d. on every £20 worth of land or rent in lay hands'.[1] In spite of the unusual nature of this tax there seems to have been no stipulation on this occasion that it should not go on record, with the result that cash receipts rose very sharply, and in fact touched their highest figure for three years. Assignment, on the other hand, fell even further than cash rose, and since there was practically no element of book-keeping of any kind, the gross total—and even the net revenue total—for the term declined to among the lowest of the reign. This may account for the partial debasing of the coinage—10% for gold and 20% for silver—which was sanctioned, as a desperate expedient, by this parliament,[2] but the immediate financial sequel is unknown, for once again all three rolls for the ensuing Easter term are missing.

EASTER 1412: No surviving roll.

		£	s.	d.	%
MICHAELMAS 1412–13:	Cash	17,666	18	10	40
	Assigned	26,045	2	11½	58
	Book-keeping	1,010	7	6	2
	Total	44,722	9	3½	100

[1] Ramsay, *Lancaster and York*, I, 133. The demesne lands of peers seem to have been liable, as they were in 1404, although they were exempt from ordinary fifteenths and tenths.   [2] Ibid., 134.

THE RECEIPT OF THE EXCHEQUER, 1377–1485

The royal chamberlain's roll is the only one which survives for this term and the marginals for about £1,900 worth of entries in it are missing: however, it has been found possible to classify most of these with a fair degree of probability, and in any case their total value is less than 4% of the whole. Cash, it will be noted, was still fairly high, while assignment returned to what may be regarded as an average level for the last three years of the reign. But the total of real revenue, though showing some improvement on recent figures, was still nothing like that reached during most Michaelmas terms during the previous century, or even in the earlier part of Henry's own reign: in short, it does nothing to bear out the wild statements occasionally encountered in the works of general historians,[1] to the effect that Henry's 'parsimony', like that of Henry VII, filled the treasury and left a substantial sum for his successor. On the contrary, he was worse off in his last years than he had ever been and almost certainly died in debt: indeed, one of his last acts (on 2 March—he died on the 20th) was to borrow another £1,000 from Whittington, while Henry V in his first term, as will be seen below, had to borrow nearly £11,000.

[1] E.g., J. J. Bagley, *Margaret of Anjou*, p. 30.

CHAPTER III

ANALYSIS, 1377-1413

Finance plays a considerable part in the tradition of 1399. The Lancastrian revolution, it has long been held, saved not only parliament and the constitution, but also the property of the subject. Henry IV was in fact the elected saviour of society, that is of the propertied classes, from an inconstant ruler who held property and promises alike in small respect. Had not Richard compelled men to seal blank charters, raised forced loans, and levied 'intolerable fines', all as the natural accompaniment of that monstrous violation both of property rights and of his own pledged word, the sequestration of the Lancastrian inheritance? Did not Henry, on the contrary, point out:

> it es noght my will that no man thynk it be waye of Conquest I wold disherit any man of his heritage franches or other ryghtes that hym aght to have?[1]

And had not the good principle, as the result of Henry's victory, triumphed finally over the bad, so that justice and security, credit and the honouring of obligations returned to England with the limitation of the monarchy? It is true that Henry's honesty made for impoverishment, but at least he was honest: he had to be. And as between the two alternatives, a rich and irresponsible monarch ruling absolutely over a bankrupt people, or a pauper government dependent on the good will of its wealthier subjects, there could be no choice: on all grounds, but especially on moral grounds, the latter was infinitely preferable. Such at any rate were the views of many men, possibly in the fourteenth and fifteenth, certainly in the seventeenth, eighteenth, and nineteenth centuries.

There is, of course, much truth in this interpretation of the events of 1399. Few will deny the arbitrary inconsequence of Richard's later years or on grounds whether of policy or morality

---

[1] *Rot. Parl.*, III, 423.

excuse his confiscation of the Lancastrian estates.[1] Again, whatever sympathy may be provoked by Richard's sensitive, art-loving temperament and the provocation he had frequently received, there will be few to claim for him any measure of real statesmanship. It has frequently been pointed out that, even if despotism can be a good, Richard had neither the genius nor the application to make a good despot. But it does not follow from this that it is necessary to concede the whole Lancastrian position. Henry's parliamentary title has been called in question,[2] and what is at least a strong presumption has been established that the revolution of 1399 was not a parliamentary revolution at all, but a successful act of selfish usurpation, on which no parliamentary conditions were in fact imposed, although it is true that there was an attempt to impose them, perhaps more than one attempt, taking into account the history of the next few years. As Tout has written, 'there was no clear-cut distinction between the monarchical policy of the fifteenth and that of the fourteenth century. Henry IV ruled by the same machinery and through the same persons as Richard II.'[3] The idea of 'Lancastrian constitutionalism' is therefore moribund, though it is not quite dead.[4] It will no doubt be found to have more and more life in it as the fifteenth century, and the study of the fifteenth century, advances, but it has little place in the revolution of 1399. It does not cause, but it is possible that it grows out of, the weakness of Henry IV.

For weakness there undoubtedly was. This weakness, to quote Tout again,[5] 'made impossible any aggressions of the sort Richard had loved'. What was the cause of this weakness, if the cause was not solely parliamentary control? One possible answer to that

[1] It is probable that personal and political should be added to financial considerations in guessing at the motives behind Richard's action, namely the desire to prevent the wide powers of the county palatine of Lancaster from passing into the hands of his rival. Cf. Armitage-Smith, *John of Gaunt*, x, esp. pp. 203–10 on the palatinate, which had been made hereditary in February 1390.

[2] By G. T. Lapsley, *Eng. Hist. Rev.*, XLIX, 423 ff., 577 ff.

[3] Tout, *Chapters in Mediaeval Administrative History*, IV, 67.

[4] Cf. T. F. Plucknett, 'Lancastrian Constitutionalism', in *Tudor Studies*, 1924. The studies of Dr. S. B. Chrimes have also helped to illuminate this problem. It does not seem that H. L. Gray, in his *Influence of the House of Commons on Early Legislation*, was justified in reverting to the older view.

[5] Loc. cit.

question is that it was primarily a financial weakness, brought about by the revolution: the real change in the financial position of the crown under Henry IV lies in the comparative weakness of its collecting power, and the rapid narrowing of the gap between the financial resources of the crown and those of its greater subjects. It is the object of this chapter to compare both the frequency and extent of Henry's borrowings with those of Richard's various governments, including the governments of the minority, and to contrast the extent to which Henry's government, in comparison with that of Richard, defaulted on its obligations. When that has been done it may be difficult to avoid the conclusion that most of Richard's later acts, while often vicious in principle, were limited in effect and even not without some shadow of precedent. It may also appear that the revolution conducted by the alleged champion of property rights in 1399 did in fact largely destroy the confidence which it is supposed to have restored. The first step in this inquiry is to produce a set of gross totals for Richard II. This will be found in the tables at the end of this book.

The most illuminating facts that emerge from such a table are as follows. In the first place, Tout's statement[1] that Richard's average annual revenue was 'in the neighbourhood of £140,000' can only be maintained if nothing whatsoever is deducted for book-keeping, that is, Tout's statement is only true of the uncorrected totals. Actually, real and fictitious loans and *prestita restituta* have to be deducted to the extent of nearly half a million pounds in all for the whole reign, and this brings the average of 'real' annual revenue for 21 full years down to £116,500, well below the 'more conservative estimate, say of £120,000', attributed by Tout to Ramsay. The total might be slightly higher, if loans not repaid were reckoned into revenue, but as I make the maximum total of these loans to be just under £36,000,[2] the effect, spread over the whole reign, is small, and still leaves the average below £120,000. Henry's 'real' average, on the other hand, is well below £90,000,

---

[1] *Chapters*, IV, 213.

[2] This is an absolute maximum. At the other extreme I should take the total amount of loans raised in and after August 1397, and not marked repaid, viz. about £18,000, as a basic minimum. Nothing less than a detailed search of the issue rolls for the entire reign, as well as for the reign of Henry IV, could determine where, between these two figures, the true total lies, but I am reasonably certain that the lower total is nearer to the truth.

and though allowance must be made for the gaps in his series, for the possibility of some loans not being repaid, for the unenrolled subsidy of 1404 and for the revenues of the Lancaster and Hereford estates, it is still very unlikely that Henry's real revenue approached an average of £100,000, i.e. it was probably about £20,000 a year less than Richard's.

The next point of comparison lies in the book-keeping totals of the two reigns. Henry's total amounts to £254,288 6s. 5½d. against Richard's £493,939 14s. 3d. This yields an average of £10,171 per term for 25 terms (the rolls for two more terms are missing entirely) against one of £11,225 for 44 terms (the roll for one term missing entirely). On the other hand, four of Henry's 25 rolls are fragmentary against one of Richard's so that Henry's average ought to be slightly higher. None the less, it is probable that the total book-keeping average sinks slightly under Henry, and it remains to determine what that means. This can best be done by analysing the book-keeping totals for the two reigns thus:

AVERAGE PER TERM	'Genuine' loans	Fictitious loans	*Prestita restituta*	Total
	£	£	£	£
Richard II	5,119	1,867	4,239	11,225
Henry IV	4,664	5,409	£98	10,171

The first of these comparisons suggests that there is not very much to choose between the borrowing activities of Richard and of Henry, particularly if it be remembered that for each reign loans not repaid are none the less calculated as true loans. If these loans are to be ruled out, Richard's average will have to come down by something between £400 and £700, and Henry's will also have to be reduced, but not by so much. That is to say, for all intents and purposes, the average borrowing activity per term of the two kings may be taken as approximately equal. It does not follow, however, that they always borrowed money from the same classes of people, and it will be necessary later on to analyse a list of each king's creditors.

The second comparison is entirely in Richard's favour. It means, briefly, that on an average his exchequer officials cut £1,867 worth per term of useless tallies, which could not be converted into cash by those who held them, while under Henry IV the average rises to no less than £5,409 worth per term. This indicates a considerable degree of financial disorganization, and in particular an inability to get in revenue on the part of local officers of the crown.[1] It also shows what is at the best a certain amount of miscalculation and misplaced optimism on the part of the exchequer, or at the worst a deliberate attempt to put off pressing creditors by means of what were known to be almost certainly worthless instruments of payment. The psychological effect of this great increase in the percentage of bad tallies cannot be neglected: repeated disappointment, whether his or theirs, can hardly have improved Henry's relations with his creditors and may even be held to have played its part in the growing discontent with his rule which marks the early years of his reign. But before guesses of that kind can be substantiated it will be necessary, as in the previous case, to make and analyse a list of those who received the largest number of bad tallies (in money value) in both reigns.

The column headed *Prestita restituta* shows a still more striking difference between the two periods, but it is a difference which, for the present purpose, I believe to be much less important than the last. The exact nature of these prests is, perhaps, rather obscure, but they clearly fall into two main categories according to their size. Small ones, though never very common, may be found occasionally at almost any date within this period, but large ones are limited to the first eighteen years of Richard's reign, i.e. they do not occur after 1395. The small prests are certainly of very little importance: they seem to represent actual cash advanced to and eventually handed back by an official, or not handed back but

---

[1] It has been suggested to me by Professor Postan that it might mean no more than a diminution in revenue from the customs, on which the great bulk of assignment was regularly made. He points out that the wool export was steadily declining and the cloth export steadily increasing during this period, and that the customs revenue to be drawn from cloth was only a small fraction of the revenue which could have been drawn from the raw wool out of which the cloth was manufactured. I do not dispute his premises, but apart from the extraordinary imbecility which the exchequer would have shown if it had not been aware of these facts, I do not think that they necessarily lead to the conclusion that the great increase in bad tallies under Henry IV is due to merely economic, unmixed with political, causes. See *Mutua per talliam*, appendix B.

merely deducted from wages, or even assigned in favour of some-one else, when the wages fall due. The large prests on the other hand, those running into several thousand pounds, are clearly con-nected with the procedure for making payments to armies in the field. The later and simpler method of financing such expeditions, i.e. the method adopted after 1395, was to make over the necessary assignments direct to the commanders themselves, who then seem to have made their own arrangements for collection or discount, whichever was employed, but before that date the practice was merely to draft the assignments in the names of the commanders, and to make officials of the household or of the receipt responsible for the actual collection and transmission of the money, which became a 'prest' while it was in their hands and a *prestitum resti-tutum* when they passed it on. One reason why this practice was abandoned during Richard's reign may have been the frequent inability of the exchequer to resist the temptation of making further assignments in favour of third parties on the balances already ear-marked for the forces while they were still in the collecting officials' hands. Perhaps it was the effort to eliminate this temptation, and the obvious confusion which must result from giving way to it, which led to the substitution of household officials for tellers and chamberlains of the receipt and to the cutting down of the danger period, during which the money was actually under the officials' control, from several months to only two or three days by the time of the first Irish expedition: after that expedition the paymaster method disappears entirely, and we must credit Richard's govern-ment with a minor administrative reform.

It will be seen that in any event all *prestita restituta* must be written off as mere book-keeping, as Ramsay has correctly pointed out,[1] and that the abrupt decrease in their number and value in the later years of Richard II's reign has no political or economic significance.[2] Once again, however, it will be necessary to look

[1] *Revenues of the Kings of England*, II, 427.

[2] I confess I cannot follow a suggestion that the change may have had much more serious effects than this merely technical one, in that it may have revealed for the first time a hitherto hidden mass of bad assignment. This, it is said, would offer yet another explanation why the total of bad tallies rises so steeply under Henry IV. The idea seems to be that the existence of paymasters of the forces under Richard not only removes a whole mass of payments out of the receipt and issue rolls, but also makes it impossible to say whether the entries in the receipt rolls represent the

more closely at the names of those who received prests and restored them before going more deeply into the question.

To sum up so far, it will appear, firstly, that Henry enjoyed only about five-sixths of the real revenue of Richard, but that he borrowed quite as freely as Richard did, though not necessarily from the same persons, and this although in the matter of assignments he defaulted much more frequently upon his obligations. This paradox demands an explanation. Secondly, in the matter of *prestita restituta*, it looks as if what is simply an important change in methods of book-keeping took place towards the end of Richard's reign. We can get no further without a more detailed examination.

Nearly all the persons concerned in credit transactions with the crown during this period fall at once into certain obvious classes. These are, firstly, the household, including the chamber, the wardrobes, the king's clerks, knights, and esquires, and the royal serjeants-at-arms. Then come the more public departments of the chancery, reckoning with it the office of the privy seal, and the exchequer. I have also placed one or two insignificant items

first or the second assignment to the king's creditor. To this I would reply: (*a*) the only payments removed out of the rolls at any time, other than a limited class which I will mention shortly, are the details of the total payment made by assignment to the commanders, whose *total* will normally appear in both series, while (paymaster or no paymaster) the details are seldom given. (*b*) If attempts were made to pay the king's other creditors by assignment of the paymaster's balances they must have been made by royal writ or tally. If by tally, they will appear in the body of the receipt rolls: if by written warrant only, they will ultimately appear as parts of what I have called 'complex' assignments, not in the body but in the right-hand margin of the roll. If they are unsuccessful assignments, i.e. if the paymaster cannot meet the writ or tally—and this is the special case that is in mind—everything depends on whether it is actually a writ alone or a tally which has been used. If it is a tally, the transaction will still be recorded (as a fictitious loan) in the receipt roll; if it is only a writ unaccompanied by a tally, it is true that all trace of the attempted transaction will probably disappear. The theory, then, is right to this limited extent, but the point is that the complete disappearance of bad writs, as distinct from bad tallies, of assignment from the records has nothing to do with the appointment or non-appointment of paymasters of the forces. It is true of all unsuccessful writs of assignment, when they are unaccompanied by tallies, except of writs or bills under the great seal. This vitiates to some extent, though not I think seriously, my figures for fictitious loans, but again the point is that it vitiates them as much under Henry IV as under Richard II. See the discussion in the first two appendices to this book.

proceeding from clerks of the signet under the same head, though at this date they belong more properly to the household. The justices, and other law officers of the crown, should come next, but their contribution to this study is so insignificant that it did not seem worth while to keep them in a separate pigeon-hole, and they have accordingly been placed under the omnibus heading of 'local officials', which includes the treasurers and victuallers of Calais, the lieutenants of Ireland, captains and constables of castles, wardens of the Scottish marches, justices of Wales and Chester, sheriffs, escheators, customs collectors, clerks of works, and clerks of the king's ships. This exhausts the classification of direct crown servants, and we come next to the Church, which appears under two main headings, viz. 'bishops' and 'religious' (i.e. ecclesiastical corporations). The second title takes its name from the great preponderance as lenders of regular monastic houses, but also includes a few secular clergy below episcopal rank, an occasional dean and chapter, friars minor or preaching friars, a hospital or two, and other charitable foundations. Laymen outside the king's immediate employ fall naturally into four classes, viz. magnates, country gentry, burgesses, and citizens of London: the last deserve a separate heading, because in both reigns their contributions easily outweigh those of all the other cities and boroughs in the kingdom put together. This leaves out only aliens, and the list is complete except for a small appendix of persons unidentified. This appendix is insignificant for both reigns, partly because the receipt rolls themselves very often give a brief description of persons they mention, while, where they do not do so, the chancery calendars, particularly the calendar of patent rolls, usually make it possible to place a name in the right compartment.

Before going any further, however, it is necessary to evolve some simple mechanism for equating two reigns of different length, viz. of $22\frac{1}{4}$ and $13\frac{1}{2}$ financial years; attested, moreover, by a slightly different weight of evidence. This could be done by taking averages, as before, but in detailed comparisons averages obscure the time factor and are apt not only to appear unreal but to be actually misleading. Another difficulty is that, while the $22\frac{1}{4}$ years of Richard's reign contain one quarter term, and one term for which the rolls are missing, Henry's reign is considerably more incomplete, containing as it does, out of a potential 27 rolls, only 21 full rolls and four fragments, the rolls for two whole terms having disappeared entirely. These difficulties are perhaps best surmounted by breaking Richard's reign into two at the appropriate date of April 1389 (the end of the Michaelmas term),[1] and treating each half of it as roughly equivalent to the whole reign of Henry IV. The effect is as follows:

	Richard II 1377–89	1389–99	Henry IV, 1399–1413
Rolls	$22\frac{1}{4}$	21	21 + four fragments
Years	$11\frac{3}{4}$	$10\frac{1}{2}$	$13\frac{1}{2}$

This approximation to equality as between the three periods and the number of rolls seems near enough to justify tabulating absolute totals for each period instead of striking averages for the whole of each reign. This method has the added advantage of comparing with each other and with Henry IV, firstly the Richard who, during the minority, the period of Michael de la Pole's ascendancy and the appellant régime, was continuously dependent on other people and, owing to his youth, was to some extent excused direct responsibility, and secondly the Richard who governed personally, if erratically, from the scene in the council at Westminster on 3 May 1389 to the day of his deposition and certainly during that time bore the full responsibility for what was done. It is also worth noting that the earlier Richard is nowhere accused of the same sort of financial depredation as the later Richard, so that the extent to which the crown at these different times in his reign did in fact borrow and default and advance money makes of itself an interesting comparison.[2]

We may perhaps begin by reviewing in rather general terms the financial operations of the crown in the period 1377–1413, together

[1] Appropriate because his personal power dated from May 1389.

[2] It is, of course, true that during the second part of Richard's reign the abnormalities tend to be concentrated in the last three years, but that seems to be no reason for depriving him of whatever credit may be due for the seven 'good' years. None the less, in what follows, the fact that the greater number of his later real and fictitious loans, though hardly any of his *prestita restituta*, do in fact belong only to the short period 1396–9 requires to be borne in mind.

with the effects upon them of the events of 1399: a more detailed survey, together with the statistical particulars, will be found later in the chapter.

In the first place such an examination makes clear that the need to borrow was not in fact so constant over both reigns as the original index numbers suggest. In round figures Richard's government borrowed £156,000 between 1377 and 1389 and only £69,000 during the rest of the reign, against Henry's £117,000 over a slightly longer period than either of these. Excluding government officials of all kinds, the 'genuineness' of some of whose loans is sometimes open to question, the figures are £121,000,[1] £53,000 and £94,000 respectively, and the averages £5,041, £2,650 and £3,750 per term. In other words, considerably less money was being borrowed by the crown in the ten and a half years immediately preceding the revolution of 1399 than at any other time in the whole period of 36 years under consideration, though, as we have seen, the averages conceal the fact that nearly four-fifths of the borrowing in the middle period is confined to the three years 1396–9.

The 'exchequer years' (Michaelmas to Michaelmas) in which 'genuine' loans[2] amount to five figures are, for Richard, 1378–9, 1381–2, 1383–8 (the appellants being in control for the last two years of that period), 1394–5 and 1396–7. Under Henry IV, for only six of whose years complete figures exist, the critical terms are 1399–1400, 1401–2 and 1406–7. Of these, 1396–7, with over £30,000, and 1406–7 with about £21,000, represent the known peaks in each reign, but in spite of their lateness it remains true to say that each king borrowed less *on an average* in his later than in his earlier years. The political occasions of these great loans are sufficiently obvious; the French war, Richard's two marriages, the first Irish expedition, the autocracy of 1397–9, the rebellions in Wales and elsewhere under Henry. But out of the nine years of really heavy borrowing and the grand total of £174,000 in Richard's reign Richard himself cannot be held personally responsible for more than five of the years and two-thirds of the total, while Henry is not only responsible for the whole of his £94,000, but

---

[1] Excluding also a so-called 'loan' (really a *prestitum restitutum*) of £14,480 3s. 10d. made by the earl of Buckingham and others in 1380. This is dealt with later.

[2] Again excluding Buckingham's.

also for a further amount, which is unknown owing to the fact that for four of his terms the rolls are fragmentary and for two entirely lost, while for the whole period of his personal rule Richard's records are complete.

To sum up, the government in Richard's early years was obliged to borrow freely, especially from aliens and from the mayor and aldermen of London; the mature Richard borrowed hardly at all in four years, very little in another three years, and really heavily in only three years out of ten; while lastly the usurper Henry tried steadily, and not unsuccessfully, to raise whatever money he could, principally from a group of individual Londoners, and as late as 1407, though perhaps not later, was still straining every nerve to raise funds.

There is, of course, little doubt that Henry could borrow as easily as Richard or, for that matter, as easily as Edward III. But it is interesting to find that in practice he often did not borrow from the same people as his predecessor. Thus, while Henry raised considerably more from individual Londoners, though not from the city in its corporate capacity, than had ever been raised before, and while he raised distinctly more from magnates, and slightly more from bishops, than Richard ever did, he raised considerably less from monasteries, country gentry and the smaller boroughs, and a very great deal less from aliens, than the government of Richard's minority had done.[1] It is clear, then, that Henry's government depended for financial backing less upon anything that might be called 'national' support than on a fairly small group of wealthy, independent Englishmen, and this conclusion throws at least a little light on the forces at work in 1399. By that date the men of property, with the exception of Henry himself, the Londoners, and the wreck of the appellant party, had not suffered appreciably from Richard's alleged depredations, but on the other hand there was a good deal of political discontent and those who felt it may have been prepared to capitalize the misfortunes of others in order to put the principal victim, Henry, on the throne and keep him there, possibly, as will be seen, at no small profit to themselves. Whether there had in fact been any real danger of a general attack on property in 1399 is much more open to question

---

[1] This may simply reflect a change in the organization of English trade. The decline begins well before the middle of Richard's reign and is clearly non-political.

than the existence of a strong contemporary belief that such a danger was a very real one.

Meanwhile, there is a second main area of comparison between the two kings in the relative value of their bad tallies or fictitious loans. It should be explained at this point that over the whole period the nominal totals under this head are inflated by repetition; that is to say, a man may be disappointed, for example, three times over in a sum of, say, £100 which is owing to him; on, for example, three successive occasions he may receive a bad tally for the same sum. Hence what is really only £100 will appear as £300 under the head of fictitious loans. However, it would not only be an endless labour to eliminate this element of repetition from the calculation of totals on the receipt rolls but it would also be to a great extent labour misapplied, for the fact that in the imaginary case just cited the king's real debt was only £100 is of less importance than the fact that the creditor had had, so to speak, £300 worth of disappointment while the receipt rolls had been falsified, according to modern ideas, not by £100 but by £300. The gross figures for fictitious loans have, therefore, been accepted in the tables and throughout this book, but it must be remembered that they do not represent the net indebtedness of either Richard or Henry but only the amount by which their promises to pay, often repeated promises to pay the same sum, fell short of their achievement,[1] and also the extent to which the undifferentiated totals in the rolls themselves must be discounted on this particular score. On the other hand, it is of course true that in estimating the volume of discontent the number of disappointed creditors is more important than the total value of fictitious loans, and accordingly in such cases numbers and names[2] will, where possible, be given.

Bearing these facts in mind we may turn to the second main division of the D tables.[3] The figures in this division are remarkable. They show that the face value of worthless tallies cut by Henry's exchequer was over three times as much as under Richard, viz. (in round figures) £135,000 against £45,000 and £37,000 respectively for the two periods of Richard's reign. Of this enormous increase

---

[1] Actually underestimated throughout the period owing to the impossibility of tracing bad writs in the same way as bad tallies of assignment. See above, p. 108, n. 2.

[2] See the later part of this chapter.

[3] See below, pp. 455–7.

in untrustworthiness and insecurity of payment under Henry a slightly larger proportion is, it is true, borne by employees of the crown, especially the household, but there is not a single one of all the headings used for the purposes of this book, from 'household' to 'unidentified', which does not show an increase, usually a very large increase, over the amount recorded in either period of Richard's reign. Apart from the household and 'local officials' the most striking examples are 'magnates', and 'London', though 'bishops', too, show a fairly heavy increase. The fact that these classes correspond to those in which there were also large 'genuine' loans in Henry's time, though not unnatural, for the two types of loan are intimately connected, is partly a coincidence; for fictitious loans were the result not only of non-repayment of real loans, but also of failure on the government's part effectively to meet other admitted obligations, such as the cost of guarding the Scottish marches or of governing Ireland. None the less it looks as if the very classes which had helped Henry to become king were precisely those which suffered most from the dilatoriness and impotence of his exchequer, and this should certainly help to explain his rapidly growing unpopularity and insecurity upon the throne. It was not that he ever repudiated what he owed—he was careful to reserve the stigma of repudiation for his predecessor—but he was apt to be an unconscionably long time in making effective payment. Men of ample means, such as Richard Whittington, substantial merchants not unaware of the intricacies of crown finance and conscious that to press the struggling government too hard would be the surest way to lose their money—these might be content to wait, especially if, as seems likely, they stood to make a handsome profit on the transaction; but magnates, like the Percys who, after making Henry king, had had to find part of their reward in defending a Scottish march for two or three years at what was virtually their own expense, might not be alive to these considerations. It certainly seems, although the gaps in his receipt rolls make guessing dangerous and, moreover, it is not wholly clear which is cause and which is effect, as if Henry's unpopularity and the value per year of his fictitious loans tended to wax and wane together: their number tends to decline steeply after 1407.

However that may be, it is absolutely certain that for some years at least nothing was gained in the matter of fictitious loans, and a great deal lost, by the action of the moneyed interests in 1399. In the last ten and a half years of Richard's reign fictitious loans were easily at the lowest figure they had reached perhaps for half a century,[1] viz. £37,000, of which, moreover, £26,000 was owed to his own household and local officials and only £11,000 to persons outside the administration. This must be contrasted with the £95,000 to the household and £39,000 to outsiders (plus an unknown quantity from the missing rolls) in the thirteen and a half years of Henry's reign.[2]

The second main conclusion must therefore be that the revolution of 1399, like many others, proved to be disappointing in its financial results, at any rate to some of its supporters, particularly among the magnates, and that of this particular feature the real weakness of Henry's position as king was both an effect and a cause.

Compared with the other two the third division in the tables, relating to *prestita restituta*, is not of great importance. The fact is that the very steep and uniform decline in the value and number of prests which clearly begins in the second half of Richard's reign probably reflects, as we have seen, merely a change in administrative method, perhaps only a change in book-keeping, rather than any matter of profound historical significance: indeed, it is likely that it was not in the least affected by the revolution. An analysis of the large 'loan' credited to the earl of Buckingham as commander of the expedition sent to Brittany in 1380[3] suggests that at the beginning of the period it was, as we have seen, the custom to finance a military or naval expedition out of a large sum in assignments to be received and forwarded to the commanders by officials of the household or of the receipt of the exchequer. These assignments would be entered in the issue roll under the names of the military or naval commanders at the date when they were actually made, which would also be regarded as the date of the original 'prest' to the officials. In the body of the receipt roll, however, they appear twice over, viz. both as assignments, and at a later date as

[1] The most casual inspection will reveal the frequency of large fictitious loans in the second half of the reign of Edward III. In 1369–70 a quarter of all the numerous tallies of assignment turned out to be bad tallies.

[2] The percentage relation of fictitious loans to (a) nominal, (b) real revenue in these periods is, for Richard: (a) nominal, less than 3%; (b) real, less than 3½%; while for Henry it is (a) nominal, 11% (b) real, 14%.

[3] For the details of this analysis see the later part of this chapter.

'prests' repaid by the financial officials when their temporary responsibility had ended, in which capacity they are entered and summed in the main column of the receipt roll as if they were real revenue. But this, of course, they are not, owing to the fact that, as already stated, they also appear in the body of the roll as ordinary assignments. It is clear that they can only be counted once as revenue, and they are more properly counted for that purpose as assignments.

We have also seen that in the second half of Richard's reign the officials of the receipt tend to disappear from this process; assignments being either made through officials of the household, as in the first Irish expedition, or immediately in favour of the persons who are actually to spend the money, i.e. without ever creating as at an earlier date the (fictitious) credit fund or 'prest'. By this time, moreover, even when prests are made, the period or term of the prest may be as short as two or three days, thus clearly indicating its artificial character. After 1395, even the officials of the household drop out and practically all assignments are made direct, so that these large prests tend to disappear entirely. The change is of technical interest, but little more; it had already begun, in the case of the second Irish expedition, under Richard II. It does not seem to affect the total volume of assignment, which was certainly heavy under Richard, as it had been under Edward III, and was even heavier under Henry IV: it merely straightens the channel through which assignment flows.

So far, then, the evidence of the receipt rolls on the purely financial point is definitely in Richard's favour. In the last half of his reign, as at no other time in the period under consideration, exchequer promises to pay substantial lenders are being met with reasonable promptitude, and borrowing is not being employed to excess. But this applies principally to the period 1389-96, and the whole gravamen of the financial charge against Richard, the charge which Henry and his supporters pressed in 1399, is that in his last three years he not only did raise abnormal sums of money but also repudiated, permanently, his obligations. The detailed accusations are too well known to quote in detail: they include forced loans, the levying of fines, the compulsory sealing of blank charters, unjust forfeitures, and a special form of blackmail extorted from the counties near London. In them, if true, may be found a substantial cause of the revolution. But little, if any, attempt has hitherto been made to inquire how far these charges may be the product of distortion, malice and exaggeration, and on this point, too, the receipt rolls have certain evidence to give.

That there was some basis in fact for all, or nearly all, these charges no one will deny: the receipt rolls make no attempt to conceal the yield of fines and forfeitures, of loans, forced or otherwise but not repaid, and of at least one of the county contributions, that of Essex: on the contrary, they are set out in detail. But the total is much smaller than we should expect after reading the lurid accounts in the chronicles. Thus, in his last three years, Richard borrowed rather under £40,000 and of this total about £18,000 may not have been repaid. Fines *coram concilio* (a new form) are easily distinguishable and amount to the relatively small sum of £2,456 6s. 8d., levied from only 26 persons in all, some of whom appear to have been royalists.[1] Forfeitures of appellant goods and chattels come to £8,496 7s. 7½d., which may be compared with £15,615 17s. 11d. worth of royalist goods and chattels forfeited in 1386–8. Both figures, of course, exclude lands, the value of which there is no means of determining from the receipt rolls, and there may be other substantial omissions which between them prevent the comparison from being very illuminating. The only county contribution which I have been able to find in the receipt rolls is that of the men of Essex who, apparently with great difficulty, discharge the entire sum of 2,000 marks, with which they have been burdened, in twelve payments made between 13 May 1398 and 30 January 1399. There is no trace of blank charters,[2] but I have found several payments *pro tot denariis in quibus recognoscunt se teneri domino Regi per recognicionem in scaccario Regis.* As far as I know, this formula occurs only during Richard's last years, and probably reflects some method of extortion such as the use of blank charters, but only five persons are involved (though there is an *et alii* with one of them) and the total is only £543 6s. 8d.

Of all these payments those which may be condemned at sight are the fines and forfeitures, the *recogniciones* just mentioned, and

---

[1] E.g., John Hermesthorpe (£250), William Glym (£133 6s. 8d.), Laurence Dru (£93 6s. 8d.).

[2] Tout, *Chapters*, IV, 48 n., remarks that he failed to find in the Public Record Office the specimens that Ramsay, *Genesis*, II, 344, asserted to be there, though he did find 'numerous indentures between individuals and royal agents, notably John Drax, covenanting to lend the king money'.

the Essex contribution, totalling in all some £12,829 7s. 7½d. This is not an unduly large sum, but the manner of its collection alone would be quite enough to cause considerable alarm and irritation in London and in the neighbouring shires, and it has to be remembered both that the chronicles make specific allegations which suggest more abandoned methods and a much larger total, and also that the silence of the receipt rolls is not evidence. The argument *ex silentio* is seldom convincing and least of all in this case, for the receipt rolls do not profess to be a complete register of anything but tallies, and money illegitimately raised by Richard may easily have been intercepted on its way to the receipt, in which case it might not figure in the rolls at all.

However this may be, many will think that at least the £18,000 worth of loans which Richard failed to repay at all should definitely be added to the sum total of his depredations, making a minimum of nearly £31,000 worth of extortion altogether. But there is something odd about these loans. Richard began to borrow heavily in the Michaelmas term of 1396–7, but it is only the loans made in and after the close of the Easter term of 1397 which he generally fails to repay, and even among these there were several, as the detailed survey will show, which were in fact repaid before the end of his reign. If Richard had always meant to repudiate, it is difficult to find any reason for these scattered exceptions.

It is again odd, if Richard meant to repudiate, that he should have taken such especial pains to enrol these loans in the chancery as well as in the exchequer, and to issue to lenders letters patent of acknowledgment under the great seal, containing a definite promise to repay at Easter 1398. During the greater part of his reign this procedure had only been adopted when a good deal of money was being borrowed from several lenders at once: it is an especially solemn procedure, employed for example in the numerous loans raised on the advice of the great council early in 1379. There was nothing new about the outward form of it in 1397. Moreover, it may be pointed out that the sum total obtained by repudiation (say £18,000) was hardly a sum worth having, considering the risks involved in offending so many influential persons and towns.[1] After all, Richard's average income at this date was perhaps nearer

---

[1] In round numbers the figures are: bishops (2) £1,100, magnates (1) £100, country gentry (36) £1,220, London (mayor and aldermen) £6,570, other towns (71) £5,550, religious (72) £3,180, aliens (1) £330.

£120,000 than £100,000. It is indisputable that Richard did not repay on the agreed date, Easter 1398, but it was no new thing for a fourteenth-century government to keep its creditors waiting, and it is at least arguable that, though he was strictly in default, he may still have meant to repay, but that he was surprised by the necessity for the second Irish expedition[1] and by the revolution which followed it. Or, again, Richard may have thought that he had taken surety from the propertied classes in England by borrowing this comparatively modest sum, and that until he repaid it he was safe, i.e. safe to go to and remain in Ireland, which is not to say that he did not mean to repay it on his return. If he really thought that the hope of recovering the money they had lent would keep the lenders loyal he was mistaken; but so were the lenders if they thought, as they may have done, that a new king would see to their rights, for, while seizing as much of Richard's property as he could lay his hands on, Henry, unlike Richard with the Lancaster estates,[2] never made any serious attempt to honour his rival's obligations. Indeed, the financial record of the two kings suggests that Richard's word, at any rate before 1398, represented the better security.[3]

It is highly unlikely that Richard's ultimate intentions about his last great series of loans will ever be known for certain, but even if the accepted view can be shaken—which is doubtful—by such arguments as these, it may still be urged that, repayment or no repayment, these loans of Richard's were vicious because they were *forced* loans. Here again we are dependent on the well-known statement in the chronicles: there is nothing in the record evidence *per se* to suggest that these loans were any more or less 'forced' than the great loans, notably those of 1379, taken earlier in the reign. As far as one can tell, the procedure seems to have been much the same: 'pressure' of some sort was probably brought to bear in most cases. On similar occasions under Henry V special

[1] On the other hand, the main cause of that expedition, viz. the earl of March's death, occurred as late as 15 August 1398, when Richard was already over four months in default (Easter 1398 fell on 7 April).

[2] *Cal. Pat. Rolls*, 1396–9, *passim*, for a long list of Lancaster grants renewed by Richard. Tout's criticisms, in *Chapters*, IV, 53 and n., seem rather beside the mark.

[3] H. Wallon, *Richard II*, II, 467–8, takes the same line in suggesting that Richard's failure to repay these loans may have been due to his deposition. He also notes the similarity of the loans with which Henry himself began (and continued) his reign, ibid., 539–40.

commissions of eminent persons are appointed in the several shires and boroughs to 'induce' people to contribute: the only difference is that the security offered is less solemn, being no longer necessarily letters under the great seal but merely tallies of assignment, cut almost immediately the cash loan is made or at the most within a week or two.[1] The language of the commissions themselves suggests the kind of pressure that was brought to bear, e.g. in 1419 and 1421–2.[2] During a popular and 'constitutional' reign it passes unnoticed, but it is easy to imagine what it might become in the hands of a hostile chronicler. One wonders whether it was really pressure of a very different kind which was applied in 1379 and 1397.

For after all there are other possible inducements to lend besides force: there is the question of interest. Nobody now supposes that the canon law effectively excluded usury from commercial transactions, and it is almost certainly untrue that in the fourteenth and fifteenth centuries, when concealed usury was an everyday affair, English kings were really powerful enough to refuse a *quid pro quo* on that special class of loans which happened to be made to the crown. The consideration, however, seems to have varied. It might sometimes be cash or assignments; there are entries marked *dona regis* in the issue rolls, and their recipients are often merchants, especially alien merchants, who have lent money, apparently free of charge, to the crown: this, however, is more characteristic of Edward III's reign than of a later period. Other lenders on a large scale might receive their reward in the form of grants or favours; a town like Coventry might buy (in effect) a new charter with a loan technically free of interest; an individual, besides obtaining valuable contracts or the coveted licence to export wool duty free, might amass profitable keeperships of royal manors, wards, and so forth, or even, as in the case of Beaufort, establish a lien on the customs revenue of a great port over a term of years.

Even the humbler lenders of smaller amounts might expect some

---

[1] This incidentally explains the absurdly short apparent duration of these loans. They were paid off in theory, though not in fact, as soon as the tallies had been issued.

[2] *Cal. Pat. Rolls*, 1416–22, pp. 249–52, 384–6, 416–17. The commissioners are to 'induce all other sufficient secular lieges of the king . . . to pay the loan . . . and to certify thereon to the treasurer of England or his deputy' by a fixed date.

return if they happened to be officials of the crown. Many such officials had strong financial connections in London or elsewhere; they undoubtedly made a practice of discounting tallies of assignment, and were in the habit of forming syndicates to offer loans in return for the lucrative farming of royal property or revenue. Every research worker who has touched this period is familiar with these hordes of rising civil servants on the make: they are the half-clerical, half-lay successors of those still better known generations of 'Caesarian' clerks who, living before the days of the *miles litteratus*, had been more easily satisfied with the accumulation of benefices and prebends.

In so far, then, as the lenders in question were either great capitalists like Sir Robert Knolles, John Hende, Richard Whittington and bishop Beaufort, or favoured officials such as, let us say, Henry Somer, the Lancastrian chancellor of the exchequer, they secured their ample *quid pro quo* in many ways, among which lending at a heavy discount, as explained in earlier chapters of this book, was perhaps the most common. Beaufort in particular is said to have doubled his working capital by his great loans to Henry V and his successor; Whittington, too, made vast gains, though according to tradition he patriotically threw the bonds, or some of them, into the fire;[1] smaller men may have trebled and quadrupled their fortunes.

Nor does this necessarily apply only to those favoured classes among lenders who had backstairs influence through the great departments of the household, or else had become in their own right wealthy bishops, merchant princes, or successful *condottieri* gorged with ransoms, blood-money and loot. Particularly in the fifteenth century, and particularly under Henry V, though also under his two predecessors, other types of lender are found: country knights and squires, rectors, even vicars, the good men and bailiffs of little market towns, the smaller and weaker religious houses. It seems fairly clear that widespread borrowing on a comparatively small scale from financially impotent classes such as these became common in the later fourteenth century: in this period it appears as early as 1379 and could no doubt be traced back into Edward III's reign. But it was the later Lancastrians who reduced it to a fine art, appointing commissions shire by shire to 'induce' the smaller people to lend—for there was at all times

[1] See *Dict. Nat. Biog.*, sub. nom.

at least an element of 'persuasion' in these transactions—and multiplying the numbers of such unwilling lenders to ten times what they had been under Richard II. The usual Lancastrian procedure was to obtain a parliamentary grant and then anticipate its yield by borrowing on the strength of it: at first this was done without parliamentary sanction, but these anticipatory loans encountered such mounting opposition that by the middle of the century sanction had to be regularly obtained, and even then the point was reached at last when people flatly refused to contribute anything at all. Yet it is by no means clear that such lenders derived no advantage from their loans, for although the tallies of assignment which they usually received in payment seem to have been made out, in theory, for the precise amount which they had lent, they may have lent much less in fact. None the less, they were temporarily worse off than if they had not contributed, for the tallies they received were frequently uncashable, at least without that considerable delay which the government had been so anxious to avoid and had so successfully transferred to the shoulders of its more timorous or patriotic subjects.

The real point, therefore, is that, even if many small loans were in fact 'forced' in this way during this period—and the word 'forced' is too strong—the method was certainly not invented by Richard II: it was practised at least as early as his minority and perhaps under his grandfather, and was carried much farther than he ever carried it in his years of personal power by those very Lancastrians who in the sacred names of property and contract had driven him from the throne.

One last objection which may easily be made to the substance of this chapter hitherto deserves remark. What after all is the value of the evidence? If, as is probable, the receipt rolls deliberately suppress traces of what is in effect usury, may they not equally wholeheartedly suppress traces of political corruption, confiscation and extortion? Have they been edited in any way? How much do they leave out? Tout himself has rather uncertainly suggested[1] that Richard may not have issued or enrolled letters patent for all the money he borrowed in 1396–7 and points out that it was not in his interest to do so. But in that case why did he issue and enrol letters patent, with a further record on the receipt roll, for as much as

---

[1] *Chapters*, IV, 47, n. I.

£20,000 of borrowed money[1] and not for the hypothetical remainder? Total omission from the records would be much more suspicious than such half-hearted omission as Tout implies; that is, unless Richard is to be credited with a truly devilish and quite uncharacteristic ingenuity, directed principally against twentieth-century historians. There is quite enough in the receipt rolls as things are to explain the statements in the chronicles, and no actual evidence has as yet been produced that somewhere else there is something more. Nor is there any physical trace of interference: the sheer bulk and unwieldiness of this triplicate series, its technical and complex nature and utterly non-party character all make it equally unlikely as an object of editing or forgery. The receipt roll, in short, is in quite a different category from, for example, the parliament roll, if only because it is transparently not designed for continuous reading.[2]

It is in quite a different category, but it has its own drawbacks, even if the probability of material alteration is not one of them. In the first place, as I have already said earlier in this book, my apparently precise totals are illusory. It has already been explained that the totals for fictitious loans are in one sense purely nominal, while the border-line between false and true loans is sometimes so vague that it has frequently impelled me to print the word 'genuine' in inverted commas. Thus, there is the fact that something, if not much, ought to be written off entirely from the rolls on account of loans which simply represent salaries temporarily unpaid, or the use by privileged persons of exchequer processes for private ends or of the exchequer itself as a place of safe deposit for their valuables. It is not likely that the sums involved would amount to more than a few hundred pounds in each decade, but they would certainly spoil the exactness of the totals.

But when all is said and done and the approximate character of these precise-looking sums has been taken into account, it is

[1] This includes the £18,000 not repaid.
[2] This argument is directed against the likelihood of there having been any 'tampering' with the receipt rolls. It remains true that there may have been routine omissions, owing to the intercepting of money by the king at an earlier stage in its collection. Such omissions do not include successful writs of assignment, though they probably include unsuccessful writs. See above, p. 108, n. 2, and the first two appendices. The fact is that the argument from the non-political and technical nature of the series is apt to cut both ways.

claimed that the receipt rolls do illuminate one of the obscurer aspects of the revolution of 1399 and that, although the financial is only one aspect among many, it is one which is worth taking into consideration. Their evidence on the point is in fact both interesting and suggestive. They show how Richard's rather futile displays of a fitful and provocative autocracy, made mainly at the expense of the smaller men and corporations, alarmed, perhaps unnecessarily, certain men of substance in the country, notably Londoners, and supplied a weapon for the more jealous magnates to wield. They explain the ease with which the revolution was conducted and the disappointment to which it almost immediately gave rise, a disappointment undoubtedly caused in part by impatience, jealousy again, and lack of understanding. They show in *other words what many different classes of men stood to gain* financially by the revolution, which of them actually did gain, and which of them lost. They do not tend to whitewash Richard, who in the financial field as elsewhere appears unprincipled, indeed, but much too dilettante, naïve and careless to be anything but an ineffectual and spasmodic tyrant. On the other hand, they help to unmask the subtle half-truths of Lancastrian propaganda, and they show that on the whole the revolution, in its purely financial causes and results, was, purely financially, unjustified.

2

The first part of this chapter has taken the form of a general review of receipt roll evidence on the financial aspects of the revolution of 1399.

I now propose to analyse the more important payments made under the three heads of 'genuine' loans, fictitious loans, and *prestita restituta* over the three periods I have mentioned. In this way it will be possible to arrive at the crown's relations not only with classes but with prominent individuals and with certain corporate bodies, such as monasteries and municipalities, and thus to press home in greater detail the comparison between English government finance before and after the revolution. To begin with the undifferentiated household: the figures are as follows:

THE HOUSEHOLD	1377–89			1389–99			1399–1413		
	£	s.	d.	£	s.	d.	£	s.	d.
'Genuine' loans	13,139	13	2	11,840	11	3	13,153	10	11
Fictitious loans	14,006	1	1	5,914	1	7	61,381	13	11
Prestita restituta	46,924	0	4	30,127	9	7½	1,184	0	8

It will be seen at once that the household accounts for a large amount of the increase in fictitious loans and the decline in prests during Henry's reign. As compared with their condition in Richard's time it is clear that Henry's household departments were practically bankrupt: they received no prests worth mentioning, while on the other hand over £61,000 worth of bad tallies were cut for the household alone.

'Genuine' loans, on the other hand, are remarkably constant in amount over all three periods. To determine their exact nature we need a more detailed analysis, such as the following:

'GENUINE' LOANS	1377–89			1389–99			1399–1413		
	£	s.	d.	£	s.	d.	£	s.	d.
Chamber	1,333	6	8	9,325	0	0	4,676	13	4
King's knights	11,146	5	2	1,166	13	4	1,859	18	8
King's esquires	160	0	0	400	0	0	5,910	6	8
Other persons of the household	500	1	4	948	17	11	706	12	3
Total	13,139	13	2	11,840	11	3	13,153	10	11

This table suggests that the three totals, in spite of their similarity, are reached in very different ways. In the first period king's knights are responsible for eleven-thirteenths of the whole, but among these the free-lance, Sir Robert Knolles, who can only doubtfully be classed as a king's knight, is responsible for over £6,000, while Sir John Sandes, in whose name another £4,000 odd is entered, though undoubtedly a king's knight, acts in conjunction with the chamber esquire, Richard Craddock, probably on behalf of the chamber. In the totals for the next two periods chamber loans account for well over two-thirds and over one-third respectively, the large sum under king's esquires for Henry IV being due almost entirely to the support of his 'wise and wealthy esquire, John Norbury'.[1] If, as is possible, these chamber loans do not represent true financial support but merely book transfers, frequently of very short duration, it will be necessary to discount them to a very large extent and to lay the chief stress upon the proper names, to which perhaps might be added that of the king's knight, Sir Hugh Waterton, another faithful follower of Henry IV, who is responsible for over £1,100. What seems to have happened is that, when the exchequer was short of money, chamber funds, if available, were sometimes applied to exchequer purposes, and entered as a loan to the exchequer, but in every case the chamber was promptly repaid what it had 'lent', usually within a few days, in which case payment would generally be by assignment, always within a month or two. Such a transaction would be mere book-keeping, since the chamber was itself dependent on the exchequer for practically all its revenue, so that in such cases no new money was involved. This means that the only outside support worth mentioning which the government received through the household in the first period was in fact the £6,003 from Knolles, acting once with John Philpot and once with a society of Lombards, and even here the connection with the household is doubtful, though it is not easy to place Knolles under any other heading.[2] In the second part of the reign Knolles makes fresh loans totalling £800, mostly for very short periods, of which the final £400, made in 1397, was not repaid, but most of the rest is simply departmental chamber 'lending', while under Henry IV Norbury and Waterton advance rather more than half the total, and the rest comes from the chamber. In other

[1] Tout, *Chapters*, IV, 56. Norbury also contributed large sums as treasurer of England. These are reckoned under 'exchequer'.

[2] He had been master of the Black Prince's household in Angoulême in 1369, had commanded the fleet sent against the Spaniards in 1377 (Wals., *Hist. Anglic.*, I, 286), and was captain of Brest in 1378 (ibid., I, 365). According to *Eulog. Hist.*, III, 353–4, he was with Richard at Smithfield in the revolt of 1381, and for his activities on that occasion he received the manor of St. Pancras from the king. On the whole, this record seems to justify placing him in a household category as a 'king's knight' in preference to treating him as either a magnate, one of the ordinary country gentry or a 'local official', though none of these classifications is really satisfactory.

words, as far as its own immediate entourage was concerned, the crown borrowed about £6,000 between 1377 and 1389, the same between 1399 and 1413, and less than £1,000 in the intervening period.

Turning to obviously fictitious loans we get a very different story, which may be tabulated thus:

FICTITIOUS LOANS	1377–89			1389–99			1399–1413		
	£	s.	d.	£	s.	d.	£	s.	d.
Chamber	—			900	0	0	10,990	9	10½
Wardrobe	6,270	4	11	428	4	6	17,378	7	1
Great wardrobe	688	6	8	4,189	1	3	20,466	14	1½
King's knights	6,680	1	2	166	13	4	2,191	10	10½
King's esquires	2	10	0	—			1,123	12	1
Royal family	—			—			8,551	11	5½
Other persons of the household	364	18	4	230	2	6	679	8	5
Total	14,006	1	1	5,914	1	7	61,381	13	11

It will be noticed that, with one comparatively insignificant exception, chamber advances during Richard's reign were made good at the first attempt, while it was only before 1389 that the wardrobe suffered appreciably from the receipt of bad tallies. Both chamber and wardrobe, on the other hand, were constantly and heavily in arrears for this reason under Henry IV. The great wardrobe with its heavy orders of valuable materials, usually from London merchants, shows a steeply increasing deficit throughout the whole period, due to the inadequacy of the exchequer tallies it received: in fact, this department alone receives over two-thirds of all the worthless tallies issued to the household in the latter part of the reign of Richard II. The absence throughout of any 'genuine' loans worth mentioning from the wardrobe and great wardrobe shows that this growing default was not on the return of book transfers, as in the case of the chamber, but on actual revenue, which had usually been pledged in advance: neither department appears to have had any cash reserve. The same is true of the royal family (queen Joan, and the king's four sons), which makes its appearance for the first time as a unit under Henry IV. They did not lend the king money: he, on the contrary, defaulted to the extent of about £7,500 in all on their allowances, the balance being owed, of course before her repatriation, to Richard's late queen, Isabella, who may be conveniently placed under this head.

The other two items, king's knights and king's esquires, are not quite so obvious as they may seem to be. Of the large sum attributed to the former, only £1,639 odd is due to Sir Robert Knolles, who generally secured fairly prompt and successful repayment of his loans: the bulk of it (£4,346) represents a long series of disappointments in pay and allowances to the future earl of Worcester, Sir Thomas Percy, who, before he became steward of the household in 1393, had lent hardly anything except service to the crown. Similarly under Henry IV it is not so much the heavy lenders, Sir Hugh Waterton and (especially) John Norbury, who are not promptly repaid, although these contribute about a tenth and a quarter respectively towards the fictitious loans of that time: the bulk of the sum represents a steady run of worthless tallies issued for their wages and expenses to seventeen other king's knights and eleven other king's esquires.

Lastly we come to *prestita restituta*. The figures are these:

Prestita restituta	1377–89			1389–99			1399–1413		
	£	s.	d.	£	s.	d.	£	s.	d.
Wardrobe	45	0	0	—			880	8	2
Privy wardrobe	5,583	6	0	—			—		
King's clerks	35,376	10	5	197	14	5½	—		
King's knights	3,014	0	0	365	6	8	206	19	2
King's esquires	—			28,717	9	10	96	13	4
Royal serjeants-at-arms	1,246	12	0[1]	218	8	6	—		
Other accountants	1,658	11	11	628	10	2	—		
Total	46,924	0	4	30,127	9	7½	1,184	0	8

Their interpretation is probably as follows. During the first part of Richard's reign large credits were created, in connection with

[1] Including £766 13s. 10d. for the chamber.

the French war, in favour of special king's clerks, notably clerks for the payment of wages of war, clerks of the king's ships and clerks of the privy wardrobe in the Tower, which, as Tout has shown,[1] was acting as a sort of ordnance department in miniature during the hundred years' war. Funds were also allocated, as we might expect, though on a smaller scale, to knights and serjeants-at-arms. In the second period of the reign the only substantial credits made were for very brief periods for the purpose of the first Irish expedition. This was financed in part through a small group headed by the king's esquire, Laurence Dru,[2] and including a king's clerk, Ralph Branktre, and a serjeant-at-arms, John Elyngeham. After 1395 the practice of transferring money in this way disappears entirely.

This concludes our survey of the part played by the household of each king in the book-keeping transactions on the receipt rolls. It suggests that the second half of Richard's reign was much the most healthy of the three decades we have been considering as far as the household is concerned. There is in that decade no compulsion to borrow money from men like Knolles, Norbury or Waterton, while the value of dishonoured tallies issued is less than half what it was in the previous period and less than one-tenth of what it is about to be under Henry IV. In comparison with this state of affairs the household in the early part of Richard's reign is in a precarious position, but even then it can expend and repay enormous prests, and its quota of worthless tallies stands at only £14,006 against the £61,381 of Henry IV. Indeed, in Henry's reign the condition of the household is calamitous: besides the heavy burden of debt imposed upon its departments by the carelessness or collapse of the exchequer, it has to provide in large part for a greatly increased royal family and is conspicuously failing to do so. It is, moreover, failing to repay the 'foreign' money it has borrowed to a greater extent, though not to a much greater extent, than under Richard II.

Let us now turn to the secretarial offices, the chancery and privy

[1] *Chapters*, III, 53–4; IV, 449–50 ff.

[2] He reported the progress of the expedition in person to the council (letter from the king, Feb. 1395), Nicholas, *Proceedings and Ordinances* (1834), I, 57. For his activities in the autumn of 1397, when he was himself appointed to the council 'en cas courseables de la ley et non pas autrement', cf. ibid., 76–7.

seal, and to what has become by this time the main source of supply and deficit, viz. the exchequer itself. We can proceed more rapidly here and consider the figures under all three heads in quick succession.

	1377–89			1389–99			1399–1413		
	£	s.	d.	£	s.	d.	£	s.	d.
'Genuine' loans									
Chancery, etc.	2,916	13	4	1,400	0	0	2,621	13	4
Exchequer	3,363	4	0½	842	6	2	5,950	10	2
Fictitious loans									
Chancery, etc.	167	0	0	—			180	8	0
Exchequer	105	0	0	—			290	8	2
Prestita restituta									
Chancery, etc.	45	18	8	16	13	4	70	9	5
Exchequer	57,151	6	7½	4,355	6	5	212	14	11

The first set of totals does not call for much remark, but it is worth noticing that the amount borrowed from each department is at or near its highest under Henry and at its lowest in the second part of Richard's reign. Individual loans worth recording are, from the chancery, £500 in 1377, £1,000 in June 1388, and £1,000 (in two payments) under Henry IV. All these loans are entered from the chancellor for the time being *et aliis diversis clericis de cancellaria*. In the exchequer the chief lenders are Sir Hugh Segrave, as treasurer, who, without any associated clerks, contributes just under £2,000 in several payments between 1382 and 1384, and Sir John Norbury, who, in the same capacity, lends Henry IV rather less than £2,500. Fictitious loans are negligible—these departments seldom cheated themselves, which is perhaps significant—and it is worth noting that they actually disappear entirely in the latter part of Richard's reign. This fact, taken in conjunction with the apparent ability of both chancery and exchequer staffs to succour the crown in emergencies out of funds amassed on their own account, deserves remark.[1] Both departments by this time formed part of what was practically a unified, permanent civil service, which was not only unaffected to a very large degree by politics,

---

[1] Something should be written off for arrears of salary, frequently shown as 'loans', but the amounts are generally very small indeed.

but was also able and determined to safeguard its own financial interests, whatever happened to those of the crown.

This leaves only *prestita restituta*, which are negligible in the case of the chancery. On the other hand, in the case of the exchequer, while showing the usual steep decrease as the period goes on, they begin at a very high figure indeed for the early years of Richard II, though they practically disappear under Henry IV. The persons associated with these early prests, which again were obviously war prests, are mostly tellers of the receipt, viz. Thomas Durant, William Howelot, Thomas Lumbard and Thomas Restwold, but they also include the better-known John Hermesthorp, Beauchamp chamberlain of the receipt between 1376 and 1397, a post which he doubled in 1381 and 1382 with the keepership of the privy wardrobe. Hermesthorp again is responsible for nearly the whole of the prests in Richard's later years, but these are not, as might have been expected, connected with the first Irish expedition, since the only large one (£3,827) was made in November 1389, and all the others, except one item of only £44, are prior to 1394.

It seems unnecessary to labour any further this confirmation of tendencies already illustrated, and we may therefore turn to the various local officers who constitute the last group of agents and employees of the crown.

LOCAL OFFICIALS[1]	1377–89			1389–99			1399–1413		
	£	s.	d.	£	s.	d.	£	s.	d.
'Genuine' loans	1,538	6	8	1,930	0	0	1,071	5	3½
Fictitious loans	14,684	2	6	16,694	9	5	33,707	15	3
Prestita restituta	21,991	4	11	6,738	11	1	40	0	0

Of these, *prestita restituta* follow the usual course. Nearly £21,000 out of the heavy total for the first period is accounted for as wages of war by John Lincoln, clerk of the king's ships, acting with Hermesthorp and John Hatfield, who was Hermesthorp's predecessor as keeper of the privy wardrobe in the Tower.[2] The dates

---

[1] In order to save space, the necessary tabulations have from this point onward been given a slightly different form, which it is hoped will not be found confusing.

[2] Tout, *Chapters*, VI, 37.

are 1378 and 1379. In the second period nearly two-thirds of the much smaller total (actually £4,166 13s. 4d.) represents prests made to the chancery clerk, Thomas Stanley, who in 1395 was made treasurer of Calais.[1] It is reasonable to connect his two prests with that appointment, for though the heavier one (of £4,000) antedates it by two years it is probable that he was already acting in conjunction with his predecessor.

Turning to the loans we find for the first time, instead of a decrease, a slight increase under the first head and a marked increase under the second head in the later part of Richard's reign, followed by a decrease in 'genuine' and a great increase in fictitious loans under Henry. It is, at first sight, rather surprising to find any substantial entry at all under 'genuine' loans: we should not expect to find the hard-pressed local official lending money to the crown in either reign: on the contrary, we should expect what we in fact get, namely, a high proportion of 'fictitious' loans, indicating the receipt of many worthless tallies. The explanation lies in the omnibus nature of the heading: in the first and third periods there is no single accountant for as much as £500; in the second the bulk of the money comes from a judge, the well-known Sir Walter Clopton, chief justice of the king's bench, and from the captain of Cherbourg who happens to be William le Scrope, the future earl of Wiltshire. Calais bears the brunt of the fictitious loans: thus between 1384 and 1386 the exchequer defaulted on £5,529 due to Simon de Burgh, treasurer of Calais; in 1388 and February 1389 on a further £5,137 due to Roger Walden; in the rest of 1389 and during the next three years on a further sum of £6,397 also due to Roger Walden, who was still treasurer; in the first part of 1397 on £6,150 due to Thomas Stanley and in the second part of the same year on £4,515 due to John Bernard. This set an unfortunate precedent which was maintained under Henry IV, under whom between 1399 and 1403 the exchequer failed to make payment of £5,206 in all to Nicholas Usk, the treasurer, and of £2,136 in 1400, 1405 and 1406 to Reginald Curteys, the victualler, of Calais. To this Henry's exchequer added a new and even heavier series of defaults in Ireland, where from 1399 to 1401 Sir John Stanley, king's lieutenant, was kept waiting for £4,405, while in and after 1402 exchequer tallies cut for Thomas, the king's son, future duke of Clarence, acting in the same capacity, fell short in the enormous

[1] Ibid., IV, 51 n.

sum of over £18,000. The growing inability of the crown to meet its overseas expenses needs no further illustration: it is, moreover, clear that, though this source of weakness was an old one, it was aggravated rather than relieved by the change of dynasty in 1399.

Hitherto we have been dealing almost exclusively with the complicated expedients of the crown in relation to its servants and dependents, and the upshot of it all has been to suggest, on balance, some improvement in the general financial position in the second half of Richard's reign, followed by a collapse under Henry to a condition far weaker than that of Richard's own minority and early manhood. We can now turn to the rather simpler but perhaps even more important question of the credit of the crown in relation to its independent subjects and to the outside world in general. In this part of the inquiry it will be possible to take the 'genuine' loan much more seriously, since in most cases, though not quite in all, loans under this head will probably be real loans, and we have only to examine their date and amount and the question of repayment. It seems reasonable to begin with the Church, and to take the bishops separately. Their figures are shown in the following table. They speak for themselves.

BISHOPS	1377–89			1389–99			1399–1413		
	£	s.	d.	£	s.	d.	£	s.	d.
'Genuine' loans	10,005	6	7	8,666	13	4	10,993	9	1
Fictitious loans	430	6	8	240	0	0	2,558	11	2
Prestita restituta	696	17	9½	599	13	1½	10	7	6

Ruling out prests as insignificant,[1] it is clear that Henry bore more hardly on the episcopate than Richard did, both in borrowing money and in failing to repay it promptly: moreover, it is the autocratic Richard of the later years who comes out best, though it is true that £1,000 lent by the see of Winchester and £100 by that of Ely in 1397 were probably not repaid at all. Of the different sees in the three periods, Canterbury lent £2,100, £1,000 and £1,675

---

[1] They are mainly, if not entirely, connected with prelates who held either the post of chancellor or that of treasurer and should perhaps have been shown under 'chancery' and 'exchequer'.

8s. 6d. respectively, Ely £1,666 13s. 4d., and Exeter £1,126 13s. 4d. in the first period only, Salisbury £1,000 in the second period, and Winchester £2,333 6s. 8d., £4,100 and £3,306 16s. 7½d. in each of the three periods respectively. No other bishopric contributed as much as £1,000 in all to either king, except London, which contributed just under £600 in the first half and exactly £600 in the second half of Richard's reign. The sees which suffered the most heavily from Henry's difficulties in finding money with which to repay them were Durham (£709) and, as one might expect, Winchester, where William of Wykeham was long kept waiting for £1,500 of his advances. The great operations of his successor, Henry Beaufort, were just beginning in the latter part of Henry IV's reign, but his total does not touch £1,100, for which he received prompt payment.

Finally, it may be noticed that Henry IV borrowed money from all the sees which Richard had approached, except Coventry and Lichfield, Carlisle and Salisbury.

We take next the loans from the religious:

RELIGIOUS	1377–89			1389–99			1399–1413		
	£	s.	d.	£	s.	d.	£	s.	d.
'Genuine' loans	4,036	13	0	7,006	19	9½	3,838	4	0
Fictitious loans	299	3	0½	163	6	8	781	13	0
Prestita restituta	351	16	8	283	13	1½	—		

Of these, the small totals for prests and fictitious loans may be disregarded, the slight increase in the latter under Henry IV being mostly due to the dean and chapter of St. Stephen's, Westminster (£372 17s. 11d.), which was practically a household department. The genuine loans, on the other hand, are instructive, for they reveal Richard for the first time pressing on his subjects more hardly than his successor does. If, looking at the first and last totals, we take £4,000 as the average sum which the minor clergy might be expected to yield in loans over a period of twelve years, Richard in the last ten years of his reign alone nearly doubles that amount. Moreover, the matter does not rest there, for most of the £7,007 shown in the middle column was borrowed in the summer of 1397, and £2,846 13s. 4d. of it from corporations, together with £333 6s. 8d. from seven out of eight individual clerks,[1] was never repaid at all. This represents a fairly high proportion of the minimum total default for the whole kingdom of rather less than £18,000,[2] and one which contrasts strongly with the mere £1,100 lost at the same time by the bishops,[3] especially since the episcopate as a whole had lent more heavily. Again, the number of religious corporations of all sorts laid under contribution in the shorter second part of Richard's reign was 79 against 59 in the longer first part, and 64 in the still longer reign of Henry, though it is true that Richard borrowed money at that time from only eight individual clerks as against eighteen for the first part of his reign, and the sixteen of Henry IV. Finally, it is perhaps significant, though the point can hardly be pressed, that most of the loans made by the religious in Richard's reign are in round sums (reckoning in either marks or pounds), whereas in Henry's time they are much more commonly found in broken amounts, perhaps suggesting that they had been raised with greater difficulty.[4] It is even possible that some sort of roster may have been kept at the exchequer for the purpose of making periodic approaches to the different houses at regular intervals; such intervals to be calculated perhaps according to their political proclivities, but more probably according to their wealth. It is true that if the second supposition is the right one there are none the less certain glaring anomalies; for instance, the very heavy contribution of Glastonbury during Richard's reign and the relatively light contribution of St. Albans. It is also not at all clear why St. Albans, Peterborough and Croyland, alone among the unfortunate clerical lenders of 1397–8, should have been repaid in full, though this fact, taken together with the larger loans advanced to Henry by St. Albans, furnishes a curious commentary on the hostility shown to Richard by the St. Albans chroniclers.

[1] These appear to have been parish priests, who may well have been raising subscriptions under their own names to a loan from the whole neighbourhood. They were certainly doing this under Henry V and later, but there is no evidence that they were doing so at this date, and these must therefore be regarded as personal loans.

[2] Above, p. 119, n.

[3] £1,000, Winchester; £100, Ely.

[4] Possibly the new practice of anticipating clerical tenths by borrowing from the clerical collectors of them may have had something to do with this.

ANALYSIS, 1377–1413

Loans from the magnates appear as follows:

MAGNATES	1377–89	1389–99	1399–1413
	£ s. d.	£ s. d.	£ s. d.
'Genuine' loans	21,720 10 2	5,965 0 0	10,750 4 11
Fictitious loans	10,238 18 7½	9,482 7 5	19,855 16 0½
Prestita restituta	11,142 12 11	2,086 0 0	853 6 8

In the first period the earl of Warwick, John Neville of Raby, John
of Gaunt, and Thomas of Woodstock contributed over £20,000 to
'genuine' loans between them. On the other hand this includes the
very large sum of £14,480 3s. 10d. from Thomas of Woodstock,
not as a cash loan but probably representing most of the cost for
over three months of the expedition which he led to Brittany as
earl of Buckingham in 1380. Something seems to have gone wrong
with the financing of this expedition, but as all three receipt rolls
for Michaelmas 1380–1 are missing it is difficult to discover what
the trouble was. Other sources show, however, that the original
intention was to adopt the procedure usual at this date. Thus on
1 June 1380 large assignments were made in favour of Buckingham, Latimer, Basset, Thomas Percy, Calverley and other captains,
one totalling £10,000 on the recently granted clerical tenth payable
after the Nativity of St. John (24 June), and another of £4,592
14s. 2d. on the subsidy of wool, etc., payable after 1 September
next in the ports of London, Boston and Kingston-on-Hull. These
sums are to be received and transmitted by John Hermesthorp,
chamberlain, and Thomas de Orgrave, teller, of the receipt, together
with John Gildesburgh, John Philpot, and Walter Bardi.[1] They
clearly ought to figure in the lost receipt rolls of the Michaelmas
term as *prestita restituta* under the names of Hermesthorp and the
rest. Whether they ever did so or not will remain a mystery: the
disturbing feature is the sudden appearance of £14,480 3s. 10d. as
a 'loan' from Buckingham and the other captains in a hasty note
made towards the end of the receipt roll for the previous Easter
term (10 September 1380). This is clearly a 'fictitious' loan in the

[1] *Foedera*, VII, 256. Ramsay, *Revenues*, II, 310–11, points out that this
was a year of unusual stringency, so Hermesthorp and the rest may have
had some temporary difficulty in cashing the assignments.

sense that it is obviously not genuine, but at the same time there is nothing about cancelled tallies in the entry: there is no note of repayment, and it is not an ordinary fictitious loan.[1] It would therefore seem that on this occasion—unique as far as I know—the clerks of the receipt, writing hurriedly towards the end of a long term and anxious to get some record of a confused transaction into their rolls, inadvertently made the wrong type of entry, and that this large sum should more properly be reckoned as a *prestitum restitutum*, which ought to have appeared under the names of the exchequer officials and not as a 'loan' from the commanders at all.

Apart from this the other loans mentioned appear to be of the normal kind: Gaunt contributes £2,200 in all, and Warwick and Neville of Raby rather over £1,700 each. In the next period Gaunt again is the principal lender with £2,000, then the earl of Arundel with £1,333 6s. 8d. and the earl of Northumberland with £1,000, the duke of Gloucester, as he had now become, adding £450. It is worth noticing that out of the whole £5,965 lent by the great families in this period only £100 (out of £300 lent by lord de la Warr) was not repaid. Under Henry by far the heaviest lender is lord Furnival, with nearly £7,000, almost all advanced during 1405 and 1406 in his capacity as treasurer of England. This belongs more properly to 'exchequer' than to 'magnates'. The only other important lender is the Neville earl of Westmorland, with £1,600, made up of several sums advanced during 1406 and 1407, though Edward, duke of York, contributes £536 on one occasion, also in 1406. No date of repayment is entered in connection with this and several other private loans, but that is not sufficient evidence for supposing that they were never repaid.[2]

As regards fictitious loans the principal sufferers in the first part of Richard's reign were John Neville of Raby with £3,646 in all, the earl of Northumberland with £1,529, Henry Percy ('Hotspur') with £1,060, the earl of March with £1,000, and John of Gaunt with £800. It will be seen that this list does not correspond exactly with that of the 'genuine' lenders, and in fact the first two magnates

---

[1] The exact wording is: *de mutuo pro solucione secundi dimidii quarterii eorundem et aliorum secum existencium in obsequio Regis in partibus Britannie.* I know no other instance of this formula.

[2] Since it tells *against* the general sense of my argument, I have assumed that *all* Henry's loans were repaid, though in numerous instances no date of repayment is given.

on it were probably kept waiting for money spent on the defence of the Scottish marches rather than for the repayment of real loans. In the second period the earl of Nottingham heads the list with £2,682 in various sums defaulted on between August 1389 and May 1390; then comes Gaunt with £2,000 (half in 1391, half early in 1398), the earl of Arundel with £1,633, all in June 1389, and lord Bourchier with £1,173 in July of the same year. Still in the second half of 1389 the exchequer defaulted on a further £708 due to Ralph Neville, future earl of Westmorland, and at different times between May 1389 and May 1398 on £544 due to Henry Percy the younger as warden of Berwick. In general, however, there is no serious default as far as magnates are concerned after 1391, except the £100 owing to the Lancaster estates at Gaunt's death in 1398. Under Henry, on the other hand, defaults are more serious: £1,216 to Edmund, duke of York, between 1399 and 1402, £4,640 to the earl of Westmorland, spread over the first ten years of the reign, and no less than £10,778 to the earl of Northumberland and his son between 1399 and 1402, which may perhaps be fairly regarded as an additional source of aggravation, leading up to their revolt against the king they had helped to the throne.

In general it seems true to say that the nobility as a class neither lent very much, considering their resources, nor received many bad tallies in the critical second period of Richard's reign, certainly less in both respects than in the first part of it. Henry they hardly supported at all by lending money, and where they supported him by service, as the Percies did in the north, they quickly found that owing to the disorganization of his finances they would have to do it very largely at their own expense.

As a class the magnates in general may have gained in dignity and independence from the revolution, but unlike the monasteries, burgesses and smaller gentry, they had hardly suffered at all from the loans of 1397–8, and it is doubtful whether they were seriously disturbed about their property rights at the end of 1399,[1] though to those of them who were hostile to Richard on other grounds the losses suffered by other classes afforded a political lever of considerable power. The country gentry, however, were in a very different position, for their own pockets were directly affected, if only on a small scale.

[1] Except of course for the precedent created by Richard's unwise confiscation of the entire Lancastrian inheritance.

COUNTRY GENTRY	1377–89	1389–99	1399–1413
	£ s. d.	£ s. d.	£ s. d.
'Genuine' loans	819 2 11½	1,696 13 4	1,015 0 4
Fictitious loans	350 13 4	30 0 0	609 12 4
Prestita restituta	117 0 6	218 6 8	87 19 10

Here Richard in his later years more than doubled the value of the loans raised in the first part of his reign. Worse than that, £1,216 6s. 8d. out of the £1,696 13s. 4d. furnished by this class of lender were not repaid at all, and moreover even a hasty examination shows that the thirty-six disappointed persons included eleven ex-sheriffs, five justices of the peace, one commissioner of array, one ex-speaker, and one future speaker of the commons. Only seven persons were paid out of a total of forty-three, and of these only one had made his loan at the critical date of August 1397: the other six loans repaid date back to the earlier 'nineties, when all loans were being repaid as a matter of course. If Richard did this thing deliberately, it was an absurd risk to take for a most inadequate return; for, as one might expect, since the total is so small, this was a class of small lender, no individual in it throughout either reign ever contributing more than £100. This enhances the absurdity of Richard's policy, if policy it was: in order to make a profit of £1,200, which even at that time was a comparatively small sum to the crown, he was apparently ready to annoy thirty-six influential persons in all parts of England by failing to repay what to each of them individually was obviously a large sum. The same argument applies to that additional source of irritation, the contemporary fines *coram concilio*.[1]

Apart from this episode it will be noticed that, if the early part of Richard's reign be taken as normal, there is still a slight increase in borrowing under Henry IV, and Henry moreover defaults on his payments to this class much more frequently than Richard does in any part in his reign: in fact the drop in fictitious loans to only £30 between 1389 and 1399 is the principal point, as far as the country gentry are concerned, in Richard's favour. As has been said, there are no outstanding lenders, and compared with most of

[1] See above, p. 118.

the other classes everything is on an almost ludicrously small scale: in fact it is the political, rather than the financial, importance of the country gentry which seemed to justify treating them separately at all. Burgesses, on the other hand, are important financially as well as politically, and this is particularly true of London, whose leading citizens stand in the same relation to those of other towns as the magnates to the country knights and squires.[1]

LONDON	1377–89	1389–99	1399–1413
	£ s. d.	£ s. d.	£ s. d.
'Genuine' loans	44,682 12 0½	21,363 12 7	51,527 18 4
Fictitious loans	3,497 12 2½	567 13 1	11,972 16 2
Prestita restituta	1,007 12 7	1,808 1 6	—

The presets under Richard include advances made to public-spirited men like John Philpot, who, as is well known, on at least one occasion waged war on pirates at his own expense, and also to various goldsmiths and jewellers commissioned by the crown. There seems to be no special significance in the cessation of the practice under Henry IV, and in any case the figures are relatively so small that they need not detain us further. Loans, on the other hand, are a different matter. There is a spectacular drop in both classes in the second half of Richard's reign, which suggests that in the 'nineties the crown either could not, or did not need to, borrow extensively in the city. As fictitious loans sink to so low a figure the second is perhaps the true explanation, though it should be added that of this £21,363 it is almost certain that hardly anything at all out of a sum of 10,000 marks (£6,666 13s. 4d.), included in the loans of August 1397, was ever repaid.[2] This loan, together with the bulk of what was borrowed at any time under Richard,

---

[1] Cf. the assessment for the graduated poll-tax of 1379, in which the mayor of London pays as an earl and the aldermen at the same rate as the mayors of other large towns, viz. as barons, whereas even the mayors of *small* towns pay according to the condition of their estate (*Rot. Parl.*, III, 57 ff.).

[2] There is a note in the margin of the receipt roll definitely stating that part of it was paid off by the hands of William Venour in December 1397, but omitting the amount. The issue roll for the same date shows that the amount repaid was only £100.

was a corporate loan by the mayor, aldermen and good men of London: the exact figures for such loans over the three periods are £29,200, £15,000 and £10,666[1] respectively. It will be noticed that there is at first a steady decline in the amount advanced in this way: the decline is not made good by individual lenders under Richard, in whose reign the number of such lenders sinks in sympathy with the dwindling corporate loans, but under Henry IV, while the corporate loans do not greatly increase in value, individual lenders suddenly become more numerous and important. Thus in the first period the only outstanding individuals are the grocers, Nicholas Brembre[2] with £2,970, John Haddele with £1,333, John Philpot with £3,076, and William Venour with £4,988, while in the second period only two lenders get into four figures, viz. the famous mercer, Richard Whittington, whose activities now begin in a mild way with loans totalling £2,311, and the vintner, William More, with £1,443, though William Venour deserves mention for adding another £906 to his heavy advances earlier in the reign. Even so, the total number of individual London citizens lending the crown an average of £100 a year or more is only four in the early part of Richard's reign, and only two in the latter part of it. Under Henry, on the other hand, there are five men in this class. They are all mercers or drapers, by name, John Hende, who advanced £14,514 in all, or an average of over £1,000 a year; Richard Whittington, who in this reign lent £13,784 to the crown; Thomas Knolles with £3,877; Thomas Oyster with £1,507; and John Woodcock with £1,260. The inference, supported by the high level of fictitious loans, or bad tallies received by Londoners under Henry, is that the city as a unit, though notoriously in Henry's favour, thought the risks in supporting him financially to be actually greater than they had been in Richard's time, so that the mayor and aldermen, while not withholding their support entirely, left the bulk of the lending to individuals.[3] That they

---

[1] Add a further £7,400, not in the surviving receipt rolls (which are deficient for large parts of Henry's reign) but traceable elsewhere. I owe this information to Mr. G. J. de C. Mead.

[2] Miss Ruth Bird tells me that Philpot and Brembre were brothers-in-law, having married two of the four heiresses of John de Stodeye, vintner. The references are in the unprinted Hustings Rolls: R. R. Sharpe in the *Calendar of Wills* is misleading.

[3] The most probable reason for this attitude is to be found in the fact that Henry did not trouble to repay the £6,566 13s. 4d. still owing to the

were right in doing so is shown by the fact that of the £11,972 on which Henry did temporarily default, the city bore far more than its share, viz. £4,035, while Hende bore £2,894, Whittington £1,222, and a new figure, Richard Merlawe, £1,700. The whole of Merlawe's total, however, belongs to his treasurership of Calais in and after 1407 and should really increase the already large total for bad tallies under Henry's 'local officials'. Compared with these figures Richard's reign emerges creditably; the second part of it has already been discussed, and for the first part it has only to be added that out of £3,497 worth of bad tallies Richard's own ardent supporter, Brembre, received £2,166 and the mayor and aldermen as a unit only £1,071, while no other accountant was disappointed in more than £100.

To sum up, the governments of the minority were very largely assisted by substantial loans, first and foremost from the city of London as a unit, and secondly from the leading victuallers as individuals, who, up to 1381 at any rate, controlled London.[1] These loans appear to have been fully and in general fairly promptly repaid. This support by the victuallers is continued, on a reduced scale, well into the second period of the reign in the person of the grocer, William Venour,[2] but altogether less than half as much money was now being borrowed from London. Fictitious loans became negligible, but on the other hand there was almost certainly an absolute default on £6,666 13s. 4d., or by far the greater part of that sum, borrowed from the mayor and aldermen in 1397, and London as a whole notoriously welcomed the deposition of Richard and the accession of Henry IV. Under this king a group of mercers, one of whom, Whittington, had already begun to be active before 1399, contribute two-thirds of all the support received from London during the entire reign. Owing to their activity the total value of this support greatly increases, though that part of it supplied by the mayor and aldermen does not do so. A great increase in the number of bad tallies issued to London, coupled with Henry's failure to honour Richard's obligation to the city, may explain or justify this trans-

mayor and aldermen in 1399 from the loan of 10,000 marks (£6,666 13s. 4d.) raised by Richard in 1397.

[1] Unwin, *Gilds and Companies of London*, p. 137.

[2] He was elected mayor in 1389 for the following year (*Calendar of Letter-Book H*, 348 and n.).

ference from the common funds of London to individual merchants of the main risks run in lending money to the crown; but more probably the reason lies in the greater extent to which the city could resist royal importunities after 1399, for its position was far weaker under Richard than it became under Henry.

Proportionately to its wealth, then, London lost comparatively little over this period, but it is doubtful whether the same is true of smaller and weaker towns.

BURGESSES	1377–89	1389–99	1399–1413
	£ s. d.	£ s. d.	£ s. d.
'Genuine' loans	5,463 5 4	6,739 7 2½	10,366 17 10½
Fictitious loans	41 13 4	—	1,213 6 8
Prestita restituta	2 14 0	141 1 2	—

These figures fail to show that Richard borrowed less heavily from the provincial burgesses than Henry did, because Henry's apparently larger total is swollen by £8,000 from the rich merchants (mainly Londoners) of the staple at Calais, from whom Richard does not seem to have borrowed at all. If we take the figure for the first half of Richard's reign as the amount of borrowing which the smaller municipal communities might be expected to stand over a period of twelve years, we find Richard after April 1389 borrowing roughly 20 per cent more than that amount over a period of only ten years, while (not counting Calais) Henry borrows considerably less than half the supposed 'normal' yield in a period of 13 years.[1] It is true that, whereas Richard's fictitious loans are negligible, Henry kept his burgess creditors waiting for over £1,200, but against this must be set the much more serious fact that out of the £6,739 borrowed in the last ten years of his reign Richard defaulted absolutely on no less than £5,551. Moreover, whereas Henry confined his borrowing to twenty-two[2] towns in all, Richard spread his over sixty-two in the first period[3] and seventy-four in the critical second period, so that his failure to

[1] This of course makes no allowance for the wide gaps in Henry's series of receipt rolls.

[2] When we count 'genuine' loans only, the number is nineteen.

[3] For which, however, he was not personally reponsible. Most of the money was raised in 1379, when he was only twelve years old.

repay the loans of 1397–8 was widely felt. There is, however, not sufficient evidence for regarding all these borough loans as abnormal. Many of the same towns lent money to the government in 1379, and did so again under Henry V and Henry VI. Again the contraction under Henry IV probably does not represent deliberate policy on the part of the crown so much as the effects of a temporary shock to its financial and political activity as an institution, for, as has just been said, the boroughs and other small lenders resumed their loans on a larger scale than ever under the later Lancastrians. The shock in this case can only have been Richard's default (it was not necessarily repudiation), followed by the events of 1399, including Henry's bland decision not to honour the obligations of his predecessor. Whether this was good policy on Henry's part or not is open to argument: he was certainly hard-pressed for money, yet the £14,664 13s. 4d. which he paid into the exchequer in cash on 10 December 1399[1] would have gone some way towards making good the amount still owing to the small lenders of 1397, and it was a dubious act, to say the least of it, on the part of the avowed protector of property to confiscate the lot.

In actual fact it might be argued that both kings were equally guilty, but as regards Richard, even if he meant to repay eventually, he did not repay at the agreed date, or within fifteen months of it, and he must therefore be accused once more, as in the case of the country gentry, of having taken a very large risk for a very small reward.

Among the towns involved Bristol is easily pre-eminent, and it is also worth noting that practically all those towns which lent sums of any size were parliamentary boroughs.[2] Moreover, the

[1] Publ. Rec. Off., E. 401/617. Ramsay, *Lancaster and York*, I, 28, gives the sum as £14,644 13s. 4d., and states that it represented the balance of Richard's hoard, after the Percies and others had been satisfied. But in that case why was it paid in French crowns, not in English currency? There seems to be no foundation for Ramsay's suggestion, which he himself corrects elsewhere.

[2] To be exact, of the forty-four towns lending £50 or more to the crown over the whole period 1377–1413, thirty-five sent members to parliament between 1264 and 1547, and nine did not. Of those lending less than £50 in all, twenty-six sent members between the same dates and forty-two did not. Cf. *Return of Members of Parliament*, Parliamentary Papers (1878), LXII, pt. i.; M. McKisack, *The Parliamentary Representation of the English Boroughs during the Middle Ages; Interim Report of the Committee on House of Commons Personnel* (1932), appendix viii.

'roster' theory of borrowing, already advanced in the case of the monasteries, finds some further support in the list of towns, for the incidence of loans in the three periods certainly suggests arrangement on the part of the exchequer. If this in turn seems to point towards compulsory lending it must still be remembered that what may have been a strong invitation in 1379 does not, in spite of the chronicles, necessarily become an absolute command in 1397.

This concludes our survey of the crown's financial relations with its own subjects in the period 1377–1413, but there still remains the important question of aliens.

ALIENS	1377–89	1389–99	1399–1413
	£ s. d.	£ s. d.	£ s. d.
'Genuine' loans	48,294 3 9	1,268 13 4	5,242 15 1
Fictitious loans	1,138 4 5	727 0 10	2,003 11 6
Prestita restituta	150 0 0	213 15 4	—

The heavy lenders in the first period are Matthew Cheyne, Lombard, with £22,261; the Bardi with £14,272,[1] always represented by Walter, who, from 1363 to at least 1391, was master of the mint in the Tower; and Antony Bache, Lombard, with £5,300. In another category are Reginald Grill of Genoa, who contributes £1,600 in the first period, and in the second £333 6s. 8d., which it is possible he never saw again; Arnold Martyn, Lombard, with £1,250; and the agent or partner of Sir Robert Knolles,[2] Andrew

[1] Miss A. Beardwood, *Alien Merchants in England, 1350–1377*, shows that the final settlement between the Bardi and the English crown took place in 1391–2. Their gross claim since the famous 'default' in 1345–6 had amounted to £93,000, of which Edward III and his successor had in fact paid £23,000, while they themselves were found to owe £39,000 to the crown. They seem to have agreed to write off the remaining £31,000 in consideration of a promise to pay them a further £2,000 on Richard's part. Of this £2,000 about £600 was actually paid.

[2] Above, p. 127. Knolles also has relations with the Bardi. The late Dr. Previté-Orton suggested to me that this Andrew Michell may be a Michiel of Venice and Matthew 'Cheyne' a Zeno, while Reginald Grill (Rinaldo Grillo) probably belonged to a well-known family of Genoese noblemen. But Dr. E. B. Fryde tells me that there is a seal of Matthew Cheyne's in the P.R.O. bearing the legend 'S. Matte Cennin *de Florentia*' (T.R. Ancient Deeds, E.43/659).

Michell, Lombard, with £1,166. It will be seen that both default and repudiation (if any) are relatively insignificant. Genoa and Lucca are the only two foreign towns actually mentioned, though of course the Bardi, and certainly some of the other persons mentioned, came from Florence. It is, however, not easy to identify all the names in the English dress which they are habitually given, nor do any of the English sources trouble to do more than lump together 'Genoese, Florentine, Lucchese, and Lombard merchants'[1] without giving any more specific information. Some of the aliens in question are obviously not merchants, e.g. the well-known count of Denia; the count of St. Pol; an esquire of the duke of Brittany; and a few other persons of feudal standing on the Continent, but the sums with which they are charged are all comparatively small ones.

Under Henry IV these 'laymen' disappear, and we have merchants only. There is also rather more precise information about the towns from which they come, and their names are spelt more accurately. The more important towns (in terms of money relations with the English crown) are, as before, Florence, Genoa and Lucca, but we have now to add Venice, Como, Ghent, Piedmont (*sic*) and the Hanse to the list, nearly all for small amounts. For the only foreign firm which supported Henry to any noticeable degree was that of the Alberti, or Albertini, of Florence, who do not appear at all under his predecessor.[2] They are responsible for £2,442 of the 'genuine' and £566 of the fictitious loans, the next in importance being also a new name, that of Andrea Giustiniani of Genoa,

---

[1] *Cal. Letter-Book H*, p. 406, petition concerning the garbling of spicery. Many of the names in this list occur in the receipt rolls. Miss Beardwood's book on alien merchants in England only covers the period 1350–77, and approaches the subject from a different angle, viz. alien participation in trade and the legal position of aliens in England. She feels the same difficulties of identification (op. cit. p. 36), but deals at some length with the Bardi (*passim*) and also with the Bache family (which came from Genoa), though her Antony Bache is apparently of an older generation.

[2] That is, in a moneylending capacity. *Cal. Close Rolls*, 1396–9, pp. 43, 99, 101, 102, 147, 252, 326, show that they were already trading from this country under Richard, and were acting as the financial agents of Thomas Arundel. Cf. Wylie, *Henry IV*, i, 164, for a small sum transferred through them to the Byzantine emperor in 1398–9. Miss Beardwood (op. cit. pp. 10, 60) notes that they had goods in England, which were seized as reprisals for the default of two Lombards, as early as 1375, at which time they were already recognized 'factors and servants of the Roman curia'.

who lent Henry £600 which seems to have been duly repaid. The only names to appear in both reigns are those of Reginald Grill of Genoa, and Lodowicus de Port of Lucca, and of these the former lends a good deal less to Henry than to Richard and the latter rather more, but not much to either king.

To sum up, it would appear that as late as the minority of Richard II the English crown was able to draw more largely upon foreign financial help than used to be imagined, and this in spite of the way in which the fourteenth century saw the gradual elimination of aliens from the wool trade, the key position of government finance. But when the declining importance of aliens in this trade really made itself felt at last, say after 1390, their financial help was naturally no longer forthcoming, so that even Henry, who raised money wherever he could, had small recourse to it. Under Henry, moreover, the foreign merchant was kept waiting for his money to an extent (about 40% of his total loans) unparalleled even by the hard-pressed governments of Richard's minority, a fact which must have made it even more unlikely than before that really heavy borrowing from alien merchants could be successfully revived.

There remains for each reign a small residue of persons whom it has not been possible to identify. The totals are as follows:

UNIDENTIFIED	1377–89			1389–99			1399–1413		
	£	s.	d.	£	s.	d.	£	s.	d.
'Genuine' loans	329	12	4	206	13	4[1]	76	6	8
Fictitious loans	74	13	4	319	0	0	665	19	3
Prestita restituta	312	16	8	40	0	0			

This involves seventeen names under Richard and eighteen under Henry. It is curious to find that even in this chance collection *prestita restituta* steadily diminish throughout, while 'fictitious' loans are at their highest under Henry, a coincidence which would prove nothing in itself if it did not happen to agree with the general tendencies illustrated throughout both reigns.

[1] Including two loans of £26 13s. 4d. and £13 6s. 8d. made in August 1397, which have to be added to the list of those never repaid.

CHAPTER IV

CALENDAR, 1413-32

		£	s.	d.	%
EASTER 1413:	Cash	24,397	7	2½	54
	Assigned	9,778	17	4	22
	Book-keeping	10,693	6	8	24
	Total	44,869	11	2½	100

The revenue until 24 July (some £16,000) was exclusively in cash, and over half of it was paid in on only two days, 4 May and 9 June. The remaining £8,000 or so in cash came in during the last four days of business, ending with a burst on 20 September. None of it can have come from new grants, for parliament did not meet until 15 May, and, although it renewed the customs duties, the first half of the subsidy which it also voted was not to be collected until Martinmas (11 November).[1] The new king, who had begun by himself advancing £1,000 to the exchequer from the wardrobe on 4 May, was in fact short of money as early as 14 July, when Whittington advanced £2,000 and Hende £333 6s. 8d.; while on 17 July twenty-one lenders, mostly bishops and abbots, raised as much as £7,133 6s. 8d. for the crown. Conspicuous among the greater lenders were the city of London with £2,000; Hende again with another £666 13s. 4d.; and the young bishop of Winchester, Henry Beaufort, with £1,333 6s. 8d. On 24 July heavy assignment became necessary, and again on 14 August and 17 September; but the drafts were all honoured, with one insignificant exception.

		£	s.	d.	%
MICHAELMAS 1413-14:	Cash	66,988	16	9½	99
	Assigned	895	8	4½	1
	Book-keeping	—	—	—	—
	Total	67,884	5	2	100

This roll comes nearer than any in the whole series under review to being a perfectly 'normal' and straightforward record of tallies

[1] Ramsay, *Lancaster and York*, I, 165.

struck for actual cash revenue received. There was literally no book-keeping whatsoever, and although, if certain doubtful entries have been wrongly interpreted, assignment may conceivably have reached 2% or even 3%, it would still be virtually negligible and was certainly employed only on the smallest scale. It was the collection of the subsidy already mentioned—the second or Easter half of which was coming in well by the last days of the term—which explains the relatively high total of real revenue; this had only once been surpassed (in 1407–8) during the whole of Henry IV's reign.

		£	s.	d.	%
EASTER 1414:	Cash	32,905	0	6	91
	Assigned	1,000	0	0	3
	Book-keeping	2,382	19	10	6
	Total	36,288	0	4	100

The general structure of this roll is clearly much the same as that of the last one, but it is on a smaller scale owing to the halving of the real revenue. There was little left to come from the subsidy, and since no fresh grant was made by the Leicester parliament in the spring,[1] the customs and the hereditary revenue between them could not quite produce £34,000. Of this total £1,000 was successfully assigned on 17 July, but there were no other assignments in the term and no fictitious loans. Nor was there any other form of book-keeping until the last two days of business (27 August and 13 September), when the king was compelled to borrow £533 6s. 8d. from Whittington and £1,509 from the earl of Arundel, then treasurer of England, together with a further £340 from two relatively small lenders.

		£	s.	d.	%
MICHAELMAS 1414–15:	Cash	85,942	16	1	95
	Assigned	2,626	4	$8\frac{1}{2}$	3
	Book-keeping	2,133	6	8	2
	Total	90,702	7	$5\frac{1}{2}$	100

The same remarkable pattern of finance persisted for a third term running, assisted upon this occasion by the grant of a double

[1] Ramsay, *Lancaster and York*, I, 183.

subsidy made in the November parliament at Westminster as an obvious war measure, 'half to be raised on the 2nd February, 1415, and half on the 2nd February, 1416'.[1] It was this fresh money, coming in during February and March, which helped to swell the cash figure from the £25,000 collected in the earlier part of the term to the record total of nearly £86,000. Meanwhile on 11 December five genuine loans—among which Hende contributed £866 13s. 4d.—produced the only book-keeping of the term. There was also a trickle of assignment from the same day onwards at fairly widely spaced intervals, but none of this was on a large scale.

		£	s.	d.	%
EASTER 1415:	Cash	18,104	7	6	19
	Assigned	38,567	14	0½	41
	Book-keeping	38,243	11	4½	40
	Total	94,915	12	11	100

With the exhaustion of the first half of the double subsidy voted in the previous autumn the rolls resume a much more familiar appearance. Cash continued to come in on a reduced scale throughout the term. Assignment began in a small way on 11 May, but was not heavy until a month later: on 21 June, however, it reached a climax of £14,192 in a single day and thereafter got well into four figures on seven subsequent occasions. This meant, as will be seen from the tables, the sudden reappearance of numerous fictitious loans, and with the French war well under way this was not the only sign of strain upon the revenue. Heavy genuine loans were raised throughout June, on 8 July and again on 2 September, bringing the total under this head to a nominal £24,869; but even this high figure was to be surpassed twice during the next six years. On 6 June there were some twenty loans for £2,796, led by the £666 13s. 4d. advanced by Nicholas 'Mulyn' and his associates of Venice; on the 7th there were twenty-two for £2,806, of which Hende lent £1,333 6s. 8d.; and on the 8th the peak was reached with twenty-three loans for £10,399, although eleven of these bear a somewhat unusual character. The first twelve, totalling £3,830, were clearly genuine; thus the earl of Arundel produced £766 13s. 4d. and Henry Beaufort £1,963 6s. 8d. The others, however,

---

[1] Ibid., I, 188.

worth in all £6,569, are said to have proceeded from the king himself, mostly by the hands of the bishop of Norwich—though John Wodehous (royal chamberlain at the receipt), John Merbury (chamberlain of south Wales), and John Butler (one of the customs collectors in the port of London) were responsible for one payment each, totalling £1,200 in all. In most cases the money was paid out to such eminent people as the treasurer of England, the duke of Bedford (as 'keeper' of England), and John Beaufort, earl of Dorset (the high admiral)—or alternatively it was expended at Southampton or Portsmouth, clearly on fitting out the French expedition, and indeed specifically enough in two cases upon ships and Welshmen, i.e. the mercenaries who were to take part in the Agincourt campaign. In other words all these special 'loans' from the crown, raised presumably from the resources of the chamber or wardrobe, or perhaps from those of the duchy of Lancaster,[1] bear a close relation to the great prests made to paymasters in Richard II's reign, by which the Irish and other expeditions were financed, rather than to loans proper. None the less, even if no fresh money was involved, the crown was fully reimbursed for these advances in due course out of exchequer revenues. It seems then that the £6,569 referred to was simply transferred and re-transferred from one government department to another and should really be deducted from the genuine loans, which will then total only £18,300. Final contributions to this amended figure were made by the city of London, with £6,666 13s. 4d. on 8 July, and by nine separate lenders, raising £2,200 between them, on 2 September. Among the latter the Albertini, who had already contributed on a smaller scale earlier in the reign, were prominent with £666 13s. 4d.; they were followed by Whittington, with £466 13s. 4d., and lord Ferrers de Groby, with £333 6s. 8d. Turning to fictitious loans, we find the wardrobe failing to collect £667 11s. in one tally on the customs dues of Chichester (14 June), while the total for the term reaches £13,374, the highest figure for the reign. Most of this occurred on 21 June (the day of heaviest assignment) when Roger Salvayn, the treasurer of Calais, got twelve bad tallies for £8,936 on the customs of Lynn, Ipswich, Hull and London. But on the 25th John Hende also had a bad tally on London (for £1,333 6s. 8d.); and on 17 July John Weele,

---

[1] See the heavy contributions in the shape of genuine loans raised from the duchy in the period 1422–32, below.

Thomas Strange and Hugh Say[1] received two others, value £1,113 6s. 8d., levied on Southampton.

		£	s.	d.	%
MICHAELMAS 1415–16:	Cash	56,360	11	3½	80
	Assigned	11,473	0	10	16
	Book-keeping	3,037	17	1½	4
	Total	70,871	9	3	100

Cash payments were regular but small until 16 December, when the decisions of the brief November parliament began to make themselves felt. This parliament had been held at Westminster by the duke of Bedford shortly before the king's triumphant return to England, and in the full flush of the victory at Agincourt it had 'agreed to accelerate by six weeks the collection of the Subsidy granted by the last Parliament for the 2nd February, 1416':[2] it had also granted another subsidy for the following Martinmas and had given Henry the customs for life. Next month the southern clergy in their turn granted two tenths, while in January the northern clergy followed with a single tenth: finally, in March 1416, another parliament agreed to antedate the Martinmas subsidy to Whitsun (7 June).[3] In these circumstances it is not surprising that the revenue was reasonably buoyant for a time, though even so neither borrowing nor assignment could any longer be wholly avoided. The latter occurred at intervals throughout the whole term, though it was only on 30 October, 9 December and 23 January that it could be described as even moderately heavy in amount. Book-keeping was lighter still, but on 5 November Henry Beaufort

---

[1] Possibly a Shropshire syndicate: there was a John Weele or Wele who was a J.P. and active in that county about this time (*C.P.R.* 1408–13), while in 1421 Thomas Strange or le Strange is described as *armiger*, which suggests a country gentleman, in the same region (receipt roll, 13 May 1421, loan of £33 6s. 8d.). I can find no trace of any *Hugh* Say, but there were vintners with that surname in London, and the large sum involved makes it *prima facie* more likely that the headquarters of the syndicate were there, rather than in Shropshire: combinations of the sort are not uncommon throughout the whole period. However, I have rather doubtfully assigned the whole transaction to Shropshire (*Country gentry*) in my analysis of this period (Chapter v), through default of any better evidence.

[2] Ramsay, *Lancaster and York*, I, 227.

[3] Ibid. I, 227–9.

advanced another £666 13s. 4d., while on 23 January Sir John Rothenhale, keeper of the wardrobe,[1] received ten bad tallies on the customs for £1,173 6s. 8d., and Richard, lord Grey, keeper of Berwick and the east march, one on Newcastle and one on Hull, totalling £775 in all.

		£	s.	d.	%
EASTER 1416:	Cash	32,452	10	10	39
	Assigned	46,144	3	2½	55
	Book-keeping	4,931	14	2	6
	Total	83,528	8	2½	100

The antedating to Whitsun of the autumn subsidy for 1416 meant as usual an increase in the cash takings, which rose sharply in and after the first week of June. But the most striking feature in this term was the volume of well-calculated assignment. This started on 11 May and touched the record figure (for a single day) of £20,578 on 6 June, when no less than 143 assigned entries in favour of 105 persons did not cause even one fictitious loan. Thereafter the day-to-day activities, though still far from light, run in more accustomed figures. Not all these assignments, however, met with the success of 6 June; thus, on the 4th, Roger Salvayn, treasurer of Calais, was unable to cash three tallies on London, worth £2,800. But there were no other substantial disappointments, unless we include the wardrobe's £589[2] in five bad tallies on the customs (23 July), and the great wardrobe's £433 6s. 8d. in three tallies on similar sources (29 July), neither of which was a serious matter.

		£	s.	d.	%
MICHAELMAS 1416–17:	Cash	81,799	11	6	61
	Assigned	31,007	10	7½	23
	Book-keeping	21,559	1	4	16
	Total	134,366	3	5½	100

---

[1] And, incidentally, also 'keeper' of the exchequer (*not* treasurer) to the end of 1415. It is interesting to note that the treasurer for the Easter term of 1417, Sir Roger Leche, is described in his turn as 'late keeper of the wardrobe'.

[2] Suffered by Sir John Rothenhale, keeper, by the hands of the king's chief butler, Thomas Chaucer, *super providencia vini pro expensis hospicii regis*.

This roll records the highest real revenue achieved in any one term (£112,807) by any of the Lancastrians or Yorkists. Its size is clearly due to the remarkably generous grants made by the October parliament in view of the threatened renewal of the French war: these were, a subsidy and a half from 2 February and another half-subsidy from Martinmas 1417.[1] Payment of the former raised the cash total during February and March from the low figure of £12,000 received up to that point so fast that it achieved a term total surpassed only in the Michaelmas term of 1414–15, when another great expedition had been pending. But this was not all: assignment, though in no way sensational, flourished steadily from the last days of October onwards and reached a respectable term total, while in addition every effort was again made to borrow money. The impression produced is, in short, that all the resources of the kingdom were being strained to the uttermost in order to support the war, and as far as loans are concerned this effort continued, as will be seen, throughout the summer. Between 30 November and 13 March 226 loans—the vast majority of them small ones—yielded £19,539; the heaviest days were 4 February (69 loans), '11'[2] February (42 loans) and 8 March (86 loans). In addition, the mayor and aldermen of London lent £3,333 6s. 8d. on 8 January, while on 30 November, 14 December and again on 9 January the king himself advanced £666 13s. 4d., £1,000 and another £1,000 respectively, all by the hands of Richard Harowdon 'the monk' (monachi).[3] The same form of entry (for a further £1,000) reappears at the end of the long list of lenders on 11 February, but otherwise there were no really large loans either on that day or on the 4th. On 8 March, on the other hand, the bulk of the £8,577 raised by the 86 lenders was supplied in two loans of £3,333 6s. 8d. from the city of London, so that in fact more than two-thirds of the total sum borrowed during the term came from London (£10,000 in all) and from the crown (£3,666 13s. 4d.), and less than £6,000 from the numerous small lenders. Fictitious loans were not serious, but on 4 November John Vittore of Florence failed to cash £706 13s. 4d. in two tallies on Southampton, while on 20 February Robert Berde, clerk, 'supervisor' of the

[1] Ramsay, *Lancaster and York*, I, 242–3.
[2] Apparently a mistake for 12 February.
[3] This curious description conceals the abbot of Westminster, whose part in these transactions is not clear.

king's ship *Grace-dieu*, could not collect the sum of £500 in one tally on the same source. The remaining amounts, however, were not large, and the total for the whole term was only just over £2,000.

		£	s.	d.	%
EASTER 1417:	Cash	28,622	18	4	37
	Assigned	16,662	17	3	21
	Book-keeping	32,981	3	4	42
	Total	78,266	18	11	100

Cash payments during this term include the abnormal item of £5,000, paid by various hands[1] on 17 May and 12 June, for the ransom of Louis de Bourbon, count of Vendôme, who had been taken prisoner at Agincourt and was reckoned as the king's peculiar property. Assignment, though found at all stages of the term, was relatively light, and the drive to borrow money, which had marked the Michaelmas term, was therefore carried on with more intensity than ever. A further £31,595 was in fact raised in some 286 loans,[2] but, as on previous occasions, much of the big money came from a few particularly powerful lenders. On 26 April, it is true, when there were at least 179 loans, the total of just under £5,000 was fairly evenly distributed, but on 12 June well over half the £26,164 borrowed in that single day was provided by bishop Beaufort alone, who now emerges clearly for the first time as the greatest English financier of his age. There is no reason to suppose that during this term Beaufort lent any more than the £14,000 with which he is credited on this occasion, even though there is a note at the end of the royal chamberlain's roll against the term total 'item, 13,000 marks (£8,666 13s. 4d.) from the bishop of Winchester'. For the fact is that a careful adding of the whole roll, excluding this marginal entry, yields a figure some £11,655 in excess of the official total. It must therefore be assumed that the extra £8,666 13s. 4d. had already been included in the body of the roll but had somehow got omitted from the roll total, yet even so

---

[1] The Florentine financiers John Vittore and Gerard Danys paid two-thirds of the amount, while the remainder came through the well-known captain, Sir John Cornewall, second husband of the king's aunt, Elizabeth, countess of Huntingdon, and subsequently lord Fanhope. See below, Chapter VI (1443–4), p. 222, n. 1.

[2] Some of the smaller loans may have been omitted from this count.

it does not close the gap, but still leaves a deficit of nearly £3,000. Now it seems a curious coincidence that, if we allow about £100 for the normal margin of arithmetical error, this final deficit of £2,988 17s. is just about one-third of bishop Beaufort's supposedly last-minute loan.[1] This in turn suggests once more that there may be something in Mr. McFarlane's theory[2] that what was normally entered in the receipt roll as a 'genuine' loan was not the amount actually received in cash but the amount which the exchequer had agreed to repay to the lender. It may well be that in this Easter roll of 1417 we have a large loan from Beaufort, the *nominal* total of which had already appeared in the body of the roll in two separate entries on 12 June, one for £5,333 6s. 8d. and the other for £8,666 13s. 4d.; and that the latter, though not the former, had somehow got left out of the roll total; thus it may have been hastily assumed that Beaufort had made only the first of these two loans. When it was discovered that the roll total was too small, the second Beaufort loan may well have been remembered and a hurried memorandum made to include it in the roll total. The fact that the total is even then some £2,900 short may be explained by the theory that there was something odd about this second £8,666 13s. 4d.—and the only thing that can have been odd about it must have been that it was *one of the exact sums which Beaufort had actually lent*, instead of the very different sum—about 33 % larger —which he expected to be repaid! Apart from Beaufort there were a few other fairly large lenders: on the same 12 June, Bristol, for example, lent £666 13s. 4d. and London £1,860: Whittington produced £1,333 6s. 8d. and the prior of St. John of Jerusalem the same. There were also three curious entries, described in the margin as *dona* but *de mutuo* in the body of the roll. All three were from officials, viz. the receiver of Brecknock (William Butler, £773), the chamberlain of south Wales (John Merbury, £1,000) and another receiver (£100). These payments have all been reckoned as loans, but there seems to have been at least one

---

[1] It was not really last-minute: the fact is that the £14,000 known to have been lent on 12 June had been paid in two instalments, the second of which was for £8,666 13s. 4d., and it seems to me that *this* was the sum which the clerk was now reminding himself he had forgotten to add in. If so, he seems to have forgotten all or part of the remaining £5,333 6s. 8d. (some of which must have represented concealed interest) as well.

[2] *Cambridge Historical Journal*, IX (1947), 51–68.

genuine *donum* (*de dono proprio* instead of *de mutuo*)—from Henry Eyton, receiver of Kidwelly (£120 5*s*. 11*d*.). Fictitious loans were few and simple: the total was only £1,198.

		£	*s.*	*d.*	%
MICHAELMAS 1417–18:	Cash	58,744	14	0½	71
	Assigned	23,138	5	8	28
	Book-keeping	969	12	6	1
	Total	82,852	12	2½	100

This is a straightforward roll, the high cash percentage of which is easily accounted for by the payment of the first of the two subsidies, to be raised in February 1418 and February 1419, which were granted by the November parliament.[1] Assignment went on steadily throughout the term but was never very heavy: book-keeping was trifling and contained no single item of importance.

		£	*s.*	*d.*	%
EASTER 1418:	Cash	12,334	6	11½	28
	Assigned	30,538	8	10	70
	Book-keeping	857	9	10	2
	Total	43,730	5	7½	100

A period between subsidies, such as this, normally shows the steep fall in cash displayed on this occasion. Assignment, on the other hand, being well nourished by customs, rose appreciably. Much of it went to Roger Salvayn, the treasurer of Calais, and Richard Bukland, the victualler of the same fortress—notably on 19 April and 12 May. The count of Vendôme's ransom was still being paid, but on this occasion only £1,000 reached the exchequer in cash from that source (16 July) by the hands of Sir John Cornewall. Another £1,222 of it was assigned, however, through Danys and Vittore to Sir John Tiptoft, treasurer of the household, in order that he might purchase certain lands and tenements for the crown. An effort to pay for jewels bought from John Palyng, goldsmith of London, by the same means was less successful; for by the end of May Danys and Vittore had to insist that this particular account

[1] Ramsay, *Lancaster and York*, I, 253. There was also a further £1,000 paid in by the hands of Danys and Vittore on behalf of the count of Vendôme.

was overdrawn, with the result that the king was credited with a fictitious loan of £500. There was no other book-keeping of any special interest, though on 16 June Richard Whittington made the relatively small loan (for him) of £333 6s. 8d. to the exchequer.

		£	s.	d.	%
MICHAELMAS 1418–19:	Cash	50,962	15	11½	72
	Assigned	19,465	18	2½	27
	Book-keeping	710	5	9	1
	Total	71,138	19	11	100

The second subsidy granted at the end of 1417 appeared punctually during the first half of February 1419—the date originally prescribed for it—and is the main reason for the cash increase. It is noticeable that assignment, which had before then been pursuing its normal course, stopped completely during this period, and only resumed in mid-February. It was fairly heavy on the 23rd—so much so that some small fictitious loans were created[1]—but it was not more than about average for the reign when the term ended.

		£	s.	d.	%
EASTER 1419:	Cash	10,962	16	7	37
	Assigned	17,602	5	2½	59
	Book-keeping	1,201	1	5	4
	Total	29,766	3	2½	100

In this interval between grants the real revenue sank to the lowest figure of the reign. It is therefore not surprising to find that the cash total is small; that assignment is (relatively) heavy; and that some assignment went wrong. The only detail missing from the picture is the occurrence of any large-scale borrowing, but this was not a year of crisis, and, though every medieval king needed money, Henry was not so abnormally short of it at the moment that he could not be satisfied with the simple anticipation of his revenue. He himself was the only real sufferer from this policy, for out of the £1,085 worth of fictitious loans, which makes up nearly all the book-keeping, £500 in five tallies was owed to the king himself by himself, and this again was due to a repetition of the

---

[1] Total only £710—and these were the sole book-keeping entries.

mistake which he had made the year before, viz. that of drawing too freely through Danys and Vittore upon the ransom of the count of Vendôme.

		£	s.	d.	%
MICHAELMAS 1419–20:	Cash	65,719	16	3	66
	Assigned	28,909	18	5	29
	Book-keeping	4,460	12	3	5
	Total	99,090	6	11	100

Grants made by the October parliament followed previous precedents so closely that the receipt roll seems to be following a regular pattern at this stage in the reign. 'A whole Subsidy was granted, to be paid on the 2nd February, with a third of another Subsidy to be paid on the 11th November, 1420. Provisions were again made for enabling the King to raise money on the security of the deferred grant';[1] while in December and January the southern clergy voted half a tenth and the northerners a tenth and a half. The results of this policy were reflected in the rolls; cash payments jumped as usual with the incoming subsidy from February onwards. Assignment, however, was spread evenly over the entire term: book-keeping consisted mainly of genuine loans raised on 3 and 26 February (only) 'on the security of the deferred grant': fictitious loans were less than £700. The borrowing power was in fact exercised with some restraint, for the 99 loans raised during the two days in question were all small and their total only £3,791.

		£	s.	d.	%
EASTER 1420:	Cash	13,677	6	5	41
	Assigned	18,085	18	0½	54
	Book-keeping	1,536	0	8	5
	Total	33,299	5	1½	100

Again the accepted pattern holds, with a slump in cash, a smaller drop in assignment and a very low real revenue. All this was spread evenly over the roll and calls for no comment. There was practically no real borrowing, but fictitious loans rose slightly to £1,484. Only two, however, were of any real size, viz. the duke of Exeter's

[1] Ramsay, *Lancaster and York*, I, 277.

£700 for four tallies on the customs (23 May),[1] and the prior of St. John of Jerusalem's £666 13s. 4d. for two tallies on London (12 July): the second of these represented an unsuccessful attempt at the repayment of a genuine loan.

		£	s.	d.	%
MICHAELMAS 1420–1:	Cash	19,882	18	5	42
	Assigned	23,134	18	10	49
	Book-keeping	4,437	3	9	9
	Total	47,455	1	0	100

The unusual lack of buoyancy in the real revenue—for this is the lowest total for a Michaelmas term in the reign—is explained by the fact that only one-third of a subsidy remained to be collected under the grant of 1419, while the short parliament which the duke of Bedford called together in December 1420 proved extremely un-coöperative and made no grant at all.[2] It is true that cash receipts rose by 50% compared with the previous Easter term, while assignment was also up; but these increases were merely seasonal and far below the average. Both were spread evenly over the term; for the fraction of a subsidy did not produce even a trace of the usual cash 'bulge' in February, probably because most of it had already been anticipated. Yet the government still refrained from borrowing—possibly in the hope that when the king returned from France he might get better results in person out of another parliament. The book-keeping total was therefore almost wholly composed of fictitious loans (£2,015) and of *prestita restituta*—the only large entry of this type to be found under Henry V. Under the former head the only important sufferer was Henry Percy, earl of Northumberland, warden of the east march, who on 29 November and 3 December was unable to obtain payment on twelve customs tallies totalling over £1,836. There were a few small *prestita restituta*, but the only important one was the large sum of £2,300 representing a clearance of accounts by Roger Salvayn, now ex-treasurer of Calais. The entry states that this was

[1] He was keeper, or lieutenant, of Aquitaine.
[2] Ramsay, *Lancaster and York*, I, 228. The main reason seems to have been the king's prolonged absence in France, which increased the popular fear that, under the recent (but not yet ratified) treaty of Troyes, the crown would ultimately become more French than English.

part of the money which he had received for the expenses of his office—no exact date is given—and that he is now quit of it by the hands of Robert Cawode, his attorney, who was a clerk in the exchequer.

		£	s.	d.	%
EASTER 1421:	Cash	16,867	1	1	19
	Assigned	27,720	12	8½	32
	Book-keeping	41,982	8	1½	49
	Total	86,570	1	11	100

Though the total nominal revenue of this term has frequently been surpassed, this is one of the longest rolls in the entire series under review, owing to the abnormally large number of small loans. Real revenue, it will be seen, was not high, for the fact was that Henry's personal approach to parliament in May failed completely, as far as money grants were concerned, though the treaty of Troyes was ratified and there were other, less important, concessions. Yet 'the subject must have been mooted, as on the 6th May a statement was laid before the Privy Council showing the inadequacy of the Revenue to meet even the ordinary expenditure of the year'.[1] Ramsay goes on to suggest that the commons may have thought that the immense borrowing operations which they now sanctioned would be enough for the time being: they even 'spoke of the loan(s) of the Bishop of Winchester as being *pur l'aise de vostre communalté d'Angleterre*'. Or 'perhaps they thought that as the war was now merely one for the reduction of the rebels to the authority of the King of France, the French ought to bear the cost'. However this may be, the only grants proceeded from the northern and southern clergy, who each gave a tenth during the summer. The result was that cash receipts and assignments both remained relatively low, although both occurred on almost every day in the term and were distinctly heavy on 17 July. Book-keeping, on the other hand, reached an unprecedented total, nearly six-sevenths of which took the form of genuine, and rather over one-seventh of fictitious, loans. Real borrowing began in a small way on 10 May, when £1,701 was produced by 37 lenders, all of whom received successful tallies of assignment as their security within some forty-eight hours. The only large loan on this occasion was one of

[1] Ramsay, *Lancaster and York*, I, 293–4.

£866 13s. 4d. from the 'men of Norfolk and Suffolk, spiritual and temporal'. On the 13th came the major operation, when no less than £34,131 in 535 loans was borrowed in a single day—a transaction unequalled during the remainder of my period. Once again Beaufort bore the brunt of it, with three loans (the greatest for £14,000) totalling £17,666 13s. 4d. in all. The next largest lender was the city of London, with only £2,000, followed by the new queen, Katharine, with £1,333 6s. 8d. Richard Whittington and the bishop of Bath and Wells each produced £666 13s. 4d. and there were 17 other lenders of sums smaller than these but still over £100. Altogether twenty-four of these larger loans—of which, as has been seen, Beaufort was responsible for three—produced nearly £25,125, leaving only £9,000 to be found by the 501 small loans. Financially speaking, we may feel that this relatively low yield was perhaps not commensurate with the trouble taken, in appointing special commissioners and so forth, to raise the money, but it is probable that the political advantages of associating the whole country as far as possible with support of the régime outweighed any other consideration: the move might even be regarded as a sort of referendum or vote of confidence, an appeal to the moneyed classes over the head of parliament. Most of these small loans were in fact collective and were levied from whole towns and vills and districts, such as wapentakes and hundreds, as well as from individuals, so that a far greater number of persons was affected than might at first sight appear. The amount of pressure employed is difficult, if not impossible, to estimate; but there seems to have been no resistance, even though it is extremely improbable that any but the largest lenders made any profit out of their loans; and the whole episode may be held to illustrate, if not Henry's popularity, the strength of his hold upon the country. Turning to fictitious loans, we find the first serious one on 14 May, when the Londoners failed to collect their £2,000 in one tally on the collectors of their own customs: there is, however, a note that the sum was paid off in cash (*moneta*) on 13 June 1425, *per breve de privato sigillo*. Meanwhile on 15 July the same earl of Northumberland again failed to collect £1,800 in ten tallies on the customs, while on the 17th the great Beaufort himself most unusually found two London tallies which he had accepted for £2,000 temporarily uncashable; nor was he eventually paid off *in moneta*, but only with fresh tallies of assignment, and that not until February 1423.

		£	s,	d.	%
MICHAELMAS 1421–2:	Cash	32,529	4	2½	55
	Assigned	23,599	19	11	40
	Book-keeping	3,157	11	5	5
	Total	59,286	15	6½	100

The king was back in France from June onwards and the last parliament of the reign met at Westminster on 1 December in his absence: he never returned to England. None the less a grant could hardly be refused, in view of the great loans which had been found necessary and the need for eventual repayment: a subsidy was therefore given, half for February and half for November 1422. It was better than nothing, but it was not a very generous provision, especially as it was stipulated that the first half of it at any rate could be paid in light nobles, worth only 5s. 8d. a piece instead of 6s. 8d.[1] Yet it made some impression on the receipts, for during February (especially) and March the cash takings were more than doubled. Assignment was as usual well distributed and fairly steady, but the total of it was no more than average. There was some small-scale borrowing of less than £1,000 in all, towards which Whittington contributed £666 13s. 4d. on 11 March, but most of the book-keeping took the form of fictitious loans, totalling just under £2,200. Out of this Henry Percy, whose financial relations with the crown had long been following family tradition, lost £871 13s. 4d. in six tallies, and on 18 February a further £425 in four tallies on the customs, or nearly £1,300 in all. Fictitious loans for another £500 arose out of two unsuccessful efforts, made in December 1421, to pay John Spenser, lately clerk of the great wardrobe, certain sums which were still owing to him as late as 1427. These assignments (seven in all) were for once not drawn against the customs but on Edmund Mortimer II, earl of March, *de fine pro maritagio suo*, and it was the earl's default which forced Spenser to come back to the exchequer and look for other means of payment.

		£	s.	d.	%
EASTER 1422:	Cash	14,013	5	11½	32
	Assigned	21,240	18	4½	49
	Book-keeping	8,063	18	8½	19
	Total	43,318	3	0½	100

[1] Ramsay, *Lancaster and York*, I, 298.

The last term of Henry V follows the established pattern of most Easter terms during his reign—excluding, that is, the abnormal summers of 1415, 1417 and 1421. In the interval between the payment of two halves of a parliamentary grant cash as usual dropped again, and assignments, much more slowly, followed suit. Real revenue in fact was at very much the level on which the reign began, though cash was £10,000 lower and assignment £11,000 higher than in 1413. Yet book-keeping was substantially lower in 1421 than in the first term of the reign, and most of it was at least made up of genuine loans—evidence of weakness perhaps, but not of confusion. Most of this borrowing took place on 11 July, when 19 small lenders produced £1,339 between them; on 14 July, when 33 such loans came to £1,920; and on 23 July, when 17 slightly larger loans yielded £3,409. Among all these lenders the only sizeable loans were those of £666 13s. 4d. each from the archbishop of Canterbury and the bishop of Bath and Wells; and a corporate loan of £531, made on 14 July by Simon Gaunstede and other clerks of chancery. From the mayor of London, Robert Chichester, *et aliis suis concivibus eiusdem civitatis* (an unusual formula) came £520, and there were 14 other loans which reached three figures —a much higher percentage than in 1421 of a much smaller total. As for fictitious loans, the total of £980 came entirely from Sir Richard Neville, keeper of Carlisle and the west march (£500 in five tallies on the customs, 27 May), and from John, lord Greystock (£480 on the same on 8 June), who seems to have been acting under Northumberland on the east march as keeper of Roxburgh castle.

		£	s.	d.	%
MICHAELMAS 1422–3:	Cash	23,707	17	7½	63
	Assigned	10,192	6	0	27
	Book-keeping	3,574	6	8	10
	Total	37,474	10	3½	100

With the death of Henry V there was an immediate, and sustained, drop in real revenue and a sharp decline in the number of days of business done at the receipt. This contraction of activity, which lasted seven years, evidently reflected the determination of parliament to reduce both taxation and expenditure, now that Henry's strong hand and immense personal prestige had been removed. Thus in the first parliament of the minority (November 1422) 'no

Subsidy was voted, and the Customs were only granted for two years, and under decided reductions'.[1] For this first term, moreover, assignment was substantially cut down in favour of cash revenue, and the probability that all the cash was not spent as fast as it came in is suggested by a rather unusual note made at mid-term in the roll in connection with a change in treasurer. At that point the record of cash collected in a period of ten weeks stood at about £9,350, without deducting issues during the same period. The obvious inference is that the latter would already have accounted for the whole of this modest sum, but on the contrary it was specifically stated during mid-December that there was still nearly £6,000 cash remaining in the treasury *in fine exoneracionis Willelmi Kynwollmersh nuper thesaurarii Anglie*. Another not unhealthy sign was the absence of practically any book-keeping until the last day of the term, when, however, some £3,000 worth of bad tallies on the customs, and another £500 on other sources, were discovered and brought to book.

EASTER 1423:		£	s.	d.	%
	Cash	12,564	12	4½	36
	Assigned	20,412	3	4½	59
	Book-keeping	1,634	0	7½	5
	Total	34,610	16	4½	100

Real revenue was well maintained, for an Easter term, but the proportion of cash to assignment was almost reversed. Both forms of payment were spread fairly evenly throughout the period. In spite of the rise in assignment fictitious loans fell sharply to under £1,000 and there was even a little genuine borrowing. Most of the latter came, very unusually, from the treasurer of Calais, Richard Bukland, who was able to advance a trifle over £600 to the new government. On the whole the policy of retrenchment appeared to be justifying itself and even paying its way, though the fall in cash receipts was clearly dangerous.

MICHAELMAS 1423–4:		£	s.	d.	%
	Cash	11,477	6	9	19
	Assigned	34,483	4	7½	57
	Book-keeping	14,700	13	9	24
	Total	60,661	5	1½	100

[1] Ramsay, *Lancaster and York*, I, 328, for details.

Although no subsidy was granted by the November parliament of 1423 (resumed in January 1424) and accordingly cash receipts shrank by another £1,000, assignment was very considerably increased and the total real revenue was the highest for the next six years. This says much for the buoyancy of the customs, even at the reduced rates imposed in 1422, for there was now no other major source of revenue. Customs, too, actually succeeded in carrying most of the assignments made upon them; for fictitious loans, though rather higher at £2,683, were still extremely moderate, and the only really large one was a matter of £1,400, levied solely upon Hull in favour of the Percy earl of Northumberland, who was still warden of the east march and of Berwick. None the less, the revenue was now so patently inadequate that recourse had to be made, for the first time during the minority, to really large-scale borrowing. On 1 March £11,944 was raised, but this time there was no pretence of any broad national appeal; for only ten lenders contributed this sum, and Henry Beaufort alone, with £9,333 6s. 8d., was responsible for most of it.[1]

		£	s.	d.	%
EASTER 1424:	Cash	2,440	18	1½	12
	Assigned	16,610	11	5	79
	Book-keeping	1,857	14	7½	9
	Total	20,909	4	2	100

This was an extraordinarily short term, with only twelve days of business and a real revenue which was the smallest in the whole period up to date. Cash in particular had never been so low, but even assignment was more than halved, compared with the previous term. Fictitious loans fell to £1,550, divided fairly evenly between nine persons, while sundry remaining items of book-keeping added only a little over £300.

		£	s.	d.	%
MICHAELMAS 1424-5:	Cash	4,824	14	6	15
	Assigned	22,353	7	5	69
	Book-keeping	5,383	5	5½	16
	Total	32,561	7	4½	100

[1] He had 'divers jewels of the king' as security for at least £4,000 of this at any rate.

Business was still most restricted. Cash had not risen much, and, though assignment had risen more, it was accompanied by a more than threefold increase in fictitious loans, the total of which, in proportion to that of genuine, was as four to one. On 28 October Sir John Hotoft, treasurer of the household, was unable to collect £1,300 in twenty-six tallies on the customs, while on 17 February the customs again defaulted in the sum of nearly £1,500 in seventeen tallies assigned to the earl of Northumberland, together with another £100 belonging to his colleague on the east march, John, lord Greystock. There was one large genuine loan during the term, when Henry Beaufort advanced £1,000 on 13 December: all other loans were insignificant.

		£	s.	d.	%
EASTER 1425:	Cash	2,687	7	4½	7
	Assigned	19,309	12	0½	33
	Book-keeping	14,833	7	0	40
	Total	36,830	6	5	100

The same general pattern persisted as far as cash, assignment and real revenue were concerned. The percentage of cash, it is true, was the lowest in the decade, but on the other hand its gross total was slightly higher than that of the year before. Assignment was average, and what really distinguished the term was the sudden rise in book-keeping. This was primarily due to the flotation of the fresh loans which were declared necessary in the parliament of 30 April: though, so far from the projected amount of £20,000[1] being raised by Christmas, less than £10,000 had been borrowed by March 1426. Still, on 21 May £6,566 13s. 4d. was in fact produced by six lenders, among whom Henry Beaufort headed the list as usual with a loan of £4,033 6s. 8d., while the Florentines and Venetians added £500 and £333 6s. 8d. respectively. On 13 June London (corporately) lent £3,000, so that (counting smaller contributions) the term ended with a total of £9,673 in genuine loans. The book-keeping balance of some £5,000 was all in fictitious loans, of which the following were the most important:

---

[1] Ramsay, *Lancaster and York*, I, 357. No subsidy was granted, but the customs duties were extended to November 1429, and tunnage and poundage were to be payable by denizens for the first time in the reign, though only from 1 August 1425 to 11 November 1426, ibid., 358–9.

10 May, £659, earl of Northumberland, in two tallies on Hull customs.

19 July, £839, from the same in ten tallies mainly on the same.

13 June, £982, lord Greystock, keeper of Roxburgh, as above.

19 July, £600, Sir John Radclyf, keeper of Fronsac in Aquitaine
—levied on a fine *pro maritagio*, payable by the bishop of Winchester for John, son and heir of Henry de Beaumont.

2 August, £750, James, earl of Ormonde, lieutenant in Ireland, in three tallies on the customs.

		£	s.	d.	%
MICHAELMAS 1425-6:	Cash	8,977	8	6½	23
	Assigned	25,401	0	2½	64
	Book-keeping	5,221	17	11	13
	Total	39,600	6	8	100

Although the 'parliament of bats' met at Leicester in the latter part of this term, it did not bring itself to make any grants before 1 June. Yet real revenue, though still anaemic, was at least some £7,000 better than it had been a year before: cash receipts, too, were nearly doubled, compared with the previous Michaelmas, though assignment was a mere £3,000 up. This may possibly be the reason why the drive to borrow £20,000, foreshadowed by the government's action in the summer, was abandoned before half the money had been raised. However this may be, there was practically no real borrowing in this term, though fictitious loans were maintained at almost the same level as before. These included:

28 November, £637, earl of Northumberland, in twelve customs tallies.

10 December, £1,000, London (loan repayment), in three tallies on the London customs.

11 January, £901, duke of Bedford, drawn on general revenue.

1 March, £606, John, earl marshal,[1] in sixteen customs tallies.

		£	s.	d.	%
EASTER 1426:	Cash	9,099	2	0	29
	Assigned	17,112	15	4½	54
	Book-keeping	5,451	4	10½	17
	Total	31,663	2	3	100

[1] John Mowbray, duke of Norfolk.

When the Leicester parliament did at last make a grant it was no more than a prolongation of the existing customs dues for two years, and of the privilege of exacting tunnage and poundage from denizens for one year.[1] Meanwhile cash receipts actually rose about £100 above the level of the previous winter, but real revenue and assignment, though burdened with the repayment of part of Beaufort's loans, were each £8,000 down. Towards the end of the term there was a revival of the older practice of borrowing from a multitude of small lenders, 103 of whom produced £3,404 between 26 July (the heaviest single day) and 28 August. The decreased total of just over £2,000 of fictitious loans did not include any outstandingly large default, though the biggest loser was once again Henry Percy, earl of Northumberland, to the extent of £560 on 15 July in several tallies on the customs.

		£	s.	d.	%
MICHAELMAS 1426–7:	Cash	18,179	9	5½	53
	Assigned	14,308	4	11½	41
	Book-keeping	2,049	15	1	6
	Total	34,537	9	6	100

There was no parliament during this term or the next, so real revenue remained at a low level. Cash, on the other hand, was higher, and assignment lower, than either of them had been for the past four years. The policy of raising several little loans was continued; no less than thirty-two of them produced only £979, while fictitious loans, at £1,070, contained no individual item of interest. One of the cash receipts was unusual in form and again suggested that Calais during the treasurership of Richard Bukland, who had actually lent the government £600 in 1423, was again not the dead loss, financially speaking, which it generally seemed to be; for on 31 October £702 9s. 8½d. was paid into the exchequer in cash *ex parte Cales'*—apparently as an addition to revenue, since there is nothing to indicate that it was some form of *prestitum restitutum*, the only probable alternative. None the less, in spite of such very occasional small loans and in-payments and its large customs revenue, there is no doubt that Calais, with its extremely costly garrison, remained on balance what it had always been, viz. a heavy burden on the English crown.

[1] Ramsay, *Lancaster and York*, I, 368.

EASTER 1427:		£	s.	d.	%
	Cash	8,963	3	10½	37
	Assigned	14,131	15	2	58
	Book-keeping	1,130	9	9	5
	Total	24,225	8	9½	100

This was another very short term of only 17 days, with the third lowest real revenue of the decade. Assignment remained almost unchanged, but cash was well down. Book-keeping consisted almost entirely of small fictitious loans totalling just over £1,100, but none of them of any special interest.

MICHAELMAS 1427–8:		£	s.	d.	%
	Cash	15,209	12	8½	32
	Assigned	24,769	7	1	53
	Book-keeping	7,160	5	8½	15
	Total	47,139	5	6	100

Parliament sat at Westminster from 13 October to Christmas, and again from 27 January to 25 March, but as usual it was only towards the end of the session that any money grants were made, and in the meantime the tunnage and poundage leviable from denizens until November 1427 were temporarily allowed to expire. They were renewed, however, for a year from April 1428, and in the end a subsidy of sorts was also voted for the first time in the reign. It took the form of 6s. 8d. on the knight's fee and on country benefices worth less than £6 6s. 8d. per annum, plus 2s. in the £ on rated value in towns, but it does not seem to have yielded very much, and this too must have been expected, since authority was simultaneously given to the government to borrow up to £24,000.[1] As a result revenue rose slightly, but mostly in assignment. Not much advantage was taken of the encouragement to borrow money—or else perhaps lenders could not be found—for only £4,500 was raised, £830 of which came from the Genoese (£500) and the Venetians. Fictitious loans accounted for another £2,700: the chief sufferer was still the earl of Northumberland, with £923 6s. 8d. in several customs tallies on 28 October, and a further £407 upon the same on 9 February.

[1] Ibid., 1, 378.

		£	s.	d.	%
EASTER 1428:	Cash	11,755	7	4	35
	Assigned	15,413	4	4	45
	Book-keeping	6,954	11	4	20
	Total	34,123	3	0	100

The new subsidy, such as it was, was now coming in, principally in cash, but even so cash and assignments both declined, the latter quite sharply. Genuine borrowing also fell to £2,533 6s. 8d., most of which was furnished on 18 June in a single corporate loan of £2,000 from London. Fictitious loans rose to £4,400, but without including any individual item of significance.

		£	s.	d.	%
MICHAELMAS 1428–9:	Cash	5,785	11	8½	19
	Assigned	19,214	17	9	64
	Book-keeping	5,180	7	4	17
	Total	30,180	16	9½	100

Cash had not been so low since 1425, and it was only the seasonal increase in assignment which saved the real revenue. Fictitious loans remained about the same at £4,513 and there was only one genuine loan (of £666 13s. 4d.). However, with this roll the slack-water period in government finance comes to an abrupt end. There are no rolls extant for the next term, and when they resume the financial tide suddenly begins to flow again.

EASTER 1429: No surviving roll.

		£	s.	d.	%
MICHAELMAS 1429–30:	Cash	38,400	0	11½	48
	Assigned	32,912	15	6	42
	Book-keeping	7,731	11	11½	10
	Total	79,044	8	5	100

Parliament met, after an interval of eighteen months, on 22 September, and in the course of a long session, which was adjourned to 16 January and continued until 23 February, the commons made a number of really generous money grants, the first of the reign. This abrupt change of policy, which was quickly reflected in the receipt rolls, was clearly caused by the military disasters of 1429, the relief of Orleans and the coronation of Charles VII. It was decided to crown the young king of England early in November, in order that he too might ultimately be crowned in France, so as to assert his father's title against the resurgent French; and soon after his English coronation on the 6th, parliament granted a subsidy on the usual lines, to be raised in January 1430. A month later a second subsidy was granted, to be raised at Christmas 1430, while the levying of tunnage and poundage from denizens was again extended until the next parliament. Finally, in February 1430 the wool duties were prolonged until November 1433.[1] The effects of the new grants did not of course emerge until the new year, when about £31,500 in cash was added to the meagre £6,900 coming in from October to December. Heavy assignment began rather earlier, viz. on 13 and 18 December, by which time it must have been known that the financial future was temporarily assured; but even so it was practised with some moderation after the first burst, considering the unfamiliar resources now at the government's disposal. Genuine loans were also restrained at £4,232, distributed over sixty to seventy lenders: more than half the money, however, was produced by seventeen of them on 12 December 1429. Fictitious loans declined to just under £3,500, none of them of any great size, although on 1 March Sir John Hotoft, for the household, experienced £456 worth of default, largely by the customs (seven tallies) but also by Geoffrey Louther, receiver-general of the duchy of Lancaster (four tallies for just under £60).

		£	s.	d.	%
EASTER 1430:	Cash	15,319	2	2½	24
	Assigned	37,276	12	7½	57
	Book-keeping	12,624	17	10	19
	Total	65,220	12	8	100

The first of the new subsidies having been exhausted by the end of the Michaelmas term, cash experienced some contraction: assignment on the other hand expanded, two-thirds of it taking place on 28 April and 1 May respectively. In spite of this, fictitious loans fell by £1,300 to only £2,165, all of it in relatively small

---

[1] Ramsay, *Lancaster and York*, I, 411.

amounts. Real borrowing, on the contrary, was more than doubled at £10,459 and had clearly started on its way towards the climax of the following term. Nearly £8,900 was raised on 20 and 24 April alone from thirty-six lenders, but there were thirty-one more small loans, producing less than £500, on the 27th, and another sixteen, totalling well under £1,000, on the 30th—which was incidentally a Sunday, not normally a day of business at that date any more than it is now. Altogether there had been eighty-six such loans before the term ended, rather early, on 19 July.

		£	s.	d.	%
MICHAELMAS 1430–1:	Cash	12,953	13	11½	11
	Assigned	58,717	8	6½	51
	Book-keeping	44,258	18	4½	38
	Total	115,930	0	10½	100

It will be noticed that this exceptionally large gross total (large, that is, for this period) conceals a much more modest real revenue —of a size, in fact, about that of the previous winter. The difference between gross and net totals in this instance is very largely explained by genuine loans. Very unusually there is no trace in the roll of any heavy in-payments on account of the second, or Christmas, subsidy voted at the end of 1429: cash received was back to about average for the decade,[1] and even assignment would have stood only at the normal figure of £25,000 or so, but for the startling total of over £33,000 assigned (and successfully assigned) in a single day (16 March) at the extreme end of the roll. Most of this day's work took the form of paying off old debts or giving security for new ones; thus Beaufort alone received £20,000 in twenty-two tallies, all of which he seems to have cashed without difficulty; London got just over £3,750; the feoffees of the duchy of Lancaster (a new pillar of the dynasty as far as loans were concerned) £3,333 6s. 8d.; and the archbishop of Canterbury, who is often found acting in close conjunction with the Lancaster feoffees, £2,010 in fourteen tallies. This abnormal day's business must, of course, be connected with the great borrowing operation of 6 March, when £28,200 of new money had been raised from fourteen lenders: among these Henry Beaufort as usual led the way

---

[1] One entry, on 25 January, was for no more than one halfpenny! Cf. the following term, p. 176, n. 1.

with £15,673 19s. 10½d.[1] This in turn should be related to the policy of the January parliament of 1431, which was inclined to be as generous as its predecessor in view of the unsatisfactory state of things in France, but generous perhaps at slightly longer range. Thus while a subsidy and a third was granted, the major part of which could be collected in the following November, the additional one-third was not to be levied until Easter 1432. A special subsidy of 20s. on the knight's fee, together with 'the same on every £20 a year in land or rent held by socage tenure',[2] came to nothing and was not collected, but it may have left its mark on the receipt rolls in the shape of an abnormally large number of small fines for distraint of knighthood, all paid in cash about this time. Customs and tunnage and poundage were both prolonged, to 1434 and 1432 respectively, while finally 'power was again taken to give security to the amount of £50,000 for advances made or to be made',[3] and it was presumably under this last clause that the abnormal March borrowings took place. Incidentally, the list of these does not exhaust the genuine loans for this term: there had been a short burst of activity on a minor scale as early as 12–13 October, when sixty-three lenders had produced £4,154, and another on 8 February when thirty-one lenders contributed £2,715. Altogether, during the whole term, £36,382 17s. 10d. was borrowed from 120 persons —an operation which compares in magnitude only with those undertaken by Henry V, and indeed just surpasses the greatest of his loans, that of 1421. Fictitious loans naturally rose to some extent in sympathy with the increase in assignment, but only to £7,876. Of these the following stand out from the rest:

28 November, £922, earl of Northumberland, nine tallies on the customs.

8 February, £402, the same, on the same.

14 December, £1,814, William Estfeld and other staplers, fifteen tallies on the clerical subsidy.

6 March, £1,900, earl of Somerset, nineteen tallies on the customs in part, but also on the revenues of Chester, Wales and Cornwall.

[1] Of this total, £12,858 6s. 9d. was raised in England and the remainder from property acquired by Beaufort in the duchy of Normandy. Cf. Easter 1432.
[2] Ramsay, *Lancaster and York*, I, 435.
[3] Ibid., I, 436.

16 March, £1,536 6s. 8d., Sir John Radclyf, seneschal of Aquitaine, eight tallies on the Melcombe customs (only).

		£	s.	d.	%
EASTER 1431:	Cash	10,476	0	8½	20
	Assigned	30,617	0	6	58
	Book-keeping	11,728	0	0½	22
	Total	52,821	1	3	100

Since the special subsidy originally designed for June 1431 had broken down, cash receipts dropped still further.[1] Assignment, however, was still fairly heavy, especially on 20 June. Borrowing had clearly passed its peak and fell steeply, but was by no means done with: thus on 14 May a private syndicate of ministers of the crown and bishops, headed by the archbishop of York (who was chancellor of England at the time), produced £2,000, while the feoffees of the duchy of Lancaster lent £1,000 on the 16th. On the 30th the staple lent another £2,333 6s. 8d. through Estfeld and there were thirteen smaller lenders, while on 18 June another twelve loans came to nearly £2,400. Altogether, £9,875 was borrowed from some thirty-five lenders—a declining activity certainly, but as yet by no means negligible. Fictitious loans were low at £1,836 and were none of them of large size, though on 16 May the ministerial-episcopal syndicate already mentioned had difficulty over the repayment of some £537, appropriately secured upon clerical tenths, for the collection of which many of its members were no doubt in part responsible.[2]

		£	s.	d.	%
MICHAELMAS 1431–2:	Cash	7,839	13	2½	18.5
	Assigned	20,118	6	5½	47.5
	Book-keeping	14,309	3	10	34
	Total	42,267	3	6	100

[1] Including another payment of one halfpenny, made by the prior of Taunton in cash on 11 May, on account of a clerical tenth. Cf. the previous term, p. 174, n. 1, also Chapter VI (1440–1), p. 216, n. 1.

[2] This is another of the few instances I have found which does something to support Ramsay's generalizations in *Lancaster and York* to the effect that clerical tenths were *habitually* anticipated by raising loans from the collectors.

There is again no trace in the rolls of any heavy payments on account of the subsidy which should have been raised at Martinmas 1431: cash indeed fell, instead of increasing, while the fact that assignment was also considerably lower than it had been in the summer shows that the grant cannot have been assigned. Real revenue in fact was, for a Michaelmas term, the third lowest in the decade. Borrowing, too, declined slowly by another £2,000, yet was still roughly equivalent to the entire real revenue in cash: some eleven lenders produced £7,838, half of it on 1 March. Fictitious loans, on the other hand, moved sharply upwards to nearly £6,500, and were destined to go higher in the summer, but, though numerous, they were individually small.

		£	s.	d.	%
EASTER 1432:	Cash	12,969	17	3½	16
	Assigned	39,466	7	7½	48
	Book-keeping	29,668	0	10½	36
	Total	82,104	5	9½	100

Parliament met in May, but, apart from the now standard renewal of the customs, the only grant made at the end of the session was 'a meagre half Subsidy, spread in two instalments over sixteen months'.[1] As the last day of business (19 July) practically coincided with the end of the parliament the effect of this grant could not in any case have appeared upon the Easter roll, but on the other hand the one-third of a subsidy voted 18 months earlier for collection at this date should normally have produced an extra £10,000 or so. Yet, apart from a special payment made by Beaufort (below) cash receipts were actually under £7,000. Beaufort's additional payment of £6,000 on 15 July was merely a special and provisional fine with the crown, in order to recover plate and jewels seized at Sandwich on the duke of Gloucester's orders. Unless the king could show that Beaufort's property had been rightly seized, this £6,000 was to be treated as a loan, and repayment of it was in fact made to him during the Easter term of 1434.[2] Strictly speaking, therefore, this sum should be deducted from real revenue and added to book-keeping, increasing genuine loans in particular to £24,620. Assignment, on the other hand, remains unaffected at the

[1] Ramsay, *Lancaster and York*, I, 440.
[2] Ibid., I, 441–2. Cf. p. 206, below.

second highest total of the decade. The reason for this is to be found in the payments of 19 July, when no less than £19,285 worth of assignment was made, almost doubling the existing total. Genuine loans for the whole term, without counting Beaufort's special payment, reached almost the same figure, so it is clear that what was happening was simply, for the most part, the issuing of tallies of assignment as security for borrowed money. This borrowing began on 3 July, when £2,500 was raised from the Lancaster feoffees, and the whole of the remaining £16,140 was raised on the 15th, when Beaufort advanced a *second* and distinct £6,000 *de mutuo*, together with a further £6,666 13s. 4d. *de mutuo in partibus Francie*—a practice he had begun in Michaelmas 1430–1.[1] There were also other oddments of his amounting to some £1,816, while London contributed £1,666 13s. 4d. Fictitious loans at just over £11,000 were the highest since 1415: the principal sufferers were the household, with £3,960 in eight tallies on the customs (20 May), and the earl of Northumberland on 17 June, with £2,200 in twenty-two tallies—all of them on the customs except one for £20.

---

[1] See above, p. 175, n. 1.

CHAPTER V

ANALYSIS, 1413-32

The object of this chapter is to carry one stage further the analysis which was begun in Chapter III. The technique remains essentially comparative; thus the first time it was used the two halves of Richard II's reign were compared with each other and with the whole of Henry IV's, while on the present occasion Henry V's reign of nine and a half years, producing nineteen complete rolls, will be compared with the first ten years and nineteen[1] rolls of Henry VI. That is to say, two approximately equal periods are being studied instead of three. but in order to preserve continuity some reference will also be made to Henry IV's reign of thirteen and a half years with its twenty-one complete and four fragmentary rolls. It has been thought that the rough approximation to equality of evidence over these three periods will still justify, as in the former chapter, the frequent use of absolute totals instead of averages, but it will have to be borne in mind that 1413-22 and 1422-32 are both slightly underestimated in relation to 1399-1413 wherever absolute totals and not averages are used.

Obviously the first comparison to be made, however meaningless, should be between the nominal totals for these periods in the rolls. They will be found in the table at the end of this book. A comparison of these shows that, whereas Henry V's nominal revenue reaches a yearly average not far short of Richard II's (£136,642 against £139,227), there is an immediate fall in the first ten years after his death to a nominal average of only £94,937.

But nominal averages do not mean much, owing to the large sums which have to be deducted on account of loans and other book-keeping transactions. In Henry V's case we have to deduct £19,031 from the yearly average, giving a 'real' revenue of £117,611, which is again very close to Richard II's 'real' revenue and well above Henry IV's (£90,000 to £100,000 only). The same calculation produces an even more striking effect for the years 1422-32, since for this period we have to make the slightly larger deduction of £19,837 on account of book-keeping from the smaller annual average, leaving a 'real' revenue of only £75,100.

[1] There are no rolls extant for the Easter term 1429.

This result raises the question how the increase in the annual average of book-keeping entries during the first years of Henry VI should be accounted for, and this can best be answered by analysing the book-keeping totals for the two periods, thus:

AVERAGE PER YEAR	'Genuine' loans	Fictitious loans	*Prestita restituta*	Total
	£	£	£	£
1413–22	14,752	4,208	71	19,031
1422–32	12,490	7,338	9	19,837

With these may be compared the figures already given for Henry IV, which are £9,328, £10,818 and £196, total £20,342, respectively.[1] The first of these makes it clear that Henry V's reign represents a peak period of borrowing by the crown and that there is some decline in this respect, though not perhaps as much as one would expect, in the ten years after his death. The second shows that there was a marked drop under Henry V in the amount of fictitious loans or bad tallies, a fact which probably reflects the increased efficiency of government, due perhaps in its turn to the greater popularity of the king and the comparative ease with which the revenue was consequently collected. But this index figure, which may be taken as a kind of inverted barometer for the fifteenth-century exchequer, rises ominously again in the early years of Henry VI, though it fails as yet to reach the level of disorganization and confusion achieved by his grandfather. Finally it has become quite evident that as a book-keeping factor the *prestita restituta* which bulk so large during the later fourteenth century have become absolutely negligible.

To sum up, it appears so far that as compared with 1413–22 the years 1422–32 saw a 17% fall in the amount of money borrowed by the crown, together with a 75% rise in exchequer inability to meet its obligations. The next step will be, as before, to note what changes may be found in the personnel of royal creditors, whether disappointed in fictitious loans or lending real ones. I propose to adopt the same classification as before and to follow the same order of examination, beginning with the household.

[1] Corrected to a yearly average: in Chapter III they were stated terminally.

THE HOUSEHOLD	1399–1413			1413–22			1422–32		
	£	s.	d.	£	s.	d.	£	s.	d.
'Genuine' loans	13,153	10	11	14,681	1	7	3,188	19	10
Fictitious loans	61,381	13	11	6,372	5	7	15,616	2	8½
Prestita restituta	1,184	0	8	287	9	6½	75	1	8

Apart from the steady decline in *prestita restituta*, which is universal in this period and to which no further reference will be made, the striking points about these figures are, firstly, the decline in 'genuine' loans under Henry VI and, secondly, the really sensational drop in fictitious loans under Henry V and their marked revival in the next reign.

To take the 'genuine' loans first, a more detailed analysis yields the following results:

'GENUINE' LOANS	1399–1413			1413–22			1422–32		
	£	s.	d.	£	s.	d.	£	s.	d.
Chamber	4,676	13	4		—		666	13	4
Wardrobe		—		12,086	0	0	100	0	0
King's knights	1,859	18	8	806	13	4	1,795	8	2
King's esquires	5,910	6	8		—		60	0	0
Other persons	706	12	3	1,788	8	3	566	18	4
Totals	13,153	10	11	14,681	1	7	3,188	19	10

This table suggests that, whereas Henry IV was able to support the exchequer when required with a temporary loan from the chamber, it was the practice of Henry V to rely on the wardrobe for the same purpose—and to a considerably greater extent.[1] The infant Henry VI, on the other hand, could not count upon either department having the necessary surplus funds in cash or tallies even for a short-term transfer. His one substantial household supporter (to the extent of £1,040) is an individual king's knight,

[1] The reason for this change is the fact that after 1415 the chamber was largely occupied abroad. See R. A. Newhall, *The English Conquest of Normandy*, 152–3.

Henry Brounflete, a former esquire of the chamber and later envoy to the General Council at Basle;[1] his name and money alike may have been inherited from Thomas Brounflete, controller of the household under Henry IV and before that chief butler of Richard II.[2] Henry IV in his day had possessed two individual supporters of this kind in connection with his household and on a far larger scale, viz. Sir Hugh Waterton, who accounts for £1,100 under king's knights for that reign, and John Norbury, who is responsible for nearly all the large total under king's esquires. Henry V, on the other hand, seems to have been rich enough not to have had to call in an emergency upon his own household followers; thus the only person from whom he borrows more than £1,000 is his queen, Katharine, whose £1,333 6s. 8d. swells the total under 'other persons'.[3] It therefore looks as if the £6,000 or £7,000 which Henry IV raised at different times from his immediate entourage, not counting interdepartmental transfers, sinks to between £1,000 and £2,000 in the next two decades when the chamber and wardrobe are similarly ruled out of reckoning.

Turning to obviously fictitious loans from the household we get a very different story, the gist of which may be tabulated thus:

FICTITIOUS LOANS	1399–1413			1413–22			1422–32		
	£	s.	d.	£	s.	d.	£	s.	d.
Chamber	10,990	9	10½	—			409	6	1
Wardrobe	17,378	7	1	3,369	14	5	10,126	5	9½
Great wardrobe	20,466	14	1½	2,785	17	10	1,060	12	2½
King's knights	2,191	10	10½	216	13	4	1,918	17	3
King's esquires	1,123	12	1	—			—		
Royal family	8,551	11	5½	—			2,027	1	5
Other persons	679	8	5	—			73	19	11½
Totals	61,381	13	11	6,372	5	7	15,616	2	8½

[1] *Cal. Pat. Rolls, Henry VI*, 1429–36, 337, 339, 342.
[2] *Cal. Pat. Rolls, Richard II*, 1396–9, 49, 536.
[3] She also contributes £333 6s. 8d. to her son's finances in the next period, but this is outweighed by nearly three times that amount in bad tallies—an indignity which she did not experience while her husband was alive.

It is clear from these figures that the chamber hardly suffers at all from bad tallies under Henry V and VI, and is therefore probably not an important spending department as far as England is concerned:[1] it reverts in fact from its perpetually bankrupt state under Henry IV to the easy conditions which prevailed under Richard II. The wardrobe, on the other hand, though not pressed nearly so hard under Henry V as under his father, still has more difficulty than any other household department of the day in cashing tallies, and these difficulties increase sharply after his death. In contrast to this, the great wardrobe not only shows a violent fall in the amount of bad tallies assigned to it but actually continues to shrink in this connection, even after 1422—this probably reflects a decline in its general importance and spending activities rather than a sudden display on the exchequer's part of a peculiar preference for the prompt payment of great wardrobe bills.

Among the king's knights of the minority the main lender, Henry Brounflete, is a main sufferer as well, in rather over £600 worth of bad tallies: Sir John Popham and Sir John Robessart, both destined to be household officials of importance in the next decade, are runners-up with £352 and £231 respectively. King's esquires and 'other persons' may obviously be dismissed from the consideration of this period; which leaves only the royal family as recipients of bad tallies after 1422. The strength of Henry V in securing the effective payment of his personal dependents' revenues is in violent contrast with his father's weakness in this respect, and it is hardly surprising to find fictitious loans from the royal family creeping in again during the infancy of Henry VI. But as yet the rot has not gone far and in fact it is Henry V's own executors to whom £650 of the total £2,027 is owed during this period, the balance going to the two widowed queens, £380 to Joan and just under £1,000 to Katharine.

Turning to the older household departments, which are now practically departments of state, we may group the comparatively insignificant returns from the privy seal and signet with those of the great seal, while showing the exchequer separately. Their figures are as follows:

---

[1] Its Norman activities under Henry V must not, however, be forgotten.

	1399–1413	1413–22	1422–32
'Genuine' loans	£ s. d.	£ s. d.	£ s. d.
Chancery, etc.	2,621 13 4	1,604 12 0	1,146 13 4
Exchequer	5,950 10 2	2,474 6 9	1,308 10 0
Fictitious loans			
Chancery, etc.	180 8 0	—	231 13 1
Exchequer	290 8 2	65 15 3	39 10 0

The most remarkable point about these figures is their practically uniform decrease from 1413 right through to 1432—a decrease which may well be taken to exhibit a continued growth of power and independence on the part of the great departments, this in turn being expressed in a refusal on their part to get involved themselves in the financial process which they control and thereby in the financial difficulties of the state they serve. In the case of the chancery there are no important individual lenders in either reign, but a passing reference might be made to a corporate loan of £531 odd, made by Simon Gaunstede, keeper of the rolls, et aliis clericis de cancellaria in July 1422, together with three similar loans totalling £418 and headed by the new keeper, John Frank, during the minority.[1] In the case of the exchequer the only lender of any real importance in either period is its chancellor, Henry Somer,[2] who advanced £1,000 to Henry V and a further £353 odd in the next ten years. Practically all the rest of the list is made up of thirty to forty small lenders whose 'loans' are frequently arrears of salary and nothing more, while fictitious loans proper from both departments are obviously negligible.

The next head, *Local officials*, is more interesting:

---

[1] It may also be worth recording that the well-known Thomas Haxey was able to lend as much as 200 marks in two instalments to Henry V, while John Kemp, archbishop of York, lent 500 marks as chancellor to Henry VI, a sum which ought in justice to be transferred from 'bishops' to this heading. Again, of the £233 worth of bad tallies received by William Alnwick, bishop of Norwich, in this reign the greater part was in his capacity as keeper of the privy seal and should really be included here.

[2] See *Dict. Nat. Biog.*, LIII, supplemented by Tout, *Chapters*, IV, 480, and J. Saltmarsh, *Cam. Hist. J.*, III, 207.

LOCAL OFFICIALS	1399–1413	1413–22	1422–32
	£ s. d.	£ s. d.	£ s. d.
'Genuine' loans	1,071 5 3½	3,791 18 6½	3,368 0 6
Fictitious loans	33,707 15 3	14,707 0 1½	7,818 2 10½

The trebling of the amount of 'real' loans under this omnibus heading in the last two periods is significant: it suggests the conversion (in some instances at least) into local assets of what under the first Lancastrian had been local liabilities. In Henry V's time the more important of these loans came from the chamberlain of south Wales[1] (nearly £1,300) and the receiver of Brecknock[2] (nearly £800), while one of the London customs collectors, John Butler, is also a substantial contributor with over £450. Between 1422 and 1432 the wealthy London fishmonger, Richard Bukland, lends £1,074 as treasurer of Calais, and John Leventhorp, receiver of lands and tenements in the hands of feoffees of the duchy of Lancaster, provides another £1,000. The rest of the total in both reigns is mainly made up of small loans, though another London customs collector under Henry VI contributes just under £250. If we couple this resilience with the marked and steady fall in fictitious loans throughout the period 1413–32, it is difficult to avoid the conclusion that with one or two exceptions the position of the crown's local officers was becoming considerably easier.[3]

Of these exceptions the principal, in fact the only, one under Henry V is Calais, whose treasurer, Roger Salvayn, received just over £12,000 worth of bad tallies out of the grand total of £14,707 for that reign. This is in the tradition of Henry IV, but it is remarkable that it is not sustained at all under Henry VI,[4] whose chief liabilities appear to be, firstly, Aquitaine in the person of Sir John

[1] John Merbury. [2] William Butler.
[3] But see *Magnates* for the very large sums owed through bad tallies to great men acting as wardens of the marches, etc., particularly under Henry VI. The remarks in the text apply only to what may be called the smaller professional officials, not to noblemen.
[4] On the contrary, Richard Bukland, when treasurer of Calais, actually made 'real' loans to the crown, while his fictitious loans totalled only £500. See also p. 248 below, for his increased activity under this head during the decade 1432–42.

Radclyf, seneschal and keeper of the castle of Fronsac (£3,555 in all) and, secondly, the castle of Roxburgh, commanding the east march of Scotland (Sir Robert Ogle, keeper, nearly £2,200). It is noteworthy, in view of the great difficulty which Henry IV's exchequer had had in financing the government of Ireland, that there is little or no trace of bad tallies being cut for the king's lieutenant there during either of the ensuing periods.[1]

This completes the first section of this study, in which we have been dealing with the direct dependents or employees of the crown. The 'genuineness' of their loans is always rather suspect owing to the practice of entering as loans both the small arrears of salary already mentioned and perhaps from time to time such rather larger items as expenses contracted in the king's service and ultimately recoverable. But in the case of plain subjects of the crown, whose loans remain to be analysed, these difficulties do not arise, or at any rate not so acutely: the 'genuineness' of their loans is in fact only suspect through the occasional use of the exchequer and its processes by favoured individuals, whether to recover private debts or as a place of safe deposit for valuables, and in either case the error is not serious. I propose to start with bishops as before.

BISHOPS	1399–1413	1413–22	1422–32
	£ s. d.	£ s. d.	£ s. d.
'Genuine' loans	10,993 9 1	44,243 1 5½	58,516 7 10½
Fictitious loans	2,558 11 2	2,200 0 0	1,703 2 8

The enormous and increasing inflation under 'genuine' loans is, of course, due to the activities of Henry Beaufort, bishop of Winchester from 1405 and cardinal-priest of St. Eusebius from 1426.[2] Although Beaufort had become bishop of Winchester as early as 1405, his major financial operations do not appear to have begun before Henry V's reign, since the see lent rather less to the crown under Henry IV than it had done in William of Wykeham's time during the latter years of Richard II. But from 1413 onwards Beaufort's financial activities become quite abnormal for a bishop,

[1] None under Henry V, but the earl of March (£622) and the earl of Ormonde (£770) received some in the period 1422–32.
[2] See D.N.B.

or indeed for any of his contemporaries, and he rapidly earns his reputation as the leading English usurer and financier of the later Middle Ages.[1] If we deduct his loans from the Winchester total, as we are entitled to do, for they have little connection with episcopal revenues, we find that, allowing, say, £3,000 as normal for the see of Winchester over a ten-year period, loans from the whole episcopate remain about the same under Henry V as under Henry IV at roughly £11,000, but increase to about £16,000 in the following minority. Beaufort's own loans (*including* contributions from the see of Winchester) amount to £35,630 under Henry V and £45,413 for the first ten years of Henry VI—both of them colossal figures, but both of them still to be eclipsed.

Among other bishoprics Canterbury provides £1,930 under Henry V and £6,716 (almost the entire episcopal increase, excluding Beaufort) under his son; Bath and Wells, on the other hand, drops from over £1,700 to less than £900. The only other see worth mentioning is Lincoln, which tops £1,000 under Henry V but does not appear at all in Henry VI's list. On the other hand, in May 1431 there is a curious composite loan of £2,000 which defies analysis, raised from the archbishop of York, the bishops of Bath and Wells, Ely and Rochester, and Walter, lord Hungerford, treasurer of England, collectively.

Turning to fictitious loans, it is clear that the bishops' sufferings in this respect are steadily and progressively reduced. Beaufort himself (£2,000) and the bishop of Lincoln (£200) are the only victims in Henry V's time of an inconvenience which Beaufort barely allowed to recur at all, as far as he was concerned, in the years 1422–32. In this second period Canterbury is the largest recipient of bad tallies with £597 worth; then the archbishop of York (as chancellor of England), £240, and the bishop of Norwich (as keeper of the privy seal), £233; the rest are not worth particularizing, but it may be noted that, besides Lincoln, the sees of Chichester and Durham occur only in the first list, and Carlisle and Rochester only in the second. We may say then that in general the episcopate supported the second and third Lancastrians neither more nor less than it had supported the first of the line, but that new and invaluable, if somewhat expensive, aid for the dynasty

---

[1] Rivalled only, and that doubtfully, by Richard of Cornwall in the thirteenth century. See N. Denholm-Young, *Seignorial Administration in England*, 63.

was provided by the Lancastrian cardinal Beaufort and also, on a far smaller scale, by Henry Chichele, archbishop of Canterbury from 1414 to 1443.

We must now turn to the religious, a heading which takes its name from the great preponderance as lenders, after bishops, of regular monastic houses, but also includes a few secular clergy below episcopal rank, an occasional dean and chapter lending corporately, friars minor, friars preachers, hospitals and so forth.

RELIGIOUS	1399–1413	1413–22	1422–32
	£ s. d.	£ s. d.	£ s. d.
'Genuine' loans	3,838 4 0	8,758 6 9	3,459 14 11
Fictitious loans	781 13 0	1,178 10 0	359 17 1½

There is an odd correspondence in these figures between the days of Henry IV and the young Henry VI, neither of whose governments seems to have been able to persuade or compel the minor clergy and religious to lend the crown even half as much as the amount extracted from these classes by Henry V.[1] Thus between 1413 and 1422 well over a hundred religious houses and corporations and about the same number of parish clergy were induced to lend money to the crown, together with several deans, with or without their chapters, archdeacons, *magistri* and others—perhaps thirty in all. Of the whole list the Hospitallers, who advanced over £2,000 through the English prior of their order, are easily the most important: other large lenders are the abbot of Glastonbury (£553) and the prior and convent of Christchurch, Canterbury (£466). The prior of St. John of Jerusalem in England was also the principal sufferer from bad tallies, £866 worth out of £1,178 going to him.

For the first ten years of Henry VI, on the other hand, we get a very different picture—there are now little more than eighty lenders in this class instead of 240, and while the Hospital and Glastonbury still head the list their individual contributions have

---

[1] He also used them very frequently as collectors and commissioners of corporate loans from the localities, but in this capacity I have included them with the country gentry, with whom they are always associated for this purpose.

sunk to £500 and £300 respectively, not much ahead of St. Albans and Westminster at £233 each. The remaining £2,000 or so are raised very largely among fifty-two other religious houses; the parish clergy have dropped from over a hundred to fourteen or fifteen with the cessation of commissioned loans, while the diocesan officials and other miscellaneous lenders, though not so catastrophically reduced, number a mere ten or so instead of thirty. On the other hand, the total value of the fictitious loans credited to the clergy as a whole is also much lower: it is principally accounted for by Reginald Kentwode, dean of St. Paul's, who lends £100 and is owed £200; by the two orders of friars at Oxford, both of which seem to have been long receiving somewhat irregularly paid subsidies from the crown; and by the dean and chapter of St. Stephen's, Westminster—the chapel *infra palatium*, whose finances were practically a household matter, if not a household word.

Turning to the laity we may begin most naturally with the magnate class, whose figures are as follows:

MAGNATES	1399–1413			1413–22			1422–32		
	£	s.	d.	£	s.	d.	£	s.	d.
'Genuine' loans	10,750	4	11	5,696	17	10	1,112	13	4
Fictitious loans	19,855	16	0½	9,292	11	8½	37,169	11	7

Here, of course, the sharply progressive decline in the sums of money which the crown was able to extract as loans from the nobility is evident—even Henry V could not raise much more than half the sum his father had done—but it is completely overshadowed by the really sensational increase in fictitious loans from 1422 to 1432. The details are as follows: under Henry V the only important 'genuine' lenders are Thomas, earl of Arundel, with £2,969, and perhaps Hugh, lord Burnell, with £966, while under Henry VI John Beaufort, earl of Somerset (£1,000), stands practically alone. In both periods the main brunt of the fictitious loans is borne by magnates filling local offices: already under Henry V, Henry Percy, earl of Northumberland, was owed £5,737 arrears of salary as warden of the east march on account of bad tallies, Richard, lord Grey, another £1,007 in the same capacity, and the duke of Exeter, £1,054, as keeper of Aquitaine. These figures, however, are not much higher than the corresponding amounts found in Richard II's reign, and are very considerably lower than those found in Henry IV's: it is the increase in the first ten years of Henry VI which breaks all records. In that period we find that the Percy earl of Northumberland alone received £19,836 worth of bad tallies for his salaried wardenship of the east march, an almost exactly equivalent sum to the entire total of the bad tallies cut for all the magnates during the whole of Henry IV's disturbed reign. There is nothing else quite on this scale, but the new earl of Salisbury, Richard Neville, receives just under £5,000 worth for his wardenship of the west march before and after his succession as earl; the duke of Bedford's figure stands at just over £2,000, and lord Greystock, as keeper at one time of the castle of Roxburgh; the earl of Somerset; and Thomas, the old earl of Salisbury (counting tallies cut for his executors but excluding a further £100 for the dowager countess), all attain four-figure totals, viz. £1,612, £1,500 and £1,749 (£519 on executors' account) respectively. These striking figures certainly suggest that the more public spirit a great man showed under the minority the more he had to pay for it out of his own pocket: councillors' salaries, for example that of John, duke of Norfolk, were apt to go the same way. But we may assume that the *protector Anglie*, duke Humphrey of Gloucester, took some pains to see that his fictitious loans did not total more than £543 for the ten years; while his rival the cardinal, in spite of his enormous loans, was able to keep his bad tallies down to only £28 for the same period.

The figures for the smaller gentry, on the other hand, while almost equally interesting in their way, tell an entirely different story.

COUNTRY GENTRY	1399-1413			1413-22			1422-32		
	£	s.	d.	£	s.	d.	£	s.	d.
'Genuine' loans	1,015	0	4	16,767	6	2	19,006	1	0½
Fictitious loans	609	12	4	1,140	0	0	1,533	18	11

Here the interest lies in the immense and sustained increase in 'genuine' loans after 1413: the comparatively small, if equally steady, rise in fictitious loans is of little consequence. As far as Henry V is concerned this increase is due to deliberately organized pressure brought to bear upon the country as a whole by specially appointed shire commissioners of loans, the two great occasions being the springs of 1417 and 1421. The commissioners are to 'induce all other sufficient secular lieges of the king . . . to pay the loan . . . and to certify thereon to the treasurer of England or his deputy' by a fixed date.[1] As far as the country gentry are concerned their efforts resulted in raising fourteen or fifteen thousand pounds in nearly seven hundred loans, of which about two hundred were joint loans made by whole hundreds, wapentakes and similar units or simply by a collector *et aliis de comitatu.* Variations on this theme, in which no collector's name is mentioned, include one county loan from all the men of Derbyshire (in addition to individual loans), one from the entire Isle of Wight, and two double-county loans, both Cornwall and Devon on the one hand and Norfolk and Suffolk on the other making large joint loans, in addition to their normal county contributions.

The average sum raised by each of thirty-six English counties[2] was actually, for the whole reign, in the region of £450 under usually about twenty proper names, but naturally there are wide variations. At the lower end of the scale Cumberland, with a solitary loan of £10 from a single individual, and Worcestershire, with only £10 6s. 8d. from four lenders, are hardly worth including in the list: the only other counties which do not get into three figures are Cheshire (£60), Shropshire (£83), Gloucestershire (£94) and Middlesex (£99).[3] Counties raising between £100 and £200 are Buckinghamshire, Huntingdonshire, Staffordshire and Warwickshire; between £200 and £300, Bedfordshire, Berkshire, Cambridgeshire, Cornwall and Norfolk (not counting their joint loans with their neighbours), Derbyshire, Hampshire (including the Isle of Wight), Rutland, Surrey and Wiltshire; between £300 and £400, we have Dorset, Herefordshire, Lancashire and Sussex; between £400 and £500, Hertfordshire, Leicestershire, Notting-

---

[1] *Cal. Pat. Rolls, Henry V,* 1416–22, 249–52, 384–6, 416–17.

[2] Northumberland, Westmorland and, of course, the palatinate of Durham do not appear at all.

[3] It will be noticed that, with the exception of Middlesex, whose peculiar relation to London, which lent heavily, perhaps marks it out from the others, all the 'weak' counties are in the north or west.

hamshire and Oxfordshire; from £500 to £600, Devon (separately), Essex and Somerset. Above this limit are only Kent (£678), Northamptonshire (£821), Yorkshire (£1,096) and Lincolnshire with the colossal figure of £3,663, raised in over a hundred loans, seventy-nine of them corporately by wapentakes and other units.[1] The collecting, as well as the 'inducing', of these loans seems to have been entrusted as a rule to the commissioners, but it is notable that the clergy, particularly in the counties which lend heavily, play a specially important part. Thus I have found the *et aliis* type of entry in conjunction with twelve abbots, five priors, eighteen rectors, vicars or parsons and nine clerks, while in Lincolnshire the bishop seems to have been responsible for a joint loan *pro partibus de Kesteven* and in Devon the dean and chapter of Exeter, on one occasion at least, for persons other than themselves. Two lay magnates are also concerned—Thomas, lord de la Warr, in Lincolnshire, and Thomas, lord Camoys, in Sussex, the latter in somewhat unexpected co-operation with John Cok, mayor of Chichester, *et aliis hominibus de comitatu*. Incidentally, this is not the only occasion on which vills or burgesses seem to have participated in loans raised from the countryside: for example, the men of Grimsby and Swineshead and of two smaller places in Lincolnshire make such loans, and there are joint loans from individual burgesses of Eynsham, Bury St. Edmunds and Dunwich which seem to have somehow got confused with their county loans, though normally the loans from boroughs are perfectly distinct. Another even rarer exception is the appearance of a government official in this category: I have, however, found an instance (from Northamptonshire) of an escheator acting as the collector of a joint loan, while over 90 % of the rather poor Middlesex contribution seems to have been raised by the chancellor of the exchequer already referred to, Henry Somer, acting no doubt in his capacity as country gentleman (for he had accumulated

---

[1] Possible explanations might be (*a*) abnormal prosperity in the Lincolnshire wool and cloth trade during this period, (*b*) exceptional loyalty to the crown, or (*c*) the reverse, in which case the loans become penal. Unfortunately I know no evidence in favour of any of these theories. From the point of view of mere county area the Yorkshire loans seem well proportioned to the rest, but not the Lincolnshire loans. On the other hand, as Professor E. F. Jacob has pointed out (*Henry V*, pp. 84–5) Lincolnshire was essentially the home of large numbers of sturdy and prosperous smallholders.

landed interests), together with Thomas Frowyk, Robert Warner *et aliis de comitatu.*[1]

These loans are almost without exception secured on tallies of assignment, only two of which, both for small sums, are not cashed as soon as they fall due. The balance (£1,113 6s. 8d.) is made up of two tallies cut for unexplained reasons in favour of two Shropshire gentlemen, Thomas le Strange and John Wele, acting with a third party, Hugh Say, whom I have not been able to identify. They do not represent an unsuccessful attempt to repay a large 'genuine' loan, since le Strange is the only one of these three who lends anything at all under that head, and he lends no more than £33 6s. 8d.[2]

Turning to Henry VI we get a completely different picture of the loans forthcoming from the country gentry. There are about forty-five small loans from individuals instead of several hundred, of which, moreover, only five bear the addition *et aliis* etc. Apart from these five there are very few organized loans and by far the greatest part of the very large total comes from an entirely new source, important for the first time in this reign, namely the feoffees of the duchy of Lancaster. These contribute no less than £11,295 in conjunction with the archbishop of Canterbury,[3] himself a feoffee of the duchy, and a further £4,666 without him. These large sums are secured in the same way as before and only £20 worth goes wrong in the repayment of them. It is apparent that the resources of the duchy, which do not appear in the receipt rolls of the first two Lancastrians, are now being thrown into the scale, and this can only be due to the sudden impoverishment of the crown by the shrinkage of the feudal revenue and, especially, the serious decrease in the frequency of parliamentary grants after 1422.

It will be observed that under this heading all other sources between them raise barely over £3,000—that is, appreciably less than Lincolnshire alone had raised under Henry V. Within this £3,000 the most important secondary source of strength is now East Anglia, where 'divers persons' in Norfolk raise £1,000 and 'divers persons' in Suffolk a further £500, both by the hands of

[1] I should perhaps repeat at this point that wherever I have found persons from other categories such as clergy, burgesses or magnates mentioned in conjunction with the words *et aliis de comitatu* I have taken them out of their own category for that particular payment and included them under 'Country gentry'.

[2] See Chapter IV, p. 153, n. 1, above.   [3] Henry Chichele.

the earl of Suffolk. Lincolnshire is now represented by no more than £589 odd raised by the treasurer of England, Ralph, lord Cromwell, together with John Kyme, John Barnaby *et aliis probis hominibus de partibus de Lindsey et Kesteven*: Kyme *et alii* add a further £30 elsewhere upon their own account. The only other collectors of loans one can trace are the Rikhill family in Essex (for three small loans), the dean of St. Paul's, who inveigles £50 odd from *aliis hominibus* of Middlesex, and a clerk of Shaftesbury, John Baret, who seems to have persuaded 20 marks out of the pockets of some other men of Dorset.

Altogether there is hardly any suggestion of the widespread support successfully commanded by the late king Henry V: the fictitious loans, too, in this class increase from three to eleven in number, though it is true that over three-quarters of the total £1,500 worth of bad tallies goes (at £400 apiece) to Anne, widow of Sir William Clifford and a possible pensioner of the crown, to Sir Reginald Cobham of Surrey and to another south-country knight, Sir John Pelham of either Kent or Sussex, both of whom may perhaps have been at one time or another in the direct service of the government and may therefore rank only doubtfully as country gentry.[1]

I have gone into some detail under this head because the bare totals rather obscure the facts which I believe to be suggested by analysis: viz. the firm control established over a very wide area by the strong and relatively popular Henry V and the loss of that control, in spite of a still greater need of money, by the council of the minority which follows. The same point can be illustrated less dramatically from the loans made by the burgesses, in which it will be convenient to begin, as I have done elsewhere, by distinguishing from the rest the much more important loans made by Londoners and London.

LONDON	1399–1413	1413–22	1422–32
	£ s. d.	£ s. d.	£ s. d.
'Genuine' loans	51,527 18 4	32,096 13 4	18,435 0 2
Fictitious loans	11,972 16 2	3,666 13 4	2,803 6 8

[1] Sir John Pelham had served as treasurer of war, 1404–5 (pp. 91–2, above), and was treasurer of England, 1411–13 (p. 420, below).

Here the steady decline in lending is most marked: it may perhaps have been due to a slackening of effective government pressure on the city, which appears to have profited little or nothing from such loans and, if so, would only have made them under what was more or less compulsion. Actually, for a reason which will appear in a moment, this slackening may have been largely voluntary under Henry V, but the further drop under his successor can only be explained by governmental weakness. This becomes clear if the 'genuine' loans are analysed: in each period the principal lender is not an individual citizen but the mayor, aldermen and good men of London in their corporate capacity, and it is these corporate loans which a popular government can 'induce' most easily, a weak government tending to fall back, as Henry IV had done for most of his London support, on individuals. Now under Henry V the corporate loans actually rise to over £20,000 against Henry IV's £18,000, but between 1422 and 1432 they sink to a little over £15,000. On the other hand only twelve or thirteen individual citizens are approached by Henry V, and of the additional £12,000 which they raise, over £10,000 are accounted for by those veteran supporters of the dynasty, Richard Whittington (£6,666 13s. 4d.) and John Hende (£3,533 6s. 8d.). As against this the government of the young Henry VI, apparently not being able to achieve much with the mayor and aldermen as such, was obliged to press as many as fifty-five individual citizens for petty loans totalling some £3,000 in all. But even in this category it met with nothing like the success of Henry IV with his individual lenders, for the only two London loans of any importance made to Henry VI (other than the corporate city loans already mentioned) are those made by syndicates; thus William Stokdale, draper, with three others, advances £1,000, and William Estfeld, mercer and mayor of the Westminster staple,[1] advances rather less than another £1,000 together with another mercer and a vintner. This time the appeal to individual Londoners had failed completely.

It will be noticed that there is a steep decline in fictitious loans from the conditions obtaining under Henry IV. Those under Henry V and Henry VI are principally accounted for by the mayor and aldermen (£2,000 and £2,186 for the two periods), and, in Henry V's reign, by John Hende (a further £1,666 13s. 4d.).

[1] Professor E. E. Rich in *Cam. Hist. J.*, IV, 193.

Burgesses outside London produce the following results:

BURGESSES	1399–1413	1413–22	1422–32
	£ s. d.	£ s. d.	£ s. d.
'Genuine' loans	10,366 17 10½	6,786 13 4	4,489 16 4
Fictitious loans	1,213 6 8	115 6 8	2,104 18 9½

Under Henry V the boroughs may have been 'induced' to lend money in much the same way as the country gentry, but it is clear that the pressure on them was relatively much less severe. Excluding London, seventy-two towns figure in the receipt rolls as lenders during his reign, Bristol (with just over £1,400) being easily the most important. There are in fact only nineteen other towns which reach even three-figure totals, and of these York (£654) is the only one to top the £500 mark. The loans are mainly corporate but individual burgesses also subscribe, occasionally for really large amounts, e.g. John Herryes of Cambridge (£253), Nicholas Blakborn of York (£200), and John Grene of Grantham (£143). Possibly these large subscribers had been acting as collectors and had allowed the total sums collected to stand in their names, but this is by no means certain since I have also found corporate loans from York and Cambridge, and though an *et aliis* formula is not uncommon in other towns it seems to be limited to fairly small sums, the average being about £20.[1] Coventry and Leicester stand out curiously from the rest in the relatively large number of their individual subscribers—nineteen, plus the gild of Holy Trinity at Coventry (total £276 odd in all), and nineteen again (but totalling only £63 6s. 8d.) at Leicester; in no other town do the names of more than three private citizens occur. Fictitious loans, it will be seen, are negligible, Bristol and Dartmouth being the only towns affected, and of these two Bristol naturally takes the lion's share.

Turning to the period 1422–32 we find Bristol still leading the other provincial towns (now only about twenty-eight in all), but with the much reduced total of £866. Norwich is second with £266, Salisbury (£178) third, and York not more than fourth (with

[1] The only notable exception is a certain mayor of Lincoln, Thomas Archer. from whom *et aliis* as much as £83 6s. 8d. was forthcoming.

£162). Southampton (£133) is the only other town to get into three figures and the whole burgess total would be little over £2,150 but for the reappearance of the staple as a lender by the hands of William Estfeld, from whom, *et aliis mercatoribus de Stapul'*, comes the fairly large amount of £2,333 6s. 8d.[1] The proportion of corporate loans, too, from the English towns has sunk from five-sixths in number to less than a half, while the roll of individual lenders and the frequency of the *et aliis* formula have both proportionately increased.

All this seems to suggest that the government of Henry VI's minority was finding it far more difficult than Henry V had done to cajole loans out of the English towns in their corporate capacities and was being forced back first on to individuals and then, when these failed, on to the staple in imitation of Henry IV, alone among previous kings. It is not surprising in the circumstances to find a sharp rise in fictitious loans, which now amount to nearly half the 'real' ones; the bad tallies representing these are inflicted mainly on the staplers (£1,814) and most of the balance upon Bristol as before. If the government was finding it hard to borrow it was finding it still harder to repay.

Yet if denizen merchants were experiencing these difficulties as creditors of the crown, aliens seem somehow to have obtained rather better security than before. The figures are as follows:

ALIENS	1399-1413	1413-22	1422-32
	£ s. d.	£ s. d.	£ s. d.
'Genuine' loans	5,242 15 1	3,133 6 8	4,535 6 8
Fictitious loans	2,003 11 6	1,240 8 6	290 12 8

It will be seen at once that the mild fluctuation in the value of 'genuine' loans, though not unexpected, is not marked compared with that complete collapse in foreign lending which took place in

[1] The only other appearance up to this date of the staplers as lenders to the crown is in Henry IV's reign, when they contributed no less than £8,000 out of a nominal 'burgess' total of £10,366 odd. In each case their heavy lending makes the 'burgess' total misleading, but it is difficult to see under what other heading they could be placed.

the latter half of Richard II's reign after the great activity of the years 1377–89: what is significant is the steady decline in the total of fictitious loans. In Henry V's reign Florentines, with £1,833, are the principal alien lenders, and Venetians a good second with £1,166. The only other alien is a Lucchese, Paul de Melan or Meliani (with £133), and practically the whole of the bad tallies are borne by Florentines, none at all being cut for the Venetians. It is perhaps a result of this that in the first ten years of Henry VI the Florentines (with £1,133) sink from first to third place as financiers of the English crown, though they continue to receive four-fifths of the admittedly much reduced output of bad tallies. Genoese, on the other hand, with £1,733, suddenly assume first place in the years 1422–32, thus resuming an activity suspended since the reign of Henry IV. Lucca disappears entirely and the second place is taken as before by the Venetians, but this time with the increased total of £1,636. It is remarkable that neither Genoa nor Venice, but only Florence, appears under fictitious loans, the small balance being accounted for by 100 marks owing to 'the cardinal of Navarre'.[1]

The names of the financial houses concerned are of some interest: thus the Florentine papal agents, the Albertini, so active under Henry IV, do not seem to keep up their dwindling connection with the English money-lending business after Henry V's reign, unless their friend or agent Alexander Farantyn or Farentini should be counted one of them.[2] Venice is represented principally, though not exclusively,[3] in both reigns by the Balbi (Bernard and later Peter), and under Henry VI by the Contarini, while Cataneo and Spinola in partnership, and one Vinaldo (separately), are the principal Genoese lenders.

I have taken certain risks in reducing this section to the lowest possible limits, but even so there are seven persons under Henry V and eleven under Henry VI about whom I have been unable to discover anything. It will be seen, however, that the amounts involved are so small as to be absolutely negligible.

---

[1] Possibly a slip for Stephen de Navarria, doctor of civil law, king's advocate before the consistory and at the council of Basle: in return for these services he obtained a licence to hold benefices in England to the value of £1,100 a year in 1435. *C.P.R.*, *Henry VI*, 1429–36, p. 461.

[2] J. Vittore under Henry V and 'Primacio Discresis' (*sic*) *et socii* under Henry VI also made loans.

[3] Nicholas 'Mulyn' (? Molini) *et alii merc' de Venicia* lend £666 13s. 4d. under Henry V.

UNIDENTIFIED	1399–1413	1413–22	1422–32
	£ s. d.	£ s. d.	£ s. d.
'Genuine' loans	76 6 8	115 0 0	70 0 0
Fictitious loans	665 19 3	0 0 0	2 10 0

In conclusion, it would appear from all this mass of detail, firstly, that the 'real' revenue under Henry V recovered more or less completely from the disturbing effects of the Lancastrian revolution and was as high as it had ever been. But after his death it declined by nearly 36%, while that percentage of the nominal totals which was pure book-keeping rose from 13 to 20. This increase was caused more by tallies going wrong than by plain borrowing, but borrowing remained higher in both periods than at any other previous date, and it is ominous that during the period 1422–32 there was also a 75% increase over Henry V's reign in exchequer inability to meet its obligations.

Secondly, as regards the actual persons lending money to the crown or disappointed by the crown under these two kings, there were certain marked changes after Henry V's death. The infant Henry VI's household was not unnaturally weaker and more impoverished than his father's, and even his wardrobe was of no financial use to him; on the contrary, it was itself highly embarrassed for funds and by 1432 even the royal family, at any rate in the persons of the two widowed queens, was going short of money. The older departments of the household, on the other hand, were becoming more and more departments of state, successfully detached by their own action from any vital contact with the involved finances of the crown. The same tendency towards detachment may be seen among the smaller professional officials in the localities; they may lend rather more than they used to do, but the scale of their small loans is unimportant compared with the fact that they no longer suffer from default upon the grand scale of preceding reigns. They convey in fact an impression that they, too, may succeed in disentangling their own interests from those of the crown before many years are past.

It is clear, then, that from 1422 at any rate, though the process certainly starts earlier, government in England will have to look more and more to its leading subjects for support and be dependent on their good will; it has exhausted most of the possibilities of living on its own vitals. Already under Henry V bishop Beaufort was lending over £35,000 to the crown, and he was to increase this to £45,000 and more per decade under Henry VI, while the contributions of the other bishops show, if anything, an increase, and yet they are all as a class much surer that the crown's growing obligations to them will be honoured than they have ever been before. This, however, is not true in either respect of the minor clergy and religious—only Henry V was strong enough to touch their pockets effectively, and under his successor, as in his father's day, they follow the tendency of all small lenders towards detachment, alike from the profits and the dangers of national finance.

With the laity it is on the whole a different story, for the lay magnates had always preferred to lend service rather than money to the crown, and the only difference between the first three Lancastrians is that the nobles were on the whole recouped for this service under Henry V but bilked upon a fairly large scale under Henry IV, and quite fantastically so by the government of the young Henry VI. Nor is it altogether fair to say that this is merely the reverse side of the well-known control of crown patronage and feudal revenue established by the council in those years, since the principal sufferer was the Percy earl of Northumberland, who seems to have obtained comparatively little compensation.[1] In fact, if there is any truth in the suggestion already made above that the more public spirit a great man showed during the minority the more dearly he had to pay for it out of his own pocket, it may be possible to find in this financial favouritism a contributory cause of the regional spirit and local jealousies which later helped to bring about the wars of the roses; it is at least significant to find two-thirds of the total default to noblemen in these ten years borne by magnates from the north of England.

[1] *D.N.B.*, sub nomine. He was, it is true, an active member of the council of regency, but the grants obtained by him in return for a good deal of ambassadorial work appear to be trifling. More material was the fact of his nominal salary as warden of the east marches of £5,000 in time of war and £2,500 in time of peace, but it was precisely this salary which he had so much difficulty in collecting. A cursory examination of the entries under his name in *C.P.R.*, *Henry VI*, 1422–9 and 1429–36, does little to dispel the impression that on balance he lost considerably more from all his offices together than he gained from them.

As regards the lesser gentry a close examination of the figure provides still further support for the generalization which has already been emerging, namely that, with the notable exception of Henry V's reign, the small men of the fifteenth century continued to be much less affected than the great men by the financial dealings of the crown. In Henry V's time, it is true, there is the tremendous drive for really 'national' loans which results in very widespread and substantial contributions by the gentry of all counties other than the far north and west, but this was an innovation which only a strong king could bring about and, in spite of the apparent increase in the figures after 1422, it was not in fact maintained. It is the sudden and, we may assume, compulsory appearance of the feoffees of the duchy of Lancaster, headed by the archbishop of Canterbury, which inflates this total out of all proportion after 1422—the obvious moral being that where Henry V could 'induce' loans from practically the whole of England the government of his successor could 'induce' them merely from the duchy, and that only with the archbishop's support.

London represents another dwindling source of funds and although, in view of the increasing stubbornness of successive mayors and aldermen, the council of the minority was forced back upon approaching a large number of individual citizens, it soon found that the days of Whittington and Hende were gone for ever and met in fact with little more success than in similar advances made to burgesses of smaller towns. Hence in London five-sixths of a much-reduced total came eventually from the city authorities, just as in the case of the other towns a most unsatisfactory yield was ultimately offset only by corporate bargaining with the powerful group of staplers—an expedient hitherto confined to the insolvent Henry IV. Finally, we have the small advances made by alien merchants, so small that there is little change from year to year except, significantly, in the security with which they are made.

The general picture, then, of English government finance, as reflected by the receipt of the exchequer, 1413-32, is not a happy one. In the first nine years we have a picture of a great king straining the resources of his people to the uttermost in a desperate gamble for an obsolete ideal, but the tension snaps, almost audibly, upon his deathbed and, though the liabilities he has created still remain, the means of meeting them have disappeared. It is no longer the fashion to carp at the council of his son's minority; but its members, however well meaning,[1] had been set an insoluble problem. Yet bad as things were in the upshot from 1422 to 1432, they were to go from bad to worse during the next generation.

[1] See, e.g., Jolliffe, *Constitutional History of Medieval England*, 465–6, 473–6.

CHAPTER VI

CALENDAR, 1432-52

		£	s.	d.	%
MICHAELMAS 1432–3:	Cash	10,874	4	0	18
	Assigned	35,777	0	5½	59
	Book-keeping	13,933	12	2	23
	Total	60,584	16	7½	100

The half-subsidy granted in July 1432, in spite of being spread over so long a period, may help to account for the fact that cash receipts were still substantially higher this winter than they were destined to be during the next three years. Assignment, too, was relatively high, though there were no outstanding days. Book-keeping did not begin to be interesting until 17 February, when just over £4,000 was borrowed in five large loans: this was followed on the 19th and 26th by more borrowing, amounting to rather less than £4,000 in the two days together, while a month later another £516 was raised, bringing the term total under the head of genuine loans to £8,543. Fictitious loans came to £5,390, of which the only serious item was the sum of £1,725, credited to Richard Bukland, treasurer of Calais, on 23 February in place of nine bad tallies on the customs.

		£	s.	d.	%
EASTER 1433:	Cash	2,643	15	5½	11
	Assigned	10,765	14	0½	43
	Book-keeping	11,583	17	4	46
	Total	24,993	6	10	100

There were only 16 days of business, none of them a heavy cash day. Assignment was continuous and reached four figures on three widely spaced occasions. Book-keeping mainly took the shape of large genuine loans raised at the beginning and end of term: there were sixteen of these in all, totalling over £8,000, the largest of them being one of £3,333 6s. 8d. advanced on 18 July by cardinal

Beaufort. A further £3,197 took the form of fictitious loans—none of them of any special interest—while £226 13s. 4d. represented a prest of 19 July 1432, now repaid, to Robert Gilbert, bishop of London, *de regardo pro expensis suis versus generale concilium.* This payment was marked *Denar' Restit'* in the left margin, instead of the more usual *prestitum restitutum.* More important than these details is the fact that a parliament sat at Westminster during the latter part of this term (8 July to 13 August), and though it made no grants it witnessed the appointment of a new treasurer of England in the person of lord Cromwell. The old treasurer, lord le Scrope, accounted on 18 July, not long after which the new treasurer was authorized to 'suspend all payments until he had £2,000 in hand for petty expenses'.[1] Not content with this, Cromwell did a rare thing for the middle ages[2] in attempting to produce a budget, according to which the ensuing exchequer year might be expected to bring in a revenue of £62,565. This, it is true, was subject to encumbrances totalling about £20,000, but on the other hand it took no account of the quarter-subsidy still owing from the previous year and worth between £8,000 and £9,000, which would bring the total revenue up to £71,000; and it is encouraging to note that this is the exact figure which my corrected receipt roll totals disclose as the 'real' revenue of the exchequer year 1433–4. The seriousness of the situation, as revealed by the duke of Bedford on a visit to England that summer, turned on the smallness of the genuinely 'free' income: thus, according to his mouthpiece, Cromwell, the French- and Scots-march garrisons alone absorbed nearly £53,500 annually between them, even on a peace footing—which left a deficit of £2,500 (that is, allowing for the £20,000 of charges on the revenue) before the normal expenses of the kingdom, not to mention any special war expenditure, were so much as taken into account. In addition, the 'schedule of debts' amounted to £164,000, including £59,500 due for wages of war and, if Ramsay is right, £17,800 due on loans as distinct from what he calls 'the bulk of the Tallies (£56,000) retained in the Exchequer'.[3] Yet so

---

[1] Ramsay, *Lancaster and York*, I, 453.

[2] Encouraged, so it is said, by the duke of Bedford. See S. B. Chrimes, 'John, first duke of Bedford; his work and policy in England, 1389–1435' (summary of thesis) in *Bulletin of the Institute of Historical Research*, VII, 110–13.

[3] Ramsay, *Lancaster and York*, I, 454.

little was parliament concerned at this insolvency that the new treasurer had to appeal twice for a day even to examine his accounts.[1]

MICHAELMAS 1433–4:		£	s.	d.	%
	Cash	5,137	0	6	11
	Assigned	23,788	14	4	53
	Book-keeping	16,506	9	10½	36
	Total	45,432	4	8½	100

Parliament, which had merely been adjourned on 13 August, resumed on 13 October, a week after the new exchequer year had begun. The commons' main concern was to persuade Bedford to accept the regency of England, but although they succeeded in their aim they did not render the new regent's task financially any easier. The only grant made was that of a subsidy subject to a £4,000 reduction, 'to be remitted rateably among the counties',[2] and spread over the whole of 1434 and 1435, though it is true that the existing customs duties were prolonged until November 1437 and that the dues payable by aliens were increased. Cash payments continued to be little more than a trickle, though they reached four figures on 19 December and approached them again on 4 February: assignment, on the other hand, was stepped up considerably during the same two months. Book-keeping was again represented for the most part by genuine loans from various sources totalling £11,758: outstanding among these were a single loan of £4,000, made on 4 February by the treasurer, lord Cromwell, and another of £1,333 6s. 8d. on 22 February from London. Though fictitious loans came to £4,641 the only notable sufferer was Sir John Tyrell, the treasurer of the household, who on 7 and 8 December failed to cash tallies for some £2,500, mainly on the customs but also on the farmers of the land of John, late duke of Norfolk. The term ended with an unusual refund to the exchequer of £107 8s. 2d. overpaid to the merchants of the staple on account of previous loans.[3]

---

[1] Ibid., I, 456.

[2] Ibid.

[3] Only two assignments are quoted, viz. one of £68 6s. 2d., made on 1 June, and another of £4 5s. 8d., made on 20 June. Perhaps the rest of the overpayment had been in cash.

		£	s.	d.	%
EASTER 1434:	Cash	4,264	15	10	7
	Assigned	37,837	12	1½	63
	Book-keeping	18,266	6	2	30
	Total	60,368	14	1½	100

Only three days passed without any cash revenue whatsoever, but the amounts remained small. Assignment started strongly in mid-April and reached four figures no less than eight times during the subsequent months, while on 10 June it climbed higher still and totalled £12,522. The whole of the last-mentioned sum was paid to cardinal Beaufort, and was accompanied by a marginal note to the effect that £6,666 13s. 4d. of it represented security for a recent loan (2 June), while the remainder represented money on account of jewels, etc., *tanquam forisfact'* to the king, but now restored to the cardinal by king and council.[1] Book-keeping was dominated by Beaufort: thus in addition to the large loan of 2 June already mentioned he advanced a further £2,000 on the 21st, and so accounted for about two-thirds of all the genuine borrowing in the term: the remainder came in some fifty-one smaller loans from various sources. In addition there was over £4,700 worth of scattered fictitious loans.

		£	s.	d.	%
MICHAELMAS 1434–5:	Cash	3,978	15	6	12
	Assigned	18,745	4	5½	54
	Book-keeping	11,749	3	2	34
	Total	34,473	3	1½	100

Although the cash percentage rose slightly, the gross total was lower than it had been for some time. Assignment was far heavier than cash, as had now become usual, especially between 5 and

[1] See p. 177, above, Easter 1432, for the explanation of this curious payment, which was in origin a conditional fine for the recovery of plate and jewels seized about that time by the cardinal's great enemy, Humphrey, duke of Gloucester. It was then agreed that if the king could show within six years any justification for the seizure the money would be forfeit, but otherwise it would be returned. Its repayment only two years later showed that Beaufort's star was definitely in the ascendant and that he had finally secured acquittal from Gloucester's charges. See Ramsay, *Lancaster and York*, I, 441–2.

11 November and on the last two days of the term, which between them accounted for over £7,000. The book-keeping total, on the other hand, would have been relatively small but for two large genuine loans—one of them the now regular contribution from cardinal Beaufort, this time (18 February) of £5,000, and the other (19 February) of rather over £3,000 from Richard Bukland (still treasurer of Calais) and John Langton.[1] Fictitious loans came to rather over £3,500, but were individually of small account.

		£	s.	d.	%
EASTER 1435:	Cash	3,921	6	11	7
	Assigned	22,206	4	8½	40
	Book-keeping	29,216	19	1	53
	Total	55,344	10	8½	100

Cash came in daily during this relatively short term, if only in small amounts. Assignment was equally steady at its own much higher level: thus on eleven days out of twenty it reached four figures, whereas cash never did so. The book-keeping percentage was the heaviest of the decade: three-quarters consisted of genuine and the remainder of fictitious loans. Principal lenders were the earl of Somerset with £1,333 6s. 8d. on 21 May, and of course cardinal Beaufort with £7,166 13s. 4d. in July: the cardinal was also associated with the feoffees of the duchy of Lancaster who lent £3,091 in June. Fictitious loans contained only two really large items, each of them levied as to about three-quarters on the customs and the rest on general revenue, viz. a £2,334 default to Sir John Tyrell, the treasurer of the household, on 28 May, and another of precisely the same amount on 18 July. There was also a small cash *donum* of £33 6s. 8d. made on 3 June by the abbot of Ramsey: this seems to have started life as a genuine loan, all claim to the repayment of which was in the end voluntarily abandoned.

		£	s.	d.	%
MICHAELMAS 1435–6:	Cash	24,297	13	8½	23
	Assigned	39,014	6	11½	37
	Book-keeping	41,267	2	10½	40
	Total	104,579	3	6½	100

[1] King's clerk at this date and subsequently (1442–53) king's chaplain.

This was easily the highest gross total of the decade: only that of Easter 1437 came anywhere near it. Presumably this was owing to the grants made by the October parliament in connection with the new war against Burgundy and the attempts to organize a coalition of the Germans and the Netherlanders. A whole subsidy was granted, and although it was again spread over two years and again subjected to a reduction of £4,000 it was at least supplemented by what Ramsay calls a 'graduated income-tax on freehold lands and offices':[1] moreover, both convocations gave reasonably generous grants and the customs duties were renewed with little change until November 1437. Power was also taken to borrow money on parliamentary security up to £100,000, though this was subject to the proviso that 'no-one should be compelled to lend against his will'. The refreshment of the revenue which these new grants provided is clearly visible in the cash column of my day-to-day analysis; e.g. on 31 October (£3,191), 23 November (£2,578), 9 December (£2,392), and during the last four or five days of the term. The resultant cash total was the highest in the decade, and indeed the most respectable since 1429–30: it was not exceeded before 1485. Assignment too increased, though not proportionately, reaching four figures on eight occasions and being particularly heavy on 16 November, 20 February and 1 and 6 March. Book-keeping, however, was once more the largest single item (as in four other terms in this decade and six in the following one) and once again genuine borrowing accounted for the greater part of it. Indeed the total of real loans at £33,341 was one of the highest of the century, although it is true that very nearly two-thirds of it came from cardinal Beaufort alone (15 February). Yet apart from Beaufort the merchants of the staple lent £5,333 6s. 8d. through Estfeld on 18 January, while the earl of Somerset lent £4,000 on 15 March and there were also smaller lenders. Fictitious loans (totalling just under £8,000) were more evenly distributed, and Beaufort's share, as might be expected, was negligible.

		£	s.	d.	%
EASTER 1436:	Cash	16,249	16	3	26
	Assigned	22,335	19	$11\frac{1}{2}$	36
	Book-keeping	23,206	10	$9\frac{1}{2}$	38
	Total	61,792	7	0	100

[1] Ramsay, *Lancaster and York*, I, 478–9, for details of all the grants mentioned in this paragraph.

Cash totals dropped by a third during this term as the yield of the new grants declined, but they were still well above average, and they were of course especially heavy at the beginning of the term. Assignment was relatively low: indeed, it was running below cash payments as late as 7 July and was only pulled up above cash by the large tallies which were cut during the next few days. Fictitious loans were within £300 of the previous term's total: the principal sufferers were the feoffees of the duchy of Lancaster, who received sixteen bad tallies on the lay subsidy for £2,143 on 10 May, forty-eight hours after advancing £2,180 to the exchequer. Other genuine loans of some size came from the archbishop of Canterbury (£1,642 on 15 May) and cardinal Beaufort (£6,000 on 28 August): the total was just under £15,000. The term is also remarkable in one other respect, viz. the relatively large number of cash *dona* received in July and August: there were no less than twenty of these, totalling nearly £1,750. Most of them, but by no means all, came from clerics—more particularly abbots, deans and bishops—but the only really large gift of this kind (£1,000 on 28 August) proceeded from the mayor and citizens of London. One *prestitum restitutum* is worth noting, viz. £666 13s. 4d. repaid in cash by John Kemp, archbishop of York, out of sums advanced him in the early spring of 1434 as ambassador to the pope and general council.

		£	s.	d.	%
MICHAELMAS 1436–7:	Cash	7,144	11	9	19
	Assigned	21,237	1	7½	58
	Book-keeping	8,545	1	1½	23
	Total	36,926	14	6	100

The periodic run-down of revenue obviously developed rapidly during this term, when cash, though a little was received almost daily, was more than halved. Assignment, however, was only £1,000 down—on the whole fairly evenly divided—and the biggest fall took place in book-keeping. Of this last only £1,733 6s. 8d. represented genuine loans, and even these were all raised on a single day (18 March), principally from Beaufort and the feoffees of the duchy of Lancaster, but also from the staple. Fictitious loans, on the contrary, did not decline very far—in fact only by some £800. One principal sufferer (for £1,666 13s. 4d. drawn on 29 November against the clerical tenth, and again on 4 December) was the archbishop of Canterbury, but the gross total of default was at its highest on the last day of term (again 18 March—some £2,750). By that date the revenues on which assignments were laid had become pretty mixed: thus only £700 fell on customs, while other sources placed under contribution included the chamberlains of Chester and of north and south Wales and various farmers and keepers of lordships and of the temporalities of the vacant see of London. There was only one *donum*, in contrast to the spate of the preceding term, viz. one of £100 from the men of Durham, presented on 26 November.

		£	s.	d.	%
EASTER 1437:	Cash	12,419	0	6	13
	Assigned	48,784	13	0	53
	Book-keeping	31,915	11	4½	34
	Total	93,119	4	10½	100

The sudden jump in real revenue this term was obviously due, as usual, to fresh parliamentary grants. Parliament had in fact been sitting at Westminster since the end of January, but it did not make its grants until the end of the session, as was the common practice, i.e. late in March, so that they could have had no effect on the Michaelmas receipt roll of the time. The grants themselves were not as generous as before, for while the subsidy was still subjected to the now familiar abatements there was no form of supplementary taxation, and the customs, though renewed until November 1438, remained at practically the old level. A point of minor interest is that nearly half the wool duty, viz. 20s. on the sack, was regularly earmarked from this time forward for the expenses of the garrison of Calais; finally, powers were again taken to borrow up to £100,000.[1] As far as cash is concerned, the newly voted revenue does not begin to appear in any bulk on the roll before 1 June, and by 2 July most of what the exchequer was going to receive under this head was already in—yet the total was unimpressive. The new revenue, such as it was, could however be anticipated, and assignments were in fact made from 14 May onwards to such purpose that their total was easily the highest of the decade, and indeed was not surpassed till 1463. Over £8,600 was assigned on the last two days of term alone, £6,875 on 8 July

---

[1] Ramsay, *Lancaster and York*, I., 493-4.

and £4,391 on 14 May, but by far the largest single item was an assignment of £13,333 6s. 8d. made in favour of cardinal Beaufort on 15 May, the day after he had produced a cash loan, nominally at least for that identical amount. This large loan goes a long way to explain the high book-keeping total, with its genuine loans standing at just under £21,000: there was, however, one other important lender besides Beaufort (not to mention a few smaller ones), viz. the staple, which on 19 July produced £6,782 13s. 4d. The £10,916 worth of fictitious loans was scattered between the staplers, who were the worst sufferers (£2,617 in eighteen tallies, all on the clerical tenth, 25 July) and a number of other crown creditors, but it is noticeable that Beaufort's share was as small as ever, viz. a mere matter of £666 13s. 4d., drawn on 15 May against the clerical subsidy. The feoffees of the duchy of Lancaster, on the other hand, were a good deal harder hit when on 15 July the collectors of the same grant again defaulted upon another eighteen tallies for a total of £2,108.

		£	s.	d.	%
MICHAELMAS 1437–8:	Cash	6,800	18	11	13
	Assigned	24,030	1	7½	45
	Book-keeping	22,194	9	6½	42
	Total	53,025	10	1	100

Owing to the absence of money grants this exchequer year was one of steadily falling revenue. Though there were only two days on which no cash at all was received, only one day total (30 November) reached four figures and many of the rest were very small. Assigned revenue was better maintained, the first heavy drafts being drawn on 31 October as security for a two-day-old loan of £6,150 13s. 4d. from the staple. Assignment was, however, almost equally heavy on 22 November and remained fairly high until 5 December, by which time it was already totalling over £19,000. Loans in general were still mainly 'genuine' and attained a total of some £17,000 under that head: thus, in addition to the large loan already mentioned, the staple advanced another £2,000 on 31 October; Beaufort £7,333 6s. 8d. on 26 March; and London £1,000 on the same date. The rather less than £5,000 worth of fictitious loans was more mixed in character, but nearly half of it occurred on the single day 30 November, mostly on the customs.

		£	s.	d.	%
EASTER 1438:	Cash	3,505	18	5½	9
	Assigned	18,282	9	4½	46
	Book-keeping	17,716	12	2½	45
	Total	39,505	0	0½	100

The continued fall in revenue is well marked, though it does not reach the low level of 1433, or even of 1434–5 and 1436–7. Cash in particular, although coming in in driblets every day but two, sank seriously: assignment, which, as usual, was rather heavier in the last two-thirds of the term, was better maintained. Under book-keeping, which was only a very little lower than assignment, the main feature is that the relative importance of genuine and fictitious loans was reversed and only £4,631 worth of new money was raised. Although £2,400 of this came from such familiar sources as the archbishop of Canterbury and the feoffees of the duchy of Lancaster, the rest was of rather more unusual origin: thus on 16 July just under £1,400 was obtained from Sir John Radclyf on the security of the revenues of north Wales, Chirk and 'Chirklandes', and the customs of the little ports of Melcombe, Poole, Exeter, Dartmouth, Plymouth and Fowey. Beaufort is conspicuously absent as a lender: on the contrary, nearly half the *fictitious* loans of the term (the whole of which total over £13,000) come from him, the other two principal victims being the archbishop of Canterbury and the earl of Northumberland, but only for much smaller sums. This was the first occasion on which Beaufort's security had seriously failed him, though, as usual, it looked sound enough at first sight, consisting as it did of the custom of Southampton, including £5,000 due from the Venetian galleys, and the Michaelmas proffers of all the sheriffs and escheators in England. Beaufort was also unlucky, however, in another and more mysterious respect this term, the last day of which (16 July) contains among the cash entries an item of £666 13s. 4d. paid by Beaufort *de fine . . . pro certis causis*; of this nothing seems to be known by any authority.

		£	s.	d.	%
MICHAELMAS 1438–9:	Cash	3,170	1	1½	5
	Assigned	33,470	11	11	53
	Book-keeping	26,574	2	8	42
	Total	63,214	15	8½	100

In view of the fact that there were still no new parliamentary grants it is difficult at first sight to account for the rise in real revenue, which takes place during this exchequer year as a whole, of no less than £24,000, but it must be remembered that half the reduced subsidy granted in March 1437 was only to be collected in and after November 1438, and there are other explanations covering Easter 1439. In this Michaelmas term, in any case, the increase was mainly in assignment: indeed, there were no cash payments at all on six days out of thirty-one. More than £6,000 of assignment took place on 19 November—otherwise it was fairly evenly spaced. A further £11,000 or so of it went wrong and appeared as fictitious lending, mostly rather mixed in nature, though the household, whose treasurer was now Sir John Popham, played a fairly conspicuous part. Genuine loans, on the other hand, once more outran fictitious; and again their total of nearly £16,000 was principally provided by Beaufort (£8,866 13s. 4d. on various occasions). There were, however, other heavy lenders, notably the Lancaster feoffees (sometimes, but not always, in conjunction with Beaufort), who produced £3,517 between them: London, too, lent £1,000. It is noticeable that Beaufort's lien on the customs of Southampton was still giving him trouble; thus on 21 November the collectors there, William Estcourt and William Soper, were unable to cash one large tally in his favour for the sum of £1,207.

		£	s.	d.	%
EASTER 1439:	Cash	16,098	16	9	23
	Assigned	24,012	12	11	35
	Book-keeping	28,625	11	11½	42
	Total	68,737	1	7½	100

The sharp rise in cash, both in percentage and in gross, was caused mainly by a large sale of crown lands to Beaufort. On 24 July he paid £8,666 13s. 4d. into the exchequer *pro certis maneriis, terris et tenementis per ipsum de domino Rege emptis in com' Wiltes', Dors' et alibi*, and, on the same day, a further £233 6s. 8d., making £8,900 in all, *de reversione manerii Salden in com' Buk' cum accidentibus etc. per ipsum de domino Rege empt'*. Apart from this wasting of the capital assets of the crown in favour of its principal moneylender, there was little real rise in cash revenue, though the first two days of the term show fairly heavy payments, presumably from the fag-end of the subsidy. Assignment was light until the middle of May, after which it was roughly average for this period. Book-keeping rose by about £2,000, but this was entirely owing to the sudden reappearance of *prestita restituta* as an appreciable factor at the end of the term: fictitious loans hardly changed at all in amount, and genuine were actually £1,000 down. Among the latter, loans made by Beaufort, the feoffees of the duchy of Lancaster (with and without Beaufort's support) and the staplers were conspicuous at £3,000, £4,527 and £2,000, among those of many smaller lenders. Of these larger loans, the entire security for Beaufort's £3,000, in the shape of another single tally on the customs of Southampton, miscarried once again and produced a fictitious loan: the other fictitious loans of the term were scattered among various creditors.[1] As regards *prestita restituta*, three-quarters of the total of £3,140 was repaid on 24 July, mostly by the bishop of Lisieux,[2] but a little by the London fletcher, William Crane: the remaining quarter, repaid on 27 July, came from six small accountants.

		£	s.	d.	%
MICHAELMAS 1439–40:	Cash	7,051	3	9½	10
	Assigned	38,548	10	2	57
	Book-keeping	22,567	5	2	33
	Total	68,166	19	1½	100

During this term there was a marked increase in the numbers of days of business, affecting every class of entry except prests, yet in spite of this fact nearly two-thirds of the low cash total was paid in on a single day, viz. 11 December, most of the other daily payments being very small. About the same date assignment suddenly increased from a fairly normal level to a day total of £7,454 assigned on 23 December only; one of £6,806 (almost wholly in favour of Beaufort) on 9 February; and one of £3,319 on the 28th: its total for the term was well above average for the decade. This was clearly owing to the fact that parliament was sitting again during

---

[1] Including Humphrey, duke of Gloucester, who on 22 July was presented with no less than twenty-one bad tallies on the hereditary revenues. The total value was only £170, but the effect must have been irritating in the extreme.

[2] Peter Cauchon, according to the *Cal. of Pat. Rolls*, but it may have been Basin, the chronicler. No name is mentioned in the receipt roll.

this winter—first at Westminster and then at Reading—and thus prospective money grants could be not unreasonably anticipated. These grants, when they came, were in fact slightly less ungenerous than of late: the usual reduced subsidy was increased to a full subsidy and a half for 1440 and 1441, and was supplemented by a small poll-tax on aliens, to run for three years. Although the yield of this cannot have been great, the much more important customs were also prolonged for three years instead of two, and the clergy were persuaded to make a grant. None the less, revenue was still obviously quite insufficient to meet even current expenses, not to mention the accumulated debt, now including, for example, among its smallest items, two years' arrears of certain judges' robes and salaries. In view of this the young king, who was now eighteen, offered, subject to the approval of the council (which was given), to charge all royal debts and household expenditure upon the revenues of the duchies of Lancaster and Cornwall: this gesture was no doubt well intended, but, whether Henry realized it or not, the revenues in question were wholly inadequate for such a purpose.[1] £14,000 raised in genuine loans during the term came largely from Beaufort (£6,666 13s. 4d. on 22 December), and (30 January) from thirteen miscellaneous lenders, among whom at least one, the king's clerk, master Stephen Wylton, received a jewel[2] in pledge for the £20 which he contributed. The £8,500 in fictitious loans was scattered among many creditors, but Beaufort at least seems to have secured himself this time from any major disappointment.

EASTER 1440:		£	s.	d.	%
	Cash	21,337	17	2	45
	Assigned	21,682	2	1	45
	Book-keeping	4,717	9	6	10
	Total	47,737	8	9	100

The fact that the cash total for this term was the highest for four and a half years must be attributed to a start being made with the collection of the recently granted subsidy, but it is interesting to note that, although some cash was brought in on every day but

[1] Ramsay, *Lancaster and York*, II, 19–20. (The index of this work is misleading in omitting to mention any money grants at all made by this parliament.)

[2] *Quoddam jocale, viz. unum tabernaculum.*

one, the only really large payments were those of 2 May (£4,781) and from 30 June onwards. Assignment started with a high figure (£4,276—nearly all of it for Beaufort) on the first day of term, but in the long run barely held its own with cash. Book-keeping had easily the lowest total for the decade: of this, only £1,000 represented genuine borrowing (from three lenders, all on 17 July), while the balance consisted of a large number of small fictitious loans from many different creditors.

		£	s.	d.	%
MICHAELMAS 1440–1:	Cash	23,033	13	3	32
	Assigned	33,009	12	10	45
	Book-keeping	16,540	10	9	23
	Total	72,583	16	10	100

The relatively high term total was caused only in part by the fact that cash actually rose still further, and indeed attained the second highest figure for the decade. This, however, was not owing to the still outstanding portions of the parliamentary grants—the proceeds of which were now being mostly assigned—but to a windfall of £13,333 6s. 8d., representing the ransom of Charles, duke of Orleans.[1] This money had already been paid over to the crown through a Florentine firm in London as far back as 3 November 1440,[2] although it did not reach the exchequer until 23 February 1441. Assignment, starting early with a £2,000 payment to the household, was in total not so much above average as cash was: after the initial burst just mentioned it hung fire for a while, and nearly two-thirds of it was levied in the second half of the term. Rather more than the same proportion of book-keeping was provided by genuine loans, eighteen of which produced over £5,000 on 16 January alone, including £1,633 6s. 8d. from the archbishop of Canterbury, £1,000 from Sir William Estfeld, the wealthy London mercer, and £1,000 from the earl of Huntingdon. On 20 February London added a £2,000 corporate loan; and on the

[1] Ramsay, *Lancaster and York*, II, 9, 11, 23, 25–7, for details of the history of this ransom. The sum originally contemplated by the English had been five times as much as was now paid, though it is true that Charles was also forced to give security for the payment of another £20,000 within six months. At the other extreme from this large cash payment is the one penny paid in on 18 November (in cash) by the Oxfordshire collectors of the lay subsidy: cf. 1430–1, 1431.

[2] Ibid., II, 27.

23rd Beaufort £1,000: and there were several other lenders. Fictitious loans were on the low side at just under £6,400, and were
well distributed over a number of relatively small creditors.

		£	s.	d.	%
EASTER 1441:	Cash	11,420	14	9	30
	Assigned	17,210	8	0	45
	Book-keeping	9,861	0	9	25
	Total	38,492	3	6	100

The sharp fall in the term total suggests that the proceeds of the
one and half subsidies granted fifteen months earlier had now been
exhausted: cash, it is true, was fairly well maintained compared
with assignment, but more than a quarter of it was raised on the
first two days of term alone and may well represent the tail-end of
the grant. The figure for assignment is the second lowest of the
decade and indeed would have been smaller than the cash figure
but for a great effort made on 29 May, when no less than £8,248,
or almost half the term total, was successfully assigned, largely to
assure the provisioning of Calais. In book-keeping, genuine
borrowing was represented by no more than a solitary loan of
£333 6s. 8d. and was easily the lowest total of the decade under
this head, but fictitious loans were relatively high at £9,171, a total
for which three unusually large defaults were mainly responsible.
Easily the biggest of these was one of £4,052 on 8 July, consisting
of twenty-two tallies, nearly all of them on the lay subsidy and all
in favour of Sir Roger Fenys, who for some two years or so had
been treasurer of the household. Secondly, on 1 June, Joanna,
widow of Richard Bukland, the former treasurer of Calais, failed
to collect £1,820 in twenty-one tallies, mainly on the customs;
while thirdly, on 15 July, much the same sources were unable to
provide £1,123 owing to the king's esquire, John Ransan, keeper of
Meulx in Brie. In addition to all this there was a *prestitum restitutum* of £356 13s. 4d. on 21 July by the hands of Louis de Luxem-
burg, archbishop of Rouen and chancellor of occupied France.

		£	s.	d.	%
MICHAELMAS 1441–2:	Cash	13,963	7	5½	27
	Assigned	20,745	19	9½	40
	Book-keeping	17,186	3	6	33
	Total	51,895	10	9	100

Parliament sat at Westminster during this term (from 24 January) and made certain grants—a fact which may account for a rather more than normal rate of increase in assignment during February and March, but which could not have influenced the even flow of cash receipts. The grants included one subsidy—apparently at the full rate—for 1442–3; prolongation of the customs for two years at existing rates; and also a continuance for the same period of the tax on aliens. This was all made subject to a charge of some £10,700, which was the estimated cost of the 'saf kepyng of the see', according to a detailed scheme worked out in the commons: at the same time authority was given to the government to borrow up to the unprecedented total of £200,000.[1] Not much advantage was taken of the last provision before the Easter term, but none the less over £7,500 was raised towards the end of March, most of it from Beaufort but also just under £2,000 from London. Assignment became noticeably heavier about the same time— largely in order to provide security for the Beaufort loan, though there had already been one heavy day without this excuse (£3,987 on 10 February). Fictitious loans were rather higher than in the previous term at £9,574: Sir Roger Fenys (20 November) with nineteen bad tallies totalling £3,933 6s. 8d., on the Southampton customs, was the chief sufferer: but the same source, together with a dribblet from the lay subsidy, failed to pay Beaufort nearly £2,000 on 28 March, though in this case only five tallies in all, two of them very small ones, were involved. Lastly, on 14 November, there was another and even smaller *prestitum restitutum* of £50 (described simply as *denarii*) from the bishop of Lisieux, as at Easter 1439.

		£	s.	d.	%
EASTER 1442:	Cash	5,485	9	7½	8
	Assigned	30,128	1	5½	42
	Book-keeping	36,080	1	5	50
	Total	71,693	12	6	100

The increase in the gross total for this term was mainly due to book-keeping; for although the first half of the subsidy voted early in the year must now have been in process of collection, real revenue was very little higher than in the previous term, whereas

[1] Ramsay, *Lancaster and York*, II, 41.

the book-keeping total was one of the largest of the decade. Cash receipts, though well spread over the term, were indeed remarkably low, and assignment, though higher than in the previous two terms, was no more than reasonably well maintained. Even this was only done, as on an earlier occasion, by violent efforts on one or two particular days—in this case 18 May, when £9,449 was successfully assigned, and 19 May (£4,822). Book-keeping was mainly inflated by the government's response to the commons' incitement to borrow: thus on 7 May alone there were seventeen genuine loans, producing £5,370, towards which Beaufort contributed £2,000 and the earls of Huntingdon and Suffolk £1,000 apiece. On 18 May the treasurer, lord Cromwell, lent £4,170, and on 18 July the king's chaplain and financial agent, John Langton (see Michaelmas 1434–5) £4,000, but even these large loans were eclipsed on 18 July, when the staplers supplied £10,000. All this, with smaller contributions, brought the genuine loan total for the term up to some £28,000, the second highest in the decade. As against this, fictitious loans fell below £8,000, most of which was fairly evenly distributed, with the exception of £2,000 in three tallies on the Southampton customs, which Beaufort was again unable to collect forthwith. On 18 July there were also no less than thirteen small *prestita restituta* totalling £489 6s., mostly by customs collectors and all of very recent date.

		£	s.	d.	%
MICHAELMAS 1442–3:	Cash	7,243	15	7	11
	Assigned	36,307	8	6	56
	Book-keeping	21,495	7	6	33
	Total	65,046	11	7	100

The grants made for two years early in 1442 obviously continued to come in during this winter, though the cash proceeds were small, and would barely have reached £5,000 but for a large payment of £2,134 on 27 March. Assignment was actually at its highest for ten years to come, though it would not have counted as much more than average some ten years earlier. The heaviest days were 19 January (just under £9,000) and 29 November (£4,448), but in general it was more evenly distributed. Book-keeping was about average for this period and was almost evenly divided between genuine and fictitious loans. The former were mainly accounted for by a £10,000 loan from Beaufort, made on 6 April 1443, and a loan from London on the previous 30 November of £1,333 6s. 8d. The only outstanding fictitious loans were from the king's agent, John Langton (£1,566 13s. 4d. on 8 November in six tallies, mainly on the London customs), and from the merchants of the staple (£1,133 6s. 8d. on 19 January in seven tallies on the customs of three ports). It is perhaps worth noting in addition that on 7 December there were no less than 134 small assignments, totalling only £81 13s. 4d., all of which were successful: thirty-one of these were *pro diversis clericis de scaccario* and clearly represented wages.

EASTER 1443:		£	s.	d.	%
	Cash	6,805	14	6	14
	Assigned	19,085	6	5½	39
	Book-keeping	22,818	10	9	47
	Total	48,709	11	8½	100

Though the gross revenue fell sharply, cash was only about £440 down: on the other hand, it included a windfall in the shape of six *dona* totalling £1,643, of which London alone contributed £1,323 (7 June). Assignment was almost halved, the only heavy day being '26' (actually 27) May (£4,014). Book-keeping was slightly higher than in the previous term and very different in character; for fictitious loans were halved, like assignment, while genuine increased by more than 50%. Out of the total under the latter head of just under £17,000 Beaufort contributed £11,666 13s. 4d. in three separate loans, and the Londoner, Sir William Estfeld, £1,100: the remaining loans in either category were of no special interest.[1] There were, however, sixteen *prestita restituta* totalling £894 on 6 July, the larger of which seem to have come from certain clerks and serjeants of the royal household, and the smaller from justices and serjeants-at-law. On the last day of term (10 July) the keeper of the great wardrobe, Robert Rolleston, lent £1,237 and Richard, duke of York, £666 13s. 4d. on the security

---

[1] E.g., £666 13s. 4d. which Humphrey, earl of Stafford, advanced on 18 July. This is described as a loan, but instead of a repayment date it bears the note, *pro resolucione cuius summe diversa jocalia Regis dicto comiti sunt invadiata*. However, these may have been redeemed: cf. the two following notes.

of certain crown jewels; this last loan may not have been repaid.[1]

MICHAELMAS 1443–4:		£	s.	d.	%
	Cash	9,177	11	2	22
	Assigned	10,518	1	10½	25
	Book-keeping	22,228	0	2	53
	Total	41,923	13	2½	100

The real dwindling of the revenue in this term is in fact even more marked than the gross total suggests, when book-keeping has been taken into account. Cash, it is true, was rather higher than it had been for two years, but assignment, low as it was by previous standards, would have been far lower still but for the great effort made on 21 February 1444 to find adequate security for a new loan of no less than £11,666 13s. 4d., advanced two months earlier by the duke of York in addition to his small loan of 10 July 1443.[2] This effort was only half successful, but even so it yielded over £6,000. The largeness of the book-keeping total is mainly accounted for by the same transaction, much of which appears twice over, first *in toto* as a genuine loan dated 7 December 1443, and secondly as a fictitious loan of rather over £6,000, when the attempt made on 21 February to pay off the original loan, plus something extra,

[1] Cf. the preceding and following notes. On 6 June, John, duke of Somerset, is credited with a similar loan of £333 6s. 8d., secured on various crown jewels, pledged specifically to Michaelmas 1444, and, as in the other two cases quoted, there is no note of repayment.

[2] The very large new loan was made on 7 December 1443. The curious feature about the attempt at repayment made on 21 February 1444 is that the total sum assigned is actually £478 6s. 8d. in excess of the December loan, viz. £12,145 in all. It might be thought that the previous loan of 10 July is being taken into account, but in that case the assignments of 21 February are £188 6s. 8d. *short* of the whole. As the July loan was secured on crown jewels, however, it is possible that the duke retained some, to the total value of the short-fall. On the other hand the February assignments are all clearly marked *pro den' mut'* 7 Dec', without reference to the previous July. If this is to be taken literally the exchequer was endeavouring to overpay the duke by £478 6s. 8d., but this sum is too small to represent anything in lieu of interest at the current rates upon so large a loan, quite apart from the open disregard of the usury laws, and I am therefore inclined to think it more probable that, in spite of the precise words to the contrary, it is none the less connected with the July loan. At any rate the smaller loan does not carry any other date of repayment.

resulted in fifty-six of the tallies struck—mainly tallies on the Hull and Boston customs—being returned to the exchequer. Nearly all the rest of the book-keeping total was provided by six genuine loans of 22 February, totalling over £4,000: of these, the city of London, the executors of lord Fanhope,[1] the feoffees of the duchy of Lancaster, and cardinal Beaufort, advanced £333 6s. 8d., £1,333 6s. 8d., £1,000 and £1,333 6s. 8d. respectively. There were also fourteen small *prestita restituta* by Peter Bowman, king's serjeant-at-arms, on 19 February, but the total (£13 9s. 4d.) was negligible. They appear to have been advances for the hire of sundry small ships, the masters of which returned the money, for reasons not stated, through Bowman to the household.[2]

		£	s.	d.	%
EASTER 1444:	Cash	20,685	4	10	47
	Assigned	10,268	14	8	23
	Book-keeping	13,532	4	10	30
	Total	44,486	4	4	100

Although there were no fresh parliamentary grants in either 1444 or 1445, the gross and net revenues both showed some improvement during this and the next two terms. The reason for this is not altogether clear, but seems to be connected with the buoyancy of customs: thus cash, whose total was the largest for the decade, was drawn mainly from that source. For example, about £3,000 was paid in on 8 May; £3,780 on 15 July; and £4,169 on the 23rd —to take only the three heaviest days—and in all these payments customs contributions predominated. Assignment, on the contrary, continued to be very low: nearly half of it was drawn in the last fortnight of July alone, but the rest fairly evenly over the remainder of the term. Under book-keeping, genuine loans were halved at £7,728, but fictitious loans fell by only £650. The former were all raised from approximately eighty lenders, among whom only the executors of lord Fanhope (viz. the archbishop of Canterbury and lord Cromwell) produced as much as £1,333 6s. 8d. (for the second term running). There were no particularly large fictitious loans in the total of £5,803 under that head, but there were two small *dona* during August, the second of which (£20 from the

---

[1] Formerly Sir John Cornewall of Burford—see above, Easter 1417, p. 156, n. 1.

[2] See Michaelmas 1446–7, p. 228, below.

citizens of Worcester) seems to have started life as a genuine loan, any hope of the repayment of which was subsequently abandoned.

		£	s.	d.	%
MICHAELMAS 1444–5:	Cash	10,762	17	5	24
	Assigned	23,387	10	4	52
	Book-keeping	10,884	9	9	24
	Total	45,034	17	6	100

Parliament was summoned to Westminster for 25 February 1445 in anticipation of the king's marriage to Margaret of Anjou, which took place on 23 April, after some delay. By that time parliament had adjourned without granting the subsidy demanded by the king's minister, the earl of Suffolk, towards the expense of the wedding and the queen's coronation. It is true that half a subsidy had been conceded, in addition to the earlier grants of 1444 for that year and for 1445, but this was little enough in view of the fact that the queen's journey to England had alone cost £5,500: moreover, the half-subsidy was not to be collected until the following November.[1] It could not therefore affect revenue, except possibly by encouraging assignment, during either the Michaelmas or Easter term of the exchequer year 1444–5. None the less in the Michaelmas term in question real revenue again increased, though only at a much reduced rate. Three fairly heavy cash days, in September, October and January[2] respectively, helped to swell the cash total: this was in fact little more than half the abnormally large total for the previous term, but was still above average for the decade. Increased assignment more than filled the place of cash, though it was very evenly distributed, only one day-total (for 9 November) just topping £2,000. Book-keeping reverted to the pattern of the previous Michaelmas, with fictitious loans three to four times as heavy as genuine, though the two together came to less than £11,000. The only genuine loans of any size came from two Londoners, Estfeld and Venour, who subscribed £500 each on 29 October—nearly half the term total under this head of £2,474. The only large fictitious loan came from Henry Percy, as

[1] Ramsay, *Lancaster and York*, II, 64–6, for the details in this paragraph.
[2] Including a single tally for £1,374 in cash from the customs of Southampton.

keeper of Berwick and the east march, on 12 November, when he was disappointed in twenty-eight tallies, mainly on the customs, value £1,067. On the other hand, the fact that on literally two days out of three there were now fictitious loans from somebody, even if they were only small ones, must have been disquieting to the government.

		£	s.	d.	%
EASTER 1445:	Cash	2,098	4	7	5
	Assigned	30,601	10	11	67
	Book-keeping	12,923	4	6½	28
	Total	45,623	0	0½	100

In spite of the continued collection of the scanty remains of the older parliamentary grant for 1445 (made in 1444) cash fell sharply during this term to the second lowest total of the decade, although small sums were still being paid in on two days out of three. Assignment almost made up for the fall in cash receipts, however, and real revenue on balance was only £1,450 down. The amounts were well spread, though tending to be rather heavier in the first five weeks of the term, which was unusual: the reason may be that the term began, as will be seen, with some fairly heavy borrowing, and security was immediately given for these loans in the shape of tallies of assignment. However, this rising trend ended abruptly on 11 May in a peak of £4,329, much of it on account of old loans of Beaufort's. The new loans already mentioned had reached a total of £7,353 by the end of the term, Sir William Estfeld of London being especially prominent during the first week or so with no less than £4,800.[1] Beaufort lent £1,000 on the last day (21 July) but was otherwise unrepresented, and all the remaining loans were well distributed. The same was true of the fictitious loans throughout; although they reached a gross total of £5,569 there was no particularly outstanding victim. Finally, it is worth noting that parliament was again sitting for the greater part of this

[1] He lent £2,666 13s. 4d. on 8 April and £2,133 6s. 8d. on the 14th. On 9 April he received tallies (all of them successfully cashed) exactly corresponding to his first loan, and on the 19th £2,234 0s. 5d. in seven tallies marked *pro den' ab eo mut' 14 Apr' ult' pret'*, for his second loan. The odd thing is that in this second instance the assignment is £94 4s. 9d. too much, especially as this seems too small a sum to represent any consideration in lieu of interest.

term, but made no additional grant, in spite of the new queen's state entry into London on 28 May and her coronation on the 30th.

		£	s.	d.	%
MICHAELMAS 1445–6:	Cash	2,667	15	10½	9
	Assigned	16,479	10	8	53
	Book-keeping	11,542	15	1½	38
	Total	30,690	1	8	100

The parliament which had originally met at the end of February, and had now been twice adjourned, met again in October, but once more without result. On 15 December it was adjourned for the third time, and it was not till 9 April 1446, after a fourth session of nearly eleven weeks, that it at last conceded a subsidy and a half, though only with an abatement per subsidy of £6,000. 'Moreover, the whole was made payable by three yearly instalments; so as to furnish just the usual half Subsidy for the years 1446, 1447 and 1448. Prolongations of Tunnage and poundage and the wool duties for four years, at existing rates, were announced at the same time.'[1] Clearly none of these measures came in time to save the royal finances for the Michaelmas term of 1445–6, when the only special nourishment they received came from the half-subsidy granted in the spring. Whatever the reason, real revenue now fell below even the disastrous level of Michaelmas 1443–4. Cash, as might be expected, remained low, though it was actually a few hundreds up on the previous term. The main fall was in assignment: there were drafts on every single day of business, it is true, but the day-totals only twice managed to touch four figures. Genuine loans contracted to £2,474, the bulk of which (£2,100) was found on 5 February by the staple. The same loan went to swell the total of fictitious loans as well as genuine, for when repayment was attempted on 20 February through the customs, the entire sum miscarried and the merchants of the staple were credited with it for the second time. Apart from this, fictitious loans, though rising slightly in gross to £9,068, contained no item of interest. There was, however, a *donum* on the last day of term (7 March) for the

---

[1] Ramsay, *Lancaster and York*, II, 68. Tenths were also granted during this exchequer year by the convocations of both York and Canterbury.

insignificant sum of £2, as if to emphasize the limited extent to which the king's subjects were prepared to assist him at the very moment when his needs were greatest.

		£	s.	d.	%
EASTER 1446:	Cash	16,612	9	3½	22
	Assigned	26,209	14	10	35
	Book-keeping	32,573	19	7½	43
	Total	75,396	3	9	100

During this term the new life injected into the revenue by the grants of April 1446 is manifest: real revenue rose at once to the second highest figure of the decade. Cash advanced to a respectable total once again, the bulk of it paid in from 30 June onwards: unexpectedly, the four heaviest days' payments were all made from the customs, and each time from a different port. Two-thirds of the assignment, which was running at a more normal rate, came from the last six or seven days of term, more especially on 20 and 21 July, when very heavy drafts were made in favour of Richard, duke of York: indeed, the duke got over £14,000 out of the sum total of assignment. But the greatest increase came under book-keeping, which was suddenly almost three times as high as it had been during the previous year or two. Moreover, less than £2,000 of this enlarged total was now due to genuine borrowing, and even out of this small figure Beaufort alone was responsible for as much as £1,333 6s. 8d. on 18 August, receiving tallies of assignment for that precise amount upon the following day. All the rest represented fictitious loans, among which the following were conspicuous:

		£	s.	d.		Tallies on customs of
30 May	Queen Margaret	1,000	0	0	5	Southampton
	Sir Roger Fenys					
	(household)	1,475	0	0	16	Various ports
	The chamber	1,000	0	0	6	London (tunnage and poundage only)
1 July	The chamber	995	0	0	12	Southampton
	The earl of Shrewsbury	1,827	6	8	13	London and Boston

		£	s.	d.	Tallies on customs of
5 July	John Noreys (great wardrobe)	1,566	13	4	20 London and Southampton
6 July	Sir Roger Fenys (household)	1,848	8	2	28 Various ports[1]
7 July	Sir Roger Fenys (household)	1,200	0	0	19 London and Southampton
9 July	Henry Percy (warden, east march)	1,283	17	1	20 Various ports[1]
20 July	Richard, duke of York	4,866	7	2½	70 Various ports[2]
21 July	Richard, duke of York	6,769	16	0	51 Various ports

		£	s.	d.	%
MICHAELMAS 1446–7:	Cash	15,670	1	11	26
	Assigned	14,494	16	1½	24
	Book-keeping	30,392	0	2	50
	Total	60,556	18	2½	100

The very high book-keeping percentage in this roll betrays a substantial fall in real revenue, which the April grants failed to make good. Less than £3,000 cash had come in by 23 November, but after that the flow improved and a fairly respectable total was eventually achieved. Assignment, on the contrary, besides being actually below the cash figure—which is most unusual by this date —was little more than half what it had been at Easter, and indeed reached four figures, with some difficulty, on only three occasions.[3] But book-keeping, though it fell by some £2,000, was still at an abnormally high level, and once again this was very largely owing to the size and number of fictitious loans. Real loans totalled little over £4,000, and among them the bishop of Carlisle's loan of £1,333 6s. 8d., made on 24 January 1447, was the only one of any real importance. The £26,000 or so in fictitious loans was also

[1] £2 (in each case) *not* assigned on customs.
[2] Not entirely customs.
[3] The first and most notable of these was 3 November, when £1,100 was successfully assigned to Richard, duke of York, out of the Hull customs.

rather widely distributed over numerous crown creditors, though the household was as usual in the lead, as the following summary table of the principal defaults makes clear:

		£	s.	d.		Tallies on the customs of
11 Nov.	Sir Roger Fenys (household)	4,176	7	8	22	Various ports
22 Nov.	Sir John Stourton (household)	1,000	0	0	3	Lynn, Boston, Hull
3 Feb.	Bishop of Carlisle	1,166	13	4	7	Southampton, London
17 Feb.	Sir John Stourton (household)	1,260	0	0	13	Various ports

In contrast with this insouciance about their major creditors the clerks of the exchequer were again careful to see that their own small salaries were paid effectively: thus on 17 February there were twenty-eight small assignments for this purpose, totalling £49 19s. 9d., not a single one of which went wrong. Finally on 7 December there was a *prestitum restitutum* by a royal serjeant-at-arms, Peter Bowman, of some interest—not for its amount, which was only £40 7s.—but because the entry explains a relic of the fourteenth-century paymaster system still in vogue at this date.[1] It appears that in the regnal year just completed this minor court official had been entrusted with various small sums *pro vadiis div' magistror' et marinar' arrestat' ad serviend' domino Regi*, and it is for some, if not all, of these that he is now accounting, though not, I think, repaying anything in cash: this last point is, however, doubtful, and it may possibly be unexpended surpluses which are now physically 'restored'.

		£	s.	d.	%
EASTER 1447:	Cash	4,241	14	10	7
	Assigned	25,388	18	0½	45
	Book-keeping	27,317	17	5½	48
	Total	56,948	10	4	100

The downward tendency continued during this term, though as yet at no great pace. Cash, it is true, dropped abruptly, and nearly

[1] See Michaelmas 1443–4, p. 222, above.

a quarter of it was brought in on a single day (1 July), but assignment rose in compensation by almost the same amount, being especially heavy between 15 and 25 July inclusive. Book-keeping was well maintained, owing to the fact that fictitious loans actually increased again to over £27,000, although genuine loans dropped to only £700, the second lowest total for the decade. It must be noted, however, that the fictitious loans were now of two types—those in which a nominal 'loan' was actually created as before, and the amount paid off by fresh tallies of assignment, and those in which the original entries in the receipt roll were merely cancelled with a note to the effect that the creditor had later received letters patent for that amount, as recorded in the memoranda rolls on such and such a date. In the latter case the fiction of a new 'loan' is not expressed in words, but on the other hand the scribe includes these cancelled items for the first time in his day totals, so that a 'loan' is at any rate implied, and the amounts have therefore as a rule been included in my own totals. The most outstanding examples under both heads during this term were as follows:

		£	s.	d.		Tallies on the customs of
2 May	Sir Roger Fenys (household)	3,449	13	4	11	(Not recorded)
17 May	William Clyff (clerk of works)	1,000	0	0	35	Various ports
15 July	Henry Percy (warden, east march)	1,700	0	0	19	Hull, Boston, Newcastle
18 July	William Clyff	1,403	6	8	17	Various ports
	Henry Percy	1,818	0	0	18	Same (and hanaper)

In addition, on 25 July, there were eight specially cancelled tallies on seven different ports, all assigned to Sir John Stourton, the new treasurer of the household, with the following note attached to them: *vacantur iste viij tallie et dampnantur cum foliis pro eo quod J. Stourton miles Thes' Hosp' Regis nullam inde habet solucionem sive contentacionem* . . . . Since the total value of these eight tallies (£2,055 3s.), unlike that of so many other cancellations, was carefully *not* included in the roll totals, this was evidently a genuine cancellation, and I have therefore omitted it from my own totals as well.

		£	s.	d.	%
MICHAELMAS 1447–8:	Cash	16,603	11	8½	37
	Assigned	15,014	7	5½	34
	Book-keeping	12,701	0	7	29
	Total	44,318	19	9	100

The sharp decline (of nearly £15,000) in book-keeping this term meant a small, but real, increase in net revenue. Cash, indeed, rose buoyantly to its fourth—and very nearly its third—highest total of the decade: most of it was brought in during November. Assignment, which took place for the most part rather later in the term, was considerably down, but this was more than compensated for by the big cash advance. The greatly reduced amount of book-keeping was almost evenly divided between genuine and fictitious loans—the former, which were slightly the more valuable, being wholly accounted for by a loan of £6,666 13s. 4d., made on 7 December by the merchants of the staple. The only important fictitious loan came from the Percies on 16 February 1448 and totalled nearly £1,100: all but £10 of it was in tallies on the customs. There was also a trifling *prestitum restitutum* of 6s. 8d. during the term (Peter Bowman, 7 December).

		£	s.	d.	%
EASTER 1448:	Cash	3,305	1	2	14
	Assigned	14,214	15	6	62
	Book-keeping	5,503	8	3½	24
	Total	23,023	4	11½	100

This time the fall in revenue was real, and even catastrophic, and although cash was principally affected it also touched assignment. Rather exceptionally, the heaviest day of the latter (30 May) was almost entirely devoted to drafts on the scanty remains of the subsidy voted two years earlier instead of on the customs: the recipient was Edmund Beaufort, marquis of Dorset. No cash at all was received on the last four days of business, though nearly £5,000 was assigned, and the only cash day-total which just reached four figures was that for 26 June. Genuine loans sank to £600—all on 4 May—while fictitious stayed at nearly £5,000, spread so evenly over the entire term that not a single individual default approached £1,000. After book-keeping has been deducted, real revenue finally stands at the lowest figure for fifteen years, the inadequacy of which needs no comment.

		£	s.	d.	%
MICHAELMAS 1448–9:	Cash	19,930	19	1	45
	Assigned	19,623	11	8	44
	Book-keeping	4,810	14	0	11
	Total	44,365	4	9	100

Although parliament met at Westminster on 12 February 1449 the grants made during the first session were extremely meagre, and for the most part not effective until the following autumn. Existing tunnage and poundage dues were renewed for five years, but a new half-subsidy (reduced by a £3,000 abatement and spread over two years) was to be collected only at Martinmas 1449 and 1450.[1] None the less the last scrapings of grants made as far back as April 1446, together with the ever-buoyant customs, not only brought real revenue up to the third highest total of the decade but even caused a relatively large amount of actual cash to flow into the exchequer. Three-quarters of this came in between 11 November and 2 December inclusive; and in the end the term total for cash not only managed to exceed the total for assignment but was actually the second highest in ten years. Assignment, which took place on every business day but one, calls for little comment, except on 7 April, when it reached the rather large figure of £5,616, all drawn against the lay subsidy but containing only one big individual item, viz. £2,100 for Calais. Book-keeping was distinctly low again, and, with the exception of two or three *prestita restituta* for a few shillings each, it consisted *wholly* of fictitious loans, none of them of any individual importance. (It is perhaps worth noting in this connection that there had not been a complete absence of genuine loans from any surviving roll since 1422–3.)

		£	s.	d.	%
EASTER 1449:	Cash	1,721	14	9½	6
	Assigned	16,794	8	7	52
	Book-keeping	13,569	13	8	42
	Total	32,085	17	0½	100

[1] Ramsay, *Lancaster and York*, II, 89.

Parliament continued sitting, off and on, during this term, but it was not until it had removed to Winchester for its third session (16 June to 16 July) that it could be induced to supplement the extremely inadequate financial provision made in its first session. This it did by an additional half-subsidy for the years 1449–50; some increase of the poll-tax on aliens (particularly if they happened to be merchants or merchants' clerks); and a prolongation of the wool duties (with substantial reductions for the produce of the four northern counties ravaged by the Scots) to as late as April 1454.[1] This slight easing of the purse-strings may have been brought about partly by the private petitions made to this parliament by royal creditors unable to obtain effective payment, but as the bulk of these came from the royal household[2] it is doubtful whether their influence on the commons was very great. In any case the new grants came far too late to save the existing situation —for real revenue was more than halved this term, and cash in particular fell to a mere trickle, never reaching as much as £300 a day. Assignment, too, was lower, and would have been a good deal lower still but for a determined attempt made on 28 August to find some sort of security for heavy borrowing—the first for eighteen months—some four weeks earlier. This return to genuine loans accounts for £7,170 of the book-keeping total: it was fairly evenly distributed on the whole between some fifty lenders. Fictitious loans account for a further £4,455, the most prominent item in which was an entry on 2 July of £1,887 for Sir John Stourton, the treasurer of the household, in 28 bad tallies on the customs of seven ports. The rest of the book-keeping (£2,043 6s. 8d.) represents the return by Beaufort's executors on 29 July of crown jewels formerly pledged to the cardinal (who had died on 11 April 1447). This is described as a *prestitum restitutum*, and, although on 28 August the said executors received tallies of assignment for the full amount, the description seems correct, since the loan could equally well have been made, like so many others, without the pledging of the jewels and their subsequent return—in itself a transaction which merely inflated the nominal totals on the receipt rolls even

[1] Ramsay, *Lancaster and York*, ii, 89.
[2] E.g., £3,449 in old arrears (1439–46) owed to the gentlemen and yeomen of the household: Ramsay, *Lancaster and York*, ii, 90. Cf. the figures under *Household* in Table E7 at the end of this book: also Chapter vii below, pp. 242–6.

more than usual. The term ended (23 September) with four *dona* in cash of £66 13*s.* 4*d.* each from the archbishop of York, the bishops of Norwich and Winchester and the abbot of Selby, together with a further £20 from the bishop of Salisbury.

		£	s.	d.	%
MICHAELMAS 1449–50:	Cash	2,689	2	4½	4
	Assigned	35,237	15	11	54
	Book-keeping	27,527	15	7½	42
	Total	65,454	13	11	100

The grants made at midsummer 1449 had evidently had some effect by March 1450, for although the more than doubling of the gross total was mainly caused by book-keeping, real revenue did increase. The rise was, however, almost wholly in assignment: cash payments were less than £1,000 up and were very feebly maintained during the second half of the term. Assignment, on the other hand, reached its second highest total for the decade and was much more evenly distributed once more: thus on twelve days out of twenty-five it attained four figures without ever exceeding £4,340. The jump of £14,000 in book-keeping was entirely caused by a rise of £17,000 in genuine loans, which completely offset the fall under the other two book-keeping heads: this time there were 120 lenders of £24,203. Among these the executors of cardinal Beaufort were pre-eminent with £8,333 6*s.* 8*d.*, lent on five separate occasions between 30 September and 13 December inclusive; but the doomed duke of Suffolk[1] and the treasurer of England, lord Saye, also lent £1,773 and £1,600 respectively—the former on 18 November and the latter at various dates between 18 November and 4 March. In addition, Richard Joynour, a London silversmith,[2] lent £1,877 on 25 February, secured on letters patent and on £500 worth of crown jewels. *Prestita restituta*, however, disappeared again, while even fictitious loans declined to £3,054: under this head the only bad tallies of any interest were a set of fourteen in favour of Henry Percy on the customs of six ports (25 February) to a total value of £970.

[1] He was formally impeached on 7 February 1450 and murdered in the same year.

[2] And collector of the London petty custom. See below, Easter 1451, p. 238, and Chapter VII, p. 249.

s   233

		£	s.	d.	%
EASTER 1450:	Cash	4,062	6	1½	27
	Assigned	7,533	16	2	48
	Book-keeping	4,040	17	4	25
	Total	15,636	19	7½	100

Owing to the formal renewal of the war by France only a fortnight after the end of its third session in July, the first parliament of 1449 had been almost immediately succeeded by another, which met at Westminster on 6 November. The first two sessions of this new parliament—which had occupied the entire Michaelmas term of 1449–50—had been taken up with a somewhat violent change of ministers, ending in the impeachment (and subsequent murder) of the duke of Suffolk, and it was not until parliament resumed at Leicester for a third session on 29 April 1450 that the financial situation, only temporarily patched up during the preceding summer, could be reconsidered. The new ministry alleged that the king's debts now amounted to £372,000 and his 'livelihood' to no more than £5,000 a year. Ramsay[1] is certainly right, however, in maintaining that, whatever may be thought of the first figure, which was probably exaggerated for obvious reasons, the second (and much more commonly quoted one) was far too low: it was, moreover, an error in tactics to produce it, for the commons instantly retorted in effect that if the hereditary revenues had really shrunk to that extent the proper remedy was not a subsidy, but a general resumption of crown lands. To this the king ultimately had to agree, though he hedged the necessary act about with no less than 186 clauses of exemption. In return, the commons offered an experimental income-tax, to which both the lords in general and Welsh landlords in particular were to be liable; this was graduated from 6d. in the £ for incomes between £1 and £20 to 2s. in the £ for incomes of over £200, and was to be paid over to special treasurers of war for the defence of the realm. This arrangement had numerous disadvantages, not the least of which was the fact that it seems to have started a rumour that ordinary fifteenths and tenths would henceforth be abolished. Moreover it did nothing for the time being towards paying the king's debts or helping him with the existing deficit in ordinary revenue, which during this

---

[1] *Lancaster and York*, II, 122–4.

term again reached alarming proportions: the gross total indeed was the lowest of the decade, though the net total was not quite the lowest. Possibly the restriction of the revenue was not wholly involuntary but designed to impress parliament, for the slump occurred entirely in assigned, that is deliberately anticipated, income, which was not only nearly £28,000 down but easily at its lowest point between 1432 and 1452. Cash, it may be noted, actually rose some £1,400, mainly owing to a large payment from the London wool customs on 1 July and a windfall of about £500 on 29 August from the goods of Sir John Mortimer, who had been executed as a traitor as far back as 1424. Little attempt was made to borrow money this term, and only £2,159 was raised; while fictitious loans shrank in sympathy with assignment to £1,741. *Prestita restituta* reappeared for the last time for thirteen years to come, but there were only three relatively small ones, totalling £140.

	£	s.	d.	%
MICHAELMAS 1450–1: Cash	8,022	3	5	30
Assigned	9,088	7	3½	34
Book-keeping	9,409	4	11½	36
Total	26,519	15	8	100

It is obvious from the gross total for this term that the financial position got very little better during the winter, especially as almost half the apparent improvement of £11,000 was due to book-keeping. Cash, it is true, was nearly doubled, but this was only owing to the payment of £3,000 from the Boston wool customs on 13 November and of £4,000 from the Hull and London customs on 4 December, not to any new source of revenue. Assignment only rose very slightly through the fact that at the last minute as much as £1,555 was assigned on 8 April, actually the last day of term. Genuine loans, on the other hand, jumped to £8,208, but practically the whole of this increase was due to a single loan of £5,866 13s. 4d. from the staple on 27 February,[1] and not any general increase in the borrowing power of the government. Somewhat surprisingly, fictitious loans did not follow the slight rise in assignment, but actually dropped still further to £1,200, the lowest figure in the decade; and this was perhaps the only encouraging

[1] The security for this loan consisted of letters patent *in diversis portubus Anglie*, i.e., a charge on the customs.

feature of the situation. All this time yet another parliament was sitting at Westminster (from 6 November 1450), but it was more concerned with the armed retinues and open rivalry of Yorkists and Lancastrians than with finance, and it was not until its second session (20 January to 29 March 1451) that the position was seriously considered.[1] Even then it was assumed that the king's difficulties were caused by the complete ineffectiveness both of the 1450 income-tax, concerning which it was admitted 'lak of diligence' had been shown, and of the crown's own unwilling act of resumption. There was therefore some tinkering with both measures, the only result of which was to make them even more useless than before.[2] The requirements of the crown were also given priority for two years from Christmas 1450 over all assignments on the customs of London and Southampton up to a total of £20,000, with exceptions in favour of the garrison of Calais and also of genuine lenders to the government—more especially the staplers, who were to receive a guaranteed annual income of £2,666 13s. 4d. in return for their financial support.[3] The contortions entered into by this extremely hostile parliament to avoid making any fresh grant to the crown could hardly have gone further, and may be placed in direct relation to the disastrous course of the French war during the next two or three years. With the exception of the brief summer session of May 1451, parliament did not meet again until March 1453, when, under temporary Lancastrian influence, generous grants were at last made; but by that time the English rule in France was *in extremis*, and within six or seven months everything but Calais had been lost for good.

EASTER 1451:		£	s.	d.	%
	Cash	13,706	14	1	27
	Assigned	20,282	16	1½	40
	Book-keeping	16,957	18	1½	33
	Total	50,947	8	4	100

[1] Ramsay, *Lancaster and York*, II, 139–40.

[2] The limit of exemption from the income-tax was actually raised, while the king was allowed to add to the resumption act forty-three new clauses of exemption.

[3] Miss W. I. Haward does not mention this arrangement in her valuable 'Financial Relations between the Lancastrian Government and the Merchants of the Staple, from 1449 to 1461', in *Studies in English Trade in the Fifteenth Century*, ed. Power and Postan, pp. 294–320.

In spite of parliament's refusal to give any positive financial support outside the customs, real revenue rose unexpectedly high this term, and indeed was well above the average for the decade. There were two reasons for this: under cash, firstly, the increase occurred wholly on the last day of term (9 August) when £9,090, nearly all of it from abnormal sources, reached the exchequer: without this windfall, cash would only have been little over half the figure for the previous term. The more extraordinary of the two special payments in the total for 9 August was a sum of £5,140 *de domino Rege* . . . *in moneta proveniente de quodam mercimonio vocato alom (sic) per dominum Regem empto de mercatoribus de Janua et per predictum dominum Regem vendito certis mercatoribus civitatis Lond'*. Of this transaction perhaps all that need be said is that Edward IV has commonly been credited with augmenting the crown revenues by trading on his own account, but not Henry VI: here, as so often in the fifteenth century, the practices of a later generation have already been anticipated. In addition to this no doubt profitable speculation in alum,[1] there was also a substantial sale outright —not a mere pledging, as on earlier occasions—of crown jewels in two lots, one worth £2,107 to John Wynne, jeweller, of London, and the other worth £1,438 to an esquire called John Grenacre.[2] In short the whole business of 9 August suggests a really desperate and creditable effort by the crown to raise money by any legitimate expedient and at any cost. Unfortunately the proceeds were still hopelessly inadequate and it proved necessary to step up assignment, which had been kept at a reasonably low level for two terms, to over £20,000.[3] The only possible recourse remaining was to raise loans, which were in fact screwed up, with some difficulty, to £10,608. It was fitting that half of this should be advanced (on 17 June) by the favoured merchants of the staple:[4] the rest proceeded at various dates during the term from thirty or forty different lenders. The most active day in this connection was again 9 August, when thirteen of these lenders produced £2,100: among

[1] We do not know what the crown originally paid for the consignment, but it seems unlikely that it made a loss.

[2] I have not been able to identify this character.

[3] All the larger drafts were unexpectedly on the hereditary revenues: customs were to a great extent reserved to swell the cash total, to which they contributed over £3,000.

[4] Again secured on letters patent *in diversis portubus Anglie*, with special reference this time to Ipswich (£666 13s. 4d.).

them the archbishops of Canterbury and York took care to see that their own contributions, of £100 and £666 13s. 4d. respectively, were secured on 'certain vessels of silver' belonging to the king, while the latter even got letters patent acknowledging the debt as well. Similarly, the London silversmith and collector of the petty custom, Richard Joynour, whom we have met before,[1] lent £300 on 21 July on the security of 'a jewel called the spiceplate'. The much increased volume of assignment during this term was almost certain to inflate fictitious loans, but in fact they only rose to the moderate total of £6,349, under which head the misfortunes of Henry Percy, still warden of the east march, alone call for notice. On 16 July he received eighteen bad tallies, mainly, but by no means exclusively, on the customs of Berwick, Newcastle-on-Tyne, Hull and Boston, for a total of £1,110; and although this was easily the largest it was by no means the only disappointment of the kind during this term which he was called on to endure.

		£	s.	d.	%
MICHAELMAS 1451–2:	Cash	6,510	10	8	34
	Assigned	9,302	19	2	49
	Book-keeping	3,127	5	8½	17
	Total	18,940	15	6½	100

In this term the final, inevitable slump of the decade arrived in good earnest: the evil day could no longer be postponed and real revenue sank rapidly towards danger level. Cash, it is true, was still relatively well maintained, all the large payments coming from the customs and including the substantial sum of £1,333 6s. 8d. (19 February 1452) from the wool dues payable not in England but at Calais. Assignment, however, went back to its old low figure, all very evenly and steadily distributed throughout the term, with only two day-totals failing to reach three figures and none reaching four. Book-keeping shrank in sympathy to its lowest point in the decade, for the fourteen genuine loans which were raised were all small and totalled only £1,139: individually, fictitious loans were very little bigger, though they came to nearly £2,000. It was obvious that the financial machine was now barely ticking over, though it was to be made to run at an even slower rate in the coming Easter term.

---

[1] Above, p. 233, Michaelmas, 1449–50.

		£	s.	d.	%
EASTER 1452:	Cash	2,291	19	7	12
	Assigned	8,581	10	1½	46
	Book-keeping	7,865	6	3	42
	Total	18,738	15	11½	100

The general debility increased alarmingly, real revenue sinking to the lowest point so far. What is especially significant of disaster is that this was the first occasion on which both the Michaelmas and the Easter terms of the same exchequer year had shown such weakness: the result was that the total real income for the year, at less than £26,700, was barely half what it had been at its lowest in the past. The same is true of cash and assignment: in previous terms, if one had been weak, the other had usually been strong, but now both of them, though not quite at their absolute lowest, were well below par. Cash was now drawn very largely from such secondary sources as the issues of the hanaper (especially 24 May), and that only in the first half of the term; while assignment, though more evenly distributed, was also weak. A desperate attempt was made to fill the gap by borrowing, but only £4,774—again from some fourteen or fifteen lenders—could be raised: the most important of such loans were one of £1,333 6s. 8d., made on 14 June by William Chadworth, receiver of lands and tenements in the hands of feoffees of the duchy of Lancaster,[1] and another of £2,000 on 4 August from William Port and other executors of Beaufort: thus even from his grave the great cardinal was still coming to the support of the tottering Lancastrians. Another unhealthy sign, however, was the rise in fictitious loans to £3,091: this does not seem much at first sight, and there were no individual creditors of outstanding importance, but it was nearly three-eighths of the reduced value of successful assignment, and the relation between these two headings is often a useful index of financial well-being or the reverse at any given moment. It is true that there was to be some measure of recovery during the next five terms, but the point at which the Lancastrian dynasty had virtually lost France, and had touched financial bottom for the first time, is none the less an appropriate one at which to end this decade, and so pause, before entering on the wars of the roses and Henry's final years.

[1] He had letters patent as security—though this was nothing unusual.

CHAPTER VII
ANALYSIS, 1432–52

The second two decades of Henry VI's reign afford the most perfect basis of comparison achieved so far, since at least one (and generally more than one) complete receipt roll survives for every exchequer term in the entire period. In order to preserve continuity it may be helpful, as before, to make some reference to the last of the preceding decades (1422–32) as well, but whenever this is done it must be remembered that only nineteen terms are represented in the figures given for the first ten years of Henry VI, which are therefore slightly underestimated in comparison with the two succeeding periods. While this remains true of gross totals, it hardly affects averages, which however are of such relatively little interest and importance that in calculating them we may be content from this point onwards to take the annual totals to the nearest £1,000, which will be found in the Table C series at the end of this book.

It will be remembered[1] that the gross nominal revenue for Henry's first decade worked out at a yearly average of £96,700 on a summary basis, or just under £95,000 on a rather closer calculation, and his real revenue at something between £75,100 and £75,700 annually. In his second ten years, when he was still not of age most of the time—and in any event had little influence on policy—Henry's average *nominal* revenue rose appreciably, viz. to £115,000 or so, though his real revenue lagged behind at £75,000, practically unchanged. In Henry's third phase, when the Lancastrian party was being formed and Suffolk and queen Margaret of Anjou were in power, the average gross revenue fell sharply to a new low level of only £85,000, while real revenue declined in sympathy to only £54,000, since the percentage, though not of course the gross total, of book-keeping remained almost the same in both periods. The simplest explanation of these broad general movements, which are only very roughly calculated (since averages are apt to be misleading anyway), is that 1432–42 was a period of such military disaster that it shook the council, and in time even the commons, into abandoning the cheap and niggardly finance, which had marked the 1420's, together with the attempt

[1] Above, Chapter v, p. 179.

240

to make the French conquests pay the whole cost of their own administration. But the damage had been done—financially as well as militarily—and although the dwindling personal and feudal revenues might be made good by rather more taxation than before, the best that could be achieved was to borrow more than ever for immediate emergencies and to arrest, but not reverse, the downward movement of real revenue. By the 1440's it was becoming pretty obvious that the French possessions, or at least the greater part of them, must be written off completely before long: the Burgundian alliance was allowed to lapse, and disaster was followed by disaster. Such confidence as the unwilling commons, and the equally unwilling men of property outside the commons, had possessed in the administration ten years earlier had disappeared, and, damaging as the quarrels of cardinal Beaufort and duke Humphrey and other leading councillors had been, they were as nothing in comparison with the disgust and hatred felt by large sections of the community for such new figures as the earl, or later duke, of Suffolk, and the foreign queen. And so grants were reduced again, if not withheld entirely, just when they were needed more than ever, while the process of party building stripped the crown of more and more capital resources in the shape of lands and tenements, with the result that the hereditary revenues themselves began to disappear. Only the customs remained buoyant, and became in fact the main financial stand-by of the dynasty, but precisely for that reason they were deluged with assignments and exemptions, grants and licences, which heavily reduced their yield. In these conditions, the serious, though not yet catastrophic, fall in revenue, not to mention the increased recourse to borrowing and to anticipation, are easily accounted for.

We may now take a rather closer look at these phenomena, which emerge clearly enough if we proceed to analyse the bookkeeping totals for the first thirty years of Henry VI's reign.

AVERAGE PER YEAR	'Genuine' loans	Fictitious loans	*Prestita restituta*	Total
	£	£	£	£
1422–32	12,490	7,338	9	19,837
1432–42	25,171	14,440	474	40,085
1442–52	13,815	16,657	320	30,792

From this table there appears very clearly, first, the frenzied attempt of the 1430's to raise money in order to prevent the loss of France. The average for genuine loans, made mostly by cardinal Beaufort, is in fact not only more than double that of the preceding decade but also nearly £11,000 *per annum* more than under Henry V (the previous peak period) and certainly higher than at any other time in the whole century between 1377 and 1485; while even the much lower figure for the succeeding decade is still the third highest on record. When we turn to fictitious loans on the other hand—a heading which invariably reflects with some accuracy the degree of financial strain to which a government is being subjected—the picture is somewhat different. The average for 1432–42 is exactly doubled, it is true, compared with the early minority, and is nearly £4,000 *per annum* higher than the previous peak figure reached under this head, namely that for Henry IV: but, unlike genuine loans, it does not decline again during the later 1440's but goes even higher still. Indeed the figure for 1442–52 is the highest for the whole period of 108 years, and that for 1432–42 the second highest—a fact which speaks for itself. Since *prestita restituta*, though substantially larger than they had been so far during the fifteenth century, were still virtually negligible, the only remaining point to stress is the high *total* average of all book-keeping as a whole during these two decades; it is in fact first 100% and then 50% higher than at any other time between 1377 and 1485. Or, confining the comparison to 1422–32 only, 1432–42 showed a 100% increase in default on bad tallies, and a more than 100% increase in money borrowed, while 1442-52 showed almost 20% *further* increase in default, but a decline in genuine borrowing, which fell to a point about half-way between that achieved by the councillors of the infant king Henry in his early years, and by his father, Henry V.

We must now see how these figures were distributed in detail among the various classes of royal creditor, again beginning at the centre with the household. Here the figures are as follows:

HOUSEHOLD	1422–32			1432–42			1442–52		
	£	s.	d.	£	s.	d.	£	s.	d.
'Genuine' loans	3,188	19	10	996	13	4	9,186	19	8
Fictitious loans	15,616	2	8½	39,846	2	5	63,661	16	1½
Prestita restituta	75	1	8	466	10	0½	686	12	3

The most remarkable point about these figures is, of course, the rapid and enormous increase in fictitious loans: it is clear where most of the bad tallies were going under Henry VI. The figure for 1442–52 is in fact £2,000 higher than that for the whole of Henry IV's reign, though it is drawn from only 20 rolls, as against 21 rolls and four fragments. *Prestita restituta* are clearly not worth bothering about, so the only remaining problem is the curious fluctuation in 'genuine' loans. For this, as usual, a rather closer investigation will be necessary. Resolved into their component parts the household figures are as follows:

'GENUINE' LOANS	1422–32			1432–42			1442–52		
	£	s.	d.	£	s.	d.	£	s.	d.
Chamber	666	13	4	—			—		
Wardrobe	100	0	0	133	6	8	1,386	13	4
Great wardrobe	—			—			1,403	13	0
King's knights	1,795	8	2	266	13	0	693	6	8
King's esquires	60	0	0	—			686	13	4
King's clerks	—			496	13	4	4,926	13	4
Others	566	18	4	100	0	0	90	0	0
Total	3,188	19	10	996	13	4	9,186	19	8

The first point of interest in this table is that the wardrobe, which had been so important under Henry V, is now insignificant throughout, though it improves in 1442–52; while the chamber's loans disappear entirely. The great wardrobe, on the other hand, achieves a separate mention for the first time in the last of these three periods, when its clerks, or keepers, like the keepers of the wardrobe proper, seem to have had enough cash in hand to be able to make a small loan to the crown (if only by forgoing a legitimate demand for the time being) on occasion. King's knights, after a good start, followed by some fluctuation, end with roughly half the total lending power of the great wardrobe—a state in which they are joined for the first time by king's esquires, though only in the latest period. The most remarkable addition to the table, compared with that in Chapter v, is the large sum apparently advanced in 1442–52 by the group known as king's clerks: £4,200, however, of the total £4,926 came from Master John Langton, the king's chaplain, who for some time past seems to have been acting as a regular financial agent of the crown.[1] This being so, it is likely that many of the sums he handled were not his own property, and that his 'loans', though regularly described as such in the receipt roll, were more properly a kind of *prestitum restitutum*, as was the case with the great 'loan' of £14,480 3s. 10d. supposed to have been made by the earl of Buckingham and others in the summer of 1380.[2] If Langton is ruled out on these grounds, the remaining sums advanced were not beyond the probable capacity of the half-dozen clerks concerned in each period: for example, the king's secretary is regularly included, and it is more than likely that a man in that position could make enough money on the side to lend the crown a hundred marks or so (£66 13s. 4d.), especially if a profit could be made on the transaction. Finally, it should be noted that king's clerks were not considered worth distinguishing from 'other persons' when the table for 1422–32 was originally drawn up, and their subsequent extraction from that category in later tables explains why 'other persons' shrink so in the years 1432–52.

The real interest of the household, however, obviously lies in its relation to fictitious loans, for if not a lending it was most certainly a spending department (or collection of departments), and perhaps the easiest of all for the exchequer to fob off with doubtful tallies.

FICTITIOUS LOANS	1422–32			1432–42			1442–52		
	£	s.	d.	£	s.	d.	£	s.	d.
Chamber	409	6	1	180	0	0	6,822	10	11
Wardrobe	10,126	5	9½	30,006	18	5½	35,013	3	2
Great wardrobe	1,060	12	2½	1,962	17	10	9,299	3	10½
King's knights	1,918	17	3	1,752	18	4	1,727	8	3½
King's esquires	—			415	1	1	1,161	2	3
King's clerks	—			505	13	4	4,465	1	6
Royal family	2,027	1	5	4,930	6	0½	3,111	4	7
Others	73	19	11½	92	7	4	2,062	1	6½
Total	15,616	2	8½	39,846	2	5	63,661	16	1½

---

[1] Above, Chapter VI, p. 207 (1434–5).
[2] Above, Chapter III, pp. 137–8.

This table shows in the first place that if the chamber had ceased to function as a lender it was still capable of spending heavily and receiving numerous bad tallies of assignment—at any rate in 1442–52, the age of 'personal' Lancastrian government. Some £1,600 out of the total shown really represents default upon the wages of the chamber's staff, but the great bulk of it (£5,221) stands for failure to pay its bills. The same is even more true of the wardrobe, though under Henry VI this seems to have remained rather more of a department of state than the chamber. It was perhaps especially concerned with the French war, as it had always been, and decade by decade was becoming more unable to meet even its accepted obligations. The great wardrobe, too, with its heavy stores of all kinds, was becoming much concerned with material of war and garrison supplies for Calais and the other French fortresses; it is significant that the bad tallies it receives are more than quadrupled in value in the last of these three decades. King's knights, on the contrary, remain extremely steady, and in fact it is unlikely that their number or commitments could be much increased. King's esquires, it is true, rise considerably, but they start from such a low level that their total is still relatively small by 1452. The more remarkable increase during the same period in the value of bad tallies cut for king's clerks is again mainly due to the obscure activities of Master John Langton, who is responsible for £3,570 worth in all, or more than three-quarters of the whole. If his 'genuine' loans are chiefly prests, as has already been suggested, these fictitious loans may simply represent some abortive attempts to place more funds (by assignment) at his disposal: but if he really did lend money to the crown, they are probably efforts at repayment. On the whole I prefer the former theory.

The fairly large sums noted under 'royal family' in the last two decades are accounted for, as in 1422–32, by queens—the two dowager queen-mothers Joan and Katharine (five-sixths for the latter) in 1432–42, and a small sum from the late queen Katharine's estate,[1] but the bulk from Margaret of Anjou (£2,424) in 1442–52. I have included nothing under this head except sums assigned personally to the royal ladies themselves, and have omitted from the total various additional defaults on wages for sundry officers of the household of queen Margaret in particular, all of which go to swell the king's household under 'others'. Some of them are

[1] She died at the beginning of January 1437.

245

considerable—for example, £340 for valets and £200 for boys and pages of the new queen's chamber. The only other really large item under 'others' in 1442–52 is a somewhat similar one of £670 for boys and pages of the *king's* household: as the king's chamber was not specified, I did not feel I could place this item under that heading. The remaining items in this omnibus category are exceptionally numerous at this late period, but mainly very small: they include a wide variety of officers and functions, the mere recital of which affords a vivid picture of the household at this date, while their number and extent suggest that practically all household wages were hopelessly in arrears during this Lancastrian hey-day, before the civil wars broke out. Thus there are numerous king's serjeants, both at-law and at-arms, including the yeoman usher of the hall and keeper of the clock in Westminster palace; ushers of the great council chamber (*sic*); the king's physician, arrow-maker, apothecary and attorneys; the queen's master of the horse; the ferreter to the household; the yeoman or 'trayer' of the cellar; and numerous body servants, valets, boys and pages. There were also several pensioners, mainly widows of king's knights and the like, whom, however, I have generally included in their late husbands' categories, where these are stated, which is not always the case. All this motley crowd of court servants and hangers-on had one thing in common—the receipt of bad tallies of assignment in lieu of pensions or wages.

Next in order to the household come the two great departments of state, namely exchequer and chancery (including the office of the privy seal). Their figures, though interesting, are on such a comparatively small scale that they can be taken together—the more so as the two departments were so closely related.

	1422–32			1432–42			1442–52		
	£	s.	d.	£	s.	d.	£	s.	d.
CHANCERY									
'Genuine' loans	1,146	13	4	2,295	0	0	1,116	13	4
Fictitious loans	231	13	1	1,937	1	3½	2,313	4	3
EXCHEQUER									
'Genuine' loans	1,308	10	0	4,976	13	4	4,085	17	2½
Fictitious loans	39	10	0	527	9	9	2,695	5	6½

From this it is clear that the continuous decline in both sets of figures which marked the reign of Henry V and the first ten years of Henry VI was sharply arrested about 1432, and indeed reversed. Both departments suddenly began to lend rather more money to the crown,[1] and in fact their figures under 'genuine' loans for 1432–42 are approximately the same as under Henry IV. There is, however, a difference in make-up, for whereas the doubling of the chancery's loans merely meant a proportionate increase in the relatively small sums lent by the chancellors themselves and by about a dozen individual clerks, the opposite is true of the exchequer. Here the sums found by the fourteen smaller lenders actually decline by 25%, and the considerable gross increase is entirely the work of one man, Ralph, lord Cromwell, who produced £4,000 during the decade in his capacity as treasurer of England. When we turn to 1442–52 the picture is again much the same: the small chancery lenders receive even less support from the chancellor than before, and in fact return to their 1422–32 level, while the exchequer loans are again mainly carried by the treasurers, two of whom, viz. Marmaduke Lumley, bishop of Carlisle, and James Fenys, lord Saye, produce £2,633 6s. 8d. between them.

With fictitious loans the case is a little different and the steady increase in amounts for both departments is unchecked. In the earlier of the two periods now under review, however, it is true that more than half the chancery defaults are borne by the keeper of the privy seal, William Lynwode, and, if he is excluded, the fictitious loans credited to chancery officials proper, though greater than they had been, come to little more than the increased, but still extremely modest, total credited to the staff of the exchequer. In 1442–52 the growing chancery defaults are spread over a generous number of officials, but the even larger amount borne by the exchequer is attributable for the most part to a single one of the two treasurers already mentioned, viz. the bishop of Carlisle: if we ignore his £1,166 13s. 4d. worth of bad tallies, the remaining officers of the exchequer were not so badly treated. To conclude, it is obvious that both chancery and exchequer were no longer finding it quite as easy as it had been in the previous twenty years

---

[1] This is partly explicable by the theory that more members of their staffs were simply kept longer waiting for their wages: when these fell due they were credited with 'loans' for the appropriate amounts, which were eventually 'repaid'.

to get paid promptly and easily, and so to keep themselves virtually free from the embarrassments which grew upon the state; but neither of them was as yet really heavily involved. This is true of ordinary staff at any rate: as far as heads of departments were concerned, it was admittedly becoming rather common at this epoch for the government to call upon the treasurers personally for financial aid from time to time, if not yet upon the chancellors. Local officials are another and a sadder story.

LOCAL OFFICIALS	1422–32	1432–42	1442–52
	£ s. d.	£ s. d.	£ s. d.
'Genuine' loans	3,368 0 6	6,878 10 6	10,682 9 11
Fictitious loans	7,818 2 10½	30,082 19 11½	47,276 10 3½

Here the trend of the first thirty years of the fifteenth century is much more spectacularly reversed. It is true that 'genuine' loans from this source had been climbing slowly ever since 1413, but now they are first doubled, and then more than trebled, in comparison with the still quite modest level of the decade ending in 1432. As far as 1432–42 is concerned, this is principally caused by Richard Bukland,[1] who as treasurer of Calais and the French march was now able to advance £3,469 6s. 8d.—for all but £250 of which he was indebted to the assistance of that curious *éminence grise*, the king's clerk, Master John Langton, whom we have encountered before.[2] But in addition Sir John Radclyf, seneschal of Aquitaine and keeper of the castle of Fronsac, produced £1,398, leaving only some £2,000 to be accounted for from other sources. More than half this balance was produced by various customs collectors in the port of London, and the rest by the chamberlains of Chester and south Wales and the receiver-general of the duchy of Cornwall, not to mention yet another treasurer of Calais. Probably the French 'loans' represent no more than the temporary assumption of responsibility for garrison supplies and 'wages of war', though some of the other loans, especially from the London customs collectors, may have been genuine enough. It is much the same story in 1442–52, though by then the customs collectors'

[1] Above, Chapter v, p. 185.
[2] Above, p. 244, and Chapter III, pp. 137–8.

loans are larger: for example, Richard Joynour, collector of the London petty custom, lends as much as £3,126, and John Poutrell, collector of the wool custom in the same port, £1,559. Another large loan which has a genuine ring about it in this later period is one of £1,333 6s. 8d. from Thomas Chadworth, receiver of lands and tenements in the hands of feoffees of the duchy of Lancaster, but a further £1,300 from Robert Manfeld, victualler of Calais, and some oddments still on Bukland's account (though by this time he was dead), are open to the same doubts as before. It will be noted that the large sums mentioned add up to over £7,300, leaving only some £3,350 to be accounted for by smaller lenders. There are thirty-three of these, and no less than twenty-six of them are customs officers in a large number of different English ports: the remaining seven contributors include an escheator, a sheriff, a controller and surveyor of mines, a royal justice of assize (for the large sum of £396 13s. 4d.), the captain of Caen town and castle, the chamberlain of Chester, and the keeper of Carlisle and the west march (now the earl of Salisbury).

The great increase in fictitious loans from local officers is less surprising than this crop of 'genuine' loans. As the war worsened and the court expenses grew, while parliamentary support and confidence diminished, it was obvious that local officials would be more and more pinched for money and that the quality of tallies hopefully assigned to them would probably degenerate. But that the total in bad tallies for 1422–32 should be first almost quadrupled, and then multiplied by more than six, considerably exceeds expectation. Calais, of course, again accounts for a good deal of this development—viz. £7,150 by the hands of Bukland and his successor Robert Whityngham in 1432–42, though only £2,525 in the following decade. Then there were the other French garrisons, such as Fronsac, Crotoy, Caen and Meulx in Brie, all of which received between them in bad tallies some £3,455 and £4,574 in the two periods respectively; the Scottish marches, which got £6,361 in the earlier, and the prodigious sum of £26,773 in the later, period; Ireland (now some £5,957 and £4,097, though in the immediate past not a very large recipient of bad tallies); and, finally, various clerks of the works, who got £2,777 and £6,822 in the one decade and the other. All these figures—which incidentally omit shillings and pence—are admittedly only approximate, but they serve to illustrate the rapidly increasing tempo of financial breakdown. No local official could be certain of receiving tallies he could cash, except at a ruinously heavy discount, and yet these dubious instruments were practically all the means he ever got from the exchequer with which to meet his multiplying dangers and commitments. In this connection the financial state of Berwick, Roxburgh and the east march was particularly scandalous: France in a sense mattered less, for the soldiers were losing it anyway and it may be that the soundest of finance could not have saved it: moreover, as will be seen under *Burgesses*, it was greatly to the interest of the rich society of staplers that at any rate Calais and its hinterland should remain safely in English hands, and they themselves possessed the funds, even if the government did not, to see that this desirable object was achieved. Neither the Scottish marches nor the Irish pale possessed protective influences of this kind, and of course the same may be said of the multitude of smaller victims. Among these last we may note no less than eight judges and fifteen customs officers: there was also the same captain of Caen town and castle (his name was Sir Andrew Ogard, or Outgard) whom we have met before;[1] an ambassador; and several small fry. The most picturesque of the little men is a certain Edmund Bryan, who was an Irish agent, informer, and later pensioner, of the crown; he is succinctly described in the patent roll of 1444 as 'in great fear of his life, and probably will be'. He was, however, still alive in 1448 and ready to enjoy his small pension, if only he could have cashed the tallies in which it was paid!

Altogether, personal dependants, courtiers, and direct employees of the crown increased the value of their rather dubious 'loans' from £9,012 in 1422–32 to £15,146 and £25,072 in the two following decades, while their fictitious loans mounted steadily from £23,751 to £72,393 and, eventually, £115,946.

The numerous categories of persons and institutions *not* directly dependent on the crown tell a very different story, for, as might be expected, their much more 'genuine' loans are considerably larger than those of the first group, while their fictitious loans, though starting at a higher rate than the others, first subside to an approximate equality with them, and then fall far below them. The figures for the two sorts of loan in relation to this 'general public' over the three periods under discussion are as follows: £109,625,

---

[1] Above, p. 249.

£236,566 and £113,075 for 'genuine', and £45,967, £72,008 and £51,619 for fictitious loans. The more detailed distribution of these large amounts is interesting.

We may begin, as usual, with the bishops, who are easily the most important lenders up to 1452.

BISHOPS	1422–32			1432–42			1442–52		
	£	s.	d.	£	s.	d.	£	s.	d.
'Genuine' loans	58,516	7	10½	110,747	11	10	45,166	1	8
Fictitious loans	1,703	2	8	25,064	18	4	5,026	1	10

As before, the obvious reason for the huge figures under 'genuine' loans is to be found in the financial operations of cardinal Beaufort, which reached their peak of £91,500 in the decade 1432–42, even without reckoning his association as a lender of a further £15,225 in the same period with the feoffees of the duchy of Lancaster (see *Country gentry*). An average of £9,150 a year from the resources of a single man is not only almost fantastic by the standards of the day but, incidentally, more than double Beaufort's own high rate of lending during the preceding twenty years. Indeed, in the thirty years starting with 1413 Beaufort's loans show a most suspicious and unvarying increase—viz. from £35,630 in the first ten years of that period to £45,413 in the second, and finally to the £91,500 already mentioned in the third. I say 'suspicious', because such a rate of growth irresistibly suggests the snowballing effect produced by heavy profits promptly reinvested in still further and more profitable loans to the crown. It is true that Mr. McFarlane, the leading authority on Beaufort, has not been able to detect him in the overt act of taking interest on these loans, but if they did *not* show a profit it is difficult to see how this amazing growth of liquid capital was brought about. Moreover, we have Mr. McFarlane's own theory, even though in Beaufort's and in other cases he cannot positively prove it, that the exchequer may have recorded, not the sums actually received by way of loan, but those which they had consented to repay, and that the difference in favour of the lender may have been considerable. I have offered some contributory evidence in support of some such theory for the first part of

Richard II's reign,[1] and I can imagine no satisfactory explanation of Beaufort's record as a financier which excludes it. It is true that in his last five years (he died in 1447) his loans only amounted to £25,333 in all—or an average of only £5,100 a year—but this is explicable in terms of age and satiety in preference to those of *lucrum cessans*, and in any case my gross total of all the loans made by Beaufort during his entire career—a matter of about £200,000 —errs, if anything, in the conservative direction. Thus Mr. McFarlane strikes the same total for the years 1417 to 1444 alone,[2] whereas I have included in my estimate some £4,000 lent in 1413–17 and £2,333 from the years 1444 to 1447. On the other hand, I have excluded (and I assume that Mr. McFarlane has done the same) the £11,333 lent by Beaufort's executors between 1447 and 1452. If we add this in, and if we also add to it the £2,000 or so which Beaufort is known to have lent Henry IV, we arrive at a grand total of over £213,000. Much of this money was, of course, lent over and over again, and, large as it must have been, Beaufort's fluid capital at his richest cannot have approached this startling figure, yet it seems likely that at the height of his career —for example in the spring and early summer of 1443—he could always find, say, £20,000 or so to lend, without straining his resources, at fairly short notice. To exclude usury from the methods by which a working capital on this scale was built up, merely because there is a lack of definite evidence to that effect— to rely, that is, upon the argument *ex silentio* when *silentium* (at the least) was called for by the canon law—seems to me to be an excess of what I can only describe as *pudor academicus*.[3]

During the period 1432–42 Beaufort seems to have developed something of a financial rival on the bench of bishops, though hardly a very serious one, in the person of Henry Chichele, archbishop of Canterbury. Chichele, who died in 1443, lent no less

---

[1] Above, Introduction, pp. xxxvii–xxxviii, and (especially) Chapter I, pp. 18–20. Cf. Chapter II, pp. 39–45.

[2] *Cambridge Medieval History*, VIII, 388. Mr. McFarlane may perhaps have reckoned as an additional loan the £8,666 13s. 4d. mentioned in a hasty jotting by one scribe at the end of a roll for Easter 1417, whereas I have taken the view that this is simply a memorandum to allow for a loan already made: above, Chapter IV, pp. 156–7.

[3] I must hasten to make it clear that I am not accusing Mr. McFarlane or anyone else of this hypothetical complaint—far from it. I am merely refusing to indulge in it myself.

than £14,218 to the crown during the last ten or eleven years of his life, and, like Beaufort himself, he was also associated with the large loans made during that period by the Lancaster feoffees—in his case to the extent of an additional £7,000. All the other bishops between them did not produce more than another £5,000 or so, and the only one of them to reach four figures was Edmund Lacy, bishop of Exeter, with £1,179. As contrasted with earlier periods this suggests a certain change in the make-up of episcopal loans to the crown: instead of the £1,000 to £1,500 a year or so all told, which was traditional, we get a much larger total for each decade, but it nearly all comes from two or three specially favoured individuals or sees. In 1442–52 this impression is confirmed: the total, though lower than it has been, is still at the high figure reached during Henry V's reign—but when we have deducted Beaufort's final loans (£25,333) and those made by his executors (£11,333) we have accounted for all but £8,500 of the whole and there are only two or three moderately important lenders out of the seventeen bishops who are left. These are John Kemp, the cardinal archbishop of York, with £2,040, and William Aiscough, bishop of Salisbury, with £1,602: we might perhaps add Adam Moleyns, bishop of Chichester, who produces £593 in that capacity and nearly as much again as keeper of the privy seal (see *Chancery*), while his executors—for he died during this decade—produced yet a third £500. Then there was Chichele's successor, John Stafford, in the see of Canterbury, who lent £833 from that source and £136 more as chancellor of England. But that is all.

In the case of fictitious loans, even the most influential prelates were no longer able to secure the virtual exemption from bad tallies which had marked their earlier years. In particular 1432–42 was obviously an unsatisfactory decade in this respect, but it is noteworthy that the main loss was borne for the first time by the two great moneylenders themselves, Beaufort and Chichele, who account for £18,346 and £4,141 respectively. A further £1,663 in bad tallies went to Marmaduke Lumley, the militant bishop of Carlisle, in his capacity as warden of the west march, so if we deduct these three special cases, less than £1,000 worth of fictitious loans remains to be accounted for. In short, the burden on the ordinary bishops or archbishops, as distinct from the financiers and the captains, was actually heavier in 1442–52, for although the gross total for the whole decade had by then descended to a mere £5,000 or so, it was much more evenly distributed among the smaller sees. It is particularly noticeable in this connection that the executors both of Beaufort and of Chichele are not troubled at all seriously in this way, nor is Beaufort himself in his last years: the main burden of default is borne by the archbishops of York and Dublin (£1,068 and £1,081), with the poor see of Rochester a close third at £1,042. Some ten other sees are also inconvenienced, though none to anything resembling this extent.

When we turn to the minor clergy, somewhat inaccurately described for purposes of this book as 'the religious', since, although monastic houses always preponderate, the heading also includes a few secular priests, the figures are as follows:

RELIGIOUS	1422–32	1432–42	1442–52
	£ s. d.	£ s. d.	£ s. d.
'Genuine' loans	3,459 14 11	6,822 6 8	4,377 4 10
Fictitious loans	359 17 1½	546 11 9½	1,866 16 8½

The fluctuation in the total amount lent 'genuinely' does not seem to be of any special significance; for the rise in the middle period shown and subsequent decline is characteristic of many other types of lender. What is interesting is that the total number of lenders again sinks as it had done before—this time from eighty to only fifty-eight in 1432–42, in spite of the increased amount of money lent, whereas it rises again to ninety-one with the rather smaller money total of 1442–52. This is partly owing to the fact that in the middle period there are three or four exceptionally heavy lenders, whereas in the last period there are none. In particular, the abbot of Westminster lent as much as £1,800 in 1432–42, and was easily the heaviest lender: but in the following decade Westminster lent only £66 13s. 4d. Similarly the prior and brothers of St. John of Jerusalem in England lent £633 6s. 8d. in 1432–42, as against £200 thereafter: while Reginald Kentwode, the dean of St. Paul's, who had begun to lend to the crown at the beginning of the reign, increased the amount of his loans from £100 to £633 6s. 8d. in 1432–42, but does not appear at all in the last period. The Hospitallers in fact had been lending pretty steadily to the crown ever since 1413, and so had the abbot of Glastonbury, whose contribution now rose from £300 to £400, though it returned to £300 in 1442–52. Only one minor churchman lent more than this at the later date, viz. the prior of St. Swithin's, Winchester, who produced £316 13s. 4d.

All this suggests that the normal contribution of this class ranged from about £3,500 to £4,500 per decade, apart from special efforts made occasionally by the richer orders or conventual houses and, occasionally, a wealthy dean or prior, with or without his chapter. Incidentally, the sum total of these loans is at no time enough to cover more than a small fraction of the clerical subsidies raised in any given decade, yet it is precisely persons such as these who acted as collectors of those subsidies. Hence Ramsay's theory that the clerical tenths were regularly anticipated in bulk by more or less forced loans from the collectors finds little general support in the receipt rolls.

Of the fifty-eight clerical lenders in 1432–42 about thirty-nine represent religious houses—a proportion which rises slightly to sixty-six out of ninety-one in the next decade. It is seldom clear, however, whether the abbots and abbesses, priors and prioresses mentioned are lending from their own or from conventual funds: the latter are occasionally referred to, but only rarely. In addition there are about ten lenders in the earlier, and thirteen in the later, period who represent other forms of clerical organization, ranging from the Order of St. John of Jerusalem to deans and chapters, provosts of collegiate churches, wardens or masters of hospitals, and, in one instance, the rectors of the Bristol churches, lending corporately. Individuals who are not described as rectors—the most common term—are sometimes prebendaries or canons but more commonly 'parsons' or plain 'clerks'. A provost of Eton, Master Henry Sever, who was also a canon of Chichester, is perhaps the most interesting of these people: he lent £16 13s. 4d. in the period 1442–52.

When we turn to fictitious loans in this connection, the continuous increase between 1422 and 1452 at once strikes the eye, though the figures are never large. Only eight persons or institutions are concerned between 1432 and 1442, and of these the only important ones are, as before, the dean (£80) and chapter of St. Stephen's, Westminister, with £185 odd in all; the master of the London hospital of St. Anthony (£133 6s. 8d.) and the abbot of Glastonbury (£100). Things are much worse ten years later, when the number suffering default has risen from eight to forty-six, though, as might be expected, the individual amounts are generally rather smaller. The largest (£200) was borne by the president and fellows of the Cambridge college of St. Margaret and St. Bernard,[1] and one of the smallest (£6) by the scholars of another Cambridge college, King's Hall, subsequently absorbed in Trinity. Other victims of some interest from the value of the bad tallies they received, or for some other reason, are the abbess of Barking (£100); the abbots of Glastonbury (again) and Gloucester (£100 and £144 6s. 8d.); the dean and chapter of Salisbury (£100); the lepers of St. Giles (£3); and, as usual, the preaching friars, ranging from their chief provincial in England (£14) to their houses in London (£8) and at Oxford (£26), where however their discomfort was surpassed by that of the friars minor (£43). All these last were in receipt of regular payments from the crown, but it can be seen that they had difficulty in collecting them: the Cambridge friars, who usually figure in the list, for once do not appear.

Summing up, we are left with the general impression that the minor clergy and religious decidedly increased their rather humble contribution to the support of crown finances in the 1430's, though they did not reach the level of lending they had touched in Henry V's reign. In the 1440's, on the other hand, a larger number of them lent distinctly less, and, like other persons in the community, they were appreciably more harassed as a class (though still not seriously) by receiving more and more bad tallies of assignment.

Among these other persons the magnates are perhaps pre-eminent, though indeed all categories of laymen tend to be conspicuous in one or both of these periods for the size and number of their loans. The magnates' figures are these:

MAGNATES	1422–32 £ s. d.	1432–42 £ s. d.	1442–52 £ s. d.
'Genuine' loans	1,112 13 4	20,266 1 4	21,746 18 1
Fictitious loans	37,169 11 7	26,288 3 7½	35,734 14 6

The enormous increase in genuine loans between 1432 and 1452

[1] Better known today as Queens' College—then, of course, Queen's.

is obviously the most striking feature in this table: it is to be associated, I believe, with the disasters of the French war, for it changes radically in character after 1452, by which date France was virtually lost, and it can be seen above that it was not a feature of the early minority, when France was erroneously believed to be secure in English hands. But it became evident in the 1430's that, great as were the temporary sacrifices and burdens assumed by the nobility, or some of them, during the previous decade in filling local offices of trust largely at their own expense (because financed by thoroughly unsound assignment), they must now begin to make a much more positive contribution in the shape of real loans to the crown, if the tottering English dominance, in which their interest and honour were bound up, was going to be maintained. The group is not a large one—about twenty persons in 1432-42—and it is dominated by half a dozen men, but between them they found £20,000. John Beaufort, earl of Somerset, was the largest lender with £6,666 13s. 4d. on his own account and a further £2,000 advanced jointly with his brother Edmund, earl of Dorset, and Thomas Courtenay, earl of Devon: to this the earl of Dorset added £833 6s. 8d. during the decade from his own pocket. Next comes that stalwart financier, Ralph, lord Cromwell, who lent another £4,170 of his own in addition to the £4,000 he advanced at various other times during the same period as treasurer of England (see *Exchequer*). John Holand, earl of Huntingdon, king's councillor and future duke of Exeter, acting with Henry Percy, earl of Northumberland, produced another £2,000; while William de la Pole, earl of Suffolk, with some others of less social standing, found £1,200 in all. The only other lender nearly approaching these figures was the veteran lord Fanhope, formerly Sir John Cornewall, with £886 13s. 4d.

In 1442-52 there are twenty-one lenders from this class for a total which is £1,500 larger: the average therefore remains about the same, though the distribution is different. Most conspicuous among them is Richard, duke of York, with no less than £12,333 6s. 8d., which suggests that this kind of support may have been regarded by the magnates at any rate as in the general interest and not yet a party question. This theory is strengthened by the fact that the next largest lender was actually York's greatest enemy, William de la Pole, successively earl, marquis and duke of Suffolk, who advanced £3,140. Next to these came John Holand, duke of

Exeter from 1444, with £1,816, and James Fenys or Fiennes, first lord Saye and Sele, who lent just under £1,100 in addition to his £1,200 (see *Exchequer*) as treasurer of England. No other magnate lent sums of this order: for example, Edmund Beaufort's contribution dropped to £433 6s. 8d. in this period, and the duke of Somerset's (as he now was) to £333 6s. 8d.,[1] so it will be seen that the number of large lenders had become slightly smaller.

It is somewhat the same story with the even larger figures involved under fictitious loans, though here the number of individuals concerned is greater—thirty-one in the first period and twenty-five in the second. As usual, the custodians of the Scots marches head the list in 1432–42; viz. Henry Percy, earl of Northumberland, with £6,064, as regards £4,066 of which he was associated in office with the duke of Exeter, who added another £2,018 on his own account. Then there is Sir Richard Neville, earl of Salisbury in virtue of his Montacute marriage, who received £5,653 in bad tallies as warden of the marches, and a further £523 in his own right, making £6,176 in all. Next to these comes Humphrey, duke of Gloucester, who received bad tallies to the value of £2,083; and John Mowbray, duke of Norfolk, with £1,857, more than half of which was associated with his own turn of duty on the marches towards Scotland.[2] To these we must add Richard Beauchamp, earl of Warwick, whose executors[3] were temporarily left some £1,463 out of pocket, in addition to the £560 worth of bad tallies (£2,023 in all) received by this earl when alive; also £1,503 for Leonard, lord Welles, though this, it is true, was in connection with his lieutenancy in Ireland, and should perhaps have been transferred to *Local officials*. Richard, duke of York, who had made no genuine loans by 1442, is credited with £909 in fictitious ones, while finally the Beaufort earls of Somerset and Dorset were £801 and £796 to the bad respectively.

[1] He died in 1444, and was succeeded, after an interval, as duke of Somerset by his brother Edmund, who had just been advanced from earl to marquis of Dorset (1443).

[2] All the figures for wardens of the marches, like that for lord Welles in his capacity as lieutenant in Ireland, should really be added to the sums appearing under these heads in *Local officials*, but where such officers are specifically stated to be magnates, and not humbler paid officials of the crown, I have thought it gave a better picture of the general situation to include them under the present head. Naturally I have done my best to avoid any duplication of my results.

[3] He died in 1439.

It would be tedious to pursue the list any further—the more so as there are much the same details to be recited for 1442–52. In this period everything is dwarfed by the enormous sum of £21,008 transmitted in bad tallies to the duke of York: this was such a poor return for his large genuine loans in the same decade that it may not be too fanciful to see in it an additional reason for the revolution which he planned and carried out in the 1450's. No other loser approached this figure, but the executors of lord Fanhope (viz. the archbishop of Canterbury and lord Cromwell) were disappointed in £2,666 13s. 4d.; and Edmund Beaufort, now marquis of Dorset and also duke of Somerset from 1448, in £2,038. Humphrey, duke of Gloucester, though he died in 1447, had received £1,522 in bad tallies in five years; while Henry, the last Beauchamp earl and first duke of Warwick, who died the year before, had already accumulated £1,046 in the same dubious currency. This leaves as representatives of the only other great family worth a mention—more for its future interest than for its present importance—Richard Woodville, first lord Rivers, and his wife Jacquetta, relict of the late duke of Bedford, who between them got bad tallies to a total of £872 in this decade, and were to get many more later.

More than enough has been written in these paragraphs to show how intimately the leading magnates as a class were now bound up with the financial fortunes of the crown, and it is certainly suggestive to discover that, whereas both Yorkists and Lancastrians had made large genuine loans by 1452, the bulk of the fictitious loans in the ten preceding years had fallen to the Yorkists. But the figures for the minor country gentry tell a very different story.

COUNTRY GENTRY	1422–32			1432–42			1442–52		
	£	s.	d.	£	s.	d.	£	s.	d.
'Genuine' loans	19,006	1	0½	31,953	12	5½	1,829	14	1
Fictitious loans	1,533	18	11	7,089	7	1	449	9	3½

Here the loss of interest as the national effort to preserve the French conquests merged into the prelude to the civil wars is apparently very marked. One might think that this class, which had certainly made a great effort to help the country in Henry V's day (£16,767), had, unlike most of the others and notably the magnates, deliberately increased that effort in the ten years after his death, while in the period of real military crisis in the 1430's their patriotic contribution stood at nearly double the high figure it had reached even under Henry V. But there, we might be tempted to add, it ends abruptly: once faction had begun to rear its head, the willingness of the country gentry to subsidize the French war, though the need was still great, dies away.

Unfortunately this romantic and sentimental picture is utterly misleading. On closer analysis it appears that while the first effort —that of Henry V's time—was truly national, the second (1422–32) depended almost wholly on the feoffees of the duchy of Lancaster; while that is even more true of the third. If national sentiment and patriotism are to be the test, these feelings disappear with the death of Henry V, and all that is happening in the first twenty years of Henry VI's reign is a ruthless exploitation of the resources of the duchy by a conciliar government to whom its ultimate exhaustion was of small concern. Why this exploitation came to such an abrupt end when Henry came of full age, formed his own friends and began to govern for himself (or at any rate for them), remains something of a mystery, but the more probable explanation is that Henry and his Lancastrian friends either could not or would not maintain this continuous pressure on the chief source of loyalty to the dynasty. It is, of course, equally possible that the financial exhaustion of the duchy and the lavish land grants had something to do with it—or it may be a combination of all these reasons—but the fact remains that the moment that this source of strength was removed in the 1440's the impressive figures for the country gentry collapse like a pricked balloon.

Consider the details. In 1432–42 there are thirty-six lenders other than the Lancaster feoffees, but only four of these reach (and they only just reach) as much as three figures apiece in their genuine loans, while the feoffees produce no less than three huge sums—£8,119 16s. 8d. on their own account; £7,000 in association with archbishop Chichele; and as much as £15,224 17s. 8½d. in association with cardinal Beaufort; total £30,344 out of £31,953. In the next period there are only sixteen lenders—only three of whom reach three figures—producing £829 in all, with no more than a further £1,000 from the Lancaster feoffees. The conclusion is inescapable: whoever was concerned with saving Henry V's

French conquests from recapture or keeping the Lancastrians on the throne, it was not the English country gentry as a whole, but only those of the duchy, and even the duchy either ceased to care or was exhausted after 1442. Fictitious loans are what we should expect in these conditions: £6,693 out of £7,089 credited to the feoffees in 1432–42, and nothing at all in 1442–52, when however other perons in this class account for £449, or about their ordinary figure. Clearly there was no wide measure of support among the rich and powerful middle classes in the shires for the Lancastrians once Henry V was dead, and we can begin to understand the difficulties which successive governments experienced in obtaining money grants from the commons, where the knights of the shire were still supreme.

But what was true of the shires need not necessarily have been true of cities, towns and boroughs, and here we may begin, as usual, with the most important, though also the most individual and in a sense unrepresentative, town of all, namely the city of London.

LONDON	1422–32	1432–42	1442–52
	£ s. d.	£ s. d.	£ s. d.
'Genuine' loans	18,435 0 2	27,569 0 5½	15,046 14 2½
Fictitious loans	2,803 6 8	2,992 17 4	899 13 4

Evidently London made something of an effort in the middle of the three periods shown above, even if it was not sustained; but it is also most striking that in the very decade when fictitious loans were at their height the city succeeded in reducing so effectively its already inconsiderable losses under this head. As it happens, in dealing with the genuine loans made by London for most of the last two periods we are for once enabled to apply a check to the receipt roll information in the shape of some research on city sources done by the late Miss E. Jeffries Davis and Miss M. I. Peake, and entitled 'Loans from the city of London to Henry VI, 1431–49'.[1] The authors of this short but interesting article were concerned only with corporate loans—or, more precisely, with

---

[1] *Bulletin of the Institute of Historical Research*, IV, 165–72.

official city loans, for the two do not seem to have always coincided. They point out that such loans were made in answer to a series of definite requests from the government; that the amount granted by the common council was 'almost invariably less than that demanded'; and that the grant was raised compulsorily from individual citizens by setting 'the ordinary machinery for collecting a fifteenth [*sic*] in motion', ward by ward. The total of these semi-forced loans, every one of which can be found in the receipt roll, comes to less than the receipt roll total, and I think that it is fair to argue that the balance represents the *voluntary* contribution of the Londoners, either corporately, in private syndicates or in individual loans, probably for a (concealed) profit motive; whereas the semi-forced loans may have been at strict face value and unpopular on that account. Miss Davis and Miss Peake found four such loans,[1] totalling £10,000, for the period summer 1435 to spring 1442, and four more, totalling £4,432 19s. 6½d., from autumn 1442 to autumn 1449: they also note that out of all these loans only £3,230 remained not repaid at the latter date (where their researches stop). As all these loans but one can be identified in the receipt roll for the exact amount stated as paid over by the city sources, my already mentioned belief that there was normally no question of concealed interest in such cases seems to be confirmed. There is, however, one exception, for when Miss Davis and Miss Peake record a loan of £2,000 as made in 'spring 1442 . . . grant for repayment, December 1443', the receipt rolls for once seem to know nothing of the London figure of £2,000 but do record one loan of £1,894 16s. 1½d. as paid over on 19 March 1442 and 'repaid' (that is, by assignment) on 14 April, together with a *second* loan of £666 13s. 4d. (of which the city records apparently say nothing), paid on 18 July 1442 and 'repaid' in the same way as the first one upon 1 December. Here the question of concealed interest may well arise: for if Miss Davis and Miss Peake are correct in saying that £2,000 was all that London lent between March and November 1442 (when a quite different loan, which is not in question, started), the receipt rolls are equally emphatic in saying that £2,561 9s. 5½d. was repaid by the exchequer in two

---

[1] I exclude the first in their series, which was raised during the winter of 1430-1, as belonging to an earlier 'decade' in my own scheme: it appears, however, quite correctly in the receipt rolls at the right time for the precise amount (£3,333 6s. 8d.).

instalments for loans made during this same period—and the difference between £2,000 and £2,561 9s. 5½d. would represent about the same rate of 'interest' as that which I detected for 1384–6 in the case of certain aliens.[1] Even if this conclusion is justified, however, I am still inclined to believe that most of these official city loans were free of interest, though there is no reason to suppose that this is equally the case with the larger number which were not official and, presumably, quite voluntary.

Turning to the details in the receipt roll, we find that in 1432–42 genuine loans totalling £16,852 are credited to the 'mayor and citizens' of London, as against the £10,000 mentioned in the London sources which we have just been dealing with. The difference of £6,852 can perhaps be accounted for on the supposition that, though corporate, these were not 'official city' loans—just as all the colleges of a federal university may occasionally act together for some intercollegiate purpose without necessarily acting as a university. Of the twenty-five citizens who lend the balance (some £11,000) individually, easily the most important in both periods is Sir William Estfeld, mercer, who in 1432–42 alone lends £2,389 on his own account, and a further £5,333 6s. 8d. in conjunction with Hamo Sutton and Hugh Dyke (evidently a private syndicate). No one else is in the same class with Estfeld, though another mercer, William Flete, lends £500 and both Ralph Holand, draper and later alderman, and John Melbourn, 'merchant', lend £400 apiece. It is true that, if executors are included, Robert Large, alderman, who died during the period, may be credited with £633 6s. 8d. in all, of which £300 was paid over in his lifetime; but the rest are really small fry. All but some £456 of the fictitious loans are borne, as we should expect, by the city lending corporately—viz. £2,536 out of £2,992.

The next period (1442–52) is, however, rather different. To begin with, there is an exact correspondence, down to the last half-penny, with the London figure of £4,432 19s. 6½d. arrived at by Miss Davis and Miss Peake for the official city loans of 1442–49; and, secondly, this is of course a much smaller proportion of the reduced London total. Indeed, in this decade, Sir William Estfeld is easily the biggest lender of all with £6,400: Ralph Holand, alderman, is now a very poor second at £900, and is closely followed

---

[1] Above, Chapter II, pp. 48–55.

by the well-known William Cantelowe,[1] himself an alderman, with £856: Cantelowe is also associated with yet another alderman, William Chalton, in a further £333 6s. 8d. An old London family, active in Richard II's time, is represented by another William Venour (£500), now described curtly as 'gentleman', not grocer, and there is a figure of some future importance in Alexander Haysant, draper, though his loans are small (£200). Perhaps Philip Malpas, alderman, who lends £463 odd, should also be mentioned. In the greatly reduced, indeed now almost negligible, fictitious loans the main sufferer and the only one worth notice is, oddly enough, William Cantelowe, who gets £561 13s. 4d. in bad tallies against Sir William Estfeld's £100, while the city lending corporately gets none at all.

On the whole we must conclude that both London as a city and a few leading individual Londoners were reasonably generous in supporting Henry VI, but that they showed considerable skill in avoiding any payment in bad tallies, usually by managing that it should be the London customs on which their assignments were made. With one or two exceptions, however, they did become distinctly less ready to lend money after 1442, and also more careful than ever—and not without reason—about the nature of their tallies of assignment.

What is true of London is never necessarily true of other towns, and the figures for other burgesses are in fact somewhat different, though, as we shall see, there was a special reason for this.

BURGESSES	1422–32			1432–42			1442–52		
	£	s.	d.	£	s.	d.	£	s.	d.
'Genuine' loans	4,489	16	4	31,006	19	9	20,203	19	5
Fictitious loans	2,104	18	0½	7,791	13	8	2,810	8	3

There is, firstly, the huge increase in genuine loans—proportionately much larger than that of London—between the first and second of the three periods shown, and though the total falls again

[1] See Power and Postan, *Studies in English Trade in the Fifteenth Century*, index, under Cantelowe, also for Estfeld. Though Londoners, they were both intimately concerned with the affairs of the Calais staple, which was coming to be more and more a London merchants' colony.

during the third period, it falls rather less steeply than the London total. In fictitious loans these burgesses start appreciably below Londoners but rise well above them in both the later periods: evidently they were not so successful in avoiding bad tallies, but, at first sight at any rate, they were even more willing (after 1432) to make genuine loans to the crown.

The picture is, however, as misleading in its way as the *prima facie* appearance of the figures under *Country gentry*, and for much the same reason. Just as in the one case they are principally accounted for by one great corporate lender, viz. the Lancaster feoffees, so in this case it is the merchants of the Calais staple, and no others, who produce the really large totals—£28,393 out of £31,006 under genuine loans in 1432–42, and £18,673 out of £20,203 in 1442–52. It will be seen that this leaves only £2,613 and £1,530 respectively for other lenders, of whom there are thirty-one in the first period and forty-two in the second: the average amounts lent by small men are obviously dwindling. Outside the staple, the only important loans in 1432–42 came in fact from Bristol (£1,100 —of which £400 may have come from the mayor individually) and Norwich (mayor and citizens, £300): in 1442–52, however, Bristol sinks to £173 and Norwich to only £38, while the largest single contribution from any source in England is as little as £200 (mayor and citizens of Lincoln). In fictitious loans the staple is responsible for all but £613 (£400 of which is borne by Bristol) in the first period, and for all but £550, fairly evenly distributed among the smaller lenders, in the second. It is a dispiriting picture on the whole, showing only too clearly that the burgesses would be well disposed, as usual, to follow any lead towards retrenchment given in the commons by the knights of the shire; and it is evident that we need concern ourselves with no one but the staplers.

Here once more there has been recent research of much value in external sources, though dealing, for the most part, with a slightly later period. It is to be found in Miss W. I. Haward's contribution to Power and Postan's *Studies in English Trade in the Fifteenth Century* under title of 'The Financial Relations between the Lancastrian Government and the Merchants of the Staple, from 1449 to 1461'. It is obvious that I shall have occasion in a later chapter to refer more fully to this interesting study, but for present purposes the overlap is small. Thus the earliest loan mentioned by Miss Haward is one of £6,666 13s. 4d. made on 7 December 1447, which duly appears in the receipt roll, together with two others made on 27 February and 7 June 1451, for £5,866 13s. 4d. and £5,333 6s. 8d. respectively. These three totals are identical in both sources and neither Miss Haward nor I have been able to find any traces of concealed interest about them. Where Miss Haward's work becomes particularly interesting, however, is in her discovery of large further loans, amounting to at least £15,233 6s. 8d., and possibly to very much more, which never found their way on to the receipt rolls at all.

For the first of these—a matter of £10,700, advanced 'at divers times' before 1449—she is able to quote detailed evidence from the treaty rolls (especially) and from the calendar of patent rolls:[1] two others are not quite so fully documented, but I see no reason to reject them. They are a further £4,533 6s. 8d., advanced 'at divers times' before 1451, together with a £1,000 loan made in 1450,[2] which may or may not be distinct from the larger loan just mentioned. In addition, some part at least of the huge sum of £40,943 odd, said to have been advanced by the staplers to the second duke of Somerset between 1451 and 1455 to pay the Calais garrison,[3] must fall within this period. If this is so—and there seems to be no reason to dispute Miss Haward's general conclusions—such major omissions from the receipt rolls, especially upon their book-keeping side, which after all has been my special theme, are obviously so serious a matter that the question whether they are any longer worth analysis along the lines I have evolved will soon require an answer. None the less this question may be temporarily deferred until a later chapter, when other instances of gross omission will appear, and we may now proceed, with somewhat shaken confidence, to examine the last categories for 1432–52, viz. *Aliens* and *Unidentified*.

ALIENS	1422–32			1432–42			1442–52		
	£	s.	d.	£	s.	d.	£	s.	d.
'Genuine' loans	4,535	6	8	7,900	17	9	4,685	4	0
Fictitious loans	290	12	8	1,566	13	4	3,557	2	0

[1] Op. cit., 295–6.   [2] Ibid., 397, n. 11.
[3] Ibid., 303.

Apart from the small rise in fictitious loans, these figures are of relatively little interest, though the genuine loans do in fact tend to run at a rather higher rate than at any time since the first part of Richard II's reign. In 1432–42 the first place is still held by Genoese houses (as in the previous decade) with £3,183, and Venetians as before take second place, somewhat raising their total once again to £2,333. Florence remains third with £2,184, though this is now nearly twice that city's previous contribution; while John Michele of Milan takes the place of the solitary Lucchese of the previous decade, though only for a small amount. Ten years later Lucca reappears, again at the bottom of the list, in the person of a certain 'Nicholas Giles' (£333 6s. 8d.), and, while Genoa remains the most important lender with £1,931, Venice and Florence change places at £1,166 and £1,253 respectively. Individuals mentioned in the rolls still include Cataneo and Spinola of Genoa in 1432–42, and also the Venetian Contarini, now supported by a house called the Cornerii: new names also include the Lomelini of Genoa and one 'George Luke' of Florence, who with other Florentines finds as much as £1,110. In 1442–52 the Contarini are still there, but the other names have all disappeared, and in their place the principal lender is one 'Lodowicus Scot' and his associates, merchants of Genoa (£1,665 in all). This syndicate also bears the main burden of the fictitious loans (£1,645), together with 'Angelo Tany' and others, of Florence (£1,000); but there are no such special cases in the first period, where the smaller total of bad tallies is more evenly distributed. Incidentally, this rise in fictitious loans reverses the downward trend under this head which had become quite marked since Richard II's time, and, together with the unfortunate tax on aliens, it may even have done something to impair Lancastrian foreign credit—though the civil war probably did more—in the succeeding period.

Finally, we are left with nine or ten persons in each decade whom I cannot satisfactorily identify: it will be seen, however, that the sums involved, though larger than they had been, are still small.

UNIDENTIFIED	1422–32			1432–42			1442–52		
	£	s.	d.	£	s.	d.	£	s.	d.
'Genuine' loans	70	0	0	300	0	0	20	0	0
Fictitious loans	2	10	0	667	17	4	274	16	6½

Among these I can offer no suggestions for the 'genuine' lenders, but there is a little light that might be thrown upon the biggish total for fictitious loans in 1432–42 (only). This is nearly all made up of two large sums—the first of which is a matter of £400 credited to John, lord of 'St. Pey'. I cannot identify this place-name, and may possibly have failed to expand some contraction or have otherwise misread it,[1] but I am inclined to think that, as in certain other cases, it may perhaps be the French title of some king's knight, taken from estates acquired during the French wars, in which event it ought to be transferred to *Household*. The other major entry is a sum of £261 in bad tallies owed to Thomas Bonour and others for bringing the dukes of Bedford and Gloucester and members of the king's council to and from Calais: the man was evidently a shipmaster and the expense again would normally be charged against the household. But, in this case, unlike others, the entry does not definitely say any of these things, and I have therefore thought it better to leave this master and his mates where they are.

To come to general conclusions; the real revenue did not improve in 1432–42 and actually sank by 20% during the ensuing decade, while the book-keeping percentage of gross totals rose from 20% to 30% for both periods. This increase in book-keeping was caused mainly by the doubling of both kinds of loan in 1432–42; but in 1442–52 genuine loans diminished sharply (if we exclude the money from the staplers not recorded in the receipt rolls), whereas fictitious loans rose still further. There was, in other words, an obvious loss of confidence in the later period, accompanied by an ever greater stringency of revenue. When we come to details we shall see that some impressions left by the preceding decades have to be corrected, while others are maintained and even strengthened.

For example, the extravagance and overspending of the royal household obviously increase in geometrical progression as we move towards 1452—a trend which causes no surprise and had in fact been noted, in its embryonic stages, in the previous period. On the other hand, the hopeful tendency observed in 1422–32 for

---

[1] Possibly 'Saintpère'. Mr. Lander (loc. cit.) mentions a lord Saintpère, who was a member of Louis XI's embassy to Edward IV many years later, viz. in 1478. This Saintpère cannot, however, be identified with any certainty with my 'St. Pey'.

not only chancery and exchequer but even local officials to detach themselves successfully from the financial troubles of the crown is emphatically reversed: the two great departments of state come to be involved again in lending and default, though on nothing like the scale of local officials, whose difficulties soon became enormous. This was bound to happen if a policy of peace abroad and economy at home could not be followed, for in the last resort these persons and departments were dependent on the second of these things for their resources and on the first for limiting expenditure. In particular the naïve belief that foreign conquests and border marches would be left undisturbed and could be expected somehow to finance themselves could not long be maintained. The disastrous turn taken by the French war and by relations with the Scots; the weakness of the young king, and the growth of the acquisitive Lancastrian party, not to mention the inadequacy of parliamentary grants, made policies of this sort quite impracticable —however much the commons might refuse to face the facts, and thereby make them far worse than they need have been. Even during the minority the council was invariably left struggling for the barest minimum of necessary supplies, and the attitude of parliament towards the adult Henry and his wife was even more unsympathetic. It was not, in short, government officials, whether locally or at Westminster, who could and did detach themselves from all responsibility from what was happening, but, as the figures show and as the parliamentary record might suggest, it was the smaller burgesses and gentry of the shires. Compared with these even the minor clergy's instinct towards detachment, noted in the previous decade (1422–32), was weak: indeed they seemed to show a somewhat less selfish spirit than the middle-class laymen, and, both by lending and by making grants in convocation, actually increased their rather humble contribution towards the national necessities.

Where the commons failed, however, the minor clergy could do little, for the gap between resources and expenditure was far too wide. There remained only the great men, lay and clerical; the wealthy corporations, such as London and the staple; the limited resources of the duchy of Lancaster itself; and perhaps the alien merchants, if their pockets could be touched. The last of these expedients was the only one not seriously attempted under Henry VI, though the first half of Edward IV's reign was to show how much could be achieved in that direction by a stronger government. Henry VI's time on the contrary was the age of taxes upon aliens—an irritating pin-prick, meant to satisfy the jealousy of the commons, whom it completely failed to move to any greater show of generosity, while in itself it brought in very little and only helped to aggravate the lack of confidence in the Lancastrians felt by wealthy foreigners to whom the crown might otherwise have turned with some effect. It is not that alien loans were discontinued, but rather that they failed to be (appreciably) increased, and that there seemed to be no sense of their potentialities, such as Edward later realized.

This left only the great churchmen with substantial funds in hand—in practice only Beaufort and, to some extent, Chichele—together with the Lancaster feoffees, the Londoners, the staple, and a handful of the wealthier and more public-spirited, or perhaps politically ambitious, laymen. Beaufort and Chichele played their parts magnificently until their dying days—not, it may be, without profit to themselves, but it is only fair to say that it is difficult to see how the government could have been maintained so long without them; nor did it in fact survive their deaths for many years without disaster. It is noticeable, too, that both these great ecclesiastical financiers seemed to operate from time to time in close connection with the feoffees of the duchy of Lancaster, almost as if the full exploitation of the resources of the duchy—a policy which, for one reason or another, ceased to be pursued not long before their deaths—had been practically a condition of their later loans. This is fanciful, no doubt, but it is at least a strange coincidence that the loans from all three sources seem to wax and wane together.

The staplers and the Londoners, whose leading figures, as in Estfeld's case, were frequently identical, had an obvious financial interest in the maintenance of order over anarchy, coupled with the safeguarding, for general trading purposes, of Calais and its hinterland. They were therefore an abiding source of comfort to the crown, and both of them had long been accustomed in emergency to come to its support: both indeed, as will be seen a little later in this book, were ready for another twenty years at least to go on giving that support, whoever sat upon the throne.

Still it was not enough: a government cannot continue indefinitely to live on borrowed money without adequate taxation revenues, more especially when it is continually wasting what small capital resources it may still possess for political and private ends. The spasmodic injections of new money, all of which had got to be repaid, and some of it quite possibly with interest—money coming not only from the sources I have mentioned but also from great men like John and Edmund Beaufort or William de la Pole on one side, or the duke of York upon the other; the more disinterested contributions of financiers and public servants like lord Cromwell or lord Saye and Sele—all these were merely drugs, and dangerous drugs, by which the failing organism was barely kept alive. The same may be said of the willingness of many of these magnates to do service on the marches, or in Ireland, or in France, very largely from their own resources, when they could no longer cash the tallies of assignment they received. It was perhaps a generous gesture and a help for the time being, but these men were not really altruists to that extent: in due course they demanded new and more effective tallies for their service and expenses, and continued to demand until they got them; and so from all these causes the vicious spiral of Lancastrian insolvency began to turn and twist and spin like a tornado.

What was worse, the money question came to be bound up with personal ambitions, fears and hatreds; government of any sort was grudged and regularly denied support, and yet the absence of all 'governance' was found by most to be intolerable. When things came to this pitch only the explosion of a civil war could solve the problem, for if the decadent Lancastrian dynasty could not govern —principally because it had become too weak and selfish, too impoverished and too unpopular to do so—there were others who could claim to take its place. In 1452 the wars of the roses had begun in everything but actual fighting—and the first battle of St. Albans was only three years away.

CHAPTER VIII

CALENDAR, 1452–85

		£	s.	d.	%
MICHAELMAS 1452–3:	Cash	10,685	18	8½	28
	Assigned	14,652	9	0½	38
	Book-keeping	13,337	10	7	34
	Total	38,675	18	4	100

There was obviously some recovery this term from the first Lancastrian collapse, but over a third of the larger gross total was merely book-keeping. Cash, it is true, showed a steep rise, most of it coming from the wool customs of Boston and elsewhere, but it would never have attained its relatively high total—incidentally much the highest for the new decade—without a windfall of £2,463 on 31 January 1453 in the shape of fifty-seven *dona*. There was nothing particularly remarkable about assignment, except that, for a fairly prosperous term, it was distinctly on the low side: only two days topped £1,000 and one £2,000. Though *prestita restituta* disappear for the whole of this decade, book-keeping too might be described as average: it was in fact pretty evenly divided between £7,319 in genuine and £6,017 in fictitious loans. Most of the former was raised in 162 loans (an unusually large number for this period) totalling £5,234, on 31 January (the day of the free gifts), but a further twenty-nine came in on 5 March, yielding another £1,839. By way of contrast, fictitious loans were very evenly distributed over the entire term in relatively small packets: there were in fact only four days on which no tally went wrong.

		£	s	d.	%
EASTER 1453:	Cash	2,656	17	1	4
	Assigned	42,209	17	2½	64
	Book-keeping	21,259	5	5	32
	Total	66,125	19	8½	100

This was the last reasonably prosperous term in the whole of Henry VI's unhappy reign: thanks to it, real revenue in his thirty-first year, taken as a whole, reached the respectable total of £70,000, or just double the most optimistic average that can be obtained for the remainder of the decade, and three or four times as much as he was getting in its later years. There were two closely connected reasons for this temporary improvement—viz. the crisis in the French war, and the fact that the parliament which met at Reading on 6 March was Lancastrian in sentiment and voted him some real money, in order, if possible, to stave off disaster, both at home and abroad. In just over three weeks it had granted, firstly, a whole subsidy (subject to the now established abatements): half of this was to be raised in November 1453 and half a year later. Secondly, tunnage and poundage were granted to the king for life at the existing rates, and the wool duties at increased rates: indeed the latter were so sharply increased, especially for aliens, that the increment could not be collected, and had to be remitted for five years in 1454. The poll-taxes on aliens were also granted to the king for life, and those on alien merchants in particular were raised and made to include not only travellers staying more than six weeks in the country but even naturalized persons. In addition, both convocations gave tenths and an elaborate scheme was worked out by which the country was to provide the king with up to 20,000 archers for six months' home service at its own cost. As the lords, Wales and Cheshire did not pay the ordinary fifteenths and tenths, it was agreed during the second, or summer, session of this parliament that they should find 6,000 of these men between them, leaving 14,000 (reduced to 13,000 later by the king's special grace) for the shires and boroughs to raise. But the needs of Aquitaine were so urgent in this summer of 1453 that the king eventually sacrificed the whole arrangement, which Ramsay calculates[1] was equivalent in value to as much as three subsidies, for an additional half-subsidy, payable in the spring of 1454. In spite of this, the accumulated charges on the royal revenue had now reached such a point that all these grants together could have made little impression on them: for example, £41,000 was owing to the staplers on account of Calais alone—£19,000 by the hands of the duke of Buckingham for former services there, and the balance by the

[1] *Lancaster and York*, II, 160–2, for the whole of this passage.

hands of the existing captain of Calais, now the duke of Somerset.[1] The new grants were all immediately anticipated as far as possible: thus, though real revenue was almost doubled, actual cash receipts fell heavily, while assignment was nearly trebled. In fact, if it had not been for a large cash payment of £1,000 or so from the Hull customs on 1 May, cash would have been negligible. Most of the assignment took place during the last fortnight in July, together with 8 and 12 June and 8 July: on practically all of these occasions it was the lay and clerical subsidies of the coming exchequer year which were being heavily anticipated, very often in favour of Calais (e.g. £6,000 on 25 July). 'Genuine' loans were doubled at £14,771: of this amount the treasurer of England, John Tiptoft, earl of Worcester, provided £2,333 6s. 8d. on 18 May, and some forty-four other lenders no less than £10,401 on 16 July: the remaining loans were small but numerous, e.g. fifty-six in one day (11 April) produced only just over £1,000. In spite of the great increase in assignment, fictitious loans remained creditably low at only £6,487, and though there were only three days in all on which no tallies went wrong, there were no outstanding sufferers. Finally, there were two or three small *dona* during the term, but only for minute amounts.

	£	s.	d.	%
MICHAELMAS 1453–4: Cash	1,780	7	11½	6
Assigned	21,405	4	11½	68
Book-keeping	8,146	19	5½	26
Total	31,332	12	4½	100

Although the Lancastrian parliament of the first half of 1453 entered on its third session in November, it was immediately adjourned again till February, and, eventually, to Westminster. Here it proved to be much less amenable than it had been at Reading: in fact it fell under Yorkist influence, and, in the case of the new wool duties already mentioned, actually reduced grants previously voted instead of making any new ones.[2] As most of the

[1] *Lancaster and York*, II, 160–2. Cf. Miss W. I. Haward, op. cit., 303; she says that £41,000 in all was put at the disposal of the duke of Somerset alone by the staplers for the purpose of paying the garrison's wages, 1451–5—most of which does not figure in the receipt rolls.

[2] Ramsay, *Lancaster and York*, II, 163, 167, 169–74.

new revenue had in any case been anticipated during the preceding term, it is not surprising to find that the real revenue is dropping once more—to a point indeed actually below, though not far below, the level reached before any of the new grants had been made. Cash payments in particular were much debilitated, and there were six days on which no cash at all appeared. Assignment was still practised valiantly and on the whole successfully, though only at just half the previous rate. Some of it, however, showed a curious affinity to the obsolescent prest system: for example, on 19 February about £3,000 was assigned to Master William Clyff, clerk of works, *de remanencia compoti sui*, which suggests that this large sum was simply written off an even larger amount that had already been advanced to him. Not much was achieved in the way of borrowing this term: for 'genuine' loans fell to £3,500, including a sum of £1,163 6s. 8d. lent on 20 October by the treasurer of England *et aliis*. Fictitious loans, however, again shrank, rather encouragingly, to £4,646, evenly distributed over every day but two and never very large at any one time: it is interesting to note among them the receipt of three bad tallies for £135 on the customs of London, Boston and Ipswich, on 30 November by the president and fellows of Queen's[1] College, Cambridge.

		£	s.	d.	%
EASTER 1454:	Cash	1,508	13	1½	4
	Assigned	23,480	9	3½	59
	Book-keeping	14,774	5	7	37
	Total	39,763	8	0	100

The additional half-subsidy, payable this spring, which had been obtained in return for surrendering the grant of archers, may have done something to increase the gross total again, but real revenue was very little up. Cash in fact continued to shrink slowly, and again none at all was paid on six days. Assignment, however, rose by rather more than cash had fallen and was again fairly successful, the most outstanding achievement being the transfer to the staple on 12 July of £4,666 13s. 4d., all assigned on the clerical tenth, normally not a very safe security, without a single tally going wrong. 'Genuine' loans, too, reached their last respectable figure of

[1] Not yet Queens' (in the plural).

the reign with £9,906, half of which came from the staple on 6 June (viz. the £4,666 13s. 4d. already mentioned as repaid *via* the clerical tenth), and the rest from a variety of smaller lenders. Among these may be mentioned the Londoner, Philip Malpas, who advanced £1,000 in all on 24 and 29 May. Fictitious loans rose by £200, as might be expected, but their total of £4,868 was still not large and was for the most part well distributed, though on 25 May the earl of Oxford failed to collect £831 assigned on the lay subsidy in twenty-two tallies, *pro custodia maris*.

		£	s.	d.	%
MICHAELMAS 1454–5:	Cash	3,122	9	3	12
	Assigned	17,207	15	5½	66
	Book-keeping	5,731	17	5½	22
	Total	26,062	2	2	100

No parliament sat during this term and the revenue began to sag a little ominously. Book-keeping, however, was relatively low, so that the large apparent fall in gross revenue was not as bad as it looks. Cash in fact was more than doubled, though assignment fell rather heavily: the latter continued to be spread evenly throughout the term. Genuine loans were more than halved at £4,163, £1,500 of which came from the earl of Worcester on 5 December, and £2,193 on 28 March in nineteen loans, the largest of which was one of £800 from the earl of Wiltshire. Fictitious loans fell to £1,568 and were none of them of importance: moreover, there were actually ten days out of twenty-seven on which none at all occurred.

		£	s.	d.	%
EASTER 1455:	Cash	1,307	15	3	10
	Assigned	7,711	7	8½	57
	Book-keeping	4,460	13	11	33
	Total	13,479	16	10½	100

Although there were to be four terms with even lower totals in this disastrous decade, the figures show that the final catastrophe had begun. For the first time on record real revenue was under £10,000; there were only eleven days of business at the receipt;

and the first battle of St. Albans was fought on 22 May, in the middle of the term. Cash reached a new low level, and even assignment sank to £7,711, £1,100 of which was marked *ad dampnandum* on 7 July, at any rate in one of the two chamberlains' rolls.[1] There were still a few genuine loans, but these came mainly from Yorkist sources after the battle, in order to keep the captured government alive and functioning: thus £1,100 was lent on 31 May by the new treasurer of England, lord Bourchier, who was brother-in-law to the victorious duke of York.[2] There were twenty-eight other lenders, however, eight of whom produced £1,044 before the fight, and twenty (apart from Bourchier) about another £1,000 after it, so that genuine loans from all sources finally stood at well over £3,000; fictitious, on the other hand, were only £1,040.

		£	s.	d.	%
MICHAELMAS 1455–6:	Cash	1,823	1	9	11
	Assigned	13,891	14	6	80
	Book-keeping	1,551	3	5	9
	Total	17,265	19	8	100

The first battle of St. Albans was quickly succeeded by the summoning of a Yorkist parliament, which met at Westminster just before the end of the Easter term 1455. Three weeks later it was prorogued to 12 November, and, after a second session of a month's duration, was again prorogued to 14 January 1456. This third session, which lasted until early March, was the only one in which the financial situation—supposed to have been eased by the ending of the French war—was so much as considered: needless to say, no grants were made. It was thought sufficient to repeal the Lancastrian resumption act of 1453, together with the numerous exemptions made in 1451, and then to pass a new act of resumption. Apart from this, and from some unsubstantiated grumblings in the commons about alleged extortions practised by the exchequer, the only financial event of any importance was the making of an arrangement under which the merchants of the staple would receive security for the large advances made by them on account

---

[1] That of the royal chamberlain, usually the more accurate of the two.
[2] Ramsay, *Lancaster and York*, II, 184. On 15 July Bourchier lent a further £566 13s. 4d.

of wages for the garrison of Calais.[1] In this particular term, however, hardly any money was raised, for genuine loans amounted to
only £793 6s. 8d. Fictitious, too, came to no more than £757,
although assignment was fairly high again, considering that cash
was still well under £2,000 and the total real revenue for the term
only £15,714. It is obvious that in this first year of civil war it was
only anticipation of such income as there was which kept the
temporarily Yorkist-controlled government going—partly with the
help of customs (e.g. £2,094 on 16 October alone) and partly from
a sum of £3,933 19s. 4d. *per parliamentum anno xxxiv pro expensis
hospicii appunctuat'*. Yet this last allocation depended not only on
the depleted resources of the duchy of Lancaster but actually on
customs revenue as well:[2] £1,700 was drawn against it on 16
December, and this, together with £1,537 on 18 March, represented the only other single days of sizeable assignment.

		£	s.	d.	%
EASTER 1456:	Cash	2,031	18	2	16
	Assigned	7,028	3	8	57
	Book-keeping	3,311	9	9	27
	Total	12,371	11	7	100

The ascendancy of Richard, duke of York, continued throughout
this term and the revenue dwindled accordingly: net income in
fact was only a few pounds more than the low level of the previous
summer, when there had been actual fighting. Cash, however,
again came up a little, mainly owing to a windfall of £940 on
17 July from Gervase Clifton, treasurer of Calais, *in obligacionibus
divers' merc' de portu Cales' eidem Thes' auctoritate parliamenti pro
Cales' assignat' et ad Receptam Scacc' per dictum Thes' liberat'*—
according to the original arrangement, of course, this sum should
have been paid over to the Calais garrison direct as wages, and not

---

[1] *Lancaster and York*, II, 190–1. Large sums had already been advanced
by the staplers for this object, according to Ramsay, quoting Enrolled
Accounts, 33–8 Henry VI (1454–60), which, he says, show a total for
these six years of £49,580. The receipt rolls do not record anything like
this amount, but cf. Miss Haward, op. cit., for some additions to them.
Even so, nothing like this total can be reached without generous allowance
for the last two years of Somerset's alleged borrowings of 1451–5: above,
p. 274, n. 1.

[2] *Lancaster and York*, pp. 190–1.

into the exchequer. The main fall in the term came in assignment, which was nearly halved, and reached four figures on only two days. Book-keeping would have been completely negligible but for a genuine loan on 2 July of £2,530 from the staple: this sum, to which perhaps should be added the £940 already mentioned, seems to have been the first-fruits of the new scheme for financing Calais, though it is possible it was merely additional thereto.

		£	s.	d.	%
MICHAELMAS 1456-7:	Cash	1,996	13	4½	16
	Assigned	6,474	15	9½	53
	Book-keeping	3,720	8	11½	31
	Total	12,191	18	1½	100

This winter saw the more or less peaceful extrusion of the leading Yorkists from the king's council by the efforts of queen Margaret, but no improvement in the revenue, in spite of a few very small attaints, the proceeds of which, totalling only some £75, were all assigned on 27 January 1457. Real revenue in fact was down again, and indeed within £225 of its lowest for the reign. Thanks to a single tally for £865,[1] paid in from the London customs on 10 February, cash was still about its usual level, and the burden of decrease was again borne almost wholly by assignment. Book-keeping was little different in amount from what it had been, but this time the staple found only £1,100 (on 23 November) out of genuine loans totalling £2,707. Of the rest, the new Lancastrian treasurer of England, the earl of Shrewsbury, produced £533 13s. 4d. on 19 February, and the rest came in driblets through the whole term from some sixteen smaller lenders. All the larger fictitious loans occurred on 8 February (£775), but the term total under this head, though double what it was at Easter, was still only £1,013.

		£	s.	d.	%
EASTER 1457:	Cash	1,930	9	1	9
	Assigned	13,607	6	8	65
	Book-keeping	5,558	14	3	26
	Total	21,096	10	0	100

[1] Contrast a tally for one penny on 27 January, paid in by the Berkshire collectors of the last fifteenth and tenth (now extremely overdue).

The Lancastrians seem to have continued in control throughout this summer, and in spite of the sacking of Sandwich by the French and the plundering of Fowey by the Bretons,[1] real revenue rose appreciably. Most of the increase took place in assignment, which was more than doubled at £13,607, over half of it on three days in the middle of July alone. Cash was down a trifle, while book-keeping rose: about three-fifths of the latter consisted of genuine, and the balance of fictitious, loans. In the first of these two classes the staple now produced only £500 (on 1 June): though of all the other nineteen or twenty lenders none seems to have produced more than this, it was certainly far less than was expected. Fictitious loans again more than doubled their total for the preceding term: the principal sufferer, rather oddly, was the treasurer himself the earl of Shrewsbury, with £972 in five tallies.

		£	s.	d.	%
MICHAELMAS 1457–8:	Cash	2,068	17	6	9
	Assigned	12,825	14	3	56
	Book-keeping	7,880	15	4	35
	Total	22,775	7	1	100

Gross revenue continued to mount, though very slowly, this term, during the latter part of which a great council at Westminster resulted in the acceptance of a royal award designed to 'heal the blood feud of the day of St. Albans'.[2] The most interesting feature of this agreement from the financial point of view was the transfer by the duke of York of royal tallies of assignment worth £3,333 6s. 8d. to the widowed duchess of Somerset and her children, and of £666 13s. 4d. in tallies held by the earl of Warwick to the Cliffords.[3] The duke of York at least was able to recoup himself by shipping a quantity of wool duty-free,[4] thereby still further weakening the customs, the last remaining pillar of the revenue. Real income was in fact already down by some £640, entirely in assignment: cash rose a little and book-keeping by a good deal

[1] Ramsay, *Lancaster and York*, II, 202.
[2] Ibid., II, 209.
[3] Tallies of assignment seem to have been freely transferred and discounted from a much earlier date, but the fact is seldom so openly avowed.
[4] Ramsay, *Lancaster and York*, loc. cit.

móre. The only details of any interest fall under the latter head: thus, of the £4,621 in genuine loans the loyal earl of Shrewsbury (who was still treasurer) provided £1,559 early in December, while the balance came on various days during the term from some thirteen other lenders. Fictitious loans at £3,259 again showed an increase, but they had risen to over £3,000 for the last time in the reign and none was of any special consequence, though it is interesting to find the celebrated Sir John Fortescue among the recipients of bad tallies, if only for the small sum of £10.

EASTER 1458:		£	s.	d.	%
	Cash	873	1	8	4
	Assigned	16,388	15	8½	81
	Book-keeping	2,951	18	2	15
	Total	20,213	15	6½	100

During this summer the prestige of the Yorkists was increased by the earl of Warwick's naval depredations at the expense of Germans and Castilians, and by their opening of negotiations on a party basis with the duke of Burgundy; but as far as the Lancastrians were concerned there was a continuance of the uneasy truce in the civil war. Real revenue actually rose again, but entirely in assignment: cash indeed almost disappeared in this term and the next, hardly any at all being received after the first five days of term. Assignment was spread fairly evenly over the whole summer. Book-keeping was greatly reduced, and was almost equally divided between genuine and fictitious loans. The staple produced the only large contribution in the former category, with £843 6s. 8d. on 15 May: there were no details of any significance under fictitious loans.

MICHAELMAS 1458–9:		£	s.	d.	%
	Cash	793	7	10½	4
	Assigned	11,556	18	5	65
	Book-keeping	5,549	10	6	31
	Total	17,899	16	9½	100

The division of the realm into two armed camps continued steadily throughout the winter, but there was still no open fighting. The

Lancastrians dared not summon parliament and subsisted miserably on the life grant of the customs, subject to such deductions as that made early in 1458 in favour of the duke of York—and these were very numerous. Naturally the revenue began to sink again: the net figure in fact fell some £5,000. Cash reached its lowest figure for the reign, and even assignment was over £4,800 down.[1] Recourse was had to genuine loans, which rose to £3,431, but there were only two of any size, viz. £1,000 from the staple on 28 December and the same from the new treasurer of England, the earl of Wiltshire, on 17 February: nineteen other lenders could raise only £1,431. Fictitious loans at £2,118 were slightly up again for the last time in the reign, but as usual they were small and numerous, rather than few and large, well scattered over the entire term and extremely miscellaneous in character.

EASTER 1459:		£	s.	d.	%
	Cash	1,060	11	6½	11
	Assigned	7,418	17	2½	76
	Book-keeping	1,271	1	8½	13
	Total	9,750	10	5½	100

Open fighting was resumed this summer, although the only important engagement, the battle of Blore Heath, did not take place until 23 September, long after the brief Easter term was over. None the less the violence and uncertainties of the time were such that it is not surprising to find the gross revenue at its lowest for the entire reign, and the real revenue almost at its lowest. Cash receipts were indeed a little up, but assignment, though practised on every one of the eighteen days of business, was a further £4,000 down.[2] The small book-keeping total was almost wholly accounted for by a single genuine loan made by the staplers on 21 June: the rest consisted of nothing but a lot of small fictitious loans.

[1] One special feature of this term is the large number of very small forfeitures of an average value of about £1 found towards the end of the roll, and all of them assigned.

[2] Over a third of the reduced total was for the protection of the marches against the Scots: thus nearly £1,100 was assigned to Henry Percy for the east march on 9 May alone, and the only other large assignment was one of much the same size, made on 22 June for the earls of Salisbury and Warwick as wardens of the west march.

		£	s.	d.	%
MICHAELMAS 1459–60:	Cash	1,463	18	11	10
	Assigned	7,399	12	10½	51
	Book-keeping	5,637	13	1	39
	Total	14,501	4	10½	100

In spite of the Yorkist victory at Blore Heath, the defection of certain professional soldiers in October[1] led to one of those sudden reversals of fortune characteristic of the period, and to the summoning of a Lancastrian parliament, which sat at Coventry during the last weeks of the year. This parliament was almost entirely given over to the attainder of the Yorkists and the establishment of the Lancastrian succession: no grant was made, or even asked for, and, though gross revenue was up, real revenue was little more than in the previous term. Such increase as there was came under the head of cash: assignment was at practically its Easter total, though this time there were three fairly big days (23 February and 1 and 3 March) instead of two. The inflation of the gross total was mainly caused by a jump of some £4,400 in book-keeping, and this again was wholly in genuine loans. A few of these were scattered through the early part of the term, but they were mostly raised on 3 March, when fifty-seven lenders, chiefly magnates and churchmen, produced £4,686 *per consilium*—which may be regarded as the Lancastrian investment in the campaign of 1460. Fictitious loans came to only £201, leaving the 'genuine' total for the whole term £5,436, produced by seventy-six lenders.

		£	s.	d.	%
EASTER 1460:	Cash	1,210	12	1	12
	Assigned	7,039	8	7½	72
	Book-keeping	1,584	17	0	16
	Total	9,834	17	8½	100

This term is rather odd in that it virtually ends on 11 June, a full fortnight before the Yorkist landing at Sandwich which ushers in their victory and period of direct rule; but then adds the solitary day of 4 September. In the interval the decisive battle of Northampton had been fought (10 July) and the government had changed

---

[1] Ramsay, *Lancaster and York*, II, 216.

hands, so that the Yorkists must be regarded as responsible for the last day, but the Lancastrians for the remainder of the roll. Even with the Yorkist appendix, however, the totals are fantastically low: real revenue was the smallest for the reign, and even gross revenue was very little above the low point of 1459. Cash and assignment were both down—the latter to its second lowest figure of the decade—while without the special Yorkist contribution of 4 September book-keeping would have been practically negligible. This contribution took the form of twenty-six genuine loans totalling £1,182 and bringing the term total under that head to £1,409: fictitious loans (all of them Lancastrian) were only £175 in all.

		£	s.	d.	%
MICHAELMAS 1460–1:	Cash	2,078	0	11½	10
	Assigned	11,240	10	2	51
	Book-keeping	8,675	2	5½	39
	Total	21,993	13	7	100

After the victory of Northampton a Yorkist parliament had been summoned and met at Westminster on 7 October. It was mainly concerned with the duke of York's claim to the throne, his recognition as Henry's legitimate successor and his proclamation as protector of the realm; no grants were made. Hearing of the Lancastrian revival engineered by queen Margaret in the north, the duke caused this parliament to be dissolved early in December and marched to meet her—only to be routed and killed at Wakefield before the year was out. The Lancastrians advanced towards London and won the second battle of St. Albans on 17 February, but, contenting themselves with the recovery of the king's person, they retired again, leaving London to the Yorkists. On 4 March duke Richard's son, Edward, assumed the crown at Westminster and within a fortnight was marching northward in pursuit of his antagonists—but by this time the exchequer term which had coincided with these great events was over. It is obvious that during it the Yorkists were in full financial control of Westminster and London, and at least of southern England, which may account for a net revenue increase to the highest figure since 1458. The smallish rise in cash was mainly owing to a £1,000 fine paid by Eleanor Broune, the widow of an attainted Lancastrian, but assignment rose much more spectacularly. This in turn was partly caused by the fact that on 8 October, the first day of term, the new Yorkist treasurer, lord Bourchier, had made a loan of £2,538, for which security had to be found in the shape of tallies of assignment. These were duly provided on the 15th and helped to raise the total of assignment for that day to £4,771—a quite exceptionally high figure at this date. Apart from these points there is little else to note about this term, except that a fresh set of five large genuine loans (worth £2,161 in all) made on 27 January helped to bring the total under that head to £7,790, the highest for seven years. Fictitious loans came up again a little to £884 and contained one interesting detail, viz. the subsequent honouring by Edward IV of three bad tallies for £300 in favour of the treasurer of Henry VI's household: administrative continuity could hardly be carried further.

		£	s.	d.	%
EASTER 1461:	Cash	3,537	19	6½	11
	Assigned	9,174	4	7	28
	Book-keeping	19,680	3	10	61
	Total	32,392	7	11½	100

Edward IV's great victory at Towton on 29 March had broken all opposition for the time being and assured him his possession of the throne. The summer was taken up with the coronation, followed by a royal progress through the south and west of England; and if it was not possible to restore the revenue at such short notice and without parliamentary assistance, at least the opportunity was taken to replenish the exchequer with some really large loans. It is these which bring book-keeping up to its highest figure for the past eight years, and it is mainly this book-keeping which in turn inflates gross revenue: real revenue was actually about £600 down. This fall took place entirely in assignment, which was not sufficiently offset by a cash increase. Most of the genuine loans were raised on 22 June, just a week before the coronation, when London finally committed itself to the Yorkists in no uncertain manner, the mayor and aldermen advancing £11,000. About eighty other lenders had produced another £6,679 by the end of the term, and on 26 September there was even a *donum* of £266 13s. 4d. from Henry's own foundation at Eton, or at any rate from its provost,

William Westbury. The staple also showed its political catholicity by contributing a loan of £1,000 (included in the above figures) on 23 July: the church in general was also a conspicuous lender. Although assignment fell, fictitious loans rose to £1,910, but there was no special victim.

MICHAELMAS 1461–2: No surviving roll.

EASTER 1462:		£	s.	d.	%
	Cash	1,093	12	11½	6
	Assigned	10,899	2	4	56
	Book-keeping	7,526	10	2	38
	Total	19,519	5	5½	100

Edward IV's first parliament had sat from November to December, but had been almost exclusively concerned with recognizing Edward's title to the throne, attainting the Lancastrians and annexing their historic duchy to the crown: no grant was made, and it remained doubtful whether the customs dues conceded to Henry VI for life could legally be collected by the new, if 'rightful', king.[1] In fact the only financial assistance other than loans which Edward had received in 1461 came from the convocation of Canterbury, which had given him a tenth; and though parliament had merely been prorogued on 21 December to May 1462 no grant seems to have resulted, even during the latter year. Hence the revenue sagged again towards Lancastrian levels: the main difference in the new picture lay simply in rather more book-keeping, made up chiefly of fictitious loans. The substantial increase to £4,226 under the last-named head may perhaps be explained in part by the rise in assignment: however, the only really heavy cancellations were those of 14 July, when lord Montagu received seven bad tallies on Sandwich worth £1,563. Genuine loans were down to £3,299, provided by about thirty-five miscellaneous lenders at various dates spread over the entire term: they would have been more than doubled (and assignment too would have been greatly increased) if the treasurer of England, now once more the earl of Worcester (who had changed sides), had been able to carry out his intention of advancing £4,000 to the crown on

[1] Ramsay, *Lancaster and York*, II, 285.

20 May. But, it is noted, *istud mutuum cancellatur hic pro eo quod nulla inde fuit recepta ad Receptam. Ideo omnes tallie cum foliis earundem pro eodem mutuo assignate sunt restitute et dampnate et non est infra summam huius diei.* Following this, thirty tallies of assignment, intended as security for the loan, were vacated on 1 June.[1]

		£	s.	d.	%
MICHAELMAS 1462–3:	Cash	323	9	4	4
	Assigned	6,959	8	11	73
	Book-keeping	2,218	18	4½	23
	Total	9,501	16	7½	100

Unfortunately the only surviving roll for this term—that of the treasurer, John Tiptoft, earl of Worcester—is so fragmentary that the above totals have little meaning: perhaps half the roll is missing. It includes only part of one day before the end of 1462, and although it then runs continuously to the end of 5 March 1463 it is finally cut off so abruptly that it is possible some more days may be missing. What is left shows a cash receipt of negligible amount, but reasonable figures in other respects: of the book-keeping it may be worth mentioning that £981 came from genuine, and £1,237 from fictitious, loans, none of them in either category of any individual interest.

		£	s.	d.	%
EASTER 1463:	Cash	2,500	4	11	3
	Assigned	49,794	19	6	71
	Book-keeping	18,119	12	6	26
	Total	70,414	16	11	100

The substantial recovery which took place in this term is remarkable: both gross and net totals were the second highest of their kind in the whole period 1462–75.[2] This recovery was clearly due

[1] The treasurer's roll for this term ends in the middle of 21 July, and the royal chamberlain's roll is fragmentary. Warwick (or Beauchamp) chamberlain adds 21 August, but this too is incomplete, although it is probable that there is not much missing which is not to be found in any of these three surviving rolls.

[2] It should be noted, however, that the gross total recorded in the only complete roll for this term is £8,032 less than mine. I can only explain this (after repeated checking) by supposing that this lower total—which

to the financial help given by the parliament which, after two adjournments, met at Westminster on 29 April. It is true that the commons' grant of a full subsidy (at first, without deductions, worth £37,000) was not announced until 18 June, and was made payable only on 1 August for the first half, and 22 November for the second. But it could be, and was in fact, anticipated by assignment the moment that the existence of such a grant was known: moreover, both Canterbury and York had given clerical tenths (York in fact a tenth and a half) during the previous summer, and these were still in process of collection. It was unfortunate that the commons at the last moment postponed collection of the second half of their new grant to March 1464, and furthermore repented of their resolution not to deduct from it the £6,000 abatement which had become traditional since 1433. But the ill effect of these decisions was at least delayed for a term or two: in the meantime the immediate results of the grant were reflected in the receipt roll. Cash, as might be expected in these circumstances, remained low, and might not have reached £1,000 but for a handsome profit on the king's personal trading account in wool and cloth, recorded on 23 June, when the day total was raised to £1,872 by the sale of two large shipments, one of cloth and one of wool, *ut fact' Regis per licenc' ipsi domini Regis*. Assignment remained virtuously low until after the commons' announcement of their grant, after which, however, daily totals rose at once to four figures. The heaviest days were 7 July, when over £14,000 was assigned on the new subsidy —£10,000 of it in favour of Calais; nearly as much again during the next week; and finally just under £11,000 on 18 August: the total for the term was thus impressive. Although fictitious loans rose to nearly £4,000, the highest figure for the decade, they were well distributed and individual losses were not high: the bulk of the book-keeping in any case came from the £14,053 received in genuine loans. Something like seventy to eighty lenders were involved, but the only heavy contributors were Sir Ralph Verney,

after all is only a marginal note in the royal chamberlain's roll—was based on rough day totals of a similar kind, many of which have obviously been subjected to erasure and correction—presumably *after* the scribe's term total had been reached. The sum of these day totals in their final form has also been carefully checked by me and is only £173 7s. 9d. less than my own term total, which is more or less the normal margin of error on the scribe's side, or mine.

alderman of London, and his associates, who put up £1,000 on
27 June, and the mayor and merchants of the staple, who advanced
£3,436 on the same date: in addition, the new treasurer of England,
lord Grey of Ruthin, produced £1,164 on 27–28 June, £67 on
23 July, and £2,000 on 18 and 23 August (£1,000 each day), and
was ultimately repaid one penny too much—a fact which is carefully noted in the roll! Finally, it may be worth mentioning that
there was a small cash *donum* of £17 on 18 August, and that
prestita restituta make their only appearance in twenty-five years
on 23 June, with the restoration of a prest of £125 odd by John
Tiptoft, earl of Worcester, possibly in connection with his resigna-
tion of the treasurership, which took place at approximately that
time.

MICHAELMAS 1463–4.   No surviving roll.

		£	s.	d.	%
EASTER 1464:	Cash	1,677	7	4	11
	Assigned	7,419	16	1	48
	Book-keeping	6,436	16	3	41
	Total	15,533	19	8	100

Although the second half of the subsidy voted in June 1463 must
have been in process of collection throughout the Easter term of
1464, it had now become subject to a last-minute abatement of
£6,000, which must have reduced its total yield to not more than
£12,500 (assuming that the whole abatement was borne by the
second half-subsidy alone). It is also possible that most of this had
been anticipated by assignment during the intervening Michaelmas
term, for which no rolls survive: in any case there is little trace of
the grant in the scanty real revenue for Easter 1464. Of the small
cash element this contained, nearly half was produced by more
royal trading profits on wool and cloth shipments, recorded on
18 May. Assignment was also very low, and much of it was
arranged on 7 May alone as security for a loan of £3,000, raised
from Sir Walter Blount, the treasurer of Calais, on the 4th. This
was the only really large loan of the term, though genuine loans
came in all to £5,054, produced by some twenty-one lenders.
Fictitious loans were again on the low side, and well distributed,

at £1,382, while the only other items of interest were two cash *dona*, made towards the end of the term—one, it is true, of no more than £2, but the other of £100, from one 'Robert' Nottingham, of whom there is no trace; but the name is possibly a slip for Sir William Nottingham, king's councillor and attorney-general.

		£	s.	d.	%
MICHAELMAS 1464-5:	Cash	598	5	2	2
	Assigned	7,719	11	1½	29
	Book-keeping	18,400	2	2	69
	Total	26,717	18	5½	100

The sudden jump in the gross total is obviously entirely due to borrowing: in the absence of any parliament, real revenue was in fact slightly lower than before, with cash down to the second lowest figure for this period. Assignment remained steady, and was more evenly distributed: thus from 6 November 1464 to 2 March 1465 there were five days on which it just about reached, or slightly exceeded, £1,000. Fictitious loans were only a little higher than before at £1,665, but genuine loans rose to £16,735. The staplers contributed the most to this total with £11,629 in three tallies, mostly on 10 but also on 27 November: Sir Walter Blount, now treasurer of England, was runner-up with £4,500 contributed at various times between 27 November and 25 January: compared with these, the eight or nine other lenders were of no importance.

EASTER 1465: No surviving rolls.

		£	s.	d.	%
MICHAELMAS 1465-6:	Cash	2,503	10	0½	5
	Assigned	25,865	2	10½	48
	Book-keeping	25,560	5	8½	47
	Total	53,928	18	7½	100

Once again the large apparent increase in the revenue was to some extent illusory, since nearly half of it was book-keeping. None the less there was a genuine, if short-lived, improvement; for a real income of £28,368, though far from satisfactory, was at least £20,000 more than the surviving rolls of 1464-5 and 1466-7 record; in fact it was the fourth highest total of this kind in the period. This may be attributed in part to the reorganization of the customs carried out by what Ramsay calls[1] 'the oft-adjourned Parliament of 1463' as late as January 1465. The main point about this measure was that Edward's right to collect customs at all was at last given parliamentary sanction in the shape of a specific grant for life at much the same levels as in Henry's reign —except that the prohibitive duties nominally payable by aliens were reduced by about 25%. But this was all: no subsidy was granted, and its place was taken by the favourite parliamentary measure of a lands resumption act, rendered futile, as usual, by no less than 288 clauses of exemption. On the other hand, the years 1464–6 saw another financial expedient—apparently carried out without consulting parliament at all—in the shape of a debasement of the currency. According to Ramsay,[2] the recoinage involved earned a profit for the crown of £15,428 between 1 September 1464 and 29 September 1466, and this may well help to explain the sharp rise in real revenue in this, the second of the two receipt rolls, which are all that survive for the whole of those two years. When the figures for 1465–6 are more closely examined, however, the first thing that strikes the eye is the relatively meagre increase in cash—much of which was not brought in until the very end of the term, e.g. a fine of £666 13s. 4d. paid on 3 March by Thomas Frowyk of London, gentleman, et aliis (the reason is not given). Assignment, on the other hand, reached its third highest total for the 1460's. Some of this, it is true, was really of a book-keeping nature: thus two or three thousand pounds were assigned to the treasurer, Sir Walter Blount (now lord Mountjoy), from the *remanencia* of his own account while treasurer of Calais. But the bulk of it was genuine enough, e.g. the £6,200 on 14 December alone, wholly assigned upon the customs. The further rise in book-keeping is mainly accounted for by a jump in genuine loans to £24,144: fictitious loans rose only a little to £2,166,[3] in sympathy

---

[1] *Lancaster and York*, II, 308, for details.

[2] Ibid., 312–13. See A. E. Feaveryear, *The Pound Sterling*, pp. 36–42, for a more professional and up-to-date treatment.

[3] It should be noted that (rather exceptionally at this date) there was at least one large fictitious loan, viz. on 10 March, when yet another treasurer of England, lord Rivers, was unable to cash six tallies on the customs of Southampton (principally) and London, totalling £1,035 1s. 8d.

with assignment. Among the real lenders, the treasurers of England, viz. the new lord Mountjoy and his successor, lord Rivers, were pre-eminent: the former lent £6,200 on 7 December and the latter £11,273 6s. 8d. on 8 March. There were, however, over forty other lenders (thirty-seven, counting lord Rivers, on 8 March alone), who produced the balance of some £6,671 between them.

EASTER 1466: No surviving rolls.

N.B. This is the year of the 'act of retainer', by which the Calais staple assumed the privilege of collecting all the Calais customs, together with the responsibility for paying the garrison out of the proceeds. For details, see Professor Eileen Power, *Studies in English Trade in the Fifteenth Century*, pp. 74–5.

		£	s.	d.	%
MICHAELMAS 1466–7:	Cash	1,164	1	6	8
	Assigned	7,774	6	11½	48
	Book-keeping	6,957	14	11	44
	Total	15,896	3	4½	100

As no new parliament had met since the last surviving roll had been compiled and any profit that there may have been on the recoinage was now exhausted, it is not surprising to find ourselves confronted with a steep fall in both gross and real revenue. Assignment, of course, had much more to lose than cash, and duly lost it; but both were well down. Book-keeping, though also reduced, was almost wholly made up of genuine loans: fictitious loans were scattered, small and generally negligible. Most of the real lending was done for the first time for very many years by aliens, for Edward, like his namesake nearly two centuries earlier, was having recourse to the Italians: thus early in November the Florentine house of the Caniziani advanced him £5,255. The remaining half-dozen loans of the term were all obviously on a much smaller scale than this and do not call for any separate comment.

EASTER 1467: No surviving rolls.

MICHAELMAS 1467–8: No surviving rolls.

		£	s.	d.	%
EASTER 1468:	Cash	6,478	1	4½	7
	Assigned	47,648	5	3	55
	Book-keeping	33,077	2	0	38
	Total	87,203	8	7½	100

The parliament of June 1467 merely passed another ineffective resumption act,[1] but when it met again in May 1468 it proceeded to make the first real grants for years, in answer to the chancellor's announcement that the king intended to renew the war with France. No less than two subsidies were voted, to be raised by half-yearly instalments beginning in November, while the convocation of Canterbury also granted a tenth. The moment that these grants were known large loans were raised on the strength of them and heavy assignment began: thus on 10 and 13 June £7,500 was assigned, mainly on the clerical subsidy, while throughout July, August and September heavy drafts on the impending lay subsidy,[2] made by way of security for repeated borrowings, brought the term total for assignment to what was not only the highest figure since 1463 but easily the highest for the rest of the whole Yorkist régime. Cash payments, on the contrary, were, with one exception, trifling: indeed there were none at all on ten days out of nineteen. The exception was on 2 August, when the huge fine of £5,333 6s. 8d. was collected in a single cash payment from Sir Thomas Coke, or Cook, alderman and former mayor of London, who was incriminated in an alleged intrigue of the Lancastrians, details of which had been extracted under torture from the servant of a well-known Lancastrian refugee caught with letters at Queenborough. The fact that Coke had previously been acting as Edward's own financial agent, and had been knighted at the coronation of queen Elizabeth, may account for the size of the fine.[3] The large book-keeping total was again mainly due to genuine loans, which, with the excuse of war, reached their highest total for the first part of Edward IV's reign. Some 176 lenders

[1] Ramsay, *Lancaster and York*, II, 324–5.
[2] On 5 and 11 July large sums were also assigned on the profits of the Tower exchanges, kept by Sir Thomas Montgomery.
[3] On the whole affair see Ramsay, *Lancaster and York*, II, 332, also Cora L. Scofield, *Edward IV*, vol. II, index, sub. nom., 'Cook, Sir Thomas', numerous refs. It is almost worthy of the twentieth century.

produced in all £32,216: among them aliens were still conspicuous, e.g. the Grimaldi of Genoa and the Prioli of Venice, in addition to the Caniziani of Florence, whom Edward had approached before. Altogether, these three Italian houses lent £2,000, £1,000 and £1,000 respectively, on either 9 August or 12 September: during the term Sir Ralph Josselyn, alderman of London, also lent £1,200.

		£	s.	d.	%
MICHAELMAS 1468–9:	Cash	2,219	16	3	6
	Assigned	19,470	14	4	57
	Book-keeping	12,636	3	8½	37
	Total	34,326	14	3½	100

Although parliament had made a reasonably generous war grant during the summer, and collection of it should have proceeded during the winter, the fact was that most of the yield had been anticipated in the heavy assignments of the Easter term, and there was therefore another spectacular fall at Michaelmas in both gross and real revenue. In each case there was something like a 60% reduction: real revenue, it will be seen, was only £21,690. Cash would have been even lower than it was but for the free gift of £1,000 by the duke of Brittany on 29 March, the last day of the term. Assignment continued steadily, fluctuating between £1,000 and more than £3,000 on nine days out of fifteen. Fictitious loans, though individually inconspicuous and in fact trivial in total (by the standards of the preceding reigns) were none the less the second highest for this period at £2,414; but the bulk of the book-keeping was again due to genuine borrowing, although the total of £10,221 was less than a third of the amount raised during the Easter term. This time only the Florentine Caniziani and the Genoese Grimaldi made important loans, with £5,835 in November and January and £1,000 in November (only) respectively; but there were also about seventeen smaller lenders.

		£	s.	d.	%
EASTER 1469:	Cash	1,068	0	8½	6
	Assigned	5,978	4	0	35
	Book-keeping	10,099	6	7½	59
	Total	17,145	11	4	100

The figures for this term offer no real basis of comparison, since the only surviving roll breaks off after 19 May and probably fails to represent more than half the true total. However, the eight days of business which remain on record suggest no important changes in the scale or pattern of the revenue, except perhaps some rise in book-keeping at the expense of assignment. This again was due to borrowing, some forty-three genuine lenders having already by 19 May produced £8,513, whereas fictitious loans up to that date remained unimpressive at £1,585. These entries are all easily identifiable, but the distinction between cash and assignment is frequently obscured (though the forty-four entries in question are mostly low in value), owing to mutilation of the right margin and, in the case of three more entries, to stains at the end of the roll.

		£	s.	d.	%
MICHAELMAS 1469–70:	Cash	897	13	5	4
	Assigned	15,290	16	11½	61
	Book-keeping	8,771	18	2	35
	Total	24,960	8	6½	100

This term may also be incomplete, though, as the record runs to 28 February, very much less is likely to be missing than for the previous Easter term. Real revenue at £16,188, compared with less than a half to only a quarter of that sum before and after it, is not likely to be far off its true total, and if cash was badly down, assignment was fairly well up—for these years of stringency, at any rate. It must be remembered that there was no parliamentary grant in the disturbed years between 1468 and 1472, and also that the grant of 1468 had almost certainly been exhausted by the winter of 1469–70. Genuine loans, it is true, were perhaps suspiciously low, considering recent activities in this field, at only £6,819, but the fact that they came from fifty-seven relatively small lenders, mainly churchmen, between 22 January and 23 February inclusive, with no outstanding individual loans, may suggest that Edward was scraping the bottom of the barrel, and it is not necessary to presume any large loans during March in a hypothetically lost portion of the roll. Fictitious loans were slightly up at £1,952, but their average amount remained small, while the remarkable cancellations (omitted from the marginal day totals) of the previous exchequer year—cancellations which may possibly be held to have been coming into fashion in place of fictitious loans—dropped to only two in number. Finally, there was one small *donum* on 23 February, of only £20, made by the abbot of Tewkesbury.

		£	s.	d.	%
EASTER 1470:	Cash	1,195	12	10	9
	Assigned	3,283	17	1½	25
	Book-keeping	8,786	0	4	66
	Total	13,265	10	3½	100

During this term the troubles between Edward and the earl of Warwick, which had already reached a crisis in 1469,[1] were intensified by Warwick's junction with the Lancastrians. There was fighting from March onwards, and Warwick was in France and angling for a French and Lancastrian alliance as early as the beginning of May. The expected invasion did not take place until September and was not certain of success until the first five days of October, when Edward at last took refuge in the Low Countries, but the whole of this Easter term 1470 may be regarded as having lain under the shadow of acute civil war. In these circumstances it is not surprising that the real revenue collapsed to its lowest figure of the period so far: cash, it is true, was slightly up, but assignment fell dramatically to what was again the lowest total up to date, and there were only nine days of business in all. In fact the mainstay of the Yorkist dynasty this term was the private lending of the earl of Worcester, who took over the treasurership during it and lent the crown £5,311 between 5 June and 24 July; some forty-three Yorkist lenders brought the total of genuine loans to £8,017, which must have helped substantially to tide Edward over the summer, and there was also one *donum*, but only of £60. Fictitious loans, on the other hand, fell to no more than £768.

		£	s.	d.	%
MICHAELMAS 1470–1:	Cash	413	8	10	6
	Assigned	5,913	15	5	85
	Book-keeping	631	15	2	9
	Total	6,958	19	5	100

[1] Warwick had risen against Edward and defeated him at Edgecote in July 1469, and had even held him prisoner for some weeks, but he had not yet gone over to Henry VI.

The whole of this term falls in the period of the brief Lancastrian restoration: it was not until 14 March that Edward entered the Humber, and it was another month before he was safely on the throne again. Exchequer processes none the less seem to have continued automatically, whatever king was on the throne, though naturally at a much reduced tempo. Real revenue was actually almost £2,000 up, and though this was practically all assignment, there is nothing to show that these Lancastrian assignments were not honoured in due course: fictitious loans fell to £132 and there were no suspicious cancellations. On the other hand, there were only eight days of business altogether, and little money could be borrowed to eke out Lancastrian finances: not more than ten lenders in fact (seven of them bishops) could be induced to find between them a bare £500.

		£	s.	d.	%
EASTER 1471:	Cash	7,983	6	9½	18
	Assigned	24,444	5	0	54
	Book-keeping	12,492	0	0	28
	Total	44,919	11	9½	100

The battle of Barnet, which assured Edward's immediate repossession of the throne, was fought on 14 April and the crowning Yorkist mercy of Tewkesbury on 4 May; by the second date the exchequer term had just begun. Not unnaturally it was abnormal in most respects; thus, to start with, such a relatively large sum of money had never previously been raised and, up to 1485, never was so again, in such a very short time. There were only six days of business, ranging from 1 May to 13 July, yet real revenue soared and the entire balance took the form of genuine borrowing, so that Edward had the useful sum of nearly £45,000 (over £20,000 in cash, counting loans, and the rest in assignment) with which to re-establish himself firmly in power. The fact that property was on the side of the Yorkists was convincingly demonstrated, not only by the loans but also by the unique feature of no less than twenty-six cash *dona*, e.g. from London and (again) from several bishops, totalling as much as £5,971 and accounting for all but £2,000 of the whole cash total for the term. Moreover, although most of the borrowed money was advanced by the staplers, who had never deserted Edward, and by his old friends, the Caniziani

(£6,600 on 13 July), thirty-one other Yorkist sympathizers could be found to advance the balance of nearly £6,000, partly on the security of crown jewels pledged on 1 May. Most of the £24,444 of assignment was drawn in ninety-five tallies on the customs, principally those of London, on the single day of 12 June (£23,129), while finally—to complete this curious term—there were no fictitious loans at all. Against this last feature, however, must be set the fact that on this same 12 June an additional fifty-six tallies of assignment for no less than £22,281 in all (with a further two tallies worth £1,000 on 24 June) were 'restored' and cancelled and omitted from the day totals; and it is probable that, in Henry VI's reign and earlier, such transactions would in fact have been represented by fictitious loans. We are therefore faced with the possibility that the apparently low gross totals in some terms under the Yorkists may merely reflect the partial abandonment of certain traditional procedures by the clerks of the exchequer, and that for purposes of comparison with earlier periods either all fictitious loans should be omitted from the gross totals or all cancellations included in them. These considerations, however, do not apply to the corrected totals, even if they may explain the apparent, though, apart from this term, the seldom quite complete, disappearance of the fictitious loan during the later Yorkist period.

MICHAELMAS 1471–2:		£	s.	d.	%
	Cash	6,098	11	11	82
	Assigned	319	1	10	4
	Book-keeping	1,043	6	8	14
	Total	7,461	0	5	100

The tremendous efforts made to render the Yorkist dynasty secure again during the summer of 1471 naturally produced some reaction in the following Michaelmas term, when all that the receipt rolls record is virtually a small cash revenue, partly from crown lands and partly from customs, supplemented by five small genuine loans and a trifle of assignment: *both* fictitious loans *and* cancellations are conspicuous by their absence. Ramsay, it is true, points out[1] that, according to the tellers' roll, 'a fresh levy was made to the amount of £12,094' at the beginning of this term in loans and *dona*, and recites particulars: he notes, however, that 'not one of

[1] *Lancaster and York*, ii, 391 and n.

these sums appears on the Pell Receipt Rolls; an inexplicable discrepancy'. It does not occur to him to ask whether, in that case, the sums he mentions were ever actually raised at all, but it seems permissible to wonder whether the tellers' notes were not in fact an estimate which was not fulfilled, rather than a record of sums actually paid: the point, of course, raises the whole important issue of the relation between the two series at this date, and of the amount of income which may perhaps by now have been avoiding record on the receipt rolls. At first sight this possibility seems plausible enough, especially when it is remembered that the receipt rolls did not aim at any time at being a complete record of the revenue, but on the contrary merely constituted a record of acknowledgment of payments made into the receipt. They were, so to speak, a list of counterfoils or 'receipts' in the modern domestic sense, given in return for payments, evidence of local payments, or deposits, so that if such a 'receipt' happened not to be issued on occasion in return for an in-payment, there was no reason why the receipt roll should contain any record of it. As against this, however, must be set the natural eagerness of any man making payments for any purpose to the crown to secure in return at least some written acknowledgment of his action, and if such an acknowledgment were given it would be the receipt rolls which would naturally, and indeed automatically, record it. Hence, if we are to accept Ramsay's theory of what happened in the autumn of 1471, we must assume that such alleged lenders or donors as Sir John Arundel, the bishops of Winchester and Lincoln, and the men of Kent and Essex either did not ask for any formal recognition of the large sums they lent or advanced, or were content with what they must have well known to be the highly informal and irregular recording of that recognition in the tellers' rolls alone. This seems so improbable that we are driven back to the conclusion that, in spite of the tellers' roll, these amounts— while very possibly discussed, even negotiated, with the tellers —may never have been actually paid in at all.

		£	s.	d.	%
EASTER 1472:	Cash	5,256	12	0½	20
	Assigned	10,779	16	9	40
	Book-keeping	10,658	13	8½	40
	Total	26,695	2	6	100

Although a clerical tenth had been granted in January 1472,[1] writs were not issued for a parliament until the Easter term was over. It was therefore all the more remarkable that real revenue went up again. This increase was not reflected in cash, which even fell a little, but entirely by assignments—nearly half of them providing the security given on 18 June for a large loan by the staplers a week earlier. Genuine loans, in fact, rose again to £10,610 in all from some forty-one lenders, including the staple: second only in importance to the latter were some citizens of London, lending individually and including William Shore, the husband of Edward's mistress: he advanced £147 on 15 July. It is interesting to find that there are again no cancellations of the type made in some recent terms, but that on the contrary fictitious loans appear again, though there are only five of them, totalling a bare £49.

		£	s.	d.	%
MICHAELMAS 1472–3:	Cash	8,124	19	3	64
	Assigned	1,221	6	9	10
	Book-keeping	3,304	8	1	26
	Total	12,650	14	1	100

The first parliament for four years met at the beginning of this term, and was immediately informed that the king intended to renew the war with France. In response the commons offered to supply 13,000 archers for one year[2] on the analogy of 1453; together with a special grant towards the cost of this levy, consisting of a tenth on landed revenues for one year—'the money to be raised by special commissioners and kept in hand till the army was actually on foot; all contributions to be refunded if the expedition had not sailed by Michaelmas 1474'.[3] It was admitted that the lords were not liable for subsidies of this sort, but in practice they voted a similar tenth of their own, without the stipulation about the special commissioners: hence their contribution, unlike that of the commons, seems to have been paid into the exchequer in the normal way. However, according to the tellers' roll,[4] it amounted

---

[1] Ramsay, *Lancaster and York*, II, 391.
[2] Ramsay, *Lancaster and York*, II, 392, points out that this offer was calculated to be worth as much as £118,625.
[3] Ramsay, *Lancaster and York*, loc. cit.
[4] Quoted by Ramsay, *Lancaster and York*, II, 393–4.

to no more than £2,461 3s. 4d.—obviously as the result of evasion
and inaccurate assessment—and it is to be presumed that, for
similar reasons, the commons' tenth was not much more satisfactory: these abnormal grants, for the collection of which no
adequate machinery existed, seldom were. Anyhow, when parliament resumed on 8 February, after an adjournment at the end of
November, it was recognized that the special tenth was not in fact
enough to meet the cost of the archers, and an ordinary subsidy,
less the traditional abatement of £6,000, was granted in addition,
but only on the same terms as regards the special commissioners:[1]
hence of all these grants only that made by the lords, as already
stated, was liable to appear in the receipt rolls. Finally, the customs
yield was burdened with a new charge of £4,333 6s. 8d., which the
staplers were to be allowed to retain annually for fifteen years in
settlement of ancient debts; and they were also allowed to go on
keeping back a further annual sum of £10,022 6s. 8d. from the
same source as wages for the garrison of Calais, in accordance with
the arrangement made in 1466.[2] In view of all this it is clear that
a substantial part—one might almost say the bulk—of the revenue
was not passing through the receipt rolls at all in these years, and
it is therefore not surprising to find that real revenue, as recorded
there, drops to £9,346—of which, however, by far the greatest
part is now in cash. Assignment was little more than nominal
again, while the much reduced book-keeping total consisted almost
entirely of genuine loans (fictitious came to only £11). Among the
real lenders, the duchess of Suffolk, who also made a *donum* of
£66 13s. 4d., was outstanding, with an advance of £1,966 13s. 4d.
made on 3 November: the remaining £1,326 was raised from
fourteen other lenders on four other occasions.

		£	s.	d.	%
EASTER 1473:	Cash	1,536	3	0½	49
	Assigned	77	11	6	3
	Book-keeping	1,503	17	10	48
	Total	3,117	12	4½	100

[1] Ibid.

[2] Ramsay, *Lancaster and York*, loc. cit., and II, 325. The date of the
original arrangement is given as 1466 in the first of these two references,
and as 1467 in the second. For the details see Professor Eileen Power
(who adopts the first date), *Studies in English Trade in the Fifteenth
Century*, 74–5.

The diversion of the parliamentary subsidies to special commissioners outside the receipt of the exchequer, and also of the customs (very largely) to the staplers at Calais, seems to have left the crown this term with hardly any receipt roll revenue at all. The figures are indeed the lowest for the whole series 1377–1485: the microscopic real revenue, as can be seen above, was nearly all in cash, and even book-keeping was only about as much again. This last was entirely confined to seven genuine loans; while business of any kind was in fact limited to six days between 11 May and 17 July inclusive.

		£	s.	d.	%
MICHAELMAS 1473–4:	Cash	5,223	1	1	28
	Assigned	7,184	3	3	39
	Book-keeping	6,210	7	10½	33
	Total	18,617	12	2½	100

The parliament of 1472, which had been adjourned for the second time in April 1473, met again on 6 October, but the financial business of this third session was confined to passing yet another resumption act, containing this time 221 clauses of exemption, but differing from its predecessors in requiring 'holders of all outstanding tallies or assignments drawn on the revenues of York, Lancaster, or Wales prior to the 10th December, 1470 . . . to bring them in for proof of the sums actually due'.[1] Following this act, parliament again adjourned to 20 January 1474; achieved nothing in its fourth session; and was once more adjourned, this time to May. The receipt roll revenue improved slightly during the winter with the help of the hereditary income, e.g. from the duchy of Cornwall, together with the yield of a clerical subsidy and of such customs as were not pledged to the staplers or to other persons; but the real total was still absurdly low. Genuine loans went up again to the moderate total of £6,186, most of which (£4,616) was found, principally on 2 March, by the Caniziani, though throughout the term, taken as a whole, there were also some thirteen other lenders. The same Florentine firm was credited with the only fictitious loan of the winter, when three tallies on the clerical tenth went wrong—to a total value, however, of less than £24.

[1] Ramsay, *Lancaster and York*, II, 396.

		£	s.	d.	%
EASTER 1474:	Cash	1,754	8	3½	11
	Assigned	7,913	7	1	48
	Book-keeping	6,830	4	10	41
	Total	16,498	0	2½	100

The much-adjourned parliament of 1472–4 met for a fifth session in May during this term, and also for a sixth in June and July, but it was only during the latter that any financial business was done. This, however, was both complicated and important: I have adopted Ramsay's form of summary.[1]

(1) The special tenth payable by commoners since 1472 had so far yielded £31,410 14s. 1½d. (which, of course, does not appear in the receipt rolls, since the money had not been handed over but merely hoarded by the commissioners). But the three northern counties, together with the palatinates of Chester and Durham, had as yet paid nothing at all, nor had anything been collected (which is much more remarkable) on account of the ordinary subsidy voted in 1473.

(2) The commons therefore proposed (a) to compel the defaulting northerners and westerners to contribute £5,383 15s. as their share of the special tenth, (b) to regrant the ordinary subsidy as from 11 November 1474.

(3) All this was now reckoned as being part of the cost of the 13,000 archers for one year originally voted in 1472, but even so it left a deficit of £51,147 on the estimated total cost of that force, which was £118,625.

(4) This deficit it was now proposed to make good by yet another special subsidy, 'to be assessed on the goods, chattels, lands and rents assessable to ordinary Fifteenths and Tenths'.[2] As the total to be raised by this means was far in excess of the yield of any ordinary subsidy, 'a table was drawn up specifying the contribution of each county, city, or borough entitled to be separately taxed'.[3] The money was to be collected half at midsummer and half at Martinmas (11 November) 1475, and was once again to be retained by special commissioners until the expedition to France

[1] Ibid., II, 400–1.   [2] Ibid., 401.
[3] Ibid., loc. cit.

was ready to sail: the time-limit for sailing was, however, extended by nearly two years, viz. to midsummer 1476.

Ramsay calculates that all these grants put together were theoretically equal to four subsidies in three years, and had been exceeded in amount only in the first four years of Henry V: they were more than Edward IV had received in all the previous years of his reign, and to them must be added no less than three and a half clerical tenths granted by Canterbury, and two tenths by York, during the same triennium. Even now the tale is not quite complete, for this parliament was adjourned for a seventh and final session, lasting from 23 January to 14 March 1475, during which, it is true, no new grants were made, but on the other hand certain changes in assessment and collection were introduced, which must interest the financial historian. These were, briefly, that the proceeds of the almost three-year-old special tenth of 1472 were found to be in such danger from the death or peculation of the collectors and their heirs that the money was called in immediately instead of waiting another year or more for the actual expedition to France; while the special subsidy of 1474 was found to raise so many difficulties that there was substituted for it a grant of one and three-quarter fifteenths and tenths of the ordinary kind, estimated to yield £53,697.[1]

It must now be calculated how much of all this abnormal activity, the whole proceeds of which in Richard II's day, or even in Henry V's, would probably have gone through the receipt rolls, can be expected to make any showing in them under Edward IV. It is doubtful, in the first place, whether any substantial part of the special tenth of 1472 was ever so recorded, though the calling-up of the proceeds of this grant early in 1475 may have meant that some part of it found its way on to the receipt rolls. The ordinary subsidy regranted as from 11 November 1474 might, however, have been recorded, at any rate in part, while the conversion of the large special subsidy of the same year into ordinary fifteenths and tenths early in 1475 makes it more likely that at least some portion of it passed through the exchequer of receipt, instead of straight into the hands of special commissioners. What is quite certain is that a most inadequate impression of the real efforts made by parliament—though not of those made by the two con-

<hr>

[1] Ramsay, *Lancaster and York*, II, 405.

vocations—during these years is afforded by the receipt rolls. It is true that by Easter 1474, the term under immediate consideration, hardly any of these measures could have had any possible effect upon the rolls, except perhaps in the making of assignments, but even under that head the total remains small and the increase from the preceding Michaelmas term is only a few hundred pounds; while the real revenue of the rolls, taken as a whole, actually falls, owing to the steep decline in cash takings. There were indeed only eight days of business at the receipt during the important summer sessions of this long parliament: book-keeping, too, was only a few hundred pounds larger, and consisted once again almost wholly of genuine loans, so that there is no trace of any attempt at much additional assignment. There were in fact only four small fictitious loans, totalling a little over £37: among the real lenders, lord Hastings, the king's chamberlain, was conspicuous with £1,566 13s. 4d. on 21 June: twenty-two others produced the remainder, viz. some £5,226. Lastly, as will be seen below, the next few terms did less than nothing to correct the impression that in practice hardly any of this new revenue ever found its way on to the receipt rolls.

		£	s.	d.	%
MICHAELMAS 1474–5:	Cash	6,462	19	11½	43
	Assigned	3,772	1	1½	25
	Book-keeping	4,851	2	6	32
	Total	15,086	3	7	100

Parliamentary developments during this winter have already been dealt with under the preceding term, and it will be remembered that early in 1475 there was a marked change in tempo and in the methods of assessment and collection, but there were no new grants. The receipt rolls remain wholly unaffected, in spite of the ordinary subsidy regranted the previous summer, as from 11 November 1474. Real revenue, it is true, was up a little, owing to a marked rise in cash, which in turn was mainly due to heavy payments from the customs, especially those of Southampton, and not to any new source of income. Assignment, which might have been expected to increase after 11 November, showed little sign of doing so, and indeed ended by achieving only half its total for the preceding Easter term; two-thirds of it, moreover, was not drawn until 13 March, when the term was almost over. Fictitious loans remained nominal (there were two for £11), but thirty-one real loans produced £4,839, among which £2,207 advanced by Richard Fowler, the king's solicitor, on 27 February 1475 was by far the most prominent.

		£	s.	d.	%
EASTER 1475:	Cash	11,945	14	7	45
	Assigned	6,718	5	6½	25
	Book-keeping	7,878	3	0½	30
	Total	26,542	3	2	100

The improved financial position is at last reflected to a moderate extent in the receipt rolls, though even now it is only the clerical tenths which make any real showing: it is these in particular—especially in heavy payments made on 23 May and 9 June—which raise cash to its highest total for the whole period since 1462. Yet assignment, though increased, was not back even to its 1473–4 level, and the total real revenue is certainly disappointing, in view of what we know parliament to have voted. Genuine loans were up a little at £7,772, of which the Medici and the treasurer of England, now Henry, earl of Essex,[1] produced the bulk, viz. £5,000 on 6 April and £1,000 on 1 May respectively. Fictitious loans at £105 reached three figures again for the first time since 1471, but there were only four of them. Altogether, the impression is confirmed that by the end of this period, if not earlier, the receipt rolls had really ceased to be a useful index to the state of crown finances, and this impression will only be strengthened as we proceed further into the last ten years of Yorkist rule.

		£	s.	d.	%
MICHAELMAS 1475–6:	Cash	3,852	8	11	29
	Assigned	9,323	11	0½	70
	Book-keeping	203	15	0	1
	Total	13,379	14	11½	100

Towards the end of the Easter term 1475 the great and long-awaited French expedition had at last got under way and Edward himself had reached Calais. Within a matter of weeks, however, he had abandoned his now discredited ally, Charles, duke of Burgundy, and had made the treaty of Picquigny with Louis XI.

---

[1] Formerly viscount Bourchier, treasurer in 1455–6.

The financial significance of this famous compact was relatively simple: Edward undertook to withdraw his formidable army immediately in return for a cash payment (which was promptly made) of 75,000 crowns, together with the promise of a further 50,000[1] annually (which was in fact regularly paid) for the remainder of his life. In addition, the unfortunate Margaret of Anjou, Henry's queen, was ransomed by Louis (who knew how to recoup himself out of territories in France to which she had a claim[2]) for a further 50,000 crowns. By the end of September Edward was back in London, where he had the grace to remit the three-quarters of a subsidy granted in the previous March for payment on and after 11 November.

In these circumstances it is obvious that the receipt rolls of the future were unlikely to record much normal revenue. In fact, during this Michaelmas term of 1475–6 Edward's real income from traditional sources fell to about the average for his reign. Characteristically, the heaviest day's assignment (5 December) was in favour of the household and was levied mainly on the revenues of the duchy of Lancaster. The only really remarkable feature of the term was the abnormally low book-keeping total, made up of one genuine loan of £100 and four small fictitious loans: this may perhaps reflect the disgust of Edward's subjects at his conduct, but is more probably a function of the comparative insignificance to which all procedure at the receipt of the exchequer was now being reduced: book-keeping in fact never recovered its old importance before 1485.

		£	s.	d.	%
EASTER 1476:	Cash	2,437	4	0½	40
	Assigned	3,637	8	5½	59
	Book-keeping	59	13	4	1
	Total	6,134	5	10	100

The pattern of the previous term was repeated even more feebly and for all the same reasons: there was a fall of nearly £5,700 in

---

[1] Roughly valued by Ramsay (*Lancaster and York*, II, 414) at £15,000 and £10,000 respectively: actually £16,250 and £10,833, if, as the receipt roll for Easter 1478 asserts, the exchange value of the French crown was 4s. 4d., not 4s.

[2] J. J. Bagley, *Margaret of Anjou*, 236–8.

assignment, but cash was also down by £1,400. Book-keeping fell to one genuine loan of £50, plus two small fictitious loans totalling only £9 13s. 4d.

		£	s.	d.	%
MICHAELMAS 1476–7:	Cash	2,231	12	5½	16
	Assigned	10,959	1	7½	78
	Book-keeping	794	9	5½	6
	Total	13,985	3	6½	100

Real revenue returned almost exactly to the level of the previous Michaelmas term. Cash, however, declined a little: it was assignment which was up by £7,322. A good deal of this was drawn against customs and the sale of wool at Calais, especially in the middle of October and also of November, and customs in general accounted for most of some £800 in cash and £1,343 in assignment on 16 January. In spite of four or five fictitious loans, book-keeping would have been negligible but for what purports to be a genuine loan of £600, made on 28 October by Sir John Say, keeper of the great wardrobe.

		£	s.	d.	%
EASTER 1477:	Cash	1,407	17	9	14
	Assigned	7,855	13	4½	76
	Book-keeping	1,011	1	1	10
	Total	10,274	12	2½	100

There was no general change in the situation, though real revenue was some £3,000 higher than in the previous Easter term. Once again, however, it was assignment which was relatively well maintained,[1] while cash fell to its lowest figure for the decade. Book-keeping touched £1,000 only because Sir John Say lent a further £700 (on 16 April); but it must be added that there were also two other genuine loans, totalling £240, on 2 July. The remaining six loans, all small, were fictitious and totalled only £91.

[1] Note especially assignments totalling £4,119 on 19 May, made mostly on the revenues of the duchy of Lancaster (as to more than £2,000) but also on the customs and on Calais, and chiefly in favour of the household.

		£	s.	d.	%
MICHAELMAS 1477–8:	Cash	2,981	9	7	30
	Assigned	6,778	8	6½	67
	Book-keeping	331	10	0	3
	Total	10,091	8	1½	100

The last parliament of the reign met on 16 January, primarily for the purpose of impeaching the king's brother, the duke of Clarence, whose conviction of high treason and subsequent murder in the Tower yielded Edward six groups of estates bringing in a net income of some £3,160 a year.[1] In the circumstances no parliamentary grant was asked for, and the real revenue remained low. It is true that cash showed its first increase of the decade, mainly owing to an in-payment of £1,445 on 17 February, but assignment continued to decline, while book-keeping dropped sharply once more and consisted wholly of fictitious loans: there are in fact no more genuine loans from now on until the last year of Edward's reign (Easter 1482 onwards). Whether the seven small fictitious loans do in fact represent all the tallies that went wrong remains open to question, for on 1 December ten other tallies, totalling £1,000, drawn against the staplers and intended for the household, were cancelled and condemned, as had sometimes happened in the previous decade, without further explanation.

		£	s.	d.	%
EASTER 1478:	Cash	17,604	14	11½	68
	Assigned	7,932	9	5	31
	Book-keeping	159	5	7½	1
	Total	25,696	10	0	100

The impressive rise in real revenue is almost wholly due to the fact that, for the first time since Edward had become a pensioner of France, substantial payments, obviously from Louis XI, suddenly make their appearance on the receipt roll and inflate the cash total by possibly £11,000 or more. There are also large assignments, worth some £2,700, made on 15 July against the clerical

[1] According to Ramsay, *Lancaster and York*, II, 425. Mr. Lander, however (loc. cit.), says that there were four groups, not six. There were six receivers, but they were not all active at the same time.

subsidies, which, unlike those of parliament, continued to be granted during this phase of the reign.[1] Finally, on 18 July, no less than £3,000 was paid in cash into the receipt from customs, mainly those of Calais, but including a contribution of £600 from London. The abnormal French entries occur on 26 August, when cash reaches a gross total for the day of as much as £12,163. About £1,071 of this seems to be ordinary revenue, though it includes a minute *donum* of 4s. and a benevolence[2] of £5 10s. The balance of £11,092, however, is clearly unusual, first in being marked *Angl'* and, secondly, in not having the treasurer's dot (showing that no tally of receipt was cut for it). It is, however, divided into three distinct portions as follows:

(1) £7,375 in fifteen payments marked *de domino Rege de denariis receptis de cofris suis per manus W. Daubeny*[3] *et al'*. There is nothing to show how this money had originally found its way into the royal 'coffers', but although the term is again used at a slightly later date, when the French pension had definitely been discontinued,[4] under Edward IV at any rate it is at least as likely that it represents royal savings from payments made by Louis XI as royal savings from private ventures in trade.

(2) A further fifteen payments, totalling £736 12s. 2d., seem to represent profit on the exchanges (*incrementum*)—for example, *de J. Pykeryng mercero Lond' £7 13s. 10d. pro summa c li. coron' sibi soluc' juxta rat' corone ad iiijs. iiijd. de incremento earundem*, and similar entries.

(3) £2,980 in one payment, openly recorded as coming from 'Louis, pretended king of France', on account of the 25,000 crowns which he had agreed to pay the king the previous Easter.

Apart from these abnormal entries there is little of importance to note about this term: assignment was about average, and was drawn mainly against the duchy of Lancaster and the clerical

---

[1] Ramsay, *Lancaster and York*, II, 463.

[2] This is one of the earliest occasions on which this term figures in the receipt rolls. According to Mr. Lander (loc. cit.) it was the household, not the exchequer, which had handled the benevolence of 1475.

[3] *Magister*, clerk of the king's jewels.

[4] See p. 318, n. 1, below, Edward V, Easter 1483, when it probably refers to the remains of Edward IV's hoard.

subsidies already mentioned, while book-keeping (all small fictitious loans) was very low again.

		£	s.	d.	%
MICHAELMAS 1478-9:	Cash	12,657	13	5½	44
	Assigned	13,679	4	1½	47
	Book-keeping	2,537	6	7	9
	Total	28,874	4	2	100

Much the same thing seems to have happened, though on a reduced scale, as in the previous term: that is to say, the receipt rolls are again inflated by payments made from France, and possibly from certain other abnormal sources. Two entries of this kind, both in cash and both made on 1 April (the last day of the term), put an extra £7,000 and more into the totals: the first of these is one of £5,000, specifically from 'Louis, pretended king of France', *in plena solucione* of £25,000 (*sic*—not crowns), at 4*s.* 'le crowne'; while the second is made up of five tallies worth £2,396 odd in all *de domino Rege de den' recept' de cofris suis*. It is notable that since the previous term the rate of exchange seems to have dropped from 4*s.* 4*d.* to 4*s.* (the figure adopted by Ramsay) and, assuming this to be the final rate, the £25,000 referred to may have been made up of the initial payment of £15,000 stipulated in the treaty of Picquigny, plus the £10,000 for the ransom of Margaret of Anjou. Unlike the annual pension of £10,000 for the term of Edward's life, these were, so to speak, capital payments, and the phrase *in plena solucione* could therefore be applied to them. However, since only £7,980 in the two terms taken together is definitely described as being paid direct by Louis in person, it is obvious that rather over £17,000 of the *plena solucio* may never have found its way on to the receipt rolls at all. This total, it is true, can be reduced by about half (£8,489) if we regard the mysterious payments *de cofris*, together with the small *incrementum* on the favourable exchange at Easter, as being all on French account, but even so there is still some £8,500—not to mention the annual pension of £10,000— which goes completely unrecorded at the receipt. There is one other less unusual, but still curious, feature of this Michaelmas receipt roll, viz. the attempt made on 17 February to assign as much as £9,653 in one day—a figure out of all proportion to the restricted totals of this period—to the household, mainly out of customs payable at Calais, London, Southampton and elsewhere. This was only about 80% successful, but the £7,833 which was actually cashed by the officers of the household more than doubled the ordinary term total for assignment at this date, and of course increased the already swollen total of all real revenue for the term by the same amount. Moreover, this ambitious operation produced fictitious loans upon a really large scale for the first time in years, when five tallies for as much as £2,515 could not be honoured and had to be returned to the exchequer by John Elryngton, the treasurer of the household. There were also four or five other fictitious loans, but these were all small, amounting to no more than another £21 odd between them.

		£	s.	d.	%
EASTER 1479:	Cash	4,864	9	4½	88
	Assigned	659	3	11	12
	Book-keeping	13	2	6	–
	Total	5,536	15	9½	100

This is one of the briefest rolls in the whole series, and it is also one of the very few to represent practically 100% real income, most of it in cash. There were only five days of business between 28 April and 6 July inclusive, during all of which cash came in, principally from the customs, in steadily increasing quantities. No comment is necessary under the other two heads.

		£	s.	d.	%
MICHAELMAS 1479–80:	Cash	5,885	12	11½	29
	Assigned	14,680	13	0½	71
	Book-keeping	5	19	0	–
	Total	20,572	5	0	100

All but four tiny fictitious loans included in this total represents real income, which therefore shows a very considerable increase: it is in fact the fourth highest figure for the decade, though there are two other totals only just below it. Cash begins in these terms a slow but steady ascent towards a peak reached at Easter 1482, though in this term at any rate the only really heavy payments were those made on 20 November by the staple. The big increase was in assignment, thanks mainly to another large draft (this time entirely successful) in favour of the household, which on 4 December received some £8,000 or more in tallies of assignment, thus bringing the sum total under this head to its third highest figure for the decade.

EASTER 1480:		£	s.	d.	%
	Cash	6,133	5	7½	61
	Assigned	3,929	8	11½	39
	Book-keeping	22	0	3	–
	Total	10,084	14	10	100

There is a clear reversion to the pattern of the previous Easter term, but although cash continues to rise slightly, thanks mainly to the Calais and other customs, assignment does not fall to anything like the low figure of Easter 1479, which was altogether exceptional in this decade. The two little fictitious loans are obviously once more negligible.

MICHAELMAS 1480–1:		£	s.	d.	%
	Cash	7,491	4	5½	35
	Assigned	12,599	9	0½	59
	Book-keeping	1,179	0	4	6
	Total	21,269	13	10	100

There is, *pace* Ramsay,[1] little trace in the receipt roll of Edward's financial preparations for the Scottish campaign of 1481. The pattern in fact is almost identical with that of Michaelmas 1479–80, viz. the steady rise in cash, mainly from Calais, London and other customs, coupled with a no more than respectable total for assignment. Over half the latter was drawn on 22 November only, nearly all of it on the forfeited estates of the duke of Clarence (for the first time) and in favour of the household. Altogether this produced a reasonable real income, only £470 less than in the preceding Michaelmas term. In fact the only real difference between these two terms is that four or five sizeable fictitious loans appeared again in 1480–1, mainly owing to failures by the customs or the

[1] *Lancaster and York*, II, 439. It is there alleged that the 'three-quarters of a Subsidy of 1474 was at last called in, with supplementary "Benevolences" ', worth £2,500. It may be so, but the receipt rolls know nothing of it.

staple. This brought book-keeping back into four figures, but, as will be seen, another full year was to pass before this tendency was definitely confirmed.

		£	s.	d.	%
EASTER 1481:	Cash	8,621	14	7	66
	Assigned	4,527	5	7	34
	Book-keeping	12	11	6	–
	Total	13,161	11	8	100

Activities against the Scots this summer were limited to a naval raid on the east coast in the spring and to military and diplomatic preparations.[1] Edward did not trouble to summon a parliament, but the Canterbury convocation was called together and granted a tenth, which, as will be seen shortly, figures in a rather unusual form in the receipt roll. There were in fact only three days out of ten on which there was any business worth mentioning at the receipt. The first of these was 7 June, when assignments up to £2,017 were made; but these were really little more than book-keeping in a disguised form, for the bulk of the sum was not only drawn against the staplers but immediately assigned back to them. On 19 June £1,890 was paid in cash, mainly from the Southampton customs but some of it from the clerical subsidy; while on 18 September a further £3,761 in cash was received from John Wode and John Fitzherbert, *coll' et receptor' cert' den' summar' unius integre decime Regi in convocat' a clero Cantuar' provinc' anno xxj*[2] *concess' sub modo et forma in eadem convoc' solvend' de ead' decima.* This bulk payment by lay collectors and receivers is unique. Book-keeping on the other hand was without interest in this term, and consisted merely of four minute fictitious loans.

		£	s.	d.	%
MICHAELMAS 1481-2:	Cash	9,020	17	9	37
	Assigned	15,165	19	2	63
	Book-keeping	16	5	0	–
	Total	24,203	1	11	100

There is again no evidence of any special financial effort in the receipt roll. Real income was, it is true, the third highest of the

---

[1] *Lancaster and York*, II, 439–41.   [2] The current year.

CALENDAR, 1452–85

decade and showed a £4,000 advance on that for the preceding
Michaelmas term, but it seems to have been drawn entirely from
the usual sources, including the Clarence estates. Cash continued
to creep upward, while assignment reached its second highest total
for the period. In each case these relatively large figures were
accounted for by activities confined to only two or three days; thus
13 and 22 November and, especially, 1 December were all marked
by heavy assignment. In particular, the last of these three days saw
what was becoming the usual draft of six or seven thousand pounds
in favour of the household about this time of year: once again, it
was drawn mainly on the Clarence estates. Heavy cash payments,
on the other hand, were reserved for the latter part of February
—notably the 14th, when nearly £4,000 was received, principally
from the customs of London and Southampton, in spite of some
substantial assignment on the former rather earlier in the term.
Book-keeping was confined to half a dozen small fictitious loans
totalling little over £16, so to all intents and purposes the nominal
revenue was once more identical with the real revenue.

		£	s.	d.	%
EASTER 1482:	Cash	10,978	19	9½	50
	Assigned	7,411	7	10½	34
	Book-keeping	3,571	11	7½	16
	Total	21,961	19	3½	100

Preparations for the long-deferred major military effort against the
Scots are at last reflected in the rolls during this term, in the shape
of certain loans and benevolences referred to by Ramsay;[1] and an
expedition under the duke of Gloucester's command, which
started in July, achieved its main object with the surrender of
Berwick castle on 24 August.[2] But the real revenue, though high
for an Easter term at this date, was still under £20,000, since no
special grant had been demanded. Cash was stepped up once more
—evidently with some difficulty—to the highest figure it had
reached for three and a half years, more than half of which came
from the staplers, acting as collectors of the Calais customs; while

[1] *Lancaster and York*, II, 442.
[2] Berwick town had fallen some weeks earlier: both town and castle had
been surrendered to the Scots in 1461 by Henry VI as the price of their
support, and had been held by them ever since.

the much-famed benevolences, of which only nine are recorded, produced only £12![1] Assignment, on the other hand, was not much more than average for an Easter term, and less than half the total it had reached during the winter. Moreover, the biggest single day's transactions (those totalling £2,733 on 20 May) were rather dubious in that they consisted for the most part in assigning back to Elryngton, the treasurer of the household, the remnant of his own account. However, there were forty-five genuine loans which, with fictitious loans for £78, revived the book-keeping total: eighteen and twenty-six of these loans took place on 10 and 21 June respectively, and one more on 30 August, but although their total came to nearly £3,500 none of them individually is worth a mention.

		£	s.	d.	%
MICHAELMAS 1482–3:	Cash	3,617	3	7	17
	Assigned	14,627	2	1	67
	Book-keeping	3,526	7	8	16
	Total	21,770	13	4	100

Success (of a sort) had hardly been achieved against the Scots when there was trouble with the French. During the first part of the Michaelmas term news arrived of the treaty of Arras 'between Louis XI and the Dauphin of the one part, and Maximilian, his children, and their subjects of the other part',[2] which, as far as Edward was concerned, meant the ending of the French 'tribute' in the very near future and the repudiation of his daughter Elizabeth, who, at any rate in his own opinion, was already as good as affianced to the dauphin. Since the whole settlement with France was thus once more in the melting-pot the only possible remedy appeared to be war, and for that purpose parliamentary grants would be essential. A parliament was accordingly summoned and met on 20 January 1483, when 'the question of war with France must have been laid before the Houses, as the Commons voted a Subsidy to be raised at Midsummer':[3] they also reimposed the

---

[1] The formula for these benevolences is: *Regi erga viagiam suam contra Scotos conc'*, etc. It looks as if only a very few of the least important of them had found their way on to the receipt rolls.

[2] Ramsay, *Lancaster and York*, II, 448–9.

[3] Ibid., 449.

trifling, but annoying, subsidy or tax on aliens. However, Edward did not live to see come in the money which had thus been voted to him, or to carry out any of his hostile intentions, for on 9 April he was dead. There had not by then been time for any of the new measures to make any impression on the receipt roll, except perhaps by way of anticipation through assignment,[1] and even that did not occur. Financially in fact the term is a completely normal one for this late Yorkist period: the total of real revenue was indeed a little down rather than up, and there was a sharp fall in cash in particular. Assignment, it is true, was somewhat above average, but this was mainly caused by a £5,000 draft on general revenues made on 10 February in favour of the household. Indeed the only distinctive feature of the term is that the borrowing begun the previous Easter was continued. Genuine loans were almost unchanged at £3,430, though they were less than half as numerous (twenty-one in all) and therefore individually more valuable. Most of the money was in fact raised on 21 February (£2,906) from a syndicate of Londoners headed by Henry Colet. Conversely, fictitious loans were much more numerous than of late, but very small; there were in fact nineteen of them, totalling only just over £96. It should be noted, however, that the entries for 5 March lead off with seven cancellations worth over £2,000—all of them, of course, originally assigned—and that at an earlier date these cancellations might well have given rise to further fictitious loans.

		£	s.	d.	%
EASTER 1483:	Cash	2,438	2	10	29
	Assigned	5,127	12	4	61
	Book-keeping	830	0	0	10
	Total	8,395	15	2	100

The troubled weeks of Edward V's pathetically short reign have not unnaturally left comparatively little trace in the receipt rolls, although the whole of this Easter term lies well within them.[2]

---

[1] This would not have been usual before the grant actually fell due, though the rule was occasionally broken.

[2] He reigned from 9 April to 25 June, when he was deposed, but he was not murdered until August. The exchequer term ran from 25 April to 21 June 1483 inclusive.

There were in fact only seven days of business, yet the real revenue, low as it may seem, was at least higher than that for Easter 1476 or Easter 1484. It is true that the now dwindling cash total would barely have reached four figures had it not been for two abnormal payments on 28 May—one of £670 *de domino Rege de den' recept' de cofris suis*,[1] and the other of £600 paid by a syndicate of four persons (including three bishops) *super jocalia Regis*.[2] The total for assignment similarly depends for the most part on the entry for a single day, viz. £4,577 on 4 June, consisting mainly of large drafts in favour of the household on every sort of royal revenue, including the Clarence estates. Most surprising of all, there is a kind of hang-over of Edward IV's borrowing in the shape of eleven genuine loans worth £636 13s. 4d. on 28 May, and four more worth £193 6s. 8d. on 4 June, thus producing the complete book-keeping total of £830: there were no fictitious loans.

MICHAELMAS 1483–4: No surviving roll.

		£	s.	d.	%
EASTER 1484:	Cash	1,656	2	2½	19
	Assigned	4,967	0	4½	57
	Book-keeping	2,152	2	0	24
	Total	8,775	4	7	100

The only parliament of Richard III sat at Westminster from 23 January to 20 February 1484, and was naturally concerned first and foremost with the regularization of the usurper's position and his establishment in power. The only grant made by it was that of customs duties at the existing rates for life, and even this was

---

[1] This suggests that this curious formula, which is first met with in Edward IV's reign (Easter 1478, p. 310 above), did not necessarily have anything to do directly with the French pension. On the other hand, the reference here is almost certainly to the remains of Edward IV's hoard, which the French pension had been chiefly instrumental in building up.

[2] Unless this was an outright sale of crown jewels, which seems to be implied, these entries should be treated as loans, though they were certainly not entered as such in the roll. The bishops were those of Durham and Chichester, with the archbishop of York. The layman was a Londoner, John Baker, collector of tunnage and poundage there.

retrospective only so far as the first day of the parliament.[1] Hence, although no receipt roll survives for Richard's first Michaelmas term, it may be assumed that revenue, both net and gross, must have been very small. It had not recovered even during the Easter term of 1484, as the figures above show, though, such as it was, it was fairly evenly distributed over eleven days of business: its main sources were the customs, clerical subsidies and issues of the hanaper. Book-keeping entirely consisted of twenty-two genuine loans, none of them of any individual interest.

		£	s.	d.	%
MICHAELMAS 1484–5:	Cash	4,781	11	8½	26
	Assigned	9,042	19	3½	48
	Book-keeping	4,896	7	0	26
	Total	18,720	18	0	100

Real revenue was more than doubled this term, mainly owing to more money coming in from the customs: thus a large cash payment of nearly £2,000, made on 17 February, was practically all from the Southampton customs only. The cash total was in fact the best since 1482, and assignment was also fairly well up. Here, too, the main source was the customs, though at least one of the five really heavy days (26 November) was made so by the assignment of a single large fine of £1,000, levied on Sir William Say for not preventing the marriage of Isabel Cheyney (presumably a royal ward). Seven fictitious loans for seventeen bad tallies accounted for £411 under book-keeping, but fifty-four genuine loans produced £4,485,[2] though without any individually outstanding lender. One point possibly worth noting under the head of loans, both genuine and fictitious, is that hardly any of them carry any reference to repayment during the ensuing reign, which looks as if for the first time in the troubled century since 1384–5 exchequer continuity, usually so imperturbable, may at last have been affected by civil war and revolution—unless the real cause is to be found in the strong personality, intense interest in exchequer matters, and overwhelming parsimony of Henry VII.

[1] Ramsay, *Lancaster and York*, II, 520.
[2] Ramsay (ibid., II, 533) makes it only £4,165. He suggests that these loans were forced, but under royal covenant of repayment.

		£	s.	d.	%
EASTER 1485:	Cash	2,387	5	8½	10
	Assigned	17,655	5	4	72
	Book-keeping	4,453	14	8	18
	Total	24,496	5	8½	100

Real revenue continued to rise strongly, in spite of being based on little else but customs and clerical subsidies:[1] most of it, however, as can easily be seen, took the shape of assignment. This is indeed the highest point assignment ever reached in the whole of this last Yorkist decade: it of course reflects the fact that Richard was straining every nerve against Henry Tudor's expected invasion. Incidentally, the greater part of something like £10,000 in assignments during May and June was drawn against the clerical subsidy, so Ramsay must be wrong in suggesting[2] that the £5,120 which he believes was borrowed from the clergy during this term, was 'the usual, in fact the invariable anticipation of the clerical half-tenth': for the same grant cannot have been anticipated in two different ways simultaneously, and if this sum was really raised from churchmen (of which I myself can find no evidence) it was almost certainly *in addition to* the subsidy. In actual fact the receipt roll shows a total of only some £4,420 borrowed in seventy-six genuine loans, lay and clerical combined—a figure which Ramsay himself would reduce even further to only £4,293,[3] though he explains away this inconsistency with his previous statement by saying that the roll is 'defective'.[4] He believes that the total of the forced loans which Richard III was trying to raise in order to finance a fleet and army against Henry was as much as £29,125, 'besides twenty letters for the city of London, on which the amounts to be borrowed are not given'. If the London letters are calculated at about £2,000,

[1] Canterbury convocation had voted another tenth in February: Ramsay, *Lancaster and York*, II, 532.

[2] Ibid., 533.

[3] Loc. cit.

[4] This it certainly is, in the sense that it exists in three long fragments only. But as far as I can judge only three days are partly incomplete, and there is nothing to suggest that any whole days are missing: for the whole period (20 April to 30 July inclusive) is well covered, and there are as many as sixteen days of business, which is 50% above average for this period.

the total would then be that of a parliamentary fifteenth and tenth (less £6,000 abatement)—which Ramsay does not regard as accidental. But it seems that only about ten or eleven thousand pounds' worth of bonds, accompanied by letters of 'request', were ever actually addressed to named individuals (including the £5,120 already mentioned as having been expected from the clergy). £18,600 was in the form of blank bonds, to be placed by the king's agents where they could.[1] How much of all this money was really raised and how much of it simply represented paper 'expectations' it seems impossible to determine, but what is quite clear is that less than one-seventh of the hoped-for total ever made any appearance whatever on the receipt roll, where the total for the whole of book-keeping, including one fictitious loan for £33 6s. 8d., is only £4,453 14s. 8d., as shown above. Three or four weeks after the rolls in which these loans are shown had ended, on 22 August 1485, the battle of Bosworth brought an abrupt end to Richard's life and reign, as well as to his would-be borrowings. In view of that other revolution—in financial technique—associated with Henry VII, the same event may also be taken as the point at which the long decadent receipt rolls lost much of their remaining meaning—or, perhaps it would be more accurate to say, were 'modelled new' in the beginning of another and much greater financial era.

---

[1] Ramsay, *Lancaster and York*, II, 532–3, for this passage.

CHAPTER IX

ANALYSIS, 1452–85

The last three 'decades' of this work are so different from their seven predecessors that I have given up the practice followed in Chapters V and VII of preserving continuity by linking them in my tabular comparisons with the decade which immediately preceded them. But if, for causes which will soon emerge, they are not comparable with 1442–52, they are at least, like my first three decades (1377–1413), fully comparable with each other. Theoretically they ought to represent the climax or dénouement of this book, but in practice they are something of an anti-climax, though they are not without a certain macabre interest of their own. It is not only that there are obvious gaps in the series of receipt rolls for the first half of Edward IV's reign, though these gaps are appreciably worse than those of Henry IV's time: it is rather that the first of these three decades was one of civil war and utter administrative collapse, for which there was no precedent, while, when government was restored and gradually strengthened in the next two decades, the whole character of the rolls begins to change. Important sources of revenue are now, in part or whole, habitually omitted, where omissions had before been quite exceptional; fictitious loans virtually disappear; and the totals, even of complete rolls, fluctuate wildly between normal and absurdly small figures before settling down in the last decade to a more plausible, but still suspiciously low, level. Admittedly, some of these changes can be traced back into possibly the second, and certainly the third, decade of Henry VI, when large loans from the staplers and certain parliamentary grants were now and then omitted,[1] and simple cancellations on a massive scale occasionally replaced fictitious loans, but in spite of such aberrations one feels that the machine at that time was still running for the most part along more or less familiar lines. This modest confidence is lost in the ensuing decades, when in many terms and even years it is becoming hard

---

[1] This of course had also been done, rather exceptionally, in Henry IV's time.

to say exactly what, if anything, the receipt rolls really do mean. It is the period again when the obscure tellers' rolls assume an unexplained and rather dubious significance: in fact the time is obviously ripe for that complete overhaul of the exchequer and of the financial system generally which was carried out by Henry VII, who, if he did not make all things new, at least did quite enough to make the evolution of a new technique by the historical research worker, and the beginning of a new volume, absolutely necessary.

In this last chapter of analysis I shall none the less adhere to the methods I have followed so far, beginning with the usual brief calculations of nominal and 'real' receipt roll revenues. I should, however, mention at this point that, as the rolls for 1461–2 and 1483–4 are missing, in addition to no less than five rolls between 1462 and 1468, and because I have invariably tried to keep my 'decades' as equal as I could in weight of evidence, I have curtailed my first decade, containing 19 complete rolls, at 1462, and prolonged the second one, containing nineteen plus two substantial fragments, as far as 1475, while my remaining decade again contains exactly 19 rolls, since, as I have just remarked, all those for 1483–4 are missing.

But to come back to the calculations: in his last eight full years (1452–60) Henry's nominal revenue declined under the impact of the civil war, and from other causes mentioned in my previous chapters, to an average of just under £47,000, while his real revenue was only a little over £33,000 *per annum*.[1] The first half of Edward's reign is very difficult to deal with on this basis, owing to the fact, as I have said, that there are as many as five terms for which no rolls survive, while in two more (1462–3 and 1469) the one surviving roll is obviously deficient. This makes the construction of any satisfactory annual average for the period quite impossible, but if we base ourselves upon the six years 1469–75, for every term in which we have at least one roll which seems to be complete, we get an average for that period of just over £36,000 gross and £24,000 real revenue. Finally, the eight years 1475–83, only the last term of which does not belong to Edward IV's reign,

---

[1] Both these figures would have been considerably lower if the two immediately pre-war years 1452–4 had been excluded. It is better to omit the two odd Easter terms, 1461 and 1462, which are separated by a complete blank for Michaelmas 1461–2, and in any case belong to Edward IV.

yield an average of just under £32,000 and £30,000 (real) respectively: Richard III's reign must unfortunately be omitted from this particular calculation, owing to the absence of any surviving roll for 1483–4. In other words, gross revenue declined throughout the thirty years under review, eventually by some 32%, while real revenue fell by 26% or so in the middle decade, but had practically returned to the late Lancastrian level by 1483. Book-keeping percentages of gross revenue did not vary much from their 30–33% in the first two decades, but sank to only 6% in Edward's last eight years. We are thus left with the general impression that the Yorkist kings were always even worse off than Henry VI had ever been, though they showed some recovery in the last part of Edward IV's reign, and yet we know that this conclusion is absolutely untrue!

The fact is that averages are hopelessly misleading in themselves, quite apart from the certainty that there were great omissions from the rolls in the Yorkist epoch, and very few omissions that we know of, except perhaps in staplers' loans, from Henry's latest series. In any case the real collapse came not in 1452 but in 1455–60, and for those five years Henry's averages are only £31,600 gross and £23,800 net, which puts him just below the Yorkists at all periods. Averages in short depend entirely on the years that happen to be chosen, and on the number of them, but before abandoning this crude technique it may still be worth while to apply it, as before, to an analysis of book-keeping, since for this purpose it is perhaps more legitimate to include a great deal of material contained in single isolated terms and parts of terms which had to be omitted from averages limited to unbroken years, and we may thus be somewhat less arbitrary in our conclusions.

AVERAGE PER YEAR	'Genuine' loans	Fictitious loans	*Prestita restituta*	Total
	£	£	£	£
1452–62	9,598	4,343	—	13,941
1462–75	18,523	1,983	12	20,518
1475–85	2,048	528	—	2,576

These results are unexpectedly interesting. They show how after Henry VI's time fictitious loans gradually follow *prestita restituta* along the path towards oblivion; how the Lancastrian borrowing power fell over 30% from their average for 1442–52, and was considerably exceeded by the early Yorkist; and finally how in their securer, later years the Yorkists managed to get on with far less borrowing than any previous kings of England—at any rate according to the receipt rolls. The average for total book-keeping also moves significantly: it was bound to be inflated in the second period by the initial Yorkist loans, though even so it was less than half the high peak reached by the Lancastrians in 1432–42. In the last period it almost disappears, and if the receipt roll totals had not been so small by then that even this low figure forms a quite appreciable proportion of them, we might have been tempted to ignore it altogether and to admit that the receipt roll totals at long last really do mean what they say.

This concludes, as usual, the more general and introductory part of my analysis, and we must now turn to the detail for the household.

HOUSEHOLD	1452–62			1462–75			1475–85		
	£	s.	d.	£	s.	d.	£	s.	d.
'Genuine' loans	1,881	13	4	11,436	12	5½	2,710	0	0
Fictitious loans	14,305	12	5½	4,869	3	0½	4,471	14	6½

Here the increase in genuine loans under the Yorkists, especially in the first half of Edward IV's reign, calls for closer investigation: the steady fall in fictitious loans, on the other hand, is much more characteristic of the period as a whole and probably reflects a change in book-keeping methods as much as anything. Incidentally the figures given above under the latter head obscure the fact, which will emerge more clearly later, that by 1475–85 the officers of the household were practically the sole recipients of bad tallies, though this is by no means true of the middle 'decade'. There were no *prestita restituta* whatsoever from this department in any of the three periods. A more detailed analysis under genuine loans yields the following results:

'GENUINE' LOANS	1452–62			1462–75			1475–85		
	£	s.	d.	£	s.	d.	£	s.	d.
Chamber	110	0	0	1,766	13	4	40	0	0
Wardrobe	1,220	0	0	256	13	4	100	0	0
Great wardrobe	10	0	0	—			1,600	0	0
King's knights	153	6	8	3,182	9	9	—		
King's esquires	26	13	4	779	4	8	146	13	4
King's clerks	250	0	0	398	6	8	233	6	8
Others	111	13	4	5,053	4	8½	590	0	0
Total	1,881	13	4	11,436	12	5½	2,710	0	0

The difference between the Lancastrian first column and the two Yorkist columns is striking: indeed the only point of resemblance is the comparative unimportance of king's clerks and, except perhaps in the middle period, king's esquires. Under king's clerks it might be mentioned that Master John Langton, whose obscure activities were entirely responsible for the great inflation under this head in 1442–52, reappears in the following 'decade' (only), but is evidently confined to his proper function of king's chaplain, for this time he advances only £66 13s. 4d. and his category therefore returns to what is obviously its normal level. I do not think the relatively slight rise in king's esquires in the first part of Edward IV's reign has any special significance: they had been almost as high as this in 1442–52. Nor is the transference of emphasis from the Lancastrian wardrobe to the Yorkist chamber,[1] and ultimately to the Yorkist great wardrobe, particularly remarkable: it seems to have been almost a matter of chance as to which department of the household had a temporary surplus at any given

---

[1] Mr. Lander (loc. cit.) points out that the chamber was one of the principal spending departments under the Yorkists, though no accounts survive. The issue rolls show that the exchequer of receipt paid it £15,000 in 1461, nearly as much in 1467–8, and over £21,000 in 1471—not to mention large but irregular sums in other years. Some of the Clarence forfeitures and farms of other estates, temporalities of vacant bishoprics, etc., were also paid direct into the chamber in the early 1480's. The formula used is generally *de privatis expensis*, but in 1464 it was *pro custubus guerre*.

time to put at the disposal of the crown. In fact the only remarkable figures are those of £3,182 for king's knights and £5,053 for 'others' in 1462–75, both of which are obviously abnormal and must represent some genuine lending to the crown.

To take the second total first: this figure is largely explained by the inclusion in it of loans amounting to no less than £3,016 from the holder of a new, or comparatively new, household office— Richard Fowler, the king's solicitor, and chancellor of the duchy of Lancaster.[1] Another fairly large lender is the Welshman Geoffrey Kidwelly, with £709, who is called a king's serjeant and was probably a serjeant-at-law, since his relative Morgan[2] Kidwelly in the next decade, who is similarly described, held the office of attorney-general in all the king's courts of record in England and Wales. Another lawyer who lent an appreciable sum (£376) to the crown in 1462–75 was John West, coroner and king's attorney in the court of king's bench; but there are at least twelve other persons whom I have had to place under this omnibus heading in this period—for example, the king's apothecary, who lent just under £300. In spite of this, however, it is clearly the law officers of the crown (other than the judges) who are now emerging for the first time as a wealthy class of person capable of advancing large sums to the government —in itself a new and interesting feature of the Yorkist régime.

All but £100 or so of the other curiously large total for this period, viz. king's knights, is accounted for by Sir John Say, who produced as much as £1,775 from his own pocket and a further £1,300 in association with Richard Fowler (the king's solicitor just mentioned) and Hugh Fenne.[3] In 1476 Say was made keeper of the great wardrobe, and the £1,600 which that department lent during the last decade appears under his name. This may perhaps

---

[1] Mr. Lander (loc. cit.) has made a very full investigation of Richard Fowler and his family. In addition to holding the offices named above, he was chancellor of the exchequer from 1469 (with one brief interval) to his death in 1477, and seems also to have been under-treasurer for at any rate part of that time. The next character mentioned in the text, Geoffrey Kidwelly, was ultimately attorney-general to Richard III and married Edward IV's former mistress, Jane Shore, much to Richard's indignation (Lander, loc. cit.).

[2] Erroneously described as 'Maurice' Kidwelly by Mr. Lander.

[3] Auditor of accounts in the exchequer. For Sir John Say see the long and interesting account in *D.N.B.* and (for his trading activities) Cora L. Scofield, *Edward IV*, ii, 419–20. He was repeatedly speaker of the commons and an ex-Lancastrian with strong landed interests in Herts.

imply that the sum in question was a real loan after all, and not merely an interdepartmental transfer, since Say was obviously a man of means. Altogether one is left with the impression that Edward IV, unlike Henry VI, did perhaps succeed in borrowing some new money from the more middle-class members of his household or immediate entourage, instead of merely changing impressive-sounding sums from one pocket to another.

When we come to fictitious loans the household is, as always, the main victim, but the figures are much reduced. The details are as follows:

FICTITIOUS LOANS	1452–62			1462–75			1475–85		
	£	s.	d.	£	s.	d.	£	s.	d.
Chamber	2,059	14	5	1,167	19	8	51	10	0
Wardrobe	7,613	2	4½	2,304	12	6	4,366	13	10½
Great wardrobe	3,401	14	9	731	0	5	5	11	8
King's knights	428	15	10	209	13	8	—		
King's esquires	79	7	4	128	7	9	20	0	0
King's clerks	—			28	13	4	13	6	8
Royal family	85	2	10	193	5	4	—		
Others	637	14	11	105	10	4½	14	12	4
Total	14,305	12	5½	4,869	3	0½	4,471	14	6½

It is obvious that, apart from the first three heads, there is hardly anything worth discussing in this table; and there is not much to be said under the first three. As usual, the wardrobe is the main recipient of bad tallies in all three periods, and the fact that its total actually rises in the last decade, when fictitious loans were out of fashion, is a tribute to the conservative instincts of the exchequer where the oldest of its clients and potential rivals was concerned. The steady decline in chamber and great wardrobe totals also calls for little comment, except that it does not necessarily imply that these departments were either doing less business or becoming more insolvent; but merely that they were more quickly affected than the wardrobe by the gradual change in book-keeping methods which was almost certainly going on. The relatively large total in the first period under 'others' contains no item of any special interest but is made up of seventeen small figures consisting chiefly of arrears of wages, or rather wages which had not been effectively paid. The picturesqueness of this salary list, on which I commented under 1442–52, is maintained by an extraordinary miscellany of small household offices, referred to in these later periods in addition to the better-known departments or categories already mentioned. Thus in 1452–62 we have a king's knight who had been on embassy to Denmark, Garter king of arms, Lancaster king of arms, the king's physician, who continues into the next period, the master of the king's ordnance and purveyor of workmen for the king's works, the king's carver and the under-clerk of the kitchen—to name only a few—among the unfortunate recipients of bad tallies, while in 1462–75 (though not in 1475–85) the list is even longer and more varied. It includes the king's apothecary (who also appears under genuine loans), a king's messenger, the deputy coroner of the household court of the marshalsea, the serjeant of the cellar, the purveyor of ale, a purveyor of fowls, another of meat and fish, the yeoman of the king's pantry, a gentleman usher of the chamber, and the usual rout of valets, servitors, esquires of the body, boys and pages. Most of them again appear only because they have received tallies which they could not cash in lieu of wages or allowances, but it is noticeable that two or three of them besides the king's apothecary—for example, the humble purveyor of ale—make what seem to be real loans to the crown. Indeed the serjeant of the cellar is credited with as much as £153 in this respect, and even if that only meant that he paid for the king's wine out of his own resources until money could be found to recoup him, his action was none the less a form of genuine lending.

However, it is time to leave the household and turn to those departments which had long 'gone out of court', viz. the chancery and exchequer.

	1452–62			1462–75			1475–85		
	£	s.	d.	£	s.	d.	£	s.	d.
CHANCERY									
'Genuine' loans	1,856	0	0	1,346	13	4	650	0	0
Fictitious loans	871	18	5	131	15	10	—		
EXCHEQUER									
'Genuine' loans	23,052	5	9	38,427	11	7½	2,271	19	4
Fictitious loans	3,286	1	11½	5,092	4	4½	191	3	9½

While chancery is obviously of not much importance in this connection, we are here confronted with figures of the first magnitude as far as genuine loans from the exchequer are concerned. The fact is that the device first noted in Chapter VII of appointing rich men treasurers, so that they could tide the exchequer over any pressing emergency out of their own resources, was being exploited by both sides to the full in the crises of the 1450's and 1460's, though after 1475 at least there is a reversion to a more normal state of affairs. Even the chancellors are now being drawn into these arrangements on a rather greater scale than before, though their contributions are still very modest compared with those of the treasurers. Thus George Neville, the Lancastrian bishop of Exeter, who was chancellor from 25 July 1460 until 1467, and again during Henry VI's brief restoration in 1470,[1] joined with the Yorkist treasurer, viscount Bourchier, to advance £1,333 6s. 8d. in 1461, though this is the only important element in the chancery's small total under genuine loans for the decade ending 1462. The same Neville, while still chancellor, was the principal lender from that department in the following decade (£400 out of £1,346 in all): in 1475-85, on the other hand, there are no chancery loans of any real significance.

George Neville's modest contributions are of course completely dwarfed by the performance of successive treasurers of England —both Lancastrian and Yorkist—in the whole period of the civil wars. For example, Henry viscount Bourchier's total effort in the first period (1455-6 and 1460-1) came to £4,524; James Butler, earl of Wiltshire and of Ormonde's to £2,541 (for 1455 and 1458-60); John Talbot, earl of Shrewsbury's (treasurer 1456-8) to £3,295; and John Tiptoft, earl of Worcester's (1452-5 and 1462) to £3,819 upon his own account, together with a further £2,000 in conjunction with the treasurer's clerk, John Wode, himself an important official in the receipt, and yet another £1,333 6s. 8d. with Thomas Thorp, the treasurer's remembrancer, assisted by two knights, Sir William Lucy and Sir Thomas Brown, who may have been outsiders. The total of all these, adding in the shillings and pence I have omitted, comes to £17,514 7s. 9½d., which

[1] He seems to have been completely non-party: thus he was a Lancastrian bishop (from 1458) and a Yorkist archbishop (appropriately of York, 1464-76), besides serving as chancellor under both dynasties in turn.

leaves little more than £5,500 of the entire exchequer contribution for 1452-62 unaccounted for. Of this the same John Wode found £1,516 unaided, and a further £626 in conjunction with a wealthy group of London citizens who were also collectors of customs, while John Brown, clerk of the estreats, acting with at least one of Wode's London associates, produced £1,983. If we add £494 from another treasurer's clerk who held office in this decade, Thomas Rothewell, and £360 from Ralph, lord Cromwell, who, though he had served as treasurer from 1433 to 1443, was now acting as royal chamberlain of the exchequer, we shall not have much left over for the sixteen other exchequer officials who also made loans during this period.

In 1462-75 these conditions continue and even assume a still more exaggerated form. This time, it is true, the earl of Worcester (treasurer 1462-3 and 1470) advanced only £1,196 on his own account, with another £255 in conjunction with Sir John Say and John Wode; but Edmund lord Grey of Ruthin (1463-4) found £3,297; Walter Blount, lord Mountjoy (1464-6) £10,700; Richard Wydville, first earl Rivers as he now was (treasurer 1466-9) £12,259; William Gray, bishop of Ely (treasurer 1469-70) £2,751; and Henry, viscount Bourchier, now earl of Essex (treasurer from 1471 to 1483) £2,010 (all before 1475). The rapid rotation of treasurers up to 1471 and the large sums which many of them advanced during a comparatively short term of office are especially worthy of note: the total of these treasurers' loans— again reckoning shillings and pence omitted previously—comes to £32,470 19s. 1d. out of an exchequer total of £38,427 11s. 7½d. The balance of rather under £6,000 is principally accounted for by the same Hugh Fenne, auditor of accounts in the exchequer, who has already been noted under *Household* as acting in other loans with Richard Fowler and Sir John Say: as an exchequer official pure and simple, he is credited in this period with genuine loans amounting to £3,357 13s. 4d. More than half the remaining £2,000 is advanced by a chief baron of the exchequer, Richard Illyngworth (£618), and by yet another treasurer's clerk, John Rogger (£666 13s. 4d.): the remainder again comes from exactly sixteen smaller lenders, and in six cases the names are the same as before.

This intense activity on the part of the exchequer staff and treasurers in shoring up the national finances during these years, whichever side was in power, is extraordinarily interesting, though it is not maintained on anything like the same scale in 1475-85. By that time treasurers' loans fall to less than £1,000 and there are only two of them: the only other sizeable loan making up the small total is one of £827 from John Fitzherbert, the king's remembrancer in the exchequer; and this is the largest single contribution in the decade. There are, however, ten or eleven smaller contributions (excluding the two treasurers), and at least three or four of the familiar names recur among them.

As might be expected, neither treasurers nor the more permanent staff of the exchequer figure largely under fictitious loans: they must have been too well aware of the probable value of tallies which their own department was cutting, or at any rate they should have been. The only treasurers who did not take fully adequate precautions in this respect were John Talbot, earl of Shrewsbury, in the first decade (£1,438), and lord Rivers (£1,863) in the following period. No one else had to endure the receipt of bad tallies totalling anything like £1,000, though Hugh Fenne of all people accumulated as much as £710 worth in 1462-75; lord Grey of Ruthin £669; lord Mountjoy £509; and the earl of Worcester £424. There was also an unexpected amount of petty default in this respect at the expense of smaller men, thirty-seven of whom appear for mostly rather modest sums in 1452-62, and twenty-four (including two treasurers) for similar amounts in the next period. In 1475-85 the number is still as high as twenty, though the amounts in every case have now become very small. Chancery in general, with its much smaller commitments in the dangerous field of government finance, obviously suffered rather less, as the figures show: the number of its officials concerned in these three periods is in fact eight, four and none respectively; and the only considerable amount is a matter of £577 in three bad tallies credited to Richard Neville, earl of Salisbury, when he was chancellor in 1454 to 1455.

General conclusions are fairly obvious, viz. that while the chancery and its employees, from the chancellor himself downwards, never counted for very much in the financial sphere, exchequer experts and financiers, following the lead of specially appointed, wealthy treasurers, played a major part in keeping the machine of state in motion in the period of the wars of the roses. Their activity in this respect was almost, though not quite, unprecedented, and was certainly unprecedented on that scale, but it was confined to the two war 'decades' lying between 1452 and 1475: after the latter date it dies right away, and is in no sense out of the ordinary in the ten years before 1485.

The figures under *Local officials* show a mild, but only a very mild, tendency to move slightly in the same direction.

LOCAL OFFICIALS	1452–62	1462–75	1475–85
	£ s. d.	£ s. d.	£ s. d.
'Genuine' loans	13,540 8 10½	14,102 5 9	3,720 0 0
Fictitious loans	10,993 14 11	3,696 9 6	438 17 6

The movements of both genuine and fictitious loans under this head are in logical continuity with those of the two previous decades. Thus the rise in genuine loans which marks the whole twenty years from 1432 to 1452 moves steadily onwards to its peak in 1462–75, and then falls away in the last decade, as so many of these book-keeping figures do. Fictitious loans, on the other hand have passed their highest by 1452 and decline with equal steadiness to 1485. *Local officials* form a crowded category for both types of loan: thus the number of them making genuine loans during the three periods is as high as seventy-six, fifty-five and twenty-one respectively, while those credited with fictitious loans—many of them, of course, the same persons—number forty-seven, twenty-eight and eight.

In 1452–62, as in the earlier Lancastrian periods, all but eighteen of the genuine lenders are connected in one way or another with the customs, as collectors, controllers, troners and pesers and so forth. It is probable, as has been said before, that these people represent the most 'genuine' element in all this alleged lending, though, with the exception of two or three outstanding loans, the individual amounts lent are seldom very large. The first of these exceptions is the £3,549 advanced, with the minimum of outside help, by John Poutrell, citizen and collector of customs in London: he is one of the group already mentioned as supporting some of the great exchequer loans, e.g. those of John Wode and the earl of Worcester, in this decade. Next to him in importance comes the curiously named Richard Tomyou, 'merchant', of Cornwall: this man was a collector of the lay subsidy in those parts and, possibly in that capacity, advanced £1,780. Most of the remaining loans of any size, however, are again associated with the London customs, as in Poutrell's case: for example, Nicholas Sharp and John Smyth, collectors, produce £841 and £403 respectively. But in addition, Sir Gervase Clifton, treasurer of Calais, lends £553, most of it in conjunction with Sir John Cheyne;[1] and one or two customs collectors from other ports, notably Southampton, lend over £400 apiece. The largest fictitious loans, on the contrary, are credited to a clerk of the king's works, Edward Blake (£1,084); to the keepers of the Castle of Roxburgh, William Neville, lord Fauconberg, Sir Ralph Grey and Sir Robert Ogle (£1,329 between them); to the 'keepers of the sea', John de Vere, earl of Oxford (£1,416) and Richard Neville, the famous earl of Warwick (£640); to the Percy, keepers of the east march towards Scotland, father and son (£896); and to another clerk of the works, Thomas Stratton, esquire (£955).

From 1462 to 1475 the pattern is much the same: four-fifths of the genuine lenders are still persons connected with the customs, but as a rule it is again only the Londoners among them who produce any really large amounts; for example, John Brampton, collector of tunnage and poundage in London, who lends £933 6s. 8d. on his own, and another £133 6s. 8d. with a colleague, and Thomas Pounde, collector, with his friend William Kerver (£534): Sir Henry Waver, on the other hand, who lends £717, collected customs at Ipswich. Apart from men connected with the customs, large sums were lent by Sir Walter Blount in 1463–4 as treasurer of Calais: this is the Sir Walter Blount whom we have already met as treasurer of England at a slightly later date (1464–6) and first lord Mountjoy (cr. 1465): in this earlier phase of his career he lent £3,000. Sir Thomas Montgomery, keeper of the exchanges in the tower of London, was another useful servant of the crown: together with two friends, he found as much as £1,553 in genuine loans. Finally, that protean figure, John Tiptoft, earl of Worcester, who has already appeared once in this chapter as treasurer of England,

[1] I cannot identify this Sir John Cheyne with any certainty: it is a surprisingly common name in England in the fourteenth and fifteenth centuries. There is a Sir John Cheyne of Kent, who lends £400 in 1452–62, but he is not necessarily the same man. There were also two Gervase Cliftons (Lander, loc. cit.) of whom this is the elder (a Lancastrian beheaded after the battle of Tewkesbury). His Yorkist nephew of the same name is found acting as a receiver of lands in the north midlands in 1477 and became a knight of the body by 1484.

and will appear again as a magnate in his own right, must be credited with no less than £4,145 lent while constable of England, keeper of the tower of London and deputy lieutenant to the duke of Clarence for the government of Ireland. The much-reduced total of fictitious loans, on the other hand, was fairly evenly distributed, and would not have come to anything very much but for £1,027 in bad tallies received by one John Wode as master of the king's ordnance, and £667 by another man of the same name as victualler of Calais.[1] The earl of Worcester's is the only other name worth noting in this context; he received in fact no less than forty-three bad tallies in this period, but their total value was only £508.

The third period (1475–85) can be rapidly dismissed. The only large genuine loans came from Thomas Cotton, collector of the London tunnage and poundage (£1,160), and Sir Thomas Bryan, chief justice of the king's bench (£800), who only qualifies rather doubtfully as a local official for want of a more suitable category to put him in; and there were no fictitious loans worth mentioning. Summing it all up, we can say that after 1452 the burdens upon local officials were progressively relaxed, partly through the loss of France, and partly through the outbreak of the civil war at home, which put an end to such central government control and interference as there might have been, and even led to rival factions bidding one against the other for the local officer's support. In 1461 the Lancastrians even sold out to the Scots in return for their alliance, and by that date no one bothered very much about the government of Ireland. Local liabilities, in other words, were much reduced by national disaster, and wherever any sizeable amount of money was still being collected, for example in the great ports and in markets such as Calais, it was possible for local officials to retain or divert a proportion of it for lending to the faction in power. With the restoration of something like efficient government, however, after 1475, these conditions disappeared, and neither the

[1] The various John Wodes in circulation at this date are somewhat baffling. In addition to these two, if they really are distinct, there is the John Wode who held the important post of treasurer's clerk in the receipt of the exchequer during the previous decade, and so can hardly be identical with yet another John Wode who was a mere usher of the receipt in 1462–75—not to mention the well-known Sir John Wood who was speaker of the commons in 1483 and treasurer of England in 1483–4.

financial necessities nor lending powers of local officers were any longer of much interest to the crown. This impression is confirmed by looking at the total figures in these three periods for all categories dependent on the government, when it will appear that household, chancery, exchequer and local officials put together first increased their genuine loans from the £25,072 of 1442–52 to £40,330 and then to £65,313 during the civil wars, while in 1475–85 they drop to only £9,351. Their fictitious loans, on the other hand, had reached their peak at £115,946 in 1442–52, and then drop sharply to £29,397, £13,789 and £5,101 during the ensuing decades. Exactly the same rhythm is followed, but even more dramatically, by the seven remaining categories of persons to be considered, viz. those who were not primarily dependent for their income or employment on the crown.

We must begin, traditionally, with the bishops.

BISHOPS	1452–62	1462–75	1475–85
	£ s. d.	£ s. d.	£ s. d.
'Genuine' loans	3,177 0 4½	7,290 6 6½	2,159 2 9
Fictitious loans	1,163 0 0	468 13 4	42 6 8

The great days of cardinal Beaufort and archbishop Chichele have obviously gone for ever, and in fact the bishops, whose normal average had been about £10,000 a decade under Richard II and Henry IV, had never lent so little to the government. Yet, unlike the lay magnates, they do go on lending on this lower level to the end, thereby showing perhaps something of the same sense of social responsibility, vis-à-vis the lay lords, as the minor clergy showed, and went on showing, in relation to the commons. Except in the middle period, when Thomas Bourchier, archbishop of Canterbury (and a cardinal from 1467) lent £2,940, no see at any time advanced as much as £1,000 per decade, yet fourteen or fifteen of them are regularly represented in each period. In 1452–62 John Chedworth, bishop of Lincoln, was the most generous, with £466; but in the middle period this was surpassed not only by Canterbury but also by Durham (Laurence Booth, £919), Norwich (£733)[1]

[1] Advanced by either Walter Lyhert (le Hart) or his successor James Goldwell, who replaced him in 1472.

and Winchester (William of Waynflete, £962).[1] In 1475–85 the only see to touch £400 was that of Ely, which was occupied by William Gray to 1478 and thereafter by the famous John Morton, subsequently archbishop of Canterbury, cardinal and minister of Henry VII. Under fictitious loans there is nothing worth recording for the bishops at any period.

If the bishops showed a steady, but subdued, generosity, religious houses and the minor clergy showed a 75% increase on their genuine loans for 1442–52 in the immediately ensuing decade; and moreover they maintained a decent standard in the last two periods; in fact they actually lent some £2,000 more in aggregate than the bishops did between 1452 and 1485.

RELIGIOUS	1452–62			1462–75			1475–85		
	£	s.	d.	£	s.	d.	£	s.	d.
'Genuine' loans	7,985	1	3	3,472	6	8	3,296	1	3½
Fictitious loans	463	13	4	188	2	5½	17	13	4

It is at first sight rather curious that this should be one of the few classes whose genuine loans do not reach their highest level in the first half of Edward IV's reign, when their contribution is in fact no more than it had been in 1422–32, and considerably below what had been advanced, decade by decade, to Henry VI during the intervening thirty years. There is in fact more than a suspicion of Lancastrian sympathies prevailing with the minor clergy, who may have been more impressed than the episcopate with Henry's reputation as a holy man. It is not that they were more politically minded than the bishops as a class, but rather less so; they were perhaps simpler, more naïve, more sentimental, and much slower to change sides. All this is guesswork, but the fact remains that in 1452–62 at least ninety-one religious houses or their heads—in this decade the community is often specifically included—made loans; not to mention the master of at least one hospital, four colleges—including Oriel and New College, Oxford, and the college of St.

¹ Possibly the £2,751 6s. 5d. lent by William Gray, bishop of Ely, 1454–78, in his capacity as treasurer of England, 1469–70, ought to be mentioned. There were, however, no other loans from Ely in this period.

Mary Winton[1]—the prior of St. John of Jerusalem in England, the dean of St. Paul's, three other deans with their chapters, and at least fifteen individual canons, prebendaries and ordinary priests. The amounts in every case but one, while generous in relation to the resources at the disposal of the lender, were not really large: the exception was another John Say, *magister*, dean of the king's chapel of St. Stephen *infra hospicium* (Westminster), who advanced the large sum of £2,056 on his own account, with a further £40 from his canons. If the Sir John Say, who is financially active in much the same way at Edward IV's court in the following decade, had not been such a well-known layman, who is moreover specifically described as a king's knight, I should have been tempted to identify the two, but it seems absolutely certain that, though they may have been related, they were different persons. Incidentally, it is worth noting that after Master John Say's loan has been deducted the mass of small clerical lenders could still produce nearly £5,900. Two or three of the small loans are, it is true, associated with the laity of the town or even county concerned, but these are quite exceptional, and there seems to be no doubt that to all intents and purposes the whole of this amount was raised from clerical sources.

It is also clear that in 1462–75 not only the total amount lent but also the number of lenders suffered sensible diminution. The number of religious houses concerned falls to forty-one, and of other clerical institutions to two, viz. the Order of St. John and the dean and chapter of Wells. Five other deans are mentioned without their chapters, including a new dean of St. Paul's, Master Roger Radclyff, who lent £426, and five other individual clergy, two of them, however, represented by executors. Apart from the dean of St. Paul's only the abbot of Glastonbury, with £556, can be described as making loans of any individual significance, and it is clear that Edward IV all in all is receiving less than half the volume of support and good will which went out from the minor clergy to his predecessor. 1475–85 is even more convincing in this respect: the number of religious houses drops to twenty-seven; that of other institutions, viz. colleges, free chapels and so forth, to three; and that of individual clergy or religious to five. The last group includes yet another dean of St. Paul's, Master Robert Worsley, who makes the greatly reduced offering of £40, and also

[1] Better known today as Winchester College.

an individual nun of good family, viz. lady Elizabeth Yorke, *deo vota*, £66 13s. 4d.

The totals under fictitious loans for this class are so small that individual items can clearly be of no particular importance, yet some of them retain a general interest which makes them worth mentioning. In 1452–62, for example, all the friars, both preaching and minor, not only of Oxford and of London, but also of Cambridge, received numerous bad tallies in lieu of their small annuities. Queen's College, Cambridge, reappears under this more familiar name,[1] with three bad tallies for £135, and even the rector of the king's free chapel within the tower of London has difficulty in collecting his small stipend. In 1462–75 friars everywhere, of both orders, are again the most regular recipients of bad tallies—a feature which persists even into the period 1475–85, when they are about the last survivors in this category among the minor clergy. However, we must leave these petty figures and return to the larger sums of all kinds still associated under the late Lancastrians and the Yorkists with the greater laymen of the country.

MAGNATES	1452–62	1462–75	1475–85
	£ s. d.	£ s. d.	£ s. d.
'Genuine' loans	4,023 0 0	2,666 13 4	40 0 0
Fictitious loans	10,226 18 3½	1,365 9 1½	—

These figures are, of course, misleadingly small for the first two periods, when so many magnates made genuine loans as treasurers of England (see *Exchequer*) and also, in a few instances, as local officials. If we include, for example, as we should, contributions made in the first of these capacities between 1452 and 1462 by viscount Bourchier and the earls of Wiltshire, Shrewsbury and Worcester, the total under genuine loans from magnates rises to £21,537, or very much what it was in the preceding decade; while in 1462–75 the addition of the treasurers' loans made by the same earl of Worcester, by lord Grey of Ruthin, lord Mountjoy, earl Rivers and again viscount Bourchier (now earl of Essex) will bring the total up to £32,386—or even to £36,531 if we include the earl

---

[1] But still Queen's, not Queens'.

of Worcester's loans under *Local officials* as well.[1] It is true that these considerations do not arise in the third period, when the magnates' loans, whether in or out of any kind of office, die right away; but it will be agreed that the picture under genuine loans for at any rate the first two periods has been utterly transformed.

If we consider magnates individually on this basis, taking into account, that is, not only loans made by them as officers of the crown but also those made in their private capacities, John Tiptoft, earl of Worcester, leads the field in 1452-62 with £5,319 on his own account and £2,000 in association with other persons. Viscount Bourchier comes next with £4,524, followed by James Butler, earl of Ormonde as well as of Wiltshire, with £3,358, and finally the earl of Shrewsbury with £3,295. The rest are nowhere, and it is, I think, rather significant that such magnates as the duke of Norfolk, the earl of Oxford, the second duke of Somerset, the Neville earl of Warwick, and (in this decade at least, unlike 1442-52) Richard, duke of York, go on record for only trifling sums. In 1462-75 what we might call the official loans from magnates rise still further, but, with one exception, there is now hardly any support at all from such persons in their private capacities. Among those who held office the ill-fated earl Rivers[2] lent the most with his £12,259 as treasurer of England: then came lord Mountjoy with £10,700 in the same official post, and a further £346 after his death by the hands of his executors; the earl of Worcester with £5,402 in his own right and another £255 with an associate; lord Grey of Ruthin with £3,297; and finally the earl of Essex (viscount Bourchier) with £2,010, to which he rather significantly added nothing from any source during the next decade, though he remained treasurer until 1483. The only loans comparable to these made by any member of the magnate class as a private person were two totalling £2,033 6s. 8d. from Alice, duchess of Suffolk: in the third period (1475-85), as already mentioned, there were practically no magnates' loans at all.

With fictitious loans the case is somewhat different, since with two or three exceptions those magnates holding offices received comparatively few bad tallies, while those in semi-private life got

---

[1] We can, I think, exclude the £3,000 advanced by lord Mountjoy under this head in 1463-4, when he was still only plain Sir Walter Blount, treasurer of Calais.

[2] Beheaded 12 August 1469.

340

more. In 1452–62 the exceptions under the first head are, first and foremost, the Percy earl of Northumberland, whose £1,909 in bad tallies as warden of the marches should be added to the £896 which appears under *Local officials* in the Percy family's name;[1] the earl of Shrewsbury, who, though treasurer in 1456–8, accumulated a total of over £1,441 in fictitious loans; and the earl of Oxford, who as 'keeper of the sea' was credited with £1,416 of the same. Against these we may set as comparatively private persons John Neville, lord Montagu, who got £1,563; lord Rivers (not yet an earl or an office-holder) who, with his wife Jacquetta, got £1,908, and at least fifteen or sixteen other members of the peerage, who between them all were credited with fictitious loans for nearly £5,000, or an average of about £300 apiece. Among these the only persons of the first political importance were Richard, duke of York, whose fictitious loans drop abruptly from the enormous total of the previous decade to as little as £785, and Richard Neville, earl of Warwick, whose £232 in private life should be added to his £640 as 'keeper of the sea', making £872 altogether.

In 1462–75 those magnates who held offices were on the whole rather less fortunate in the matter of fictitious loans then those who did not; for, as we have seen, earl Rivers, as he now was, when taking his turn as treasurer was £1,863 to the bad in this respect, to which must be added £120 for himself and his wife as private persons; again, the fictitious loans of lord Mountjoy and lord Grey of Ruthin, though not large, are greater than those of any private magnate other than lord Montagu; while the earl of Worcester's £61 in private rises to £993 when his £424 under *exchequer* and £508 under *local officials* have been taken into account. In contrast with this only John Neville, lord and (in 1470) marquis Montagu, got as much as £530 in bad tallies under his old title, and a further £210 for himself and members of his family as the new and interloping earl of Northumberland (1464–1471). The only other peer worth mentioning in this context for this decade is lord Scales, who was credited with £337 for four bad tallies, as against only

---

[1] It is not always very easy to distinguish father from son in the decade 1452–62, since they were both called Henry Percy and seem both to have been acting as wardens of the marches. The younger Henry Percy succeeded his father as earl of Northumberland in 1455 and died and was attainted in 1461, but he was certainly active on the east march before 1455.

£100 in the previous period. In 1475-85 the whole of this category is completely empty, so there is nothing more to be said.

The general conclusion of the whole matter is, however, fairly obvious. It is that in the period of the civil wars government was sustained by a group of not more than a dozen great nobles, among whom may be found men prominent on either side and at least two who changed their colours. Their support almost invariably took the form of service in one office or another, and was accompanied, as regards two-thirds of them, by heavy lending to the crown: as far as the remaining three or four men were concerned their chief contribution was to do their job and to be content, for the time being, with getting bad tallies in return. Outside these few public-spirited, or politically ambitious, or financially acquisitive types—for they seem to have included all three, and anyhow it is doubtful whether many of them lost money on their loans—there stood a much larger magnate class which remained almost completely apathetic towards the death-throes of the medieval *regnum*, or merely used its extremities to advance their private wars. Although a fair proportion of these people passively accepted quite considerable numbers of bad tallies without protest, only one among the whole lot—and that one a woman—made any large loans to the crown. After 1475 even this degree of interest in 'governance' died away, and for the next ten years no magnate had any financial relations of any kind worth mentioning with the king—or at least none which went on record in the exchequer. In this indifference, however, they had long been anticipated, and indeed far exceeded, by the smaller landowners, as will now become clear.

COUNTRY GENTRY	1452-62	1462-75	1475-85
	£ s. d.	£ s. d.	£ s. d.
'Genuine' loans	3,310 15 4½	2,760 12 9½	844 3 6
Fictitious loans	45 6 1½	156 0 0	—

Now that the Lancaster feoffees have disappeared it is evident that this class falls away into insignificance. It is true that there is at first some revival in the number of lenders, and even an increase of some £1,500 in the total amount lent, as compared with 1442-

52, but this effort does not come to anything very much and it is not sustained. In 1452–62 the total under genuine loans is produced by sixty-two lenders at an average of about £53 per head, and they are widely distributed over the length and breadth of England. Many of them, however, are not really individuals but communities represented by an individual, frequently a knight—e.g. a hundred, a group of vills, or 'divers persons' in some particular shire. The greatest effort seems to be made in Northamptonshire, partly under the leadership of a Londoner, Robert Tanfeld, who was probably a commissioner of loans; at any rate there is a total of £518 under his name, at least some of which is associated with 'divers persons' in that county, and there is another entry, about which there is no doubt, specifically crediting 'divers persons spiritual and temporal' of Northamptonshire with just under another £118. Altogether this midland county, together with its neighbours, Warwickshire and Leicestershire, seems to have raised more than most parts of England. What is going on is obviously a last attempt to raise money on a national, not merely a Lancastrian, scale, through commissioners of loans, as had been done with such success in Henry V's time, but compared with the £16,767 raised in that reign the result is not impressive, and in fact suggests that this appeal from the commons at Westminster to the commons in the shires did little but confirm the general lack of interest felt by this class in providing money for the crown.

In 1462–75 we do not find appeals of this sort being launched, and the eighteen lenders with their rather higher average of about £150 apiece are all genuinely individual persons, occasionally with one or two associates but never really representing anyone but themselves. The largest individual loan is one of £584 from John Glyn of Morval, Cornwall, but there are as many as ten others which attain three figures. Nearly all these loans come from southern and south-western England, which recalls the triumphal tour of those districts undertaken by Edward in the summer of 1461:[1] only two, and both for small amounts, come from as far north as Derbyshire and Lincolnshire. In the decade 1475–85 loans of this sort fall to only eleven, none bigger than £100 and more than half of them from east Anglia: two worth notice for their general interest and associations, though not for their amounts,

[1] See above, Chapter VIII, p. 285.

343

come respectively from William Paston[1] (£200) and Edmund Bedingfeld (£66 13s. 4d.) of Oxburgh Hall in Norfolk, where, until very recently, descendants of the same name still inhabited this unspoilt specimen of a fifteenth-century fortified manor house—and, incidentally, prefixed the name of Paston to their own.

Under fictitious loans the figures—or the lack of them—speak for themselves, and in conclusion it can only be repeated that the general results for *Country gentry* in the three periods under review could not more convincingly demonstrate the virtually complete withdrawal of this vitally important class of person from taking any part or lot in the financial struggles of the crown.

The same cannot be said of Londoners, though, as can be seen below, even their figures fall very steeply during the last period.

LONDON	1452–62			1462–75			1475–85		
	£	s.	d.	£	s.	d.	£	s.	d.
'Genuine' loans	18,924	12	4	35,852	9	4	3,044	2	1
Fictitious loans	852	8	11½	2,137	1	1	7	6	8

The first of the three figures under genuine loans reverts in fact to the fairly respectable total of 1422–32, while the second actually surpasses by some £3,800 the amount lent by London to Henry V. Only Henry IV in fact and Richard II (in the first half of his reign) succeeded in borrowing more from Londoners than Edward IV did between 1462 and 1475, quite apart from the fact that heavy lending in 1461 must also be credited, as we shall see, to his account.

In 1452–62 corporate loans from the mayor, aldermen and citizens as a body do in fact amount to exactly £11,000, as against £4,433 in the preceding decade, but whereas the £4,433 went to the Lancastrian, in default of any other, government, the whole of the £11,000 represents a single large loan made to Edward IV in the summer of 1461 in order to establish him in power. Nearly all the remaining loans for 1452–62, however, seem to be to the Lan-

---

[1] This is probably William Paston, son of judge Paston: see James Gairdner, ed., *Paston Letters*, III, index, sub. nom., also for Edmund Bedingfeld.

castrians—certainly all large ones. Among the bigger individual lenders alderman Philip Malpas, who appeared for only £463 in 1442–52, now increases his contribution to £3,213 and thus becomes Henry's main London support: no one else indeed even approaches four figures, except the executors of Ralph Holand, now described as 'tailor',[1] who provided the Lancastrian government with £933 from his estate. There are, however, thirty-two other lenders, including five small syndicates, for the remaining £3,778, and in general the names are new, though William Venour (still 'gentleman') recurs for a small sum, and Alexander Haysant is the principal sufferer (£400) under fictitious loans. The fishmongers perhaps are slightly more conspicuous than other gilds, though most of the leading fraternities are represented. Robert Tanfeld, who was found raising loans in Northamptonshire (see *Country gentry*) and was also an associate (under *Local officials*) for a small sum with the customs collector, John Poutrell, now joins with Hugh Wyche, alderman and later mayor (1462), in a loan of £500, but that is about all there is worth mentioning. The intimate connection between London and the Calais staple is emphasized by the fact that two lenders of small amounts are specifically described as 'merchants of the staple of Calais' in addition to being citizens of London, members of London gilds, and in one case sheriff and alderman of London.

In the first half of Edward IV's reign a very special effort was made by Londoners to help him, quite apart from the great corporate loan of 1461, and no less than 108 names, including nine syndicates, appear between 1462 and 1475 as those of persons lending him money, many of them considerable amounts. One very striking point is that there are practically no more corporate loans (only £647 worth in this period and none in the next), leaving no less than £35,205 to be found by private individuals. Among these we may note a goldsmith, John Barker, acting with Henry Massy (£1,830); another goldsmith, Hugh Brice, who not only lends £2,850 himself but is also a member of a syndicate advancing another £800; Robert Colwych, draper and chamberlain of London (£1,747); Sir William Hampton, fishmonger, who finds £1,143 on his own and a further £1,026 with friends; alderman Sir Ralph

---

[1] 'Draper' and alderman, lending £400, in 1432–42: alderman only, lending £900, in 1442–52.

Josselyn, who advances £240 alone and £1,000 with Thomas Tremayle; and William Kerver, who finds £1,302 6s. 1d. alone, £770 with Thomas Pounde,[1] and £545 17s. 3½d. with Geoffrey Kidwelly[2]—or £2,618 in all. Kerver, who is described elsewhere as a mercer, is also found in a rather mysterious but suggestive association with a certain Reginald or Roger Appleton, who seems to have been an auditor of the exchequer, and with John Rogger, variously described as 'of London' and as holder of no less an office than treasurer's clerk at the receipt; and this association seems to have produced, first and last, as much as £2,583 in genuine loans to the crown. The circumstances are obscure, but if the identities of Appleton and Rogger as exchequer officers can be taken as established, it certainly looks as if one function of Edward IV's senior clerks in that department—not to mention the livelier members of his household, like the Welshman Kidwelly— was to persuade their wealthy London friends, with whom they must have been in constant contact, to lend him money, or, quite possibly to join with them themselves in a profitable syndicate for the purpose—for I think it may be assumed that, whatever may have been the case with corporate loans, all this private lending by Londoners was done according to Mr. McFarlane's theory, that is, for a substantial but concealed consideration not appearing in the exchequer rolls.

However that may be, with this loan we reach almost the end of this long list: there only remain to be added to it John Parys, pewterer (£1,112), and a syndicate headed by alderman Sir Ralph Verney, who produced £540 himself and a further £1,000 in conjunction with two friends. It will thus be seen that some £18,489, or more than half the gross total lent by all London, was found by seven syndicates and the same number of individuals, most of whom take part in at least one syndicate as well. Excluding the small amount advanced corporately by the city, this leaves £16,716 for the remaining lenders, who numbered nearly a hundred and therefore lent, upon an average, about £160 apiece. Two or three of these names are interesting—for example, Anne Boleyn, widow of Geoffrey Boleyn (a former mayor), lent £200: and

---

[1] These two have already been found lending money in association elsewhere: see *Local officials* under Pounde, who was a collector of the London customs, above, p. 334.

[2] Prominent at the court of Edward IV—see *Household*, above, p. 327.

William Shore, mercer, that *mari complaisant*,[1] more than £540; while lady Alice Wyche, probably the widow of Hugh Wyche, lent as much as £838 6s. 8d. Only one stapler is specifically mentioned this time, viz. Sir John Yonge, who was also mayor of London in 1467 (£250). With all this lending fictitious loans naturally show some increase, but they are fairly well distributed, for the most part in comparatively small packets: only Sir William Hampton is credited with as much as £529 in bad tallies on his own account, and with a further £400 in association with his friend, John Brampton, alderman and collector of the London tunnage and poundage: William Kerver, too, gets £325 worth of bad tallies and Robert Colwych £240, but there are no other large fictitious loans.

In 1475-85 the picture is as usual very different; the total of genuine loans is enormously reduced, while fictitious loans practically disappear, and there are only fifteen genuine lenders. Among these, two-thirds of the entire total is found by a syndicate of citizens (unspecified in names or numbers) headed by Henry Colet and William Bracebrigge (£2,000, with a further £50 from Colet separately). There are no corporate city loans, and the only other loan which perhaps deserves mention is one of £233 6s. 8d. from a leading goldsmith, Sir Edmund Shaa, alderman. It is evident that Londoners no longer thought the Yorkist dynasty in need of such support as it had received during the preceding decade; or perhaps Edward IV, with his French pension and the ransoming of Margaret of Anjou,[2] did not think it worth his while to apply for what was possibly rather an expensive form of accommodation. The virtually complete disappearance of corporate loans from the city after 1461 is another interesting feature of his reign, especially if the theory that such loans were normally free of interest, while those from private individuals and syndicates were not, can be upheld. It must be remembered, however, that the last great loan of this nature, the £11,000 of 22 June 1461, though falling in my rather arbitrarily arranged scheme of decades in the period 1452-62, was not of course an investment in the failing Lancastrians but in the rising Yorkists. The city of London, which, if we deduct

---

[1] His wife Jane was notoriously Edward IV's mistress from about 1470 to 1482. It must, I think, be the same man, though he is described as a goldsmith in *D.N.B.* ('Jane Shore'). For Jane Shore's subsequent marriage to Geoffrey Kidwelly, see p. 327, n. 1, above.

[2] See above, Chapter VIII, pp. 306-7.

this £11,000, had done comparatively little between 1452 and 1461 to help Henry VI, was now definitely committed to the Yorkist cause, but it was left to private citizens to confirm Edward in power and so ensure the full repayment, whether with or without interest, of London's loans during the first half of his reign.

The same sort of private citizen or burgess outside London and the Calais staple, which was so closely associated with London, did very little, however, to help either Yorkists or Lancastrians. Once more the totals are misleading at first sight, because they include the staplers' loans.

BURGESSES	1452–62	1462–75	1475–85
	£ s. d.	£ s. d.	£ s. d.
'Genuine' loans	17,653 11 11	25,402 19 7½	875 11 8
Fictitious loans	706 4 6	49 5 9	94 1 4

Out of the above figures, it is obvious that only the genuine loans for the first two periods given are of any real interest, and when we come to look at these more closely we find that nearly all of them are accounted for by the staple or by staplers—for there are a few individual contributions described as such, in addition to the corporate staple loans. Thus between 1452 and 1462 the receipt rolls record loans amounting to £13,140 15s. 8d. from the society, and £2,080 from the mayors, of the staple, to which must be added £223 6s. 8d. from four individual staplers, making £15,444 2s. 4d. in all. This leaves only £2,209 from all the other seventy-four lending burgesses put together, or an average of only £30 per head. At least three-quarters of these, and probably even more, are community loans raised from cities, boroughs, vills and market towns as such, evidently on the same basis and at the same time as the numerous small loans from the shires and rural communities recorded under *Country gentry* for this period. In other words, commissioners of loans had been at work in the towns and boroughs as well as in the shires—and with about the same lack of success. Thus large and wealthy cities like Norwich[1] and Bristol could only

[1] For the internal politics of Norwich in this period see another useful study by Miss Haward, viz. 'Economic Aspects of the Wars of the Roses in East Anglia', *English Historical Review*, XLI (1926), 170–89. More regional studies on this excellent model are very badly needed.

be persuaded to lend £66 13s. 4d. and £100 respectively, and of the seven loans which reach three figures no less than four, including the two largest, are contributed by individuals or by private syndicates. Admittedly these two larger loans both came from citizens of Bristol, viz. William Canynges or Canyng, merchant (£333 6s. 8d.), and Thomas Yonge (£266 13s. 4d.), which may be held to increase the Bristol total to £700, but as against this Nottingham could not produce more than £153 3s. 2d. (corporately); two private merchants of York £101 4s. 1d. between them; and Lincoln (corporately) only £100. As in the case of the country gentry, the nation-wide appeal to wealthy burgesses through commissioners of loans had obviously been even more of a failure than the appeal to the same classes, the commons, in parliament. Indeed the one stronghold of the burgess class (outside London) which was willing to lend freely was the Calais staple, and the contrast is heightened by the fact that in that case even the large figures I have already quoted do not tell the whole story.

For this we must return to Miss W. I. Haward's chapter on 'The Financial Relations between the Lancastrian Government and the Merchants of the Staple, from 1449 to 1461' (*Studies in English Trade in the Fifteenth Century*, pp. 294–320). Miss Haward, it is true, does not take into account the loans from mayors of the staple and other individual staplers which I have included; and moreover, at first sight her figures even for corporate loans between 1452 and 1461 are some £2,000 short of mine. This, however, is easily explained by the fact that, as she herself points out, the £1,000 lent corporately on 28 December 1458 was only the first instalment of 'a loan of £1,000 a quarter which they (sc. the staplers) had just undertaken to lend to the king'. Miss Haward thinks that there may possibly have been one more quarterly payment of £1,000—and apparently one only, viz. at Michaelmas 1459. As she seems to be in some doubt about this, however, I have not included it in my summary of the totals she gives, but on the other hand I *have* included two quarterly instalments of £1,000 each lent on 21 June 1459 and 23 July 1461, both of which, though they are recorded in the receipt rolls, Miss Haward seems to have missed. The first at least of these was evidently paid under the arrangement of 1458, and I think it quite likely that the last payment, though made to Edward IV and not to Henry VI, was an echo of the same: as we shall see, what the staplers wanted was

349

'governance' and protection, and they were prepared to pay for it, whatever king was on the throne. In any case, the £2,000 in question makes up the difference between Miss Haward's figures and my own.

But again this is by no means all the story, for Miss Haward proceeds to mention an enormous loan of which the receipt rolls apparently take no account at all. This was the huge amount of £40,943—already referred to under *Burgesses* in my Chapter VII above—which the staplers are said to have advanced to the second duke of Somerset between 1451 and 1455, to pay the Calais garrison. If we suppose that a quarter of this can be added to my previous decade (1442-52) we are still left with well over £30,000 to be added to the recorded staple loans for 1452-62—in other words, just twice as much again as appears in the receipt rolls. I am not very clear about Miss Haward's authority for the existence of this vast addition to the help given by staplers to the crown, but she seems to be in no sort of doubt about it and I do not feel I can challenge her conclusions. After all, a total of £46,000 lent to the government in one decade should not have been beyond the staplers' powers: London lent over £51,000 to Henry IV, and over forty years later the resources of the staplers—many of whom in any case were themselves leading Londoners—cannot have been much smaller. Moreover there was a special reason for their help in the great mutiny of the Calais garrison (for want of wages) which took place in 1454. Miss Haward stresses at some length the alarm and inconvenience caused by this mutiny to staplers and the home government alike, and asserts that it was the staple which finally paid off the garrison's arrears, though it was not able to complete the task until 1456. One other alleged addition of considerable size to the receipt roll record of the staplers' loans is, however, rejected by Miss Haward, viz. the story told by the Tudor chronicler Fabyan that around 1460 the staplers lent the Yorkists about £18,000, which, if true, would have meant that they were largely instrumental in placing Edward IV upon the throne and had thereby set a precedent to the Londoners for the latter's large recorded loan of June 1461, which was certainly aimed at keeping him there. But Miss Haward considers that the contemporary evidence, which she examines at some length, makes the existence of this £18,000 loan highly improbable, though she does not mention the fact that between 1462 and 1475, as the receipt rolls show, the staplers really did lend not £18,000 but over £23,000 to Edward, quite apart from the 'act of retainer' of 1466,[1] under which they assumed the privilege of collecting all the Calais customs for a period of years, together with the responsibility for paying the garrison in future out of the proceeds.

The exact total of the staplers' loans in 1462–75 is £23,208 9s. 6½d., of which £22,231 16s. 2½d. was advanced corporately and a further £976 13s. 4d. by six individual staplers. (I can find no record of mayors of the staple lending separately in this period, and if they did so their contributions may be taken as included in my figure for corporate loans.) It will be noticed that this leaves only £2,194 10s. 1d. for other burgesses, of whom this time there were no more than eleven, all of whom were single individuals averaging just under £200 apiece. There are not even any private syndicates on this occasion—much less any corporate community loans. The largest lender is Richard Hert, mercer, of Lincoln with £637; he is followed by Thomas Lye, Ligh or Alegh, tailor, of Kyngstrete by Westminster,[2] with £545; John Robert, mercer, of Tregoney, Cornwall, with £246; William Canynges again, of Bristol, with £200; and Thomas Bounde, merchant, of Exeter, with £150: the rest are considerably smaller. In fact, as far as ordinary burgesses outside the staple are concerned, the picture under Edward IV is the same for them, if on an infinitely smaller scale, as for the Londoners: a few rich individuals supported him, but community loans were either withheld or, more probably, not asked for. In the last period (1475–85) all activity in this field dies away, and the society of the staple is practically the only lender with a mere £812 out of £875: there are only two other loans. As for fictitious loans, they are not worth serious consideration in any one of the three periods, though the staplers did get a couple of bad tallies for £500 in all between 1452 and 1462.

Generally speaking, then, there is nothing unexpected about the results under *Burgesses*: they merely confirm one trend (reliance on the staple) which had begun far back under the Lancastrians, and help to establish others which have already been explained and noted under *London, Country gentry* and elsewhere. What is interesting and demonstrable from the figures is the political

---

[1] Above, Chapter VIII, pp. 292, 301 and n. 2.

[2] Still perfectly distinct from, and outside the walls of, London, of course, so this is technically not a London loan.

catholicity of the staplers; the continued lack of any wide-based popular support for either of the rival dynasties outside London and Calais; and the growing unreliability of receipt roll evidence —at any rate in the 1450's—where the latter is concerned. So much at any rate is true of denizens: when we turn to alien merchants the picture changes yet again.

ALIENS	1452–62	1462–75	1475–85
	£ s. d.	£ s. d.	£ s. d.
'Genuine' loans	1,033 6 8	38,128 15 6	753 6 8
Fictitious loans	500 0 0	1,606 12 6	—

In this table for the first time we have really only one total worth considering, viz. that of genuine loans for 1462–75. The two small totals for 1452–62 can be eliminated, since they consist of five little genuine loans made at the very end of that decade not to the Lancastrians but to Edward IV, together with two fictitious loans credited in the same year (1461–2) to two of the lenders. Henry VI in short had no relations of any kind with alien merchants in his last few years; the political danger and discredit of his position, together with the futile tax on aliens and the not inconsiderable numbers of bad tallies which aliens had received during the previous twenty years, had done their work. They lent him no money at all; but they were prepared to invest heavily in his rival Edward, who in fact succeeded in borrowing far more from aliens in the critical first half of his reign than any previous English government had done since the minority and youth of Richard II, or the still palmier days of Edward III.

Edward's chief friends in this category were the Florentines, who provided him with no less than £30,472, and among these again by far the most prominent was the well-known Gerard de Caniziani,[1] who alone found as much as £24,705. Next to him came the great

---

[1] Mr. J. R. Lander (loc. cit.) says he was 'naturalized', i.e. had letters of denization—a special favour accorded to a very few aliens. An additional reason for this privilege may be found in a further statement by Mr. Lander, viz. that he was Edward's principal factor for his private trading.

house of Medici, mentioned for the first time in the receipt rolls, with £5,000; while the smaller of the remaining two Florentine lenders reflected the fallen fortunes of the Bardi. From 1422 to 1452 it had been the Genoese who had led the way in Italian lending to the English crown; after ten years' interval they now resumed the practice with loans totalling £4,500—a rather higher level than before. They were still represented for this purpose by a Spinola, coupled this time with one of the Grimaldi. Venice contributed £2,956, the greater part of which was found by Marco de Prioli (£1,000) and Marco de Pesero (£840) and their associates: three Lucchese lenders brought up the rear with less than £200 between them. In view of the large total it is not surprising to find a small revival in fictitious loans: over half of these (£820) were credited to an anonymous Venetian syndicate, which had also made real loans totalling only £666 13s. 4d.,[1] and most of the remainder to Gerard de Caniziani (£616). About 1475–85 all that need be said is that the same four Italian cities, and many of the same firms, reappear for relatively minute sums, but the biggest single amount is one of £266 13s. 4d. from 'Harman Plowgh' (sic) and other merchants of the Hanse—an organization last heard of in this connection under Henry IV.

There remains only the limbo of the unidentified, which contains an embarrassingly large number of persons in the first half of Edward IV's reign. The figures are:

UNIDENTIFIED	1452–62			1462–75			1475–85		
	£	s.	d.	£	s.	d.	£	s.	d.
'Genuine' loans	142	13	0	4,340	13	6	116	13	4
Fictitious loans	70	17	11	73	4	5	13	6	8

I do not think we need concern ourselves with the first and last of these periods or with fictitious loans in the middle one, since in each case the total value is so small. But the figure for genuine

---

[1] Just possibly this may represent another instance of concealed interest —viz. £666 13s. 4d. lent in actual cash, but £820 repaid (at any rate in intention). The proportion of the two sums is about right, compared with 1384–5.

loans, 1462–75, certainly requires some comment, though I am afraid that in spite of much research in chancery calendars—my main source of information about individuals where the receipt rolls provide none—I cannot give a satisfactory explanation. It is true that Thomas Godelok, lender of the largest single sum (£1,473), may perhaps have been a burgess of Southampton, but I cannot be reasonably sure of this. Of John Trymland, the next largest lender (£612), I can find no trace at all: the third largest, Thomas Tomeowe (£470), may, however, be some relation to Richard Tomyou, whom we have encountered about this time as a merchant of Cornwall. Of the remaining lenders who achieve three figures—and there are nine of them—I can again find absolutely no trace, so that at the best the total cannot be reduced by more than £1,943, which may possibly belong to *Burgesses*: this, however, still leaves nearly £2,400 unaccounted for, concerning which I can only offer my regrets and pass on.

When we consider the subject matter of this chapter as a whole, not much in fact remains to be said which has not been said before, but it may be convenient to repeat it here in summary form. Real revenue for this last abnormal period of thirty years, 1452–85, seems to fluctuate between £24,000 and £33,000 *per annum*—the lowest it had ever been—but whereas Henry's figures are probably fairly accurate, these low totals take little or no account of important external sources of income created or acquired by Edward IV. We must add liberally in the latter's case for benevolences, most of which were obviously omitted from the receipt rolls; for the whole, or at the very least a large portion of, the French pension (from 1475); and very probably for the profits upon trading ventures undertaken by the crown, which must have been much more frequent and have come to much more than the receipt rolls will allow; besides which there are important parliamentary grants[1] whose proceeds for one reason and another were not included in the rolls, and the Calais customs (and expenses) made over from 1466 to the staplers.[2] All this must be considered to have been real income; and it must also be remembered that, owing to the trans-

---

[1] Above, Chapter VIII, pp. 303–5 (Easter 1474).

[2] Mr. J. R. Lander (loc. cit.) adds that under the Yorkist kings the hereditary Yorkist lands were not accounted for at all in the exchequer but, if anywhere, in the chamber. He thinks the same to be true of forfeited lands, but here I am inclined to think he overstates his case.

mutation of the French relationship from a heavy debit to an asset, Edward IV had nothing like the expenses of the unfortunate Henry VI. In the 1460's, it is true, and indeed until the early 1470's, he was still menaced with further civil war and insurrection, while these new sources of relief were as yet in only part operation, but in his last ten years at least, if not earlier, he was very much more prosperous than his predecessor—a fact which the receipt rolls disguise.

It may be that this period of prosperity alone accounts for the steep fall in the book-keeping percentage in the rolls from a steady 30% or more to only 6% after 1475: there was no longer any need to borrow money or to pay creditors with doubtful tallies of assignment. Had Richard III won the battle of Bosworth, of course, the picture might have changed again; for the French pension had ceased and the civil wars had been renewed, and there is little reason to suppose that the usurper would have shown the financial and political ability of Henry Tudor.[1] It is significant that even during the two years through which he clung to the throne (for which, moreover, only three receipt rolls out of four survive) there is a distinct rise in genuine, though not in fictitious, loans. Whether this rise would have gone on, however, depends not only on the chances of the civil war but also on the interesting question whether the habit of omitting major items from the receipt rolls had become so well established under Edward IV that, in face of competition from the tellers and the *scriptor talliarum*, the three clerks of the receipt would never have regained their old importance or have been encouraged to revive upon a large scale

[1] On the other hand Mr. Lander (loc. cit.) points out that a financial memorandum long in print (*Letters and Papers of Ric. III and Hen. VII*, I, 81-5, ed. James Gairdner) was originally drawn up, out of Yorkist experience, for Richard III's use in 1485. It was never put into effect, but it is believed to have anticipated many of Henry VII's still mysterious exchequer reforms on the receipt and issue side (see A. P. Newton in *Eng. Hist. Rev.*, XXXIII, 352-3). If this could be proved, it would lend force to Mr. Lander's claim at the conclusion of his thesis that 'the "new monarchy" of Edward IV and Henry VII was a movement of conservative "economical reform" and the last and most successful effort after stabilization and order'. In other words there was no real break in exchequer history in 1485, and Henry VII was no innovator but merely carried out the intentions of the Yorkists. However, we know far too little at present of Henry VII's exchequer reforms to be able to say this with any certainty, and personally I do not believe it.

THE RECEIPT OF THE EXCHEQUER, 1377-1485

such obsolete procedures as those of the fictitious loan.

But these are speculations on the might-have-been—never a very profitable mode of writing history. To return to facts: the change from Lancastrian to Yorkist is marked by many other things, one of which is the increased adventurousness and rather shady prosperity of certain members of the royal household. Under Henry we have impecunious, hag-ridden officials who can offer nothing but their service to the crown; but under Edward there is clearly coming into existence a type of courtier—generally a common-lawyer—on the make, who is evidently encouraged in his dubious activities by a king who was able and unscrupulous enough himself in such respects to appreciate these qualities in others. The one condition laid upon these Says and Fowlers and Kidwellys seems to have been that of lending from their profits to the crown; but, provided that they did so, their private financial relations with the Londoners, for example, may well have been encouraged. On the whole they were small fry, but they were doing well for themselves: indeed, the lifting of the Yorkist stone by Henry Tudor must have revealed a host of creeping, thriving things beneath it.

Some of these men held office in the exchequer, but in general the great loans made by that department were the work of magnate treasurers who had already been employed for just such a purpose, and with similar success, by the Lancastrians. Their activities in both periods—though, of course, the individual magnates concerned are apt to change—easily explain why the totals under *Magnates* (that is, in their private function) come to be so small: those of them who were prepared to lend money to the crown were doing so as office-holders and were assuming large administrative responsibilities as well. One of them—John Tiptoft, earl of Worcester—even has a triple instead of a dual role, for he lends still further sums in more official capacities than one; but with this exception, and that of an occasional treasurer of Calais, the moneylenders among what I have called *Local officials* are usually customs officers of some sort, who were after all about the only persons in that category by that date in the least likely to have any money in hand. Customs in fact, pledged, abated and remitted and assigned as they now were, had become about the only steady sources of revenue and it is indeed remarkable that they went on being collected with such comparative efficiency right through the period of the civil wars, and even during some years in the 1460's when Edward had as yet no parliamentary title to them at all. Probably the explanation lies precisely in the fact that not only the king but so many other powerful persons and corporations, such as the staple, stood to gain by their collection: the position was hopelessly confused, but there was at least a majority interest in keeping the collection of the customs going, whichever side was uppermost in the civil war.

Bishops, broadly speaking, cease to be financiers in this epoch, with the possible exception of George Neville, bishop of Exeter, and William Gray, bishop of Ely; in any case, whatever these two did, they did as chancellor and treasurer respectively, and no other bishop made more than what one might call small routine loans to the government. In proportion to their much smaller wealth the minor clergy did a good deal more, especially in aid of the Lancastrians, when their contribution was actually more than twice as much as that of the episcopate. The country gentry and smaller burgesses, on the other hand, outside London and Calais, were unwilling to take risks of any kind for either dynasty, and refused in their own homes as steadfastly as they did through representatives at Westminster to provide adequately for the financial needs of government.

We are left with the three great groups of powerful merchants— the first two closely interlocked—who lived in London, Calais and north Italy. Of these the first and last showed a pronounced Yorkist bias; aliens in particular now utterly refused to help the tottering Lancastrians. Londoners were rather more generous, but reserved their main effort to set up and fortify the Yorkists; while the staplers seem to have thought, in their own interest, that any form of English government in any hands was better than none, and to have subsidized all and sundry indiscriminately to the limits of their power.

But all that I have said in these paragraphs applies only to the last Lancastrian and the first Yorkist 'decade': after 1475 the ingenious Edward is secure, and so the powerful assistance of magnate treasurers, staplers, Londoners and Italian finance houses, which had done so much to put him where he was and keep him there, falls right away. Even the staplers' contract to collect the Calais customs and pay the Calais garrison is not exempt, in time, from this development. Yet the structure which Edward had so painfully assembled was a personal one: it had already cracked and

357

was collapsing at his death, and though the usurper Richard did his best to shore the ruins by reviving some at least of the traditional expedients, it was only on a small and feeble scale and the effort was predestined to defeat. Not least in matters of exchequer records and financial cunning the establishment of Henry Tudor on the throne meant the beginning of a new and stabler world.

CONCLUSION

We have travelled a long way from the simple inquiry whether entries marked *sol'* in the receipt rolls do or do not disappear to all intents and purposes in the course of the fifteenth century: as the tables show, the answer is broadly in the negative. It is to be hoped, however, that they show much more than that—if not, perhaps, with the same degree of conviction. Looking back on my researches as a whole, I am first of all impressed with the majestic downward movement of the revenue during these hundred and eight years, as portrayed in graph I at the end of this book. It seems clear that, if the receipt rolls can be trusted to display a tolerably accurate effect, fourteenth-century kings—even Edward III—dealt in figures of a wholly different order of magnitude from those of their successors, excluding Henry V. It is true that income must be measured against expenditure and that war is the greatest of extravagances: consequently, neither of the two kings I have just mentioned was comfortably placed, in spite of the large sums which flowed into their exchequers. The same may be said of the minority of Richard II, when the French war was dragging on from bad to worse and engulfing large amounts of money. But the period of Richard's personal rule tells a very different story, and, thanks to the peace policy which he so successfully pursued and for which he is seldom given full credit, the finances of the crown at that time achieved a prosperity and buoyancy unequalled in the whole middle ages. Unfortunately Richard's political sense at home did not match his comparatively enlightened foreign policy; he was guilty of a feeble attempt at despotism, and it became possible for his numerous enemies to maintain that the financial success which he enjoyed was really built upon a general attack on private property. There was much truth in this, but the attack was probably a good deal less lucrative and necessary for Richard's ends than was asserted at the time, though quite as ill-judged. It destroyed him; and destroyed with him for the time being the stability of English foreign relations and the financial independence, and indeed the solvency, of the English crown. Henry IV was hopelessly enmeshed in theories about a parliamentary title to the throne, imposed retrospectively after the event; he was also

359

continuously harried by rebellion at home and hostility abroad; by financial needs and commitments, in other words, which far outran his means. It needed all the strength and popularity of Henry V, and the brilliant victories which marked his renewal of the French war, to put the revenue back on to a fourteenth-century standard and even then it was the standard not of Richard II but of Edward III.

With Henry's death and the long minority of his son the natural reluctance of the English people, like that of all peoples, to pay taxes had free play, and only the loss of all Henry's French conquests forced them in the long run, when it was already much too late, to make some belated provision of the sort which they should have made many years earlier. The modern world suffers from an excess of 'governance' and exploitation of the individual, which brings its own evils and very terrible they are; but the late Lancastrian period shows equally decisively the perils of the opposite extreme. Conditions of this sort usually result in civil war, the main effect of which is to set the pendulum swinging again in the opposite direction. In the Yorkist period it did not swing very far, but it swung far enough for Edward IV to evolve, after a prolonged and shaky start, an interesting compromise by which the legitimate demands upon the private citizen were not much increased but other, and more dubious, means were found to satisfy the king's financial necessities. The policy was a personal one and was beginning to collapse even before Edward's death, but the renewal of the civil war was brief, and since Henry Tudor chanced to be a man of altogether exceptional powers he was able to found a stable dynasty.

Such at any rate is the picture of the age presented by the receipt rolls. To what extent can we accept it? I do not think that the comparative prosperity which the rolls suggest in Richard II's later years is very far from the mark, though it is not unlikely that they obscure the details of his illegitimate exactions: such things, as in the case of Edward IV and his benevolences, were apt not to find their way into exchequer records, except in such small amounts as to disguise their true importance. As to Henry IV, the rolls tend slightly to exaggerate his money difficulties—for example, parliament allowed no record to be made in them of the abnormal subsidy of 1404—yet in his reign and in that of Henry V the broad outlines of the picture are probably fairly accurate. The same may be said of Henry VI's reign; for though certain technical changes begin in the middle of that long period which somewhat shake one's confidence in the series in other respects, they do not go so far as to affect the genuineness of the impression one receives of a steeply, almost catastrophically, falling revenue. Under Edward IV, however, the rolls cease to be a trustworthy guide, since not only benevolences but parliamentary grants upon a large scale, much of the large income derived from Louis XI, and probably the bulk of Edward's trading profits, are omitted from them.

However, it was not the main object of this book to arrive at an approximate statement of the gross royal revenues, or even of that proportion of them which is recorded in the receipt rolls: it was merely a first step in the analysis to discover how much of the apparent revenue actually recorded there was genuine; not to find out how much unrecorded revenue must be added to it. The second step, as already indicated at the beginning of this epilogue, was to determine how much of the net recorded revenue was actually paid in cash into the exchequer and how much was anticipated or 'assigned'. There were great technical difficulties, which have been dealt with as far as possible in Chapter I and in appendix A, in distinguishing with any certainty between the two types of revenue, but at any rate approximately accurate results have been recorded in graph II and in the B series of tables. It will be seen from these that, while assignment generally predominates, there were periods of extremely high cash frequency under Richard II and Henry V, while an appreciable amount of cash continued to be paid direct into the exchequer even in the Yorkist epoch: indeed, in no less than four terms out of nineteen in the period 1475-86 cash actually exceeded the volume of assignment —and the last of these terms is as late as 1482.

But, proceeding in order of increasing difficulty, the analysis reached its main problem only when it came to deal with the large margin of difference in the receipt rolls between all recorded real revenue, whether paid in cash or assigned, and the usually much larger total of nominal revenue; and it was in the attempt to break down that margin into its component parts that the real difficulties began. If various interesting but minor elements are now excluded, it can be said that the principal ingredients of this margin turned out to be three in number during Richard II's reign, viz. loans, genuine and fictitious, and *prestita restituta*, but that only the first two of these were found in sizeable amounts during the remainder of the period. Again it was not easy to distinguish even these principal ingredients from each other; to decide which loans were really genuine; to differentiate between types of fictitious loan; to be quite certain of the difference between loans and prests, which deceived even the clerks of the exchequer themselves on at least one occasion. The results must therefore once more be regarded as approximate, but such as they are they are offered to the reader in graph III and in the D series of tables, while the distribution of the amounts between different classes in the community is recorded in the tables marked E.

To begin with genuine loans: it was discovered that the governments of Richard II's minority relied mainly on Italian merchants and the Londoners for this form of support; that Richard II in his later phase did not really borrow very much from anyone but Londoners, and, although there was a new and unpleasant element of compulsion in his later loans, they were in fact less than half the amount raised between 1377 and 1389. London again, and this time on a very large scale, was the main—indeed the only considerable—supporter of Henry IV. Henry V also borrowed fairly freely from the Londoners, but he went further than his father in laying the country gentry of England under heavy contribution as well, though bishop Beaufort was his chief financial source. For the first half of Henry VI's reign cardinal Beaufort, as he had now become, was easily the main stand-by of the government, followed, at some distance, by Henry Chichele, archbishop of Canterbury, and other feoffees of the duchy of Lancaster; the Calais staplers; and the Londoners. It is noteworthy that London loans declined from 1422 to 1432, and though they rose again in the next decade their rise was not proportionate to the efforts made by other lenders: indeed by this time it was the staplers who, although they had lent only some £8,000 to Henry IV, were now the chief supporters of the government. In fact 1432-42 marks the peak of all genuine borrowing, with just over a quarter of a million pounds, but this total falls away rapidly during the next ten years, when Lancastrian credit was sinking, and only Beaufort, Chichele, the staplers, and a small group of wealthy magnates continued to support the failing dynasty in a vain effort to avert the loss of France. The next period is one of civil war, in which only a few rich magnates, acting as treasurers, some individual Londoners, and the staplers sought to keep some sort of government in being. In the first half of Edward IV's reign, however, loans rise again, viz. from magnate treasurers once more; alien merchants (for the first time since the minority of Richard II); the Londoners, who now support Edward almost as vigorously as they had once supported Henry IV; and finally the staple. After 1475, however, genuine loans from any source practically disappear from the receipt rolls.

It must surely be admitted that this pronounced rhythm of lending to the crown is of sufficient interest in itself—illustrating, as it does, the varying relations between government and the community—to justify the four chapters of detailed analysis which have been given to it in this book. But it raises other points as well, for example the question of motive, and how far that was influenced by the possibility of defying the canon law on usury and deriving profit from these loans. I confess I have been much attracted by Mr. McFarlane's theory, to which I have already frequently referred, that the simplest possible method of defeating canonist prohibitions was followed in most cases: viz. that of entering on the receipt rolls as repayable (and in many cases as actually repaid) a sum greater by, say, 25% or more than that actually received in cash in the exchequer. By this means no record of any kind would be left of the usurious side of the transaction, and that aspect of it becomes *ex hypothesi* all the more difficult for the modern historian to prove. I believe, however, that I have found some contributory evidence, which I have quoted in this book, apropos of certain loans from aliens and others in 1384-6—evidence which supports, although it may not prove, Mr. McFarlane's theory. I have also found hints to much the same effect in the case of a London loan of 1442 and in that of another loan made by an anonymous Venetian syndicate at the extreme end of my period. Personally I feel little doubt that Mr. McFarlane is right, but there is another consideration which, unlike the foregoing, I have not yet mentioned in these pages; and this unfortunately detracts somewhat from the profit-making motive of the lenders, or, alternatively, explains the high rate of discount supposed to have been offered on their loans by the exchequer. It is this.

When genuine loans were accepted at the exchequer they were frequently 'paid off' or, as we should say, security was given for their repayment, within a very short period, sometimes only a day

THE RECEIPT OF THE EXCHEQUER, 1377-1485

or two. In most cases this security took the form of tallies of assignment, i.e. drafts upon future revenue in the hands of local collectors of one kind or another. Now these tallies were themselves not only inconvenient to cash—if drawn, as they often were, on some official at the other end of the country—but also very frequently dishonoured, in which case the creditor had to bring them back to the exchequer and ask for new and better tallies in their place, which again might be dishonoured in their turn. This meant that the whole tedious process could be repeated almost indefinitely until the creditor was satisfied, and might actually extend over years. As a result of this, the practice of discounting tallies of assignment in or near Westminster for sums very much less than their face value is known to have sprung up, and there is little doubt that it was practised by many of the very people who received such tallies in return for genuine loans made to the crown. It is important to note that in such cases the profit which the original lenders may have expected (under Mr. McFarlane's theory) to have made out of their loans, was extinguished by the discount which they in turn had to agree to if they wanted quick results from their tallies of assignment: in other words, the two discounts cancel one another out and the profit (if any) is passed on to the professional discounter of tallies, usually a citizen of London or perhaps a small Westminster official, not uncommonly himself on the staff of the exchequer. I do not say that this happened every time, or anything like it, but it is a possible cycle of events which should be taken into account, if only because it helps to explain the rapid rise to wealth of at least some Londoners and of certain Westminster officials or civil servants. It must be remembered that the investment was foolproof; for the exchequer would always see that the tally was paid off in the end, and it was only a question of patience on the discounter's part, coupled with the possession of enough cash reserves in the first instance for some of them to be frozen, possibly for years, before they could bear fruit.

This business of discounting tallies of assignment also affects the next sub-head, viz. fictitious loans. When a tally of assignment was dishonoured the person who had accepted it in satisfaction of some claim against the crown was usually credited with a fictitious 'loan' until his claim was effectively satisfied. Each fictitious loan therefore represents a temporary default on the part of the exchequer, and this, to say the least of it, might prove exceedingly annoying, especially to a creditor who had shut his ears to the discounters and had perhaps been to a great deal of trouble and expense to try and cash what had finally turned out to be a bad tally. It is for this reason that I have thought it worth while to extract the totals of fictitious loans from the rolls and to analyse them in the same way as genuine loans, viz. by showing their weight of incidence on different classes in the community. It seemed to be a convenient measure of frustration, which, as it was so often practised on a really large scale, might even have political effects.

But if in the majority of cases the recipient of a tally of assignment hastened to discount it before he knew whether it was in fact a bad tally or not, it is obvious that he would not be affected if the tally, which no longer concerned him, was eventually returned to the exchequer. The only person to suffer any inconvenience—possibly renewed, as bad tally succeeded bad tally—would be the discounter, and his discount was obviously designed to meet precisely this contingency. This being so, it is clear that when, let us say, Henry Percy, earl of Northumberland, received large numbers of bad tallies of assignment in his capacity as warden of the east march against Scotland, he may in fact have discounted them immediately and so, at a sacrifice, have obtained some real money. But as the receipt rolls invariably go on using the name of the earl of Northumberland in this hypothetical example, whoever may in fact be handling the tallies, until the original assignment has been made good, we may be receiving a completely false impression of the true situation. Moreover, it must be remembered that fictitious loans were repetitive and cumulative; that is to say, a single obligation admitted by the exchequer could give rise to a whole series of fictitious loans in succession for the same original amount in the same person's name, as effort after effort to satisfy the original obligation failed: in fact, the whole process might continue to repeat itself almost indefinitely, causing a new fictitious loan each time, until the original debt was paid off. Hence simply to add up the total of fictitious loans, as I have done, may be held to represent a great inflation of the actual default of the exchequer, although, as I have said earlier in this book, the persons who accepted these bad tallies, provided that they were also the actual persons who kept on trying to cash them, would at least have had their full fictitious loans' worth of annoyance and disappointment!

And even if the would-be cashers were not the men whose names stand in the receipt and issue rolls as the recipients of these tallies, still the actual recipients (e.g. in my hypothetical case, the earl of Northumberland in person) would at least have been subjected to another and still irritating experience, viz. that of being forced to accept a heavy and completely irrecoverable discount on sums urgently needed and genuinely due, as the sole alternative to going through the weary processes associated with the fictitious loan.

None the less it may still be felt that my totals of these 'loans' will not really bear the full weight of the interpretation which I have placed upon them. In reply to this I would urge that, in addition to the corrective factors I have already mentioned, there are yet others which perhaps will tip the scales. In the first place, by no means every tally of assignment was discounted; most of them in fact were undoubtedly accepted by the persons for whose benefit they were made out. Those which are doubtful are usually marked in the margin of the receipt roll with some formula containing a *per manus* element, and, although these *per manus* entries are certainly very common, they are by no means universal: moreover, as I have explained in appendix A and elsewhere, it is not at all certain that all of them refer to the discounting of tallies of assignment. Secondly, there is reason to believe, as I have again suggested in the same appendix, that assignments could be made by writs and other instruments distinct from tallies—perhaps even by word of mouth—and that when assignments such as these went wrong no trace whatever would be left in the receipt rolls, which are primarily a register of tallies and of little else. The value of such assignments may well have been considerable, and the proportion of them which failed (without, of course, giving rise to a fictitious loan, since they were not entered on the roll) must have been rather greater, if anything, than that of ordinary assignments. *Ex hypothesi* they are very difficult to trace, yet the total amount of default they represent, whatever that may be, ought really to be added to that of the fictitious loans on record, and this unknown sum should go a long way towards reinflating the existing totals, if no confidence is felt in them. Finally, there is the fact that from the middle of Henry VI's reign there are large numbers of assignments in the rolls which have been cancelled *without* giving rise to so much as one fictitious loan. These, too, I have discussed in Chapter I and in appendix A, but it must be stressed that I have neither summed them nor added them to my total of bad tallies, so that here is another natural corrective to any possible inflation in my total of fictitious loans—or, more strictly, a justification of that total. In Henry VI's time these heavy cancellations co-exist with even heavier fictitious loans, made for other cancellations: under the Yorkists, however, it is possible that such uncorrected cancellation *takes the place of* the fictitious loan to a considerable extent, though never quite completely. This may possibly explain the heavy fall in totals under that head, especially during the first half of the Yorkist period—a fall which in that case represents a very considerable underestimate on my part of this kind of default.

Subject to these warnings and qualifications the totals for fictitious loans are interesting enough, reign by reign, to justify much the same sort of summary as that which I have already given for genuine loans. In the first part of Richard II's reign the main victims are household and local officials (about equally), and to a less degree magnates; in the second part of the reign, local officials only. Under Henry IV there is an enormous inflation of these figures for the household, which received almost as many bad tallies as it did in the peak period (1442–52 for this purpose) under Henry VI. Local officials are again left badly off in 1399–1413, and so are magnates, especially those occupying any administrative post. Under Henry V the more favourable conditions of 1389–99 are largely reproduced; but under Henry VI crown finances deteriorate so rapidly that many magnates suffer from the start from this abuse; though when the king grows up it is again household and local officials who tend to take an ever larger and larger share of those tallies which could not at first be cashed. In 1432–42 bishops—that is, principally cardinal Beaufort and Henry Chichele —also get a great many of them, though that is the only decade in the whole hundred and eight years in which bishops are major victims. The peak figure for fictitious loans is reached, as has already been said, in 1442–52, but by this time more than two-thirds of them are for the account of local officials and the household. In the abnormal civil war period which follows, the same two classes receive most of the reduced total, with magnates running very near to them; but in 1462–75 we enter on an age when, as I have said, the technique of the fictitious loan is becoming obsolete and the figures are no longer of the same order of significance. It is interesting to find that, for the first time, the exchequer itself heads the much-reduced list, mainly on account of treasurers' loans, but the household is still a good second and provides the only class of person of any consequence whatsoever in this connection between 1475 and 1485. I do not think it necessary to point out here what moral, if any, can be drawn from this brief survey; but I again hope that at any rate enough may have emerged from it for the reader to agree that the more detailed treatment of the subject given in my four chapters of analysis has been worth while.

We are left with *prestita restituta*, which account for very large sums appearing in the receipt rolls of Richard II and his predecessors, but practically wither away after 1395. Most of these were simply large credits, often in assignments, held by clerks or minor household officers for a shortish period on behalf of commanders in the field in war-time—to whom they were eventually transferred for the purpose of acquiring material of war and, more especially, of paying soldiers' and sailors' wages. When this happened and the paymasters' accounts were cleared, they were entered on the receipt roll as 'prests'—that is, credits or advances —now 'repaid' (or, more properly, accounted for), though the revenue they represent must have figured once already in some earlier roll. The inflation thus created is considerable in the first eighteen years of my period, but apart from this not unimportant fact *prestita* have small significance. They represent indeed little more than a somewhat clumsy book-keeping device, the real object of which is obscure; but in any case it went out of fashion well before the close of Richard II's reign, and, unlike loans of all kinds, throws very little light on the financial problems of the crown. It is a minor key on which to end, but it is none the less the logical ending.

If there is one thing to be learned from the long and intricate analysis embodied in this book—approximate, and indeed impressionist, as most of its results are bound to be—it is that of exchequer continuity throughout the whole period, and indeed far beyond. Methods might change; *prestita* might dwindle; fictitious loans might ultimately fall into disfavour; abnormal grants of revenue, once faithfully recorded (cf. the poll-taxes of Richard II), might be banned from the receipt rolls by Lancastrian parliaments; Henry IV, that saviour of society, might omit to repay Richard's forced loans; Richard III, too, might try to clean the slate; but

CONCLUSION

the exchequer went on, for century after century, through war and
revolution, without suffering any purge of personnel and with the
major lines of its technique unchanged. It might develop an
internal struggle of its own between auditor and tellers on the one
side and the 'treasurer of the receipt', or treasurer's clerk, assisted
by the chamberlains' clerks, upon the other; but it never wholly
ceased to function and it never lost important ground to its old
enemies, the wardrobes and the chamber, even when household
finance was vigorously revived alongside it by the Tudors. Tallies
went on being cut (and growing steadily in size); assignments
made; receipt rolls written; until the time of Pepys—indeed until
the time of George III—and nobody can understand the full
intricacies of Stuart finance or appreciate the niceties of the
Hanoverian treasury and its placemen, without steeping himself in
the procedure of the medieval clerks of the exchequer, in which
the clerks of the receipt played no small part. Such an understanding must involve a maddening juggle with interminable figures,
most of which do not even begin to mean what they appear to say:
yet this too has a fascination of its own. I return to the quotation
from that great and much-lamented historian, Marc Bloch, which
I have placed upon my title page. *Laissons d'abord parler les chiffres.*
Ils ont une sorte de brutale éloquence.

APPENDIX A

MARGINALIA OF THE TREASURER'S RECEIPT ROLLS, 1349-99

INTRODUCTION

In the course of an investigation into the proportion borne by the so-called *sol'* entries to the *pro* entries in the receipt rolls of the period 1349-99,[1] I was struck by the multiplicity and variety of the general marginalia of these rolls. These marginalia strayed so often and so far from the simple *sol'* and *pro* formulae which I had set out to observe that, while carrying out my original purpose, I endeavoured to make a few rough notes of the principal variants I encountered on my way. When I came to analyse the results I had obtained in this fashion, it seemed to me worth while to draft them into a supplementary study in the hope that, while establishing little on their own account, they might still prove of some use to other workers in this field. It is obvious that not much can be definitely proved from a partial and hurried examination of the evidence contained in a set of rolls which really require to be checked in detail by the complementary issue rolls at least, and indeed by as many other allied classes of record as possible. So elaborate an investigation I have not undertaken, but I hope I have at any rate indicated certain points from which it might begin. I have permitted myself some inferences of a highly hypothetical character, but they can in the nature of things be little more than shots in the dark, and if they are occasionally couched in too dogmatic terms, that is merely because the continued use of the conditional clause and the qualifying epithet soon becomes equally tedious to writer and reader alike.

I should explain that, whereas the paper I have already mentioned was based upon an examination of every extant receipt roll of the period, the following observations are confined to the treasurer's rolls alone. The reason for this is simply the idle one that the treasurer's roll is for various reasons much easier to analyse in a given time than either of the two chamberlains' rolls. The latter are supposed to be approximately duplicates of the treasurer's roll and of each other, but they habitually omit much of just that sort of detail of which I was in search. Their chief use is that they bridge the sometimes not inconsiderable gaps in the treasurer's series, but even for that purpose I have

---

[1] *Eng. Hist. Rev.*, XLIII, 172.

not consulted them on this occasion. My excuse is that this particular inquiry is more selective than statistical: I have, that is to say, been interested in noting the different types of marginalia rather than the number of occasions on which they occur. Whenever I do mention figures of that sort it should be remembered that they exclude approximately two-fifths of the treasurer's rolls for this period, which have disappeared. The proportion may sound a high one, but the only continuous gaps of more than three terms in length are from Easter 1365 to Easter 1368 and from Michaelmas 1374–5 to Michaelmas 1376–7 inclusive. Moreover, the general impression I obtained when examining the chamberlains' rolls, though admittedly from the point of view of *sol'* and *pro* alone, was not such as to make me think that much would be gained by extending the present inquiry in the same fashion.

My results fall roughly into twelve divisions, as follows. To begin with the *pro* entries, I soon discovered that there was a whole class of entry in which the word *pro* was followed either by more than one name, or by certain other and even more convincing indications that the payment in the body of the roll was being, or had been, assigned to more than one purpose. This class, whose mere existence breaks most of the accepted rules, I grouped together under the provisional title of *Complex assignment.*[1] The simpler, but still abnormal *pro* entries, namely those which appeared to refer to only one assignment but were unusual in form, then fell naturally into the category of *Simple assignment.* A third main variety of assignment was furnished by the discovery that a large number of entries were assigned under a standard formula to the very persons who were supposed to have made the payments in question; these I have headed *Reflex assignment.* I then proceeded to group all apparent varieties of *sol'*, which were not nearly so numerous, under one head. Following this, I noticed that a large number of the cancelled entries, which I had omitted entirely from my previous inquiry, bore a series of notes often embodying some cross-reference and usually explaining the reasons for cancellation, which were not always the same. I collected these under the head of *Cancelled entries.* It then occurred to me that the number of entries which did not carry on the left-hand margin the dot associated with the actual levying of a tally was sufficiently remarkable to bear classification.[2] I soon found that not only returned prests and fictitious loans, to the second of which I assigned a separate, but as it proved rather unsatisfactory, section, were without

---

[1] See examples below under that head.

[2] This dot occurs only in the treasurer's rolls: it is mentioned and its purpose explained by Sir Hilary Jenkinson in *Archaeologia*, LXXIV, 299. Sir Hilary adds in a footnote that fictitious loans and 'advances which had been returned' (*prestita restituta*) are not marked with this marginal.

the dot, but that what seemed to me to be genuine loans, together with entries marked *remissiones*, were in the same position. This gave me four more heads, to which I subsequently added a fifth or omnibus heading of entries other than those I have mentioned which were still without the dot, and for which no tally had therefore been levied[1]. Even now there were many marginalia, both right and left of the main body of the roll, which would not fit into any of the groups I had adopted: these I brigaded together under the heading *Miscellaneous*. I decided to omit innovated tallies, which would have given me yet another head, since these are recorded separately on special and still extant rolls.[2] Finally, as I proceeded, certain clear-cut rules of enrolment followed by the clerks in the receipt emerged. These rules were, however, occasionally broken, and I kept a note of such cases under the heading *Irregularities*.

Such results as I obtained from this inquiry are therefore presented in what follows section by section under the above heads. I can only repeat that the examination from which they are derived has been hurried as well as incomplete, that there is inevitably a certain amount of cross-division, and that not only my comments, but even the rather unstable material upon which they are based, must be regarded as the results of no more than provisional observation.

Complex assignment

In 1349 five entries carry the marginals *inde sol'*, *inde pro*, and in the following year these simple forms develop into the slightly more complicated *pro . . . inde sol'*, *pro N £x et sol' £y*, etc. Within a few terms more, and onward well into Richard II's reign, every conceivable change is being rung in single marginals upon the words *inde*, *sol'*, *pro* and a host of proper names. The term *per billam* occurs (rarely) in the medley from 1351–2, and the phrase *per manus* in and after 1361, while *pro exp' hosp' R'* joins in from the following winter. *Inde pro X et Y et Z pro A et pro B et sol'; inde pro X et Y et per manus Z* are moderate instances from 1364: in one entry from the same term *pro* is repeated with no less than nine different names in succession, and the entry concludes with an *et sol' inde*. *Inde pro X per man' Y et pro eodem A* (a 'vertical' reference[3]) *et pro Z* is a good example from Richard II (1383–4), but many more complicated specimens might be quoted. The amounts allotted to each person named are normally given—sometimes they exhaust the sum in the body of the roll; if not, the balance is usually marked *et sol'*.

---

[1] See this sub-section for fresh proof of Sir Hilary Jenkinson's contention (loc. cit.) that the dot and tally come and go together.

[2] Miss Mabel H. Mills tells me that the later plea rolls of Edward III's reign show that claims for innovated tallies were brought before the exchequer of pleas before fresh tallies were issued.

[3] See *Reflex assignment*, below, pp. 381–4.

Any kind of payment, whether normal revenue payments by bill or tally, *prestita restituta*, loans, or even in one case a *remissio* (1355–6), can be treated in this fashion, and reflex assignments and assignments on behalf of the household (*pro hosp' R'*) quite commonly form elements in the complex entries thus created. Their numbers, too, are considerable: I have counted 564 in 33 rolls of Edward III and 780 in 29 of Richard II. These numbers, particularly for the second reign, are liable to certain deductions: thus I do not think the formula *pro X et Y*, whose appearances average six per term from 1349 to 1364, need be anything other than a simple assignment in favour of a single accounting unit, e.g. a man and his wife or the like.[1] Unfortunately, however, I have reckoned the formula as 'complex' for the latter part of Edward III and for the whole of Richard II. But even after deducting such entries at the rate of 20% of the complex total, which is the figure at which they are more or less constant in the period 1349–64, over which I kept a separate list, we are still left with over 500 entries in the earlier reign, and over 600 in the later, which cannot possibly be explained on the principles of simple assignment.[2]

The difficulty is roughly as follows. An ordinary tally of assignment is given to a single creditor, the main entry in the receipt roll taking the form of what is really an advance receipt from some local body, office or official likely to have money in hand. In the margin, after 1349, is normally recorded the name of the person X, to whom such a tally is given, under the simple formula *pro X*, X being then left to find the assignees and cash the assignment. If we examine the issue roll for the same day we find that X is duly charged with the precise amount of the tally he has received, *unde respondebit*. All this is well known, and the conditions of the process have given rise to an apparently axiomatic rule, stated by Sir Hilary Jenkinson,[3] that 'one line on the (receipt) roll should mean one tally'. Nor is this rule affected by any variants, such as *pro per billam*, *pro per manus*, noted under *Simple assignment*, for these only affect the identity of the single recipient X, and it is only when we begin to multiply the number of recipients that trouble begins.

But this multiplication is precisely what the very common complex assignment of the type we are discussing forces us to accept. If we take

[1] E.g., *pro Galfrido Chaucer et Philippa Chaucer* (1384–5), *pro X et Y super reparat'* (1379); collectors of the customs and subsidies in the ports (*passim*) and the sheriffs of London.

[2] I should add that, apart from my slip about *pro X et Y*, I have included no doubtful entries whatsoever in this reckoning—thus the not very common *pro . . . sol'*, *sol' . . . pro* types have been excluded and will be discussed separately under *Varieties of sol'*.

[3] *Archaeologia*, LXXIV, 298. He adds in a footnote that *per duas tallias* is sometimes postulated, but that does not affect my argument.

a *pro X et Y et Z et sol'* entry and follow it on to the issue roll, we find there separate entries recording that X, Y and Z have each received the quota mentioned in the receipt roll marginal, while the balance (*et sol'*) is of course ignored, for that was an immediate cash receipt, not a disguised issue of a future receipt. On most days which I have examined in detail, all at the beginning of the period, there is not an exact correspondence between receipt and issue roll, nor is there any reason why there should be. The only entries that correspond in names and in amount in each roll are the entries marked *pro*, or which should have been marked *pro* and are left blank, in the receipt roll margin. Apart from these there are frequently many cash entries (*sol'*) on the receipt roll, the separate amounts and sum total of which bear no relation to those of the surplus non-assigned issues in the issue roll. What is interesting, and disturbing, is that a single receipt roll entry, when assigned in a 'complex' way, can be broken up into several assignments on the issue roll, plus (very often) a cash balance, which does not appear on the issue roll at all and was presumably paid into the treasury. This looks as if one entry on the receipt roll can in such cases no longer mean one tally, for no tally could be split up in this way.[1] At the same time there is no indication on the receipt side in these cases that more than one tally was used. For the only explanation of these difficulties that I can see we must return to our consideration of the general nature of assignment.

Let us approach the practice from the assignee's point of view. Two collectors, let us say, of the customs and subsidies, while engaged in their task, are constantly being invited by writ and tally to satisfy crown creditors who have been given a tally of assignment on their office. When they come to account at the exchequer they will bring with them so much money in cash, and so much evidence, in the form of writs or tallies, of money already spent locally. The money they bring in cash will be entered on the receipt rolls '*de N et M*, collectors of the customs and subsidies, x pounds, shillings and pence', and in the margin *sol'*. The tallies they bring with them will already have been entered months or even years before, at the time when they were levied and given to the creditor X. To verify this, the clerks of the receipt need only look at the date on each tally proffered by the collectors, turn up the day on the receipt roll, and find the entry '*de N et M* etc., x pounds etc.,

---

[1] But cf. Miss Mills's account of the (much earlier) *tallia dividenda* in her introduction to *Surrey Record Society*, vol. VII, *Pipe Roll for 1295, Surrey Membrane*. The principle there given can hardly, however, be applied to anything but immediate cash receipts, whereas the late fourteenth-century issue rolls show that the complex entries discussed in the text are invariably assignments, though of a special kind.

pro X'. So much for the collectors who can produce such tallies: that is their end of the process of simple assignment. It will be noticed that the assigned entry in the receipt roll had reference to a *future* receipt.

But what if the collectors N and M have spent money locally for which, when they are called to account, they can produce evidence *other than* tallies of assignment? The exchequer, though perhaps the sole ultimate authority, at least after 1365, is not the only immediate authority that can order them from time to time to disburse upon the spot: the king himself, or his officers of the household, or indeed any individual showing adequate cause, can compel them to do so, while the exchequer itself may occasionally use some method other than the normal writ and tally of assignment. True, the collectors will be held responsible at Westminster for the full amount due from them, and will therefore not be satisfied with less than unimpeachable authority for any spending they may be obliged to do before they get there, but none the less such authority they repeatedly seem to have had. For in no other way can we account for the entry '*de N et M* etc., x pounds etc., *pro X et Y et Z et sol*' ' than by the assumption that that is what was really written on a tally first levied and given to them direct at the actual time when they came themselves to Westminster, a tally which represents, not a future payment, but a general receipt to the collectors for a number of local payments which they have already made. They produce, in short, evidence that they have paid X so much, Y so much, and Z so much, and have so much left over in cash, which they now pay in (*et sol'*). X, Y and Z are duly charged with the amounts on the issue roll the same day, and the cash balance disappears into the treasury. There has been assignment but, unlike simple or direct assignment, it has been under some authority other than that of a tally, and it is all over long ago: the entry on the roll in fact represents what is, at the time it is made, a past and not a future transaction.

It only remains to consider what authority other than the exchequer writs and tallies of direct assignment our collectors N and M can have received. The problem really lies outside my present field; indeed I can advance but little further than the *a priori* argument by which I have insisted on some such authority's existence. An obvious example would be the wardrobe debenture; for through most of this period wardrobe officers were authorized to draw on local officials for their needs up to the fixed total of a large credit, which their department had received at the exchequer. But I do not think that household activity, though it explains much, explains everything. The number of what we may now call indirect assignments—assignments, that is, which the exchequer only indirectly authorized—is much too large. Household activity is now known to have decreased considerably in the last quarter of the

fourteenth century,[1] whereas the amount of indirect assignment shows
a slight but steady increase under Richard II. Decentralization seems
to have proceeded steadily through the comparative order of the fourteenth to the chaos of the fifteenth century; more and more revenue
came to be spent as it was collected, locally; less and less cash, and more
and more of what a modern might call 'receipted bills' arrived at the
exchequer. There is nothing new in that, but under what authority, if
not of that of the household, did that growth of indirect assignment,
which represents one aspect of these tendencies, go on? We shall find
traces under *Genuine loans* of letters patent under the great seal, letters
obligatory, writs of privy seal, and bills under the seal of the exchequer
being used for a similar purpose, and it would seem to be instruments
of this kind, as well as those of the wardrobe or household, to which
we must look for an explanation.[2]

Simple assignment

The normal formula is *pro X* in the right-hand margin, but X (a
proper name) alone, and *alloc'*, *allocac'*, *alloc' pro X*, or even *X pro y*,
where y = an object of expenditure, e.g. the king's dogs, occur occasionally in the earlier rolls. X can be the person or persons by whom
the payment is made, in which case of course the assignment is really
an allowance made direct to a future accountant, as the *alloc'* found in
early entries of this sort would suggest. X may also be in the plural,
e.g. *pro probis hominibus* of some town such as Lincoln or Bristol, which
at first sight suggests a complex assignment, but really represents a
single accounting unit—cf. *pro Staple* (1363)—and is normal enough.
Sometimes X (the beneficiary) has been erased entirely, but unless the
word *pro* has also been erased I have reckoned such cases[3] as assignments: it is possible that the issue rolls might explain the reason for the

---

[1] Cf. Tout, *Chapters*, IV, 212–13.

[2] Tout (ibid., IV, 319–20) records payments by the collectors of
customs in three of the chief ports direct into the chamber in the years
1380–2. These collectors had the sums they paid allowed to them in their
account at the exchequer on production of the sub-chamberlain's receipts.
Cf. *pro hosp' per man' Y per bill'* (1383–4). *pro hosp' per bill' Y* (1386–7),
pro hosp' per ii bill' per man' Y et alterius (1385), *pro hosp' per divers' bill'*
(1386–7)—all apparently cases from a slightly later period in the receipt
rolls, in which money was similarly advanced to some department of the
household direct and allowance subsequently claimed at the exchequer
on the strength of the receipt or 'bill' obtained from the household
authorities. But even so, occasional arrangements like this do not explain
the steady growth of indirect assignment on a very large scale under
Richard II.

[3] In my article in *Eng. Hist. Rev.*, XLIII (April 1928).

erasures. There are not many instances in this period of the old marginal *Gard'* or *pro Gard'*; at least I have only found three, varied by a more explicit *alloc' per bill' de Gard'* in 1356. Cf. a solitary *pro div' min' de Gard'* (1383–4). The great wardrobe appears once in *pro offic' magn' Gard'* (1363–4), and the chamber rather more often, but still infrequently, viz. *pro exp' cam'* (1353–4), *pro cam' R'* (1383), *pro cam' R' per man' Y* (1384–5, 1385). A unique entry runs *pro familia R' per breve de priv' sig' de term' Mich' anno ii* (1390). The household in general, besides appearing rather rarely in the *pro hosp'* entries already mentioned, blossoms out into a whole crop of entries, with which I intend to deal a little later, under Richard II.

After Easter 1353 there is a marked rise in the number of unusual *pro* entries of a 'simple' type, and several new varieties occur. One class of these consists of what one might call concrete objects, *pro palefr', pro pergam', pro domicella, pro plumbo, pro vesselament'* etc. The question arises whether these entries are not assignments at all, but simply notes of objects on which cash coming into the exchequer was spent. Reference to the issue rolls, however, suggests that in most cases they were real assignments in favour of the departments, persons or officials responsible for buying these objects, though loosely classified by the names of the objects instead of by the names of the officials. This is almost certainly the explanation of the vaguer *pro op'*—cf. *pro X pro* (or *super*) *op'*, e.g. 1361—which begins abruptly in the Michaelmas term 1353–4 and remains quite common down to the end of the period. Such entries were assignments in favour of the various clerks of the works in different places,[1] and we may class a solitary *pro rep'* along with them. A few other *pro* entries, however, such as *pro div' soluc' ut patet in exitu isto die* (1370, 1382, 1383), or *pro div' soluc' ipso die*, are probably not assignments, but these again are rare. They should be distinguished from such entries as *pro divers' soluc' per ipsum faciendis* (1370), *pro div' sol' per X* (1386), where the concluding words make all the difference.

Wages also appear about this time and seem to fall into much the same group as the *pro op'* assignments—we have *pro sagittar' R', pro carrettar' R', pro vad' marinar', pro X pro custod' Berwick*, but it seems to me questionable whether *pro ministris de mag' scacc'* (1362–3) represents an assignment. *Pro Caleys* appears for the first time in 1358 and *pro vict' pro Caleys* in the following winter: *pro Staple* (1363) we have already had. A late type of entry which we might mention here is *pro X de superplusagio*, of which I shall have more to say under *Reflex assignment*: it is apparently peculiar to three years (1383–5) of Richard II's reign.

---

[1] The locality is sometimes given, e.g., *pro op' castr' de Corf'* (1377, Edw. III).

There is a lull in the number of abnormal entries round about the year 1360, followed, however, by a renewed activity and the appearance of at least two new forms of importance. *Pro hospic'*, *pro hosp' R'*, *pro exp' hosp' R'* represents one group of these: the other is a *pro X per man' Y* group, while a formula combining both in *pro exp' hosp' R' per man' Y* also begins to be common. Sir Hilary Jenkinson has explained the *per manus* entry of the issue roll as having reference to a wardrobe transaction,[1] and it is a fact that the right-hand margin of the receipt roll, whose composition we are studying, bears a very close relationship to that series. This type may therefore be interpreted *pro X* (a wardrobe official) *per man' Y* (a tradesman, or the like), and it may record a simple act of purveyance, which is being paid for by the exchequer on behalf of the wardrobe in the form of an assignment in favour apparently of X, but really of Y. As X is in fact frequently represented by the name of some well-known wardrobe official, this seems to me in such cases the correct explanation, though it may be noted *en passant* that the form *pro X per man' Y per man' A per man' B* occurs at least once (1361) and that raises fresh difficulties.[2] Moreover, though we may agree that *pro exp' hosp' R' per man' Y* is sufficiently explained by the wardrobe analogy, what of *pro diversis per man' Y*? How can X, which normally = a wardrobe official, or a department of the civil service, suddenly come down to mean the vague *diversis*, whether masculine or neuter? How can *diversi* (or *diversa*) authorize Y to demand money from the exchequer on the strength of their (unmentioned) name or names?[3] But just as the term X can break down in this mysterious formula, so can the term Y dissolve into *per man' Y per man' A per man' B*, as we have seen above, while, as we shall see below, the nexus *per man'* can also be quite casually included in what I have called a complex assignment. What does *per manus* mean? It should be noted that the wardrobe use is not what we might call the face value of the term—a person ignorant of it would naturally assume that the formula *pro X per man' Y* meant that X was receiving money, or a tally for money, through the medium of Y, whereas, as we have seen, the actual meaning is that Y is receiving money or its equivalent in repayment of a debt formerly contracted with him by X. Now I do not think it is necessary to abandon this interpretation, which certainly holds good for the reign of Edward III, when

[1] *Archaeologia*, LXXIV, 305.
[2] See note on p. 381 below.
[3] We are helped towards a solution by the entry *pro plumbo per man' X* (1362–3), which is clearly only a new form of the early *X pro Y* (object of expenditure) noted above. Cf. the obvious identity of *pro X pro exp' hosp' R'* and *pro hosp' R' per man' X*. The two forms overlap in the last years of Edward III, but the second eventually displaces the first.

wc come to the more difficult phenomena of the reign of Richard II. The difficulty is briefly this. In Edward III's reign, we know from the late Professor Tout that the wardrobe was particularly active as 'War Office, Admiralty and Foreign Office rolled into one'; yet the highest number of *pro . . . per man'* entries I have noticed for any one term is 11 (1361–2), and that is the only term in which they reach double figures. Again the total number of such entries in the 33 rolls examined was only 45, giving an average of 1.3. Conversely, we know that in Richard II's reign wardrobe activities declined, and yet in 1382 there are 13 such entries, 45 a year later, 101 in 1383–4, and no less than 164 the following Michaelmas. The numbers do not sink below 30 again until 1395–6, when they touch 18, only to rise again to 131 in 1397 and 171 in 1397–8. Thence they decline gradually to 17 in the last term of the reign. The total from the rolls examined is no less than 1590 and the average per term 54.8 for 29 rolls.

To my mind these remarkable figures, taken together with those of Edward III's reign, largely dispose of the possibility that the formula *pro . . . per man'* should be limited to the use of the wardrobe, or even to the household in general, for though it is true that the formula *pro hosp' R' per man' Y* and its variants account for two-thirds or so of the first peak period above, that proportion steadily diminishes. I would still retain the interpretation 'that Y is receiving money or its equivalent in repayment of a debt formerly contracted with him by X', but what I am inclined to abandon is the suggestion that X must always be a government official or department. Let X be a private person, who has by service or otherwise established some sort of claim against the government. We know how slow fourteenth- and fifteenth-century governments were in settling their obligations.[1] X therefore sells his claim to, or has it discounted by, Y, who presumably produces proof of the transaction at the exchequer, and receives a tally *pro X per man' Y*. This hypothesis is strengthened by the occurrence of what I think can only be explained as immature versions of the perfect form. Thus as early as 1361 we have *pro per lit' de amicis, pro per lit' de amicis carissimis* —these it is true are, as far as I am aware, unique, but from 1370 onwards they are superseded by a form, *pro per bill'*, which is found occasionally as early as 1350–1, 1351–2, 1358–9 and quite commonly in the terms 1383, 1383–4, 1388–9, 1390, 1391–2 and 1392. On one occasion (1378) the exchequer apparently made an assignment of this sort for special causes without the usual authority, and carefully recorded the fact thus, *pro X sine billa*. Now all this continued and careful reference to documentary authority seems to me to be precisely an effort to cope with the increasing number of applicants for exchequer moneys

[1] Cf. *Bulletin of the Institute of Hist. Research*, IV, 165–72.

who were not the original creditors themselves but the financial agents who had obliged them. The exchequer is in short insisting on some evidence of identity and good faith and recording such evidence—not only in the receipt roll, for there is reason to believe that the original 'bills' were filed—whenever it obtains it. But before long the process becomes a tedious one, and the clerks are satisfied with the old formula *pro X per man' Y*, which simply records the name of Y, the beneficiary, and leaves it at that. In this way the old wardrobe use was diverted to a new purpose, and after co-existing for some time with the clumsier *pro per bill'* type, eventually superseded it.[1]

If my general hypothesis be correct, the *pro per man'* figures quoted above indicate little of political or administrative, but much of economic, importance, viz., even allowing for the larger number of household entries, a marked increase in the sale of debts and credit towards the close of the fourteenth century. This is, it is true, what other sources have recently led us to expect we might find, but the point is, as far as I am aware, incapable of proof from the receipt and issue rolls alone. For, having dealt after a fashion with the receipt roll entries, it only remains to add that the issue rolls normally record payments merely to X in such cases with a complete and incurious uniformity.

Reflex assignment

The normal formula *pro eodem* (*eadem, eisdem*) is open to some ambiguity. In the first place the reference might lie to the person or persons making the payment in the body of the roll. I have called this type, which is by far the commonest, a horizontal reference; it is, of course, a true reflex assignment. But where the embryonic column of right-hand marginals is well developed in the roll, it sometimes happens that *pro eodem* has a vertical reference to the last person in favour of whom an assignment was made. The effect of this is to convert the entry into the same sort of assignment (usually a simple type) as the one above it, and to rule out any implication of such *pro eodem* entries being *per se* reflex assignments. Finally we get a third class of apparent

[1] As for the solitary *pro X per man' Y per man' A per man' B* (1361) noted above, reference to the issue rolls shows that a large assignment was made to the keeper of the wardrobe *per man' X* [*sic*] for divers reasons, as set forth in a bill which he presented: the names of Y, A and B do not occur on the issue roll, but the total assignment corresponds with the sum total of the amounts set opposite their names in the receipt roll. Now X is described in the issue roll as *nuper camerarius R*, and the whole transaction is probably the same as that which would later be expressed by the formula *pro hosp' per bill'*—see note on p. 377 above. This would perhaps account for its extreme rarity in this form; I have noted no other instance of it.

reflex assignments, in which the ambiguities of the context are such that, without consulting the issue rolls in every case, it is impossible to say with any certainty which sort of reference is intended.

I did not think it necessary to carry this particular investigation any further than to note the total numbers of apparent reflex assignments in the rolls examined, the number therein of horizontal references, the number of vertical references, and the number of those references which were doubtful. The total number of apparent reflex assignments remained extraordinarily constant for the whole period: thus it averaged 14.95 per term for the 33 terms examined in Edward III's reign, and 15.17 per term for the 29 terms examined under Richard II. The total numbers of horizontal references, i.e. undoubted reflex assignments, were 313 and 364 respectively, but the apparent increase is deceptive, for on the other hand the doubtful cases diminished from 179 to 69 and the vertical references increased from 8 to 23. We may therefore assume that the practice of paying local officials by assignment on the revenues which they themselves are in process of collecting[1]—for that is what it amounts to—remained approximately constant in the later fourteenth century with, if anything, a slight tendency to increase under Richard II. The device must have saved much time and trouble and illustrates still further the way in which the exchequer was becoming more and more a clearing-house and less and less the scene of cash transactions. Reflex assignment was not open to many of the objections which may be brought against the principle of assignment in general, and was frequently applied to cases other than those of local officials— e.g. that of the queen Philippa herself (1363–4)—in which a past or future debt to the crown could be used to extinguish a royal obligation. Thus from 1351–2 to 1398–9 *passim* we find *prestita* being treated in this way: an advance, that is, becomes due for repayment, but meanwhile the recipient proves that he is entitled to a credit with the crown, with the result that he is excused the repayment of his prest, or of an equivalent proportion of it, and the transaction appears in the receipt roll as a restored advance (*prestitum restitutum*) assigned back to the payer; loans and *remissiones*, with both of which I hope to deal later,

---

[1] *Pro eisdem coll'*, sometimes *de regardo* and/or *et contrarotulator'* (from 1384–5 especially) is one of the commoner types of reflex assignment. Interesting variants are *pro eisdem* (coll') *pro uno anno*, and again *pro conductu dom' et pro X* (both 1396–7), *pro eodem super officio suo* or *de dono R'* (including one 'bill' from south Wales) in 1391, *pro eisdem de regardo per cedulam* (1390), *per breve de privato sigillo* (1391, 1391–2), and *inde pro eodem per breve de priv' sig' et pro . . . per cedulam* (1394). For another complex assignment embodying this element, cf. *inde sol' et pro regardo eorundem* (1394–5).

APPENDIX A

are often treated in the same way. An abnormal *restitucio billarum*[1] too, assigned back to the payer, like another *restitucio* . . . *pro eadem camera R'* (1383), has obvious affinities with this group, and there is one case (1361–2) of an entry being assigned back to the 'payer' which has subsequently been cancelled and made the subject of a fictitious loan, presumably because the 'lender' had proved that he was not in debt to the crown at the time the entry was made, and that therefore the crown was now in debt to him. With this may be associated a curious *pro eodem* (1378) *per sex tallias damnatas vto die Nov' 51 Ed. III.* The opposite state of affairs is reflected in *pro eodem de superplusagio* (1383–4, 1391) or *in parte superplusagii sui* (1392), in which presumably the accountant is having his adverse balance reduced. Both types are illustrated by cases recorded in comparative detail, once in the Easter term 1398 and once in the following Michaelmas term. On both occasions payments in the name of W. Dynys, clerk of the works to the king, are first assigned back to him, then cancelled, and fresh tallies for the same amount levied on him *de den' sup' ipsum oneratis.*[2] Here I imagine it was thought by the exchequer that as much was due to Dynys as he had in hand, and consequently he was entered in the first place as having paid in the money and as having had it assigned back to him to square the account. Subsequently it was discovered that nothing had been due to him, though he still had large sums in hand,[3] forming in fact a *superplusagium*, or balance against the accountant. Consequently the original entries were cancelled and tallies for the exact amount levied on him in the form given. The latter might, however, equally well have been *de superplusagio suo*, though it should be noticed that in this case the new marginal entries are still *pro Dynys* and that therefore Dynys is being relieved of his 'surplus' on account of further expenses which he had incurred.

That reflex assignments were neither dependent on, nor yet always independent of, the levying of tallies, is shown by the fact that, though tallies are employed in the whole 'collector' or 'local official' class of reflex assignment, none is used for the equally common *prestita restituta*, for loans, or for the rarer *remissiones*, while from 1390 onwards we find that entries from north and south Wales, Chester and Ireland which, perhaps as royal possessions, were represented by bills instead of tallies, could be assigned reflexively as freely as any others.

Finally, it will be seen from some of the examples quoted that reflex assignments, like the *per manus* entries, can form elements in a complex

[1] See *Entries without tallies*, and cf. *Avantag'* (1364–5) and prize-money (1374) used for reflex assignment, ibid.
[2] Cf. *inde in onere X et sol'* (1360).
[3] Two Michaelmas tallies are for £40 and £80 respectively.

383

assignment, though they are more commonly found alone. I have instances of the former from 1353 to 1396–7.

Varieties of sol'

Any kind of entry in the receipt roll may be marked *sol'*[1] but it is unusual for any names or further information to be supplied: *sol'* in the vast majority of cases stands alone. Its meaning is, of course, that the main entry should be taken at its face value: so much hard cash has actually been paid by the person or persons mentioned, and for the reason given, into the treasury. *Sol' in recept'*, which I have found three times, and *sol' in thes'*, which I have found once, both only in the period 1349–54, merely drive the point home. *Sol' X, sol' pro X*, where X often = the treasurer, are in a slightly different category, but are very uncommon—I have noticed no more than six, all in the period 1349–53, and two or possibly three under Richard II. The explanation probably lies in the subsequent conversion of a cash payment into an issue on account of wages or allowances to the staff of the exchequer. Cf. *sol' vad' argent'* (1353–4). The entry is of course irregular, for it ought to appear on the issue rolls alone, but it is predominantly early and very rare. The still rarer *sol' versus X*, which only occurs twice in the whole period (again 1351, 1352–3), may perhaps be referred to something of the same kind, as may also the rather commoner *in man'* formula. *In man' thes' et sol'* occurs in 1351, *in man' X* in 1358, 1383–4 (twice) and 1384–5. The first of these entries seems to suggest that *in man'* was different from *sol'*, so the fact that the 1358 entry appears simply as *sol'* on one of the chamberlains' receipt rolls may merely go to show that the latter as usual has been more carelessly made up—or it may be that they really were identical and the treasurer's entry tautologous. It is significant that the majority of these entries appear very early in the period chosen, before the marginalia had been standardized. *Pro . . . sol'* is also found from time to time but, though I have refrained from including it under *Complex assignment*, I am inclined to think that it is merely a looser version of *pro . . . inde sol'* or the like, and that that is the section to which it belongs. See above, Chapter I, p. 16.

A curious set of entries found only between 1355–6 and 1378, and only common in the altogether abnormal roll of Easter 1370, presents a rather stiffer problem. These are the *sol' per man' X* (once *sol' per man' attorn'*, 1355–6) and the *sol' per X* entries. The explanation of the first class at any rate is, I think, that the payments in question had been made by proxies or agents other than the actual persons from whom they were due. The solitary *sol' per man' attorn'* practically states this,

[1] See my 'Distribution of Assignment in the Treasurer's Receipt Roll, 1364–5', *Camb. Hist. Journal*, II (1927).

and in 1363 we have a *sol'* payment on account of the ransom of France (John II) made by the hands of the mayor of the staple, which exactly fits the theory, the latter presumably being one of the agents by whom successive instalments of the ransom were forwarded.[1] Whether there really were absolutely no cash payments by agent or proxy except within the period 1355–78 I am inclined to doubt, though it is true that the exchequer always insisted very strictly on the actual appearance of accountants in person, whenever possible. But it is perhaps more likely that on most occasions when the accountants themselves could not appear the clerks compiling the receipt roll did not trouble to record the fact, as long as they got the money. Thus on 22 October 1379 an order was made by the council by bill of the treasurer to all admirals, customers, keepers of seaports and so forth, to allow James Walterson and Peter Petreson, merchants of Holland, to load and export wool and woolfells from the port of Kingston-upon-Hull, because they had paid all the customs, duties, etc., on the said cargo in advance, while a like order issuing the same day to the collectors in that port bade them 'allow James and Peter to load and export wools, as above, receiving from them the king's tallies levied under the names of the said collectors in respect of the sums aforesaid, whereby and by this present order they [the collectors] shall have due allowance in their account at the exchequer'.[2] I have quoted this case in full because it seems to me to point towards the existence in the *sol'* class of an unexpected type, namely the advance payment. As it was evidently cash which James and Peter paid into the exchequer under the collectors' names the entry would obviously be *sol'*, and it would be a *sol'* tally or tallies which they would bring to Hull to authorize their free departure. This use of the *sol'* tally as a sort of clearing-ticket by exporting houses is something new, but it is such an obvious convenience to all parties concerned that I cannot believe that this was the only occasion on which it was used. In this case there was apparently nothing in the receipt roll to show that the *sol'* entry in question was different from any other, but I suggest that it was an early consciousness of this difference that produced the *sol' per man'* entries in cases of much the same type, and that it was the realization that no exchequer purpose was really served by such a record which led to their discontinuance just the year before this case, viz. in 1378. The probability on the other hand that proxies or agents were expected to, and normally did, produce some evidence of their authority is shown by three *sol' defic'* (or *sine*) *billa* entries (1378,

---

[1] Cf. 'Ransom of John II', *Camden Miscellany*, xiv, by Dr. Dorothy M. Broome. Miss Broome prints the actual entry in question, ibid., p. 8.

[2] P.R.O., *Cal. of Fine Rolls*, 1377–83, pp. 176–7. This important reference is omitted from 'Exchequer, tallies of', in the index.

twice, and 1379—the precise transition period just mentioned above). The first of these is particularly illuminating: it runs *sol' defic' billa per man' X pro suis op'* and is, I think, explicable on this hypothesis.

Sol' per X is practically limited to 1370 when, however, it occurs pretty often. The similarity between the abbreviations for *pro* and *per*, when hastily written, is so great that I have some doubts about the solitary example (1356) I have found outside this term, but there is no doubt about twenty-one of those in 1370, though seventeen more from that term might conceivably be intended for *sol' . . . pro*. In many cases these entries are associated with payments on account of a clerical subsidy by some abbot or prior, the said payments then being cancelled and replaced by loans from the same person or persons. The only explanation I can suggest is on the following lines. All the indications in the receipt roll point to the fact that the crown was never quite so hard pressed for ready money as in the Easter term of 1370. The roll for that term is unusually long and quite extraordinarily confused, while nearly one in four of the *pro* entries turned out to be worthless.[1] True, the parliament of 1369 had granted an increased custom on wool for three years, and the clergy had supplemented the grant with a tenth for the same period, but on the other hand the war had been renewed, there was evidently an urgent need for cash, and the money was apparently not coming in quickly enough. Among other expedients the government seems to have had recourse to the collectors of the clerical tenth, and to have borrowed all it could from them in cash on the security of the grant they were collecting. Whenever this was done a dotted entry was originally made showing the receipt of such and such a sum on account of the clerical subsidy. All that was then necessary was to mark the entry *sol'* and hand the *sol'* tally to the collector for him to present again in his account. There would then have been an advance payment, essentially of the type described above for 1379, the collector naturally recouping himself from the subsidy as it came in. But the exchequer was soon disturbed by the loan element entering into the transaction. It was not the clergy of York or Bedfordshire or London who had paid their quota in advance: it was the collectors of the clerical subsidy in those places who had advanced the money before they had collected it, and it soon appeared that in many cases they could not recover the large sums they had lent from the proceeds of the grant, and were so much out of pocket. The bishop of London, for example, had lent 700 marks and only collected 200; what was to be done about it? Possibly at the time of entry, possibly at this stage, the note *mutuum* had been added on the extreme left of all such entries, while on the right was written not plain *sol'*, but *sol' per X*, X being

[1] See *Fictitious loans*, below, pp. 391–2.

the person making the payment. The difficulty now was that, in spite of all these cautionary marginalia, the sums in question had actually been entered in the body of the roll as definite receipts on account of the clerical tenth and the clerks, though acknowledging the obligation which had arisen, were reluctant to change the totals. In the end such entries were cancelled and the tallies presumably surrendered, but the totals were saved, for the unfortunate collectors, instead of receiving payment at once, were merely credited by interlineation with their ill-considered loans, and had to wait until money was more plentiful at Westminster or until trustworthy tallies of assignment could be levied for them. Only the bishop of London succeeded in getting 200 marks which he had actually collected assigned back to him on account of his loan, and remained a mere 500 marks out of pocket.

It should be noticed that all this trouble might have been saved if the collector's loans had been properly entered as such in the first place without any reference to the subsidy, and it is to be supposed that some such course was followed thenceforward:[1] at any rate I have come across no more *sol' per* or *sol' per man'* entries (but for the solitary example of the latter, already quoted, from 1378).

One or two other curiosities from round about this period may be noted briefly under this head. In the same term (1370) a solitary *sol'* entry bears the legend *inde hab' lit' R' pat' de mag' sigillo*. The combination with *sol'*, though the two entries are on different margins, is, as far as I am aware, unique; what had happened was simply that letters patent for the marriage of a royal ward had been purchased from the king direct.[2] From a chamberlain's roll of the term before (1369–70) we have another unique entry, *sol' per ii vices*: this is apparently a note of the fact that one joint tally of receipt was levied for payments made on two separate occasions. If so, this is very unusual; but it may also mean no more than that the chamberlain's clerk had omitted to make a separate entry for an earlier payment by the same accountant and, on finding out his mistake, had included it in this one. It is quite normal to find that entries on the treasurer's roll are omitted from one or both of the chamberlains' rolls. One more point concludes the list, viz. a reference, unique under *sol'*, to the L.T.R. memoranda roll (1359–60).

Cancelled entries

I have counted 106 cancelled entries in the rolls examined for Edward III's reign—of these, 19 are cancelled without explanation, 83 bear the legend *quia tall' restit' et dampn' cum fol'*, and four are definitely

---

[1] As it already had been in the past: cf. my article *Camb. Hist. J.*, II, p. 80.
[2] *C.P.R.*, 1367–70, p. 407, grant to Thomas de Lodelowe.

abnormal. Under Richard II the rolls were better kept—no entry seems to have been cancelled without explanation, and the total is only 59, of which moreover 31 are special cases, mostly due to the troubles of 1386–8 or 1397–9, while 28 carry the same *quia tall' restit'*, etc. I have excluded from the reckoning in both reigns the large number of tallies cancelled on account of the ordinary fictitious loan, as their numbers will be shown separately under that head. There is, however, some possibility that the common form *quia tall' restit'*, etc., may also be an indication of a fictitious loan, though one of a slightly different kind. Sir Hilary Jenkinson has described[1] three different courses in use during the short period 1357–9, any one of which the clerks of the exchequer might follow whenever, as was not uncommon, a tally of assignment duly entered in the roll could not be met by the assignee, with the result that the beneficiary had been obliged to bring it back to the exchequer.

The first of these was simply to cancel the tally and alter the receipt roll totals, marking the cancelled entry with the formula under discussion. This would spoil the roll and cause a certain amount of trouble in the way of elementary arithmetic: moreover, in strict logic the corresponding entry in the issue roll, and the issue roll totals, would have to be altered as well. I am, however, by no means satisfied that the clerks did all this in every case in which I have noticed that the formula was applied.

The second method was the well-known use of the fictitious loan, by which the original entry was cancelled, but an interlineation made recording the receipt of a 'loan' from the beneficiary for the precise amount in question. This 'loan' would of course be paid off later in cash or in fresh tallies of assignment; meanwhile it would not be necessary to touch the totals.

The third method was the most complicated of all and ran as follows. The original assignment was not cancelled in the receipt roll, though the stock and foil representing it were destroyed. Their places were then taken by two new tallies—one on the assignees who had so far failed to pay for as large a fraction of the whole as they could manage, and another representing a fictitious loan for the balance only from the beneficiary. Sir Hilary Jenkinson adds that the second, but not the first, of these new tallies was then entered on the roll.[2] The advantages of this method seem to me very dubious. It has not the pristine simplicity of

---

[1] *Proceedings of the Society of Antiquaries*, 2nd series, xxv, 29–39.

[2] I have followed Sir Hilary Jenkinson's account, loc. cit. But I cannot reconcile it with the fact that no loan—fictitious or otherwise—normally carries the dot in the treasurer's roll which indicates the levying of a tally. This makes it look as if the real substitutes employed were (*a*) tally, but no entry, (*b*) entry, but no tally.

the first method, which, though troublesome and untidy, avoids all book-keeping complications. At the same time it does not possess the chief virtue of the second method, namely that of keeping the totals at least technically correct without any alteration. The root of this weakness is the failure to cancel the original entry: if this be done, all the worst objections disappear, and the device merely becomes a convenient and elastic variant on the fictitious loan, suitable for covering all those cases in which the assignees had neither completely defaulted nor yet completely paid up. Finally, if one supposed that the first and third methods could be and were combined, it should be noticed that nearly all the drawbacks disappear. It would not matter then that in many cases the cancelling of an entry *quia tall' restit' et dampn' cum fol'* does not seem to be followed by the change of totals required by Sir Hilary Jenkinson's explanation, because no such change would be necessary, while the mere effect of cancellation in itself redeems the third method from confusion. I am therefore inclined to suggest, though with much diffidence, that the formula should be associated with the partial use of the fictitious loan, and with the partial rather than the complete dishonouring of a tally of assignment.

Turning to Richard II we find the formula *quia tall' restit'*, etc., speedily recurs, but is only about one-third as common. It is interesting, however, to find that record is now being kept of tallies levied to pay off a debt contracted by the dishonouring of an earlier tally—*pro X per Y tall' damn'* is the formula, together with the exact reference. It is quite common from the first term of the reign, whereas I have no note of it under Edward III. Another small point is that bills, when used in certain districts, such as north Wales, instead of tallies, can be cancelled (e.g. 1386, 1387) under the standard formula, thus confirming the impression gained elsewhere that they are exactly similar to tallies in every respect. Finally, in 1392-3, comes the first of a whole series of cancellations, continued in almost every term up to 1399, for special causes explained in the early issue rolls of Henry IV, the exact references always being given. I have noticed nothing else abnormal under this head, except the peculiar 'Dynys' cancellations of 1398, 1398-9, with which I have already dealt under *Reflex assignment*.

Prestita restituta

The nature of the *prestitum restitutum* is suggested by what is apparently a clerical error in the roll of 1355, where we find an otherwise normal entry of this type labelled *restitucio den'*. Mr. J. H. Johnson, however, in his study of the wardrobe of Edward II[1] takes us further than this. He points out that though the word 'prest' originally meant

---

[1] *Trans. Royal Hist. Soc.*, 4th series, XII, 75–104 (1929).

no more than an advance of money, to be repaid at some future date, it was subsequently used to cover any sum of money due, even when not originally 'advanced' to the accountant: the term was in short a convenient one for describing sums of money owing for whatever cause. It is improbable that this lax use was limited to the wardrobe but, be that as it may, the word was also used more legitimately, and I think in the exchequer as well, to cover an advance of money on account of expenses, even though, if the latter were proved in the process of account to have absorbed the former, no repayment would be made. It should be noticed that prests in the wider sense were not necessarily made in cash—thus prests on account of wages often took the form of provisions or of cloth, and were naturally not repayable.

Of the four kinds of prest I have mentioned only the first two types are at first sight likely to produce the entry (*prestitum restitutum*) under review. It might conceivably happen in the last two cases, but only if excessive allowances had accidentally been made, and even then the *restitucio* would only represent the difference between the original advance and the true wage or legitimate expense. Mistakes of this kind may, however, have been common during the hundred years' war, and it is probable that all four types of prest are represented in the 900-odd instances of 'restoration' which I have noticed in the rolls examined for this period. For the original creation of real prests the receipt rolls naturally yield hardly any evidence; but I am inclined to think that issues of that type were seldom differentiated from any others until the account was cleared at the exchequer. If it were otherwise one would expect to find more entries of the type *pro . . . inde . . . et res' prest'*, of which, however, I have no more than this one instance (1361–2).

The common form of the restored prest runs as follows: *de X de prestito restituto £y*. There is normally, as Sir Hilary Jenkinson has already observed,[1] no dot in the left-hand margin, thus showing that no tally was levied. Nevertheless the flexibility of the entry is complete.[2] Approximately 33% of them—the percentage is slightly higher under Richard II—are marked *sol'* and therefore represent cash payments. The rest, with the exception of some 150 doubtful entries from Edward III's reign, are assigned, and moreover assigned in every conceivable way. Most varieties of simple assignment include specimens of *prestita restituta*; they are often assigned back to their 'payers'; and they can even take the shape of complex or indirect assignments. Their use for simple or direct assignment shows that that process did not necessarily depend upon the tally, for *ex hypothesi* in such cases some

---

[1] *Archaeologia*, LXXIV, 299 n.

[2] For the significance of this fact see *Genuine loans*, below, pp. 393–5.

other instrument must have been used.[1] In the case of reflex assignment we have a pleasant piece of book-keeping: X has a claim on the exchequer which is extinguished by cancelling his obligation to repay an advance made to him at an earlier date. Similarly in complex assignments of this type, what has happened is presumably that the accountant's list of local payment is offset by a previous obligation, and all he gets in return for his proofs of local expenditure is the writing off of the earlier debt in question. It will therefore be seen that *prestita restituta*, at least when legitimately used, are book-keeping entries pure and simple, though this is not, I think, as at first sight might appear, the reason why they are not honoured with a tally.[2]

Note.—They may also represent from time to time the use of exchequer processes to recover private debts: see below, p. 393, n. 2.

Fictitious loans

The character and object of the fictitious loan has been described more than once, and this section contains little more than a note on its apparent frequency. It should be noticed that a single one of these 'loans' normally covers several dishonoured tallies: in my attempt to arrive at an average per term for both reigns I have therefore provided a separate note of the number of such tallies as well as one of the number of fictitious loans. These loans nearly always carry a reference to the date of their subsequent repayment, but I have not troubled to follow these up. They are without the treasurer's dot, and therefore no tally was levied for them. It is of course inconceivable that a cash payment (*sol'*) could be cancelled and made the subject of a fictitious loan, and the rare instances in which this apparently occurs have therefore been classed under *Irregularities*. Before we come to the actual figures two small points are perhaps worth noticing. The first is a curious little piece of book-keeping. In 1361-2 it was apparently discovered that the 'lender' of a fictitious loan was in debt to the crown, so he was promptly paid off by the marginal *alloc' pro eodem*, neatly cancelling the one obligation with the other. But circumstances of this sort must have been rare and I have found no other instance of the kind. Secondly, we find that in this sphere, too, the bill can and does replace the tally in relation to Wales and neighbouring districts—thus we find dishonoured bills of assignment (1385, 1386) on those parts being made the subject of fictitious loans, just as if they were tallies.

---

[1] I have found one note *inde habet billam sub sig' off'* opposite a *prestitum restitutum* (1381), but only one. Cf. another entry, *certificatur in cancellaria* 10 *Jul' 49 Ed. III* (1373-4).

[2] See *Entries without tallies*, below, pp. 397-400.

The actual figures for the respective reigns are 169 loans, cancelling 254 bad tallies, in the 33 terms examined under Edward III, giving an average per term of approximately 5 loans for 8 tallies, and 218 loans, cancelling 382 bills and tallies in 29 terms under Richard II, averaging 7 loans for 13 tallies. It should be remembered that these figures are exceedingly conservative. They exclude one or two instances of an allied form of procedure, which will be found under *Remissiones*, and above all they exclude the very large class of tallies which were only partly dishonoured, and for only part of which in consequence smaller fictitious loans were made. Their method of entry[1] made it all but impossible to trace these without an elaborate investigation, and it would therefore be inadmissible at present to hazard even a guess at their total numbers. But even without this important element the more or less legitimate addition of the other cancelled entries to tallies totally dishonoured brings the numbers up to 360 for Edward III and 441 for Richard II, and that throws a certain amount of light on the degree of security attained by the process of assignment. On the figures I have been able to obtain, that is, figures for totally dishonoured tallies only, I have calculated that, of the *pro* tallies levied, approximately 1 in 40 during the reign of Edward III and 1 in 28 during that of Richard II were returnable as uncashable to the exchequer. This average, however, does not hold for the abnormal term of Easter 1370, when no fewer than 107 *pro* tallies (very nearly 1 in 4) were brought back and converted into 73 fictitious loans. To run a normal risk of 1 in 40, or even of 1 in 28, a risk, too, merely of postponement, not of absolute uncashability, for the exchequer never seems to have repudiated a *bona fide* claimant with a dishonoured tally, does not seem a very grave affair. True, the ratio would be altered considerably by the inclusion of the unknown percentage of partially dishonoured tallies, and it is, as it stands, liable to a certain amount of adverse modification when one remembers that an appreciable proportion, though a relatively small one, of the *pro* figures on which it is based represents complex or indirect assignments, all of which should have been excluded from the count. But when all is said and done it must be confessed that the ultimate percentage of assigned bills and tallies which went astray looks as if it would not be high enough, except in the one chaotic term mentioned, to constitute a serious charge against the general practice of assignment, at any rate under Edward III. It is, however, significant, in view of what we may safely assume to have happened in the fifteenth century, that, in spite of the more orderly character of the rolls, the average risk in question, even without the disturbing effect of any one term comparable with that of 1370, was considerably accentuated under Richard II.

[1] See *Cancelled entries*, above, pp. 387-9.

Genuine loans

Under this head are reckoned all entries marked *mutuum* in the left margin, except those which specifically refer to dishonoured tallies and are therefore only fictitious loans. Unfortunately, as we have seen, the division is not watertight, since a fictitious loan for the balance of a tally only dishonoured in part frequently seems to bear all the outward characteristics of a genuine loan.[1] The following figures therefore err considerably on the generous side, and are only of qualified interest, since the means to rectify them are lacking.

	Total	Average per term
Edward III . . .	554	17
Richard II . . .	466	16

Terms of special activity (over 50) are 1351, 1356, 1370, 1386-7, 1394-5, 1397-8. The figures for 1351 and 1370 are as high as 118 and 147 respectively; the next highest (1386-7) reaches 66 only. The political significance of the Ricardian dates looks like something more than a coincidence, and encourages the hope that these figures, relatively to each other at any rate, may be more accurate than I had supposed. So, too, the slight decline in the frequency of borrowing under Richard II might be countered by the magnitude of the sums borrowed; on the other hand this argument might tell the other way.

As opposed to this unsatisfactory result, the classification of these totals into *sol'* (cash), *pro* (assigned) and 'doubtful' does yield some interesting information. Under Edward the proportions are $\frac{1}{4}$, $\frac{1}{4}$, $\frac{1}{2}$ respectively; under Richard $\frac{3}{4}$, $\frac{1}{4}$, o. Now a cash loan (*sol'*) could hardly be anything but genuine[2] and, unless we put all the doubtful Edwardian entries into the cash class, which seems unwarranted, we have, after dividing them equally between the two classes, an appreciable frequency-increase in *sol'* under Richard. The corresponding decline in *pro* loans (probably about 30%) may be put down to the unsatisfactory system of classification adopted above—thus, if we adopt the Ricardian figure as something like the normal level of the *pro* loan, and write off the remaining half of the doubtful Edwardian entries as

---

[1] Moreover, as Dr. Dorothy M. Broome has pointed out to me, many apparently genuine loans simply represent the use of exchequer processes to recover private debts, the sum in question being 'lent' to the crown, extracted from the debtor and repaid to the creditor. The treasurer and other officials of the exchequer often seem to have done this, and the fact modifies the figures in the text still further. Cf. too the use made of the exchequer by prominent persons as a place of safe deposit for valuables, treated as 'loans', below, p. 398.

[2] This statement must be modified, for the reasons given in the last note ([1]).

disguised fictitious loans for partly paid assignments, we arrive at the following readjustment:

	Sol'	Pro	Doubtful
Edward III . . .	$\frac{2}{3}$	$\frac{1}{3}$	o
Richard II . . .	$\frac{3}{4}$	$\frac{1}{4}$	o

This hypothetical change in emphasis, which is probably underestimated, is accompanied by a slight rise in loans of all kinds, bookkeeping and otherwise, from an average of 22 per term in the first reign to one of 23 per term in the second.

Something may now be gained by examining the reputedly genuine loan in greater detail. In the first place it should be recalled that the normal entry—whether fictitious or genuine—has no dot, thus showing that a tally was not levied. There are a few instances to the contrary, but they are so rare that they are almost certainly clerical errors. Another normal feature common to all types of loan is the presence of a note, made later, of repayment, together with a precise reference to the day on which this was carried out. That genuine loans could be assigned we have already seen: it is perhaps worth noting that, in the case of a simple assignment, this might sometimes be equivalent to a forced loan, since it is necessary to suppose that the assignee's consent was always obtained in advance. However, the decreased proportion of *pro* loans under Richard II, just when we might expect them to rise in number for this reason, makes the hypothesis *prima facie* rather unlikely and, as we shall shortly see, there are other reasons against it.

The not uncommon case of a complex or indirect assignment being paid wholly by loan is still more difficult: one can only suppose that in such cases the 'lender' discharged official obligations locally under direct instruction from some competent authority other than the exchequer, or if at the command of the exchequer, under some instrument other than a tally:[1] otherwise there is no motive. It is significant in that connection that several entries, principally from 1350–2, but also from all parts of Richard II's reign, bear the note *inde hab' lit' R' pat' sub magno sigillo*, while beside one at least is written *certific' in canc' pro lit' R' oblig' in'* [?] *habend'* (1351–2, cf. 1384). Later variations on the same theme are *inde hab' bill' sub sig' offic'* and *inde hab' indent' sub privato sigillo* (both 1370), and *inde hab' lit' oblig' sub sigillo Thes' et J. Innocentii clerici* (1396, 1396–7). The fact, moreover, that many *sol'* and ordinary *pro* loans, i.e. loans directly assigned in the ordinary manner, share these legends makes it look as if written authority was normally used to raise a loan, irrespective of the way in which it might be spent. The receipt of such authority, though possibly tantamount to an unwelcome

---

[1] See *Complex assignment*, above, pp. 375–7.

command, by the lender would afford adequate notice in the case of an ordinary *pro* loan, and makes the theory just put forward, that such loans were 'forced' *because* assigned, intrinsically improbable.

Finally, there is the assignment of part of an apparently genuine loan back to the lender, of which I have collected eight examples ranging from 1357–8 to 1386. This is certainly connected with the problem of inducement, and may represent the interest paid to the lender. It is gratifying to receive this final confirmation of my belief that a loan could be manipulated in just the same way as any other payment. If this be true of loans, of all entries, except perhaps *remissiones*, in the term 1364–5 and, as we shall see, of *prestita restituta* at all times, it is likely enough that any sort of payment at any time could be either made in cash or directly or indirectly assigned with equal facility.[1]

Remissiones

Loans of all kinds and *prestita restituta* are not the only entries which lack the treasurer's dot: I have in fact been able to enlarge this class considerably.[2] Of the recruits, however, only one occurs frequently enough to merit a separate heading, and that is the *remissio*. In comparison with the *prestitum restitutum* and the loan the *remissio*, it is true, is almost rare: I have, however, found about 81 in my 33 Edwardian rolls, and 41 in those of Richard II. Most of these entries appear to be assigned simply, while a substantial minority are specifically assigned back to their 'payers'—I have found only one complex assignment (1355–6) of a very elementary kind, and one reputed *sol'* (1373–4), the authenticity of which I mistrust for reasons which will appear when we come to examine the structure of the entry.

The original nature of the *remissio* is suggested by the form it takes in, for example, two entries of 1364–5. One of these runs, *de X et Y £z de vadiis suis guerre gratanter R. remissis . . . pro eisdem*, and the other *de X £y de den' sibi deb' per bill' . . . pro (? Z)*. From this it is clear that the *remissio* lies halfway between the genuine loan and the *donum*: it records, in short, something which may have started as a loan but ended as a gift, viz. the voluntary abandonment of a claim against the crown.

We must now turn to the occasions on which a lien on the crown might be abandoned. Of the two cases quoted one is a claim for wages, and the other apparently a loan: the latter can be paralleled by a long

---

[1] See my 'Distribution of Assignment in the Treasurer's Receipt Roll, 1364–5', *Cambridge Historical Journal*, II, 178–85. The value of the figures given in my article in *Eng. Hist. Rev.*, XLIII, 172, depends largely on this argument.

[2] See *Entries without tallies*, below, pp. 397–400.

entry from 1397, recording in unusual detail how Thomas Coggeshall, the prior of Dunmowe, Richard Knychbole, Thomas Brichle and the good men of Branktre of their own free will remitted and relaxed four loans which they had made the crown, restoring letters patent which they had previously received in acknowledgment thereof to be cancelled at the receipt of the exchequer. All this is perfectly straightforward, even though the stock *gratanter*, *mera voluntate*, etc., may possibly be somewhat suspect. But meanwhile an extended use of the *remissio* had sprung up in connection with dishonoured tallies of assignment. Thus from 1370 onwards, viz. in 1382, 1385, 1386–7, 1388–9, 1390 and 1399, we find cases in which a disappointed assignee apparently resigned all hope of payment and (always *gratanter*) returned his worthless tallies for cancellation and remitted the debt. The entries corresponding to the dishonoured tallies were then cancelled in the usual way, but instead of the ordinary fictitious loan, which would have indicated that the creditor still pressed his claim, the accounts were squared by a *remissio*, or note to the effect that he had abandoned it. The entry is a bookkeeping one in the sense that its *raison d'être*, like that of the fictitious loan, is to prevent the alteration of the totals, but unlike the loan it does represent a genuine accession of revenue, even though no tally is levied for it. *Remissiones* of this kind really form a class by themselves: it is noticeable that I have found only one such specimen in Edward III's reign, and that in the abnormal Easter term of 1370, while only one *remissio* (1397) is *not* of this type under Richard II.

It is difficult to understand how a *remissio* could ever be assigned directly to a third party, and in this case the difficulty cannot be disposed of by the simple argument that there is only one known instance of it and that that is probably a clerical error, for *remissiones* apparently assigned in this way are much too common. What had X to gain by accepting a note to Z which, so far from getting money out of Z, merely told him that his claim for the repayment of a sum previously advanced by him was (*gratanter* on his part!) remitted? The exchequer ought to have had the money long before and X could not have it again. Possible solutions seem to be either that X and Z are really identical or in partnership, in which case we have what we should expect to find and do find in a great many cases, viz. an ordinary reflex assignment, or else that Z had not really paid the exchequer anything at all until instructed to pay X, and that apparently without reason and without the prospect of account! Neither explanation is satisfactory, but I prefer the first: indeed I am inclined to think that all *remissiones*, like fictitious loans, should be classed as reflex assignments for the present purpose or not classed at all. The solitary complex assignment of 1355–6 affords an exception to this rule: it is explicable on the assumption that the accountant, after proving his local expenditure in the usual way, took the extraordinary step of resigning his claim either to repayment or to the usual allowance for the sum total off his account. There may have been special reasons for such a course of which we know nothing in the one instance I have found.

In conclusion it should be noticed that the *remissio*, though sufficiently interesting, and certainly baffling enough, to have deserved this special treatment, is probably of little real importance. In proportion to the total number of entries it is easily the rarest type as yet under discussion, and the sums involved in it are in most cases comparatively small.

Entries without tallies

The following marginals may be used to confirm Sir Hilary Jenkinson's statement[1] that the levying or otherwise of a tally may be determined by the presence or absence of the treasurer's dot in the receipt roll. Against undotted entries we have in 1349 the notes *non fiat tallia quia alloc' in magno rotulo*, and again *non fiat tallia quia habet litteras de mag' sig'*; in 1350 *non debet fieri inde tallia quia habet acq' de mag' sig'*, and in 1360 *non fiat inde tallia quia non debet inde computari*. Finally in 1394–5 the dot against seven cognate entries has been carefully erased and the note made *inde habet alloc' sine tallia*, the inference from which is conclusive. Of the reasons given for the absence of the tally that alleged in 1360 is perhaps the most illuminating, but unfortunately it will by no means cover every case. As it happens, we have entered here on a sub-section which might be entitled 'entries without tallies for special cause given', and it may be as well to complete it before proceeding to deal with the more standard types of entry from which the dot and tally are missing. Thus in 1356 no tally was levied for a certain entry owing to reasons given in the memoranda roll, a precise reference to which follows. In 1363–4 no reason at all is alleged—the note runs simply *inde non fiat tallia*—but in the following term (1364) another case is set out at full length, thus:

Arg' forinsec' — *Lond'* —	*De Reg' de Sholdam scrutatore*
Inde non fiat tall'	*dni R' in port' Lond' 222 li.*,
quia hab' alloc' in	*de pretio 27 pec' arg' in massa*
comp' suo ad scacc'	*forinsec'.*
de pec' arg' subscriptis	
et non de den' liberatis.	(Right margin blank).

This entry again stands alone, as does the following, which concludes

---

[1] *Archaeologia*, LXXIV, 229.

THE RECEIPT OF THE EXCHEQUER, 1377–1485

the list of special entries, from 1364–5: *inde non fiat tall' quia subscripta n[omina?] onerantur inde ad scacc' comp'*. Before leaving this group, however, it should be mentioned that out of the whole period some 182 entries of an otherwise normal type omit the dot for no apparent reason whatever: I shall recur to this under *Irregularities*.

Turning to entries which, whenever they occur, are regularly without the dot and tally, we find the following groups, viz. *dona, avantagia, incrementa, hostagia* and ransoms under Edward III, while *dona* again, prize-money, money made by the arrest and sale of forfeited goods, forfeitures in general and fines made before the council predominate under Richard II. This list is by no means exhaustive. A solitary *restitucio billarum* (assigned) from 1361 may probably be dismissed as a species of *remissio*, but entries bearing the legend *inde habet billam sub sig' off'* on the other hand are both individual enough and pretty common: I have counted 155 in all, mainly from Richard II's reign, to which should be added 31 of the allied late Edwardian type *inde habet indenturam sub sig' off'*, and 17 *inde habet acq' de mag' sig'*, which are mostly earlier. A few entries of receipts apparently more or less normal in themselves, but drawn from unusual sources or difficult to classify, are also undotted, e.g. *Janua* (2) (freightage), *Franc'* (4), *Normann'*— *inde non fiat tall'* (2) and *Angl'* (1), the last of which refers to issues of the hanaper, becomes standardized, and ultimately receives the dot. Finally three unique entries of 1398–9 remain undotted—viz. one payment of £200 in cash by the duke of Surrey on account of a circlet or coronet of gold; and two book-keeping credits, assigned back to him, for the bishop of St. David's on account of certain vestments. Both these probably refer to the function of the exchequer as a bank and place of safe deposit[1] and it is not surprising to find no tallies levied for them.

Before attempting to find any guiding thread through this mass of detail it may be as well to say a little more of certain individual items. *Dona* appear to be gifts pure and simple, though whether strictly voluntary, especially towards the close of Richard II's reign, I cannot tell.[2] Thirteen out of fifteen, however, are in cash and look more innocent than the two assignments. *Avantagia* and *incrementa* are related—they refer to windfalls or unexpected profits made either on minting (the more usual use of *avantagium*) or on the exchange. They are very infrequent and appear indifferently as cash or as assignments. *Hostagia*

[1] Stressed by Miss Broome in a letter to *History*, July 1928. Cf. Tout, *Chapter*, IV, 321 n.
[2] A *donum* of 1377 (Ed. III) takes the form of a sum which the payer *recognoscit se Regi debere*. Is this the medieval equivalent of 'conscience money'?

only appear six times in all (five *sol'* and one doubtful) and only in the two terms 1370 and 1372. The sole entry under this head in the former term bears the note *certificatur in cancellaria sub sig' off' . . . sol'*. I am a little vague about their meaning, but am inclined to suppose that they may be ransom payments on account of persons of minor importance as distinct from the equally undotted and much commoner payments on account of the three great ransoms of France,[1] Burgundy, and Scotland. To these we might add two payments on account of the ransom of the count of St. Pol, both made and assigned in 1379. Any ransom payment could be either assigned or paid in cash—the one other thing they have in common being the absence of the tally. Some of the French payments are marked *inde hab' bill' sub sig' off'* (or *acq' de mag' sig'*), and the former at least are subject to the same indifferent treatment, but the majority bear no notes of this kind. Prize money, that is, profit of prizes taken at sea, first appears in 1374 and continues spasmodically under Richard II: it is twice paid in cash and five times assigned. Receipts on account of forfeitures, sale of arrested goods and fines before the council become fairly common in the later years of Richard II, and are nearly always paid in cash. This is true of over a hundred entries under the three heads; while six are doubtful, I have noticed only three assignments.

Entries in which bills are systematically used in place of tallies, especially under Richard II, are associated with certain specially 'royal' areas, e.g. Wales (north and south), Chester (with Flint on one occasion) and Ireland. One or two entries from Devon and Cornwall, and one from Somerset and Devon (probably a slip for Dorset) are treated in the same way, but this is rare. Bills of this sort seem to have taken the place of tallies for all purposes in the districts concerned and to have been treated in exactly the same way or ways. Thus we have 61 *sol'*, 94 assigned and 20 doubtful. In and just after 1360 a similar experiment seems to have been tried with the English shires in general—thus we find at that time over thirty undotted, but otherwise normal, entries from all parts of England marked *inde hab' indent' sub sig' off'*, the majority of them being *sol'*. The experiment, if such it was, seems to have been abandoned, or at any rate confined subsequently to the western half of the British Isles.

In conclusion, these notes suggest to me two things. The first is the ease with which instruments other than the tally, e.g. the exchequer bill, the indenture, letters under the great seal, etc., could be used to take the tally's place: this may confirm in part some of my earlier guesses under *Complex* and *Simple assignment*. The second is that the one thing nearly all these entries, except those from Chester, Wales and Ireland,

---

[1] See Miss Broome's careful study, *Camden Miscellany*, XIV.

have in common is their more or less abnormal character. I do not mean that they are abnormal simply because no tallies are levied for them, but that in nearly every case they were abnormal to begin with and that *therefore* no tally was levied. They are not abnormal because they never end in an account, for many of them do; nor again because they represent book-keeping totals only and no real accession of revenue —ransoms and gifts alone disprove it. It is simply that they are entries which either in source or character cannot be brought under any standard head of revenue, and therefore require special instruments and special treatment. It should, however, be remembered that the entries summarized above are all, like *remissiones*, relatively rare in comparison not only with the vast mass of normal entries and their orthodox, ordinary instruments, the tallies, but even with the other three standard entries without tallies which have already been treated individually, viz. the *prestitum restitutum* and the 'genuine' and fictitious loans.

Miscellaneous

Most of the entries included in this section are made very faintly on either the extreme left or extreme right of the roll. Their unusually small size, irregular position and comparative illegibility distinguish them from the normal marginalia and make it doubtful whether they were ever meant to be used at all, unlike the text and the ordinary marginal, for purposes of future reference. I noticed them first in the roll of 1373–4, from which term up to 1385 many, but not all, subsidy payments are marked on the extreme left, according to their character, *Xve*, *subs' per laic'*, *subs' gross'*, *subs' vjd. de lib'*, *subs' cleri*, etc. No other entries appear to be marked in this way, nor does it seem to matter whether the entries in question were *sol'* or *pro*. Nearly ten years later the same sort of thing occurs on the extreme right of the roll, but this time it is a succession of proper names which we find, e.g. 'hilton', 'more', 'preston', 'Wyltes', 'Isaak', 'Gelr', 'Godmaston', 'blyth', 'wax-combe', 'burgh', etc. The series is extremely intermittent in character and appears only between 1394 and 1398 inclusive; it is associated especially, but not I think exclusively, with *sol'* payments. One of these names may perhaps be identified as that of Thomas More, who about this time was general receiver of the late queen Anne's effects, and seems to have had a good deal of money in hand, out of which he made several payments into the receipt during this period; at the same time one of his own *sol'* payments is marked 'more' which, if the identity holds, is puzzling, since in no other case does there seem to be any relation between these ultra-marginals and either the text or the mar-ginals proper. The only explanation that occurs to me is that these names may be those of financial agents resident at Westminster and

London acting in some sense as intermediaries[1] between accountants proper and the exchequer. Rough castings of totals often appear in the same position (e.g. in 1398–9) and all such notes in any case appear to be quite ephemeral in character.

Another interesting detail, the general object of which is clearer, though its development is rather obscure, first appears on the chamberlains' rolls of 1365–8,[2] but is not well established on the treasurer's roll till 1384–5. This is a small dot in the immediate neighbourhood of the words *pro* and *sol'*. It is undoubtedly connected with some process of checking the entries or tallies or both, but it is not until it is adopted with modifications by the treasurer's clerk in the last fifteen years of Richard II that it becomes really interesting. It is often accompanied or replaced on this series from 1384–5 by what appears to be a highly formalized 'e' and sometimes by an erasure: again, unlike the earlier dots on the chamberlains' rolls, it is now associated as a rule with *pro* alone. Thus we have intermittent dots to the left of many *pro* entries in 1387, then erasures to the left of *pro*, followed later by a dot in between the two, in 1388–9; the 'e' sign on top of an erasure, then the dot only, then the erasure only, then the dot again, all in 1390; dots *or* erasures, apparently as alternatives, in 1391 and 1391–2; 'e' on top of an erasure for many *sol'* [*sic*] entries and dots for *pro* entries, then erasures only again, in 1392; followed by a new sign, the 'e' struck through and followed by an erasure, in 1392–3. The changes are then rung on these elements for the rest of the period, but the practice is more or less confined to *pro* entries and it seems probable that the 'e' stands for *exitus*, and indicates that any entry marked with it on the receipt roll is to be found as an issue on the issue roll.

Some other general characteristics of these late receipt rolls may be mentioned before we go on to deal with individual entries. A ruled right-hand column of a formal type begins to appear for the *sol'* and *pro* marginals proper in 1388–9, and about the same time a tendency begins, which unhappily does not persist, to confine *pro* and *sol'* entries as far as possible to different days: thus one day's entries will be all assignments and the next day's all cash, and it is not until the 'mid-term' entries at the end of these rolls that the old haphazard confusion of *pro* and *sol'* returns again. Again, towards the end of Richard's reign there is a marked tendency towards the concentration of business on much fewer days in the term: the total number of entries for a term, it is true, is somewhat higher, but the average number of entries per day is now considerably higher still. In general the rolls are not only larger but

---

[1] Cf. my discussion of *sol' per*, under *Varieties of sol'*, and of *pro . . . per man'* under *Simple assignment*, above, pp. 379–81, 384–7.

[2] A period for which all the treasurers' rolls are missing.

tidier and more carefully kept under Richard than under his grandfather.

This brings us to the half-dozen individual entries which are possibly worth record. The first of these is a note *in man' div' merc' per lit' oblig'* (1359–60), which apparently displays the exchequer in the somewhat unusual role of a moneylender. The second is a unique instance of a schedule, the purport of which is not explained, being attached to the foil of a *sol'* tally (1392). It reads, *a la foile de ceste taille est une cedule liee de quele cedule doit estre avisez quant la taille est monstree*. There is a similar, but less explicit, reference to a schedule apropos of one payment by More in 1396–7. Another curious entry tends to confirm the hypothesis that *pro* tallies were negotiable.[1] In this case the tally had been dishonoured, and we find the new one being levied for the claimant X *per tall' assign* Y *dampn' et restit'* (1384–5). It adds something to the interest of this case to find that Y was a Lombard. Finally, we have three entries from 1397–8 which apparently defied classification and for which no tallies were levied: they are

(a) a payment on account of certain victuals found in the king's ship *la Gràcedieu de la Tour*.

(b) *moneta inventa in mag' Thes' R' de den' Anne nuper regin' Angl'*.

(c) *de Drugone Barantyn de pretio unius chapelletti venditi*.

They do not seem to me to be of any great significance, but I record them for the sake of their unusual character, which seems to have puzzled the clerks of the receipt. The last of them might be classed with the entries of 1398–9 affecting the duke of Surrey and the bishop of St. David's,[2] while the first two seem rather to resemble *prestita restituta* in type.

Irregularities

Intentional irregularities are rare, and are either explained by the conservative clerks of the receipt upon the spot, or else marked with a reference to another place where the explanation may be found. We have had several of these references: to these may be added one of 1398, made because an apparently normal assignment had not been entered in the issue roll of the same day as it should have been. Hence the note *exitus ist' particule fit xj. Jul' prox' sequenti*, which incidentally illustrates the close relationship and complementary character of the receipt and issue rolls, an omission in one requiring an *ad loc.* explanation in the other. Another apparently intentional irregularity, which is fairly com-

---

[1] See *Simple assignment*, above, pp. 380–1.

[2] See *Entries without tallies*, above, p. 398.

mon, may not perhaps have been regarded as altogether irregular by the clerks themselves—this is the multilinear entry. It is usually assumed that an entry in the receipt roll should not exceed one line in length, but I have collected some 39 entries out of the whole period—and more could probably be found—which break the rule, and of these 29 are two lines, 6 three lines, 3 four lines, and 1 as many as eight lines, long. The sole argument against the practice seems to be the difficulty of inscribing a very long entry on a tally, but that is answered by the fact that the majority of these multilinear entries belong to the various classes of entry for which no tally was levied—that of eight lines in length, for example (1356), being a single *prestitum restitutum* paid in 18 separate sections on behalf of queen Philippa. It is true that 16 out of my 39 entries do not belong to any of these classes, but nearly all of them are irregular in another sense, viz. in that very absence of the dot and tally which makes possible their abnormal length. In addition to these 16 entries I have noted altogether some 166 perfectly normal ones, making 182 in all, for which the dot is unaccountably lacking, and can only suggest that in these cases its absence is the result of mere carelessness in the checking stage, since the total average is barely three per term, while the entries in question are freely assigned or paid in cash, just like any others.

The allegation of carelessness against the clerks of the receipt has been used before in order to explain certain difficulties, and it requires substantiation. No careful student of these rolls, however, will long be disposed to deny that mistakes of all kinds, though creditably rare in comparison with the immense bulk and complexity of the whole series, do occur and are to be found in almost every roll. Small arithmetical mistakes in the daily, weekly and terminal totals are at once apparent to anyone who takes the trouble to check them, while mistakes in date are to be found in no less than seventeen of the rolls I have examined. Thus it is quite common for a clerk to write 'Monday 2 May', 'Tuesday 3 May', 'Thursday 6 May', or the like, and then go on for a fortnight without discovering his mistake, which he eventually corrects without comment: I have even found cases in which the dates were for some time two or more days out. When mistakes of this sort occur, it is hardly surprising to find mere dots omitted or displaced, and it is unnecessary to puzzle oneself over the fact that four 'genuine' loans, for example, receive one when four hundred do not. What is extraordinary over so long a period is not that the mistakes are so many but that they are so few. The wrong manipulation of the dot is naturally the commonest; thus, in addition to the examples I have quoted, half a dozen 'bill' entries unexpectedly receive it under Richard II, as do four fictitious loans. Three more fictitious loans are nonsensically marked *sol'* at the beginning of the period, and another is recorded in 1386 in which the offending tallies have been left uncancelled. All things considered, the record of the clerks is wholly admirable, but at the same time they remained only human, and I contend that there is in that fact alone sufficient justification, especially in the vexed matter of the dot, for cutting the Gordian knot of certain difficulties with the convenient sword of 'clerical error'.

Conclusions

I have ventured to devote a final section to a brief recapitulation of the few hypotheses I have allowed myself to make in the course of this inquiry.

(1) The steady growth of indirect assignment all through the fourteenth century indicates the increased use of letters patent, letters obligatory, writs of privy seal, bills under the exchequer seal, etc., as substitutes upon occasion for the tally.

(2) At the same time the much more violent increase in the number of *per manus* entries under Richard II suggests that a great deal of discounting is now being done, i.e. that much of this new 'paper', especially that of the household, is now changing hands before presentation (when it is frequently met by fresh 'paper') at the exchequer. This development is not surprising in view of the matter-of-course traffic in wardrobe debentures characteristic of Edward III's reign at least, and probably of Edward II's,[1] while both tendencies are probably accelerated by what seems to be an increasing decentralization of government finance.

(3) This somewhat hypothetical decentralization, which has been thought (erroneously) to have ended by reducing the exchequer to a clearing-house at which by the fifteenth century little actual cash ever appeared, is further illustrated by a slight increase in the already well-established habit of paying local officials by drafts or assignments on the revenues which they themselves are in process of collecting, and in the general application of this principle to all cases in which a past or future debt to the crown could be used to extinguish a royal obligation.

(4) Even the ordinary *sol'* entry has been found to veil upon occasion an advance payment, the *sol'* tally in return for which was sometimes used, for example, in connection with the customs, as a sort of clearing-ticket by exporting houses. The practice of accepting such payments was probably confined to cases of this type after 1370, when some confusion appears to have arisen over what were really loans from the collectors of a clerical subsidy being treated in this way.

---

[1] See my 'Negotiation of Wardrobe Debentures in the Fourteenth Century', *Eng. Hist. Rev.*, XLIV, 439.

(5) The roll for Easter, 1370, is in fact quite abnormally confused in character.[1] Thus, apart from the case just quoted, nearly 1 in 4 of the *pro* entries upon it turned out to be worthless, whereas the normal ratio for the reign is 1 in 40. No less than three entries again from this one term carry the very rare reference, probably indicating something badly amiss, to processes recorded in the memoranda rolls; while the number of 'genuine' loans is more than twice as great as that of any other term but one (1351) in the whole period, and even 1351 is 20% short of 1370. It is in this term, too, that we find for the first time the extended use of the *remissio*, so common under Richard II, in connection with dishonoured tallies of assignment.

(6) 1370, however, marks the nadir of the receipt rolls: there is an abrupt change to clarity and order, and the rolls are much more tidily kept all through the next reign. This is illustrated by a drop of 33% in the number of entries cancelled without sufficient explanation, by the adoption of a new formula which distinguishes tallies levied to pay off a debt or debts contracted by the dishonouring of earlier tallies, by improvements in checking entries and in methods of reference to other classes of record, by the full development of the regular *sol'* and *pro* columns, by the better classification of business at the receipt, and by experiments with certain 'ultra-marginals'.

(7) This improvement in the actual keeping of the rolls, however, does not seem to have carried with it much improvement in the general state of government finance. It is true that the appearance for the first time under Richard II of money made by the arrest and sale of forfeited goods, by forfeitures in general on a large scale, and by fines made before the council may reflect what is primarily political rather than financial degradation. But on the other hand such purely financial causes as we have noted above in the growth of decentralization, the partial displacement of the tally, and the increased traffic in negotiable instruments, evidently enhanced the dangers of assignment[2] and correspondingly accelerated the transition to the financial chaos of the fifteenth century. At any rate we find that whereas the average risk run by a person who accepted an exchequer *pro* tally was only 1 in 40 under Edward III, it had become 1 in 28 under Richard II, while the number of 'genuine' loans had, to say the least, not declined as it should have

---

[1] The term 1369–70, for which only chamberlains' rolls survive, is much the same. No other term even approaches comparison with these.

[2] The two documents which I published in *Eng. Hist. Rev.*, XLIV, 439, indicate that forgery of the instruments in question probably became common: it is treated as a normal offence as early as the beginning of this period. Dr. Dorothy Broome has also drawn my attention to three separate cases of forged tallies on the memoranda rolls, 11–15 Ed. III!

done,[1] in view of the increased prosperity of the country and the marked relaxation in the prosecution of the war. Lastly, the use of the *remissio* to register the complete abandonment of a claim for a dishonoured tally became rather more common in and after 1385, thereby indicating an approach towards that acute embarrassment which is so characteristic of late Lancastrian finance.

[1] Loans of all sorts, fictitious and otherwise, average 22 per term under Edward III and 23 under Richard II. However, these are only straws in the wind, and although I have let this final paragraph stand substantially as it was written many years ago, I now feel that the conclusions it embodies are somewhat over-emphasized.

APPENDIX B

'MUTUA PER TALLIAM,' 1377–1485

I

It has long been well known that many of the 'mutua' (loans) recorded in the English receipt rolls of the later middle ages are fictitious, that is, they do not represent a real loan to the crown. What has happened is that the exchequer has tried to anticipate revenue by issuing to a creditor a kind of cheque or draft upon some local official or debtor of the crown in the shape of an advance tally of receipt made out in the name of the payer, and this draft has not been honoured, whereupon instead of merely cancelling the entry in the receipt roll the clerks have interlineated a 'loan' from the disappointed creditor. Another draft in the form of a writ or writ-and-tally will then be made, until by this means or sometimes by payment in cash, if there is, by chance, enough cash in the receipt, the creditor is finally satisfied. It will be noticed that one advantage of this rather cumbrous proceeding is that it makes it unnecessary to alter the nominal totals in the receipt roll, though at the same time it helps, with similar devices, to rob such totals of any real meaning.

The undoubted existence of a large number of these *mutua per talliam*, as they come to be called in the margin of the roll during this period, is obviously of the highest importance to any student of finance and of the larger questions of government policy and government embarrassment which lie behind finance. In the first place, the nominal revenue must clearly be reduced for this cause alone (and there are other causes) by many thousands of pounds. In the second place, any fluctuation in the number and value of such entries (and there is violent fluctuation) should clearly be related to, and may illuminate, general economic and even political history.

For this purpose further inquiry is necessary: we want to know the nature of the fluctuation and what particular revenues failed to bear the strain imposed on them. Broadly speaking, the answer to the first question, namely: What is the nature of the fluctuation?—is as follows: For the first half of Richard II's reign such *mutua* amount to well over £47,000 in 456 tallies; for the second half of the same reign to over £34,000 in 214 tallies; and for Henry IV's reign to just under £135,000 in 1,246 tallies.[1] Of these periods Henry IV's reign is clearly the longest,

---

[1] Average value of such tallies, £104, £165 and £108 respectively.

but the accident of manuscript survival makes it possible to equate it fairly closely with each of the two halves of Richard's reign, reckoning, that is, by weight of surviving evidence instead of by years. In other words, if we count the three periods as roughly equipollent, fictitious loans are seen to decline steadily under Richard, notably in the period of his personal rule, while they jump remarkably with the revolution of 1399.

So much for the first question: it will, I hope, be agreed that the figures are large enough to merit some discussion and that there is a peculiar fluctuation in them. It is, however, the second question, namely, what particular revenues failed to bear the strain, with which this appendix is concerned. If it can be shown that assignments which went wrong were almost exclusively assignments on the wool custom, then it might be argued that the great increase in the number of bad assignments early in the fifteenth century does not necessarily reflect any general financial confusion, corruption, or mismanagement, but was simply due to the established fall in the value of the wool custom during this period, owing to the declining export of wool-sacks and wool-fells and the increasing export of English-made cloth, which yielded a far lower duty than the equivalent amount of wool or fells.[1] Apart from this suggestion, the examination of which was the original object of this inquiry, it has turned out to be a matter of some interest in itself to see from the point of view of the payer rather than of the receiver how bad assignments were distributed at this time. But before coming to a summary of results it is necessary to say something about the nature of the evidence.

In the first place there were certainly bad assignments other than those recorded as *mutua per talliam* in the receipt rolls. The reason for this is that these rolls are primarily registers of tallies, hence an assignment made by writ alone often found no corresponding entry in the

---

[1] H. L. Gray, 'Production of English Woollens in the Fourteenth Century', *Eng. Hist. Rev.*, XXXIX, 13–35; *Studies in English Trade in the Fifteenth Century*, ed. Eileen E. Power and M. Postan, especially the tables of enrolled customs and subsidy accounts, pp. 330–60. I do not propose to deal here with still another suggestion, namely, that the great increase in fictitious loans under Henry IV may only be an apparent one because of the technical change which occurred some time between 1395 and 1399 in the method of making payments to the armies. It is argued, I think wrongly, that the older method, which was last employed in the first Irish expedition of 1394–5, may have effectively concealed a large number of bad assignments, and that it is merely the change in method which reveals a great number of these for the first time and so produces the impression of an absolute increase under Henry IV. The arguments against this theory, which I have given elsewhere in this book, are to my mind decisive.

body of the roll. On the other hand, when the official who received the writ came up to Westminster to account in the exchequer, his nominal 'payments' into the receipt would include sums already paid out locally under writs or like authority, which he would of course produce in evidence. He would then be entitled to a tally of receipt involving an entry in the roll, but in order to distinguish this entry from a cash payment it would be annotated in the margin with some such formula as *inde pro X et Y et Z*, ending possibly *et sol'*, that is, if there happened to be a small cash balance to be paid in after all the writs of assignment the official could produce had been allowed to him.[1]

This was the 'ideal' process, but it might be that the local official could not meet the writ of assignment out of balances in hand any more than he could meet the more formal (and I think more usual) tally of assignment. It seems to me that in that case the odds are heavily in favour of all record of the attempted transaction being lost. It might sometimes appear in the issue roll, but I do not think it would necessarily do so,[2] and when it did it is probable that it could only be detected by establishing its complete absence from the receipt roll, involving a heart-breaking search for a negative result not infrequently impossible to achieve with any certainty owing to gaps in the series. The tracing of unsuccessful writs, as distinct from unsuccessful tallies, of assignment must therefore be given up as a bad job, except perhaps in individual instances, and it must be admitted that, as no trace at all of them would appear on the receipt rolls, any calculations of the total volume of bad assignments based only on receipt roll evidence are vitiated to an unknown, but not I think to a very serious, extent. Successful writs of assignment, on the other hand, leave traces on the receipt rolls, namely, in the margin as items of 'complex' assignment, a fact which is not always realized.

Allowing, then, that the receipt roll *mutua per talliam* do not fully exhaust the number of bad assignments and that the true total of such assignments is probably irrecoverable, we may now turn to the existing *mutua* themselves. They are generally easy to recognize by the very

[1] I am convinced that this is the correct explanation of these entries, which I have elsewhere called 'complex assignments' (see appendix A, above, pp. 373–7, for a full analysis).

[2] Not, for example, if the writ were issued locally under one of the small seals, no contemporary registers of which survive. If issued under the great seal it would probably be enrolled, but then it would probably be in the issue roll as well, and in any case the same exhausting test of the receipt roll for a negative reaction would have to be applied. (This is exclusive of the fact that in certain areas at this time, such as north and south Wales, bills under the great seal habitually replace tallies and are regularly treated as such.)

obvious cancellation of some entries coupled with the interlineation of others. But it will sometimes be found that the totals of the cancelled and interlineated entries do not exactly correspond, as in theory they ought to do. There are two reasons for this. Where the total of the cancelled entries is the higher of the two, the probable explanation is that there had in fact been only part payment on one or more of the cancelled tallies of assignment; where the interlineations, on the other hand, total up to more than the total of the cancelled entries the explanation is simply clerical carelessness. This can often be detected when more than one copy of the receipt rolls—in theory a series kept in triplicate—survives, but we are frequently dependent on only one surviving roll for any one term, and in such cases it is sometimes impossible to detect which entries ought to have been cancelled but have not been so. Throughout this article only entries which have actually been cancelled have been taken into account, whereas elsewhere, when I have been primarily considering the recipients of the bad tallies rather than the persons on whom they were drawn, I have given only the total of the interlineations. There is therefore some discrepancy, variable either way, between the grand totals of *mutua per talliam* from the two points of view, and the totals given in this appendix are, for example, plus 5% for the first half and minus 8% for the second half of Richard II's reign, but minus only 0.2% for the reign of Henry IV.[1]

On examining the cancelled entries, that is those cancelled *per talliam* —there are a few cancelled for other reasons, clearly stated in the roll, which do not concern us here—certain well-defined classes immediately appear. In the first place, small unsuccessful assignments are fairly commonly made on speculative farmers and keepers of crown property and other lucrative interests, whether temporary or permanent, that is not only of manors, lands, castles, vills, boroughs, and even counties (in Wales), but also of royal wards, alien priories, and the temporalities of vacant sees. More and more of the feudal revenue of the crown was being farmed out at this period and many small men, clerks, esquires, or even yeomen in the service of the great, were forming syndicates to take up these contracts, when they were too big for one of them alone to handle, and were laying out of the profits the substantial basis of many a county family.[2] This group shades off into the second, namely,

[1] The comparatively large errors for Richard may be due to a mistake (though I cannot trace it) in distribution between the two halves of the reign. Actually the plus error for the first half almost cancels the minus error for the second half, so that the total error, taking the reign as a whole, is infinitesimal, namely (minus) only 0.005%.

[2] See *Cal. of Fine Rolls*, vols. IX–XI, *passim*, and an article of mine on

APPENDIX B

royal officers, each strictly accounting *de exitibus ballive sue*—of these
the most important are sheriffs, escheators, bailiffs, reeves, constables
(as distinct from farmers) of castles, receivers, for example the receivers-
general of the duchy of Cornwall and (under Henry) of the Lancaster
estates, chamberlains of Wales, and (again under Henry only) the clerk
of the hanaper. Some of these people, for example certain sheriffs, might
appear in both groups, but the tallies drawn on them, say as farmers of
royal manors, have been carefully distinguished from those drawn on
the issues of their bailiwicks.

All the remaining feudal revenues of the crown can be conveniently
placed under a third head comprising fines and forfeitures of all kinds,
aids (Henry's aid *pur fille marier* of 1402 is the only one of these) and (under Richard) prizes of war, to which we should have to add ransoms in
Henry V's time. Of the three headings so far none is of great importance,
but the first two attain a respectable total in at least two periods out of
three. After the aids come the gracious aids, namely the lay and clerical
subsidies regularly granted in parliament and convocation. The clerical
tenths seem to have been freely assigned and consequently their proportion of bad tallies reaches the highest figure treated so far, though
only in the first part of Richard's reign. The lay fifteenths and tenths,
on the other hand, seem to have been very infrequently assigned at this
time considering the large sums raised by this means during the period,[1]
and consequently both the number and value of the bad tallies struck
on them are of small account, and even sink to nothing in the second
half of Richard's reign.

With the wool custom, however, we at once reach a different order
of magnitude and it is quite clear that this is where the great bulk of
the assignment, and therefore of the bad tallies, lies. It is also clear,
however, that the wool custom has a rival, namely, 'customs unspecified'. This rivalry, however, is only apparent: for although, to be on the
safe side, I have calculated 'customs unspecified' separately, I believe
them to be identical with the wool custom. Thus both of them are
never heavy at the same time, and it is the specified wool custom which
easily preponderates until 1392, after which there are practically no
fictitious loans of any kind for a period of nearly five years. When
fictitious loans become common again in the final crisis of Richard II's

the sheriffs of Cambridgeshire and Huntingdonshire in the time of
Richard II, printed in the Cambridge Antiquarian Society's *Proceedings*,
XXXVI, 1–34.
[1] See, for example, the specimen term totals for Richard II analysed
by Sir James Ramsay in his *Revenues of the Kings of England*, vol. II. The
figures of course are largely nominal, being given at face value only, but
they afford some idea of the relative yield of different branches of the
revenue.

reign we hear nothing of the wool custom, but we have very heavy entries *de collectoribus cust' et subs' Regis in portu de X, Y, Z*, and yet these entries remain distinct from those recording tallies struck on tunnage and poundage and the petty custom, even though in the smaller ports the names of the collectors of all three kinds of custom are often identical. Then, after a life of eight years, 'customs unspecified' suddenly diminish and are replaced in 1404–5 by heavy assignments on the specified wool custom, a practice which continues without intermission into the reign of Henry VI.

I believe, therefore, that we have here simply a temporary change in nomenclature, and this belief is strengthened by the fact that, especially in the transitional periods 1396–7 and 1404–5, it is quite common to find mentioned on successive days, or even on the same day, collectors for the same port both of 'customs unspecified' and of the specified wool custom, and even in the largest ports the names of the two sets of collectors are always identical. It is therefore suggested that the two heads should be added together for the purposes of this article. If this is done, we find that whereas the wool custom alone accounts for $67\frac{1}{2}\%$, 48% and 24% of the total of unsuccessful assignments in the three periods, the figures rise to 77%, 86% and 92% respectively when 'customs unspecified' are added—a remarkably steady increase, though it may be noted here in passing that they drop back slightly to 84% without and 86% with 'customs unspecified' under Henry V.

The remaining heads, tunnage and poundage, the petty custom, and the subsidy on cloths for sale in England, can be rapidly dismissed, for they are never of much importance, though the first two increase steadily throughout the three periods and tallies on tunnage and poundage do, in fact, go on increasing in number and value, proportionately to other entries, up to 1422.

We seem, then, to have arrived at an answer to the main question raised by this appendix: what were the causes of the great increase in *mutua per talliam* under Henry IV? It has been found that probably 92% of the bad tallies struck in that reign were meant to be levied on the wool custom; it is known that the value of the wool custom was then rapidly diminishing as the volume of the cloth export, equally rapidly, went up; and it therefore looks at first sight as if we simply have here yet another reflection of an entirely non-political economic change in the nature of English industry and trade.

None the less I believe this to be the wrong view. In the first place, it does not explain why the gross total of unsuccessful assignment was falling in the second half of Richard's reign at a time when the percentage of such assignment on the wool custom (counting in 'unspecified') was actually rising, and the change-over from wool to cloth export was proceeding most rapidly.[1] In the second place, the vast increase from £34,000 in the second half of Richard's reign to £135,000 in Henry's is much too abrupt to be explained by what seems to have been a fairly steady economic process suffering no such violent acceleration as this in and after 1399, but rather (if at all) before that date.[2] Thirdly, and most important of all, the increase is not maintained under Henry V or even in the early years of Henry VI. Yet it ought to have been maintained if the transition from wool to cloth export or the abandonment of fourteenth-century methods of paying the armies were the real cause. On the contrary, under Henry V, for whose reign a complete set of 19 receipt rolls[3] survives, Henry IV's gross total of £135,000 worth of *mutua per talliam*, extracted from not more than 21 rolls and four fragments, drops to less than £39,000, little more than Richard's second period (21 rolls) and £6,000 less than his first period (22¼ rolls). Or, putting it in averages calculated on the surviving evidence, the average amount of unsuccessful assignment per term is about £2,000 from 1377–89, £1,760 from 1389–99, over £6,000 from 1399–1413, and only a little over £2,000 again from 1413–22: we have already seen that under Henry V even that percentage of bad tallies which is levied on the wool custom drops back to what it had been in the last ten years of Richard II.

On these grounds I must conclude that the great temporary increase in unsuccessful assignment during Henry IV's reign is political rather than economic in origin and reflects what Professor Postan has called[4] 'a greater shortage of liquid reserves in the hands of the exchequer and the principal receivers of the royal revenue'. This in turn can only be due to the dislocation caused by the revolution of 1399 and the high price paid, in more ways than one, by Henry for his successful usurpation of the throne. Professor Gray himself has written of the cloth trade:

'In the second half of the fourteenth century, annual shipments of English woollens had expanded until the average for the years Mich., 1392, to Mich., 1395, amounted to 43,072 broadcloths. With the reign of Henry IV came a sharp contraction, the average annual exportation from Mich., 1410 to Mich., 1415 being only 26,958 cloths. Recovery attended the substitution of victorious foreign war for the civil disorders which had followed the coming of the new dynasty.[5]

Here Professor Gray boldly made the causal connection between civil

[1] See especially Professor H. L. Gray's article, *Eng. Hist. Rev.*, XXXIX, p. 35.
[2] This is certainly true of the growth in cloth exports, but rather less true of the decline in wool exports. The figures are given later.
[3] In triplicate.
[4] In a private letter (quoted with his permission).
[5] *Studies in English Trade in the Fifteenth Century*, p. 361.

413

war and declining trade which he made only with some reservation apropos of the wars of the roses.[1] I believe that he was right to make it *sans phrase* about Henry IV, and I believe, too, that what he says may be safely applied not only to the cloth export but also to the general finance of the customs and subsidies at large—a subject with which he intentionally does not deal—and, finally, to the whole of government finance. The average annual exportation of wool had been about 32,000 sacks at the beginning of Edward III's reign; between 1410 and 1415 it was down to 13,625 sacks, it is true, and this is just when *mutua per talliam* are increasing, and yet between 1392 and 1395, when there were no such *mutua* whatsoever on the wool custom, the export average in sacks was no more than 19,359,[2] and again when *mutua* drop sharply under Henry V the wool export, instead of expanding, or at least remaining stationary, continues to contract and by 1446–8 has shrunk to 7,654 sacks.[3] These figures seem to me conclusive: there is no correlation between *mutua per talliam* and either cloth or wool exports. From 1377 to 1413 the vast bulk of assignment was certainly (and steadily) made on the customs, under Henry IV as under other kings: but that such assignments went wrong to an unprecedented degree under Henry IV alone was due, not to any change in the character of what was exported, but to 'civil disorder' and the general contraction of all trade which resulted from that disorder. And that seems to be a serious reflection, as I have shown elsewhere, on the nature and effects of the Lancastrian revolution.

2

Although it hardly affects the argument in this appendix, which is virtually complete as it stands, it may be worth while to add a note on the distribution of *mutua per talliam* between 1413 and 1485, together with a word or two on the different ports principally affected by overdrafts upon the customs during the whole period from 1377 onwards.

I have already mentioned that in Henry V's time only 14% (in money value) of his *mutua per talliam* were levied on sources other than the wool customs, and I need only add that tunnage and poundage, fines and forfeitures, and ransoms (in that order) account for most of this small balance. If 'customs unspecified' are reckoned from this point as synonymous with wool customs and added to them, the four decades of Henry VI's reign show the following results.

(1) 1422–32: 87% wool customs; with the rest fairly evenly distributed between farmers and keepers, officials of many kinds, fines and

---

[1] *Studies in English Trade in the Fifteenth Century*, p. 1.
[2] Ibid., pp. 10–11.   [3] Ibid., p. 401.

APPENDIX B

forfeitures, the clerical subsidies, tunnage and poundage, and the petty custom (in that order). The lay subsidies, which come last but one, are responsible for only £483 in *mutua*, and the subsidy on cloth for sale in England, which makes its first appearance in this decade, for as little as £33.

(2) 1432–42: 59% wool customs; officials, 13%; farmers, keepers, 8%; clerical and lay subsidies about 6.5% each; and the remaining 7% divided between fines and forfeitures, tunnage and poundage, the petty custom, and the subsidy on cloth (in that order). There is also one new source of income, viz. the subsidy on aliens (*mutua per talliam*, £258, bottom of the list).

(3) 1442–52: 79% wool customs; tunnage and poundage, 6%; farmers, keepers, 5%; officials, 4%; remaining 6% divided between fines and forfeitures, petty custom, clerical subsidies, subsidy on cloth, lay subsidies, and subsidy on aliens (in that order).

(4) 1452–62: 55% wool customs; farmers, keepers, 14%; officials, 10%; fines and forfeitures, 5%; lay and clerical subsidies, tunnage and poundage, subsidy on cloth, and petty custom (in that order) all between 3% and 2%; subsidy on aliens a bad last.

The two Yorkist periods, similarly treated, yield the following results:

(1) 1462–75: 29% lay subsidies; wool customs, 22%; officials, 18%; farmers, keepers, 11%; tunnage and poundage, 6%; and the remaining 14% divided between clerical subsidies, fines and forfeitures, the subsidy on cloth, the petty custom, and the subsidy on aliens (in that order).

(2) 1475–85: 56% wool customs; tunnage and poundage, 19%; farmers, keepers, 11%; and the remaining 14% divided between officials, fines and forfeitures, petty custom, and the subsidy on cloth (in that order): the clerical and lay subsidies come last, with only 1% and 0.5% respectively, while the subsidy on aliens has disappeared entirely.

As I have said, these figures merely confirm the argument put forward in the first part of this appendix. The value of the wool customs went on declining through the fifteenth century as the volume of the cloth exports increased, but so far from a further rise in the admittedly extremely high percentage of bad tallies levied on the wool customs in Henry IV's reign (92%), the percentage actually drops by about 5% to 6% during the twenty years after his death, and then falls away to 59% in the decade 1432–42. The next decade was the heaviest in the whole century under review as regards the gross total of all *mutua per talliam*, yet the percentage levied on the wool customs only goes up to

79, while with the much lower gross totals of 1452-85 it settles down in the middle 50's: its temporary collapse to only 29% in 1462-75 may be associated with the handing over of the Calais customs to the staplers and the special privileges in other ports which they and other persons received.

There is of course something odd about the movements of the gross totals of *mutua per talliam*, which ought to have gone on rising steadily throughout the fifteenth century, if the theory which I was attacking in the first part of this appendix is to be maintained. They do indeed rise for the first thirty years after Henry V's death, viz. from £39,000 during his reign (or an average of just over £2,000 per term) to £72,000, £142,000 and £165,500 (the highest figure ever reached) in 1442-52; the relevant averages are £3,700, £7,100 and £8,275 per term respectively. Yet, as we have seen, the percentage of bad tallies on the wool customs actually declines during the first twenty years of this period when the gross totals are increasing so enormously, and though they rise again in 1442-52 they never go as high as before. After 1452 *mutua per talliam* fall away to only £43,000, £20,000 and finally £5,000 in round figures (averages per term, £2,260, £952 and £251 respectively). Now this remarkable change, the causes of which I have tried to analyse elsewhere in this book, was certainly not produced by further fluctuations in the wool customs and cloth exports, which, if they had had any influence at all, would *ex hypothesi* have had precisely the opposite effect. My argument, as I maintain, is therefore vindicated without even bringing into play the low percentages of *mutua per talliam* on the wool customs in this final epoch.

There remains only the incidence of unsuccessful customs assignments on the ports, for reckoning which we must include not only wool but customs of all kinds—that is, tunnage and poundage and the petty custom. Perhaps this is a purely academic question, but at least some curious reader may be interested to know which ports received bad tallies and which were most habitually affected by these overdrafts upon their customs revenues. The complete list for 1377-1485 is as follows, and in fact most, though not quite all, of the ports mentioned in it appear in every decade, viz. Berwick-on-Tweed, Boston, Bridgwater, Bristol (tunnage and poundage and the petty custom only), Chichester, Dartmouth (always with Exeter as one unit), Fowey (always with Plymouth), Hull, Ipswich, London, Lynn, Melcombe (often with Poole), Newcastle-on-Tyne, Rye (very rarely), Sandwich, Scarborough, Southampton and Great Yarmouth—to which may be added a single large tally on Calais in the period 1475-85. Most of these places can be ignored, since there were always, decade by decade, four or five ports which in this connection far outstripped the rest. As the order, and even

APPENDIX B

the identity, of these large ports tended to change from time to time, it is easiest to place them in a table, arranged in each decade in order of importance: the actual number of bad tallies received in each of them is shown immediately below the total sum involved. Small ports are omitted.

1377-89 London, £11,273; Boston, £8,618; Southampton, £5,962;
           53   56   48
         Hull, £5,186; Great Yarmouth, £2,100; Lynn, £1,279.
           42   23   15

1389-99 Hull, £7,509; London, £6,982; Boston, £6,532;
           34   53   32
         Southampton, £5,571; Lynn, £3,516; Bristol, £800.
           20   19   7

1399-   London, £33,295; Hull, £24,362; Southampton, £21,622;
1413   308   163   157
         Boston, £19,978; Lynn, £9,267; Ipswich, £9,244.
           128   103   77

1413-22 London, £14,800; Hull, £5,862; Southampton, £4,624;
           22   26   22
         Boston, £3,857; Lynn, £1,685; Newcastle-on-Tyne, £1,259.
           37   13   7

1422-32 Hull, £19,674; Boston, £12,839; London, £8,738;
           215   139   108
         Ipswich, £5,204; Southampton, £4,259; Chichester, £2,139.
           74   37   38

1432-42 Hull, £21,923; Southampton, £19,623; Ipswich, £16,986;
           237   47   210
         London, £13,182; Boston, £9,136; Sandwich, £1,633.
           169   131   24

1442-52 London, £33,694; Southampton, £31,524; Hull, £22,674;
           478   395   319
         Boston, £17,345; Ipswich, £13,055; Bristol, £9,178.
           200   238   163

1452–62   London, £8,635; Southampton, £3,957; Hull, £2,799;

               145   47   66

        Boston, £2,680; Ipswich, £2,519; Sandwich, £2,226.

              58   64   20

1462–75   Southampton, £2,023; London, £1,356; Sandwich, £961.

               17   20   11

1475–85   Southampton, £1,620; London, £1,121; Calais, £1,000.

                3   10   1

APPENDIX C

I

This list is based on that in the *Handbook of British Chronology* edited by F. M. Powicke, Charles Johnson and W. J. Harte for the Royal Historical Society, 1939. (By permission of the Society.)

TREASURERS OF ENGLAND (RICHARD II TO RICHARD III)

RICHARD II

1377 22 June Henry Wakefield, bishop of Worcester 1375–95 (appointed 11 January 1377), remained in office.

1377 19 July Thomas Brantingham, bishop of Exeter 1370–94. Formerly keeper of the wardrobe: treasurer of England 27 June 1369 to 27 March 1371.

1381 1 Feb. Sir Robert Hales, prior of the hospital of St. John of Jerusalem.

1381 10 Aug. Hugh Segrave.

1386 17 Jan. John Fordham, bishop of Durham 1382–8, bishop of Ely, 1388–1425.

1386 24 Oct. John Gilbert, bishop of Bangor 1372–5, bishop of Hereford 1375–89, bishop of St. David's 1389–97.

1389 4 May Thomas Brantingham. (*See under* 1377.)

1389 20 Aug. John Gilbert. (*See under* 1386.)

1391 2 May John Waltham, bishop of Salisbury 1388–95.

1395 20 Sept. Roger Walden, formerly king's secretary, archbishop of Canterbury 1398, bishop of London 1405–06.

1398 22 Jan. Guy de Mone, bishop of St. David's 1397–1407.

1399 3 Sept. John Norbury (esquire of Henry of Lancaster).

HENRY IV

1399 30 Sept. John Norbury, formally appointed.

1401 31 May Laurence Allerthorp.

1402 27 Feb. Henry Bowett, bishop of Bath and Wells 1401–07, archbishop of York 1407–23.

1403 between 14 July and 16 Sept. William Ros, lord Ros of Hamelak.

1404 13 Dec. Thomas Neville, lord Furnival.
1407 15 April Nicholas Bubwith, bishop of London 1406–07; of Salisbury 1407; of Bath and Wells 1407–24.
1408 14 July Sir John Tiptoft, 1st lord Tiptoft 1426.
1410 6 Jan. Henry, 3rd lord Scrope 1406; resigned 16 December 1411.
1411 ?20 Dec. Sir John Pelham.

HENRY V

1413 21 Mar. Thomas Fitzalan, 5th earl of Arundel and Surrey 1400.
1415 9 Aug. John Rothenhale (acting).
1416 10 Jan. Hugh Mortimer.
1417 17 April Sir Roger Leche.
1417 before 7 July Henry Fitz Hugh, 4th lord Fitz Hugh 1386.
1417 8 July William Kynwolmerssh, dean of St. Martin-le-Grand, acting during Fitz Hugh's absence in France.
1421 26 Feb. William Kynwolmerssh.

HENRY VI

1422 30 Sept. William Kynwolmerssh reappointed.
1422 18 Dec. John Stafford, bishop of Bath and Wells 1425–43; archbishop of Canterbury 1443–52.
1426 16 May Sir Walter Hungerford, 1st lord Hungerford January 1426.
1432 26 Feb. John, 4th lord Scrope 1426.
1433 11 Aug. Ralph Cromwell, 3rd lord Cromwell 1417.
1443 7 July Ralph Butler, lord Sudely.
1446 18 Dec. Marmaduke Lumley, bishop of Carlisle 1430–50; bishop of Lincoln 1450.
1449 22 Sept. James Fiennes, 1st lord Saye and Sele 1447.
1450 22 June John Beauchamp, 1st lord Beauchamp of Powick 1447.
1452 15 April John Tiptoft, 2nd lord Tiptoft, earl of Worcester 1449.
1455 15 Mar. James Butler, earl of Wiltshire 1449, and earl of Ormonde 1452.
1455 29 May Henry Bourchier, viscount Bourchier, cr. earl of Essex 1461.
1456 5 Oct. John Talbot, 2nd earl of Shrewsbury 1453.
1458 30 Oct. Earl of Wiltshire. (*See under* 1455.)
1460 28 July Viscount Bourchier (appointed by the Yorkists).

EDWARD IV

1461 18 Mar. Viscount Bourchier. (*See under* 1455.)
1462 14 April Earl of Worcester. (*See under* 1452.)

1463 24 June Edmund Grey, lord Grey of Ruthin 1440, cr. earl of
              Kent 1465.
1464 24 Nov. Walter Blount, cr. lord Mountjoy June 1465.
1466 4 Mar.   Richard Woodville, lord Rivers 1448, cr. 1st earl Rivers
              1466. Beheaded 1469.
1469 16 Aug. John Langstrother, prior of the hospital of St. John of
              Jerusalem.
1469 25 Oct. William Gray, bishop of Ely 1454–78.
1470 10 July Earl of Worcester. (*See under* 1452.)
1470 20 Oct. John Langstrother, appointed by Henry VI during his
              brief restoration, 'by word of mouth'. (*See under*
              1469.)
1471 22 April Earl of Essex. (*See under* 1455.)

EDWARD V

1483 17 May   Sir John Wood, speaker of the house of commons
              1483.

RICHARD III

1483 2 July   Sir John Wood, reappointed.
1484– 6 Dec. John Tuchet, lord Audley 1459.

APPENDIX C

2

This list is based on a manuscript list compiled many years ago for use in the Public Record Office by the present Deputy Keeper from the sources named, with added material compiled for the Department by M. Pierre Chaplais.

CHAMBERLAINS OF THE RECEIPT (RICHARD II TO EDWARD IV)

Abbreviations

I.R.   Issue Roll
M.R.   Memoranda Roll
K.R.   King's Remembrancer
L.T.R.   Lord Treasurer's Remembrancer
C.P.R.   Calendar of Patent Rolls

CHAMBERLAINS OF THE RECEIPT: KING'S CHAMBERLAINS

RICHARD II

Robert Crull	Letters for admission: 4 Oct. 1376.	M.R., K.R. 153, Mich. Rec. rot. i. (51 Edw. III).
	Appointed 26 June 1377.	C.P.R. 1377–81, p. 3.
	Admitted 27 June 1377.	M.R., K.R. 153, Trin. Rec. (1 Ric. II).
John Bacon	Appointed 28 Aug. 1377.	C.P.R. 1377–81, p. 23. M.R., K.R. 154, Mich. Rec.
Thomas de Orgrave	Appointed 27 Jan. 1385.	C.P.R. 1381–85, p. 517. M.R., K.R. 161, Hil. Rec.
John Lincoln de Grimsby	Appointed 5 Nov. 1386.	C.P.R. 1385–89, p. 236. M.R., K.R. 163, Mich. Rec.
Arnold Brocas	Appointed 6 Jan. 1388.	C.P.R. 1385–89, p. 382. M.R., K.R. 164, Hil. Rec.
John Godmanston	Appointed 25 Feb. 1396. Admitted 18 Mar. 1396.	C.P.R. 1391–96, p. 695. M.R., K.R. 172. Easter Rec. Black Book, fo. 14r.

HENRY IV

John Godmanston	Appointed 30 Sept. 1399.	C.P.R. 1399–1401, p. 8.
John Ikelington	Appointed 8 June 1401.	C.P.R. 1399–1401, p. 501. M.R., K.R. 177, Trin. Rec. rot. i.
John Legburn	Appointed 9 Sept. 1403.	C.P.R. 1401–05, p. 259.

HENRY V

John Ikelington	Appointed 30 Mar. 1413.	C P.R. 1413–16, p. 2.
John Wodehous	Appointed 6 July 1415. Letters for admission: 10 July 1415.	C.P.R. 1413–16, p. 336. Black Book, fo. 49v. M.R., K.R. 191, Trin. Rec. rot. xvi.

HENRY VI

John Wodehous	Appointment confirmed: 27 Jan. 1423.	C.P.R. 1422–29, p. 69.
John Hotoft	Appointed 1 Feb. 1431. Admitted 6 Feb. 1431.	C.P.R. 1429–36, p. 102. Black Book, fo. 59v. M.R., K.R. 207, Hil. Rec. rot. i.
	Appointment confirmed: 17 Dec. 1439.	C.P.R. 1436–41, p. 359. M.R., L.T.R. 218, Hil. Rec. rot. xvii.
(James Fenys	Appointed 2 July 1440 in the event of the death of John Hotoft; he never performed any duties, as he surrenders his letters of appointment in favour of Ralph, lord Cromwell.)	M.R., L.T.R. 218, Hil. Rec. rot. xvii.
Ralph, lord Cromwell	Appointed 24 Nov. 1442.	C.P.R. 1441–46, p. 158. M.R., L.T.R. 218, Hil. Rec. rot. xvii.
Thomas Neville and *Humphrey Bourchier*	Appointed 2 Mar. 1456.	C.P.R. 1452–61, p. 275.
Richard Tunstall	Appointed 19 Dec. 1459. Admitted 6 Mar. 1460.	C.P.R. 1452–61, p. 533. Black Book, fo. 60r.

EDWARD IV

Humphrey Bourchier, lord Cromwell	Appointed 4 Mar. 1461.	I.R. 822–832. M.R. K.R. 242, Hil. Rec. rot. x.
	Pardoned and reappointed 17 July 1464.	Ibid.
John Leynton, deputy of Humphrey Bourchier	Appointed by Humphrey Bourchier: 31 Aug. 1465.	Ibid. I.R. 835–842.
William Hastings, lord Hastings	Appointed for life: 27 June 1471. Admitted 3 July 1471.	M.R., K.R. 248, Trin. Rec. rot. iv. Black Book, fo. 50.
Henry Grimsby	Admitted 20 Feb. 1483.	

CHAMBERLAINS OF THE RECEIPT: BEAUCHAMP CHAMBERLAINS

RICHARD II

John Hermesthorp	Presented and admitted: 20 Oct. 1376.	M.R., K.R. 153, Mich. Rec.
John Oudeby	Appointed by the earl of Warwick: 4 Sept. 1396. Admitted 20 Dec. 1396. Reappointed by the king after the earl's forfeiture: 27 Sept. 1397.	Black Book, fo. 14r. C.P.R. 1396–99, p. 196.

HENRY IV

John Oudeby	Appointed by the king: 14 April 1401.	M.R., K.R. 177, Easter Rec. rot. ii.

HENRY V

John Oudeby		
Nicholas Calton	Appointed by Richard Beauchamp: 14 July 1414.	M.R., K.R. 190, Trin. Rec. rot. ii. Black Book, fo. 15r.
John Throckmarton	Enters office between 11 Dec. and 11 Mar., 6 Hen. V.	I.R. 638.

HENRY VI

John Throckmarton	Still in office during the Mich. term, 23 Hen. VI.	I.R. 756.
John Nanfan	Admitted 26 May 1445.	Black Book, fo. 61v. I.R. 757.

John Brown	Appointed by Henry, duke of Warwick: 3 June 1446. King's letters for his admission: 4 July 1446. Still in office during the Mich. term, 29 Hen. VI.	M.R., K.R. 222, Trin. Rec. rot. xxviii. I.R. 781.
Thomas Colte	Enters office 6 Dec. 1451 as the deputy of Richard Neville, earl of Warwick.	I.R. 295, M.R., K.R. 230, Hil. Rec. rot. iv. C.P.R. 1446-52, p. 409.

EDWARD IV

Thomas Colte	Still in office during the Easter term, 7 Edw. IV.	I.R. 822–838.
Richard Neville, earl of Warwick and *Walter Wrottesley*		I.R. 840–842.
John, earl of Worcester	Appointed 30 April 1470.	C.P.R. 1467–77, p. 207.
Richard, duke of Gloucester		
John Pilkington, deputy of the duke of Gloucester	Appointed 14 April 1477. Admitted 16 May 1477.	Black Book, fo. 50v. M.R., K.R. 254, Easter Rec. rot. iii.
James Tyrell, in the same capacity	Appointed 14 Jan. 1479. Admitted 28 April, 1479.	Black Book, fo. 50v. M.R., K.R. 252, Easter Rec. rot. i.d.

APPENDIX D

TABLE A1

RECEIPT ROLL TOTALS, RICHARD II, 1377–89

Date	My total			Total in roll			My variation		
	£	s.	d.	£	s.	d.	£	s.	d.
1377	15,369	9	11	15,367	19	11	+	1	10	0
1377–8	165,335	0	3	165,335	0	3				
1378	46,478	0	1½							
1378–9	65,941	14	1½	66,151	10	1½	—	209	16	6
1379	73,352	2	6	70,363	5	5	+	2,988	17	1*
1379–80	82,908	12	8	83,087	2	9	—	178	10	1
1380	173,012	7	3½							
1380–1										
1381	61,976	10	3	61,876	10	3	+	100	0	0
1381–2	62,496	6	9½	62,836	8	2½	—	340	1	5
1382	28,125	2	10	28,114	12	10	+	10	10	0
1382–3	87,187	1	0½	87,085	9	11½	+	101	11	1†
1383	41,983	2	2	41,813	12	9	+	79	9	5
1383–4	85,020	9	11½	84,917	9	10½	+	103	0	1
1384	64,321	10	3½	64,521	12	3½	—	200	2	0
1384–5	88,551	1	7	88,451	8	8	+	99	12	11
1385	94,932	14	11	94,932	15	0	—			1
1385–6	126,993	0	9	127,515	5	0½	—	522	4	3½
1386	63,035	5	8	63,285	11	8½	—	250	9	0½
1386–7	71,016	12	9	71,454	6	11	—	437	14	2
1387	40,060	0	0½	40,321	6	9	—	261	6	8½
1387–8	57,526	5	4½	57,535	5	5½	—	9	0	1
1388	84,486	4	5½	84,485	14	5½	+		10	0
1388–9	67,669	19	2½	67,869	19	2½	—	200	0	0‡

* After repeated checking I am still unable to explain this large discrepancy.

† At least one day total in this roll is demonstrably £50 less than it should be.

‡ The difference is exactly accounted for by a cancellation which is ignored by the roll total.

TABLE A2

RECEIPT ROLL TOTALS, RICHARD II, 1389–99

Date	My total			Total in roll			My variation			
	£	s.	d.	£	s.	d.		£	s.	d.
1389	53,573	4	1½							
1389–90	53,075	3	1½	53,466	2	11½	−	390	19	10
1390	27,234	16	6	28,168	3	2	+	933	6	8*
1390–1	71,330	9	3							
1391	27,111	11	8							
1391–2	54,605	5	2	54,530	9	9½	+	74	15	4½
1392	50,593	6	2	50,393	6	2	+	200	0	0
1392–3	58,799	15	7½	58,801	15	8½	−	2	0	1
1393	62,908	11	10							
1393–4	74,745	13	3							
1394	38,792	15	0	39,292	15	0	−	500	0	0*
1394–5	120,620	3	3½	120,920	13	2	−	300	9	10½
1395	51,870	5	11							
1395–6	64,484	16	9	64,664	16	9	−	180	0	0
1396	57,382	5	3½	57,382	5	3½				
1396–7	71,291	17	11½	71,968	11	3½	−	666	13	4*
1397	74,793	6	3	74,794	6	3	−	1	0	0
1397–8	67,601	9	10	69,529	1	4	−	1,927	11	6†
1398	54,475	4	2½	55,003	0	8	−	527	16	5½†
1398–9	74,798	15	8	75,749	9	7½	−	950	13	11½†
1399	62,408	16	5½	63,473	0	1½	−	1,064	3	8‡

* These differences are exactly accounted for by cancellations which are ignored by the roll total.

† These differences are partly accounted for by cancellations which are ignored by the roll total.

‡ It is possible that a few days are missing where the roll has been cut in two between 13 and 30 May.

TABLE A3

RECEIPT ROLL TOTALS, HENRY IV, 1399–1413

Date	My total			Total in roll			My variation		
	£	s.	d.	£	s.	d.	£	s.	d.
1399–1400	66,886	16	8	66,686	16	8 ?	+ 200	0	0
1400	42,354	15	0	42,354	10	6½	+	4	5½
1400–01	57,083	15	6½	57,083	15	6½			
1401	70,987	16	4						
1401–02	66,733	10	5½						
1402	60,158	17	10½						
1402–03	73,540	8	7½	73,539	2	10	+ 1	5	9½
1403*	16,814	10	1½*						
1403–04	67,330	19	6						
1404*	7,477	1	8*						
1404–05*	17,915	16	2½*						
1405	51,683	10	4½						
1405–06*	18,296	1	8½*						
1406	48,735	14	6½						
1406–07	63,087	5	2						
1407	42,913	9	9	42,913	9	9			
1407–08	90,399	17	7	90,399	17	9	−		2
1408	42,287	10	6½						
1408–09	66,001	3	3	65,991	3	3	+ 10	0	0
1409	41,910	8	5	41,910	7	5	+	1	0
1409–10	44,106	4	1½	44,304	11	8½	− 198	7	7
1410	45,283	0	2½	45,283	?	?			
1410–11	36,592	18	6½	36,592	18	6½			
1411									
1411–12	32,753	18	5	33,797	1	6	− 1,043	3	1†
1412									
1412–13	44,722	9	3½						

* Roll incomplete.

† The discrepancy is limited to the last five days of the roll, but repeated checking (and collation of the two surviving rolls) has failed to explain it.

Table A4

RECEIPT ROLL TOTALS, HENRY V, 1413–22

Date	My total	Total in roll	My variation
	£ s. d.	£ s. d.	£ s. d.
1413	44,869 11 2½		
1413–14	67,884 5 2		
1414	36,288 0 4		
1414–15	90,702 7 5½		
1415	94,915 12 11		
1415–16	70,871 9 3		
1416	83,528 8 2½	? 82,647 5 5	+ 881 2 9½*
1416–17	{ 15,589 19 2 / 118,776 4 3½	118,776 ? ?†	
1417	78,266 18 11	66,611 8 7	+ 11,655 10 4‡
1417–18	82,852 12 2½	82,853 2 2½	— 10 0
1418	43,730 5 7½		
1418–19	71,138 19 11		
1419	29,766 3 2½		
1419–20	99,090 6 11		
1420	33,299 5 1½		
1420–1	47,455 1 0		
1421	86,570 1 11	86,570 (13 4)	— 11 5§
1421–2	59,286 15 6½	59,292 4 11½	— 5 9 5
1422	43,318 3 0½	43,505 14 5½	— 187 11 5

* Total in roll not clearly decipherable.

† Change of treasurer. The first of my totals refers to the outgoing treasurer: the only total given in the roll is expressly stated to refer only to the new one, and coincides with my second total, except for shillings and pence (which are indecipherable).

‡ Total in roll as stated, with note, *Item*, 13,000 *marc' de episcopo Wynton'*, which reduces my surplus to £2,988 17s. For a possible explanation see the discussion in Chapter IV, 'Calendar 1413–32', under Easter 1417, pp. 156–7 above.

§ Shillings and pence in roll not clearly decipherable.

TABLE A5

RECEIPT ROLL TOTALS, HENRY VI, 1422–32

Date	My total			Total in roll			My variation		
	£	s.	d.	£	s.	d.	£	s.	d.
1422–3	37,474	10	3½						
1423	34,610	16	4½	34,574	15	4½	+	36	1	0
1423–4	60,661	5	1½	60,661	5	0½	+			1
1424	20,909	4	2	20,919	4	2	−	10	0	0
1424–5	32,561	7	4½						
1425	36,830	6	5	36,830	8	5½	−		2	0½
1425–6	39,600	6	8	39,416	16	11	+	183	9	9
1426	31,663	2	3	31,582	8	8½	+	80	13	6½
1426–7	34,537	9	6	33,576	7	2	+	961	2	4
1427	24,225	8	9½	24,224	18	9½	+		10	0
1427–8	47,139	5	6						
1428	34,123	3	0						
1428–9	30,180	16	9½						
1429*									
1429–30	79,044	8	5						
1430	65,220	12	8						
1430–1	115,930	0	10½						
1431	52,821	1	3	55,986	17	11	− 3,165	15	8†
1431–2	42,267	3	6						
1432	82,104	5	9½						

* No surviving roll.

† I can find no explanation of this wide variation, in spite of repeated checking.

Table A6

RECEIPT ROLL TOTALS, HENRY VI, 1432–42

Date	My total			Total in roll			My variation		
	£	s.	d.	£	s.	d.	£	s.	d.
1432–3	60,584	16	7½						
1433	24,993	6	10						
1433–4	45,432	4	8½	45,807	13	8½*	− 375	9	0 *
1434	60,368	14	1½	60,369	3	7	− .	9	5½
1434–5	34,473	3	1½	34,473	3	1½			
1435	55,344	10	8½	54,267	18	11½	+ 1,076	11	9
1435–6	104,579	3	6½	106,375	9	8½†	− 1,796	6	2 †
1436	61,792	7	0	61,782	7	0	+ 10	0	0
1436–7	36,926	14	6	36,917	2	1	+ 9	12	5
1437	93,119	4	10½	93,098	3	11½	+ 21	0	11
1437–8	53,025	10	1	53,225	9	11	− 199	19	10
1438	39,505	0	0½	40,572	13	5½	− 1,067	13	5
1438–9	63,214	15	8½	63,215	5	8½	−	10	0
1439	68,737	1	7½	68,669	6	11½	+ 67	14	8
1439–40	68,166	19	1½	68,166	9	0½	+	10	1
1440	47,737	8	9	47,747	8	9	− 10	0	0
1440–1	72,583	16	10	72,583	16	6‡	+		4
1441	38,492	3	6	38,492	0	6½§	+	2	11½
1441–2	51,895	10	9	51,893	10	9	+ 2	0	0
1442	71,693	12	6	71,693	11	6	+	1	0

* Including £375 8s. 11½d. brought forward from the previous term. If this is disregarded, my total is ½d. short.

† The roll total has been much cancelled and corrected.

‡ Item £1,000, after total.

§ Item £7 3s. 9½d., after total.

TABLE A7

RECEIPT ROLL TOTALS, HENRY VI, 1442–52

Date	My total			Total in roll			My variation		
	£	s.	d.	£	s.	d.	£	s.	d.
1442–3	65,046	11	7	65,037	2	7	+	9	9	0
1443	48,709	11	8½	48,711	1	8½	−	1	10	0
1443–4	41,923	13	2½						
1444	44,486	4	4						
1444–5	45,034	17	6						
1445	45,623	0	0½						
1445–6	30,690	1	8	30,692	1	8	−	2	0	0
1446	75,396	3	9						
1446–7	60,556	18	2½						
1447	56,948	10	4	56,900	18	8	+	47	11	8
1447–8	44,318	19	9	44,398	11	9	−	79	12	0
1448	23,023	4	11½						
1448–9	44,365	4	9						
1449	32,085	17	0½	32,299	2	8	−	213	5	7½
1449–50	65,454	13	11	65,909	14	1½	−	455	0	2½
1450	15,636	19	7½	15,633	6	8	+	3	2	11½
1450–1	26,519	15	8						
1451	50,947	8	4						
1451–2	18,940	15	6½						
1452	18,738	15	11½	18,8(01)(18		0)*	−	63	2	0½*

* Latter part of roll total barely decipherable.

APPENDIX D

TABLE A8

RECEIPT ROLL TOTALS, 1452–62

Date	My total			Total in roll			My variation		
	£	s.	d.	£	s.	d.	£	s.	d.
1452–3	38,675	18	4						
1453	66,125	19	8½						
1453–4	31,332	12	4½						
1454	39,763	8	0						
1454–5	26,062	2	2						
1455	13,479	16	10½						
1455–6	17,265	19	8						
1456	12,371	11	7						
1456–7	12,191	18	1½						
1457	21,096	10	0						
1457–8	22,775	7	1						
1458	20,213	15	6½						
1458–9	17,899	16	9½						
1459	9,750	10	5½						
1459–60	14,501	4	10½						
1460	9,834	17	8½						
1460–1	21,993	13	7						
1461	32,392	7	11½						
1461–2*									
1462	19,519	5	5½						

* No surviving roll.

433

TABLE A9

RECEIPT ROLL TOTALS, 1462–75

Date	My total			Total in roll			My variation		
	£	s.	d.	£	s.	d.	£	s.	d.
1462–3†	9,501	16	7½†						
1463	70,414	16	11	62,381	19	1½‡	+ 8,032	17	9½‡
1463–4*									
1464	15,533	19	8						
1464–5	26,717	18	5½						
1465*									
1465–6	53,928	18	7½						
1466*									
1466–7	15,896	3	4½	15,896	4	4½	—	1	0
1467*									
1467–8*									
1468	87,203	8	7½						
1468–9	34,326	14	3½	34,226	4	4½	+	100	9 11
1469†	17,145	11	4†						
1469–70	24,960	8	6½						
1470	13,265	10	3½						
1470–1	6,958	19	5						
1471	44,919	11	9½						
1471–2	7,461	0	5						
1472	26,695	2	6						
1472–3	12,650	14	1						
1473	3,117	12	4½						
1473–4	18,617	12	2½						
1474	16,498	0	2½						
1474–5	15,086	3	7						
1475	26,542	3	2						

* No surviving roll.

† Seriously deficient—each about half a roll.

‡ The roll total is a marginal entry only and may be inaccurate. In view of the large variation I have made a special check of the day-to-day marginal totals and have found that, when added, they are only £173 16s. 9d. less than my own total for the term. I am unable to explain the very different term total in the roll. See above, pp. 287–8, n. 2.

TABLE A10

RECEIPT ROLL TOTALS, 1475–85

Date	My total	Total in roll	My variation
	£ s. d.	£ s. d.	£ s. d.
1475–6	13,379 14 11½		
1476	6,134 5 10		
1476–7	13,985 3 6½		
1477	10,274 12 2½		
1477–8	10,091 8 1½		
1478	25,696 10 0		
1478–9	28,874 4 2		
1479	5,536 15 9½		
1479–80	20,572 5 0		
1480	10,084 14 10		
1480–1	21,269 13 10		
1481	13,161 11 8		
1481–2	24,203 1 11		
1482	21,961 19 3½		
1482–3	21,770 13 4		
1483	8,395 15 2		
1483–4*			
1484	8,775 4 7		
1484–5	18,720 18 0		
1485†	24,496 5 8½†		

* No surviving roll. † Roll not quite complete.

TABLE B1

ANALYSED TOTALS, 1377–89

Date	Rolls*	Cash			Assigned			Book-keeping			%	%	%
		£	s.	d.	£	s.	d.	£	s.	d.			
1377	T C²	14,227	16	6	649	5	1	492	8	4	93	4	3
1377–8	T C¹ C²	127,541	1	7	28,528	12	0	9,265	6	8	77	17	6
1378	T† C¹ C²	33,779	17	11	9,961	11	1½	2,736	11	1	73	21	6
1378–9	C¹ C²	49,111	3	4	15,086	18	3½	10,743	12	6	61	23	16
1379	T C¹ C²	43,501	3	10	13,429	9	6	16,421	9	2	59	18	23
1379–80	C²	17,180	8	8	54,410	4	3½	11,317	19	9	21	65	14
1380		81,958	15	6	32,051	13	5½	59,001	18	4	47	19	34
1380–1	T C¹ C²	28,965	4	2½	17,298	12	7½	15,712	13	5	47	28	25
1381	C¹ C²	7,137	13	6½	47,501	2	7½	7,857	10	7½	11	76	13
1381–2	T C¹ C²	7,094	3	10	14,948	18	7	6,082	0	5	25	53	22
1382	T C¹ C²	39,230	17	2½	45,808	6	3	2,147	17	7	45	53	2
1382–3	T C¹ C²	16,412	6	4	19,927	3	10	5,553	12	0	39	48	13
1383	T C¹ C²	25,681	9	9	47,111	13	3½	12,227	7	3	30	56	14
1383–4	T C¹ C²	8,456	19	5½	35,157	10	5½	20,707	0	6½	13	55	32
1384	T C¹	15,990	3	3	53,569	1	11	18,991	16	10½	18	61	21
1384–5	T C¹	33,475	15	1	37,341	19	10	24,114	19	11	35	39	26
1385	T C¹	35,125	17	11½	57,643	17	8	34,223	4	11½	28	45	27
1385–6	T C¹	11,458	18	3	29,914	11	0	21,661	12	7	18	48	34
1386	T C¹	25,583	6	9	33,548	14	5	11,884	11	4	36	47	17
1386–7	T	30,759	0	2½	6,211	15	9	3,089	4	10	77	15	8
1387	T C¹	18,324	19	10½	31,563	0	5	7,637	16	1	32	55	13
1387–8	T C¹	33,493	12	5	27,010	4	0½	23,982	8	0	40	32	28
1388–9	T C²	22,365	3	2½	37,665	11	11½	7,639	4	0½	33	56	11

* T = treasurer; C¹ = Beauchamp chamberlain; C² = king's chamberlain. † Incomplete.

TABLE B2
ANALYSED TOTALS, 1389–99

Date	Rolls			Cash £	s.	d.	Assigned £	s.	d.	Book-keeping £	s.	d.	%	%	%
1389	T	C¹		29,034	18	0	12,301	11	5	12,236	14	8½	54	23	23
1389–90		C¹	C²	18,802	8	10½	29,044	18	6½	5,227	15	8½	35	55	10
1390	T	C¹	C²	13,528	1	10½	11,765	4	9½	1,941	9	10	50	43	7
1390–1	T	C¹	C²	40,609	0	7½	20,467	18	1½	10,253	10	6	57	29	14
1391	T	C¹		6,912	18	5½	15,583	8	7	4,615	4	7½	26	57	17
1391–2	T	C¹	C²	15,264	10	5	32,428	17	10	6,911	16	11	28	59	13
1392	T	C¹	C²	38,539	0	9	11,738	3	9	316	1	8	76	23	1
1392–3		C¹		20,430	16	9½	38,089	10	9½	279	8	0½	35	65	—
1393	T	C¹		40,171	6	10	19,839	16	3½	2,897	8	8½	64	31	5
1393–4	T	C¹	C²	45,273	15	7	20,915	17	2	8,556	0	6	61	28	11
1394	T	C¹		23,131	4	7½	14,773	8	11½	888	1	5	60	38	2
1394–5	T	C¹	C²	35,765	19	11½	35,819	1	5½	49,035	1	10½	29	30	41
1395		C¹		36,791	7	9	13,202	4	10	1,876	13	4	71	25	4
1395–6	T	C¹		55,047	9	2	9,156	16	5	280	11	2	86	14	—
1396	T	C¹		28,711	17	8½	25,178	9	10	3,491	17	9	50	44	6
1396–7	T	C¹		20,857	13	4½	36,189	4	7½	14,244	19	11½	29	51	20
1397	T	C¹		9,583	19	0	41,728	13	9	23,480	13	6	13	56	31
1397–8	T	C¹		12,343	17	4½	44,927	4	8	10,330	7	9½	18	67	15
1398	T	C¹	C²	14,698	4	5	33,393	15	2½	6,383	4	7	27	61	12
1398–9	T	C¹		46,706	10	8½	26,396	9	2½	1,695	15	9	63	35	2
1399	T	C¹		35,560	7	9½	26,354	8	9	493	19	11	57	42	1

TABLE B3

ANALYSED TOTALS, 1399–1413

Date	Rolls	Cash £	s.	d.	Assigned £	s.	d.	Book-keeping £	s.	d.	%	%	%
1399–1400	C^1* C^2	20,860	4	2	36,011	3	6½	10,015	8	11½	31	54	15
1400	T C^2	5,988	10	7	17,077	3	3	19,289	1	2	14	40	46
1400–01	C^3	6,357	9	4½	28,706	16	7½	22,019	9	6½	11	50	39
1401	C^2	20,904	12	5	32,933	7	6½	17,149	1	4½	30	46	24
1401–02	C^1 C^2*	14,530	3	10½	39,823	5	0½	12,380	1	6½	22	60	18
1402	T* C^1	4,076	7	7½	29,209	7	4	26,873	2	11	7	48	45
1402–03	T C^1 C^2	19,910	9	11	32,455	4	11	21,174	13	9½	27	44	29
1403	T*†												
1403–04	T*† C^1*†	7,222	13	0	39,470	14	9	20,637	11	9	11	58	31
1404	T*†												
1404–05	T C^1*† C^2												
1405	C^1*†	6,632	17	10	34,304	17	5	10,745	15	1½	13	67	20
1405–06	C^1*†												
1406	T C^2	10,922	1	8	24,644	10	3½	13,169	2	7½	22	51	27
1406–07	T C^2	40,025	5	8	15,915	7	8½	7,146	11	9½	63	26	11
1407	T C^2	21,022	19	5	4,716	13	4	17,173	17	0	49	11	40
1407–08	C^2	33,166	2	7½	47,272	11	9½	9,960	13	2	37	52	11
1408	C^2	27,830	0	6½	13,616	19	3	840	10	9	66	32	2
1408–09	T C^2	22,880	16	3	37,737	17	4	5,382	9	8	35	57	8
1409	T	10,201	4	9	25,815	11	11½	5,893	11	8½	24	62	14
1409–10	T C^1	6,909	14	3	21,871	13	10½	15,324	16	0	16	49	35
1410	T	7,974	12	10½	26,652	13	8	10,655	13	8	18	59	23
1410–11	T C^2	10,670	13	10	25,256	19	5½	665	5	3	29	69	2
1411													
1411–12	T C^2	19,877	16	3½	12,773	17	1½	102	5	0	61	39	—
1412													
1412–13	T C^2	17,666	18	10	26,045	2	11½	1,010	7	6	40	58	2

* Mutilated or unfit.

† These solitary surviving rolls are so fragmentary that analysed totals obtained from them are meaningless.

TABLE B4

ANALYSED TOTALS, 1413–22

Date	Rolls		Cash			Assigned			Book-keeping			%	%	%
	T	C	£	s.	d.	£	s.	d.	£	s.	d.			
1413	T	C²	24,397	7	2½	9,778	17	4	10,693	6	8	54	22	24
1413–14	T	C²	66,988	16	9½	895	8	4½				99	1	—
1414	T C¹	C²	32,905	0	6	1,000	0	0	2,382	19	10	91	3	6
1414–15	T C¹	C²	85,942	16	1	2,626	4	8½	2,133	6	8	95	3	2
1415	T* C¹	C²*	18,104	7	6	38,567	14	0½	38,243	11	4½	19	41	40
1415–16	T C¹	C²	56,360	11	3½	67,833	12	1½	3,037	17	1½	80	16	4
1416	T C¹	C²	32,452	10	0	46,144	3	2½	4,931	14	2	39	55	6
1416–17	T* C¹	C²*	81,799	10	6	31,007	10	7½	21,559	1	4	61	23	16
1417	T C¹	C²*	28,622	18	4	16,662	17	3	32,981	3	4	37	21	42
1417–18	T C¹	C²	58,744	14	0½	23,138	5	8	969	12	6	71	28	1
1418	T	C²	12,334	6	11½	30,538	8	10	857	9	10	28	70	2
1418–19	T* C¹	C²	50,962	15	11½	19,465	18	2½	710	5	9	72	27	1
1419	T* C¹*	C²	10,962	16	7	17,602	5	2½	1,201	1	5	37	59	4
1419–20	T		65,719	16	3	28,909	18	5	4,460	12	3	66	29	5
1420	T C¹	C²	13,677	6	5	18,085	18	0½	1,536	0	8	41	54	5
1420–1	T	C²	19,882	18	5	23,134	18	10	4,437	3	9	42	49	9
1421	T*		16,867	1	1	27,720	12	8½	41,982	8	1½	19	32	49
1421–2	T	C¹* C²	32,529	4	2½	23,599	19	11	3,157	11	5	55	40	5
1422	T*	C¹* C²	14,013	5	11½	21,240	18	4½	8,063	18	8½	32	49	19

* Mutilated or unfit.

TABLE B5

ANALYSED TOTALS, 1422–32

Date	Rolls	Cash £ s. d.	Assigned £ s. d.	Book-keeping £ s. d.	%	%	%
1422–3	T C²	23,707 17 7½	10,192 6 0	3,574 6 8	63	27	10
1423	T* C²	12,564 12 4½	20,412 3 4½	1,634 0 7½	36	59	5
1423–4	T* C²	11,477 6 9	34,483 4 7½	14,700 13 9	19	57	24
1424	C²	2,440 18 1½	16,610 11 5	1,857 14 7½	12	79	9
1424–5	C²	4,824 14 6	22,353 7 6	5,383 5 5½	15	69	16
1425	C²	2,687 7 4½	19,309 12 0½	14,833 7 0	7	53	40
1425–6	C²	8,977 8 6½	25,401 0 2½	5,221 17 11	23	64	13
1426	T C²	9,099 2 0	17,112 15 4½	5,451 4 10½	29	54	17
1426–7	C²	18,179 9 5½	14,308 4 11½	2,049 15 1	53	41	6
1427	C²	8,963 3 10½	14,131 15 2	1,130 9 9	37	58	5
1427–8	C²	15,209 12 8½	24,769 7 1	7,160 5 8½	32	53	15
1428	C¹* C²	11,755 7 4	15,413 4 4	6,954 11 4	35	45	20
1428–9	C²	5,785 11 8½	19,214 17 9	5,180 7 4	19	64	17
1429†							
1429–30	C²	38,400 0 11½	32,912 15 6	7,731 11 11½	48	42	10
1430	C²	15,319 2 2½	37,276 12 7½	12,624 17 10	24	57	19
1430–1	C²	12,953 13 11½	58,717 8 6½	44,258 18 4½	11	51	38
1431	T* C¹* C²	10,476 0 8½	30,617 0 6	11,728 0 0½	20	58	22
1431–2	C¹* C²	7,839 13 2½	20,118 6 5½	14,309 3 10	19	47	34
1432	C²	12,969 17 3½	39,466 7 7½	29,668 0 10½	16	48	36

* Mutilated or unfit.   † No surviving roll.

TABLE B6

ANALYSED TOTALS, 1432–42

Date	Rolls	Cash £ s. d.	Assigned £ s. d.	Book-keeping £ s. d.	%	%	%
1432–3	C²	10,874 4 0	35,777 0 5½	13,933 12 2	18	59	23
1433	C²	2,643 15 5½	10,765 14 0½	11,583 17 4	11	43	46
1433–4	C¹* C²*	5,137 0 6	23,788 14 4	16,506 9 10½	11	53	36
1434	T* C¹* C²*	4,264 15 10	37,837 12 1½	18,266 6 2	7	63	30
1434–5	T C¹* C²	3,978 15 6	18,745 4 5½	11,749 3 2	12	54	34
1435	C¹* C²	3,921 6 11	22,206 4 8½	29,216 19 1	7	40	53
1435–6	T C¹ C²	24,297 13 8½	39,014 6 11½	41,267 2 10½	23	37	40
1436	C¹* C²	16,249 16 3	22,335 19 11½	23,206 10 9½	26	36	38
1436–7	C¹* C²	7,144 11 9	21,237 1 7½	8,545 1 1½	19	58	23
1437	T* C¹* C²*	12,419 0 6	48,784 13 0	31,915 11 4½	13	53	34
1437–8	C¹* C²	6,800 18 11	24,030 1 7½	22,194 9 6½	13	45	42
1438	T C¹* C²*	3,505 18 5½	18,282 9 4½	17,716 12 2½	9	46	45
1438–9	T* C¹ C²	3,170 1 1½	33,470 11 11	26,574 2 8	5	53	42
1439	T* C¹ C²	16,098 16 9	24,012 12 11	28,625 11 11½	23	35	42
1439–40	C¹ C²	7,051 3 9½	38,548 10 2	22,567 5 2	10	57	33
1440	T* C¹ C²	21,337 17 2	21,682 2 1	4,717 9 6	45	45	10
1440–1	T* C¹ C²	23,033 13 3	33,009 12 10	16,540 10 9	32	45	23
1441	T* C¹* C²	11,420 14 3	17,210 8 0	9,861 0 9	30	45	25
1441–2	T C¹ C²	13,963 7 5½	20,745 19 9½	17,186 3 6	27	40	33
1442	C¹ C²	5,485 9 7½	30,128 1 5½	36,080 1 5	8	42	50

N.B. For two terms only (Easter 1439 and Michaelmas 1439–40) the P.R.O. notation is reversed, C¹ referring to the royal and C² to the Warwick, or Beauchamp, chamberlain.

* Mutilated or unfit.

TABLE B7

ANALYSED TOTALS, 1442–52

Date	Rolls	Cash £ s. d.	Assigned £ s. d.	Book-keeping £ s. d.	%	%	%
1442–3	T C²	7,243 15 7	36,307 8 6	21,495 7 6	11	56	33
1443	C¹ C²	6,805 14 6	19,085 6 6	22,818 10 9	14	39	47
1443–4	C¹ C²	9,177 11 2	10,518 1 5½	22,228 0 2	22	25	53
1444	C¹ C²	20,685 4 10	10,268 14 10½	13,532 4 10	47	23	30
1444–5	C¹ C²	10,762 17 5	23,387 10 4	10,884 9 9	24	52	24
1445	T C²	2,098 4 7	30,601 10 11	12,923 4 6½	5	67	28
1445–6	C²	2,667 15 10½	16,479 10 8	11,542 15 1½	9	53	38
1446	C	16,612 9 3½	26,209 14 10	32,573 19 7½	22	35	43
1446–7	T* C¹ C²	15,670 1 11	14,494 16 1½	30,392 0 2	26	24	50
1447	C¹ C²	4,241 14 10	25,388 18 0½	27,317 17 5½	7	45	48
1447–8	C¹ C²	16,603 11 8½	15,014 7 5½	12,701 0 7	37	34	29
1448	C¹* C²	3,305 2	14,214 15 6	5,503 8 3½	14	62	24
1448–9	T† C¹ C²	19,930 19 1	19,623 11 8	4,810 14 0	45	44	11
1449	C¹ C²	1,721 14 9½	16,794 8 7	13,569 13 8	6	52	42
1449–50	C¹ C²	2,689 2 4½	35,237 15 11	27,527 15 7½	4	54	42
1450	T* C¹ C²	4,062 6 1½	7,533 16 2	4,040 17 4	27	48	25
1450–1	C¹ C²	8,022 3 5	9,088 7 3½	9,409 4 11½	30	34	36
1451	C¹ C²	13,706 14 1	20,282 16 1½	16,957 18 1½	27	40	33
1451–2	C¹* C²	6,510 10 8	9,302 19 2	3,127 5 8½	34	49	17
1452	T† C¹* C²	2,291 19 7	8,581 10 1½	7,865 6 3	12	46	42

* Mutilated or unfit.   † Occasional deficiencies.

TABLE B8

ANALYSED TOTALS, 1452–62

Date	Rolls	Cash £ s. d.	Assigned £ s. d.	Book-keeping £ s. d.	%	%	%
1452–3	C¹ C²	10,685 18 8½	14,652 9 0½	13,337 10 7	28	38	34
1453	T† C¹ C²	2,656 17 1	42,209 17 2½	21,259 5 5	4	64	32
1453–4	T C¹ C²	1,780 7 11½	21,405 4 11½	8,146 19 5½	6	68	26
1454	T* C¹* C²	1,508 13 1½	23,480 9 3½	14,774 5 7	4	59	37
1454–5	T C¹ C²	3,122 9 3	17,207 15 5½	5,731 17 5½	12	66	22
1455	T* C¹ C²*	1,307 15 3	7,711 7 8½	4,460 13 11	10	57	33
1455–6	T* C¹* C²	1,823 1 9	13,891 14 6	1,551 3 5	11	80	9
1456	C¹ C²	2,031 18 2	7,028 3 8	3,311 9 9	16	57	27
1456–7	C¹ C²	1,996 13 4½	6,474 15 9½	3,720 8 11½	16	53	31
1457–8	T* C¹ C²	1,930 9 1	13,607 6 8	5,558 14 3	9	65	26
1458	T C¹ C²	2,068 17 6	12,825 14 3	7,880 15 4	9	56	35
1458–9	C¹ C²	873 1 8	16,388 15 8½	2,951 18 2	4	81	15
1459	C¹ C²	793 7 10½	11,556 18 5	5,549 10 6	4	65	31
1459–60	T* C²	1,060 11 6½	7,418 17 2½	1,271 1 8½	11	76	13
1460	C¹ C²	1,463 18 11	7,399 12 10½	5,637 13 1	10	51	39
1460–1	T C¹ C²	1,210 12 1	7,039 8 7½	1,584 17 0	12	72	16
1461	C¹* C²	2,078 0 11½	11,240 10 2	8,675 2 5½	10	51	39
1461–2‡		3,537 19 6½	9,174 4 7	19,680 3 10	11	28	61
1462	T† C¹ C²†	1,093 12 11½†	10,899 2 4†	7,526 10 2†	6	56	38

* Mutilated or unfit.   † Incomplete.   ‡ No surviving roll.

TABLE B9

ANALYSED TOTALS, 1462–75

Date	Rolls	Cash £	s.	d.	%	Assigned £	s.	d.	%	Book-keeping £	s.	d.	%
1462-3†	T†	323	9	4¼	4	6,959	8	11†	73	2,218	18	4½†	23
1463	C¹† C²	2,500	4	11	3	49,794	19	6	71	18,119	12	6	26
1463-4*													
1464	C²	1,677	7	4	11	7,419	16	1	48	6,436	16	3	41
1464-5	C²	598	5	2	2	7,719	11	1½	29	18,400	2	2	69
1465*													
1465-6	T‡	2,503	10	0½	5	25,865	2	10½	48	25,560	5	8½	47
1466*													
1466-7	T	1,164	1	6	8	7,774	6	11½	48	6,957	14	11	44
1467*													
1467-8*													
1468	T C²	6,478	1	4½	7	47,648	5	3	55	33,077	2	0	38
1468-9	T C²†	2,219	16	3	6	19,470	14	4	57	12,636	3	8½	37
1469†	T C²†	1,068	0	8½‡	6	5,978	4	0†	35	10,099	6	7½†	59
1469-70	T C²	897	13	5	4	15,290	16	11½	61	8,771	18	2	35
1470	T	1,195	12	10	9	3,283	17	1½	25	8,786	0	4	66
1470-1	T C²	413	8	10	6	5,913	15	5	85	631	15	2	9
1471	T C¹† C²†	7,983	6	9½	18	24,444	5	0	54	12,492	0	0	28
1471-2	T C¹ C²	6,098	11	11	82	319	1	10	4	1,043	6	8	14
1472	T C²	5,256	12	0½	20	10,779	16	9	40	10,658	13	8½	40
1472-3	T C²†	8,124	19	3	64	1,221	6	9	10	3,304	8	1	26
1473	T C¹†	1,536	3	0½	49	77	11	6	3	1,503	17	10	48
1473-4	T C¹ C²	5,223	1	1	28	7,184	3	3	39	6,210	7	10½	33
1474	T C¹† C²	1,754	8	3½‡	11	7,913	7	1	48	6,830	4	10	41
1474-5	T† C²	6,462	19	11½	43	3,772	1	1½	25	4,851	2	6	32
1475	T C¹ C²	11,945	14	7	45	6,718	5	6½	25	7,878	3	0½	30

* No surviving roll. † Deficient, mutilated or unfit. ‡ Deficient individually, but the two rolls are complementary enough to present a reasonably good composite record for the term.

TABLE B10

ANALYSED TOTALS, 1475–85

Date	Rolls	Cash £ s. d.	Assigned £ s. d.	Book-keeping £ s. d.	%	%	%
1475–6	C¹ C²	3,852 8 11	9,323 11 0½	203 15 0	29	70	1
1476	C¹ C²	2,437 4 0½	3,637 8 5½	59 13 4	40	59	1
1476–7	C¹ C²	2,231 12 5½	10,959 1 5½	794 9 5½	16	78	6
1477	C¹ C²	1,407 17 9	7,855 13 7½	1,011 1 1	14	76	10
1477–8	T C¹*	2,981 9 7	6,778 8 4½	331 10 0	30	67	3
1478	T C¹	17,604 14 11½	932 9 6½	159 5 7½	68	31	1
1478–9	T C²	12,657 13 5½	579 4 5	2,537 6 7	44	47	9
1479	T C¹	4,864 9 4½	559 3 1½	13 2 6	88	12	—
1479–80	C¹	5,885 12 11½	580 13 11	5 19 0	29	71	—
1480	C² C²*	6,133 5 7½	929 8 0½	22 0 3	61	39	—
1480–1	C¹	7,491 4 5½	12,599 9 11½	1,179 2 4	35	59	6
1481	C¹	8,621 14 7	4,527 5 0½	12 11 6	66	34	—
1481–2	C²	9,020 17 9	15,165 19 7	16 5 0	37	63	—
1482	T* C¹* C²	10,978 19 9½	7,411 7 2	3,571 11 7½	50	34	16
1482–3	T C‡	3,617 3 7	14,627 2 10½	3,526 7 8	17	67	16
1483	T	2,438 2 10	5,127 12 1	830 0 0	29	61	10
1483–4†			4				
1484	C²	1,656 2 2½	4,967 0 4½	2,152 2 0	19	57	24
1484–5	C²	4,781 11 8½	9,042 19 3½	4,896 7 0	26	48	26
1485	C‡	2,387 5 8½	17,655 5 4	4,453 14 8	10	72	18

* Incomplete.
† No surviving roll.
‡ Incomplete chamberlain's roll—uncertain whether C¹ or C².

TABLE CI

ANNUAL TOTALS (TO NEAREST £1,000) AND
PERCENTAGES, 1377–89

Date	Nominal receipts (£1,000)	Real receipts (£1,000)	Cash %	Assigned %	Book-keeping %
1377–8*	227*	215*	81*	14*	5*
1378–9	139	112	57·5	23·5	19
1379–80	256	186	34	42	24
1380–1†	62†	46†	47†	28†	25†
1381–2	91	77	18·5	64	17·5
1382–3	129	121	42	50·5	7·5
1383–4	149	116	21·5	55·5	23
1384–5	183	140	26·5	50	23·5
1385–6	190	134	23	46·5	30·5
1386–7	111	96	56·5	31	12·5
1387–8	142	110	36	43·5	20·5
1388–9†	68†	60†	33†	56†	11†

* 1⅛ years (2¼ rolls).   † Half-year (1 roll) only.

TABLE C2

ANNUAL TOTALS (TO NEAREST £1,000) AND PERCENTAGES, 1389–99

Date	Nominal receipts (£1,000)	Real receipts (£1,000)	Cash %	Assigned %	Book-keeping %
1389*	54*	41*	54*	23*	23*
1389–90	81	74	42·5	49	8·5
1390–1	98	84	41·5	43	15·5
1391–2	105	98	52	41	7
1392–3	122	119	49·5	48	2·5
1393–4	114	104	60·5	33	6·5
1394–5	172	122	50	27·5	22·5
1395–6	122	118	68	29	3
1396–7	146	108	21	53·5	25·5
1397–8	122	105	22·5	64	13·5
1398–9	137	135	60	38·5	1·5

* Half-year (1 roll) only.

TABLE C3

ANNUAL TOTALS (TO NEAREST £1,000) AND
PERCENTAGES, 1399–1413

Date	Nominal receipts (£1,000)	Real receipts (£1,000)	Cash %	Assigned %	Book-keeping %
1399–1400	109	80	25	49	26
1400–01	128	89	21	49	30
1401–02	127	88	15	54	31
1402–03†	74†	52†	27†	44†	29†
1403–04†	67†	47†	11†	58†	31†
1404–05*	52*	41*	13*	67*	20*
1405–06*	49*	36*	22*	51*	27*
1406–07	106	82	58	19	23
1407–08	132	122	46	46	8
1408–09	108	97	31	59	10
1409–10	89	63	16	54	30
1410–11†	37†	36†	29†	69†	2†
1411–12†	33†	33†	61†	39†	
1412–13†	45†	44†	40†	58†	2†

* Easter term only.   † Michaelmas term only.

APPENDIX D

TABLE C4

ANNUAL TOTALS (TO NEAREST £1,000) AND
PERCENTAGES, 1413–22

Date	Nominal receipts (£1,000)	Real receipts (£1,000)	Cash %	Assigned %	Book-keeping %
1413–14	113	102	80	10	10
1414–15	127	122	93	3	4
1415–16	166	125	45	30	25
1416–17	217	191	53	35	12
1417–18	161	127	54	25	21
1418–19	115	113	55	43	2
1419–20	129	123	60	36	4
1420–1	81	75	42	51	7
1421–2	146	101	34	35	31
1422*	43*	35*	32*	49*	19*

* Easter term only. (The regnal, not the exchequer, year has been followed in the above table: i.e. each year starts with the Easter and ends with the Michaelmas term.)

449

TABLE C5

ANNUAL TOTALS (TO NEAREST £1,000) AND
PERCENTAGES, 1422–32

Date	Nominal receipts (£1,000)	Real receipts (£1,000)	Cash %	Assigned %	Book-keeping %
1422–3	72	67	49·5	43	7·5
1423–4	82	65	15·5	68	16·5
1424–5	69	49	11	61	28
1425–6	71	61	26	59	15
1426–7	59	56	45	49·5	5·5
1427–8	81	67	33·5	49	17·5
1428–9*	30*	25*	19*	64*	17*
1429–30	144	123	36	49·5	14·5
1430–1	169	113	15·5	54·5	30
1431–2	124	80	17·5	47·5	35

* Michaelmas term only. No surviving roll for Easter term.

TABLE C6

ANNUAL TOTALS (TO NEAREST £1,000) AND
PERCENTAGES, 1432–42

Date	Nominal receipts (£1,000)	Real receipts (£1,000)	Cash %	Assigned %	Book-keeping %
1432–3	86	60	14·5	51	34·5
1433–4	106	71	9	58	33
1434–5	90	49	9·5	47	43·5
1435–6	166	102	24·5	36·5	39
1436–7	130	90	16	55·5	28·5
1437–8	93	53	11	45·5	43·5
1438–9	132	77	14	44	42
1439–40	116	89	27·5	51	21·5
1440–1	111	85	31	45	24
1441–2	124	70	17·5	41	41·5

APPENDIX D

TABLE C7

ANNUAL TOTALS (TO NEAREST £1,000) AND
PERCENTAGES, 1442-52

Date	Nominal receipts (£1,000)	Real receipts (£1,000)	Cash %	Assigned %	Book-keeping %
1442-3	114	69	12·5	47·5	40
1443-4	86	51	34·5	24	41·5
1444-5	91	67	14·5	59·5	26
1445-6	106	62	15·5	44	40·5
1446-7	118	60	16·5	34·5	49
1447-8	67	49	25·5	48	26·5
1448-9	76	58	25·5	48	26·5
1449-50	81	50	15·5	51	33·5
1450-1	77	51	28·5	37	34·5
1451-2	38	27	23	47·5	29·5

TABLE C8

ANNUAL TOTALS (TO NEAREST £1,000) AND
PERCENTAGES, 1452–62

Date	Nominal receipts (£1,000)	Real receipts (£1,000)	Cash %	Assigned %	Book-keeping %
1452–3	105	70	13	54	33
1453–4	71	48	5	63·5	31·5
1454–5	40	29	11	61·5	27·5
1455–6	30	25	13·5	68·5	18
1456–7	33	24	12·5	59	28·5
1457–8	43	32	6·5	68·5	25
1458–9	28	21	7·5	70·5	22
1459–60	24	17	11	61·5	27·5
1460–1*	22*	13*	10*	51*	39*
1461–2†	32†	13†	11†	28†	61†
1462‡	20‡	12‡	6‡	56‡	38‡

* Half-year only (end of Henry VI's reign, excluding 1470–1).
† Easter 1461 only (Michaelmas 1461–2 missing: no surviving roll).
‡ Easter 1462 only (regnal year broken at this point to secure balance of 'decades', and exchequer year used for rest of Edward IV's reign).

TABLE C9

ANNUAL TOTALS (TO NEAREST £1,000) AND
PERCENTAGES, 1462–75

Date	Nominal receipts (£1,000)	Real receipts (£1,000)	Cash %	Assigned %	Book-keeping %
1462–3*	80*	60*	3*	72*	25*
1463–4†	16†	9†	11†	48†	41†
1464–5†	27†	8†	2†	29†	69†
1465–6†	54†	28†	5†	48†	47†
1466–7†	16†	9†	7·5†	48†	44·5†
1467–8†	87†	54†	7†	55†	38†
1468–9*	51*	29*	6*	46*	48*
1469–70	38	21	6·5	43	50·5
1470–1	52	39	12	69·5	18·5
1471–2	34	22	51	22	27
1472–3	16	11	56·5	6·5	37
1473–4	35	22	19·5	43·5	37
1474–5	42	29	44	25	31

* Incomplete, but about three-quarters of a year.
† Incomplete: half a year.

TABLE C10

ANNUAL TOTALS (TO NEAREST £1,000) AND
PERCENTAGES, 1475–85

Date	Nominal receipts (£1,000)	Real receipts (£1,000)	Cash %	Assigned %	Book-keeping %
1475–6	20	19	34·5	64·5	1
1476–7	24	22	15	77	8
1477–8	36	35	49	49	2
1478–9	34	31	66	29·5	4·5
1479–80	31	31	45	55	
1480–1	34	33	50·5	46·5	3
1481–2	46	43	43·5	48·5	8
1482–3	30	26	23	64	13
1483–4*	9*	7*	19*	57*	24*
1484–5†	43†	34†	18†	60†	22†

* Half-year only: no surviving rolls for Michaelmas term.
† Second term (Easter 1485) not quite complete.

454

TABLE D1

ANALYSIS OF BOOK-KEEPING, 1377–89

Date	Loans						Prestita restituta		
	'Genuine'			Fictitious					
	£	s.	d.	£	s.	d.	£	s.	d.
1377*	361	13	4*	50	0	0*	81	5	0*
1377–8	8,551	13	4	323	6	8	390	6	8
1378	160	6	8	2,450	0	0	126	4	5
1378–9	3,897	17	0	160	0	0	6,685	15	6
1379	13,229	2	2	92	8	0	2,941	6	6
1379–80	143	8	4	1,694	10	0	9,480	1	5
1380	18,463	18	9	1,578	5	0	38,959	15	2
1380–1				·					
1381	4,830	7	10	375	17	6	10,506	8	1
1381–2	5,718	0	8	1,896	18	8½	242	11	3
1382	4,273	6	8	893	5	11	915	7	10
1382–3	200	0	0	1,116	13	4	831	4	3
1383	3,103	2	2	699	19	7	1,750	10	3
1383–4	7,830	16	1	3,227	17	10	1,168	13	4
1384	9,976	7	6½	489	4	0	10,241	9	0
1384–5	7,113	9	9	3,914	0	11½	7,964	6	2
1385	14,813	12	4½	7,092	5	6½	2,209	2	0
1385–6	19,120	7	2	8,643	7	9	6,459	10	0½
1386	10,626	12	4½	1,873	5	2	9,161	15	0½
1386–7	9,205	8	10	2,525	5	10	153	16	8
1387	1,546	0	0	914	15	2	628	9	8
1387–8	6,305	0	0	998	18	8	333	17	5
1388	7,132	7	11	4,010	16	3	12,839	3	10
1388–9	1,788	16	3½	3,388	0	0	2,462	7	9

* Quarter-term.

TABLE D2

ANALYSIS OF BOOK-KEEPING, 1389–99

Date	Loans 'Genuine'			Loans Fictitious			*Prestita restituta*		
	£	s.	d.	£	s.	d.	£	s.	d.
1389	200	1	1½	3,341	3	4	8,695	10	3
1389–90	243	0	0	3,632	4	2	1,352	11	6½
1390	428	19	6	897	7	0	615	3	4
1390–1	120	19	4	3,254	4	2	6,878	7	0
1391	616	13	4	1,541	18	10	2,456	12	5½
1391–2	336	4	8	5,870	6	8	705	5	7
1392				120	0	0	196	1	8
1392–3							279	8	0½
1393	2,785	13	4				111	15	4½
1393–4				50	0	0	8,556	0	6
1394	37	1	8	156	17	10	694	1	11
1394–5	37,190	18	4½	200	0	0	11,644	3	6
1395							1,876	13	4
1395–6							280	11	2
1396	2,703	6	8				788	11	1
1396–7	11,963	6	8½	2,100	0	0	181	13	3
1397	18,392	2	6	4,980	15	4	107	15	8
1397–8	4,574	10	0	5,173	15	6	582	2	3½
1398	3,074	9	6½	3,051	1	8½	257	13	4
1398–9	1,681	6	8				14	9	1
1399							493	19	11

Table D3

ANALYSIS OF BOOK-KEEPING, 1399–1413

Date	Loans 'Genuine'			Fictitious			Prestita restituta		
	£	s.	d.	£	s.	d.	£	s.	d.
1399–1400	3,526	18	5½	6,455	10	6	33	0	0
1400	11,257	8	10½	8,014	13	1½	16	19	2
1400–01	5,049	13	5½	16,810	6	1	159	10	0
1401	2,339	4	6½	14,235	18	10	574	13	0
1401–02	2,390	1	5½	9,900	0	1	90	0	0
1402	16,823	19	3½	9,983	8	9½	65	14	10
1402–03	5,634	4	1½	15,487	3	0	53	6	8
1403*									
1403–04	5,032	8	9½	15,590	2	11½	15	0	0
1404*									
1404–05*									
1405	5,681	17	9	4,730	10	8½	333	6	8
1405–06*									
1406	12,725	0	5	444	2	2½			
1406–07	5,094	10	1	2,052	1	8½			
1407	15,929	19	0	1,243	18	0			
1407–08	1,930	1	4	7,544	5	2	486	6	8
1408	60	10	4	659	15	4	120	5	1
1408–09	5,266	13	4	115	16	4			
1409	653	11	8½	5,240	0	0			
1409–10	7,676	11	0	7,475	15	0	172	10	0
1410	7,826	10	0	2,819	3	8	10	0	0
1410–11	75	14	4½	589	10	0½			
1411†									
1411–12				102	5	0			
1412†									
1412–13	1,000	0	0				10	7	6

* These solitary surviving rolls are so fragmentary that analysed totals obtained from them are meaningless.

† No surviving roll.

TABLE D4

ANALYSIS OF BOOK-KEEPING, 1413–22

Date	Loans		Prestita restituta
	'Genuine'	Fictitious	
	£ s. d.	£ s. d.	£ s. d.
1413	10,626 13 4	66 13 4	
1413–14	0 0 0	0 0 0	
1414	2,382 19 10		
1414–15	2,133 6 8		
1415	24,869 6 8	13,374 4 8½	
1415–16	742 15 1	2,283 15 6½	11 6 6
1416	455 0 0	4,417 10 6½	59 3 7½
1416–17	19,539 5 7	2,010 17 4	8 18 5
1417	31,595 15 8	1,198 16 8	186 11 0
1417–18	453 6 8	482 19 2	33 6 8
1418	343 6 6	514 3 4	
1418–19		710 5 9	
1419	113 3 0	1,085 8 5	2 10 0
1419–20	3,791 9 6½	658 6 0½	10 16 8
1420	12 0 0	1,484 0 0	40 0 8
1420–1	68 0 0	2,015 3 10½	2,353 19 10½
1421	35,836 5 8	6,146 2 5½	
1421–2	911 13 4	2,197 16 4	48 1 9
1422	7,043 5 3	980 6 8	40 6 9½

TABLE D5

ANALYSIS OF BOOK-KEEPING, 1422-32

| Date | Loans | | Prestita restituta |
	'Genuine'	Fictitious	
	£ s. d.	£ s. d.	£ s. d.
1422–3		3,574 6 8	
1423	669 4 11½	964 15 8	
1423–4	11,944 0 0	2,633 6 8	73 7 1
1424	292 13 9½	1,550 11 10	14 9 7
1424–5	1,066 18 5½	4,316 7 0	
1425	9,673 13 4	5,159 13 8	
1425–6	105 0 0	5,116 17 11	
1426	3,404 9 10	2,046 15 0½	
1426–7	979 5 1	1,070 10 0	
1427	20 0 0	1,110 9 9	
1427–8	4,497 0 0	2,663 5 8½	
1428	2,533 6 8	4,421 4 8	
1428–9	666 13 4	4,513 14 0	
1429*			
1429–30	4,232 13 4	3,498 18 7½	
1430	10,459 13 9	2,165 4 1	
1430–1	36,382 17 10	7,876 0 6½	
1431	9,875 9 10½	1,836 0 2	16 10 0
1431–2	7,838 11 8	6,470 12 2	
1432	18,620 0 0	11,048 5 10½	

* No surviving roll.

459

TABLE D6

ANALYSIS OF BOOK-KEEPING, 1432–42

Date	Loans 'Genuine'			Loans Fictitious			Prestita restituta		
	£	s.	d.	£	s.	d.	£	s.	d.
1432–3	8,543	10	0	5,390	2	2			
1433	8,159	6	8	3,197	17	4	226	13	4
1433–4	11,758	0	0	4,641	1	8½	107	8	2
1434	13,497	18	1	4,758	8	1	10	0	0
1434–5	8,219	8	8	3,529	14	6			
1435	21,813	4	2½	7,403	14	10½			
1435–6	33,341	14	8	7,925	8	2½			
1436	14,906	0	5	7,633	16	11	666	13	5½
1436–7	1,733	6	8	6,811	14	5½			
1437	20,999	6	8	10,916	4	8½			
1437–8	17,370	13	4	4,823	16	2½	20	0	0
1438	4,631	8	6	13,085	3	8½			
1438–9	15,784	3	2	10,789	19	6			
1439	14,474	10	2	10,737	16	4	3,140	5	5½
1439–40	14,014	4	5	8,553	0	9			
1440	1,000	0	0	3,717	9	6			
1440–1	10,143	6	0	6,397	4	9			
1441	333	6	8	9,171	0	9	356	13	4
1441–2	7,561	9	5½	9,574	14	0½	50	0	0
1442	27,842	7	0	7,748	8	5	489	6	0

TABLE D7

ANALYSIS OF BOOK-KEEPING, 1442–52

Date	Loans 'Genuine'			Loans Fictitious			Prestita restituta		
	£	s.	d.	£	s.	d.	£	s.	d.
1442–3	11,049	8	4	10,445	19	2			
1443	16,918	9	1½	5,006	0	10½	894	0	9
1443–4	15,766	13	4	6,457	17	6	13	9	4
1444	7,728	19	6½	5,803	5	3½			
1444–5	2,590	0	0	8,294	9	9			
1445	7,353	6	8	5,569	17	10½			
1445–6	2,474	11	8½	9,068	3	5			
1446	1,995	10	0	30,578	9	7½			
1446–7	4,394	9	1	26,286	4	0	40	7	0
1447	700	0	0	27,317	17	5½*			
1447–8	6,666	13	4	6,034	0	7	0	6	8
1448	600	0	0	4,903	8	3½			
1448–9				4,775	2	0	2	5	4
1449	7,170	13	4	4,455	13	8	2,043	6	8
1449–50	24,203	1	1	3,054	14	6½			
1450	2,159	2	8	1,741	14	8	140	0	0
1450–1	8,208	18	1	1,200	6	10½			
1451	10,608	8	8	6,349	9	5½			
1451–2	1,139	6	9½	1,987	18	11			
1452	4,774	5	1½	3,091	1	1½			

* Of this total £3,628 6s. 8d. represents entries cancelled with a special note recording or implying later payment by other means, but not actually a fictitious loan, such as might have been expected. These entries are, however, clearly assignments which have gone wrong in some way which is later put right, and it therefore seems fair to classify them with fictitious loans, whose object was after all the same. See pp. 25–6 above.

TABLE D8

ANALYSIS OF BOOK-KEEPING, 1452–62

| Date | Loans | | Prestita restituta |
	'Genuine'	Fictitious	
	£ s. d.	£ s. d.	£ s. d.
1452–3	7,319 14 3	6,017 16 4	
1453	14,771 6 9	6,487 18 8	
1453–4	3,500 13 4	4,646 6 1½	
1454	9,906 2 8	4,868 2 11	
1454–5	4,163 13 4	1,568 4 1½	
1455	3,420 11 10	1,040 2 1	
1455–6	793 6 8	757 16 9	
1456	2,793 15 4	517 14 5	
1456–7	2,707 0 0	1,013 8 11½	
1457	3,326 2 4	2,232 11 11	
1457–8	4,621 13 10½	3,259 1 10½	
1458	1,313 6 8	1,638 11 6	
1458–9	3,431 6 8	2,118 3 10	
1459	1,000 0 0	271 1 8½	
1459–60	5,436 11 4	201 1 9	
1460	1,409 10 9	175 6 3	
1460–1	7,790 10 0	884 12 5½	
1461	17,769 16 3½	1,910 7 6½	
1461–2*			
1462	3,299 15 10	4,226 14 4	

* No surviving roll.

TABLE D9

ANALYSIS OF BOOK-KEEPING, 1462–75

Date	Loans 'Genuine'	Loans Fictitious	Prestita restituta
	£ s. d.	£ s. d.	£ s. d.
1462–3†	981 13 11†	1,237 14 5½†	
1463	14,055 8 2½	3,938 12 0	125 12 3½
1463–4*			
1464	5,054 16 10	1,381 19 5	
1464–5	16,734 17 10	1,655 4 4	
1465*			
1465–6	24,144 4 1	2,166 1 7½	
1466*			
1466–7	6,312 6 6	645 8 5	
1467*			
1467–8*			
1468	31,216 4 7½	1,860 17 4½	
1468–9	10,221 9 0	2,414 14 8½	
1469†	8,513 19 5½†	1,585 7 2†	
1469–70	6,819 17 6	1,952 0 8	
1470	8,017 15 7	768 4 9	
1470–1	499 19 4	131 15 10	
1471	12,492 0 0		
1471–2	1,043 6 8		
1472	10,609 12 10	49 0 10½	
1472–3	3,292 18 0	11 10 1	
1473	1,503 17 10		
1473–4	6,186 10 9	23 17 1½	
1474	6,792 18 2	37 6 8	
1474–5	4,839 19 5	11 3 1	
1475	7,772 16 4½	105 6 8	

* No surviving roll.
† Incomplete—about half a term in each case.

TABLE D10

ANALYSIS OF BOOK-KEEPING, 1475–85

| Date | Loans | | Prestita restituta |
	'Genuine'	Fictitious	
	£ s. d.	£ s. d.	£ s. d.
1475–6	100 0 0	103 15 0	
1476	50 0 0	9 13 4	
1476–7	600 0 0	194 9 5½	
1477	920 0 0	91 1 1	
1477–8		331 10 0	
1478		159 5 7½	
1478–9		2,537 6 7	
1479		13 2 6	
1479–80		5 19 0	
1480		22 0 3	
1480–1		1,179 0 4	
1481		12 11 6	
1481–2		16 5 0	
1482	3,493 6 8	78 4 11½	
1482–3	3,429 19 1	96 8 7	
1483	830 0 0		
1483–4*			
1484	2,152 2 0		
1484–5	4,485 5 11½	411 1 0½	
1485†	4,420 8 0†	33 6 8†	

* No surviving roll.   † Not quite complete.

TABLE E1

INCIDENCE OF LOANS AND PRESTS, 1377–89

| | Loans | | | | | | Prestita restituta | | |
| | 'Genuine' | | | Fictitious | | | | | |
	£	s.	d.	£	s.	d.	£	s.	d.
Household	13,139	3	2	14,006	1	1	46,924	0	4
Chancery	2,916	13	4	167	0	0	45	18	8
Exchequer	3,363	4	0½	105	0	0	57,151	6	7½
Local officials	1,538	6	8	14,684	2	6	21,991	4	11
Total	20,957	17	2½	28,962	3	7	126,112	10	6½
Bishops	10,005	6	7	430	6	8	696	17	9½
Religious	4,036	13	0	299	3	0½	351	16	8
Magnates	21,720	10	2*	10,238	18	7½	11,142	12	11*
Country gentry	819	2	11½	350	13	4	117	0	6
London	44,682	12	0½	3,497	12	2½	1,007	12	7
Burgesses	5,463	5	4	41	13	4	2	14	0
Aliens	48,294	3	9	1,138	4	5	150	0	0
Unidentified	329	12	4	74	13	4	312	16	8
Total	135,351	6	2	16,071	4	11½	13,781	11	1½
Add	20,957	17	2½	28,962	3	7	126,112	10	6½
Total	156,309	3	4½	45,033	8	6½	139,894	1	8

* £14,480 3s. 10d., though entered as an ordinary loan from magnates in the receipt roll, should strictly be transferred to *prestita restituta* under the same head (above, pp. 43, 137–8).

TABLE E2

INCIDENCE OF LOANS AND PRESTS, 1389–99

	Loans						*Prestita restituta*		
	'Genuine'			Fictitious					
	£	s.	d.	£	s.	d.	£	s.	d.
Household	11,840	11	3	5,914	1	7	30,127	9	7½
Chancery	1,400	0	0				16	13	4
Exchequer	842	6	2				4,355	16	5
Local officials	1,930	0	0	19,694	2	5	6,738	11	1
Total	16,012	17	5	25,618	11	0	41,238	0	5½
Bishops	8,666	13	4	240	0	0	599	13	1½
Religious	7,006	19	9½	163	6	8	283	13	1½
Magnates	5,965	0	0	9,482	7	5	2,086	0	0
Country gentry	1,696	13	4	30	0	0	218	6	8
London	21,363	12	7	567	13	1	1,808	1	6
Burgesses	6,739	7	2½				141	1	2
Aliens	1,268	13	4	727	0	10	213	15	4
Unidentified	206	13	4	319	0	0	40	0	0
Total	52,913	12	11	11,529	8	0	5,390	10	11
Add	16,012	17	5	25,618	11	0	41,238	0	5½
Total	68,926	10	4	37,147	19	0	46,628	11	4½

466

TABLE E3

INCIDENCE OF LOANS AND PRESTS, 1399–1413

	Loans						Prestita restituta		
	'Genuine'			Fictitious					
	£	s.	d.	£	s.	d.	£	s.	d.
Household	13,153	10	11	61,381	13	11	1,184	0	8
Chancery	2,621	13	4	180	8	8	70	9	5
Exchequer	5,950	10	2	290	8	2	212	14	11
Local officials	1,071	5	3½	33,707	15	3	40	0	0
Total	22,796	19	8½	95,560	5	4	1,507	5	0
Bishops	10,993	9	1	2,558	11	2	10	7	6
Religious	3,838	4	0	781	13	0			
Magnates	10,750	4	11	19,855	16	0½	853	6	8
Country gentry	1,015	0	4	609	12	4	87	19	10
London	51,527	18	4	11,972	16	2			
Burgesses	10,366	17	10½	1,213	6	8			
Aliens	5,242	15	1	2,003	11	6			
Unidentified	76	6	8	665	19	3			
Total	93,810	16	3½	39,661	6	1½	951	14	0
Add	22,796	19	8½	95,560	5	4	1,507	5	0
Total	116,607	16	0	135,221	11	5½	2,458	19	0

TABLE E4

INCIDENCE OF LOANS, 1413–22*

	'Genuine'			Fictitious		
	£	s.	d.	£	s.	d.
Household	14,681	1	7	6,372	5	7
Chancery	1,604	12	0			
Exchequer	2,474	6	9	65	15	3
Local officials	3,791	18	6½	14,707	0	1¼
Total	22,551	18	10½	21,145	0	11½
Bishops	44,243	1	5½	2,200	0	0
Religious	8,758	6	9	1,178	10	0
Magnates	5,696	17	10	9,292	11	8½
Country gentry	16,767	6	2	1,140	0	0
London	32,096	13	4	3,666	13	4
Burgesses	6,786	13	4	115	6	8
Aliens	3,133	6	8	1,240	8	6
Unidentified	115	0	0			
Total	117,597	5	6½	18,833	10	2½
Add	22,551	18	10½	21,145	0	11½
Total	140,149	4	5	39,978	11	2

* *Prestita restituta* remain so small in this period that they have little significance and are therefore not tabulated. The only large one is the sum of rather over £2,300 from Roger Salvayn, treasurer of Calais, which should be placed under the head of *Local officials*. All the rest come to less than £450 in all for the entire reign. (See Table D4.)

TABLE E5

INCIDENCE OF LOANS, 1422–32*

	'Genuine'			Fictitious		
	£	s.	d.	£	s.	d.
Household	3,188	19	10	15,616	2	8½
Chancery	1,146	13	4	231	13	1
Exchequer	1,308	10	0	39	10	0
Local officials	3,368	0	6	7,818	2	10½
Total	9,012	3	8	23,751	13	3
Bishops	58,516	7	10½	1,703	2	8
Religious	3,459	14	11	359	17	1½
Magnates	1,112	13	4	37,169	11	7
Country gentry	19,006	1	0½	1,533	18	11
London	18,435	0	2	2,803	6	8
Burgesses	4,489	16	4	2,104	18	9½
Aliens	4,535	6	8	290	12	8
Unidentified	70	0	0	2	10	0
Total	109,625	0	4	45,967	18	5
Add	9,012	3	8	23,751	13	3
Total	118,637	4	0	69,719	11	8

* *Prestita restituta* have almost disappeared. (See Table D5.)

TABLE E6

INCIDENCE OF LOANS AND PRESTS
1432–42

	Loans						Prestita restituta		
	'Genuine'			Fictitious					
	£	s.	d.	£	s.	d.	£	s.	d.
Household	996	13	4	39,846	2	5	466	10	$0\frac{1}{2}$
Chancery	2,295	0	0	1,937	1	$3\frac{1}{2}$			
Exchequer	4,976	13	4	527	9	9	370	10	9
Local officials	6,878	10	6	30,082	19	$11\frac{1}{2}$	281	4	8
Total	15,146	17	2	72,393	13	5	1,118	5	$5\frac{1}{2}$
Bishops	110,747	11	10	25,064	18	4	3,487	19	$5\frac{1}{2}$*
Religious	6,822	6	8	546	11	$9\frac{1}{2}$			
Magnates	20,266	1	4	26,288	3	$7\frac{1}{2}$			
Country gentry	31,953	12	$5\frac{1}{2}$	7,089	7	1			
London	27,569	0	$5\frac{1}{2}$	2,992	17	4	26	13	4
Burgesses	31,006	19	9	7,791	13	8	107	8	2
Aliens	7,900	17	9	1,566	13	4			
Unidentified	300	0	0	667	17	4			
Total	236,566	10	3	72,008	2	6	3,622	0	$11\frac{1}{2}$
Add	15,146	17	2	72,393	13	5	1,118	5	$5\frac{1}{2}$
Total	251,713	5	5	144,401	15	11	4,740	6	5

* These prests principally consist of a single payment of £2,464 12s. 8d. from the bishop of Lisieux, together with the esquires John Montgomery and John Denyssh, about which I have been able to discover nothing.

APPENDIX D

TABLE E7

INCIDENCE OF LOANS AND PRESTS
1442-52

| | Loans | | | | | Prestita restituta | | |
| | 'Genuine' | | | Fictitious | | | | | |
	£	s.	d.	£	s.	d.	£	s.	d.
Household	9,186	19	8	63,661	16	1½	686	12	3
Chancery	1,116	13	4	2,313	4	3			
Exchequer	4,085	17	2½	2,695	5	6½	201	11	2
Local officials	10,682	9	11	47,276	10	3½	272	2	4
Total	25,072	0	1½	115,946	16	2½	1,160	5	9
Bishops	45,166	1	8	5,026	1	10	2,043	6	8*
Religious	4,377	4	10	1,866	16	8½			
Magnates	21,746	18	1	35,734	14	6			
Country gentry	1,829	14	1	449	9	3½			
London	15,046	14	2½	899	13	4			
Burgesses	20,203	19	5	2,810	8	3			
Aliens	4,685	4	0	3,557	2	0			
Unidentified	20	0	0	274	16	6½			
Total	113,075	16	3½	51,619	2	5½	2,043	6	8
Add	25,072	0	1½	115,946	16	2½	1,160	5	9
Total	138,147	16	5	166,565	18	8	3,203	12	5

* This is all one prest representing the value of crown jewels pledged to cardinal Beaufort and returned by his executors after his death. See Chapter VI, p. 232.

TABLE E8

INCIDENCE OF LOANS, 1452–62*

	'Genuine'			Fictitious		
	£	s.	d.	£	s.	d.
Household	1,881	13	4	14,305	12	5½
Chancery	1,856	0	0	871	18	5
Exchequer	22,452	5	9†	3,286	1	11½
Local officials	13,540	8	10½	10,933	14	11
Total	39,730	7	11½	29,397	7	9
Bishops	3,177	0	4½	1,163	0	0
Religious	7,985	1	3	463	13	4
Magnates	4,023	0	0†	10,226	18	3½
Country gentry	3,310	15	4½	45	6	1½
London	18,924	12	4	852	8	11½
Burgesses	17,653	11	11	706	4	6
Aliens	1,033	6	8	500	0	0
Unidentified	142	13	0	70	17	11
Total	56,250	0	11	14,028	9	1½
Add	39,730	7	11½	29,397	7	9
Total	95,980	8	10½	43,425	16	10½

* There are no *prestita restituta* during this decade.

† Four magnates make loans totalling £21,537 in their capacity as treasurers of England: these are shown under *Exchequer* but might almost as well appear under the other head.

Table E9

INCIDENCE OF LOANS AND PRESTS
1462–75

| | Loans | | | | | | *Prestita restituta* | | |
| | 'Genuine' | | | Fictitious | | | | | |
	£	s.	d.	£	s.	d.	£	s.	d.
Household	11,436	12	5½	4,869	3	0½			
Chancery	1,346	13	4	131	15	10			
Exchequer	38,427	11	7½*	5,092	4	4½			
Local officials	14,102	5	9†	3,696	9	6			
Total	65,313	3	2	13,789	12	9			
Bishops	7,290	6	6½‡	468	13	4			
Religious	3,472	6	8	188	2	5½			
Magnates	2,666	13	4*	1,365	9	1½	125	12	3½
Country gentry	2,760	12	9½	156	0	0			
London	35,852	9	4	2,137	1	1			
Burgesses	25,402	19	7½	49	5	9			
Aliens	38,128	15	6	1,606	12	6			
Unidentified	4,340	13	6	73	4	5			
Total	119,914	17	3½	6,044	8	8	125	12	3½
Add	65,313	3	2	13,789	12	9			
Total	185,228	0	5½	19,834	1	5	125	12	3½

* Five magnates make loans totalling £32,386 in their capacity as treasurers of England: these are shown under *Exchequer* but might almost as well appear under the other head.

† £4,145 of this total must be credited to the earl of Worcester in various capacities, and should perhaps have still further reinflated the unnaturally low total under *magnates*.

‡ This total could be brought up to £10,041 12s. 11½d. by transferring to it £2,751 6s. 5d., at present shown under *Exchequer*, which was advanced by William Gray, bishop of Ely, in his capacity as treasurer of England.

TABLE E10

INCIDENCE OF LOANS, 1475–85*

	'Genuine'			Fictitious		
	£	s.	d.	£	s.	d.
Household	2,710	0	0	4,471	14	6½
Chancery	650	0	0			
Exchequer	2,271	19	4	191	3	9½
Local officials	3,720	0	0	438	17	6
Total	9,351	19	4	5,101	15	10
Bishops	2,159	2	9	42	6	8
Religious	3,296	1	3½	17	13	4
Magnates	40	0	0			
Country gentry	844	3	6			
London	3,044	2	1	7	6	8
Burgesses	875	11	8	94	1	4
Aliens	753	6	8			
Unidentified	116	13	4	13	6	8
Total	11,129	1	3½	174	14	8
Add	9,351	19	4	5,101	15	10
Total	20,481	0	7½	5,276	10	6

* There are no *prestita restituta* during this decade.

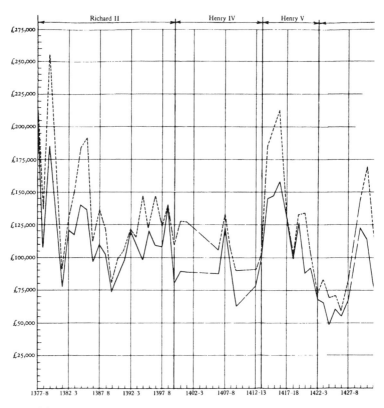

'Exchequer' years, Michaelmas to Michaelmas

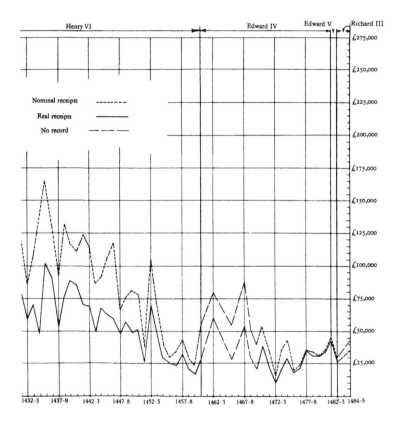

£275,000

£250,000

Nominal receipts --------   £225,000

Real receipts ————

No record — — —   £200,000

£175,000

£150,000

£125,000

£100,000

£75,000

£50,000

£25,000

1432-3   1437-8   1442-3   1447-8   1452-3   1457-8   1462-3   1467-8   1472-3   1477-8   1482-3   1484-5

APPENDIX E, GRAPH I. NOMINAL AND REAL RECEIPTS

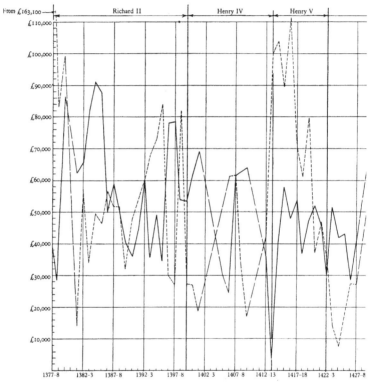

From £163,100 —→ | Richard II | Henry IV | Henry V

'Exchequer' years, Michaelmas to Michaelmas

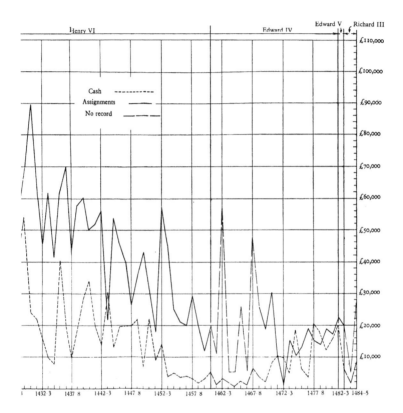

£110,000

£100,000

Cash   — — — — — — —
Assignments   ————
No record   — — — —

£90,000

£80,000

£70,000

£60,000

£50,000

£40,000

£30,000

£20,000

£10,000

1432-3   1437-8   1442-3   1447-8   1452-3   1457-8   1462-3   1467-8   1472-3   1477-8   1482-3 1484-5

APPENDIX E, GRAPH II. CASH AND ASSIGNMENTS

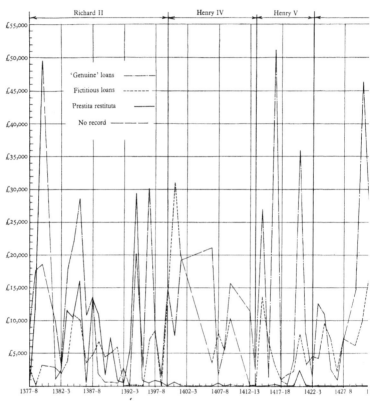

'Exchequer' years, Michaelmas to Michaelmas

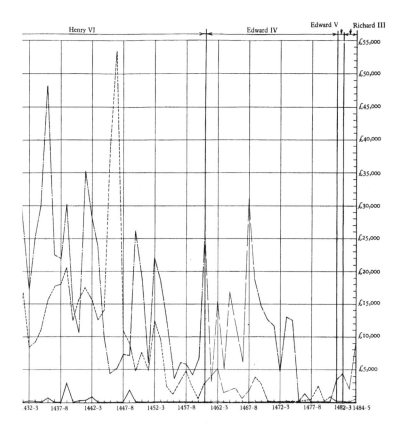

APPENDIX E, GRAPH III. LOANS AND *PRESTITA RESTITUTA*

INDEX

OF PERSONS AND PLACES

No attempt has been made to give the complete *cursus honorum* of any person mentioned in this index. The names of modern authorities are given in italics.

Burgh, Simon de, treasurer of Calais, 50, 133
Burgh, Thomas, esquire, 9
Burgundy, alliances with, 241, 281, 306; war against, 208; ransom of, 399; dukes of see Charles the Bold
Burley, Simon, king's knight, 71
Burnell, Hugh, lord, 189
Bury St. Edmunds, men of, 192
Butler, James, see Ormonde (earl of), Wiltshire (earl of)
Butler, John, collector of customs, London, 152, 185
Butler, William, receiver of Brecknock, 157, 185
Byzantine emperor, the, see Constantinople

Caen, town and castle, captain of, 249; and see Ogard (Sir Andrew)
Calais, 236, 245, 250, 266, 268, 270, 273, 278-9, 306, 350, 357
assignments to, 38, 43, 45, 49-51, 53-4, 56, 58, 61, 65-7, 69, 70, 73-9, 82, 133, 217, 231, 236, 249, 288
part of wool custom (local) pledged to, 210
whole of local wool custom assigned to, 292, 301-2, 351, 354, 416
high cost of, 99, 170
receipts from (mainly customs), 170, 238, 308, 310, 312-13, 315, 335, 354; assigned, 416, 418
garrison, mutiny of, 350; special methods of financing the, 292, 301, 351, 354, 357
captains of, see Calverley (Sir Hugh), Somerset (Edmund, duke of)
treasurers of, 21, 41-2, 46, 48, 51, 58, 61-2, 73, 77, 110, 356; loans from, 170, 248; and see Bernard (John), Blount (Sir Walter), Bukland (Richard), Burgh (Simon de), Clifton (Sir Gervase), Folkyngham (Robert), Merlawe (Richard), Salvayn (Roger), Selby (Robert), Stanley (Thomas), Usk (Nicholas), Walden (Roger), Whityngham (Robert)
victuallers of, 110; and see Bukland (Richard), Curtays (Reginald), Manfeld (Robert), Wode (John)
See also Staple (merchants of the)
Calton, Nicholas; Beauchamp chamberlain of the receipt, 424
Calverley, Sir Hugh, 137; captain of Calais, 40-1
Cambridge, burgesses of, 196; and see Herryes (John)
colleges of, see Queen's (Queens'), King's Hall (Trinity)

Cambridge, parliament at, 60-1
And see Friars
Cambridge, Edmund, earl of, 44; and see York (Edmund, duke of)
Cambridgeshire, men of, 191; with Huntingdonshire, sheriffs of, 411
Camoys, Thomas, lord, 192
Caniziani, the, of Florence, 31, 292, 294, 297, 302
Gerard de, 352-3
Cantelowe, William, alderman, of London, 264
Canterbury, archbishop of, 71, 134, 165, 174, 187, 201, 209-10, 212-13, 216, 222, 238, 259, 336; and see Arundel (Thomas), Bourchier (Thomas), Chichele (Henry), Morton (John), Stafford (John)
Canterbury, prior and convent of Christchurch, 188
Canyng(es), William, merchant, of Bristol, 349, 351
Carisbrooke (Isle of Wight), alien priory of, 90, 95
Carlisle, bishop of, 135, 187, 227-8; treasurer of England, 247, 420; warden of the west march towards Scotland, 253
And see Lumley (Marmaduke)
Carlisle, garrison of, 55; keepers of, and of the west march towards Scotland, see Lumley (Marmaduke), Neville (John, lord, of Raby), Neville (Sir Richard), Warwick (Richard, earl of), Westmorland (Ralph, earl of)
Carp, John, keeper of the wardrobe, 81
Castile (Castilians), 55, 281; and see Spain
Cataneo, of Genoa, 68, 267
Cauchon, Peter, bishop of Liseux, 214
Cawode, Robert, clerk in the exchequer, attorney for Roger Salvayn (q.v.), 162
Chadworth, William, receiver of lands etc. in the hands of feoffees of the duchy of Lancaster, 239, 249
Chalton, William, alderman, of London, 264
Charles the Bold, duke of Burgundy, 306
Charles VII, king of France, 173
Chaucer, Geoffrey, xxxiv, 63, 65; with Philippa, his wife, 374
Chaucer, Thomas, king's chief butler, 154
Chedworth, John, bishop of Lincoln, 336
Cherbourg, 43-5, 50-1, 56; captains of, see Harleston (John), Kent (Thomas, earl of), Scrope (William le), Windsor (William de)

Wyclif, John, xxxv
Wykeham, William of, bishop of Winchester, 71, 74, 76, 84, 135, 186
Wylie, J. H., xxvi, 77, 86, 96, 147
Wylton, Master Stephen, king's clerk, 215
Wynne, John, jeweller, of London, 237

Yarmouth, Great, customs of, 65, 416–17
Yonge, Sir John, stapler, and mayor of London, 347
Yonge, Thomas, of Bristol, 349
York, archbishop of, 43, 91, 233, 238, 254, 318; also acting as chancellor of England, 71, 176, 187; *and see* Arundel (Thomas), Kemp (John), Neville (George)

York, citizens of, 196, 349; *and see* Blakborn (Nicholas)
York, duchy of, attempt to protect the revenues of the, 302
York, dukes of,
Edmund, 139; *and see* Cambridge (Edmund, earl of)
Edward, 138; *and see* Rutland (Edward, earl of)
Richard, 220–1, 226–7, 257–9, 271, 277–8, 280, 282, 340–1; protector of the realm, 284
Yorke, lady Elizabeth, *deo vota*, 339
Yorkists, the, xii, xx–xxii, xxviii, xxxviii, 3, 5, 22, 28–31, 35, 155, 236, 259, 274, 277–9, 281, 283–5, 293, 296–8, 306, 317, 320, 324–7, 330, 334, 339, 347–8, 350, 354–7, 360–1, 367, 415
Yorkshire, men of, 192

SUBJECT INDEX

Abbeys,
abbots, abbesses (collectively), 149,
192, 209, 255; *and see* Barking,
Croyland, Glastonbury, Gloucester,
Peterborough, Ramsey, Reading,
Selby, Tewkesbury, Westminster;
see also Monastic houses, etc.
Admirals, 'keepers of the sea', 385; *and
see* Dorset (Thomas Beaufort, earl
of), Oxford (John de Vere II, earl
of), Warwick (Richard Neville,
earl of)
Advocate, the king's, before the consistory and at the council of Basle;
see Navarria (Stephen de)
Agents, 381, 385, 400–1
royal, *see* Bryan (Edmund), Caniziani
(Gerard de), Coke (Sir Thomas),
Langton (Master John)
Aids, royal, 411
Ale, the king's purveyor of, 329
Alien priories, 410; *and see* Carisbrooke,
Lodres
Aliens (collectively), xiii, 110, 113, 119,
121, 146–8, 197–8, 201, 266–7,
269–70, 292, 294, 352–3, 357,
362–3; fines on, 94; poll-taxes
(subsidy) on, 215, 218, 232; special
customs levied on, 80–1, 273,
reduced, 291
Alum, trading venture in, by Henry VI,
237, *and see* Genoa, London
Ambassadors, the king's, to Arras,
33; to the council of Basle, 182, 209;
to Denmark, 329; to the papal
curia, 53; *and see* Brounflete (Sir
Henry), Dagworth (Sir Nicholas),
Godebarne (Master Henry), Kemp
(John), Northumberland (Henry
Percy II, earl of)
Apothecary, the king's, 246, 327, 329
Appellants, lords appellant, 58–9, 64,
111–13, 118
Archers, 42, 44; 'grants' of, by parliament, 273, 275, 300–1, 303
Array, commissioners of, 140
Arrears of salaries, 83–4, 96, 124, 131,
185–6, 250; in chancery and exchequer, 247; of councillors, 190;
in household, 246, 329; of judges
(and of robes), 215
Arrow-maker, the king's, 246
Assignment, general description of, viii,
xxix–xxxiv, xxxvii–xxxviii, 364,
366, 374–6; king's requirements

given priority over, 236; practice of,
passim; *and see* Complex assignment, Simple assignment, Reflex
assignment, Tallies, Writs of assignment
Attorney-general, the king's 29, 290
Attorneys, the king's, 246, 327; *and see*
West (John)

Bailiffs (bailiwicks), 411
'Balance-sheets', national, xxiii–xxiv,
204
Beauchamp chamberlain of the receipt,
3, 4, 10–12, 287, 424–5, 441; *and
see* Brown (John), Gloucester
(Richard, duke of), Hermesthorp
(John), Oudeby (John), Warwick
(Richard, earl of), Worcester (John,
earl of)
deputies of the, *see* Pilkington (Sir
John), Tyrell (Sir James)
Benevolences, xxxix, 1, 34, 310, 313,
315–6, 354, 360–1
Bills of exchange, of the exchequer, 23,
33, 374, 377, 381–3, 389, 391, 399,
403–4; of the household, 377; on
Rome, 53; of the treasurer of
England, 385
Bishops (collectively), xiii, 110, 113,
115, 119, 122, 134–6, 149, 176, 184,
186–8, 200, 209, 251–4, 297, 318,
336–7, 357, 367; *and see* Canterbury, York (archbishops of), *and
individual dioceses*
Blank charters, 103, 117–18
'Blank' entries, on the receipt rolls,
xiv–xvi, xxxi, 14–15, 79, 102
Body, the king's, esquires of the, 329;
knights of the, 334; servants of the,
see Household
Bonds, blank, 82, 321
Boroughs, 410; parliamentary, 145; *and
see* Burgesses
Boys and pages, *see* Chamber (the
queen's), Household
Budgets, *see* 'Balance-sheets' (national)
Burgesses, xiii, 110, 113, 119, 122, 125,
139, 141, 144–6, 163, 192–4, 196–7,
201, 250, 261, 264–6, 269, 338,
348–52, 354, 357
Business, days of, in the receipt,
tendency to dwindle, 2, 3, 92–3,
165, 167, 174, 276, 282, 297, 302
305, 312, 318–20, 401

492

SUBJECT INDEX

Farmers (keepers), 58. 60, 65, 121–2, 205, 210, 410–11, 414–15
Ferreter, the king's, 246
Fictitious loans, xiii–xv, xviii, xxv, xxvii, xxxi–xxxiii, 1, 12, 13, 17, 18, 20–2, 24–6, 30–2, 229, 298, 364–8, 372, 383, 386, 388–9, 391–4, 396, 400, 403, 407–8, 411, 461, *et passim*; *see also Mutua per talliam*
Fines, 103, 117, 284, 291, 293, 411, 414–15; *coram concilio*, 78, 118, 140, 398–9, 405; for distraint of knighthood, 175; *pro maritagio*, 164, 169, 319; special (*see* cardinal Beaufort), 177, 206, 212
Fishmongers, of London, 345; *and see* Bukland (Richard), Hampton (Sir William)
Fletchers, of London, *see* Crane (William)
Forced loans, 17, 103, 117–18, 120, 123, 146, 262, 319–20, 362, 368, 394–5; parliamentary provision against, 208
Foreign exchange, profit on, 68, 75, 82, 145, 307, 310–11, 397–8
Forfeitures, 59–60, 64–5, 76–7, 83, 117–18, 282, 354, 398–9, 405, 411, 414–15; *and see* Beauchamp (Sir John), Brembre (Nicholas), Clarence (George, duke of), Mortimer (Sir John), Northampton (John of), Northumberland (Henry Percy I, earl of), Percy (Sir Henry), Perrers (Alice)
Forgeries of debentures, tallies, etc., 122, 405
Fowls, the king's purveyor of, 329
Freightage, 398
Friars, minor, 110, 188; of Cambridge, 339; of London, 339; of Oxford 189, 256, 339
preaching, 188; of Cambridge, 339; of London, 256, 339; of Oxford, 189, 256, 339; chief provincial in England of, 256
And see Religious (the)

'Genuine' loans, xii, xiii, xv, xviii, xxv, xxvii–xxviii, xxxi, xxxvii–xxxviii, 1, 16, 17, 20, 26, 33, 373, 390, 393–5, 400, 405, *et passim*; disguising arrears of salaries, 131, 184, 186, 247; disguising deposit of valuables in the exchequer, 16, 186; disguising exchequer processes used by privileged persons, 124, 186; disguising expenses contracted in the king's service, etc., 186, 248; not repaid, 105–6, 118–20, 138, 140–8, 262

Gifts, free, *see Dona*
Goldsmiths, of London, 141, 347; *and see* Barker (John), Brice (Hugh), Palyng (John), Shaa (Sir Edmund), Tildesley (Christopher)
Goods, arrested, sale of, 398–9, 405
Great councils, 39, 119, 280; ushers of their chamber, 246
Great seal, letters under the, xxx, xxxvii, 17, 18, 26, 119–20, 183, 377, 399, 409; writs or bills under the, 25–6, 28, 109, 409
Great wardrobe, the, 26, 41, 44–6, 49, 51, 67–8, 70, 73–5, 77–8, 86–8, 109, 128, 154, 182–3, 243–5, 326–8, 369, 378; keepers of, *see* Clifford (Richard), Loveney (William), Macclesfield (John), Noreys (John), Rolleston (Robert), Say (Sir John), Spenser (John), Stokes (Alan)
Grocers, of London, *see* Brembre (Nicholas), Haddele (John), Philpot (John), Venour (William I)

Hanaper, issues of the, 47, 66–7, 69, 73, 78–80, 100, 229, 239, 319, 398; clerks of the, 411; *and see* Claydon (Robert)
Horse, the queen's master of, 246
Hospitallers, *see* St. John of Jerusalem
Hospitals, 110, 188; wardens and masters of, 255, 337; *and see* London (St. Anthony), Lepers (of St. Giles)
Hostagia, 398
Household, the, 115–16, 122, 125–8, 130, 180–2, 199, 215, 232, 242–6, 268, 310, 325–9, 331, 336, 346, 356, 367–9, 376–7, 380–1, 404; accounts of, xxv, xxx; assignments to, 38–9, 41, 43–5; 47, 50–1, 53, 63–9, 73–81, 100, 109, 178, 216, 228, 278, 307–9, 311–13, 315, 317–18; bills of, 377; body-servants of, 246; chapel of, *see* Westminster (St. Stephen's); gentlemen and yeomen of, 232, 246; pages, boys and valets of, 246, 329; petitions from, to parliament, 232; prests handled by officials of, 108, 116–17; ships hired by, 222; stewards of, *see* Percy (Sir Thomas); treasurers (controllers) of, 285, *and see* Brounflete (Thomas), Elryngton (John), Fenys (Sir Roger), Fogge (Sir John), Hotoft (Sir John), Popham (Sir John), Stourton (Sir John), Tiptoft (Sir John I), Tyrell (Sir John)
See also Wardrobe (keepers of the)
Household, the queen's, 245–6

SUBJECT INDEX

Incrementa, 398

Indentures, 394, 398–9; covenanting to lend the king money, 118

Inducement, to lend money to the king, problem of, xxxvii, 18–20, 33, 40, 44, 48–9, 51–2, 54–5, 121–3, 157, 191–2, 195–6, 201, 221, 224, 251–2, 262–3, 342, 346–7, 353, 363, 395; *and see* Forced loans, Interest, Usury

Informers, *see* Bryan (Edmund)

Innovated tallies, 22–3, 373

Interest on loans, 121, 262–3, 271, 348, 353, 395; *and see* Inducement

Issue rolls, xix, xxv–xxvii, xxxi, 7, 8, 38, 40, 105, 116, 141, 326, 355, 371, 374–9, 381–2, 384, 388–9, 401–2, 409, 422, 424–5

Jewellers, of London, *see* Wynne (John)

Jewels, plate, etc., the king's, pledges or sales of, 38, 40, 42, 44, 46, 87, 167, 215, 220–1, 232–3, 237–8, 298, 318, 471
  purchases of, 158
  clerks of, *see* Bacon (John), Daubeny (Master William)
  cardinal Beaufort's, 177, 206

Judges, justices, 84, 110, 220, 250, 327; of assize, 249; of Chester, 110; of the exchequer (chief baron), *see* Illyngworth (Richard); of the peace, 140; of Wales, 110; salaries (and robes), arrears of, 215; *and see* Common bench, King's bench, Fortescue (Sir John), Paston (William)

Keepers, of lands, vills, etc., *see* Farmers

King's bench, coroner and king's attorney in, *see* West (John); justices of, 83; chief justices of, *see* Bryan (Sir Thomas), Clopton (Sir Walter), Fortescue (Sir John)

King's chamberlain, of the receipt, 4, 10, 11, 12, 93, 102, 156, 277, 287–8, 305, 422–4, 441; *and see* Bacon (John), Brocas (Arnold), Cromwell (Ralph, lord), Hastings (William, lord), Hotoft (Sir John), Lincoln (John), Orgrave (Thomas de), Wodehous (John)

Kitchen, the king's, under-clerk of, 329

Knights, the king's, 109, 126–30, 181–3, 243–6, 268, 326–9; *and see* Brounflete (Henry), Burley (Simon), Knolles (Robert), Peytevyn (Thomas), Sandes (John), Say (John), Waterton (Hugh)

of the shire, 261, 265; *and see* Commons (the)

Lancastrian inheritance, the, 81, 103–4, 106, 120, 139

Lepers of St. Giles, 256

Letters, obligatory, 377, 404; patent, 76, 95, 119, 123, 229, 233, 235, 237–9, 377, 396, 404, *and see* Great seal; 'of request', 320–1

Loans, 394, 406; commissioners of, 121–2, 163, 188–9, 191–2, 343, 348–9; *and see* 'Genuine' loans

Local officials, xii, 110, 115–16,127, 132–3, 143, 184–6, 199, 248–50, 257–8, 269, 333–6, 339–41, 345–6, 356, 367, 376, 382–3, 404, 407, 409, 414–15

Lords, the (collectively), *see* Magnates

Magnates, xiii, 110, 113, 115–16, 119, 125, 127, 137–9, 141, 185, 189–90, 193, 200–1, 256–60, 269, 271, 283, 336, 339–42, 356–7, 362–3, 367, 465, 472–3; exempt from ordinary fifteenths and tenths, 273, and from similar grants, 300; *see also* Peers

Manors, the king's, 410–11; *and see* Mereworth (Kent), St. Pancras, Salden (Bucks.)

Marches, the,
  French, 248.
  towards Scotland, 53, 62, 69, 93, 115, 139, 249–50, 258, 269, 271, 282; high cost of, 204, 250; keepers (wardens) of, 110, 185–6; *and see* Grey (Richard, lord), Lumley (Marmaduke), Neville (John, lord, of Raby), Neville (Sir Richard), Norfolk (John Mowbray II, duke of), Northumberland (Henry Percy I, II and III, earls of), Percy (Sir Henry), Warwick (Richard, earl of), Westmorland (Ralph, earl of)
  See also Wales

Marshalsea, court of, 329

Medium tempus (mid-term), 2, 401

Memoranda rolls, xix, xxv, 23, 25–6, 90, 229, 397, 405; of king's remembrancer, 422–5; of treasurer's remembrancer, 387, 422–3

Men-at-arms, 42, 44

Mercenaries, Welsh, 283

Mercers, of London, 143, 195, *and see* Estfeld (William), Fauconer (Thomas), Flete (William), Kerver (William), Pykeryng (John), Shore (William), Whittington (Richard); of Cornwall, *see* Robert (John); of Lincoln, *see* Hert (Richard)

FORMULARY

For EU product safety concerns, contact us at Calle de José Abascal, 56–1°,
28003 Madrid, Spain or eugpsr@cambridge.org

 www.ingramcontent.com/pod-product-compliance
Ingram Content Group UK Ltd.
Pitfield, Milton Keynes, MK11 3LW, UK
UKHW042210180425
457623UK00011B/127